RHCSA®

Red Hat® Enterprise Linux® 10

Training and Exam Preparation Guide

Exam Code: EX200

Fourth Edition | December 2025

Asghar Ghori

www.ingramspark.com

Technical Reviewers: Many of author's students and peers
Editors: Zainab Ghori with GenAI-assisted editing
Cover Design: Nid n Nad Graphics Printing Inc. (www.nidnnad.ca)
Printers and Distributors: IngramSpark Inc.

Printed in the United States of America and other countries.

ISBN-13: **978-1775062189**
ISBN-10: **177506218X**
Library of Congress Control Number: **2025923522**

For information on bulk purchases or special sales for corporate training programs, please contact the author directly at *asghar_ghori2002@yahoo.com*

Disclaimer:
The author and publisher have made every effort to ensure the accuracy and completeness of the information contained in this book; however, they make no warranties, express or implied, regarding the content herein. This book is provided "as-is", without warranty of any kind, including but not limited to the warranties of merchantability, fitness for a particular purpose, or non-infringement.

Neither the author nor the publisher shall be held liable for any loss or damages, including but not limited to incidental, consequential, or other damages, in connection with or arising from the furnishing, performance, or use of this material.

This publication is an independent study guide and is not affiliated with, sponsored by, or endorsed by Red Hat, Inc. It is not a replacement for the official Red Hat curriculum courses (RH124 and RH134). While this book is designed to prepare candidates for the RHCSA (EX200) exam based on the published RHCSA 10 objectives, neither the author nor the publisher guarantees that using this book will result in exam success.

Preface

The journey to becoming a Red Hat Certified System Administrator (RHCSA) is a challenging and rewarding pursuit. It tests not just your knowledge, but your ability to think critically and solve problems. With the release of Red Hat Enterprise Linux (RHEL) 10, this journey incorporates the latest innovations of the platform. This guide was written to be your definitive companion on that path.

My approach in this book is built on a principle I've seen proven time and again in both the classroom and the data center: true expertise is forged through practice. You cannot simply read about Linux administration; you must *do* it. Consequently, this book is filled with hands-on exercises and challenging labs designed to build the muscle memory and troubleshooting skills essential for the exam and your future career.

You will notice that the Do-It-Yourself (DIY) challenge labs do not include solutions. This is intentional. The ability to research, reason, and resolve issues independently is the hallmark of a competent system administrator. Embrace these challenges; overcoming them is where the deepest learning occurs.

I encourage you to visit www.nixeducation.com for errata, updates, and additional learning resources. Your feedback is invaluable to me. Please share your thoughts, report any errors, or suggest improvements at **asghar_ghori2002@yahoo.com**.

I wish you the best of luck in your studies and on your exam. The skills you build here will serve you well.

Good luck in your endeavors.

Asghar Ghori | December 2025 | Toronto, Canada

Acknowledgments

First and foremost, I am grateful to God for the strength and guidance to complete this work.

My sincere thanks to the students, colleagues, and readers of my previous publications on RHCSA, RHCE, CompTIA Linux+, and HP-UX. Your valuable feedback has been instrumental in shaping this edition and making it a better resource.

I recognize the constructive feedback I had received from the readers of my previous publications. I have used their comments toward the improvement of this edition.

A special and heartfelt thank you to my wife and children. Your patience and unwavering support during the many hours of my "mental absence" made this book possible. This accomplishment is as much yours as it is mine.

Finally, I offer my enduring tribute to my late parents and sisters, whose memory continues to inspire me.

Asghar Ghori

About the Author

Asghar Ghori is a seasoned Linux, Cloud, and DevOps consultant, curriculum designer, trainer, and author with over 30 years of industry experience.

As a consultant, he has architected, implemented, and supported complex IT environments across both public and private sector organizations. As an educator with more than 25 years of teaching and curriculum development experience, he has designed, authored, and delivered structured training curricula, hands-on labs, and assessment materials covering Linux/UNIX administration, RHCSA, RHCE, cloud platforms (Microsoft Azure and AWS), automation (Terraform and Ansible), high-availability systems, and enterprise infrastructure operations.

Asghar is the author of 12 published books on Linux, RHEL, UNIX, and CompTIA Linux+, widely used by students, instructors, and professionals worldwide.

He holds numerous industry certifications across Linux, UNIX, Microsoft Azure, AWS, and is a Project Management Professional (PMP) and Microsoft Certified Trainer (MCT). A strong advocate of hands-on, outcomes-driven learning, Asghar brings real-world expertise directly into the classroom and onto the exam.

Asghar lives in Toronto, Canada with his wife and children. He can be reached via email at asghar_ghori2002@yahoo.com or LinkedIn: https://www.linkedin.com/in/asghar-ghori-0315632/

Publications of Asghar Ghori including this are:

1. RHCSA Red Hat Enterprise Linux 10: Training and Exam Preparation Guide (EX200) (ISBN: 978-1775062189 | RHEL version 10 | December 2025
2. RHCSA Red Hat Enterprise Linux 9: Training and Exam Preparation Guide (EX200) (ISBN: 978-1775062165 | RHEL version 9 | February 2023
3. RHCSA Red Hat Enterprise Linux 8 (UPDATED): Training and Exam Preparation Guide (EX200) (ISBN: 978-1775062141 | RHEL version 8 | November 2020
4. RHCSA Red Hat Enterprise Linux 8: Training and Exam Preparation Guide (EX200) (ISBN: 978-1775062127 | RHEL version 8 | January 2020
5. CompTIA Linux+/LPIC-1: Training and Exam Preparation Guide (Exam Codes: LX0-103/101-400 and LX0-104/102-400) (ISBN: 978-1775062103 | 2017
6. RHCSA & RHCE Red Hat Enterprise Linux 7: Training and Exam Preparation Guide (EX200 and EX300) (ISBN: 978-1495148200 | RHEL version 7 | 2015
7. Red Hat Certified System Administrator & Engineer: Training Guide and a Quick Deskside Reference (ISBN: 978-1467549400 | RHEL version 6 | 2012
8. Red Hat Certified Technician & Engineer (RHCT and RHCE) Training Guide and Administrator's Reference (ISBN: 978-1615844302 | RHEL version 5 | 2009
9. HP-UX: HP Certified Systems Administrator, Exam HP0-A01, Training Guide and Administrator's Reference (ISBN: 978-1606436547 | HP-UX 11iv3 | 2008
10. HP Certified Systems Administrator, Exam HP0-095, Training Guide and Administrator's Reference (ISBN: 978-1424342310 | HP-UX 11iv2 and 11iv3 | 2007
11. Certified System Administrator for HP-UX: Study Guide and Administrator's Reference (ISBN: 978-1419645938 | HP-UX 11iv1 | 2006
12. Fundamentals of UNIX: published 2002

Conventions Used in this Book

This book uses several typographic and layout conventions to help you distinguish between different types of information.

Book Antiqua Italic 10 pt. is used in text paragraphs to introduce new terms. For example:

> "Red Hat renamed the Red Hat Linux operating system series *Red Hat Enterprise Linux* (RHEL) in 2003."

Times Roman Italic 10 pt. is used in text paragraphs to highlight names of files, directories, commands, daemons, users, groups, hosts, domains, and URLs. This font also highlights file and directory paths. For example:

> "To go directly from */etc* to a subdirectory *dir1* under *user1*'s home directory, create *dir1*, as . . . ."

Times New Roman 9 pt. is used to segregate command output, script/file contents, and information expected to be entered in configuration files from the surrounding text. It is also used in tables, index, and side notes.

Times Roman Bold 10 pt. is used to highlight commands and command-line arguments that the user is expected to type and execute at the command prompt. For example:

[user1@server1 ~]$ **ls -lt**

Two white spaces (**cp -p file1 /tmp**) are inserted between parts of a typed command for clarity.

`Ctrl+x` key sequence implies that you hold down the `Ctrl` key and then press the other key. `Courier New` font is used to highlight such combinations. This font is also used to identify keystrokes, such as `Enter` and `Esc`.

. . . . Dotted lines represent truncated output in command examples.

Screenshots: Show actual terminal sessions and graphical interfaces to help readers verify their work and understand expected outcomes.

Headings: All headings and sub-headings are in California FB font, and are bolded.

Chapter Opening Images: Sourced from public domain or used with appropriate permissions. All image rights remain with their respective owners.

Times Roman 8 pt. is used for notes.

Times Roman 8 pt. is used for warning messages.

Exam Tip surrounded by a solid box is included where necessary.

The RHCSA 10 Exam and Exam Objectives

The Red Hat Certified System Administrator (RHCSA) exam (EX200) is a performance-based test conducted on a live system running Red Hat Enterprise Linux 10. Your exam environment will consist of two RHEL 10 virtual machines where you will perform all tasks. This is a closed-book exam; no external resources, including the internet, personal devices, or printed materials, are permitted. Access is limited to documentation and manual pages installed on the exam VMs.

The official exam objectives (62 in total as of this writing) are the definitive source for exam content and are subject to change. For the most current list, always refer to:
http://www.redhat.com/training/courses/ex200/examobjective

There are no formal prerequisites to attempt the RHCSA certification.

This book provides comprehensive coverage of all official exam objectives. The following list enumerates each objective and directs you to the corresponding chapter for detailed study.

Understand and Use Essential Tools

1. Access a shell prompt and issue commands with correct syntax (chapter 2)
2. Use input-output redirection (>, >>, |, 2>, etc) (chapter 7)
3. Use grep and regular expressions to analyze text (chapter 7)
4. Access remote systems using ssh (chapters 1 and 20)
5. Log in and switch users in multiuser targets (chapter 6)
6. Archive, compress, unpack, and uncompress files using tar, gzip, and bzip2 (chapter 3)
7. Create and edit text files (chapter 3)
8. Create, delete, copy, and move files and directories (chapter 3)
9. Create hard and soft links (chapter 3)
10. List, set, and change standard ugo/rwx permissions (chapter 4)
11. Locate, read, and use system documentation including man, info, and files in /usr/share/doc (chapter 2)

Manage Software

12. Configure access to RPM repositories (chapters 10 and 11)
13. Install and remove RPM software packages (chapter 11)
14. Configure access to Flatpak repositories (chapter 12)
15. Install and remove Flatpak software packages (chapter 12)

Create Simple Shell Scripts

16. Conditionally execute code (use of: if, test, [], etc.) (chapter 8)
17. Use Looping constructs (for, etc.) to process file, command line input (chapter 8)
18. Process script inputs ($1, $2, etc.) (chapter 8)
19. Processing output of shell commands within a script (chapter 8)

Operate Running Systems

20. Boot, reboot, and shut down a system normally (chapter 14)
21. Boot systems into different targets manually (chapter 14)
22. Interrupt the boot process in order to gain access to a system (chapter 13)
23. Identify CPU/memory intensive processes and kill processes (chapter 9)
24. Adjust process scheduling (chapter 9)
25. Manage tuning profiles (chapter 14)
26. Locate and interpret system log files and journals (chapter 14)

27. Preserve system journals (chapter 14)
28. Start, stop, and check the status of network services (chapter 14)
29. Securely transfer files between systems (chapter 20)

Configure Local Storage

30. List, create, and delete partitions on MBR and GPT disks (chapter 15)
31. Create and remove physical volumes (chapter 15)
32. Assign physical volumes to volume groups (chapter 15)
33. Create and delete logical volumes (chapter 15)
34. Configure systems to mount file systems at boot by Universally Unique ID (UUID) or label (chapter 16)
35. Add new partitions and logical volumes, and swap to a system non-destructively (chapters 15 and 16)

Create and Configure File Systems

36. Create, mount, unmount, and use vfat, ext4, and xfs file systems (chapter 16)
37. Mount and unmount network file systems using NFS (chapter 18)
38. Configure autofs (chapter 18)
39. Extend existing logical volumes (chapters 15 and 16)
40. Diagnose and correct file permission problems (chapter 4)

Deploy, Configure, and Maintain Systems

41. Schedule tasks using at and cron (chapter 9)
42. Start and stop services and configure services to start automatically at boot (chapter 14)
43. Configure systems to boot into a specific target automatically (chapter 14)
44. Configure time service clients (chapter 19)
45. Install and update software packages from Red Hat Network, a remote repository, or from the local file system (chapters 10 and 11)
46. Modify the system bootloader (chapter 13)

Manage Basic Networking

47. Configure IPv4 and IPv6 addresses (chapter 17)
48. Configure hostname resolution (chapter 19)
49. Configure network services to start automatically at boot (chapter 14)
50. Restrict network access using firewall-cmd/firewall (chapter 21)

Manage Users and Groups

51. Create, delete, and modify local user accounts (chapter 5)
52. Change passwords and adjust password aging for local user accounts (chapters 5 and 6)
53. Create, delete, and modify local groups and group memberships (chapter 6)
54. Configure superuser access (chapter 6)

Manage Security

55. Configure firewall settings using firewall-cmd/firewalld (chapter 21)
56. Manage default file permissions (chapter 4)
57. Configure key-based authentication for SSH (chapter 20)
58. Set enforcing and permissive modes for SELinux (chapter 22)
59. List and identify SELinux file and process context (chapter 22)
60. Restore default file contexts (chapter 22)
61. Manage SELinux port labels (chapter 22)
62. Use Boolean settings to modify system SELinux settings (chapter 22)

Taking the Exam

The following strategies will help you manage your time and focus during the 3-hour performance-based exam:

1. **Manage Your Time Aggressively:** Time is your most limited resource. Work efficiently and move on if you get stuck; you can return to challenging tasks later.
2. **Ensure Changes Persist:** Any configuration you implement must survive a system reboot. Get into the habit of running systemctl reboot after completing major tasks to verify their persistence.
3. **Choose Your Editor Wisely:** Use the text editor you are fastest and most comfortable with (vim, nano, etc.) for editing configuration files. Proficiency here saves valuable minutes.
4. **Understand the VM Structure:** The exam tasks are divided between two virtual machines. You **must** perform each group of tasks within its assigned VM. Confirming you are in the correct VM before starting a task is critical.
5. **Report Issues Immediately:** If you encounter any technical problems with the exam system or the virtual machines, inform the proctor immediately. Do not attempt to troubleshoot system-level issues on your own.
6. **Adhere to the Closed-Book Policy:** The exam is a closed-book environment. You will have no access to the Internet, personal electronic devices, or any external reference materials.
7. **Read Tasks Carefully:** Read each exam question completely and ensure you understand the requirements before you begin. Misinterpreting a task is a common and avoidable mistake.
8. **Identify Storage Devices Precisely:** For all storage-related tasks, use the lsblk command to carefully identify the correct disk (e.g., vdb, sdb) before performing operations like partitioning, formatting, or mounting.

Exam Fee and Registration

The fee for the RHCSA (EX200) exam is US$500 (plus any applicable taxes), or equivalent in local currencies. To register, visit *http://www.redhat.com/training/courses/ex200/examobjective*, select your location, and click Get Started to log in with your Red Hat account to complete the registration process. The RHCSA exam is based on RHEL 10 and it is a 3-hour, performance-based test.

About this Book

RHCSA Red Hat Enterprise Linux 10: Training and Exam Preparation Guide, Fourth Edition provides comprehensive, in-depth coverage of all objectives for the RHCSA EX200 exam based on RHEL 10. This book is strategically organized to take you from fundamental concepts to advanced system administration through a structured, logical progression.

What You Will Find Inside:

- **22 Chapters of Progressive Learning:** The book begins with building your lab environment and learning essential Linux concepts and commands, and advances through critical topics including user and group administration, software management, system initialization, storage (partitions, LVM, filesystems, and swap), networking, and security (firewalls, SELinux).
- **Proven Learning Aids:**
    - **Step-by-Step Exercises:** Guided, hands-on procedures with screenshots of actual commands and outputs.
    - **DIY Challenge Labs:** End-of-chapter labs that test your comprehensive understanding without provided solutions, building problem-solving resilience.
    - **Review Questions & Answers:** To help you self-assess your grasp of each chapter's key concepts.
    - **Exam Tips, Notes, and Warnings:** Highlight crucial information, common pitfalls, and best practices.
- **Final Preparation Tools:** Four full-length practice exams in the appendices simulate the real RHCSA testing environment, allowing you to gauge your readiness.

This Book Is Designed For:

- RHCSA 10 exam candidates using it as a self-study guide.
- Students and instructors in formal training courses (RH124/RH134 equivalents).
- IT professionals seeking a structured desktop reference for RHEL 10.
- Administrators new to RHEL who need a clear, practical introduction.

TABLE OF CONTENTS

List of Figures

List of Tables

Chapter 01

Local Installation

By the end of this chapter, you will be able to:

- Explain Linux, Open Source, and the Red Hat Ecosystem
- Plan Your RHCSA Lab Environment: A Step-by-Step Guide
- Describe the RHEL Installer Program
- Monitor the Installation: Logs and Consoles
- Install VirtualBox and Create Virtual Machine
- Perform a Custom RHEL Installation
- Access Your New RHEL System Locally and Remotely

RHCSA Objectives:

04. Access remote systems using ssh
This chapter establishes the foundational environment required to learn and practice the RHCSA exam objectives

Welcome to your journey toward the Red Hat Certified System Administrator (RHCSA) certification on Red Hat Enterprise Linux (RHEL) 10. This book is your hands-on guide to mastering the practical skills required for this exam. The philosophy is simple: the best way to learn is by doing. Every concept you encounter will be reinforced with practical exercises in your dedicated lab environment.

You will begin by building that foundation. This chapter guides you through creating a personal lab by installing RHEL in a Virtual Machine (VM) and making your first remote connection—the first of many steps toward your certification. By the end of this chapter, you will have a fully functional RHEL system, ready for the exploration and practice that lies ahead.

A Quick Look at Linux Development

Linux is a free, UNIX-like operating system (OS) that shares many of UNIX's core concepts, features, and stability and security. It powers an extensive range of computer hardware platforms, from laptop and desktop computers to massive mainframes and supercomputers. Linux also runs as the base OS on networking, storage, gaming, smart television, and mobile devices. Numerous vendors offer commercial support to Linux users worldwide.

Due to its functionality, adaptability, and cost-effectiveness, Linux serves as the primary alternative to proprietary UNIX and Windows systems. While over two hundred distinct Linux distributions exist from various vendors and communities, only a handful are widely adopted. Commercial support for these popular distributions is provided by companies such as Red Hat/IBM, Canonical, and Oracle. As a result, Linux sees extensive use in government, corporate, academic, and scientific environments, with its development and adoption continuously growing.

A Brief History of Linux

The foundation for Linux was laid in 1984 when Richard Stallman launched the GNU (*GNU's Not Unix*) Project to create a free, UNIX-compatible, open-source operating system. By 1991, the project had developed most of the necessary software components. The one critical piece still missing was the kernel—the core software that manages hardware resources and enables communication between software and hardware.

This gap was filled by a new kernel developed by Linus Torvalds around the same time. The new kernel was named *Linux*, and it was gradually integrated with the GNU software to form a complete operating system, today known as *GNU/Linux* or simply *Linux*.

Linux was released under the GNU *General Public License* (GPL). Initially written for Intel x86-based computers, the first version (0.01) was released in 1991 with little over 10,000 lines of code. The first major release (1.0.0) arrived in 1994. Since then, through contributions from tens of thousands of developers worldwide, it has evolved into a massive, complex system. The GPL ensures the source code remains freely available, allowing anyone to view, modify, and redistribute it.

Red Hat's Journey

Red Hat, Inc., pioneered commercial Linux distributions with the release of *Red Hat Linux* (RHL) 1.0 in 1994. The RHL series concluded in 2003 with version 9, which also marked Red Hat's strategic shift toward the enterprise market as Red Hat Enterprise Linux (RHEL) 3.

Originally developed in-house at Red Hat, the RHL project evolved in 2003 into the community-driven *Fedora Project*. Sponsored by Red Hat, Fedora serves as a test bed for new features and technologies. The stable, refined results from Fedora are then incorporated into successive RHEL releases.

While Fedora is a free distribution, RHEL is a commercially supported product. Table 1-1 outlines the key RHEL releases, their underlying kernels, and their source Fedora distributions:

RHEL Version	Release Date	Kernel Version	Based on Fedora
RHEL 3	Mar 2003	2.4.20	RHL 9
RHEL 4	Feb 2005	2.6.9	Fedora 3
RHEL 5	Mar 2007	2.6.18	Fedora 6
RHEL 6	Nov 2010	2.6.32	Fedora 13
RHEL 7	Jun 2014	3.10.0	Fedora 20
RHEL 8	May 2019	4.18.0	Fedora 28
RHEL 9	May 2022	5.14.0	Fedora 34
RHEL 10	May 2025	6.12.0	Fedora 40

Table 1-1 RHEL Release Information

RHEL 10 is engineered for broad compatibility, tested to run reliably on bare-metal computer hardware, major virtualization platforms, cloud-based virtual machines, graphics workstations, IBM Power servers, IBM System Z, and more.

Lab Environment for Practice

RHEL 10 is available as a free download from Red Hat for systems using Intel, AMD, and ARM processors. You must create a free Red Hat user account to download it. You can then attach the downloaded image file to a *Virtual Machine* (VM) as an ISO image, write it to a DVD for local installation on a physical computer, or place it on a remote server for network-based installations via the HTTP, FTP, or NFS protocol.

An ISO image is a file that represents the content of an entire optical disc.

Procedures for writing the image to a DVD and configuring a network-based installation server are beyond the scope of this book. This chapter focuses on local installation of Linux using an ISO image.

Lab Environment for In-Chapter Exercises

This book presents comprehensive discussions of system, network, and security topics, accompanied by practical implementation and administration examples. Each chapter includes hands-on exercises designed to reinforce your task performance and command execution skills.

To set up your practice environment, you will need a laptop or desktop computer that meets or exceeds the following specifications:

- **Processor:** A dual-core processor or better
- **Memory:** 8 GB of physical memory (16 GB strongly recommended)
- **Storage:** 50 GB of free storage space to accommodate two virtual machines

A critical prerequisite is that your computer's BIOS or UEFI firmware must have hardware virtualization support enabled. This feature is essential for installing 64-bit guest operating systems within a virtualized environment.

If you plan to assign static IP addresses via your home router, it is crucial to maintain a clear mapping between the router's assignments and the addresses used in this book to prevent configuration conflicts.

Table 1-2 summarizes the required configuration for in-chapter exercises:

Component	**Specs for VM1**	**Specs for VM2**
Host OS	Windows 11 / macOS 14 or higher	
Hypervisor	Oracle VM VirtualBox Manager (VirtualBox in short) 7.2.4 or higher	
VM name in VirtualBox	RHEL10-VM1	RHEL10-VM2
Hostname	server1.example.com	server2.example.com
IP address (static)	192.168.0.110/24	192.168.0.120/24
Memory	2048 MB	2048 MB
vCPUs	2	2
OS disk	1 x 20 GB	1 x 20 GB
Data disks	None	4 x 400 MB disks added in Chapter 15 for storage management exercises.

Component	Specs for VM1	Specs for VM2
Network	1 x Bridged adapter	1 x Bridged adapter
OS	RHEL 10	RHEL 10
Note1	Built using Exercises 1-1 and 1-2	Built using Lab 1-1
Note2	Renamed to server10.example.com in Chapter 17	Renamed to server20.example.com in Chapter 17

Table 1-2 Server Specs for In-Chapter Exercises

Check your Windows/macOS IP assignments and make sure to use the same subnet for the VMs. For instance, use 172.16.3.110/24 and 172.16.3.120/24 for the VMs if your Windows/macOS is on the 172.16.3.0/24 subnet.

Figure 1-1 illustrates the system and network specifications for the lab environment you will build in this chapter for performing all the in-chapter exercises presented in this book.

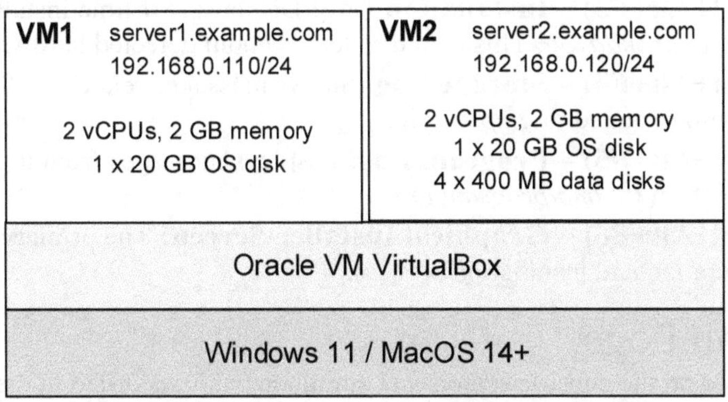

Figure 1-1 Lab Setup for In-Chapter Exercises

While you can use an alternative hypervisor like VMware or Hyper-V, all exercises, screenshots, and instructions in this book are based on VirtualBox.

Lab Environment for End-of-Chapter Labs

To perform the end-of-chapter labs, you should build a new, separate environment. This environment will consist of two new virtual machines with specifications identical to RHEL-VM1 (*server1*) and RHEL-VM2 (*server2*). You can name the new systems RHEL-VM3 (*server3*) and RHEL-VM4 (*server4*) for consistency.

Create this environment only after completing all the in-chapter exercises. These labs are designed for you to complete with minimal guidance, providing hints but not step-by-step instructions, to further solidify your understanding and skills.

The RHEL Installer Program

The RHEL installation is performed by the installer program, *Anaconda*. Anaconda provides a centralized Installation Summary screen that allows you to configure all aspects of the installation before it begins. This design ensures you can review, verify, and modify your settings efficiently. Certain configuration items are mandatory and must be completed before the installation can proceed, while others are optional and can be adjusted after the operating system is installed.

The configuration can be completed in any order. For an efficient installation, prepare the necessary information in advance. Key configuration items include language, keyboard type, time zone, software selection, disk partitioning, hostname, IP assignments, root password, and user information.

Virtual Consoles

During the installation, Anaconda provides six text-based virtual consoles for monitoring progress, viewing diagnostic messages, and troubleshooting issues. You can switch between the consoles anytime using the key combination described below:

Console 1 (Ctrl+Alt+F1) – Main Installation Screen: This is the initial console for selecting the installation language. After this step, the interface automatically switches to the sixth screen (Console 6).

Console 2 (Ctrl+Alt+F2) – Root Shell Prompt: Provides a command-line interface where you can run commands as the *root* user for advanced troubleshooting.

Console 3 (Ctrl+Alt+F3) – Installation Log: Displays real-time installation messages and logs them to */tmp/anaconda.log*. This includes details about detected hardware.

Console 4 (Ctrl+Alt+F4) – Storage Log: Shows messages related to disk partitioning and storage configuration, logged to */tmp/storage.log*.

Console 5 (Ctrl+Alt+F5) – Program Log: Displays messages from the software being installed and logs them to */tmp/program.log*.

Console 6 (Ctrl+Alt+F6) – Graphical Installer Screen: The primary interface for the graphical configuration and installation process.

Installation Logs

The logs displayed on the console screens are simultaneously recorded in the installation log files for post-installation verification or analysis. Table 1-3 describes these log files.

File	Description
/root/anaconda-ks.cfg	Records the configuration entered
/var/log/anaconda/anaconda.log	Contains informational, debug, and other general messages
/var/log/anaconda/dbus.log	Records D-Bus communication, including service activations and errors exchanged between the installer and system components such as NetworkManager, storage services, and systemd.
/var/log/anaconda/journal.log	Stores messages generated by many services and components during system installation
/var/log/anaconda/lorax-packages.log	Records packages as they are installed
/var/log/anaconda/lvm.log	Records messages generated by the LVM commands and subsystem during LVM volume creation and management process.
/var/log/anaconda/packaging.log	Records messages generated by the dnf and rpm commands during software installation
/var/log/anaconda/program.log	Captures messages generated by external programs
/var/log/anaconda/storage.log	Records messages generated by storage modules
/var/log/anaconda/syslog	Records messages related to the kernel

Table 1-3 Installation Logs

Anaconda stores the log files in the */tmp* directory during the installation process, and moves them to their permanent location in the */var/log/anaconda* directory upon successful completion.

Exercise 1-1: Download and Install VirtualBox Software, and Create a Virtual Machine

In this exercise, you will:

- Download and install the VirtualBox software
- Create a virtual machine to establish the foundational environment for installing RHEL 10 in the subsequent exercise.

> **EXAM TIP:** Downloading and installing the VirtualBox software and creating a virtual machine are not covered by the exam objectives. They are provided here solely to help you build a personal lab environment for practice.

Downloading and Installing VirtualBox

VirtualBox is freely available for download and use. This book uses version 7.2.4, which was the latest version at the time of writing. The following steps provide a guide for downloading and installing this version on a Windows 11 system.

1. Navigate to the official website, *www.virtualbox.org*, and click Download.
2. In the "VirtualBox Platform Packages" section, click the link for "Windows hosts" to download the installation package for Windows (Figure 1-2).

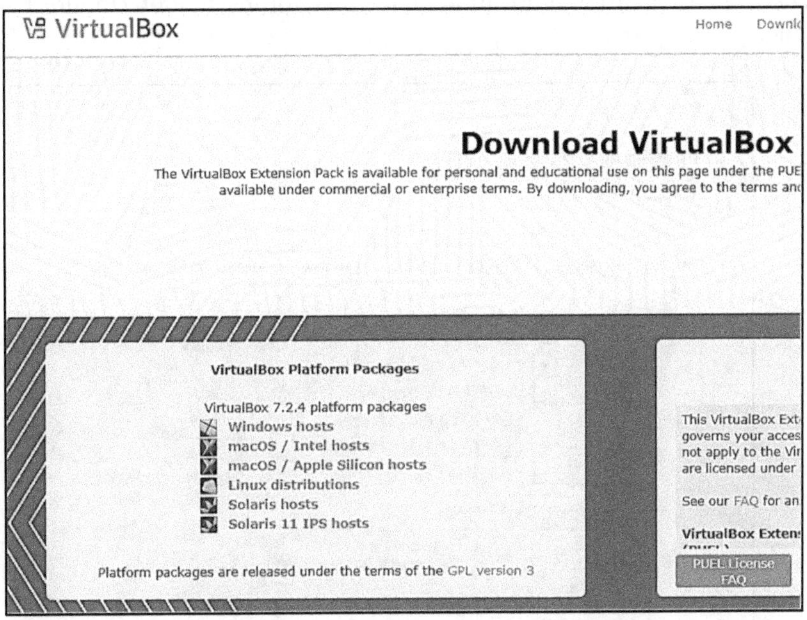

Figure 1-2 VirtualBox Download

3. Locate and double-click the downloaded VirtualBox installer executable to launch the setup wizard. Click Next on the initial welcome screen to proceed (Figure 1-3).

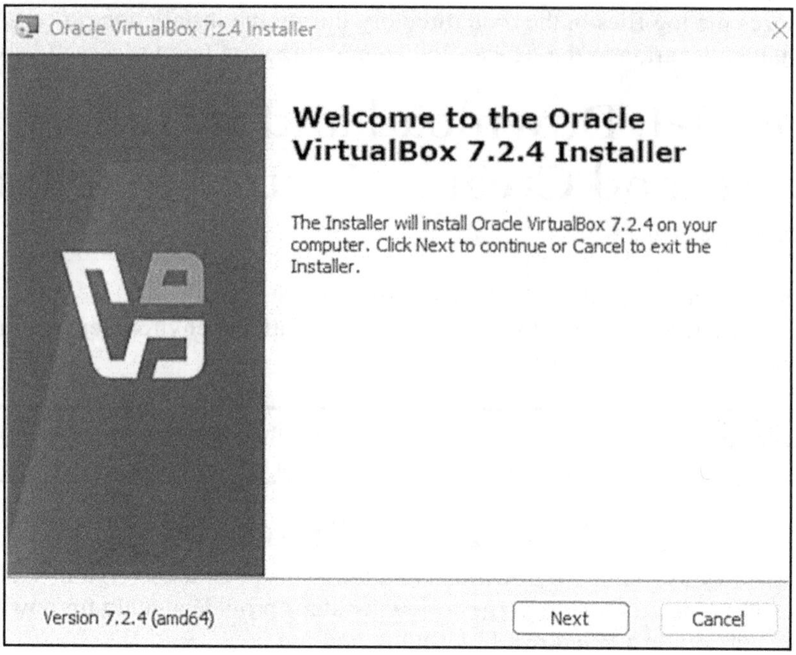

Figure 1-3 VirtualBox Installation 1

4. On the License Agreement screen, select "I accept the terms of the license agreement" and click Next.
5. If needed, choose a different location on the disk for installation (Figure 1-4). Click Next to continue.

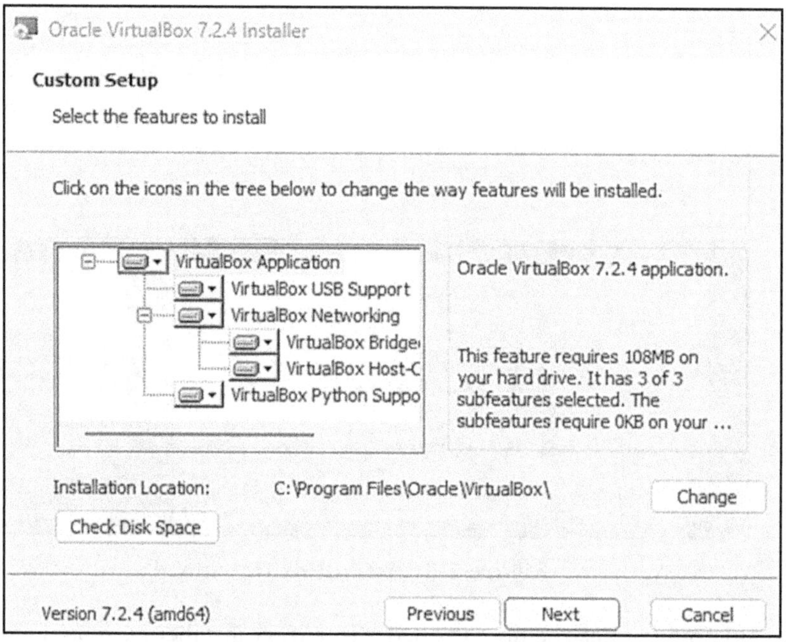

Figure 1-4 VirtualBox Installation 2

6. Accept the warning and press Yes to continue (Figure 1-5).

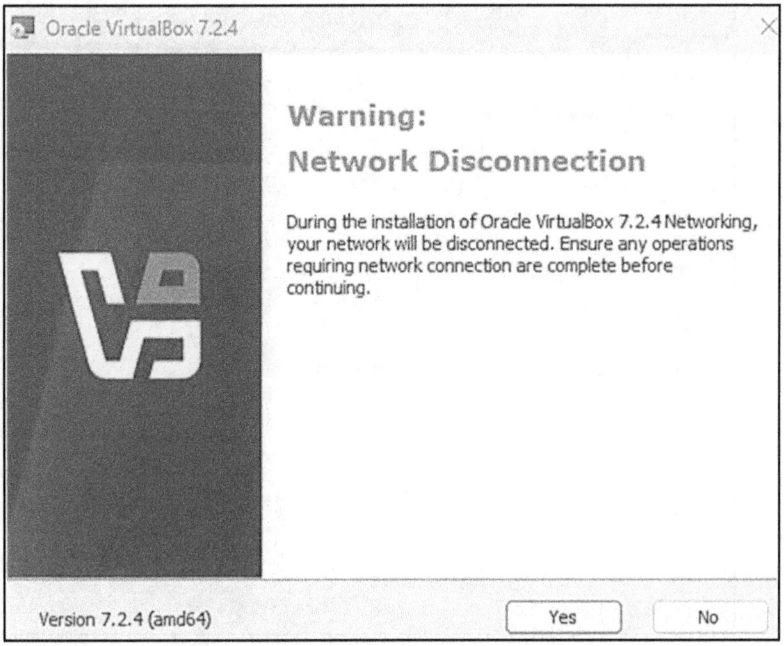

Figure 1-5 VirtualBox Installation 3

7. The installation also includes Python Core software package and win32api bindings. Click Yes to proceed (Figure 1-6).

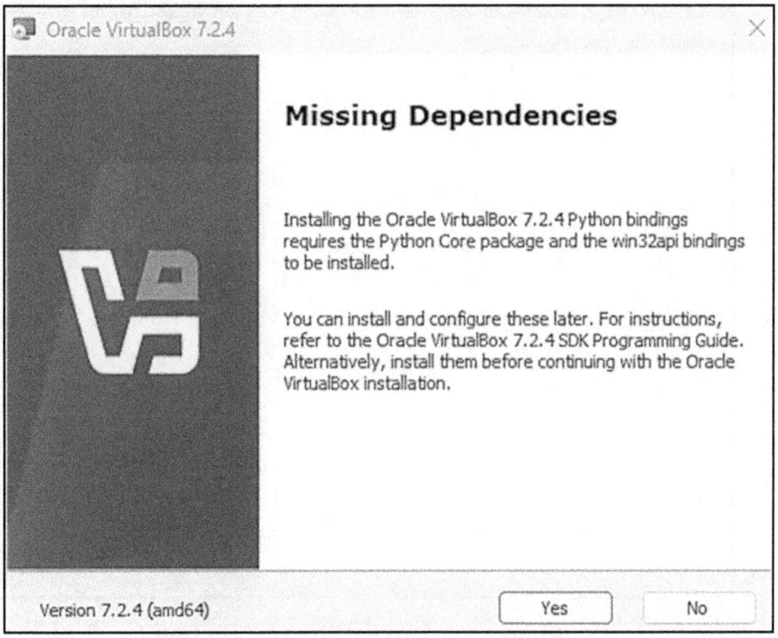

Figure 1-6 VirtualBox Installation 4

8. Select or unselect startup options as required (Figure 1-7). Click Next to proceed.

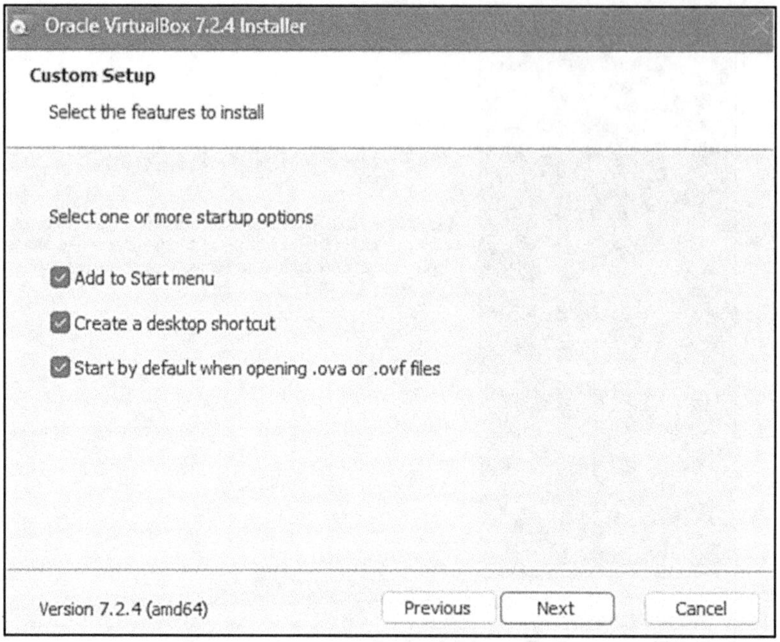

Figure 1-7 VirtualBox Installation 5

9. The setup wizard is now ready to begin the installation (Figure 1-8). Click Install to proceed.

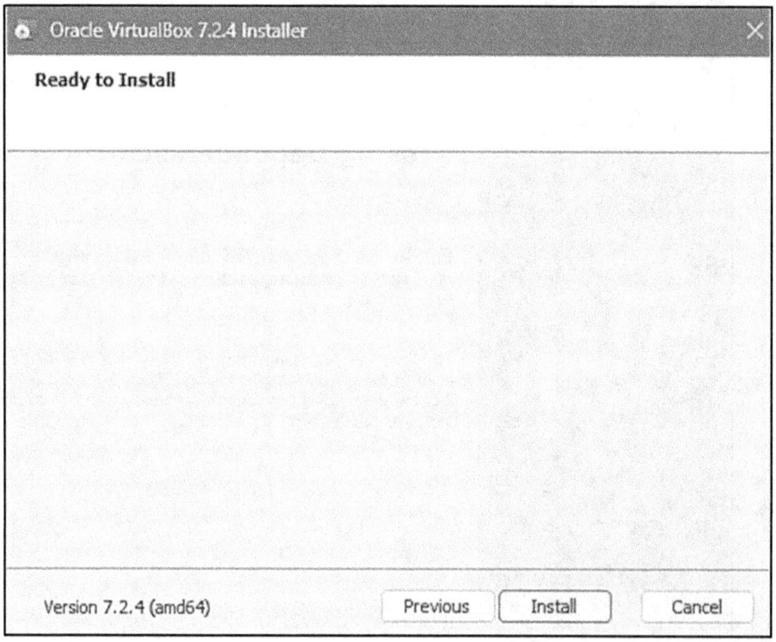

Figure 1-8 VirtualBox Installation 6

10. Once the installation completes successfully, click Finish to exit the setup wizard (Figure 1-9).

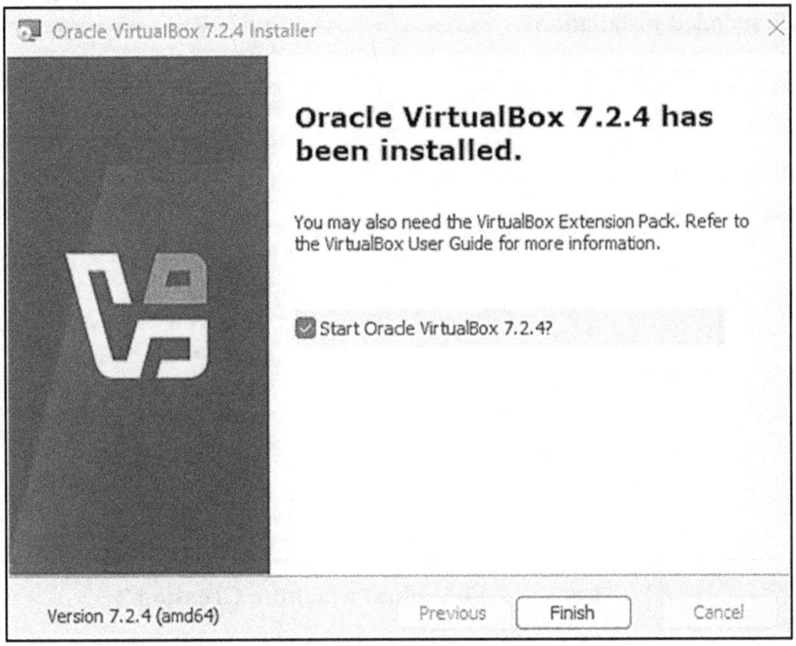

Figure 1-9 VirtualBox Installation 7

The VirtualBox program will launch when you click Finish.

Creating a Virtual Machine

Use VirtualBox to create the first virtual machine called *RHEL10-VM1* with specifications described earlier in this chapter. Here are the steps for VM creation.

1. Launch VirtualBox if it is not already running. The home screen looks similar to what is shown in Figure 1-10.

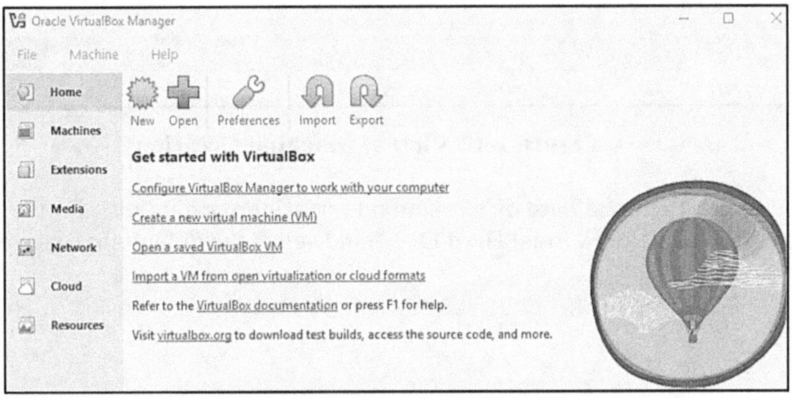

Figure 1-10 Virtual Machine Creation 1

2. Click on New on the top menu bar to launch the VM creation wizard as shown in Figure 1-11. Enter name *RHEL10-VM1*, select a location to store the VM files, choose Linux as the OS, Red Hat as the OS Distribution, and Red Hat (64-bit) as the OS version. Uncheck "Proceed with Unattended Installation".

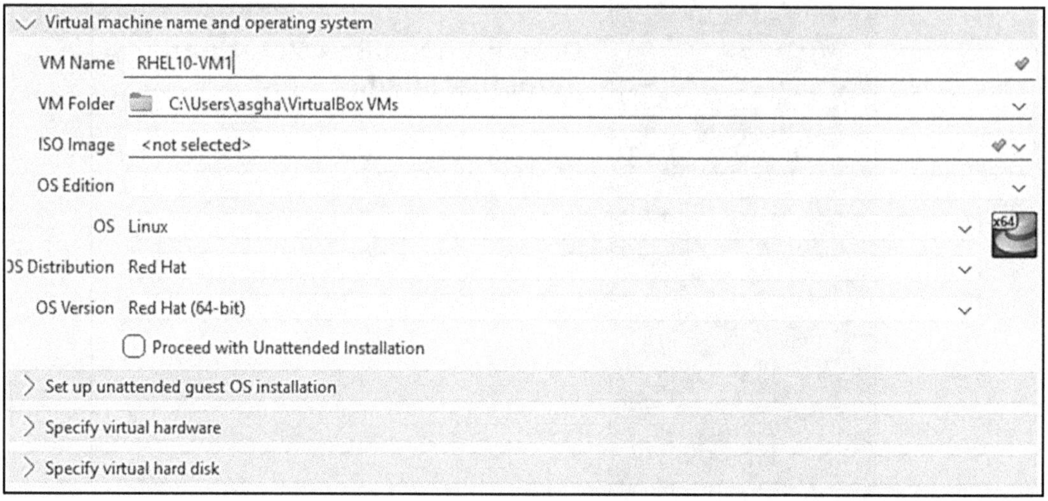

Figure 1-11 Virtual Machine Creation 2

3. Expand the "Specify virtual hardware" section, and set the memory to 2048 MB and CPU count to 2 (Figure 1-12).

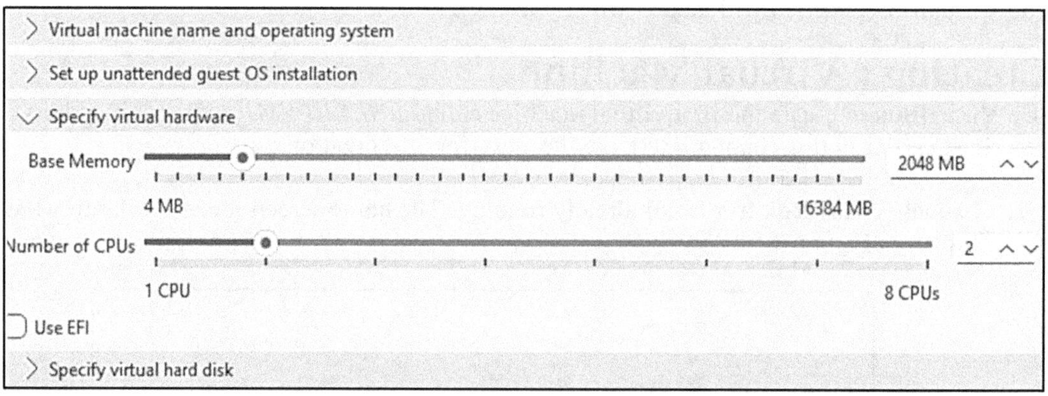

Figure 1-12 Virtual Machine Creation 3

4. Expand "Specify virtual hard disk" section to configure a hard disk for the OS (Figure 1-13). Choose "Create a New Virtual Hard Disk" and select the default disk size of 20 GB.

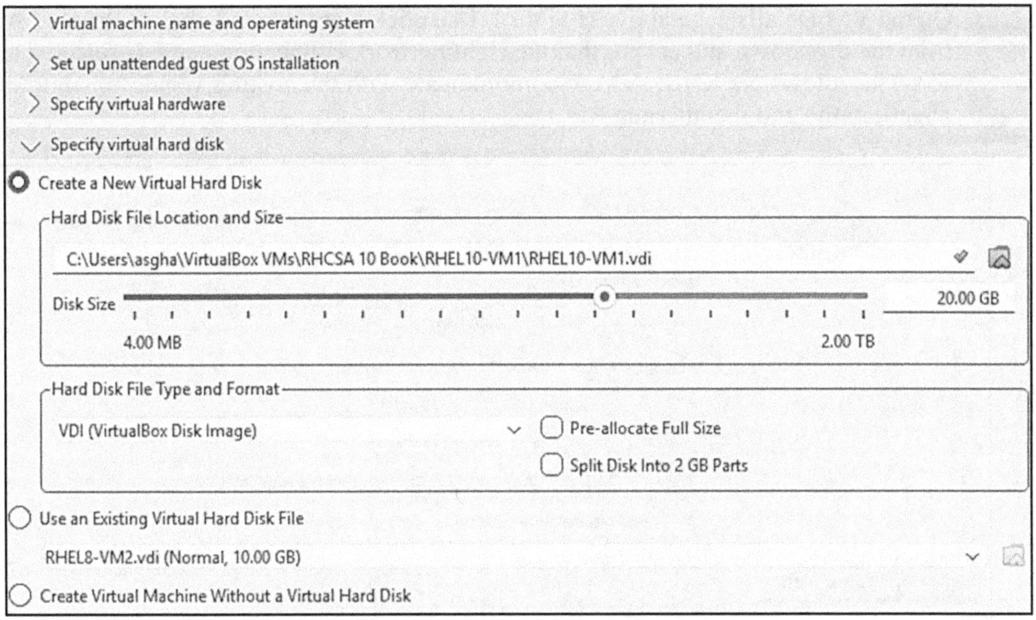

Figure 1-13 Virtual Machine Creation 4

5. VirtualBox will have the VM listed along with its configuration (Figure 1-14).

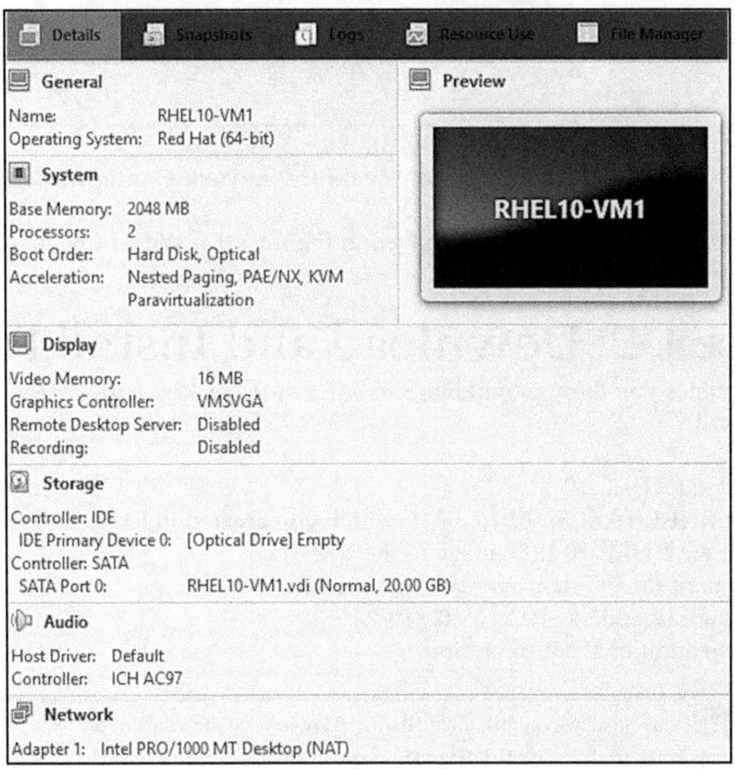

Figure 1-14 Virtual Machine Configuration Summary

6. On the VM Details page above (Figure 1-14), click Network and choose Bridged Adapter from the dropdown and ensure that the right network connection name is selected (Figure 1-15). This allows the RHEL VM to communicate with the hosting Windows computer bi-directionally, and the internet.

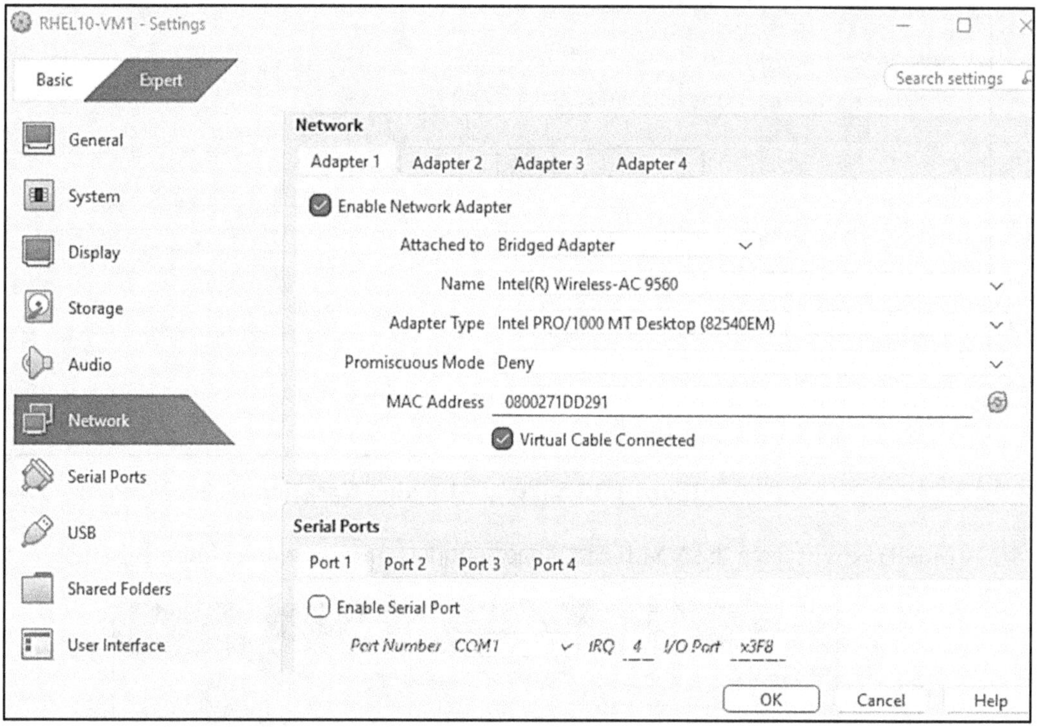

Figure 1-15 Virtual Machine Network Configuration

There are other configurable items as depicted in Figure 1-14. We will be making additional changes later.

Exercise 1-2: Download and Install RHEL

This exercise guides you through building *server1* inside the *RHEL10-VM1* virtual machine. In this exercise, you will:

- Download RHEL 10
- Install RHEL 10 in *RHEL10-VM1*, which you created in Exercise 1-1
- Attach the RHEL 10 ISO image to the VM
- Name the Linux system *server1.example.com*
- Configure IP address 192.168.0.110/24
- Perform additional configuration

EXAM TIP: Downloading and installing RHEL 10 are beyond the scope of the exam. They have been included here only to support the readers with building their own lab environment for practice.

Topics such as time synchronization, base environments, storage management, network device and connection configuration, and user creation, are not explained as part of this exercise; they are discussed in later chapters.

Downloading RHEL 10 ISO Image

RHEL 10 image is available as a free download from Red Hat Developer's website. You need to create a user account to log in and obtain a copy for yourself. You can alternatively use your GitHub, Google, or Microsoft credentials to log in. For this demonstration, you will find instructions on how to open a new account and download the software.

1. Visit *https://developers.redhat.com* and click on Login to get to the web page depicted in Figure 1-16.

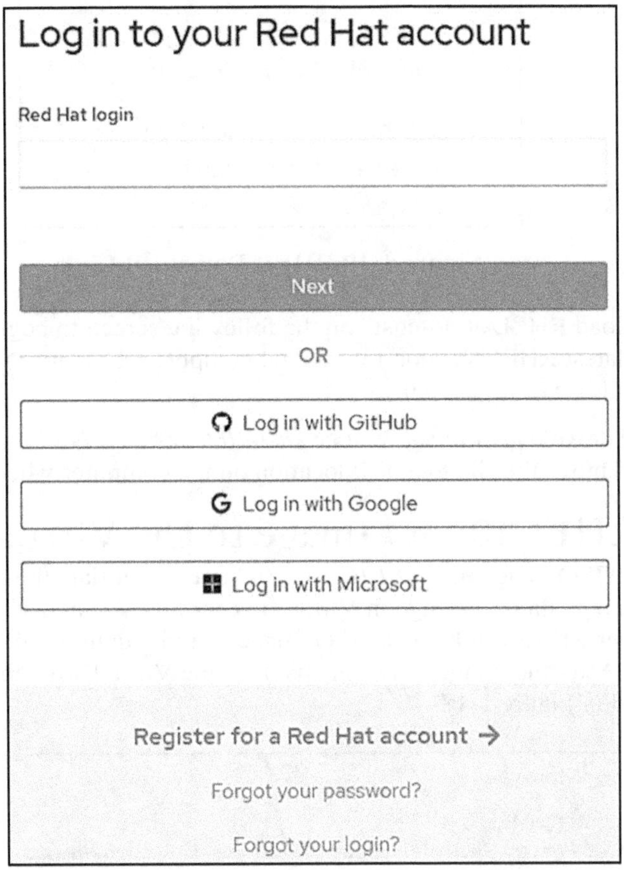

Figure 1-16 Red Hat Login / Account Creation

2. Enter the Red Hat login name if you already have one, click Next, and enter the password on the next screen to log in to the developer portal. You can register for an account if you do not already have one by clicking "Register for a Red Hat account". The third option is to use your GitHub, Google, or Microsoft account for signing in.
3. Click on "Red Hat Enterprise Linux" under "Featured products" after you have logged in (Figure 1-17).

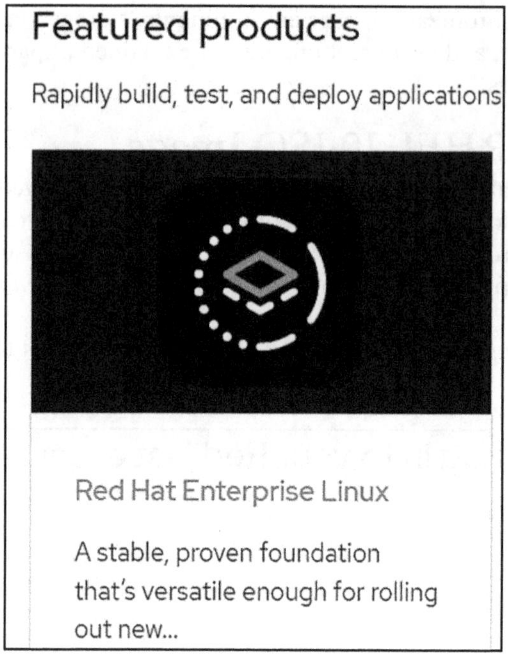

Figure 1-17 RHEL Download Link

4. Click "Download RHEL at no-cost" on the following screen to begin downloading the ISO image of the latest RHEL version for x86_64 computer. The latest version of RHEL available at the time of this writing is 10.0.

The filename of the downloaded image will be *rhel-10.0-x86_64-dvd.iso* and it will be around 8.2 GB in size. You can move the file to a disk location on the computer where you want it stored.

Attaching RHEL 10 ISO Image to the Virtual Machine

Attach the RHEL 10 ISO image to *RHEL10-VM1* to boot and initiate the installation. Click "[Optical Drive] Empty" under Storage in VirtualBox for this VM and select "Choose a Disk File". Navigate to the folder where you have the ISO image stored. Highlight the image and click Open to attach it to the VM. After the image has been attached, the VirtualBox Storage configuration will look like as depicted in Figure 1-18.

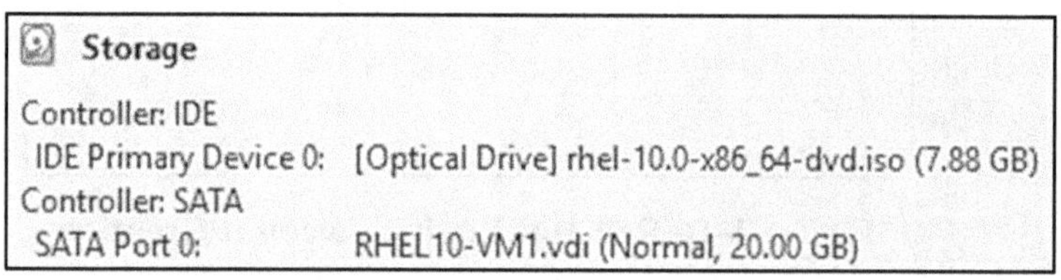

Figure 1-18 ISO Image Attached to VM

Leave the rest of the settings to their default values.

Launching the Installer Program

1. While the VM is highlighted in VirtualBox, click the Start button at the top to power it up.

2. A console screen appears displaying the boot menu with three options (Figure 1-19). Press the `Spacebar` within the 60-second countdown to halt the autoboot process. Then press the `UP` arrow key to select the first option, "Install Red Hat Enterprise Linux 10.0", and press `Enter` to boot. The installer launches in graphical mode.

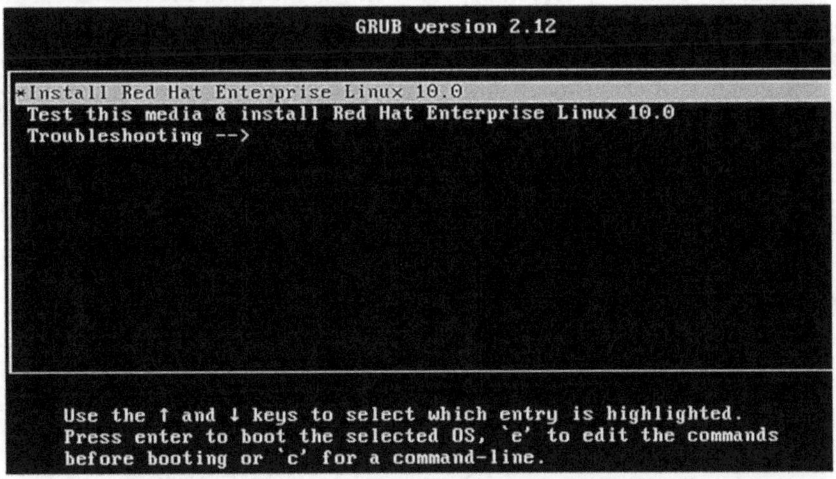

Figure 1-19 Boot Menu

If you want the installation media tested for integrity before proceeding, simply allow the countdown to expire without pressing `Spacebar`. The system continues with the default boot entry—the second option on the list—which performs the media check. The third option, "Troubleshooting", allows you to address boot-related issues that might arise during installation.

3. The installer program shows a welcome screen with a long list of supported languages that you could use during installation (Figure 1-20). The default is set to English. Click Continue to accept the default and move on.

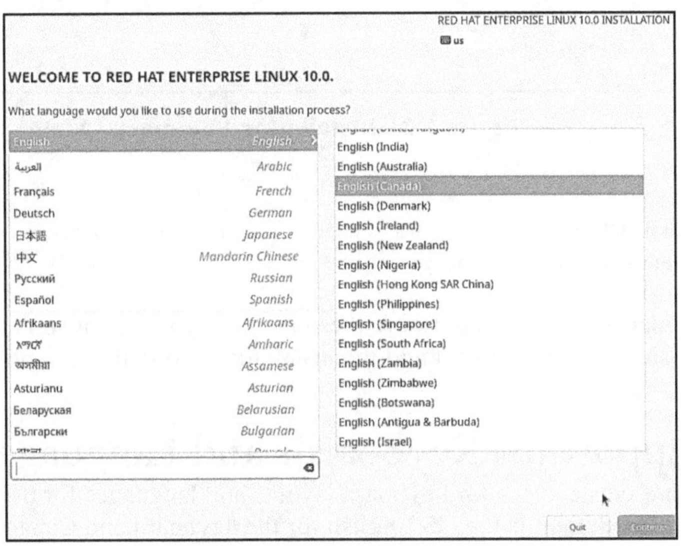

Figure 1-20 Language Selection

If all the content does not fit on the console screen, try changing the Graphics Controller to VMSVGA under Settings | Display in VirtualBox for the VM. You must power off the VM to make this change.

4. The Installation Summary screen appears next, as shown in Figure 1-21. You have the opportunity to make all necessary configuration changes prior to starting the installation. This screen presents a unified interface to configure localization (keyboard, language, date, time, and time zone), software (installation source and software selection), system (disk partitioning, network assignments, hostname setting, etc.), and user settings (root password and user creation).

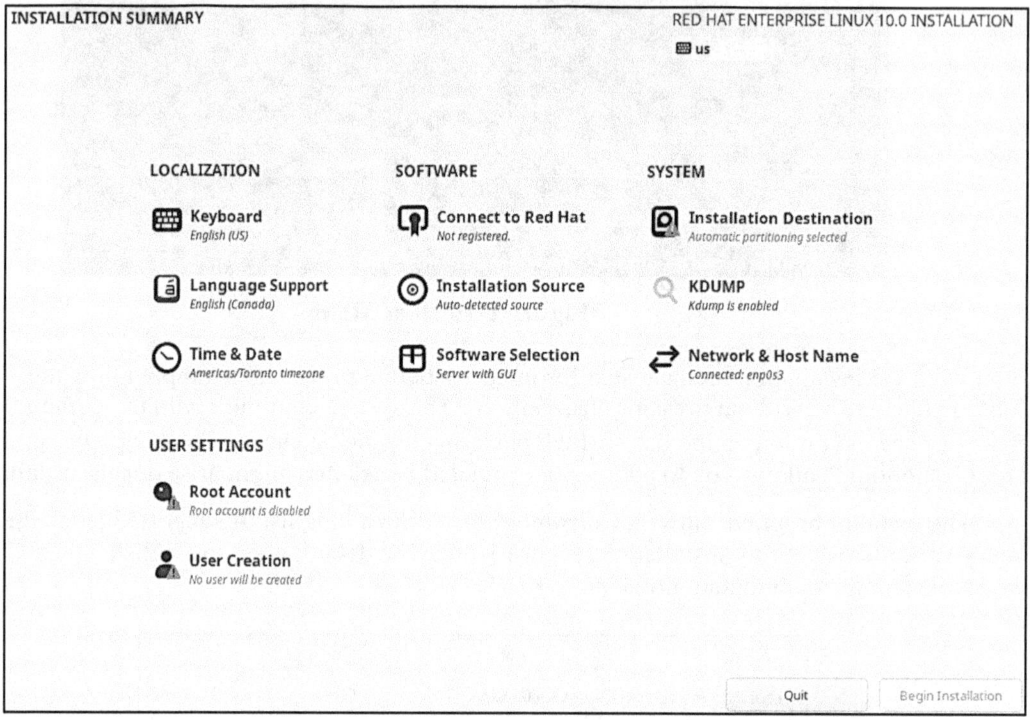

Figure 1-21 Installation Summary | Main

Any items highlighted in red and with a warning icon must be configured before the Begin Installation button at the bottom right of the screen becomes active.

There is no particular sequence to configure these items. If you do not wish to change a non-highlighted item, simply leave it intact and the installation program will apply the default settings for it.

Adding Support for Keyboards and Languages

5. Anaconda presents choices for keyboard layouts and languages for use during and after the installation. The default is the US English for the keyboard and Canadian English as the language (for my location). Go ahead and change them as required.

Configuring Time & Date

6. Click Time & Date to set the time zone (region and city), date, and time for the system (Figure 1-22). Click Done in the upper left corner to save the changes and return to the Installation Summary screen.

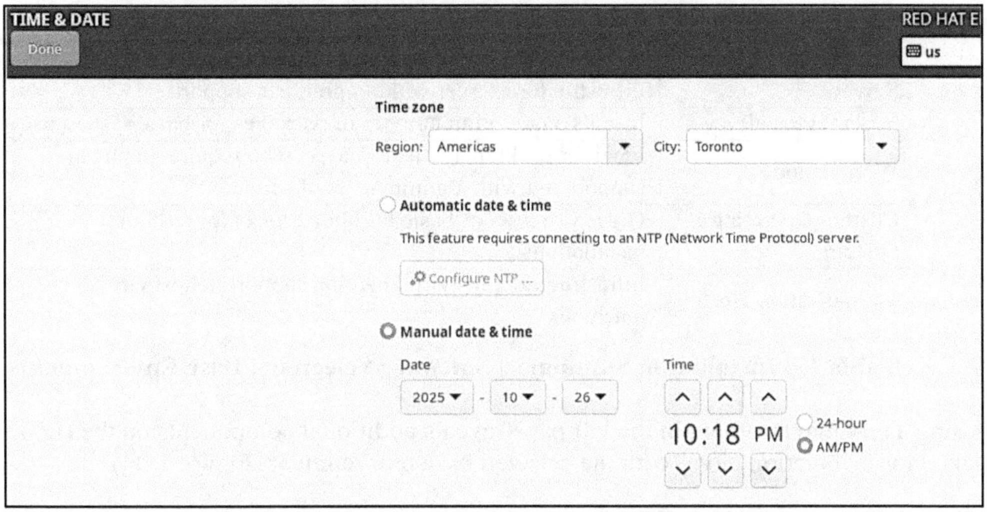

Figure 1-22 Installation Summary | Time & Date

Figure 1-22 reflects two adjustments from the default. The "Manual date & time" is selected, and the clock format is switched to AM/PM.

Choosing an Installation Source

7. You can set the installation source for RHEL 10. By default, Anaconda chooses the auto-detected installation medium (ISO image/DVD or USB flash drive) that was used to start this installation. For this demonstration, leave the installation source to the default. Click Done to return to the Installation Summary page.

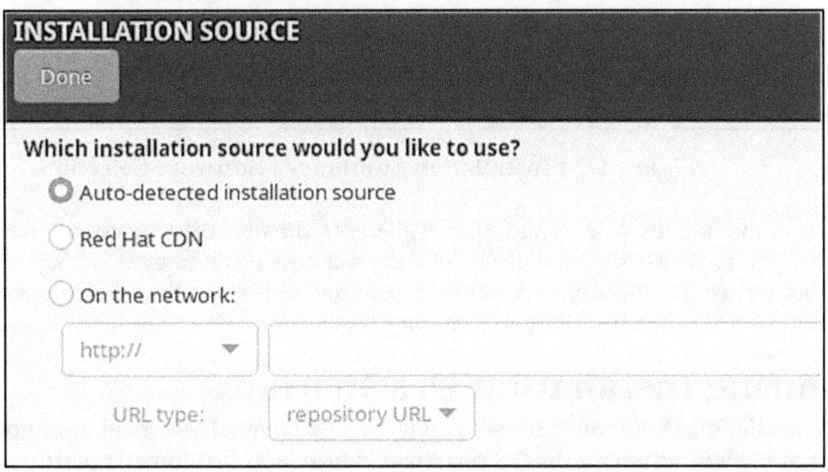

Figure 1-23 Installation Summary | Installation Source

Selecting Software to be Installed

8. You can choose the base operating environment that you want installed. Base environments are predefined groups of software packages designed for specific use cases. The six available base environments are described in Table 1-4.

Base Environment	Description
Server with GUI	Infrastructure server with graphics support
Server	Infrastructure server without graphics support
Minimal Install	Installs a minimum number of packages for basic system use
Workstation	Ideal for desktop and laptop users who require graphical support and with a minimal set of services
Custom Operating System	Gives you a set of basic building blocks for custom installations
Virtualization Host	Infrastructure plus virtualization support to host virtual machines

Table 1-4 Installation Summary | Software Selection | Base Environments

Choosing a base environment in the left pane reveals additional components on the right that may be ticked for installation along with the selected base environment (Figure 1-24).

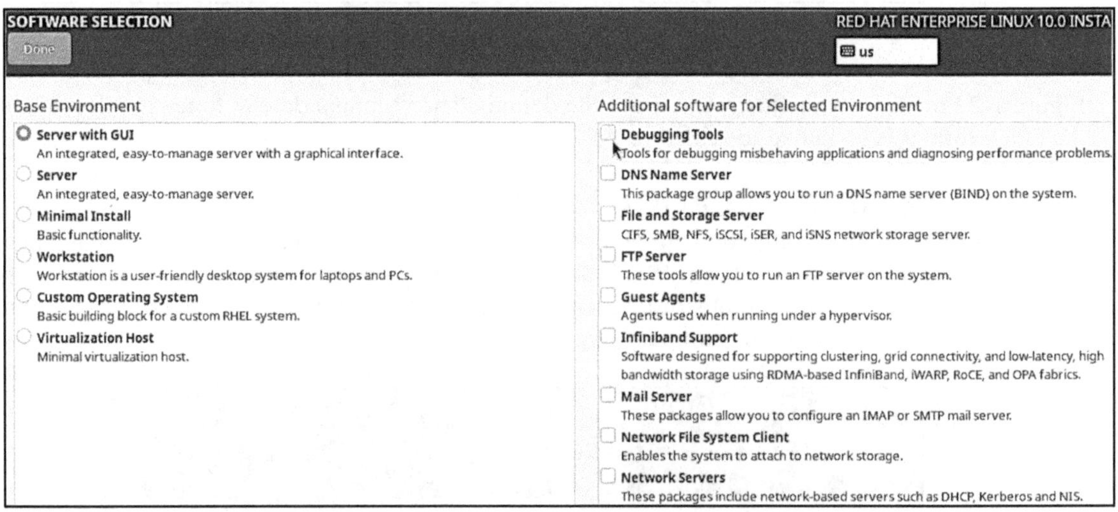

Figure 1-24 Installation Summary | Software Selection

The installer automatically selects and installs the prerequisite software components to fulfill all dependencies for a successful installation. The default base environment is "Server with GUI", which is what we use for this demonstration. Leave the add-ons at their default settings as well. Click Done to return to the Installation Summary page.

Configuring Installation Destination

9. The Installation Destination allows you to choose an available local or remote disk for partitioning and installing the OS on. Anaconda selects "Automatic partitioning selected" (highlighted in red) on the Installation Summary page (Figure 1-21 earlier), which you can

change on Installation Destination (Figure 1-25 below). By default, the 20 GB virtual disk you assigned to the VM is automatically picked up by the installer as the target and it is represented as *sda*. The "Encrypt my data" checkbox under Encryption (scroll down to see it) encrypts all partitions on the disk. If you choose this option, you will be prompted to enter a passphrase to access the partitions later. The "Full disk summary and bootloader" link at the bottom left allows you to choose a disk to place the bootloader program on. This does not need to be modified on a single disk system. The default and the only bootloader program available in RHEL is called GRUB2, and it is explained at length in Chapter 13, "Boot Process, GRUB2, and the Linux Kernel".

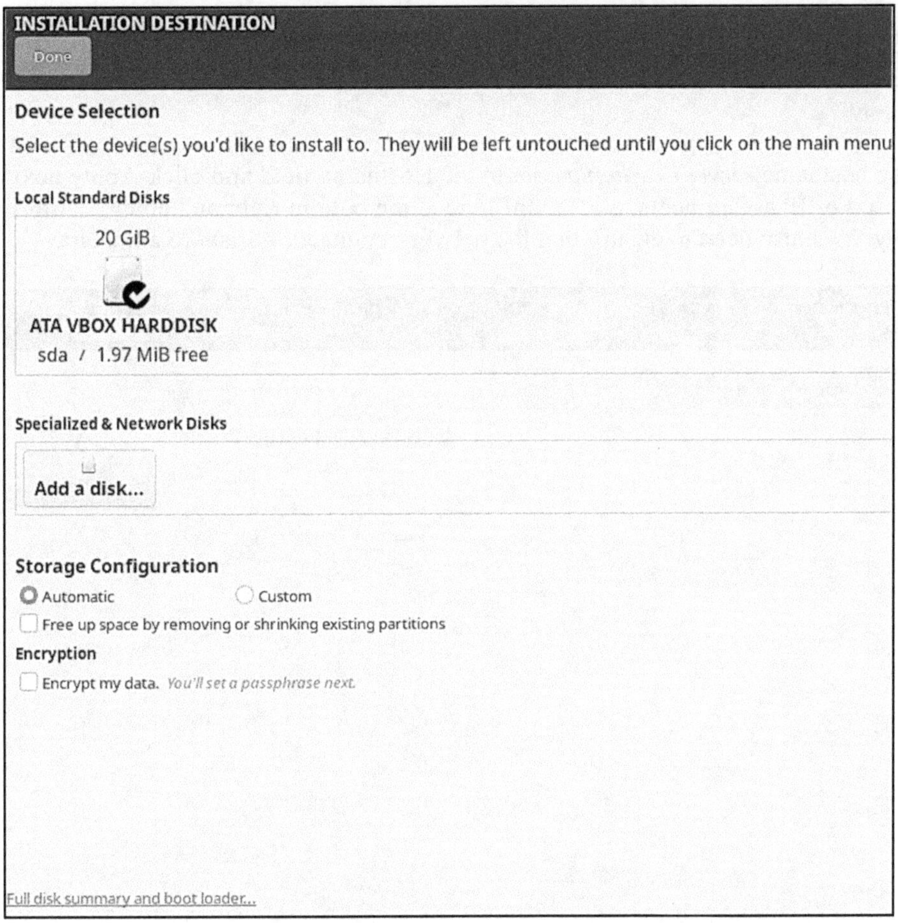

Figure 1-25 Installation Summary | Installation Destination

For this demonstration, stick to the default automatic partitioning scheme. Simply click Done to return to the previous screen. This scheme will create three partitions—*/boot*, */*, and swap—and together they will consume the entire disk space.

Configuring Network and Hostname

10. Assigning appropriate IP and hostname are essential for system functionality in a network environment. Click Network & Hostname on the Installation Summary page and a window

similar to the one shown in Figure 1-26 appears. Anaconda detects all attached network interfaces, but it does not automatically assign them IP addresses. Also, the default hostname field is empty. You need to modify these assignments so that your system can communicate with other systems on the network. Currently, there is one network device assigned to the system, which is represented as *enp0s3*.

The terms "network interface" and "network device" refer to the same physical or virtual hardware component and are used interchangeably throughout this book. These terms are different from the term "network connection", which is the software configuration applied to a network interface/device.

The default naming convention for network devices vary based on the underlying virtualization software being used.

Enter the hostname *server1.example.com* in the Hostname field and click Apply next to the field to activate it. For IP assignments, click Configure at the bottom right and enter IP information manually. You also need to ensure that the network connection is set to autostart.

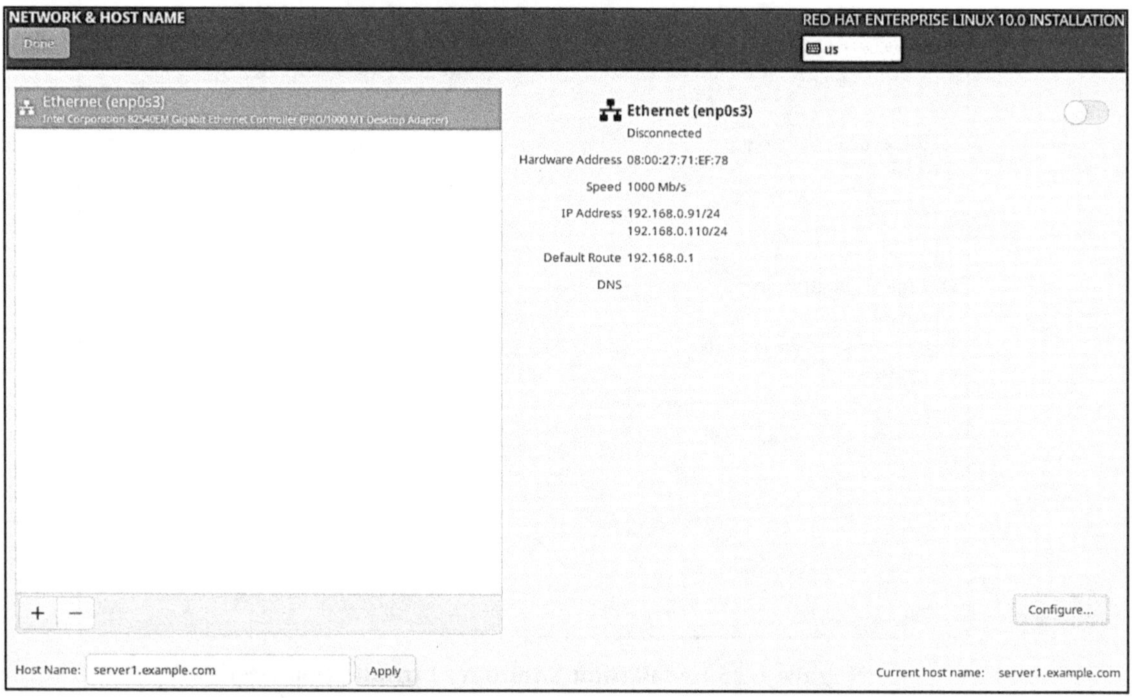

Figure 1-26 Installation Summary | Network & Hostname

There are multiple tabs available on the network connection configuration screen, as depicted in Figure 1-27. Go to IPv4 Settings and choose Manual from the drop-down list against Method. Click Add and enter address 192.168.0.110, netmask 24, and gateway 192.168.0.1. Click Save to save the configuration and return to the Network & Hostname window.

Check your Windows/macOS host computer IP assignments and make sure to use the same subnet for your RHEL VMs. For instance, use 172.16.3.110/120 for your VMs if your host system is on the 172.16.3 subnet.

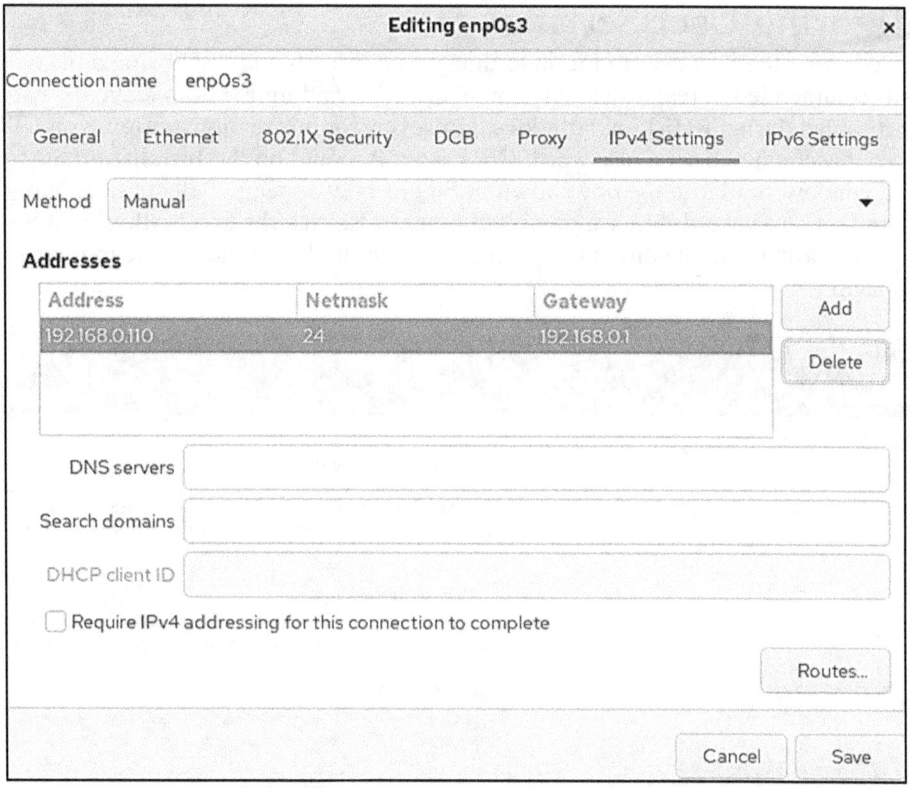

Figure 1-27 Installation Summary | Network & Hostname | Configure

On the Network & Hostname window, slide the ON/OFF switch to the ON position to activate the new assignments right away. This will also ensure that the assignments are applied automatically on subsequent system reboots.

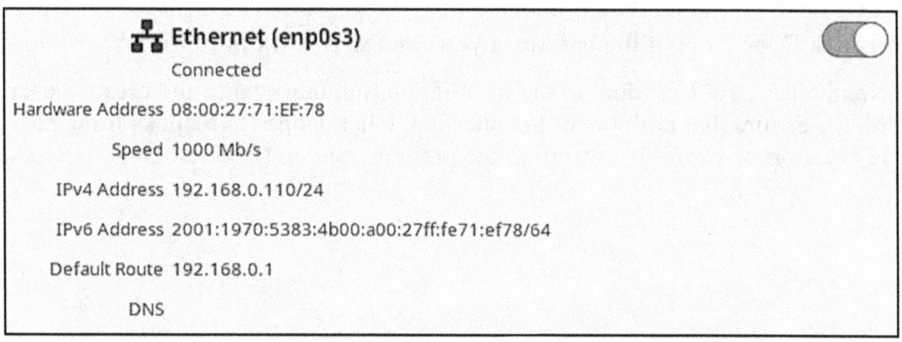

Figure 1-28 Installation Summary | Network & Hostname | Activate

Now click Done to return to the Installation Summary page. Chapter 17 "Networking Essentials and Network Connections" discusses configuring hostnames, network interfaces, and network connections in detail.

Configuring User Settings

11. Allowing the *root* user to log in to the system directly via SSH using a password is not recommended in real-world environments. Many administrators leave the *root* account disabled during RHEL installations. However, for this demonstration, you will enable the root account and set a password. Click Root Account on the Installation Summary page and a window similar to the one shown in Figure 1-29 appears. Select "Enable root account" and set a password. Enter a password twice. Also tick the box "Allow root SSH login with password" to enable direct root login access to the VM. Click Done to return to the previous page.

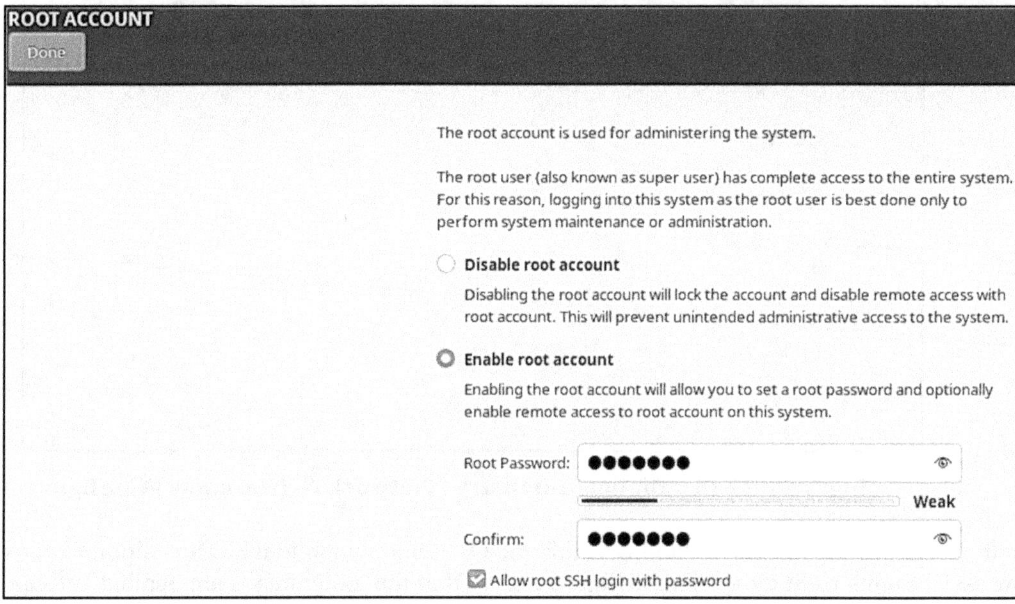

Figure 1-29 Installation Summary | Root Password

You must click Done twice if the password you entered is weak or too short.

12. Next, click User Creation on the Installation Summary page and create a user account called *user1*. Ensure that both boxes are checked. Click Done (two clicks if the password entered is too short or simple) to return to the previous screen (Figure 1-30).

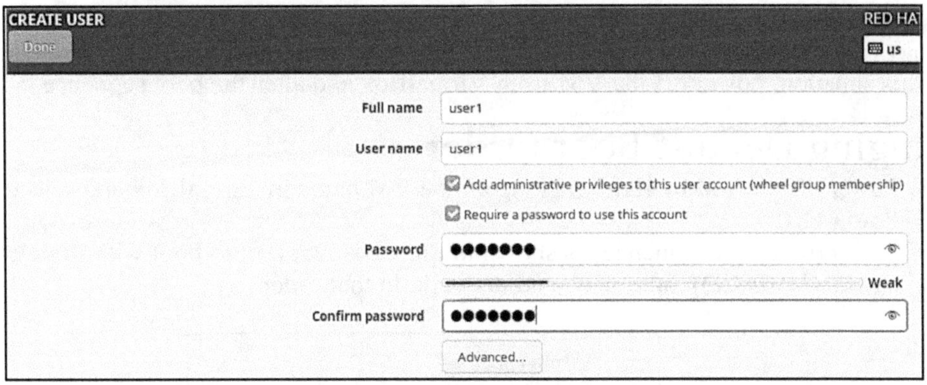

Figure 1-30 Installation Summary | User Creation

Anaconda will set the *root* user password and create the user account during installation.

Beginning Installation

13. You are now on the Installation Summary page. At this stage, you can still go back to review, configure, or reconfigure any settings you may have missed. Once you are satisfied with all configurations, click Begin Installation at the bottom-right corner to start the installation process. Anaconda will partition the selected disk, install the required software, and complete all configuration tasks. Note that any existing data on the selected disk will be permanently erased.

The Begin Installation button remains inactive until all items highlighted in red or marked with a warning icon have been properly configured.

The configuration and file copying process may take some time. The duration depends on the system's performance and the resources allocated to the VM.

Concluding Installation

14. Once the installation is complete and all software packages have been installed, the Reboot System button at the bottom right of the Installation Progress screen (Figure 1-31) will become active. Click this button to reboot the new system.

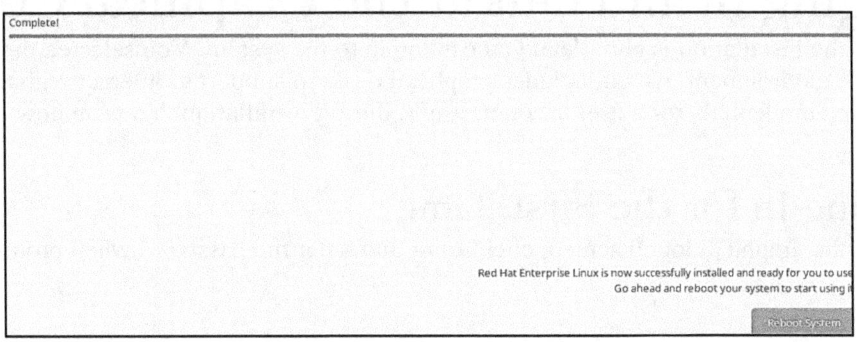

Figure 1-31 Configuration | Finishing Installation

By default, VirtualBox does not automatically change the default device boot order for the VM. This may result in rebooting the VM from the ISO image again and restarting the installation. To avoid this situation, power off the VM from VirtualBox and alter the boot sequence.

Changing Default Boot Order

15. Power off the VM by right-clicking on the VM name in VirtualBox and selecting Stop | Power Off.
16. The current boot sequence, as shown in Figure 1-32, is set to boot with floppy first and then optical (DVD/CD), hard disk, and network, in that order.

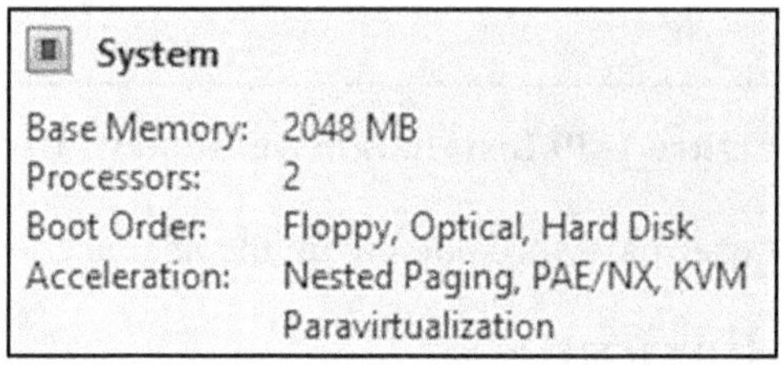

Figure 1-32 VirtualBox | System | Boot Order

17. Change this sequence to hard disk first and optical next (Figure 1-33). Untick Floppy and Network, as they are not needed.

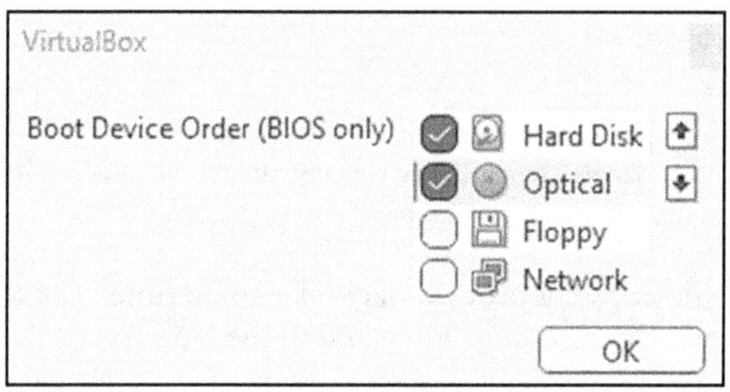

Figure 1-33 VirtualBox | System | Boot Order | Alter

Power on the VM from VirtualBox. It will boot the installed OS.

Logging In and Out at the Graphical Console

Now that the installation is complete, you can log in to the system. You selected the "Server with GUI" base environment, which includes graphical desktop support to interact with the system. You also entered credentials for a user account, *user1*, during installation. You can now use this account to log in.

Logging In for the First Time

1. On the graphical logon screen, click *user1* and enter the password when prompted.

Figure 1-34 Graphical Desktop | Sign-in Screen

2. Click "No Thanks" when prompted for a tour.
3. The default graphical desktop included in RHEL 10 is the GNOME desktop environment (Figure 1-35). You should now be able to start using the system as *user1*.

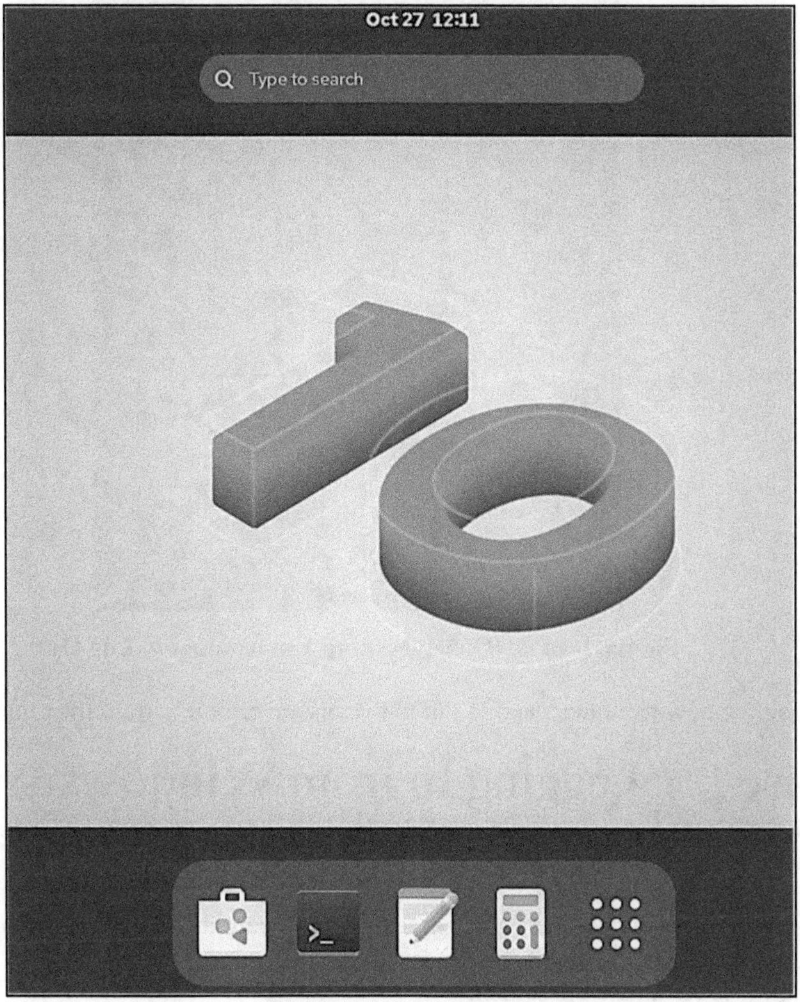

Figure 1-35 GNOME Desktop Environment

You can close the "System Not Registered" message, as you did not configure the "Connect to Red Hat" option under Installation Summary | Software during installation configuration.

GNOME stands for *GNU Network Object Model Environment*. It is the default graphical display manager and desktop environment in RHEL 10. Chapter 02 "Initial System Interaction" discusses more on this topic.

Logging Out

4. Logging out of the system is straightforward. Click on any icon in the top right corner and then on the Power Off icon (Figure 1-36). Click "Log Out" and then confirm. This will sign out *user1* in 60 seconds and present the main login screen again.

Figure 1-36 GNOME Desktop Environment | Log Out

Now, let's look at how to connect and log in to the system remotely from over the network.

Exercise 1-3: Logging In from Windows

Perform this exercise on the Windows computer hosting the virtual machine for *server1*. In this exercise, you will:

- Use a program called *PuTTY* to access *server1* using its IP address as *user1*
- Run some basic commands on the server for validation
- Log off to terminate the session

1. On Windows desktop, download PuTTY free of charge from the Internet. Launch this program and enter the target system's IP address (Figure 1-37). Leave the rest of the settings to their defaults.

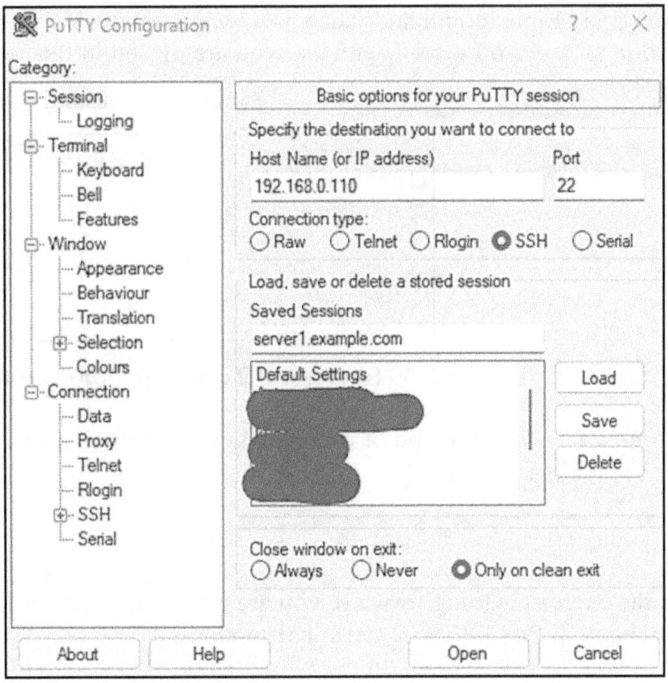

Figure 1-37 PuTTY Interface

You may assign a name to this session (typically the system's hostname is used as the session name) in the Saved Sessions field and click Save to store this information so as to avoid retyping in the future.

2. Click on the Open button at the bottom of the screen to connect.
3. Click Yes to accept a potential security breach warning. This alert only appears once.
4. Enter *user1* at the "login as" prompt and then the password to log in (Figure 1-38):

```
login as: user1
user1@192.168.0.110's password:
Web console: https://server1.example.com:9090/ or https://192.168.0.110:909

Register this system with Red Hat Insights: rhc connect

Example:
# rhc connect --activation-key <key> --organization <org>

The rhc client and Red Hat Insights will enable analytics and additional
management capabilities on your system.
View your connected systems at https://console.redhat.com/insights

You can learn more about how to register your system
using rhc at https://red.ht/registration
Last login: Sun Nov 16 09:19:53 2025

[user1@server1 ~]$
```

Figure 1-38 Remote Terminal Login Session

5. Issue some basic Linux commands such as *whoami*, *hostname*, and *pwd* to confirm that you are logged in as *user1* on *server1* and that you are placed in the correct home directory (Figure 1-39):

```
[user1@server1 ~]$ whoami
user1
[user1@server1 ~]$ hostname
server1.example.com
[user1@server1 ~]$ pwd
/home/user1
[user1@server1 ~]$
```

Figure 1-39 Successful Terminal Connection

6. Run the *logout* or *exit* command or press the key combination `Ctrl+d` to log off and terminate the login session:

```
[user1@server1 ~]$ logout
```

This concludes the exercise. Going forward, you are expected to perform all the exercises and labs presented in this book in PuTTY (SSH) terminal sessions.

Chapter Summary

This chapter has taken us from theory to practice. We began by understanding the RHEL platform, then moved to the critical preparation of our lab environment. We successfully downloaded the necessary software, created virtual machines in VirtualBox, and performed a customized installation of RHEL 10 using the Anaconda installer. The process included configuring key items like software selection, disk partitioning, network settings, and user accounts.

Finally, we verified our success by accessing the systems both through their graphical consoles and remotely via an SSH client. With both servers now operational, our lab environment is ready.

Review Questions

1. RHEL 10 cannot be installed over the network. True or False?
2. Can you install RHEL 10 in text mode?
3. You can use the */boot* partition inside an LVM volume to boot RHEL. True or False?
4. Which kernel version is the initial release of RHEL 10 based on?
5. Several log files are created and updated in the */tmp* directory during the installation process. Where are these files moved to after the completion of installation?
6. The Minimal Install base environment includes the graphical support. True or False?
7. Name the RHEL installer program.
8. How many consoles do you have access to during the installation process?
9. RHEL 10 can be downloaded from Red Hat's developer site. True or False?
10. What is the name of the default graphical user desktop if Server with GUI is installed?

Answers to Review Questions

1. False. RHEL 10 can be installed with installation files located on a network server.
2. Yes, RHEL 10 can be installed in text mode.

3. False. */boot* cannot reside within LVM.
4. The initial release of RHEL 10 is based on kernel version 6.12.
5. These files are moved to the */var/log* directory.
6. False. Minimal Install base environment does not include graphics support.
7. The name of the RHEL installer program is Anaconda.
8. There are six consoles available to you during the installation process.
9. True. RHEL 10 can be downloaded from *developers.redhat.com*. You need to open a new account or use an existing account before you can download it.
10. The default graphical desktop is called GNOME.

Do-It-Yourself Challenge Labs

The following labs are designed to reinforce most of the concepts and skills covered in this chapter. You are expected to complete these labs without external assistance. A step-by-step guide is not provided, as the required knowledge has already been presented in the chapter; however, each lab includes hints pointing to the relevant major topic(s).

Lab 1-1: Build RHEL10-VM2 (server2)

Create another virtual machine called *RHEL10-VM2* in VirtualBox, attach the ISO image to it, and install RHEL 10. Use the configuration provided in "Lab Environment for Practice" and follow the procedures outlined in Exercises 1-1 and 1-2. Follow Exercise 1-3 to connect to the new server.

Chapter 02

Initial System Interaction

By the end of this chapter, you will be able to:

- Navigate the GNOME Desktop and Wayland Display Protocol
- Explain the Linux Filesystem Hierarchy Standard
- Identify and Describe the Top-Level RHEL Directories
- Describe Command-Line Fundamentals
- Use Core Linux Commands for Navigation and Inspection
- Access Help using Native Tools and Documentation

RHCSA Objectives:

01. Access a shell prompt and issue commands with correct syntax
11. Locate, read, and use system documentation including man, info, and files in /usr/share/doc

NOW that you have a working RHEL system, it is time to learn how to communicate with it. This chapter introduces the two primary interfaces you will use: the graphical desktop for intuitive point-and-click tasks and the command-line terminal for precise control. You will explore the Linux filesystem layout, which organizes all files and directories logically for ease of administration, and understand the purpose of key top-level directories.

You will then learn the mechanics of how commands are constructed and apply that knowledge by running fundamental commands for navigation, file listing, and system inspection. Finally, you will discover how to find help when you need it—a critical skill for every Linux administrator.

Linux Graphical Environment

RHEL supports both text-based and graphical environments. While text interfaces present greater complexity, administrators and developers often prefer them for their power and flexibility. Graphical environments simplify OS interaction by abstracting the underlying complexities inherent in text-mode operation.

Wayland is a display protocol that sets up the foundation for running graphical programs and applications. It is the default and the only display protocol used in RHEL 10. Wayland provides superior graphics capabilities, features, and performance. There are two components critical to the functionality of a graphical environment: a *display manager* (a.k.a. *login manager*) and a *desktop environment*. Both are launched following the completion of the groundwork established by Wayland.

Display Manager

A display manager presents the graphical login screen, allowing you to enter credentials to log on to the system. A preconfigured graphical desktop manager appears after the credentials are verified. In RHEL 10, the default display manager is called *GNOME Display Manager* (GDM). Figure 2-1 provides an image of GDM.

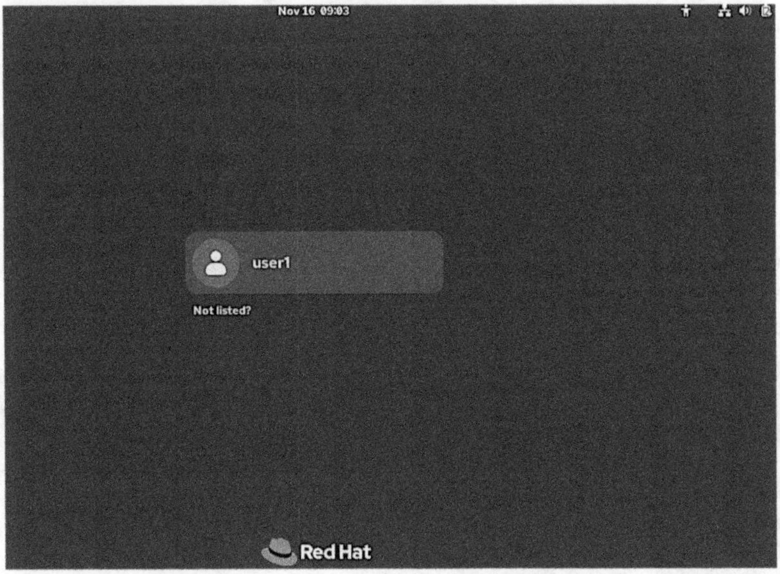

Figure 2-1 GNOME Display Manager

The login screen presents a list of all normal user accounts that exist on the system. You can log in as any one of them by selecting the desired account. To sign in as an unlisted user or the *root* user, click "Not Listed?" and enter the username and password for the desired account. The current system date and time also appear at the top of the login screen.

The human icon at the top right of the login screen provides access to accessibility features that you can enable if needed. The group of icons next to it allows you to enable or disable network connectivity, adjust system volume, and manage power options, including restarting or powering off the system. Additional controls become available after you log in.

Desktop Environment

Once your credentials are validated, the display/login manager starts your *Desktop Environment* (DE). In RHEL 10, the GNOME desktop environment is the default and the only officially supported graphical environment. GNOME provides an intuitive point-and-click interface for running applications and system tools. Figure 2-2 shows the default GNOME desktop environment.

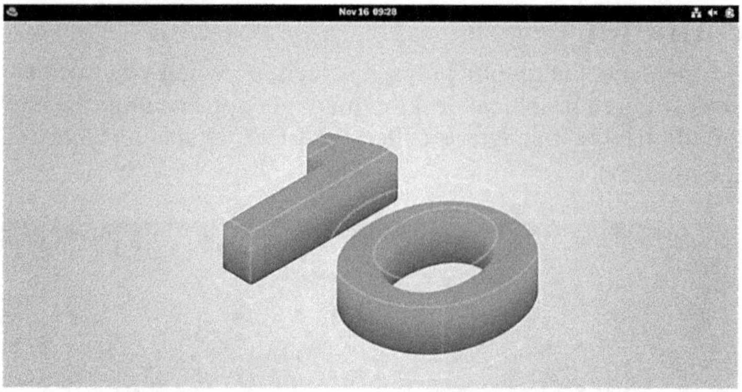

Figure 2-2 GNOME Desktop Environment | Main

If you have worked with Microsoft Windows or macOS, you should have no difficulty using this desktop. The red hat icon in the top-left corner allows you to search for and access programs. Figure 2-3 shows several application icons that appear at the bottom when you click the red hat icon.

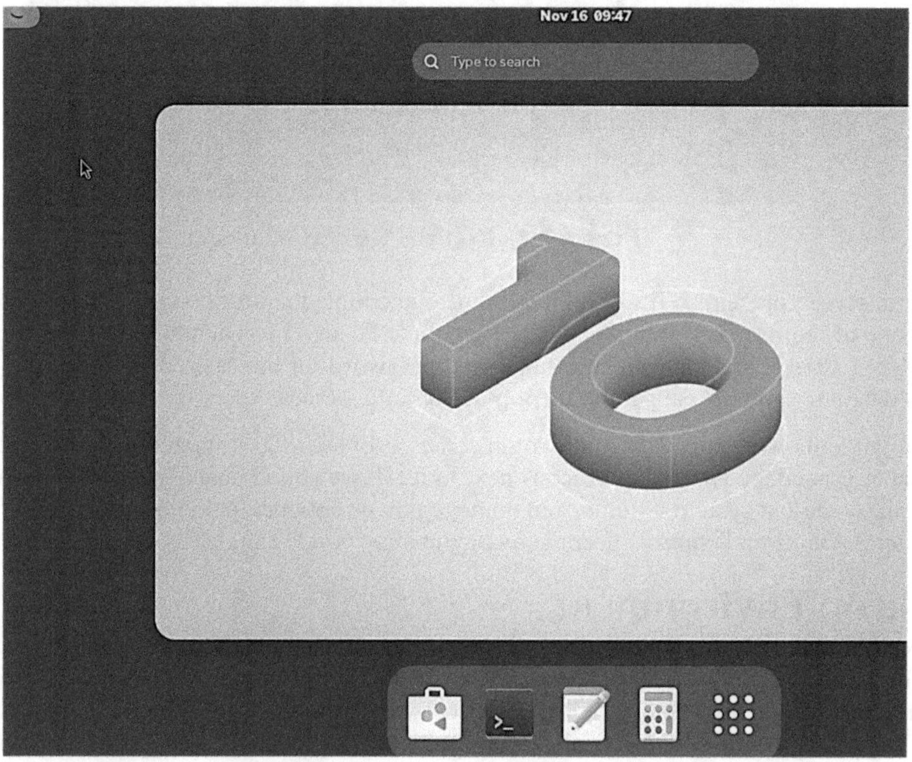

Figure 2-3 GNOME Desktop Environment | Red Hat Icon

The application icons represent, from left to right, the software manager, shell terminal, text editor, and calculator. The icon with nine dots opens a list of additional applications, including Settings. The Settings application provides both administrative and user-level options for viewing or modifying system configuration, such as Wi-Fi, Bluetooth, desktop background, notifications, regional settings, privacy, sound, power, screensaver, network, and more.

Linux Directory Structure and File Systems

Linux uses a hierarchical file structure that simplifies administration and file management. This structure comprises numerous directories organized within larger containers called *file systems*. Red Hat Enterprise Linux follows the *Filesystem Hierarchy Standard* (FHS) for file organization, which describes names, locations, and permissions for many file types and directories.

Linux file systems contain files and subdirectories. A subdirectory, also called a *child* directory, is located under a *parent* directory. The parent directory is a subdirectory of a higher-level directory. The Linux directory structure resembles an inverted tree, where the top of the tree is the root of the directory, branches are subdirectories, and leaves are files. The root of the directory is represented by the forward slash character (/), and this is where the entire directory structure is ultimately connected.

The forward slash is also used as a directory separator in pathnames, such as */etc/rc.d/init.d/README*. In this example, the *etc* subdirectory is located under /, making *root* the parent of *etc* (child), *rc.d* (child) is located under *etc* (parent), *init.d* (child) is located under *rc.d* (parent), and *README* (leaf) is located under *init.d* (parent) at the bottom.

The term *subdirectory* is used for a directory that has a parent directory.

Each directory has a parent directory and a child directory, with the exception of the root and the lowest level subdirectories. The root directory has no parent, and the lowest level subdirectory has no child.

Top-Level Directories

The key top-level directories under the root (/) directory are shown in Figure 2-4. Some of these hold *static* data while others contain *dynamic* or *variable* information. Static data refers to file content that remains unchanged unless modified explicitly. Dynamic or variable data, in contrast, refers to file content that is modified and updated as required by system processes. Static directories normally contain commands, configuration files, library routines, kernel files, device files, etc., and dynamic directories contain log files, status files, temporary files, etc.

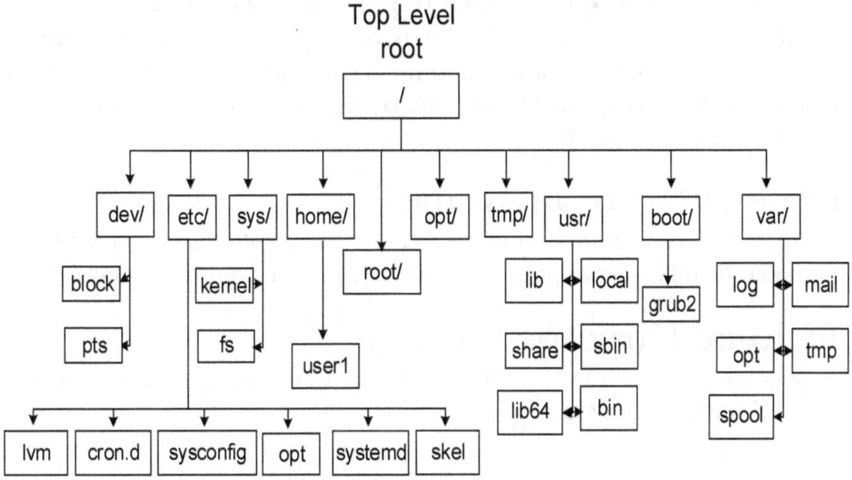

Figure 2-4 Linux Directory Structure

The hierarchical directory structure keeps related information together in a logical fashion. Compare this concept with a file cabinet containing several drawers, with each drawer storing multiple file folders.

File System Categories

RHEL supports a variety of file system types, which can be categorized into three basic groups: *disk-based*, *network-based*, and *memory-based*. Disk-based file systems are typically created on physical media such as a hard drive or a USB flash drive. Network-based file systems are essentially disk-based file systems that are shared over the network for remote access. Memory-based file systems are virtual; they are created automatically at system startup and destroyed when the system goes down. The first two types of file systems store information persistently, while any data saved in virtual file systems is lost at system reboots.

During RHEL installation, two disk-based file systems are created when you select the default partitioning. These file systems are called root and boot. Furthermore, several memory-based file systems are vital to the operation of a RHEL system.

The Root File System (/), Disk-Based

The *root* directory is the top-level file system in the FHS and contains many higher-level directories that store specific information. Some of the key directories are:

/etc: The *etcetera* (or *extended text configuration*) directory holds system configuration files. Some common subdirectories are *systemd*, *sysconfig*, *lvm*, and *skel*, which comprise configuration files for systemd, most system services, the Logical Volume Manager, and per-user shell startup template files, respectively.

/root: This is the default home directory location for the *root* user.

/mnt: This directory is used to mount a file system temporarily.

The size of the root file system is determined automatically by the installer based on the available disk space when you select the default partitioning; but can be altered at the time of installation if required.

The Boot File System (/boot), Disk-Based

The *boot* file system contains the Linux kernel, boot support files, and boot configuration files. As with the *root* file system, its size is also determined automatically by the installer based on the available disk space when you select the default partitioning; but can be set to a different size during or after the installation if required.

The Home Directory (/home)

The */home* directory aims to store user *home* directories and other user contents. Each user is assigned a home directory to save personal files, and the user can block access to other users.

The Optional Directory (/opt)

This directory is typically used for installing additional third-party software. A subdirectory is created for each installed software.

The UNIX System Resources Directory (/usr)

This directory contains most of the system files. Some of the important subdirectories are:

/usr/bin: The *binary* directory contains crucial user executable commands.

/usr/sbin: Most commands are required at system boot, and those that require the *root* user privileges to run are located in this *system binary* directory. In other words, this directory contains crucial system administration commands that are not intended for execution by normal users (although they can still run a few of them). This directory is not included in the default search path for normal users because of the nature of data it holds.

/usr/lib and **/usr/lib64:** The *library* directories contain shared library routines required by many commands and programs located in the */usr/bin* and */usr/sbin* directories, and by the kernel and other applications and programs for their successful installation and operation. The */usr/lib* directory also stores system initialization and service management programs. The subdirectory */usr/lib64* contains 64-bit shared library routines.

/usr/include: This directory contains header files for *C* language.

/usr/local: This directory serves as a system administrator repository for storing commands and tools downloaded from the web, developed in-house, or obtained elsewhere. These commands and tools are not generally included with the original Linux distribution. In particular, */usr/local/bin* holds executables, */usr/local/etc* holds configuration files, and */usr/local/lib* and */usr/local/lib64* holds library routines.

/usr/share: This is the directory location for manual pages, documentation, sample templates, configuration files, etc., that may be shared with other Linux platforms.

/usr/src: This directory is used to store source code.

The Variable Directory (/var)

The */var* directory contains data that frequently changes while the system is operational. Files in this directory contain log, status, spool, lock, and other dynamic data. Some common subdirectories under */var* are:

/var/log: This is the storage for most system log files, such as system logs, boot logs, user logs, failed user logs, installation logs, cron logs, mail logs, etc.

/var/opt: This directory stores log, status, and other variable data files for additional software installed in */opt*.

/var/spool: Directories that hold print jobs, cron jobs, mail messages, and other queued items before being sent out to their intended destinations are located here.

/var/tmp: Large temporary files or temporary files that need to exist for longer periods of time than what is typically allowed in another temporary directory, */tmp*, are stored here. These files survive system reboots and are automatically deleted if they are not accessed or modified for a period of 30 days.

The Temporary Directory (/tmp)

This directory is a repository for temporary files that are created by programs during runtime or installation. These files survive system reboots and are automatically removed if they have not been accessed or modified for 10 days.

The Devices File System (/dev), Virtual

The *Devices* (*dev file system*) file system is accessible via the */dev* directory. It stores device files (*device nodes*) that represent physical hardware and virtual devices on the system. The Linux kernel interacts with devices by reading from and writing to these device files. RHEL uses the *systemd-udevd* device management service to dynamically create or remove device files in */dev* as devices are added or deleted.

Device files fall into two main categories: *character* (or *raw*) devices and *block* devices.

Character devices: transfer data one byte at a time in a serial stream. Examples include terminals, serial ports, mice, keyboards, and sound devices.

Block devices: transfer data in fixed-size blocks and support random access. Examples include hard drives, SSDs, and optical drives.

The Procfs File System (/proc), Virtual

The *Procfs* (*process file system*) file system is accessible through the */proc* directory. It is used to maintain information about the current state of the running kernel. This includes the details for current hardware configuration and status information on CPU, memory, disks, partitioning, file systems, networking, running processes, and so on. This information is stored in a hierarchy of subdirectories that contain thousands of zero-length pseudo files. These files point to relevant data maintained by the kernel in the memory. This virtual directory structure simply provides an easy interface to interact with kernel-maintained information. The Procfs file system is dynamically managed by the system.

The contents in */proc* are created in memory at system boot time, updated during runtime, and destroyed at system shutdown.

The Runtime File System (/run), Virtual

This virtual file system stores runtime data needed by running processes and services. One of its subdirectories, */run/media*, is commonly used by GDM to automatically mount removable media, such as optical discs and USB flash drives when they are inserted.

The contents of this file system are automatically deleted at system shutdown.

The System File System (/sys), Virtual

The */sys* directory contains the sysfs virtual file system, which provides a structured view of kernel data related to devices, device drivers, and certain kernel subsystems. Sysfs exposes this information to user space to allow system tools to detect devices, load necessary drivers, and create device nodes in */dev*. The contents of this file system are generated and updated dynamically by the kernel.

Essential System Commands

RHEL provides hundreds of commands that vary in complexity, structure, and usage. You can combine these commands for innovative use cases. Some commands offer only a few options, while others offer dozens. This section introduces how commands are formed and demonstrates several basic, commonly used commands. You will encounter additional commands and their advanced usages throughout this book.

Starting a Remote Terminal Session

To issue commands and run programs at the command prompt, you need access to a terminal. Follow the steps identified in Exercise 1-3 from the previous chapter to log in to the system remotely as *user1*. Figure 2-5 shows an example of a terminal session with *user1* logged in.

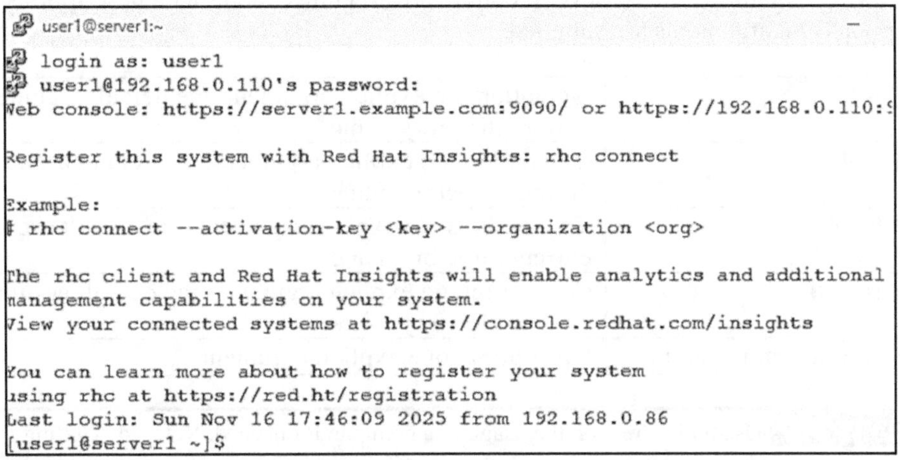

Figure 2-5 Remote Terminal Session

The header bar displays the logged-in user's name, the hostname of the system, and the current working directory.

The command prompt shown at the bottom of the figure above, "[user1@server1 ~]#", is the default format of a command prompt. It displays the logged-in username (such as *user1* or *root*), the system hostname (such as *server1* or *server2*), and the current directory, all enclosed in square brackets []. The prompt ends with a dollar sign ($) for normal users and a hash sign (#) for the *root* user, outside the closing bracket. Commands are entered at the cursor and executed by pressing the `Enter` key.

Understanding the Command Mechanics

The basic syntax of a Linux command is:

command [options] [arguments]

A Linux command functions much like a sentence. The command itself is the verb—the action you want to perform. *Options* (a.k.a. *switches* or *flags*) act like adverbs that modify how the action is carried out. *Arguments* are the nouns—the targets of the action. Understanding the command structure is the key to unlocking the power of the Linux command line.

Options are optional. You can specify zero or more options with a command. Arguments, in contrast, may be optional or mandatory depending on the command and its usage. Many commands have preconfigured default options and arguments, which you are not required to specify. Other commands require at least one option or argument to work correctly. In essence, an option modifies the behavior of the command, while an argument defines the target on which the command acts.

Options may begin with a single hyphen character (-la, for instance), which is known as the short-option format. Each individual letter in this depiction represents a separate option (l and a are two individual options in -la). This format appears frequently throughout this book.

Options may also begin with two hyphen characters (--all, for instance), which is known as the long-option format. All letters in this representation are collectively identified as a single option (--all is one option).

The following examples express several command structures, along with descriptions stating how many options and arguments are supplied:

$ **ls**	No option, no explicit argument; the default argument is the current directory name
$ **ls -l**	One option, no explicit argument; the default argument is the current directory name
$ **ls -al**	Two options, no explicit argument; the default argument is the current directory name
$ **ls --all**	One option, no explicit argument; the default argument is the current directory name
$ **ls -l directory_name**	One option, one explicit argument

EXAM TIP: Use online help on the usage of a command if needed. Refer to "Getting Help" later in this chapter for details on how to access and use help.

Now let's examine some essential Linux commands and understand their usage.

Listing Files and Directories

One of the most fundamental commands you will use in Linux is the *ls* (*list*) command, which displays the files and directories in a given location. This command supports numerous options, some of which are listed in Table 2-1 along with a brief explanation.

Option	Description
-a	Includes hidden files and directories in the output. A file or directory name that begins with the period character (.) is considered hidden.
-l	Displays long listing with detailed file information including the file type, permissions, link count, owner, group, size, date and time of last modification, and name of the file
-ld	Displays long listing of the specified directory but hides its contents
-lh	Displays long listing with file sizes shown in human-friendly format
-lt	Lists all files sorted by date and time with the newest file first
-ltr	Lists all files sorted by date and time with the oldest file first (reverse)
-R	Lists contents of the specified directory and all its subdirectories (recursive listing)

Table 2-1 ls Command Options

A grasp of the usage of this command and the output it produces is important. The following examples illustrate how different options affect the behavior of the *ls* command.

To list the files in the current directory (assuming */root* is the current directory):

```
[user1@server1 ~]$ ls
Desktop  Documents  Downloads  Music  Pictures  Public  Templates  Videos
```

To list the files in the current directory with detailed information:

```
[user1@server1 ~]$ ls -l
total 0
drwxr-xr-x. 2 user1 user1 6 Oct 27 12:10 Desktop
drwxr-xr-x. 2 user1 user1 6 Oct 27 12:10 Documents
drwxr-xr-x. 2 user1 user1 6 Oct 27 12:10 Downloads
drwxr-xr-x. 2 user1 user1 6 Oct 27 12:10 Music
drwxr-xr-x. 2 user1 user1 6 Oct 27 12:10 Pictures
drwxr-xr-x. 2 user1 user1 6 Oct 27 12:10 Public
drwxr-xr-x. 2 user1 user1 6 Oct 27 12:10 Templates
drwxr-xr-x. 2 user1 user1 6 Oct 27 12:10 Videos
```

The long listing in the output above provides detailed information about each file and directory, organized into nine distinct columns:

Column 1: The first character (- or d) indicates the file type, and the next nine characters (rw-rw-r--) represent the permissions.
Column 2: Displays the number of links (links are explained later in this chapter)
Column 3: Shows the owner name
Column 4: Exhibits the owning group name
Column 5: Identifies the file size in bytes. For directories, this value reflects the number of blocks used to store information about the directory's contents.
Columns 6, 7, and 8: Display the month, day, and time of creation or last modification
Column 9: Indicates the name of the file or directory

As an alternative to **ls -l**, you can use the shortcut **ll** for brevity and convenience, unless a specific situation requires the former.

To show the long listing of only the specified directory without its contents:

```
[user1@server1 ~]$ ls -ld /usr
drwxr-xr-x. 12 root root 144 Oct 27 10:40 /usr
```

To display all files in the current directory with their sizes in human-friendly format:

```
[user1@server1 ~]$ ls -lh
total 0
drwxr-xr-x. 2 user1 user1 6 Oct 27 12:10 Desktop
drwxr-xr-x. 2 user1 user1 6 Oct 27 12:10 Documents
drwxr-xr-x. 2 user1 user1 6 Oct 27 12:10 Downloads
drwxr-xr-x. 2 user1 user1 6 Oct 27 12:10 Music
drwxr-xr-x. 2 user1 user1 6 Oct 27 12:10 Pictures
drwxr-xr-x. 2 user1 user1 6 Oct 27 12:10 Public
drwxr-xr-x. 2 user1 user1 6 Oct 27 12:10 Templates
drwxr-xr-x. 2 user1 user1 6 Oct 27 12:10 Videos
```

To list all files, including the hidden files, in the current directory with detailed information:

```
[user1@server1 ~]$ ls -la
total 28
drwx------. 14 user1 user1 4096 Oct 27 12:57 .
drwxr-xr-x.  3 root  root    19 Oct 27 11:01 ..
-rw-------.  1 user1 user1  404 Nov 16 17:48 .bash_history
-rw-r--r--.  1 user1 user1   18 Oct 28  2024 .bash_logout
-rw-r--r--.  1 user1 user1  144 Oct 28  2024 .bash_profile
-rw-r--r--.  1 user1 user1  522 Oct 28  2024 .bashrc
drwx------. 10 user1 user1 4096 Nov 12 13:56 .cache
drwx------. 11 user1 user1 4096 Nov 16 09:47 .config
drwxr-xr-x.  2 user1 user1    6 Oct 27 12:10 Desktop
drwxr-xr-x.  2 user1 user1    6 Oct 27 12:10 Documents
drwxr-xr-x.  2 user1 user1    6 Oct 27 12:10 Downloads
drwx------.  4 user1 user1   32 Oct 27 12:10 .local
drwxr-xr-x.  4 user1 user1   39 Oct 27 10:39 .mozilla
drwxr-xr-x.  2 user1 user1    6 Oct 27 12:10 Music
drwxr-xr-x.  2 user1 user1    6 Oct 27 12:10 Pictures
drwxr-xr-x.  2 user1 user1    6 Oct 27 12:10 Public
drwxr-xr-x.  2 user1 user1    6 Oct 27 12:10 Templates
drwxr-xr-x.  2 user1 user1    6 Oct 27 12:10 Videos
........
```

To repeat the previous example with the output sorted by date and time and with the newest file first:

```
[user1@server1 ~]$ ls -lt
total 0
drwxr-xr-x. 2 user1 user1 6 Oct 27 12:10 Desktop
drwxr-xr-x. 2 user1 user1 6 Oct 27 12:10 Documents
drwxr-xr-x. 2 user1 user1 6 Oct 27 12:10 Downloads
drwxr-xr-x. 2 user1 user1 6 Oct 27 12:10 Music
drwxr-xr-x. 2 user1 user1 6 Oct 27 12:10 Pictures
drwxr-xr-x. 2 user1 user1 6 Oct 27 12:10 Public
drwxr-xr-x. 2 user1 user1 6 Oct 27 12:10 Templates
drwxr-xr-x. 2 user1 user1 6 Oct 27 12:10 Videos
```

To list the contents of the */etc* directory recursively:

```
[user1@server1 ~]$ ls -R /etc
/etc:
adjtime                 makedumpfile.conf.sample
aliases                 man_db.conf
alsa                    mcelog
alternatives            microcode_ctl
anacrontab              mime.types
asound.conf             mke2fs.conf
at.deny                 modprobe.d
audit                   modules-load.d
........
```

Run **man ls** at the command prompt to view the manual pages for the *ls* command, including all available options and their usage.

Printing Working Directory

The *pwd* (*print working directory* or *present working directory*) command displays the user's current location in the directory tree. In the following example, *user1* is currently in their home directory (*/home/user1*):

```
[user1@server1 ~]$ pwd
/home/user1
```

The *pwd* command always returns the absolute path to the current working directory.

Navigating Directories

Files are stored throughout the Linux directory structure, and a typical system contains tens of thousands of them. Each file and directory has a unique path within the directory tree. This *path*—also called a *pathname*—serves as a precise locator, defining the route through the hierarchy to reach any specific file or directory. It uniquely identifies a particular file or directory by its absolute or relative position in the directory structure.

Using an Absolute Path

An *absolute path* (a.k.a. a *full path* or *fully qualified pathname*) points to a file or directory relative to the root of the directory tree. It always begins with a forward slash (/). You can use *pwd* to view your current absolute path:

```
[user1@server1 ~]$ pwd
/home/user1
```

The output indicates that */home/user1* is the current working directory for *user1*. The leading / confirms that this is a full path.

Using a Relative Path

A *relative path*, on the other hand, specifies a location relative to your current directory. It never begins with a forward slash. A relative path may begin with two period characters (..) to indicate the parent directory, or with a subdirectory name such as *etc/sysconfig* (without a leading /).

Understanding the distinction between absolute and relative paths makes navigating the directory hierarchy intuitive. Let's run a few examples using the *cd* (*change directory*) command to move between directories and *pwd* to verify the results.

To determine the current location and then move one level up into the parent directory using the relative path:

```
[user1@server1 ~]$ pwd
/home/user1
[user1@server1 ~]$ cd ..
[user1@server1 home]$ pwd
/home
```

The above sequence of commands display the current location (the *pwd* output), then move one level up (*cd ..* is relative to the current location), and finally verify the new location (*/home*). You may alternatively use the absolute path (**cd /home**) instead for this purpose.

Using Absolute and Relative Paths to Reach the Same Directory

Now, let's switch to the */etc/sysconfig* directory. You can use either the absolute path (*/etc/sysconfig*) or the relative path (*../etc/sysconfig*):

```
[user1@server1 home]$ cd /etc/sysconfig/
[user1@server1 home]$ cd ../etc/sysconfig/
```

Similarly, to change to */usr/bin*, you can run either of the following:

```
[user1@server1 sysconfig]$ cd /usr/bin
[user1@server1 sysconfig]$ cd ../../usr/bin/
```

These examples show that an absolute path can reach a target directory directly regardless of your current position in the hierarchy, while a relative path is interpreted based on your current location.

Returning to Your Home Directory

To return to your home directory, simply run the *cd* command without any arguments, or use the *tilde* character (~) with the command.

You could also use an absolute path (**cd /home/user1**) or a valid relative path (**cd ../../home/user1**).

Switching to the Previous Directory

To switch between the current and previous directory, issue the *cd* command with a hyphen character (-). See the following example and observe the output:

```
[user1@server1 ~]$ pwd
/home/user1
[user1@server1 ~]$ cd -
/usr/bin
[user1@server1 bin]$ cd -
/home/user1
[user1@server1 ~]$ pwd
/home/user1
```

The example shows the use of a hyphen with *cd* to toggle between the current directory and the previous one.

Viewing Directory Hierarchy

The *tree* command displays a visual hierarchy of directories and files. You can specify numerous options to enhance the output. Table 2-2 describes some common options.

Option	Description
-a	Includes hidden files in the output
-d	Displays directories only (excludes files)

Option	Description
-h	Shows file sizes in human-friendly format
-f	Prints the full path for each file
-p	Includes file permissions in the output

Table 2-2 tree Command Options

To list only the directories in *user1* user's home directory:

```
[user1@server1 ~]$ tree -d
.
├── Desktop
├── Documents
├── Downloads
├── Music
├── Pictures
├── Public
├── Templates
└── Videos

9 directories
```

The output indicates that there are nine directories under */home/user1*.

To list the files in the */etc/sysconfig* directory along with their sizes (in human-readable format), permissions, and full path:

```
[user1@server1 ~]$ tree -hpf /etc/sysconfig
[drwxr-xr-x   4.0K]   /etc/sysconfig
├── [-rw-r--r--    112]   /etc/sysconfig/anaconda
├── [-rw-r--r--    403]   /etc/sysconfig/atd
├── [-rw-r--r--     50]   /etc/sysconfig/chronyd
├── [-rw-r--r--    110]   /etc/sysconfig/crond
├── [-rw-r--r--     73]   /etc/sysconfig/firewalld
├── [-rw-r--r--   1.4K]   /etc/sysconfig/irqbalance
├── [-rw-r--r--   2.8K]   /etc/sysconfig/kdump
├── [-rw-r--r--    185]   /etc/sysconfig/kernel
├── [-rw-r--r--    310]   /etc/sysconfig/man-db
........
```

The output shows permissions in column 1, sizes in column 2, and the full path of each file in column 3.

Run **man tree** at the command prompt to view the manual pages for this command, including additional options and their usage.

Identifying Terminal Device File

Linux allocates unique *pseudo* (*virtual*) device files to represent the terminal sessions opened by users. These device files allow the system to communicate with each session independently. By default, the files are stored under the */dev/pts* (*pseudo terminal slave*) directory. They are created automatically when a user opens a new terminal session and removed when the session is closed. The numbers associated with these files are reused for new sessions as needed.

You can use the *tty* (*teletype*) command to identify the device file associated with the current terminal session:

```
[user1@server1 ~]$ tty
/dev/pts/1
```

The output discloses the filename "1" and its location (*/dev/pts* directory).

Inspecting System Uptime and Processor Load

The *uptime* command is used to display the current system time, length of time it has been up for, number of users currently logged in, and the average system load over the past 1, 5, and 15 minutes. Consider the following output:

```
[user1@server1 ~]$ uptime
 07:44:48 up 22:46,  3 users,  load average: 0.00, 0.01, 0.00
```

The output shows the current time (07:44:48), up duration (22 hours and 46 minutes), number of logged-in users (3), and the load averages over the past 1, 5, and 15 minutes (0.00, 0.01, and 0.00), respectively.

The load average represents the average number of processes either running or waiting for system resources. On a single-core system, 1.00 indicates full utilization. On multi-core systems, divide the load average by the number of CPU cores to determine utilization—for example, on a 4-core system, a load of 4.00 indicates full utilization.

Clearing the Screen

The *clear* command clears the terminal screen and places the cursor at the top left corner of the screen. This command is useful for removing distracting information and continuing work on a clean screen.

```
[user1@server1 ~]$ clear
```

You can achieve the same result by pressing `Ctrl+l`.

Determining Command Path

RHEL provides several tools that help identify the absolute path of a command when you run it without specifying its full path. These tools include the *which*, *whereis*, and *type* commands. The following examples show the full location of the *uptime* command:

```
[user1@server1 ~]$ which uptime
/usr/bin/uptime
[user1@server1 ~]$ whereis uptime
uptime: /usr/bin/uptime /usr/share/man/man1/uptime.1.gz
[user1@server1 ~]$
[user1@server1 ~]$ type uptime
uptime is /usr/bin/uptime
```

As shown above, all three commands return an identical path for *uptime*, which is */usr/bin/uptime*. This means you do not need to type the entire path */usr/bin/uptime* to run the command—the system locates it automatically based on the search paths defined in your environment. Refer to Chapter 07 "The Bash Shell" for more guidance.

Viewing System Information

A RHEL system stores hardware, kernel, storage, networking, and other details about the operating system. The *uname* command displays elementary information about the system including its hostname. Without any options, the output of this command is restricted to the operating system name; however, it reports other details by adding the -a option.

```
[user1@server1 ~]$ uname -a
Linux server1.example.com 6.12.0-55.9.1.el10_0.x86_64 #1 SMP PREEMPT_DYNAMIC Tue
 Mar 25 09:14:09 EDT 2025 x86_64 GNU/Linux
```

The data returned by the second command is elaborated in Table 2-3:

Output	Description
Linux	Kernel name
server1.example.com	System hostname
6.12.0-55.9.1.el10_0.x86_64	Kernel release (version, Red Hat build, architecture)
#1	Kernel build number
SMP	Symmetric Multiprocessing support
PREEMPT_DYNAMIC	Dynamic kernel preemption model
Tue Mar 25 09:14:09 EDT 2025	Kernel build date and time
x86_64	System hardware architecture
GNU/Linux	Operating system type (GNU userland + Linux kernel)

Table 2-3 System Information

Try running *uname* with the -s (kernel name), -n (node name), -r (kernel release), -v (kernel version/build), -m (hardware name), and -o (OS name) options separately to view specific information.

Viewing CPU Specs

The *lscpu* command displays detailed CPU architecture information, including CPU type, operating modes, quantity, vendor, family, model, speed, cache sizes, and virtualization support. The following example output is from *server1*:

```
[user1@server1 ~]$ lscpu
Architecture:             x86_64
  CPU op-mode(s):         32-bit, 64-bit
  Address sizes:          39 bits physical, 48 bits virtual
  Byte Order:             Little Endian
CPU(s):                   2
  On-line CPU(s) list:    0,1
Vendor ID:                GenuineIntel
  Model name:             Intel(R) Core(TM) i7-10510U CPU @ 1.80GHz
    CPU family:           6
    Model:                142
    Thread(s) per core:   1
    Core(s) per socket:   2
    Socket(s):            1
    Stepping:             12
    BogoMIPS:             4608.01
    Flags:                fpu vme de pse tsc msr pae mce cx8 apic sep mtrr pge
                          ca cmov pat pse36 clflush mmx fxsr sse sse2 ht sysca
                           nx rdtscp lm constant_tsc rep_good nopl xtopology n
                          stop_tsc cpuid tsc_known_freq pni pclmulqdq ssse3 fm
                          cx16 pcid sse4_1 sse4_2 movbe popcnt aes xsave avx f
                          c rdrand hypervisor lahf_lm abm 3dnowprefetch ibrs_e
                          anced fsgsbase bmi1 avx2 bmi2 invpcid rdseed adx clf
                          shopt arat md_clear flush_l1d arch_capabilities
Virtualization features:
  Hypervisor vendor:      KVM
  Virtualization type:    full
Caches (sum of all):
  L1d:                    64 KiB (2 instances)
  L1i:                    64 KiB (2 instances)
  L2:                     512 KiB (2 instances)
  L3:                     16 MiB (2 instances)
NUMA:
  NUMA node(s):           1
  NUMA node0 CPU(s):      0,1
........
```

The output shows the CPU architecture (x86_64), supported operating modes (32-bit and 64-bit), number of CPUs (2), vendor ID (GenuineIntel), model name (Intel …), threads per core (1), cores per socket (2), number of sockets (1), and other information.

Getting Help

You are not expected to memorize every command or option. The mark of a skilled Linux administrator is knowing how to find information quickly. RHEL's built-in help is your first and most important resource when you need guidance. It offers extensive help via *manual* pages on commands, configuration files, etc. They are installed under the */usr/share/man* directory when associated software packages are installed.

In addition to manual pages, *apropos* and *whatis* commands and the documentation under */usr/share/doc* are also available.

> **EXAM TIP:** If you need help with a command or configuration file, do not hesitate to use the manual pages, the documentation under /usr/share/doc, or one of the other help tools.

Accessing Manual Pages

Use the *man* command to view manual pages. The following example shows the manual pages for the *passwd* command:

```
[user1@server1 ~]$ man passwd
PASSWD(1)                        User Commands                        PASSWD(1)

NAME
       passwd - change user password

SYNOPSIS

       passwd [options] [LOGIN]

DESCRIPTION
       The passwd command changes passwords for user accounts. A normal user
       may only change the password for their own account, while the superuser
       may change the password for any account.  passwd also changes the
       account or associated password validity period.

   Password Changes
       The user is first prompted for their old password, if one is present.
       This password is then encrypted and compared against the stored
       password. The user has only one chance to enter the correct password.
       The superuser is permitted to bypass this step so that forgotten
       passwords may be changed.
```

The output shows the command name, the section number in parentheses, and the command type (User utilities) on line 1. It then presents a short description (NAME), the command's usage (SYNOPSIS), and a long description (DESCRIPTION), followed by a detailed explanation of each option (OPTIONS) that the command supports and other relevant data. The status line at the bottom indicates your current position within the manual. Press h for navigation help and q to quit.

Table 2-4 summarizes the keys and commands useful for navigation.

Key	Action
Enter / Down arrow	Moves forward one line
Up arrow	Moves backward one line
f / Spacebar / Page down	Moves forward one page
b / Page up	Moves backward one page
d / u	Moves down / up half a page
g / G	Go to beginning / end of the page
:f	Displays line number and bytes being viewed
q	Quits the man pages
/pattern	Searches forward for the specified pattern
?pattern	Searches backward for the specified pattern
n / N	Finds the next / previous occurrence of a pattern
h	Gives help on navigational keys

Table 2-4 Navigating within Manual Pages

Practice *man* on the commands you have learned so far and navigate using the help shown above.

Headings in the Manual

Manual pages are organized under several standard headings. Common headings include NAME of the command or file with a short description, SYNOPSIS (syntax summary), long DESCRIPTION, available OPTIONS, usage EXAMPLES, related FILES, SEE ALSO for reference to other manual pages or topics, AUTHOR information, etc. You may find a subset of these headings or additional headings depending on what information is documented for that command or file.

Manual Sections

For organization, the manual is split into nine numbered sections based on the type of content they store. Table 2-5 describes the common sections:

Section Number	Description
1	User-level commands
4	Device special files found under /dev
5	File formats for various configuration files
8	Administrator-level commands to run by root.

Table 2-5 Common Manual Sections

The default behavior of the *man* command is to search through section 1 and each successive section until it finds a match. Some commands share names with configuration files. For example, the *passwd* command under */usr/bin* and the *passwd* file in */etc*.

When you run **man passwd**, the command scans through the manual and the first occurrence it finds is of the *passwd* command that's stored in section 1. To consult the manual pages for the *passwd* file, you must specify the section number to instruct the command to scan that particular section only. Here is example:

```
[user1@server1 ~]$ man 5 passwd
passwd(5)                   File Formats Manual                   passwd(5)

NAME
       passwd - password file

DESCRIPTION
       The /etc/passwd file is a text file that describes user login accounts
       for the system.  It should have read permission allowed for  all  users
       (many  utilities,  like ls(1) use it to map user IDs to usernames), but
       write access only for the superuser.

       In the good old days there was no great problem with this general  read
       permission.  Everybody  could  read  the  encrypted passwords, but the
       hardware was too slow to crack a well-chosen password, and moreover the
       basic assumption used to be that of a friendly  user-community.  These
       days  many  people run some version of the shadow password suite, where
. . . . . . . .
```

The header identifies this page as belonging to section 5, confirming it documents the *passwd* file.

Searching by Keyword

Sometimes you need to use a command but cannot recall its name. Linux allows you to perform a keyword search across the entire manual using the *man* command with the *-k* (lowercase) flag, or the *apropos* command. These commands search all manual sections and show a list of all entries matching the specified keyword in their names or descriptions.

Before performing keyword searches on a new RHEL installation, you need to run the *mandb* command as the *root* user to build an indexed database of the manual pages. Enter the password of *user1* when prompted by *sudo* to allow the *mandb* command to run with the *root* user privileges.

```
[user1@server1 ~]$ sudo mandb
Processing manual pages under /usr/share/man...
Updating index cache for path `/usr/share/man/man7'. Wait...mandb: warning: /usr
/share/man/man7/podman-rootless.7.gz: whatis parse for podman-rootless(7) failed
mandb: warning: /usr/share/man/man7/podman-troubleshooting.7.gz: whatis parse fo
r podman-troubleshooting(7) failed
mandb: can't resolve man7/groff_man.7
mandb: warning: /usr/share/man/man7/man.man-pages.7.gz: bad symlink or ROFF `.so
' request
........
Updating index cache for path `/usr/local/share/man/mann'. Wait...done.
Checking for stray cats under /usr/local/share/man...
Checking for stray cats under /var/cache/man/local...
130 man subdirectories contained newer manual pages.
7622 manual pages were added.
0 stray cats were added.
0 old database entries were purged.
```

The sudo command is discussed in Chapter 06 "Advanced User and Group Management".

Now you can carry out keyword lookups. For example, to find a forgotten XFS administration command, search for a string "xfs" by running either **man -k xfs** or **apropos xfs**. Both will produce an identical result.

```
[user1@server1 ~]$ man -k xfs
attr (1)             - extended attributes on XFS filesystem objects
filesystems (5)      - Linux filesystem types: ext, ext2, ext3, ext4, hpfs, i.
fs (5)               - Linux filesystem types: ext, ext2, ext3, ext4, hpfs, i.
fsck.xfs (8)         - do nothing, successfully
fsfreeze (8)         - suspend access to a filesystem (Ext3/4, ReiserFS, JFS,.
mkfs.xfs (8)         - construct an XFS filesystem
xfs (5)              - layout, mount options, and supported file attributes f.
xfs_admin (8)        - change parameters of an XFS filesystem
........
```

Once you have identified the command you were looking for, you can check its manual pages for usage.

Some commands also provide built-in help through the --help option. This displays a brief summary of available options for the specified command. For example, to get quick help on the *passwd* command, run the following:

```
[user1@server1 ~]$ passwd --help
Usage: passwd [options] [LOGIN]

Options:
  -a, --all                     report password status on all accounts
  -d, --delete                  delete the password for the named account
  -e, --expire                  force expire the password for the named account
  -h, --help                    display this help message and exit
  -k, --keep-tokens             change password only if expired
  -i, --inactive INACTIVE       set password inactive after expiration
                                to INACTIVE
  -l, --lock                    lock the password of the named account
  -n, --mindays MIN_DAYS        set minimum number of days before password
                                change to MIN_DAYS
........
```

Not all commands support the --help option.

Exposing Short Description

The *whatis* command displays the brief description of a given command or file from the manual database. It scans through the installed manual pages for the specified string and lists all the matching entries. Consider the following examples:

```
[user1@server1 ~]$ whatis dnf.conf
dnf.conf (5)         - DNF Configuration Reference
[user1@server1 ~]$
[user1@server1 ~]$ whatis passwd
passwd (1)           - change user password
passwd (1ossl)       - OpenSSL application commands
passwd (5)           - password file
```

The first command output indicates that the specified file is a configuration file for the *dnf* utility, and the second output points to three entries for *passwd* (one configuration file and two commands).

You may alternatively use **man -f dnf.conf** and **man -f passwd** for the exact same results. Both *man -f* and *whatis* produce identical output.

Documentation in the /usr/share/doc Directory

The */usr/share/doc* directory stores general documentation for installed packages, organized into subdirectories that match the package names. For example, the documentation for the gzip package includes the following files:

```
[user1@server1 ~]$ ls -l /usr/share/doc/gzip/
total 184
-rw-r--r--. 1 root root     98 Dec 31  2018 AUTHORS
-rw-r--r--. 1 root root 124368 Aug 19  2023 ChangeLog
-rw-r--r--. 1 root root  25256 Aug 19  2023 NEWS
-rw-r--r--. 1 root root   6146 Jan 10  2023 README
-rw-r--r--. 1 root root  14764 Dec 28  2022 THANKS
-rw-r--r--. 1 root root   3467 Jan 10  2023 TODO
```

These text files contain general information about the gzip package. However, manual pages are typically more useful to users and administrators.

Red Hat Enterprise Linux Documentation

Red Hat provides extensive RHEL 10 and other product documentation at *docs.redhat.com* in HTML and PDF formats (Figure 2-6).

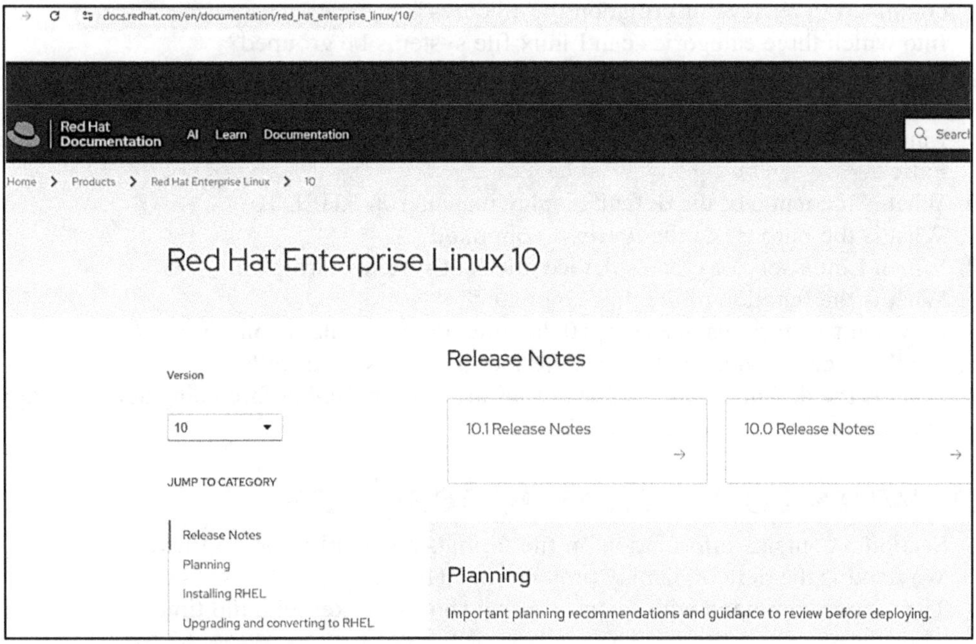

Figure 2-6 Red Hat's Webpage for RHEL 10 Documentation

This documentation includes release notes, and guides on planning, installation, administration, security, networking, storage management, virtualization, and so on. You can view the documentation online or download for free.

Chapter Summary

This chapter provided our first real interaction with the RHEL operating system. We began by exploring the modern graphical interface, understanding the roles of the Wayland protocol, the GNOME Display Manager, and the GNOME Desktop environment.

Next, we learned about the Linux directory structure and its significant higher-level subdirectories, which contain logically grouped static and variable files.

We analyzed command syntax and ran selected user-level commands for familiarity. These tools helped us list and view files, identify basic system information, and navigate the directory hierarchy.

Finally, we learned how to access online help for commands and configuration files, and how to effectively search through manual pages to find the required information.

Review Questions

1. What type of information does section 5 of the manual pages contain?
2. Which protocol is used as the default display protocol in RHEL 10?
3. Which command can be used to determine the time the kernel was built?
4. RHEL follows the Filesystem Hierarchy Standard. True or False?
5. Consider a Linux system with six processor cores. How many times must you run the *lscpu* command to retrieve information for all cores?
6. Into which three categories can Linux file systems be grouped?
7. Which three commands can be used to identify the full path of a command?
8. Which Linux command displays the hierarchical structure of a directory?
9. Linux commands may be categorized into two groups: privileged and non-privileged. True or False?
10. What is the name of the default display manager in RHEL 10?
11. What is the purpose of the *apropos* command?
12. Which Linux service creates device nodes at system startup?
13. What is the function of the *pwd* command?
14. In which two formats is RHEL 10 documentation available on *docs.redhat.com*?
15. For the *ls* command, what are the -R and -a options used for?
16. What is the default number of days files are kept in */tmp* before being automatically deleted if not accessed or modified?

Answers to Review Questions

1. Section 5 contains information on file formats and configuration files.
2. Wayland is the default display protocol in RHEL 10.
3. The *uname* command with -a or -v option shows the kernel build time.
4. True.
5. Once. The *lscpu* command displays information for all CPUs in a single invocation.
6. Linux file systems can be divided into disk-based, network-based, and memory-based categories.
7. The *which*, *whereis*, and *type* commands can be used to determine a command's full path.
8. The *tree* command shows the hierarchy of a directory.
9. True.
10. The GNOME Display Manager (GDM) is the default display manager in RHEL 10.
11. The *apropos* command searches the manual page database by keyword.
12. The *systemd-udevd* service creates device nodes at startup.
13. The *pwd* command shows the absolute path of the current working directory.
14. RHEL 10 documentation is available in PDF and HTML formats.
15. -R is used for recursive directory listing and -a to include hidden files.
16. 10 days.

Do-It-Yourself Challenge Labs

The following labs are designed to reinforce most of the concepts and skills covered in this chapter. You are expected to complete these labs without external assistance. A step-by-step guide is not provided, as the required knowledge has already been presented in the chapter; however, each lab includes hints pointing to the relevant major topic(s).

Use the lab environment created specifically for the end-of-chapter labs. See the sub-section "Lab Environment for End-of-Chapter Labs" in Chapter 01 "Local Installation" for details.

Lab 2-1: Navigate the Linux Directory Tree

As *user1* on *server3*, execute the *pwd* command to check your location in the directory tree. Run the *ls* command with appropriate switches to show files in the current directory including the hidden files. Change directory into */etc* and run *pwd* again to confirm the directory change. Switch to the previous directory and run *pwd* again to verify. (Hint: Essential System Commands).

Lab 2-2: Miscellaneous Tasks

As *user1* on *server3*, execute the *tty* command to identify your terminal device file. Observe the terminal number reported. Open additional terminal sessions and compare their terminal numbers using *tty*. Execute the *uptime* command and analyze the system uptime and load averages. Use the three commands—*which*, *whereis*, and *type*—to determine the location of the *vgs* command. (Hint: Essential System Commands).

Lab 2-3: Identify System and Kernel Information

As *user1* on *server3*, issue *uname -a* and analyze the system and kernel information. Run the *lscpu* command and examine key items relevant to the processor. (Hint: Essential System Commands).

Lab 2-4: Use Help

As *user1* on *server3*, run *man uname* and *man 5 shadow*, and review major headings and what they contain. Try *apropos ext4* and *man -k ext4*, *whatis group*, and compare their outputs. (Hint: Getting Help).

Chapter 03

File Management and Editing

By the end of this chapter, you will be able to:

- Identify Common Linux File Types
- Compress and Uncompress Files
- Create and Manage Archives
- Edit Text Files using the vim Editor
- Perform Essential File and Directory Operations
- Create Hard and Soft Links
- Differentiate between Copying and Linking

RHCSA Objectives:

06. Archive, compress, unpack, and uncompress files using tar, gzip, and bzip2
07. Create and edit text files
08. Create, delete, copy, and move files and directories
09. Create hard and soft links

At the heart of Linux administration is data management. This chapter equips you with the essential tools to handle files and directories from the command line. Linux supports different file types that are identified based on the kind of data they store. Some files save information in plain text or binary format—this type is very common. Other files store device information or simply point to file locations on the disk. A solid understanding of file types is important for your work as an administrator.

Compressing and archiving one or more large files or an entire directory hierarchy allows you to conserve disk space or copy them remotely at a faster pace. You can easily uncompress and unarchive the resulting compressed archive whenever and wherever needed. RHEL offers native tools to support both needs.

As a Linux administrator, you will need to edit text files regularly as part of your job. Linux delivers several text editors for this purpose, including the vim editor, which is popular within the Linux community. A sound, working knowledge of this tool is essential for your role.

You will perform many common operations on files and directories in addition to viewing their contents. These operations include creating, listing, copying, moving, renaming, and removing both files and directories. Normal users require higher privileges to perform these operations outside of their realm.

Finally, you will learn to demystify the concept of file linking and understand the differences between hard and soft links. Knowing when to link files or directories versus when to copy them is important for effective system administration.

Common File Types

RHEL supports seven file types: regular files, directories, block special device files, character special device files, symbolic links, named pipes, and sockets. The first two are the most common.

The two types of device files are used by the operating system to communicate with hardware and virtual devices. Symbolic links are also widely used. The last two types—named pipes and sockets—support inter-process communication.

Linux does not require a filename extension to determine a file's type. Instead, it provides commands such as *file*, *stat*, and *ls* to ascertain file types and, in some cases, the kind of data stored in a file. This chapter focuses on the first five file types; named pipes and sockets are beyond the scope of this book.

Regular Files

A *regular* files may contain text or binary data. It can hold a script, configuration, or command. When you list a directory, all line entries whose first character is a hyphen (-) represents regular files. For example, the following truncated output is from the */etc/sysconfig* directory:

```
[user1@server1 ~]$ ls -l /etc/sysconfig/
total 80
-rw-r--r--. 1 root root  112 Oct 27 11:01 anaconda
-rw-r--r--. 1 root root  403 Nov  5  2024 atd
-rw-r--r--. 1 root root   50 Nov  5  2024 chronyd
-rw-r--r--. 1 root root  110 Dec 10  2024 crond
-rw-r--r--. 1 root root   73 Jan 14  2025 firewalld
-rw-r--r--. 1 root root 1399 Mar 19  2024 irqbalance
-rw-r--r--. 1 root root 2835 Mar  5  2025 kdump
```

Notice the hyphen in field 1 of column 1 before the permissions (rw-r--r--). This character indicates that the listed file is a regular file. Run the *file* and *stat* commands on file *anaconda* and see how they report the type:

```
[user1@server1 ~]$ file /etc/sysconfig/anaconda
/etc/sysconfig/anaconda: ASCII text
[user1@server1 ~]$
[user1@server1 ~]$ stat /etc/sysconfig/anaconda
  File: /etc/sysconfig/anaconda
  Size: 112             Blocks: 8          IO Block: 4096   regular file
Device: 253,0   Inode: 2136910     Links: 1
Access: (0644/-rw-r--r--)  Uid: (    0/    root)   Gid: (    0/    root)
Context: system_u:object_r:etc_t:s0
Access: 2025-11-19 08:27:21.933132963 -0500
Modify: 2025-10-27 11:01:02.717786312 -0400
Change: 2025-10-27 11:01:02.717786312 -0400
 Birth: 2025-10-27 11:01:02.339783799 -0400
```

The two commands report the file type differently. The first command shows the specific type of content that the file contains (ASCII text), while the latter simply identifies the file type as a regular file.

Directory Files

A *directory* is a logical container that holds files and subdirectories. The following *ls* command output shows the listing of */usr*:

```
[user1@server1 ~]$ ls -l /usr/
total 216
dr-xr-xr-x.   2 root root 40960 Oct 27 10:51 bin
drwxr-xr-x.   2 root root     6 Oct 28  2024 games
drwxr-xr-x.   3 root root    24 Oct 27 10:43 include
dr-xr-xr-x.  40 root root  4096 Oct 27 10:50 lib
dr-xr-xr-x.  98 root root 61440 Oct 27 10:51 lib64
drwxr-xr-x.  43 root root  8192 Oct 27 10:51 libexec
drwxr-xr-x.  12 root root   131 Oct 27 10:40 local
dr-xr-xr-x.   2 root root 16384 Oct 27 10:51 sbin
drwxr-xr-x. 197 root root  8192 Oct 27 10:51 share
drwxr-xr-x.   4 root root    34 Oct 27 10:40 src
lrwxrwxrwx.   1 root root    10 Oct 28  2024 tmp -> ../var/tmp
```

The letter "d" at the beginning of each line entry identifies the file as a directory. Run the **file** and **stat** commands on */usr* and see how they report directory information.

Block and Character Special Device Files

Each device on the system is represented by one or more files under the */dev* directory. The kernel and Linux tools use these device files to communicate with that device. This type of file is called a *device file*. There are two types of device files: *character* (or *raw*) and *block*. In the example below, the *ls* command distinguishes between the two with a "c" for character and a "b" for block in field 1 of column 1:

```
[user1@server1 ~]$ ls -l /dev/console
crw--w----. 1 root tty 5, 1 Nov 18 16:37 /dev/console
[user1@server1 ~]$
[user1@server1 ~]$ ls -l /dev/sda*
brw-rw----. 1 root disk 8, 0 Nov 18 16:37 /dev/sda
brw-rw----. 1 root disk 8, 1 Nov 18 16:37 /dev/sda1
brw-rw----. 1 root disk 8, 2 Nov 18 16:37 /dev/sda2
brw-rw----. 1 root disk 8, 3 Nov 18 16:37 /dev/sda3
```

Use the **file** and **stat** commands on */dev/console* and */dev/sda* for additional confirmation.

Every device, such as a disk, optical drive, or terminal is associated with a device driver loaded into the kernel. The kernel communicates with the devices through their respective device drivers. Each device driver is assigned a unique *major* number that identifies the driver to the kernel.

Multiple devices may share the same driver. For example, a single SATA disk driver can control all SATA hard disks and optical drives on the system. In such cases, the kernel assigns a unique *minor* number to each device instance managed by that driver. Partitions on a disk also receive distinct minor numbers. In summary, a major number identifies the device driver, and a minor number identifies a specific device (or partition) managed by that driver.

In the long listing above, the device's major and minor numbers appear in the 5th and 6th columns. Major number 8 typically represents SCSI/SATA disk devices. Similarly (not shown in the above output), the major number 253 denotes the driver for device mapper (used for LVM logical volumes, etc.) and the major number 11 signifies optical devices. LVM is discussed in Chapter 15 "Storage Management".

Symbolic Links

A *symbolic link* (a.k.a. a *soft link* or *symlink*) is a file that points to another file or directory by its pathname. When you issue *ls -l* on a symbolic link, the line entry begins with the letter "l", and an arrow (->) shows pointing to the target. For example:

```
[user1@server1 ~]$ ls -l /usr/sbin/vigr
lrwxrwxrwx. 1 root root 4 Nov  3  2024 /usr/sbin/vigr -> vipw
```

Run the **file** and **stat** commands on */usr/sbin/vigr* to see how they describe both the link and its target.

Compression and Archiving

Compression tools reduce the size of one or more files to conserve disk space and speed up data transfers. They are commonly used together with the *tar* archiving tool to create a single compressed archive containing many files and directories. A compressed archive is smaller and faster to copy to remote systems or backup locations than a collection of uncompressed files. RHEL offers several compression tools, such as *gzip* (*gunzip*) and *bzip2* (*bunzip2*).

The *tar* command can preserve general file attributes such as the owning user, owning group, and timestamp as well as extended attributes, including SELinux contexts.

An SELinux context is a security label set on files and directories to enhance the level of protection against unauthorized access by users and processes. Refer to Chapter 22 "Security Enhanced Linux" for details.

Using gzip and gunzip

The *gzip* and *gunzip* compression utilities have been part of Linux for decades. The *gzip* command compresses each specified file and appends a *.gz* extension to identify the compressed version. It supports the -r option to compress an entire directory tree, and the -l option to display compression statistics for a gzipped file. The -l option also instructs the command to display the filename that will be assigned to the file when it is uncompressed.

For example, to compress the */etc/fstab* file, first copy it to your home directory and then compress the copied version:

```
[user1@server1 ~]$ cp /etc/fstab .
[user1@server1 ~]$
[user1@server1 ~]$ ls -l fstab
-rw-r--r--. 1 user1 user1 615 Nov 19 09:55 fstab
[user1@server1 ~]$
[user1@server1 ~]$ gzip fstab
[user1@server1 ~]$
[user1@server1 ~]$ ls -l fstab.gz
-rw-r--r--. 1 user1 user1 383 Nov 19 09:55 fstab.gz
```

The original file is replaced with a compressed version named *fstab.gz*. Run *gzip* again with the -l option to view compression information:

```
[user1@server1 ~]$ gzip -l fstab.gz
         compressed        uncompressed  ratio uncompressed_name
                383                 615  41.6% fstab
```

To decompress the file, use the *gunzip* command:

```
[user1@server1 ~]$ gunzip fstab.gz
[user1@server1 ~]$ ls -l fstab
-rw-r--r--. 1 user1 user1 615 Nov 19 09:55 fstab
```

Confirm with *ls* after decompression. The filename, size, timestamp, and all other attributes are restored as they were before compression.

Using bzip2 and bunzip2

Another common compression pair in Linux is *bzip2* and *bunzip2*. The *bzip2* command compresses each specified file and appends a *.bz2* extension for identification.

Compress the *fstab* file again, but this time with *bzip2*:

```
[user1@server1 ~]$ bzip2 fstab
[user1@server1 ~]$ ls -l fstab.bz2
-rw-r--r--. 1 user1 user1 415 Nov 19 09:55 fstab.bz2
```

The original file is replaced with a compressed version named *fstab.bz2*. To decompress the file, use the *bunzip2* command:

```
[user1@server1 ~]$ bunzip2 fstab.bz2
[user1@server1 ~]$ ls -l fstab
-rw-r--r--. 1 user1 user1 615 Nov 19 09:55 fstab
```

Confirm with *ls* after decompression. The filename, size, timestamp, and all other attributes are restored as they were before compression.

Differences between gzip and bzip2

The function of both *gzip* and *bzip2* is the same: to compress and decompress files. However, *bzip2* usually achieves a better compression ratio (smaller compressed file) but it is typically slower than *gzip*. These differences are noticeable on large files. For small files, either tool is acceptable. Both commands support several similar options.

Using tar

The *tar* (*tape archive*) command creates an archive file (often called a *tarball* or *tarfile*) from a collection of files and directories. It can also list, append to, update, and extract the contents from an existing archive. You can instruct the command to compress the tarball after its creation.

tar supports a multitude of options such as those described in Table 3-1.

Option	Definition
-c	Creates a tarball.
-C	Extracts (restores) to a different directory.
-f	Specifies a tarball name.

Option	Definition
-p	Preserve file permissions when extracting. Default for the root user. Specify this option if you create an archive as a normal user.
-r	Appends files to an existing uncompressed tarball.
-t	Lists the contents of a tarball.
-u	Appends files that are newer than the ones in an existing uncompressed tarball.
-v	Verbose mode.
-x	Extracts (restores) files from a tarball.

Table 3-1 tar Command Options

The -r and -u options cannot be used to append files to an existing compressed tarball.

The following examples illustrate the use of *tar*. Pay close attention to the syntax and options used in each command and observe the output.

Creating a Tarball of a Directory

To create a tarball called */tmp/default.tar* of the */etc/default* directory, use the -v option for verbosity and the -f option to specify the archive name with the command. The following is a truncated output:

```
[user1@server1 ~]$ tar cvf /tmp/default /etc/default/
tar: Removing leading `/' from member names
/etc/default/
/etc/default/useradd
/etc/default/grub
```

The resulting tarball does not include the leading slash (/) in the file paths, as shown on line 1 of the output, even though */home* is given as an absolute path. This default behavior of the *tar* command allows you to restore files into any directory without being forced back under */etc/default*. Use the -P option at the creation time to override this behavior.

Creating a Tarball of Selected Files and Appending Files to it

To create a tarball called */tmp/files.tar* containing only two files from the */etc* directory:

```
[user1@server1 ~]$ tar -cvf /tmp/files.tar /etc/passwd /etc/dnf/dnf.conf
tar: Removing leading `/' from member names
/etc/passwd
tar: Removing leading `/' from hard link targets
/etc/dnf/dnf.conf
```

To append files from the */etc/yum.repos.d* directory to the existing tarball */tmp/files.tar*:

```
[user1@server1 ~]$ tar -rvf /tmp/files.tar /etc/yum.repos.d/
tar: Removing leading `/' from member names
/etc/yum.repos.d/
/etc/yum.repos.d/redhat.repo
tar: Removing leading `/' from hard link targets
```

To list the updated contents of the tarball:

```
[user1@server1 ~]$ tar -tvf /tmp/files.tar
-rw-r--r-- root/root      2352 2025-10-27 11:01 etc/passwd
-rw-r--r-- root/root       108 2024-04-24 07:16 etc/dnf/dnf.conf
drwxr-xr-x root/root         0 2025-10-27 13:01 etc/yum.repos.d/
-rw-r--r-- root/root       376 2025-10-27 13:01 etc/yum.repos.d/redhat.repo
```

Restoring Files from a Tarball

To restore a single file, *etc/dnf/dnf.conf*, from */tmp/files.tar* in the home directory of *user1*, and confirm:

```
[user1@server1 ~]$ tar -xvf /tmp/files.tar etc/dnf/dnf.conf
etc/dnf/dnf.conf
[user1@server1 ~]$ ls -l etc/dnf/dnf.conf
-rw-r--r--. 1 user1 user1 108 Apr 24  2024 etc/dnf/dnf.conf
```

To restore all files from */tmp/files.tar* in *user1*'s home directory, and confirm:

```
[user1@server1 ~]$ tar -xvf /tmp/files.tar
etc/passwd
etc/dnf/dnf.conf
etc/yum.repos.d/
etc/yum.repos.d/redhat.repo
[user1@server1 ~]$
[user1@server1 ~]$ ls -l etc/
total 4
drwxr-xr-x. 2 user1 user1   22 Nov 19 12:38 dnf
-rw-r--r--. 1 user1 user1 2352 Oct 27 11:01 passwd
drwxr-xr-x. 2 user1 user1   25 Oct 27 13:01 yum.repos.d
```

Using tar with Compression

tar can call compression tools directly while creating or extracting archives. Table 3-2 summarizes the compression options.

Option	Description
-j	Compresses or decompresses a tarball with bzip2
-z	Compresses or decompresses a tarball with gzip

Table 3-2 tar Compression Options

You will use these options to create compressed archives in Exercise 3-1.

> **EXAM TIP:** Archiving and compression are frequently combined in real-world tasks. Be comfortable creating and extracting compressed tarballs.

Exercise 3-1: Create Compressed Archives

Perform this exercise on *server1* as *user1*. In this exercise, you will:

- Create a *gzip*-compressed tarball */tmp/skel.tar.gz* of the */etc/skel* directory
- Create a *bzip2*-compressed tarball */tmp/skel.tar.bz2* of the */etc/skel* directory

- List the contents of *skel.tar.gz* without decompressing it
- Extract all files from *skel.tar.gz* into the current directory
- Extract the *bzip2*-compressed archive into */tmp*

1. Create a *gzip*-compressed tarball under */tmp* for */etc/skel*:

```
[user1@server1 ~]$ tar -czf /tmp/skel.tar.gz /etc/skel
tar: Removing leading `/' from member names
```

2. Create a *bzip2*-compressed tarball under */tmp* for */etc/skel*:

```
[user1@server1 ~]$ tar -cjf /tmp/skel.tar.bz2 /etc/skel
tar: Removing leading `/' from member names
```

3. List the contents of the *gzip*-compressed archive without uncompressing it:

```
[user1@server1 ~]$ tar -tf /tmp/skel.tar.gz
etc/skel/
etc/skel/.mozilla/
etc/skel/.mozilla/extensions/
etc/skel/.mozilla/plugins/
etc/skel/.bash_logout
etc/skel/.bash_profile
etc/skel/.bashrc
```

4. Extract files from the *gzip*-compressed tarball into the current directory:

```
[user1@server1 ~]$ tar -xf /tmp/skel.tar.gz
```

5. Extract files from the *bzip2*-compressed tarball into */tmp*, which is a different directory location than the current directory:

```
[user1@server1 ~]$ tar -xf /tmp/skel.tar.bz2 -C /tmp/
```

Run **ls /tmp** to view the extracted files.

File Editing with vim

The *vim editor* is an interactive, full-screen *visual* text-editing tool that allows you to create and modify text files. It is widely available on UNIX and Linux systems, does not require a graphical environment, and is lightweight in terms of resource usage. All text editing within *vim* takes place in *registers* (small chunks of memory used to hold file updates temporarily). Changes can be written to disk, or discarded.

As a Linux administrator, it is essential for you to master *vim* editor skills. The best way to learn is by practicing: open or create files and try the commands. Consult the manual pages (**man vim**)for details, or run *vimtutor* to launch the built-in tutorial.

Modes of Operation

The *vim* editor has three primary modes of operation: command mode, insert mode, and last line mode. A fourth mode, visual mode, is not discussed in this book.

Command (Escape) Mode

This is the default mode when you start *vim*. In command mode, you can carry out tasks such as copy, cut, paste, move, remove, replace, change, and search for text, in addition to performing navigational operations. This mode is also known as *escape* mode because you press the `Esc` key to return to it.

Insert (Edit or Input) Mode

In this mode, anything that you type on the keyboard is inserted as text into registers, which you can then save to a file or discard. You cannot execute *vim* commands while in this mode. This mode is also called *edit* mode or *input* mode. You need to press the `Esc` key to return to command mode.

A common frustration for vim beginners is not knowing which mode they are in. If you start typing and get beeps or the cursor jumps oddly, you are likely in command mode. If your text appears correctly, you are in insert mode. When in doubt, press the `ESC` key. This will always return you to command mode, from which you can re-enter insert mode or issue another command.

Last Line (Command-Line or Extended) Mode

While in command mode, you can perform advanced editing tasks on text by pressing the colon character (:), which places the cursor at the beginning of the last line of the screen, and hence it is called *last line* or *command-line* mode. This mode is considered a specialized extension of command mode.

Starting vim

Start the *vim* editor by typing *vim* at the command prompt. You can optionally specify an existing or new filename as an argument. If you start *vim* without a filename, it opens an empty screen where you can enter text, which you can save in a file or discard it.

```
[user1@server1 ~]$ vim
```

Alternatively, you can supply a filename as an argument. This way, *vim* will open the specified file for editing if the file exists, or it will create a file by that name if it does not.

```
[user1@server1 ~]$ vim <filename>
```

There are additional options available that you can specify at the time of launching this editing tool. Refer to the manual pages for more information.

Inserting Text

Once *vim* is running, you can use one of the six commands to switch from command mode to insert mode. These commands are simple lowercase and uppercase letters as described in Table 3-3.

Command	Action
i	Inserts text before the current cursor position
I	Inserts text at the beginning of the current line
a	Appends text after the current cursor position
A	Appends text to the end of the current line
o	Opens a new line below the current line and enters insert mode
O	Opens a new line above the current line and enters insert mode

Table 3-3 vim Editor | Inserting Text

Press `Esc` when you are finished entering text to return to command mode.

Navigating within vim

Navigation keys are helpful in editing small and large files. They allow you to make rapid moves in the file. There are multiple key sequences available in *vim* to control cursor movement. Some of the elementary keystrokes are elaborated in Table 3-4.

Command	Action
h	Moves backward one character
j	Moves downward one line
k	Moves upward one line
l	Moves forward one character
w	Moves to the start of the next word
b	Moves backward to the start of the preceding word
e	Moves to the ending character of the next word
$	Moves to the end of the current line
Enter	Moves to the beginning of the next line
Ctrl+f	Scrolls down to the next page
Ctrl+b	Scrolls up to the previous page

Table 3-4 vim Editor | Navigating

You can precede any of these commands with a number to repeat the command action that many times. For instance, 3h will move the cursor three places to the left, 5Enter will move the cursor five lines down, and 2Ctrl+f will move the cursor two screensful forward.

In addition, you can use 0 (zero) to move to the beginning of the current line, [[(or gg) to move to the first line of the file, and]] (or G) to move to the last line of the file.

Revealing Line Numbering

While editing large files, you deal with hundreds or even thousands of lines. You may need to delete, copy, paste, or move one or more lines within the file. To perform these operations with accuracy, *vim* allows you to reveal in-editor line numbering. Table 3-5 describes the command.

Command	Action
:set nu	Shows line numbering
:set nonu	Hides line numbering

Table 3-5 vim Editor | Revealing Line Numbering

Line numbers are not written to the file when you save it; they are for on-screen reference only.

Deleting Text

vim provides several commands to carry out delete operations. Some are described in Table 3-6.

Command	Action
x	Deletes the character at the cursor position
X	Deletes the character before the cursor position
dw	Deletes the word or part of the word from the cursor position to the end of the current word
dd	Deletes the current line
D	Deletes from the cursor position to the end of the current line
:6,12d	Deletes lines 6 through 12 (last-line mode)

Table 3-6 vim Editor | Deleting Text

You can precede any of these commands, except for the last line mode command, by a numeral to repeat the command action that many times. For instance, 2X will delete two characters before the cursor position, and 3dd will delete the current line and the two lines below it.

Undoing and Repeating

Table 3-7 explicates the commands that undo the last change made and repeat the last executed command.

Command	Action
u	Undoes the previous command
U	Undoes all the changes done on the current line
:u	Undoes the previous last line mode command
. (dot)	Repeats the last executed command

Table 3-7 vim Editor | Undoing and Repeating

You can precede any of these commands, except for U and :u, by a numeral to repeat the command action that many times. For instance, 2u would undo the previous two changes, and 2U would undo all the changes made on the current and the previous lines.

Searching for Text

You can perform forward and reverse searches while in command mode using the / and ? characters followed by the string to be searched. For instance, in a file with numerous occurrences of the string "profile," you can run /profile or ?profile for a forward or reverse search, respectively. Table 3-8 summarizes these actions.

Command	Action
/string	Searches forward for string
?string	Searches backward for string
n	Repeats the last search in the same direction
N	Repeats the last search in the opposite direction

Table 3-8 vim Editor | Searching for Text

After initiating a forward search with /string, pressing "n" moves the cursor to the next occurrence of the string, while "N" moves to the previous one. Conversely, after a backward search with ?string, "n" repeats the search in the backward direction, and "N" moves to the next occurrence in the forward direction.

Replacing Text

Table 3-9 describes last-line mode commands used to perform search and replace operations.

Command	Action
:%s/old/new	Replaces the first occurrence of *old* with *new* on every line in the file.
:%s/old/new/g	Replaces all occurrences of *old* with *new* in the entire file.

Table 3-9 vim Editor | Replacing Text

For example, *:%s/profile/Profile* replaces only the first occurrence of "profile" with "Profile" on every line in the file, and *:%s/profile/Profile/g* replaces all occurrences of "profile" with "Profile" in the entire file.

To undo the change, use the last line mode command :u.

Copying, Moving, and Pasting Text

vim allows you to yank (copy) text (one or more characters, words, or lines) and then paste it to the desired location within the file. Table 3-10 describes the copy, move, and paste commands.

Command	Action
yl	Yanks the character at the cursor position
yw	Yanks the current word from the cursor position to the end
yy	Yanks the entire current line
p	Pastes yanked data below the current line
P	Pastes yanked data above the current line
:1,3co6	Copies lines 1 through 3 and pastes them after line 6
:4,6m9	Moves lines 4 through 6 after line 9

Table 3-10 vim Editor | Copying, Moving, and Pasting Text

You can precede any of the commands listed in Table 3-10, except for the last line mode commands, by a numeral to repeat the command action that many times. For instance, 2yw will yank two words, 2yy will yank two lines, and 2p will paste the yanked data twice.

Changing Text

vim offers commands to change text within a file. They are summarized in Table 3-11. Most of these commands switch to edit mode to let you complete the operation, so you will need to press the `Esc` key to return to command mode.

Command	Action
cl	Changes the letter at the cursor position
cw	Changes the word (or part of the word) from the cursor position to the end
cc	Changes the entire current line
C	Changes text from the cursor position to the end of the line
r	Replaces the character at the cursor position with the next typed character
R	Overwrites text as you type
J	Joins the next line to the end of the current line
xp	Swap the character at the cursor position with the one to the right of it
~	Toggles the letter case (uppercase to lowercase, and vice versa) at the cursor position

Table 3-11 vim Editor | Changing Text

You can precede any of the commands listed in Table 3-11 by a numeral to repeat the command action that many times. For instance, 2cc will change the entire current and the next line, and 2r will replace the current character and the next character.

Saving and Quitting vim

After editing, you can choose to save or discard your changes using the commands described in Table 3-12.

Command	Action
:w	Writes changes to the file without quitting vim
:w file2	Writes changes to another file called *file2* without quitting vim
:w!	Writes changes to the file even if the file owner does not have write permission on the file
:wq	Writes changes to the file and quits vim
:wq!	Writes changes to the file even if the file owner does not have write permission on the file, and quits vim
:q	Quits vim if no modifications have been made
:q!	Quits vim if modifications have been made, but you do not wish to save them

Table 3-12 vim Editor | Saving and Quitting

The exclamation mark (!) forces *vim* to override its internal write protections; however, you must still have appropriate file-level permissions to save your changes.

EXAM TIP: You may be required to edit configuration files or create scripts. A solid working knowledge of vim is crucial.

File and Directory Operations

This section elaborates on various management operations that you can perform on files and directories. These operations include creating, viewing, copying, moving, renaming, and deleting files and directories. You can perform these operations as a normal user if you are the owner or have appropriate permissions. If you lack sufficient permissions, the command will fail with an error. The *root* user, however, can operate on any file or directory, regardless of who owns it.

Creating Files and Directories

You can create files using several commands, but there is a single primary command for creating directories.

Creating Empty Files Using touch

The *touch* command creates an empty file. If the file already exists, it simply updates its timestamp to the current system time. Execute the following to create *file1* and then run *ls* to verify:

```
[user1@server1 ~]$ cd
[user1@server1 ~]$ touch file1
[user1@server1 ~]$ ls -l file1
-rw-r--r--. 1 user1 user1 0 Nov 20 08:11 file1
```

As expected, column 5 (the size column) shows 0, indicating that *file1* is created with zero bytes in size. If you rerun the *touch* command on this file after a minute or so, you will notice a new timestamp placed on it:

```
[user1@server1 ~]$ touch file1
[user1@server1 ~]$ ls -l file1
-rw-r--r--. 1 user1 user1 0 Nov 20 08:13 file1
```

The *touch* command has a few useful options. The -d and -t options set a specific date and time on a file; the -a and -m options enable you to change only the access or modification time on a file to the current system time; and the -r option sets the modification time on a file to that of a reference file's. Let's use a couple of these options in the examples below:

To set the date on *file1* to January 31, 2027:

```
[user1@server1 ~]$ touch -d 2027-01-31 file1
[user1@server1 ~]$ ls -l file1
-rw-r--r--. 1 user1 user1 0 Jan 31  2027 file1
```

To change the modification date/time on *file1* to the current system time:

```
[user1@server1 ~]$ touch -m file1
[user1@server1 ~]$ ls -l file1
-rw-r--r--. 1 user1 user1 0 Nov 20 08:17 file1
```

Try the other options for practice.

Creating Short Files Using cat

The *cat* command allows you to create short text files. The ending angle bracket ">" must be used to redirect the output to the specified file (*catfile1* in this example):

```
[user1@server1 ~]$ cat > catfile1
```

Nothing is displayed when you execute the above, as the system is waiting for you to input something. Type some text, and then press `Enter` to open a new line and continue typing. When you are done, press `Ctrl+d` to save the text in *catfile1* and return to the command prompt. Verify the file creation with *ls* and view its content with *cat*.

Creating Files Using vim

You can use the *vim* editor to create and modify text files of any size. Refer to the previous section in this chapter on how to use *vim*.

Making Directories Using mkdir

The *mkdir* command is used to create directories. This command produces output when you specify the -v option. The following example demonstrates the creation of a directory named *dir1*:

```
[user1@server1 ~]$ mkdir dir1 -v
mkdir: created directory 'dir1'
[user1@server1 ~]$
[user1@server1 ~]$ ls -ld dir1/
drwxr-xr-x. 2 user1 user1 6 Nov 20 08:27 dir1/
```

You can create a hierarchy of subdirectories by specifying the -p (parent) option with *mkdir*. In the following example, *mkdir* creates the hierarchy *dir2/perl/perl5*:

```
[user1@server1 ~]$ mkdir -vp dir2/perl/perl5
mkdir: created directory 'dir2'
mkdir: created directory 'dir2/perl'
mkdir: created directory 'dir2/perl/perl5'
```

Notice the placement of options in the two examples. Many commands in Linux accept either format.

Displaying File Contents

RHEL offers a variety of tools to display file contents. Directory contents are simply the files and subdirectories that it contains. Use the *ls* command as explained earlier to view directory contents.

For viewing files, you can use the *cat*, *more*, *less*, *head*, or *tail* command. These tools are explained below.

Using cat

cat displays the content of a text file in one go. It is best suited for short files. The following example shows the *.bash_profile* file with this command:

```
[user1@server1 ~]$ cat .bash_profile
# .bash_profile

# Get the aliases and functions
if [ -f ~/.bashrc ]; then
      . ~/.bashrc
fi

# User specific environment and startup programs
```

You can add the -n option to the command to include line numbers in the output.

Using less and more

Both *less* and *more* are text pagers that are used for viewing long text files one screen at a time, starting from the beginning. The *less* command is more advanced than the *more* command. Unlike *more*, *less* does not need to read the entire file before displaying its contents, which makes it faster. Additionally, *more* supports only forward text searches, whereas *less* supports both forward and backward searches. Run the *less* and *more* commands individually and observe the visual differences in their outputs:

```
[user1@server1 ~]$ less /usr/bin/znew
[user1@server1 ~]$ more /usr/bin/znew
```

You can navigate using the keys listed in Table 3-13 while viewing files with either tool.

Key	Purpose
Spacebar / f	Scrolls forward one screen
Enter	Scrolls forward one line
b	Scrolls backward one screen
d	Scrolls forward half a screen
h	Displays help
q	Quits and returns to the command prompt
/string	Searches forward for string
?string	Searches backward for string; only applies to the less command
n	Jumps to the next occurrence of a string
N	Jumps to the previous occurrence of a string; only applies to the less command

Table 3-13 Navigating with less and more

If the */usr/bin/znew* file is unavailable, use */etc/profile* instead.

Using head and tail

head displays the first few lines of the specified text file. By default, it returns the first ten lines. The example below illustrates this behavior:

```
[user1@server1 ~]$ head /etc/profile
# /etc/profile

# System wide environment and startup programs, for login setup
# Functions and aliases go in /etc/bashrc

# It's NOT a good idea to change this file unless you know what you
# are doing. It's much better to create a custom.sh shell script in
# /etc/profile.d/ to make custom changes to your environment, as this
# will prevent the need for merging in future updates.
```

The output above includes three empty lines as well. You can provide a number as an argument to limit the number of lines displayed. For example, run the following to view only the first three lines of */etc/profile*:

```
[user1@server1 ~]$ head -3 /etc/profile
# /etc/profile

# System wide environment and startup programs, for login setup
```

On the other hand, the *tail* command displays the last ten lines of the specified file by default, unless a number is passed as an argument to alter the behavior. Issue the following two commands in your terminal to observe the difference:

```
[user1@server1 ~]$ tail /etc/profile
[user1@server1 ~]$ tail -3 /etc/profile
```

The *tail* command is particularly useful for monitoring log files as they are updated. The -f (follow) option enables this behavior. The following example allows you to view updates to the system log file */var/log/messages* in real time:

```
[user1@server1 ~]$ sudo tail -f /var/log/messages
```

You may need to wait a moment before new updates appear. Press `Ctrl+c` to exit when you are finished.

Counting Words, Lines, and Characters in Text Files

The *wc* (*word count*) command displays the number of lines, words, and characters (or bytes) contained in a text file or input supplied. For example, when you run this command on the */etc/profile* file, you will see output similar to the following:

```
[user1@server1 ~]$ wc /etc/profile
  85  271 1983 /etc/profile
```

Column 1 in the output shows the number of lines (85) in the file, followed by the number of words (271), the number of characters (or bytes) (1983), and finally the filename (*/etc/profile*).

You can use the options listed in Table 3-14 to limit the output as needed.

Option	Action
-l	Prints a count of lines
-w	Prints a count of words
-c	Prints a count of bytes
-m	Prints a count of characters

Table 3-14 wc Command Options

The following example displays only the count of words in */etc/profile*:

```
[user1@server1 ~]$ wc -w /etc/profile
271 /etc/profile
```

Try running *wc* with the other options and observe the differences.

Copying Files and Directories

The copy operation duplicates a file or directory. RHEL provides the *cp* command for this purpose, along with a variety of useful options.

Copying Files

The *cp* command copies one or more files within the same directory or to another directory. To duplicate a file in the same directory, you must provide a different name for the target file. However, for copying a file to a different directory, you may keep the same filename or assign a new one. Consider the following examples:

To copy *file1* as *newfile1* within the same directory:

```
[user1@server1 ~]$ cp file1 newfile1
```

To copy *file1* to another existing directory *dir1* using the same filename:

```
[user1@server1 ~]$ cp file1 dir1
```

By default, the copy operation overwrites the destination file if it already exists, without issuing a warning. To alter this behavior, use the -i (interactive) option, which instructs *cp* to prompt for confirmation before overwriting:

```
[user1@server1 ~]$ cp file1 dir1 -i
cp: overwrite 'dir1/file1'? y
```

Press `Enter` after typing "y" to confirm or "n" to cancel.

For regular users, the *cp* command does not prompt for confirmation unless the -i option is specified; however, for the *root* user, overwrite confirmation is enabled by default due to a predefined alias.

Copying Directories

Use the *cp* command with the -r (recursive) option to copy an entire directory tree to another location. In the following example, *dir1* is copied to *dir2*, and the contents of *dir2* are listed for verification:

```
[user1@server1 ~]$ cp -r dir1/ dir2/
[user1@server1 ~]$ ls -l dir2
total 0
drwxr-xr-x. 2 user1 user1 19 Nov 20 20:46 dir1
drwxr-xr-x. 3 user1 user1 19 Nov 20 08:51 perl
```

You may also use the -i option for confirmation if the destination directory already contains matching files or subdirectories.

Try running **ls -l dir2 -R** to view the entire *dir2* hierarchy.

The *cp* command also supports the -p option, which preserves the original file or directory attributes (timestamp, permissions, ownership, etc.) during the copy. Run **cp -p file1 /tmp** and then **ls -l** on both files to compare their attributes.

Moving and Renaming Files and Directories

A file or directory can be moved within the same file system or to a different one. When a move occurs within the same file system, only directory entries are updated: a new entry is created in the target directory, and the original entry is removed. The actual data remains unchanged. However, when moving a file or directory across file systems, the data is physically copied to the new location and then removed from the source.

Renaming simply changes the name of a file or directory without modifying its data.

Moving and Renaming Files

The *mv* command is used to move or rename files. You can use the -i option to request confirmation before overwriting an existing file. The following example moves *file1* into *dir1* and prompts for confirmation:

```
[user1@server1 ~]$ mv -i file1 dir1/
mv: overwrite 'dir1/file1'? y
```

For regular users, the *mv* command does not prompt for confirmation unless the -i option is specified; however, for the *root* user, overwrite confirmation is enabled by default due to a predefined alias.

To rename *newfile1* as *newfile2*:

```
[user1@server1 ~]$ mv newfile1 newfile2
```

Verify the above operations using **ls -l**.

Moving and Renaming Directories

Use the *mv* command to move a directory and its contents or to rename an existing directory. For example, the following command moves *dir1* into *dir2* (note that *dir2* must already exist; otherwise, the operation becomes a simple rename):

```
[user1@server1 ~]$ mv dir1 dir2
```

To rename *dir2* as *dir20*:

```
[user1@server1 ~]$ mv dir2 dir20
```

Verify the above operations with **ls -l**.

Removing Files and Directories

The remove operation deletes a file entry from the directory structure and marks the corresponding data blocks as free. For directories, the operation removes their entries from the file system hierarchy.

Removing Files

You can remove a file using the *rm* command, which deletes one or more specified files. For example, run the following command to erase *newfile2*:

```
[user1@server1 ~]$ rm -i newfile2
rm: remove regular empty file 'newfile2'? y
```

For regular users, the *rm* command does not prompt for confirmation unless the -i option is specified; however, for the *root* user, overwrite confirmation is enabled by default due to a predefined alias.

You can also use the *rm* command to erase files whose names contain wildcard characters, such as an asterisk (*) or a question mark (?). Because these characters have special meaning to the shell, you must prepend filenames with a backslash character (\) so the shell interprets them as literal characters.

Careful use of the *rm* command is particularly important when you have administrative privileges. For example, if a file named * exists under the */tmp* directory (create it using **touch /tmp/***), you can remove it with **rm /tmp/***. If you mistakenly run **rm /tmp/*** instead, all files under */tmp* will be deleted.

Wildcard characters are commonly used for filename globbing and for performing actions on groups of files that match specific patterns. They are discussed further in Chapter 07 "The Bash Shell".

Removing Directories

The *rmdir* and *rm* commands erase directories. The *rmdir* command is used to delete empty directories, while *rm* requires the -d option to accomplish the same. In addition, the -r or -R (recursive) flag with *rm* will remove a directory and all of its contents. Both commands support the -v (verbose) switch to display actions as they occur.

To erase an empty directory named *emptydir* (assuming it exists), use either of the following:

```
[user1@server1 ~]$ mkdir emptydir
[user1@server1 ~]$ rmdir emptydir -v
rmdir: removing directory, 'emptydir'
[user1@server1 ~]$
[user1@server1 ~]$ mkdir emptydir
[user1@server1 ~]$ rm -dv emptydir
removed directory 'emptydir'
```

To remove *dir20* and all its contents recursively, use either -r or -R with the command:

```
[user1@server1 ~]$ rm -r dir20
```

The *rm* command also supports the -i flag for interactive deletion.

> **EXAM TIP:** Manipulating files and directories is one of the most common administrative tasks on Linux. A solid understanding of the tools covered in this section is essential for success on the RHCSA exam.

The same rules for removing files with wildcard characters in their names also apply to directories. See the previous topic for details.

File Linking

Each file within a file system has a set of attributes assigned at the time of its creation. These attributes, collectively known as the file's *metadata*, are updated whenever the file is accessed or modified. A file's metadata includes the file type, size, permissions, owning user, owning group, last access/modification time, link count, number of allocated blocks, and pointers to the data's storage location. This metadata occupies 128 bytes per file and is stored in a data structure called an *inode* (*index node*).

An inode is assigned a unique numeric identifier that the kernel uses to access, track, and manage the file. A filename is then mapped to this inode to make the file accessible to users. This mapping between a filename and an inode is referred to as a *link*. It is important to note that the inode does not store the filename; instead, filenames are maintained in the metadata of the directory in which the file resides.

Linking files or directories creates additional references that point to the same physical data on disk. Depending on the type of link, linked files may or may not share inode numbers and metadata.

RHEL supports two types of links: hard links and soft links. Links are always created between objects of the same type (file to file, directory to directory); you cannot create a link between a file and a directory.

Hard Link

A *hard* link is a direct association between a filename and an inode number. All filenames that are hard-linked to the same inode are indistinguishable from one another, sharing the same inode, same metadata, and the same physical data blocks. Any change made using any of the filenames affects the same underlying data.

Figure 3-1 shows two filenames—*file10* and *file20*—both sharing inode number 10176147. Each name is essentially a hard link pointing to the same inode.

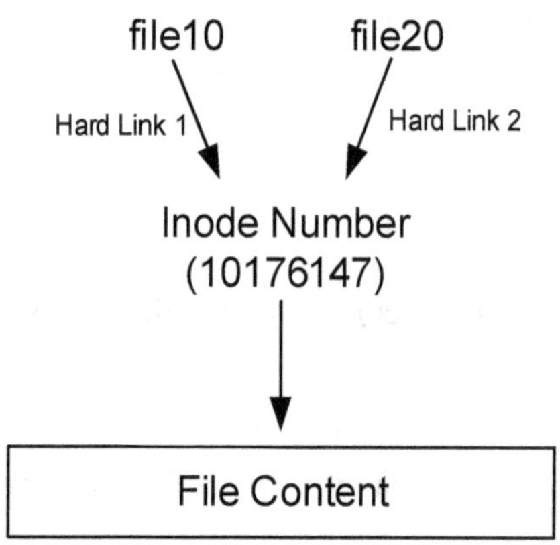

Figure 3-1 Hard Link

Hard links cannot cross file system boundaries, and hard links to directories are not permitted to prevent issues with commands that traverse file systems.

The following example creates the empty file *file10* and then uses the *ln* command to create a hard link named *file20* in the same directory:

```
[user1@server1 ~]$ touch file10
[user1@server1 ~]$ ln file10 file20
```

After creating the link, run *ls* with the -li flags as follows:

```
[user1@server1 ~]$ ls -li file*
51036324 -rw-r--r--. 2 user1 user1 0 Nov 20 21:52 file10
51036324 -rw-r--r--. 2 user1 user1 0 Nov 20 21:52 file20
```

Column 1 displays the shared inode number (10176147), and column 3 shows the *link count*. Both *file10* and *file20* point to the same inode. If you remove the original file (*file10*), the data remains accessible through *file20*. Each time you add a hard link, the link count increases by 1. Similarly, deleting a hard link decreases the link count by 1. When all hard links (files) have been erased and the link count reaches 0, the data becomes eligible for deletion by the operating system. The updated link count is reflected consistently across all hard-linked filenames.

Soft Link

A *soft* link (also known as a *symbolic* link or *symlink*) associates one file or directory with another by storing its pathname. The actual file is referred to as the *target*, while the symbolic link points to that target. The concept is similar to a shortcut in Microsoft Windows: the actual file resides in one location, while one or more shortcuts (symlinks) with different names may point to it.

With a soft link, you can access the target file either through its original filename or through any of its symlinks. Each soft link has its own unique inode, which stores only the pathname of the target. The link count of the target file does not increase when symlinks are created, because each symlink is represented by a separate inode. The pathname stored in a symlink may be absolute or relative, depending on how it was created. The size of a soft link corresponds to the number of characters in the pathname it contains.

Figure 3-2 illustrates *file10* with a soft link named *soft10* pointing to it.

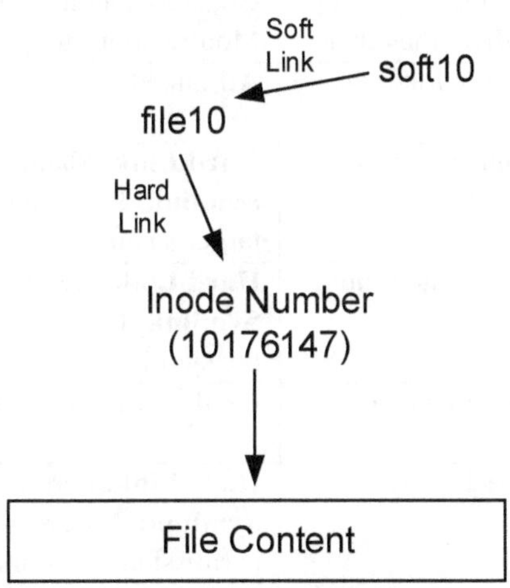

Figure 3-2 Soft Link

Soft links can cross file system boundaries, and they can be used to link directories, as they simply use pathnames of the targets.

To create a soft link named *soft10* for *file10* in the same directory, use the *ln* command with the -s switch:

```
[user1@server1 ~]$ ln -s file10 soft10
```

After creating the link, issue **ls -l** and notice the letter "l" as the first character in column 2 of the output. Also note the arrow indicating the relationship between the symlink and its target. These elements show that *soft10* is merely a pointer to *file10*. The -i option displays the associated inode numbers in the first column. See the output of **ls -il** below:

```
[user1@server1 ~]$ ls -il file10 soft10
51036324 -rw-r--r--. 2 user1 user1 0 Nov 20 21:52 file10
51035879 lrwxrwxrwx. 1 user1 user1 6 Nov 20 22:16 soft10 -> file10
```

If you remove the target (*file10*), the link *soft10* remains but points to a non-existent file.

RHEL 10 has four soft-linked directories under /. They are:

```
lrwxrwxrwx.   1 root root    7 Oct 28  2024 /bin -> usr/bin
lrwxrwxrwx.   1 root root    7 Oct 28  2024 /lib -> usr/lib
lrwxrwxrwx.   1 root root    9 Oct 28  2024 /lib64 -> usr/lib64
lrwxrwxrwx.   1 root root    8 Oct 28  2024 /sbin -> usr/sbin
```

The syntax for creating symlinked directories is identical to that of symlinked files.

Differences between Copying and Linking

Copying and linking operate very differently. Understanding these distinctions will help you determine when to use a copy and when to use a link. Table 3-15 highlights the main differences between the two:

Copying	Linking
Creates a duplicate of the source file. Modifications to one file do not affect the other.	Creates an additional reference to the file's data. Modifications to one file affects the other.
Each copy stores its own data at a separate location.	All linked files point to the same underlying data.
Each copy has a unique inode number and its own metadata.	**Hard Link:** Shares the same inode number and metadata. **Symlink:** Has a unique inode number that stores only the target's pathname.
Deleting, renaming, or moving a copy does not affect the source.	**Hard Link:** Removing one link leaves others intact. **Symlink:** Removing the target breaks the link; removing the symlink does not affect the target.
Used when you need an independent editable copy.	Used when you need multiple references to the same data.
Permissions are independent for each copy.	**Hard Link:** Permissions are identical for all files. **Symlink:** Access is governed by the target file's permissions; symlink permissions are irrelevant.

Table 3-15 Copying vs. Linking Files

Keep these differences in mind when you need to decide whether to copy a file or create a link.

Exercise 3-2: Create and Manage Hard Links

Perform this exercise on *server1* as *user1*. In this exercise, you will:

- Create an empty file named *hard1* under */tmp* and display its attributes (the inode number, permissions, link count, owning user, owning group, size, and timestamp)
- Create two hard links named *hard2* and *hard3* for *hard1*, and list the attributes for all three files
- Edit *hard2* and add some random text
- List the attributes for all three files again and observe identicalness in all attributes except for the names of files
- Remove *hard1* and *hard3* and list the attributes again for the remaining file
- Observe a decrease in the link count by 2

1. Create an empty file */tmp/hard1*, and display the long file listing including the inode number:

```
[user1@server1 ~]$ touch /tmp/hard1
[user1@server1 ~]$ ls -li /tmp/hard1
18047204 -rw-r--r--. 1 user1 user1 0 Nov 21 07:36 /tmp/hard1
```

The file listing indicates the inode number in column 1, followed by permissions (column 2), number of links (column 3), owning user and group (columns 4 and 5), size (column 6), timestamp (columns 7, 8, and 9), and filename (column 10).

2. Create two hard links called *hard2* and *hard3* under */tmp*, and display the long listing:

```
[user1@server1 ~]$ ln /tmp/hard1 /tmp/hard2
[user1@server1 ~]$ ln /tmp/hard1 /tmp/hard3
[user1@server1 ~]$ ls -li /tmp/hard*
18047204 -rw-r--r--. 3 user1 user1 0 Nov 21 07:36 /tmp/hard1
18047204 -rw-r--r--. 3 user1 user1 0 Nov 21 07:36 /tmp/hard2
18047204 -rw-r--r--. 3 user1 user1 0 Nov 21 07:36 /tmp/hard3
```

Observe the file listing. All attributes are identical.

3. Edit file *hard2* and add some random text. Display the long listing for all three files again:

```
[user1@server1 ~]$ vim /tmp/hard2
[user1@server1 ~]$ ls -li /tmp/hard*
18047204 -rw-r--r--. 3 user1 user1 51 Nov 21 07:36 /tmp/hard1
18047204 -rw-r--r--. 3 user1 user1 51 Nov 21 07:36 /tmp/hard2
18047204 -rw-r--r--. 3 user1 user1 51 Nov 21 07:36 /tmp/hard3
```

Observe the size and timestamp columns for all three files. They are identical.

4. Erase file *hard1* and *hard3*, and display the long listing for the remaining file:

```
[user1@server1 ~]$ rm -f /tmp/hard1 /tmp/hard3
[user1@server1 ~]$ ls -li /tmp/hard*
18047204 -rw-r--r--. 1 user1 user1 51 Nov 21 07:36 /tmp/hard2
```

The number of links reduced to 1, all other attributes are the same. You can still access the same data through this last file.

Exercise 3-3: Create and Manage Soft Links

Perform this exercise on *server1* as *user1*. In this exercise, you will:

- Create a soft link named *soft1* under *user1*'s home directory, pointing to */tmp/hard2*
- Display the attributes for both the symlink and its target
- Edit *soft1* and add some random text
- List the attributes again for both files
- Remove the target *hard2* and then list *soft1*
- Observe that *soft1* becomes invalid because its target no longer exists
- Remove *soft1* to complete the exercise

1. Create the soft link */home/user1/soft1* pointing to */tmp/hard2*, and display the long file listing for both:

```
[user1@server1 ~]$ ln -s /tmp/hard2 /home/user1/soft1
[user1@server1 ~]$ ls -li /tmp/hard2 /home/user1/soft1
51035878 lrwxrwxrwx. 1 user1 user1 10 Nov 21 08:02 /home/user1/soft1 -> /tmp/hard2
18047204 -rw-r--r--. 1 user1 user1 51 Nov 21 07:36 /tmp/hard2
```

The file listing displays the inode number in column 1, followed by permissions (column 2), link count (column 3), owning user and owning group (columns 4 and 5), size (column 6), timestamp (columns 7, 8, and 9), and the filename (column 10). For the soft link, the first character in column 2 is "l", indicating a symbolic link, and the filename field shows an arrow pointing to the target file. Notice the file size for *soft1* (10 bytes for the pathname */tmp/hard2*). Observe the similarities and differences between the symlink and its target.

2. Edit *soft1* and display the long listing again:

```
[user1@server1 ~]$ vim soft1
[user1@server1 ~]$ ls -li /tmp/hard2 /home/user1/soft1
51035878 lrwxrwxrwx. 1 user1 user1  10 Nov 21 08:02 /home/user1/soft1 -> /tmp/hard2
18047204 -rw-r--r--. 1 user1 user1 121 Nov 21 08:03 /tmp/hard2
```

Because *soft1* points to */tmp/hard2*, editing *soft1* modifies the target file. The size and timestamp for *hard2* have changed. The symbolic link's metadata remains unchanged.

3. Remove *hard2* and display the long listing:

```
[user1@server1 ~]$ rm -f /tmp/hard2
[user1@server1 ~]$ ls -li /tmp/hard2 /home/user1/soft1
ls: cannot access '/tmp/hard2': No such file or directory
51035878 lrwxrwxrwx. 1 user1 user1 10 Nov 21 08:02 /home/user1/soft1 -> /tmp/hard2
```

The target, *hard2*, is deleted, leaving the soft link broken. You can remove it with **rm -f soft1**.

Chapter Summary

This chapter began with an introduction to common file types in RHEL. We learned that a file's type is determined by the data it stores, with regular files for text or binary data and directories being the most common. We also explored other types, including device files and link files.

We then looked at creating and manipulating compressed files and archives, which is a common practice for data storage and transfer. Our focus shifted to the vim editor, where we examined its various operational modes and learned how to create and edit text files, navigate content, perform search operations, manipulate text, and save or discard changes.

Next, we mastered various tools for file and directory manipulation, practicing common operations like creating, listing, copying, moving, and removing them. We also examined the differences between soft and hard links, including their advantages and limitations, enabling us to choose and create the appropriate link type for specific use cases. Finally, we clarified the fundamental differences between file copying and file linking operations.

Review Questions

1. A file compressed with *bzip2* can be uncompressed with the *gunzip* command. True or False?
2. The *tar* command can be used to archive files with their SELinux contexts. True or False?
3. Which numeric identifier does the kernel use to determine the uniqueness of a device within a device driver type?
4. What two indications in the output of *ls -l* tell you if the file is a symbolic link?
5. The *rmdir* command without any switches can be used to erase an entire directory structure. True or False?
6. What would the command *tar pczf output.file /usr/local* do if executed by a normal user?
7. The *ls -l* command produces 9 columns of output. True or False?
8. Which three Linux utilities can be used to determine a file's type?
9. Two hard-linked files exist in a directory. How would you identify them?
10. Which *vim* mode allows you to execute advanced copy and move functions?
11. What would the command *wc -c file1* show?
12. What does the kernel use the major number for?
13. The *tail* command can be used to view a file while it is being updated. True or False?
14. Soft-linked directories cannot cross file system boundaries, but hard-linked directories can. True or False?
15. A file must have the *.exe* extension to run. True or False?
16. What does the command *touch file1* do when *file1* already exists?

Answers to Review Questions

1. False. The file must be uncompressed with *bzip2* or *bunzip2*.
2. True. The *tar* command supports this via the --selinux switch.
3. The kernel uses the minor number to identify the uniqueness of a device within a device drive type.
4. A symlink line entry in the *ls -l* command output begins with the letter "l" and has an arrow pointing to the target file.
5. False. The *rmdir* command erases only empty directories.
6. This command will create a gzip-compressed tar archive named *output.file* containing */usr/local* directory with permissions preserved.

7. True.
8. The *stat*, *file*, and *ls* commands can be used to determine a file's type.
9. Run *ls -li*; hard-linked files share the same inode number.
10. Last-line mode (also called extended mode or command-line mode) allows advanced copy and move operations in *vim*.
11. This command shows the number of bytes in *file1*.
12. The kernel employs the major number to identify the device driver associated with the device.
13. True. Use *tail -f* to follow a file as it is updated.
14. False. Soft-linked directories can cross file system boundaries, but hard-linked directories cannot.
15. False. Linux does not require file extensions to determine executability; permissions control execution.
16. This command updates the access and modification times on *file1*.

Do-It-Yourself Challenge Labs

The following labs are designed to reinforce most of the concepts and skills covered in this chapter. You are expected to complete these labs without external assistance. A step-by-step guide is not provided, as the required knowledge has already been presented in the chapter; however, each lab includes hints pointing to the relevant major topic(s).

Use the lab environment created specifically for the end-of-chapter labs. See the sub-section "Lab Environment for End-of-Chapter Labs" in Chapter 01 "Local Installation" for details.

Lab 3-1: Archive, List, and Restore Files

As *user1* on *server3*, execute the *tar* command to create a *gzip*-compressed archive of the */etc* directory. Run the *tar* command again to create a *bzip2*-compressed archive of the same directory. Compare the file sizes of the two archives. Run the *tar* command and uncompress and restore both archives without specifying the compression tool used. (Hint: Compression and Archiving).

Lab 3-2: Practice the vim Editor

As *user1* on *server3*, create a file named *vimpractice* in the home directory using *vim*. Type (do not copy/paste) each sentence from Lab 3-1 on a separate line (ignore line wrapping). Save the file and quit the editor. Open *vimpractice* in *vim* again and copy lines 2 and 3 to the end of the file to bring the total number of lines in the file to 6. Move line 3 to become the new line 1. Go to the last line and append the contents of the *.bash_profile* file. Substitute all occurrences of the string "Profile" with "Pro File", and all occurrences of "profile" with "pro file". Erase lines 5 through 8. Save the file and quit *vim*. Finally, use the *wc* command to display the count of lines, words, and characters in the *vimpractice* file. (Hint: File Editing).

Lab 3-3: File and Directory Operations

As *user1* on *server3*, create one file and one directory in the home directory. List the file and directory and examine their permissions, owning user, and owning group. Try moving both the file and directory to the */var/log* directory and note the results. Try again to move them to */tmp*. Duplicate the file using the *cp* command, then rename the duplicated file using any name. Erase the file and directory created for this lab. (Hint: File and Directory Operations).

Chapter 04

File Permissions and Searching

By the end of this chapter, you will be able to:

- Interpret and Modify File and Directory Permissions
- Apply Permissions with Symbolic and Octal Notations
- Change Access Rights for the Owner, Group, and Public
- Configure Default Permissions for New Files and Directories
- Locate Files and Directories using a Variety of Ways

RHCSA Objectives:

10. List, set, and change standard ugo/rwx permissions
40. Diagnose and correct file permission problems
56. Manage default file permissions

In Linux, regulating file and directory access is a fundamental administrative task. Proper permissions prevent unauthorized users from viewing or modifying sensitive data. This chapter explores the standard ugo/rwx permission model. You will learn to assign permissions to the three distinct user categories using two different methods, and calculate and apply consistent permissions on new files and directories.

Finally, you will learn to locate files at specified locations using a wide array of criteria, including name, size, time, and permissions, and how to execute actions on the results as they are found.

File and Directory Access Permissions

Linux is a multi-user operating system capable of supporting hundreds of users working concurrently. The OS has hundreds of thousands of files and directories that it must maintain securely to warrant a successful system and application operation from security and reliability standpoints. Therefore, it is imperative that you regulate file and directory access by granting users only the permissions they need to carry out their tasks, thereby maintaining system security. This control of permissions on files and directories is commonly referred to as user *access rights*.

Determining Access Permissions

Access permissions on files and directories allow administrative control over which users (permission classes) can access them and to what level (permission types). File and directory permissions discussed in this section are referred to as *standard ugo/rwx permissions*.

Permission Classes

Users are categorized into three unique classes for maintaining file security through access rights. These classes are *user* (u), *group* (g), and *other* (o, also called *public*). These permission classes represent the file's owner, the assigned group, and all other users on the system, respectively. There is another special user class called *all* (a) that represents the three user classes combined.

Permission Types

Permissions control what actions can be performed on a file or directory and by whom. There are three types of permissions bits—*read* (r), *write* (w), and *execute* (x)—and they behave differently for files and directories. For files, the permissions govern viewing or copying content (read), modifying content (write), and running the file as a program (execute). For directories, the permissions control listing its contents with *ls* (read); creating, erasing, or renaming entries within it (write); and accessing (changing into) the directory with the *cd* command (execute).

If a read, write, or execute permission bit is not desired, the hyphen character (-) is used to represent its absence.

Permission Modes

A permission mode is used to *add* (+), *revoke* (-), or *assign* (=) a permission type to a permission class. You can view the permission settings on files and directories in the long listing of the *ls* command. This information is encapsulated in column 1 of the output, a sample of which is shown below:

- rwx rw- r--

The first character indicates the type of file: - for regular file, d for directory, l for symbolic link, c for character device file, b for block device file, p for named pipe, s for socket, and so on.

The next nine characters—three groups of three characters—show the read (r), write (w), and execute (x) permissions for the three user classes: user (owner), group, and other (public), respectively. The hyphen character (-) represents a permission denial for that level.

Modifying Access Permission Bits

The *chmod* command modifies access rights and works identically on files and directories. *chmod* can be used by *root* or the file owner, and can modify permissions specified in one of two ways: *symbolic* or *octal*. Symbolic notation uses a combination of letters (ugo/rwx) and symbols (+, -, =) to add, revoke, or assign permission bits. The octal notation (often called the *absolute* mode) uses a three-digit numbering system ranging from 0 to 7 to express permissions for the three user classes. Octal values are given in Table 4-1.

Octal Value	Binary Notation	Symbolic Notation	Explanation
0	000	---	No permissions
1	001	--x	Execute permission only
2	010	-w-	Write permission only
3	011	-wx	Write and execute permissions
4	100	r--	Read permission only
5	101	r-x	Read and execute permissions
6	110	rw-	Read and write permissions
7	111	rwx	Read, write, and execute permissions

Table 4-1 Octal Permission Notation

In Table 4-1, each "1" corresponds to an r, w, or x, and each "0" corresponds to the hyphen character (-) for no permission at that level. Figure 4-1 shows weights associated with each digit position in the 3-digit octal numbering model.

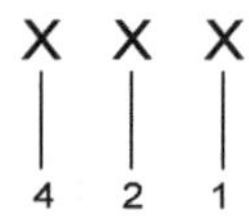

Figure 4-1 Permission Weights

As shown in Table 4-1, the octal value is derived from the sum of the weights for each permission bit that is set: read (4), write (2), and execute (1). For example, a permission of 6 (4+2) grants read and write, while a permission of 2 grants write-only.

Exercise 4-1: Modify Permission Bits Using Symbolic Form

Perform this exercise on *server1* as *user1*.

For this exercise, assume a file called *permfile1* exists with read permission for the owner (*user1*), owning group (*user1*), and other, as shown below. If the permissions vary, bring them to the desired state by executing **chmod 444 permfile1** prior to starting the exercise.

```
-r--r--r--. 1 user1 user1 0 Sep  6 20:02 permfile1
```

In this exercise, you will:

- Add an execute bit for the owner and a write bit for group and public
- Revoke the write bit from public
- Assign read, write, and execute bits to the three user categories at the same time
- Revoke write from the owning group and write and execute bits from public

Use the -v switch with the *chmod* command to display what it has changed and/or view the long listing after each command execution for verification.

1. Add an execute bit for the owner:

```
[user1@server1 ~]$ chmod u+x permfile1 -v
mode of 'permfile1' changed from 0444 (r--r--r--) to 0544 (r-xr--r--)
```

2. Add a write bit for group members and public:

```
[user1@server1 ~]$ chmod -v go+w permfile1
mode of 'permfile1' changed from 0544 (r-xr--r--) to 0566 (r-xrw-rw-)
```

3. Remove the write permission for public:

```
[user1@server1 ~]$ chmod -v o-w permfile1
mode of 'permfile1' changed from 0566 (r-xrw-rw-) to 0564 (r-xrw-r--)
```

4. Assign read, write, and execute permission bits to all three user categories:

```
[user1@server1 ~]$ chmod a=rwx -v permfile1
mode of 'permfile1' changed from 0564 (r-xrw-r--) to 0777 (rwxrwxrwx)
```

5. Revoke write bit from the group members and write and execute bits from public:

```
[user1@server1 ~]$ chmod g-w,o-wx permfile1 -v
mode of 'permfile1' changed from 0777 (rwxrwxrwx) to 0754 (rwxr-xr--)
```

Exercise 4-2: Modify Permission Bits Using Octal Form

Perform this exercise on *server1* as *user1*.

For this exercise, a file called *permfile2* exists with read permission for the owner (*user1*), owning group (*user1*), and other, as shown below. If the permissions vary, bring them to the desired state by executing **chmod 444 permfile2** prior to starting the exercise.

```
-r--r--r--. 1 user1 user1 0 Sep  6 21:12 permfile2
```

In this exercise, you will:

- Add an execute bit for the owner and a write permission bit for group and public
- Revoke the write bit from public and assign read, write, and execute permissions to the three user categories at the same time

Use the -v switch with the *chmod* command to display what it has changed and/or view the long listing after each command execution for verification.

1. Add an execute bit for the owner:

```
[user1@server1 ~]$ chmod -v 544 permfile2
mode of 'permfile2' changed from 0444 (r--r--r--) to 0544 (r-xr--r--)
```

2. Add a write permission bit for group and public:

```
[user1@server1 ~]$ chmod -v 566 permfile2
mode of 'permfile2' changed from 0544 (r-xr--r--) to 0566 (r-xrw-rw-)
```

3. Revoke the write bit for public:

```
[user1@server1 ~]$ chmod -v 564 permfile2
mode of 'permfile2' changed from 0566 (r-xrw-rw-) to 0564 (r-xrw-r--)
```

4. Assign read, write, and execute permission bits to all three user categories:

```
[user1@server1 ~]$ chmod 777 -v permfile2
mode of 'permfile2' changed from 0564 (r-xrw-r--) to 0777 (rwxrwxrwx)
```

Default Permissions

Linux assigns *default permissions* to files and directories at the time of their creation. The system calculates default permissions for a new file or directory by subtracting the *umask* (*user mask*) from a preset *initial* permissions value.

The umask is a three-digit octal value (also represented in symbolic notation) that refers to the read, write, and execute permissions for the owner, group, and public. Its purpose is to set default permissions on new files and directories without impacting the permissions on the existing files and directories. The default umask is 0022 for all users including the *root* user. Note that the leading 0 has no significance. Run the *umask* command without any options to display the current umask in octal notation:

```
[user1@server1 ~]$ umask
0022
```

Run the command again but with the -S option to display the umask in symbolic form:

```
[user1@server1 ~]$ umask -S
u=rwx,g=rx,o=rx
```

The initial permissions are 666 (rw-rw-rw-) for files and 777 (rwxrwxrwx) for directories. For security reasons, new files are never created with execute permissions, even if the umask calculation suggests otherwise (e.g., a umask of 000 results in file permissions of 666, not 777). The execute bit must be explicitly added later with the *chmod* command if required.

Calculating Default Permissions

Consider the following example to calculate the default permission values on files:

```
Initial Permissions      666
umask                  – 022   (subtract)
==========================
Default Permissions      644
```

This is an indication that every new file will have read and write permissions assigned to the owner, and a read-only permission to the owning group and others.

To calculate the default permission values on directories:

```
Initial Permissions      777
umask                  – 022    (subtract)
==========================
Default Permissions      755
```

This indicates that every new directory created will have read, write, and execute permissions assigned to the owner, and read and execute permissions to the owning group and everyone else.

If you want different default permissions set on new files and directories, you must modify the umask. You first need to determine the desired default values. For instance, if you want all new files and directories to get 640 and 750 permissions, you can set umask to 027 by running either of the following:

```
[user1@server1 ~]$ umask 027                          or
[user1@server1 ~]$ umask u=rwx,g=rx,o=
```

The new value becomes effective right away, and it will only be applied to files and directories created thereafter. The existing files and directories will remain intact. Now create *tempfile1* and *tempdir1* as *user1* under */home/user1* to test the effect of the new umask:

```
[user1@server1 ~]$ touch tempfile1
[user1@server1 ~]$ ls -l tempfile1
-rw-r-----. 1 user1 user1 0 Sep  6 21:42 tempfile1
[user1@server1 ~]$ mkdir tempdir1
[user1@server1 ~]$ ls -ld tempdir1
drwxr-x---. 2 user1 user1 6 Sep  6 21:42 tempdir1
```

The above examples show that the new file and directory were created with different permissions. The file received (666 – 027 = 640) and the directory (777 – 027 = 750) permissions.

The umask value set at the command line will be lost as soon as you log off. To retain the new setting, place it in an appropriate shell startup file discussed in Chapter 07 "The Bash Shell".

File Searching

A typical RHEL system can contain hundreds of thousands to millions of files distributed across multiple file systems. At times, you will need to look for one or more files based on certain criteria. For example, you might need to find all files owned by employees who left the company over a year ago, or search for all the files that have been modified in the past 20 days by a specific user. For such situations, RHEL offers a command called *find*. You supply your search criteria and this command gets you the result. You can also instruct this utility to execute a command on the files as they are found.

Using the find Command

The *find* command recursively searches a directory tree for files and directories that match specified criteria and can optionally perform actions on them. You can tailor this tool to look for files in a number of ways. The search criteria may include tracking files by name or part of the name, owning user, owning group, permissions, inode number, last access or modification time in days or minutes, size, and file type. Figure 4-2 shows the general syntax of this command.

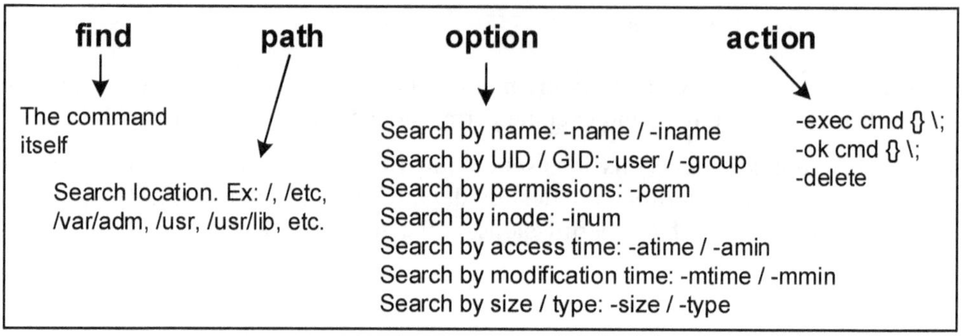

Figure 4-2 find Command Syntax

With *find*, files that match the criteria are located and their full paths are displayed.

Exercise 4-3: Perform Basic File Searches

Perform this exercise on *server1* as *user1* with *sudo* where required. The use of *sudo* is discussed in Chapter 06 "Advanced User and Group Management". In this exercise, you will:

- Search for a file by name
- Perform a case-insensitive name search
- Search for files by size
- Search for files by modification time

1. Search for a file called *file10* by its name in *user1*'s home directory. Create this file if it does not already exist.

```
[user1@server1 ~]$ find . -name file10 -print
./file10
```

-print is optional. The *find* command, by default, displays the results on the screen. You do not need to specify this option.

2. Perform a case-insensitive search in */dev* for files and directories whose names begin with the string "usb" followed by any characters (filename globbing):

```
[user1@server1 ~]$ find /dev -iname usb*
/dev/usbmon0
/dev/usbmon1
/dev/bus/usb
/dev/usbmon2
```

3. Find files in *user1*'s home directory smaller than 1 MB in size. You can issue the command from anywhere in the directory tree.

```
[user1@server1 ~]$ find ~ -size -1M
```

The tilde character (~) expands to a user's home directory.

4. Search for files larger than 40 MB in size in the */usr* directory:

```
[user1@server1 ~]$ sudo find /usr -size +40M
```

5. Find files in the */etc* directory that were modified more than 2000 days ago:

```
[user1@server1 ~]$ sudo find /etc -mtime +2000
```

Repeat the above search for files modified exactly 12 days ago; replace "+2000" with "12".

6. Find files in the */var/log* directory that have been modified (-mmin) in the last (-) 100 minutes:

```
[user1@server1 ~]$ sudo find /var/log -mmin -100
```

Repeat the above search for files modified exactly 25 minutes ago; replace "-100" with "25".

Exercise 4-4: Perform Advanced File Searches

Perform this exercise on *server1* as *user1* with *sudo* where required. The use of *sudo* is discussed in Chapter 06 "Advanced User and Group Management". In this exercise, you will:

- Search for files using owner and group criteria
- Search for files by permissions and type
- Search for files by directory depth
- Perform multi-criteria searches

1. Search for files in the */etc/sysconfig* directory with owning user set to *root*:

```
[user1@server1 ~]$ sudo find /etc/sysconfig -user root
```

2. Search the entire directory structure for files owned by *root* whose owning group is not *root* (-not -group or ! -group):

```
[user1@server1 ~]$ sudo find / -user root -not -group root
```

3. Search for block device files in the */dev* directory with permissions matching exactly 660 (that is, all other permission bits must be unset):

```
[user1@server1 ~]$ sudo find /dev -type b -perm 660
```

4. Find files in the */etc/systemd* directory that are executable by at least their owner or their group (/110):

```
[user1@server1 ~]$ sudo find /etc/systemd -perm /110
```

5. Search for all directories by the name "src" in */usr* at a maximum of two subdirectory levels below:

```
[user1@server1 ~]$ sudo find /usr -maxdepth 2 -type d -name src
```

Repeat the above search, but at 3+ subdirectory levels beneath */usr*, substitute -maxdepth 2 with -mindepth 3.

6. Search for all regular files in */usr* owned by *root* with size smaller than 4MB and with permissions granting read, write, and execute access to the owner (rwx, or octal 700):

```
[user1@server1 ~]$ sudo find /usr -type f -user root -size -4M -perm 700
```

Using find with -exec and -ok Flags

An advanced use of the *find* command is to perform an action on files as they are found based on any criteria outlined in the previous subsection and in the command's manual pages. You can perform basic file management operations such as copying, erasing, renaming, changing ownership, or modifying permissions on each file found. This is done using the -exec action. An equivalent option -ok may be used instead, which requires user confirmation before taking an action.

> **EXAM TIP:** The find command is extremely flexible and offers a wide array of options for searching files. You should know the use of the exec option well.

Exercise 4-5: Search for Files and Perform an Action

Perform this exercise on *server1* as *user1* with *sudo* where required. The use of *sudo* is discussed in Chapter 06 "Advanced User and Group Management". In this exercise, you will:

- Search for files and list them
- Search for files using a variety of criteria, and copy them to a directory

1. Search for directories in the entire directory tree by the name "core" and list them as they are discovered, without prompting for user confirmation:

```
[user1@server1 ~]$ sudo find / -name core -type d -exec ls -ld {} \;
```

The *find* command replaces {} with each matched pathname as it is found. The semicolon character (;) marks the termination of the command and is escaped with the backslash character (\).

2. Search for all files with a .conf extension in the */etc/sysconfig* directory and copy them interactively to */tmp*:

```
[user1@server1 ~]$ sudo find /etc/sysconfig -name *.conf -ok cp {} /tmp \;
< cp ... /etc/sysconfig/nftables.conf > ? y
```

The destination directory (*/tmp*) is specified between {} and \;. Replace -ok with -exec if you do not want to be prompted for confirmation.

3. Search for all regular files under */var/log* directory with a .log extension that were modified in the past 24 hours, and copy them into $HOME:

```
[user1@server1 ~]$ sudo find /var/log -type f -name "*.log" -mtime -1 \
> -exec cp {} $HOME \;
```

The *find* command is a useful and powerful tool with numerous other options. Refer to its manual pages for details. Try running this command with similar or different criteria for additional practice.

Chapter Summary

This chapter covered three fundamental areas of file management: permissions, default permissions, and file searching. We learned about permission classes, types, and modes, and applied this knowledge using both octal and symbolic notation to modify access rights on files and directories.

We also examined the concept of default permissions, explaining how to configure parent directories so that new files and subdirectories inherit specific permissions automatically. This included a detailed look at the role of the umask value in calculating these default permissions.

Finally, we explored the powerful find utility, learning to construct search criteria and use its extended -exec flag to perform actions on the results.

Review Questions

1. What would the *find / -name core -ok rm {} \;* command do?
2. Default permissions are calculated by subtracting the initial permissions from the umask value. True or False?
3. Name the permission classes, types, and modes.
4. The default umask for a normal user in bash shell is 0027. True or False?
5. The output generated by the *umask* command shows the current user mask in four digits. What is the significance of the left-most digit?
6. What would the command *find /dev -type c -perm 440* do?
7. What is the equivalent symbolic value for permissions 751?
8. What permissions would the owner of the file get if the *chmod* command is executed with 555?
9. What does *chmod a+r file1* do?
10. What does the execute (x) permission mean on a directory?

Answers to Review Questions

1. The command searches the entire file system for files named core and, for each match, prompts the user for confirmation before executing the rm command to delete that file.
2. False. Default permissions are calculated by subtracting the umask value from the initial permission values.

3. Permission classes are user, group, and public; permission types are read, write, and execute; and permission modes are add, revoke, and assign.
4. False. The default umask for bash shell users is 0022.
5. The left-most digit has no significance in the umask value.
6. The command finds all character device files under */dev* whose permissions match exactly 440.
7. The equivalent for octal 751 is rwxr-x--x.
8. The owner receives read and execute permissions.
9. It adds read permission for user, group, and other.
10. It allows entering (cd into) the directory.

Do-It-Yourself Challenge Labs

The following labs are designed to reinforce most of the concepts and skills covered in this chapter. You are expected to complete these labs without external assistance. A step-by-step guide is not provided, as the required knowledge has already been presented in the chapter; however, each lab includes hints pointing to the relevant major topic(s).

Use the lab environment created specifically for the end-of-chapter labs. See the sub-section "Lab Environment for End-of-Chapter Labs" in Chapter 01 "Local Installation" for details.

Lab 4-1: Manipulate File Permissions

As *user1* on *server3*, create file *file11* and directory *dir11* in the home directory. Make a note of the permissions on them. Run the *umask* command to determine the current umask. Change the umask value to 0035 using symbolic notation. Create *file22* and directory *dir22* in the home directory. Observe the permissions on *file22* and *dir22,* and compare them with the permissions on *file11* and *dir11*. Use the *chmod* command and modify the permissions on *file11* to match those on *file22*. Use the *chmod* command and modify the permissions on *dir22* to match those on *dir11*. Do not remove *file11*, *file22*, *dir11*, and *dir22* yet. (Hint: File and Directory Access Permissions).

Lab 4-2: Find Files

As *user1* on *server3*, execute *sudo find* to search for all files in the entire directory structure that have been modified in the last 300 minutes and display their type. Use the *find* command again and search for named pipe and socket files. (Hint: File Searching).

Lab 4-3: Find Files Using Different Criteria

As *user1* on *server3*, issue *sudo find* to search for regular files under */usr* that were accessed more than 100 days ago, are not bigger than 5 MB in size, and are owned by the user *root*. (Hint: File Searching).

Chapter 05

Basic User and Group Management

This chapter describes the following major topics:

- Monitor Current and Past User Logins
- Inspect System Reboot History
- Query User and Group Identity Information
- Decode the Structure of the Local User Authentication Files
- Manage the User Lifecycle: Creating, Modifying, and Deleting Local User Accounts
- Assign and Change User Passwords
- Create Non-Login User Accounts

RHCSA Objectives:

51. Create, delete, and modify local user accounts
52. Change passwords and adjust password aging for local user accounts (only the first part of this objective "change passwords for local user accounts" is covered in this chapter; the second part is in Chapter 06)

Every user on the Linux system is an identity with specific rights and boundaries. This chapter is about managing those identities. User login activities are monitored and recorded in various files. RHEL offers a set of tools that read the activity data from these files and display the results. In addition to user activities, a history of system reboots is also maintained, and you can view it with one of the tools. This information is useful in debugging, testing, or auditing purposes.

To gain system access, an authorized individual must have a unique user account created for them. You assign this user a password, and they can change it themselves. User account information is recorded in several files. While you can edit these files manually, if necessary, this practice is discouraged. As a Linux administrator, a solid grasp of the syntax and content of these files is paramount. You can modify user attributes later, or remove the account from the system altogether if it is no longer required.

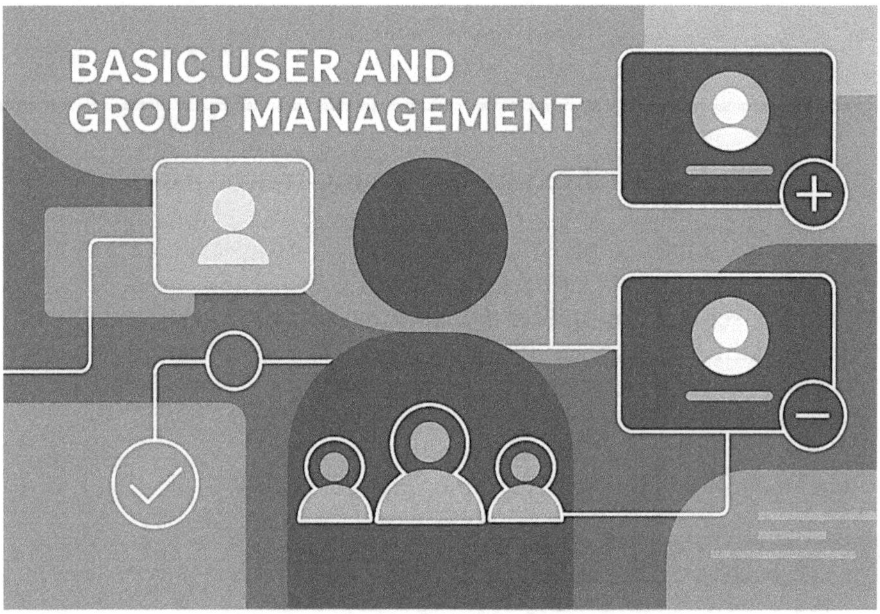

Though service user accounts are added to the system when you install a corresponding service, there may be situations when you need to add them manually. These accounts do not require login access; their presence is needed to support an installed application.

User Login Activity and Information

On a busy RHEL system, many users sign in and run commands under their own accounts, or they switch to the *root* or another user account to run tasks that only those users have the privilege to execute. As an administrator, it is your responsibility to ensure that only authorized users are allowed to access the system. You can monitor user login activity—including who is currently logged in and their previous successful and unsuccessful login attempts—to detect suspicious behavior. For instance, multiple failed login attempts for a valid user account may indicate a forgotten password or a possible break-in attempt.

RHEL maintains many log files that are continuously updated by system services as activity occurs. These logs capture login activity along with other types of events. This section focuses on the log files and tools that pertain to user logins; others logs are discussed in later chapters.

Listing Logged-In Users

A list of successfully authenticated users can be displayed using one of the two basic Linux tools: *who* and *w*.

The *who* command reads the */run/utmp* file to report users currently logged in. Here is an example from *server1*:

```
[user1@server1 ~]$ who
user1    pts/0        2025-11-23 08:57 (192.168.0.86)
```

Column 1 displays the username, column 2 shows the terminal device filename (pts stands for *pseudo terminal slave*, and tty identifies a terminal window on the console), columns 3 and 4 show the date and time of the login, and column 5 indicates if the terminal session is graphical (:0), remote (IP address), or text on the console (blank).

The *w* (*what*) command presents similar information, but it adds more detail. In addition to what *who* shows, it also lists the user's idle time (IDLE), along with the total CPU time consumed by all processes on that terminal (JCPU), CPU time for the current process (PCPU), and the command the user is currently running (WHAT). In the following example, the header line displays the current system time (08:57:44), the system up duration (4 days, 16 hours, and 20 minutes), number of users currently logged in (4), and the average number of runnable processes over the past 1, 5, and 15 minutes (0.01, 0.01, and 0.00), respectively. This header mirrors the output of the *uptime* command, which was discussed in Chapter 02 "Initial System Interaction".

```
[user1@server1 ~]$ w
 08:57:44 up 4 days, 16:20,  4 users,  load average: 0.01, 0.01, 0.00
USER     TTY        LOGIN@   IDLE   JCPU   PCPU WHAT
gdm      tty1       Tue16    4days  3:18   0.05s /usr/bin/gnome-keyring-daemon -
gdm                 Tue16   20:43m  0.00s  1.03s /usr/lib/systemd/systemd --user
user1               08:57   20:43m  0.00s  0.19s sshd-session: user1 [priv]
user1               08:57   20:43m  0.00s  0.64s /usr/lib/systemd/systemd --user
```

The load average numbers represent the system's average runnable task count over the given periods. A value of 0.00 indicates no load, 1.00 means the CPU was fully utilized, and a value above 1.00 indicates processes were waiting for CPU time.

Inspecting History of Successful Login Attempts and Reboots

The *last* command reports historical successful user login activity and system reboot events by reading the */var/log/wtmp* file. This file keeps a record of all login and logout activities, including the login time, duration a user stayed logged in, and tty (where the user session took place). Consider the following two examples.

To list all user login, logout, and system reboot occurrences, issue the *last* command without any arguments:

```
[user1@server1 ~]$ last
user1    pts/0        192.168.0.86     Sun Nov 23 08:57   still logged in
user1    pts/0        192.168.0.86     Sat Nov 22 13:50 - 01:51  (12:00)
user1    pts/0        192.168.0.86     Fri Nov 21 18:57 - 12:58  (18:00)
user1    pts/0        192.168.0.86     Fri Nov 21 15:56 - 18:57  (03:00)
user1    pts/0        192.168.0.86     Fri Nov 21 10:59 - 13:59  (03:00)
user1    pts/0        192.168.0.86     Fri Nov 21 08:49 - 10:49  (02:00)
user1    pts/1        192.168.0.86     Fri Nov 21 07:33 - 10:16  (02:43)
user1    pts/0        192.168.0.86     Thu Nov 20 22:15 - 07:33  (09:17)
user1    pts/0        192.168.0.86     Thu Nov 20 20:32 - 22:15  (01:43)
user1    pts/0        192.168.0.86     Thu Nov 20 11:15 - 14:49  (03:33)
user1    pts/0        192.168.0.86     Thu Nov 20 08:51 - 10:51  (02:00)
user1    pts/0        192.168.0.86     Wed Nov 19 10:55 - 08:51  (21:55)
user1    pts/1        192.168.0.86     Wed Nov 19 10:19 - 10:20  (00:00)
user1    pts/0        192.168.0.86     Wed Nov 19 08:23 - 10:55  (02:31)
user1    pts/0        192.168.0.86     Tue Nov 18 23:01 - 08:02  (09:00)
user1    pts/0        192.168.0.86     Tue Nov 18 16:38 - 21:38  (05:00)
reboot   system boot  6.12.0-55.9.1.el Tue Nov 18 16:37   still running
user1    pts/1        192.168.0.86     Tue Nov 18 09:42 - 12:08  (02:25)
wtmp begins Mon Oct 27 11:34:17 2025
```

For user login activity, the output shows:

Column 1: Login name of the user
Column 2: Terminal name assigned upon logging in
Column 3: Terminal name or IP address from where the connection was established
Column 4 to 7: Day, month, date, and time when the connection was established
Column 8: Log out time. If the user is still logged on, it will say "still logged in"
Column 9: Duration of the login session

For system reboots:

Column 1: Action name (reboot)
Column 2: Activity name (system boot)
Column 3: Linux kernel version
Column 4 to 7: Day, month, date, and time when the *reboot* command was issued
Column 8: System restart time
Column 9: Duration the system remained down. If the system is running, it will say "still running".

The last line in the output indicates the log filename (*wtmp*) used to record this information and the time it started to log events.

To list system reboot details only, you can issue the *last* command and pass reboot as an argument:

```
[user1@server1 ~]$ last reboot
reboot   system boot  6.12.0-55.9.1.el Tue Nov 18 16:37   still running
reboot   system boot  6.12.0-55.9.1.el Sun Nov 16 08:58 - 12:09 (2+03:10
```

This filters the output to show only system boot entries, formatted using the same column definitions described above.

Viewing History of Failed User Login Attempts

The *lastb* command reports a history of unsuccessful login attempts by reading the */var/log/btmp* file. This file records failed authentication attempts, including the username, tty (where the attempt was made), and time. Consider the following example.

To list all failed login attempts, run the *lastb* command. You must be *root* or use *sudo* to run this command.

```
[root@server1 ~]# lastb
root      ssh:notty    192.168.0.4      Fri Jan 27 14:28 - 14:28  (00:00)
root      ssh:notty    192.168.0.4      Fri Jan 27 14:27 - 14:27  (00:00)
root      ssh:notty    192.168.0.4      Fri Jan 27 14:11 - 14:11  (00:00)
root      ssh:notty    192.168.0.4      Fri Jan 27 14:11 - 14:11  (00:00)
root      ssh:notty    192.168.0.4      Fri Jan 27 14:09 - 14:09  (00:00)
root      ssh:notty    192.168.0.4      Fri Jan 27 14:08 - 14:08  (00:00)

btmp begins Fri Jan 27 14:08:57 2023
```

The output is presented in multiple columns similar to the *last* command. Here is the description for each column:

Column 1: Username who attempted to log in
Column 2: Name of the protocol used. No tty was assigned as the attempt failed
Column 3: Terminal name or IP address from where the attempt originated
Column 4 to 7: Day, month, date, and time of the attempt
Column 8: Duration the login attempt was tried
Column 9: Duration the login attempt lasted for

The last line in the output shows the log filename (*btmp*) being read and the time when it began recording events.

Reporting Recent User Login Attempts

The *lastlog* command reports the most recent login time for every user account on the system. It reads data from the */var/log/lastlog* file, which stores the most recent successful login recorded for each user, including the username, port (or tty), and time. Consider the following example.

```
[user1@server1 ~]$ lastlog
Username         Port     From             Latest
root             pts/1                     Thu Nov 20 20:59:18 -0500 2025
bin                                        **Never logged in**
daemon                                     **Never logged in**
adm                                        **Never logged in**
lp                                         **Never logged in**

........
tcpdump                                    **Never logged in**
user1            pts/0    192.168.0.86     Sun Nov 23 08:57:37 -0500 2025
```

The displayed output is organized into four columns. Here is the description for each column:

Column 1: Login name of the user
Column 2: Terminal name assigned upon logging in

Column 3: Terminal name or IP address from where the session originated
Column 4: Timestamp of the latest successful login, or the text "Never logged in" for accounts that have never authenticated.

System accounts (created to run and manage background system services) will almost always show "Never logged in", which is expected because these accounts are not intended for interactive logins. System accounts are discussed in detail in the next section.

Examining User and Group Information

The *id* (*identifier*) command displays detailed information about the calling user. This includes the user's UID (*User IDentifier*), username, GID (*Group IDentifier*), primary group name, secondary groups the user is a member of, and the SELinux security context. The following example shows typical output when this command is executed without any option:

```
[user1@server1 ~]$ id
uid=1000(user1) gid=1000(user1) groups=1000(user1),10(wheel) context=unconfined
_u:unconfined_r:unconfined_t:s0-s0:c0.c1023
```

Each user and group has a corresponding number—called UID and GID—for identification purposes. These numeric IDs are used internally by the kernel, while the names exist for human readability. These are discussed in subsequent sections. For SELinux, see Chapter 22 "Security Enhanced Linux".

The *id* command can also be used by a user to query identity information for other users. The following example shows the information for the *root* user:

```
[user1@server1 ~]$ sudo id
uid=0(root) gid=0(root) groups=0(root) context=unconfined_u:unconfined_r:unconf
ined_t:s0-s0:c0.c1023
```

The *groups* command, in contrast, lists all groups that the calling user belongs to:

```
[user1@server1 ~]$ groups
user1 wheel
```

The first group (user1) listed is the user's primary group; and the remaining entries (zero or more) are secondary or supplementary groups, which grant additional access permissions beyond those provided by the user's primary group.

You can also specify a username as an argument to the *groups* command to view the group memberships of another user. Try running **groups user2** (user2 must exist) and observe the outcome.

Local User Authentication Files

RHEL supports three fundamental types of user accounts: *root*, *system*, and *normal* accounts. The *root* user (a.k.a. the *superuser* or *administrator*) has unrestricted access to all system resources, services, and administrative functions. This user is created automatically during installation. System accounts are used by system services, such as apache, ftp, mail, chrony, and others. These accounts allow services to run with limited privileges rather than running as *root*. Normal users have standard, non-administrative privileges. They can run applications and programs permitted to them but cannot perform administrative tasks unless explicitly granted elevated rights.

Local user and group information is stored in four primary files located in the */etc* directory. These files—*passwd, shadow*, *group*, and *gshadow*—are updated when you create, modify, or delete a local user or group. They are also referenced by the system during login to validate user identity and credentials, which is why they are collectively known as user authentication files. Because these files are so critical to system operation, the system automatically maintains backup versions of each—*passwd-*, *shadow-*, *group-*, and *gshadow*—in the */etc* directory before any changes are made to them.

Here is an example showing the four files and their backups as listed from the */etc* directory:

```
[user1@server1 ~]$ ls -l /etc/passwd* /etc/group* /etc/shadow* /etc/gshadow*
-rw-r--r--. 1 root root  869 Nov  2 05:07 /etc/group
-rw-r--r--. 1 root root  850 Oct 27 10:50 /etc/group-
----------. 1 root root  703 Oct 27 11:01 /etc/gshadow
----------. 1 root root  693 Oct 27 10:50 /etc/gshadow-
-rw-r--r--. 1 root root 2352 Oct 27 11:01 /etc/passwd
-rw-r--r--. 1 root root 2306 Oct 27 10:50 /etc/passwd-
----------. 1 root root 1102 Oct 27 11:01 /etc/shadow
----------. 1 root root 1107 Oct 27 11:01 /etc/shadow-
```

Although these files are small, they grow gradually as more users and groups are added. Let's examine these files closely to understand the type of information they store and how they are structured.

The passwd File

The *passwd* file is a simple plaintext file that contains vital user account data. Each row in the file holds information for one user account. There are seven colon-separated fields per line entry. A sample row is displayed in Figure 5-1.

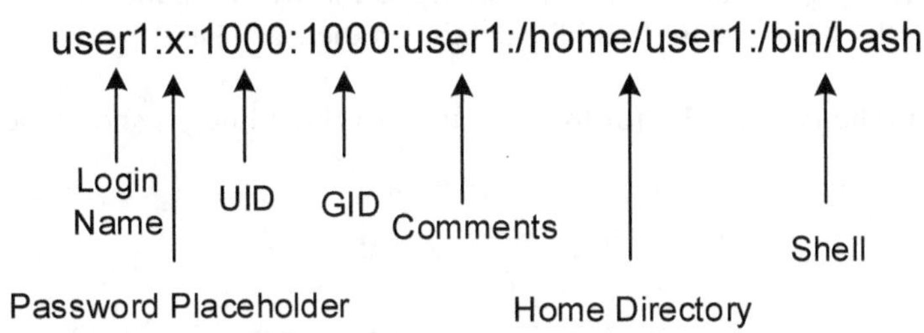

Figure 5-1 The passwd File

Here is a description for each field:

Field 1 (Login Name): Contains the login name for signing in. Login names may contain up to 255 characters, including the underscore (_) and hyphen (-) characters, but the use of special characters and uppercase letters is discouraged.
Field 2 (Password): Typically contains the letter "x", indicating that the encrypted password is stored securely in the */etc/shadow* file. An asterisk "*" in this field denotes a disabled account (commonly used for system accounts) while an exclamation mark "!" implies that the account is

locked. If this field contains a hashed password, it would use the legacy, non-shadow authentication, which is not the default in RHEL.

A hashed password is a combination of random letters, numbers, and special characters. It is an irreversible, unique, and scrambled string of characters generated from a clear-text password. It is generated by converting the password using one of the available hashing algorithms. By default, RHEL uses the SHA-512 algorithm for this purpose.

An algorithm is a set of well-defined but complex mathematical instructions used in data encryption and decryption techniques.

Field 3 (UID): Comprises a numeric UID between 0 and approximately 4.2 billion. UID 0 is reserved for the *root* account, UIDs between 1 and 200 are statistically assigned by Red Hat to core system accounts, UIDs between 201 and 999 are reserved for non-core system accounts, and UIDs 1000 and beyond are assigned to normal user accounts. By default, RHEL begins assigning UIDs to new users at 1000.
Field 4 (GID): Holds a GID that corresponds with a group entry in the */etc/group* file. By default, RHEL creates a *User Private Group* (UPG) for every new user with a name matching their login name and a GID that matches their UID. The GID defined in this field represents the user's primary group.
Field 5 (GECOS/Comments): Optionally stores general information about the user, such as their full name, phone number, or department. The name "GECOS" is a historical reference to the *General Electric Comprehensive Operating System.*
Field 6 (Home Directory): Defines the absolute path to the user home directory. A *home* directory is the location where a user is placed after signing in and it is used for personal storage. The default location for user home directories is */home.*
Field 7 (Shell): Contains the absolute path to the shell program that the user will use as their primary shell after logging in. The default shell used in RHEL is the Bash shell (*/bin/bash*). Consult Chapter 07 "The Bash Shell" for details on the Bash shell.

A *head* and *tail* from the *passwd* file for the first and last three lines is shown below:

```
[user1@server1 ~]$ head -3 /etc/passwd ; tail -3 /etc/passwd
root:x:0:0:Super User:/root:/bin/bash
bin:x:1:1:bin:/bin:/usr/sbin/nologin
daemon:x:2:2:daemon:/sbin:/usr/sbin/nologin
dnsmasq:x:981:980:Dnsmasq DHCP and DNS server:/var/lib/dnsmasq:/usr/sbin/nologir
tcpdump:x:72:72:tcpdump:/:/usr/sbin/nologin
user1:x:1000:1000:user1:/home/user1:/bin/bash
```

The output indicates the *root* user with UID 0 followed by two system accounts (*bin* and *daemon*). The last three lines display the three user accounts that were created earlier as part of some of the exercises.

Verify the permissions and ownership on the *passwd* file:

```
[user1@server1 ~]$ ls -l /etc/passwd
-rw-r--r--. 1 root root 2352 Oct 27 11:01 /etc/passwd
```

The access permissions on the file are 644 (readable by all, writable only by the owner), and it is owned by the *root* user.

The shadow File

RHEL uses a secure password control mechanism called *shadow passwords*. With this mechanism, user passwords are hashed and stored in a more secure */etc/shadow* file. This system also enforces password aging, which allows setting limits on user passwords such as expiration and warning periods on a per-user basis. These limits and other settings are defined in the */etc/login.defs* file, which the shadow password mechanism enforces on user accounts. This is called *password aging*. Unlike the *passwd* file, which is world-readable and owner-writable, the *shadow* file has no access permissions at all. This is done to safeguard the file's content.

With the shadow password mechanism active, a user is initially checked in the *passwd* file for existence and then in the *shadow* file for authenticity.

The *shadow* file contains user authentication and password aging information. Each row in the file corresponds to one entry in the *passwd* file. There are nine colon-separated fields per line entry. A sample row from this file is showcased in Figure 5-2.

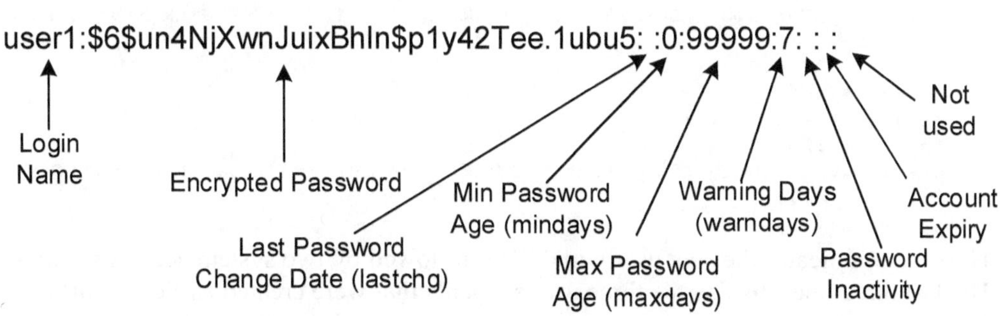

Figure 5-2 The shadow File

Here is a description for each field:

Field 1 (Login Name): Contains the login name as appears in the *passwd* file.
Field 2 (Encrypted Password): Consists of a hashed password. A single exclamation mark (!) at the beginning of this field implies that the user account is locked. If this field is empty, the user will have passwordless entry into the system.
Field 3 (Last Password Change Date): Sets the number of days since the UNIX epoch, a.k.a. UNIX time (January 01, 1970 00:00:00 UTC) when the password was last modified. An empty field disables password aging features, and a 0 forces the user to change their password upon next login.
Field 4 (Minimum Password Age, mindays): Expresses the minimum number of days that must elapse before the user is allowed to change their password. This field can be altered using the *chage* command with the -m option or the *passwd* command with the -n option. A 0 or null in this field disables this feature.
Field 5 (Maximum Password Age, maxdays): Defines the maximum number of days of password validity before the user password expires and it must be changed. This field may be altered using the *chage* command with the -M option or the *passwd* command with the -x

option. A null value here disables this feature along with other features such as the maximum password age, warning alerts, and the user inactivity period.

Field 6 (Password Warning Period, warndays): Denotes the number of days for which the user gets warnings for changing their password before it actually expires. This field may be altered using the *chage* command with the -W option or the *passwd* command with the -w option. A 0 or null in this field disables this feature.

Field 7 (Password Inactivity Period): Defines the maximum allowable number of days for the user to log in with the expired password and change it. This field may be altered using the *chage* command with the -I option or the *passwd* command with the -i option. An empty field disables this feature.

Field 8 (Account Expiry Date): Determines the number of days since the UNIX time when the user account will expire and no longer be available for logging in. This field may be altered using the *chage* command with the -E option. An empty field disables this feature.

Field 9 (Reserved): Reserved for future use.

A *head* and *tail* from the *shadow* file for the first and last three lines is shown below:

```
[user1@server1 ~]$ sudo head -3 /etc/shadow ; sudo tail -3 /etc/shadow
root:$y$j9T$nOZ7ODpmS8ejX90k/1lj6neU$pX5v4d.o60/aKHYvXvJZxMwNr7fdDlDJJaQfHbrv5f1
::0:99999:7:::
bin:*:20025:0:99999:7:::
daemon:*:20025:0:99999:7:::
dnsmasq:!:20388::::::
tcpdump:!:20388::::::
user1:$y$j9T$tWnIvsH5NKtVEbxhIVyZZx.5$t6w//hR1yzgZJ8c9Jz5B8DFdgdT5XWqBygmD9JOKeF
2::0:99999:7:::
```

The output indicates the *root* user with UID 0 followed by two system accounts (*bin* and *daemon*). The last three lines display the three user accounts that were created earlier as part of some of the exercises. Notice that login names are used as a common key between the *shadow* and *passwd* files.

Verify the permissions and ownership on the *shadow* file:

```
[user1@server1 ~]$ ls -l /etc/shadow
----------. 1 root root 1102 Oct 27 11:01 /etc/shadow
```

The access permissions on the file are 000 (no permissions for user, group, or others), and it is owned by the *root* user. There is a special mechanism in place that is employed in the background to update this file when a user account is added, modified, deleted, or the password changed. This is discussed in Chapter 22 "Security Enhanced Linux".

The group File

The *group* file is a simple plaintext file and contains critical group information. Each row in the file stores information for one group entry. Every user on the system must be a member of at least one group, which is referred to as the *User Private Group* (UPG). By default, a group name matches the username it is associated with. Additional groups may be set up, and users with common file access requirements can be added to them. There are four colon-separated fields per line entry. A sample row from the file is exhibited in Figure 5-3.

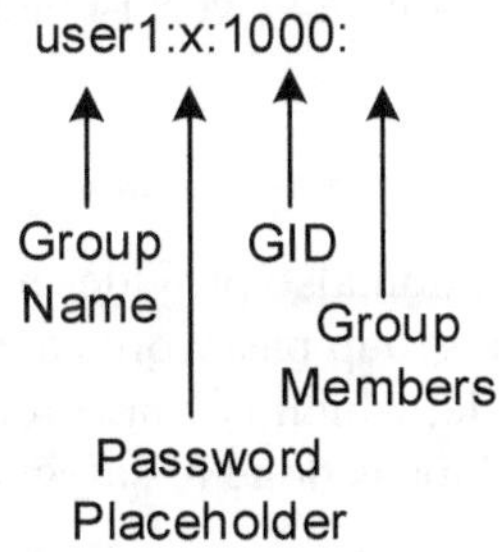

Figure 5-3 The group File

Here is a description for each field:

Field 1 (Group Name): Holds a group name that must begin with a letter. Group names with up to 255 characters, including the underscore (_) and hyphen (-) characters, are supported. It is not recommended to include special characters and uppercase letters in group names.

Field 2 (Password Placeholder): Usually contains an "x", indicating that the group password is stored in the */etc/gshadow* file. It can also be empty or contain a hashed group password. You can set a password on a group if you want non-members to be able to change their group identity temporarily using the *newgrp* command. The non-members must enter the correct password to do so.

Field 3 (GID): Holds a GID, which is also placed in the GID field of the *passwd* file. By default, groups are created with GIDs starting at 1000 and with the same name as the username. The system allows several users to belong to a single group; it also allows a single user to be a member of multiple groups at the same time.

Field 4 (Group Members): Lists the usernames of group members, separated by commas. Note that this field does not include users for whom this is their primary group; that is defined by the GID in the *passwd* file.

A *head* and *tail* from the *group* file for the first and last three lines is shown below:

```
[user1@server1 ~]$ head -3 /etc/group ; tail -3 /etc/group
root:x:0:
bin:x:1:
daemon:x:2:
tcpdump:x:72:
plocate:x:979:
user1:x:1000:
```

The output discloses the *root* user with GID 0 followed by two group system accounts (*bin* and *daemon*). The last three lines showcase the three groups that were created earlier as part of some of the exercises.

Verify the permissions and ownership on the *group* file:

```
[user1@server1 ~]$ ls -l /etc/group
-rw-r--r--. 1 root root 869 Nov  2 05:07 /etc/group
```

The access permissions on the file are 644 (world-readable and owner-writable), and it is owned by the *root* user.

The gshadow File

The shadow password implementation also provides an added layer of protection at the group level. With this mechanism in place, the group passwords are hashed and stored in a more secure file */etc/gshadow*. Unlike the *group* file, which is world-readable and owner-writable, the *gshadow* file has no access permissions at all. This is done to safeguard the file's content.

The *gshadow* file stores hashed group-level passwords. Each row in the file corresponds to one entry in the *group* file. There are four colon-separated fields per line entry. A sample row from this file is exhibited in Figure 5-4.

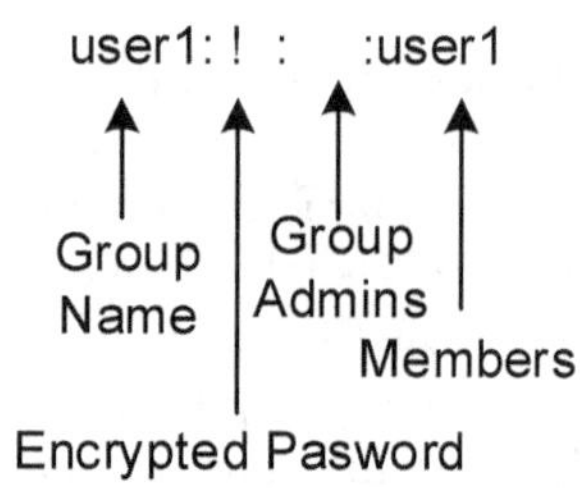

Figure 5-4 The gshadow File

Here is a description for each field:

Field 1 (Group Name): Consists of a group name as appeared in the *group* file.
Field 2 (Encrypted Password): Can contain a hashed password, which may be set with the *gpasswd* command for non-group members to access the group temporarily using the *newgrp* command. A single exclamation mark (!) or a null value in this field allows group members passwordless access and restricts non-members from switching into this group.
Field 3 (Group Administrators): Lists usernames of group administrators that are authorized to add or remove members with the *gpasswd* command.
Field 4 (Members): Holds a comma-separated list of supplementary group members.

The gpasswd command is used to add group administrators, add or delete group members, assign or revoke a group-level password, and disable the ability of the newgrp command to access a group. This command picks up the default values from the /etc/login.defs file. Additional discussion on this command is beyond the scope; however, you can view the manual pages for this command for details on its usage.

A *head* and *tail* from the *gshadow* file for the first and last three lines is shown below:

```
[user1@server1 ~]$ sudo head -3 /etc/gshadow ; sudo tail -3 /etc/gshadow
root:::
bin:::
daemon:::
tcpdump:!::
plocate:!::
user1:!::
```

The output indicates the *root* user with GID 0 followed by two group system accounts (*bin* and *daemon*). The last three lines exhibit the three groups that were created earlier as part of some of the exercises. Notice that group names are used as a common key between the *gshadow* and *group* files.

Verify the permissions and ownership on the *gshadow* file:

```
[user1@server1 ~]$ ls -l /etc/gshadow
----------. 1 root root 703 Oct 27 11:01 /etc/gshadow
```

The access permissions on the file are 000 (no permissions at all) and it is owned by the *root* user. There is a special mechanism in place that is employed in the background to update this file when a group account is added, modified, deleted, or the group password changed. This is discussed further in Chapter 22 "Security Enhanced Linux".

The useradd and login.defs Configuration Files

The *useradd* command (discussed in the next section) uses default values from the */etc/default/useradd* and */etc/login.defs* files for any options you do not explicitly provide on the command line. The *usermod*, *userdel*, *chage*, and *passwd* commands also consult the *login.defs* file as needed. Both files store several defaults including those that affect the password length and password lifecycle. You can use the *cat* or *less* command to view the *useradd* file content or display the settings with the *useradd* command as follows:

```
[user1@server1 ~]$ useradd -D
GROUP=100
GROUPS=
HOME=/home
INACTIVE=-1
EXPIRE=
SHELL=/bin/bash
SKEL=/etc/skel
USRSKEL=/usr/etc/skel
CREATE_MAIL_SPOOL=yes
LOG_INIT=yes
```

These defaults include the starting GID (GROUP) if USERGROUPS_ENAB in *login.defs* is set to no (the default is yes), home directory location (HOME), number of inactivity days between password expiry and permanent account disablement (INACTIVE), account expiry date (EXPIRE), login shell (SHELL), skeleton directory to copy user initialization files from (SKEL), and whether to create a mail spool directory (CREATE_MAIL_SPOOL). You will find a description for some of these in the next section.

The *login.defs* file comprises additional directives that set various defaults. User and group management commands consult this file to obtain information that is not supplied at the command line. A *grep* on the file with uncommented and non-empty lines is shown below:

```
[user1@server1 ~]$ grep -v ^# /etc/login.defs | grep -v ^$
MAIL_DIR          /var/spool/mail
UMASK             022
HOME_MODE         0700
PASS_MAX_DAYS     99999
PASS_MIN_DAYS     0
PASS_MIN_LEN      8
PASS_WARN_AGE     7
UID_MIN                    1000
UID_MAX                   60000
SYS_UID_MIN                 201
SYS_UID_MAX                 999
SUB_UID_MIN                  524288
SUB_UID_MAX               600100000
SUB_UID_COUNT                 65536
GID_MIN                    1000
GID_MAX                   60000
SYS_GID_MIN                 201
SYS_GID_MAX                 999
SUB_GID_MIN                  524288
SUB_GID_MAX               600100000
SUB_GID_COUNT                 65536
PASS_CHANGE_TRIES         5
PASS_ALWAYS_WARN          yes
ENCRYPT_METHOD YESCRYPT
USERGROUPS_ENAB yes
CREATE_HOME     yes
HMAC CRYPTO ALGO SHA512
```

The grep command is discussed in detail in Chapter 07 "The Bash Shell".

Most of these directives are elaborated in Table 5-1.

Option	Description
MAIL_DIR	Specifies the mail directory location
UMASK	Defines the umask value used to set permissions on new user home directories at creation
HOME_MODE	The permissions mode for new home directories. If not specified, the UMASK value is used.
PASS_MAX_DAYS, PASS_MIN_DAYS, and PASS_WARN_AGE	Define maximum, minimum, and warning period for password aging. See Chapter 06 "Advanced User and Group Management" for details.
UID_MIN, UID_MAX, GID_MIN, and GID_MAX	Define the UID and GID ranges for allocating to new normal users and groups

Option	Description
SYS_UID_MIN, SYS_UID_MAX, SYS_GID_MIN, and SYS_GID_MAX	Define the UID and GID ranges for allocating to new non-core system users and groups
ENCRYPT_METHOD	Specifies the encryption method for user passwords
USERGROUPS_ENAB	If yes, the useradd command creates a group with the same name as the user, and the userdel command deletes the user's group if no other members exist.
CREATE_HOME	Determines whether to create a home directory for new users

Table 5-1 login.defs File Directives

Many more directives are available for added control and flexibility. See the manual pages for *login.defs* for complete details.

User Account Management

Managing user accounts involves creating, assigning passwords to, modifying attributes of, and deleting local user accounts. RHEL provides a set of tools for you to perform these operations. These tools are *useradd* to add a new user to the system, *usermod* to modify the attributes of an existing user, and *userdel* to remove a user from the system. In addition, the *passwd* command is available to set or modify a user's password.

The useradd, usermod, and userdel Commands

This set of commands is used to add, modify, and delete a user account from the system. The *useradd* command adds entries to the four user authentication files for each account added to the system. It creates a home directory for the user and copies the default user startup files from the *skeleton* directory */etc/skel* into the user's home directory. It can also be used to update the default settings that are used at the time of new user creation for unspecified settings. The *useradd* command supports a variety of flags; Table 5-2 lists some common options in both short and long versions.

Option	Description
-b (--base-dir)	Defines the absolute path to the base directory for placing user home directories. The default is /home.
-c (--comment)	Describes useful information about the user.
-d (--home-dir)	Defines the absolute path to the user home directory.
-D (--defaults)	Displays the default settings from the /etc/default/useradd file and modifies them.
-e (--expiredate)	Specifies a date on which a user account is automatically disabled. The format for the date specification is YYYY-MM-DD.
-f (--inactive)	Defines the maximum days of inactivity between password expiry and permanent account disablement.
-g (--gid)	Specifies the primary GID. Without this option, a User Private Group (UPG) matching the username is created with a GID from the normal range.
-G (--groups)	Specifies the membership to supplementary groups.

Option	Description
-k (--skel)	Specifies an alternative skeleton directory (default is /etc/skel) containing default user initialization files. These files are copied to the user's home directory at the time of account creation. Three hidden bash shell files—.bash_profile, .bashrc, and .bash_logout—are available in this directory by default. You can customize these files or add your own to be used for accounts created thereafter.
-m (--create-home)	Creates a home directory if it does not already exist.
-o (--non-unique)	Creates a user account sharing the UID of an existing user. When two users share a UID, both get identical rights on each other's files. This should only be done in specific situations.
-r (--system)	Creates a system account with UID between 1 and 999, and without password expiration.
-s (--shell)	Defines the absolute path to the shell file. The default is /bin/bash.
-u (--uid)	Indicates a unique UID. Without this option, the next available UID from the /etc/passwd file is used.
login	Specifies a login name to be assigned to the user account.

Table 5-2 useradd Command Options

You can modify the attributes of a user account with the *usermod* command. The syntax of this command is very similar to that of the *useradd*'s, with most switches identical. Table 5-3 describes some key options for *usermod*, and shows them in both short and long versions. There are two additional flags of interest that are discussed in Chapter 06 "Advanced User and Group Management".

Option	Description
-a (--append)	Adds a user to one or more supplementary groups
-d (--home)	Works with the -m option to move the contents of the current home directory to the new location. The new location is created if it does not already exist.
-l (--login)	Specifies a new login name
-m (--move-home)	Used with the -d option to move the contents of the current home directory to the new location

Table 5-3 usermod Command Options

The *userdel* command is straightforward. It removes entries for the specified user from the authentication files, and deletes the user's home directory if the -r flag is also specified. The -f option may be used to force the removal even if the user is still logged in.

Exercise 5-1: Create a User Account with Default Attributes

Perform this exercise on *server1* as *user1* with *sudo* where required. The use of *sudo* is discussed in Chapter 06 "Advanced User and Group Management". In this exercise, you will:

- Create a user account *user2* using the defaults defined in the *useradd* and *login.defs* files
- Assign this user a password

- Show the new line entries from all four authentication files

1. Create *user2* with all the default values:

```
[user1@server1 ~]$ sudo useradd user2
```

2. Assign this user a password and enter it twice when prompted:

```
[user1@server1 ~]$ sudo passwd user2
New password:
BAD PASSWORD: The password is shorter than 8 characters
Retype new password:
passwd: password updated successfully
```

3. *grep* for *user2* on the authentication files to examine what the *useradd* command has added:

```
[user1@server1 ~]$ cd /etc ; sudo grep user2: passwd shadow group gshadow
passwd:user2:x:1001:1001::/home/user2:/bin/bash
shadow:user2:$y$j9T$OIUfy52/q7NZBhMT6ldlq0$GQJN5Pv66VDmUgTPwJRcVXbYpO69KNzH1Ydh8
YL055C:20417:0:99999:7:::
group:user2:x:1001:
```

The command used the next available UID (1001) and GID (1001) from the normal ranges, and the default settings for the home directory (*/home/user2*) and shell file (*/bin/bash*).

4. Test this new account by logging in as *user2* and then run the *id* and *groups* commands to verify the UID, GID, and group membership information:

```
[user1@server1 etc]$ su - user2
Password:
[user2@server1 ~]$ id
uid=1001(user2) gid=1001(user2) groups=1001(user2) context=unconfined_u:unconfir
ed_r:unconfined_t:s0-s0:c0.c1023
[user2@server1 ~]$ groups
user2
```

The above outputs confirmed the UID and username, GID and group name, and primary group name.

Exercise 5-2: Create a User Account with Custom Values

Perform this exercise on *server1* as *user1* with *sudo* where required. The use of *sudo* is discussed in Chapter 06 "Advanced User and Group Management". In this exercise, you will:

- Create an account *user3* with UID 1010, home directory */usr/user3a*, and shell */bin/sh*
- Assign this user a password
- Exhibit the new line entries from all four authentication files

1. Create *user3* with UID 1010, home directory */usr/user3a*, and shell */bin/sh*:

```
[user1@server1 ~]$ sudo useradd -u 1010 -d /usr/user3a -s /bin/sh user3
```

2. Assign password "user123". Note that supplying a password on the command line or via standard input or scripts is not recommended for production systems due to security risks, as the password may be stored in the shell history. It is, however, acceptable for lab use:

```
[user1@server1 ~]$ echo user123 | sudo passwd --stdin user3
BAD PASSWORD: The password is shorter than 8 characters
```

3. *grep* for *user3* on the four authentication files to see what was added for this user:

```
[user1@server1 ~]$ cd /etc ; sudo grep user3: passwd shadow group gshadow
passwd:user3:x:1010:1010::/usr/user3a:/bin/sh
shadow:user3:$y$j9T$tlR5Hcpvfjimrleqt5dk91$2qDDqfwTXpZJUfARHFHD5de7GqZO4Jw9kWhcE
q8WJF/:20417:0:99999:7:::
group:user3:x:1010:
gshadow:user3:!::
```

The command used the custom UID (1010), GID (1010), home directory (*/home/user3a*), and shell file (*/bin/sh*).

4. Test this account by switching to or logging in as *user3* and entering user123 as the password. Run the *id* and *groups* commands for further verification.

Exercise 5-3: Modify and Delete a User Account

Perform this exercise on *server1* as *user1* with *sudo* where required. The use of *sudo* is discussed in Chapter 06 "Advanced User and Group Management". In this exercise, you will:

- Modify certain attributes for *user2* and then delete it
- Change the login name to *user2new*, UID to 2000, home directory to */home/user2new*, and login shell to */sbin/nologin*
- Display the line entry for *user2new* from the *passwd* file for validation
- Remove this user and confirm the deletion

1. Modify the login name for *user2* to *user2new*, UID to 2000, move home directory to */home/user2new*, and set login shell to */sbin/nologin*. Notice that the options are specified in a different sequence.

```
[user1@server1 ~]$ sudo usermod -l user2new -md /home/user2new \
> -s /sbin/nologin -u 2000 user2
```

2. Obtain the information for *user2new* from the *passwd* file for confirmation:

```
[user1@server1 ~]$ grep user2new /etc/passwd
user2new:x:2000:1001::/home/user2new:/sbin/nologin
```

3. Remove *user2new* along with their home and mail spool directories:

```
[user1@server1 ~]$ sudo userdel -r user2new
```

4. Confirm the user deletion:

```
[user1@server1 ~]$ grep user2new /etc/passwd
[user1@server1 ~]$
```

Nothing is returned in the output, which means this user does not exist in the *passwd* file any longer. This confirms the removal.

No-Login (Non-Interactive) User Account

The *nologin* shell is a special purpose program typically located in the */usr/sbin* (or */sbin*) directory. This program is used for user accounts that do not require login access to the system. With this program assigned, the user is refused access with the message, "This account is currently not available." displayed on the screen. If a custom message is required, you can create a file called */etc/nologin.txt* in and add the desired text to it. The content of this file is printed on the screen upon user access denial instead of the default message.

> **EXAM TIP:** If a no-login user can authenticate, verify their shell in /etc/passwd is set to /sbin/nologin or /usr/sbin/nologin.

Typical examples of user accounts that do not require login access are the system accounts such as *mail*, *ftp*, and *sshd*. Examine the *passwd* file and list such users:

```
[user1@server1 ~]$ grep nologin /etc/passwd
bin:x:1:1:bin:/bin:/usr/sbin/nologin
daemon:x:2:2:daemon:/sbin:/usr/sbin/nologin
adm:x:3:4:adm:/var/adm:/usr/sbin/nologin
lp:x:4:7:lp:/var/spool/lpd:/usr/sbin/nologin
mail:x:8:12:mail:/var/spool/mail:/usr/sbin/nologin
operator:x:11:0:operator:/root:/usr/sbin/nologin
```

The output returns a truncated list of non-interactive user accounts. There are tens of them, and they grow as you install more services on the system.

Exercise 5-4: Create a User Account with No-Login Access

Perform this exercise on *server1* as *user1* with *sudo* where required. The use of *sudo* is discussed in Chapter 06 "Advanced User and Group Management". In this exercise, you will:

- Create an account *user4* with all the default attributes but with a non-interactive shell
- Assign this user the nologin shell to prevent them from signing in
- Display the new line entry from the *passwd* file
- Test the account by attempting to log in and observe the output

1. Create *user4* with non-interactive shell file */sbin/nologin*:

```
[user1@server1 ~]$ sudo useradd -s /sbin/nologin user4
```

2. Assign user123 as password:

```
[user1@server1 ~]$ echo user123 | sudo passwd --stdin user4
```

3. *grep* for *user4* on the *passwd* file and verify the shell field containing the nologin shell:

```
[user1@server1 ~]$ tail -1 /etc/passwd
user4:x:1011:1011::/home/user4:/sbin/nologin
```

4. Test this account by attempting to log in or switch:

```
[user1@server1 ~]$ su - user4
Password:
This account is currently not available.
```

As mentioned earlier, you may create the */etc/nologin.txt* file and add a custom message to it. The new message appears on your next login attempt.

Chapter Summary

This chapter focused on user monitoring and account management. We began by exploring system files and associated tools that track user logins and system reboots, information vital for auditing and troubleshooting. While many of these tools are accessible to regular users, some require elevated privileges for full functionality.

The chapter then provided a detailed analysis of the four core local authentication databases: passwd, shadow, group, and gshadow. We examined their structure, syntax, and the critical user and group information they store, which is fundamental to the login process and system security.

Finally, we transitioned to practical administration, employing user management commands in hands-on exercises. These tools were used to create, modify, and delete user accounts, demonstrating how to apply both default and custom attributes, including the creation of non-login system accounts for service operation.

Review Questions

1. What is the sequence of files consulted when authenticating a user login?
2. UID 999 is reserved for normal users. True or False?
3. Which file is assigned to users to deny them login access?
4. You execute the *lastb* command as a normal user. The output reports an error. What do you need to do to run this command successfully?
5. What are the default permissions for the */etc/shadow* file and why?
6. What would the command *useradd -D* do?
7. What does the *lastlog* command do?
8. What would the command *useradd user500* do?
9. The *id* and *groups* commands are useful for listing a user's group membership. True or False.
10. Name the three fundamental user account classes in RHEL.
11. Every user in RHEL gets a private group by default. True or False?
12. What does the "x" in the password field in the *passwd* file imply?
13. Name the file that the *who* command consults to display logged-in users.
14. What information does the *lastb* command provide?
15. The *who* command may be used to view logged out users. True or False?
16. What would the *userdel* command do if it is run with the -r option?
17. Name the four local user authentication files.
18. The *passwd* file contains secondary user group information. True or False?

19. What is the default first UID assigned to a normal user?
20. What is the default first GID assigned to a group?
21. What is the name of the default backup file for *shadow*?
22. Which file does the *last* command consult by default to display reports?

Answers to Review Questions

1. */etc/passwd* to check if user exists and then */etc/shadow* to verify password.
2. False. UID 999 is reserved for system accounts.
3. The */sbin/nologin* file is assigned to users to deny them login.
4. You need to run the *lastb* command as *root* or with sudo, as it requires privileged access to retrieve the data.
5. 000 (no permissions) to prevent unauthorized access to password hashes.
6. This command displays the defaults settings used at the time of user creation or modification.
7. The *lastlog* command provides information about recent user logins.
8. The command provided will add *user500* with all predefined default values.
9. True.
10. The three fundamental user account categories are root, system (or service) accounts, and normal (or regular) accounts.
11. True.
12. The "x" in the password field implies that the hashed password is stored in the *shadow* file.
13. The *who* command consults the */run/utmp* file to list logged-in users.
14. The *lastb* command reports the history of unsuccessful user login attempts.
15. False. The *who* command shows currently logged-in users only.
16. The *userdel* command with -r will delete the specified user along with their home directory.
17. The *passwd*, *shadow*, *group*, and *gshadow* files.
18. False. The *passwd* file contains primary user group information.
19. The default first UID assigned to a normal user is 1000.
20. The default first GID assigned to a normal user is 1000.
21. The name of the default backup file for *shadow* is *shadow-*.
22. The *last* command consults the */var/log/wtmp* file to display reports.

Do-It-Yourself Challenge Labs

The following labs are designed to reinforce most of the concepts and skills covered in this chapter. You are expected to complete these labs without external assistance. A step-by-step guide is not provided, as the required knowledge has already been presented in the chapter; however, each lab includes hints pointing to the relevant major topic(s).

Use the lab environment created specifically for the end-of-chapter labs. See the sub-section "Lab Environment for End-of-Chapter Labs" in Chapter 01 "Local Installation" for details.

Lab 5-1: Check User Login Attempts

As *root* on *server3*, execute the *last*, *lastb*, and *lastlog* commands, and observe the outputs. Check which users have recently logged in and out successfully (*last*) and unsuccessfully (*lastb*). List the timestamps of recent system reboots (*last*). Check the last login status for each user (*lastlog*). Use the *vim* editor to record your results. (Hint: User Login Activity and Information).

Lab 5-2: Verify User and Group Identity

As *user1* on *server3*, run the *who* and *w* commands and compare their outputs. Execute the *id* and *groups* commands and compare the outcomes. Examine the additional information that *id* displays but *groups* does not. (Hint: User Login Activity and Information).

Lab 5-3: Create Users

As *root* on *server3*, create user account *user4100* with UID 4100 and home directory under */usr*. Create another user account *user4200* with default attributes. Assign both users passwords. Examine the *passwd*, *shadow*, *group*, and *gshadow* files and observe the entries added for the two new users. (Hint: Local User Authentication Files, and User Account Management).

Lab 5-4: Create User with Non-Interactive Shell

As *root* on *server3*, create user account *user4300* with login disabled. Assign this user a password. Attempt to log in as this user and note the message displayed. Examine the *passwd* file to identify what prevents this user from logging in. (Hint: Local User Authentication Files, and User Account Management).

Lab 5-5: Modify and Analyze User Authentication Files

As *root* on *server3*, create user *user4400* with default settings. Examine and compare the entries for this user across all four authentication files. Use *usermod* to change the user's shell to */bin/sh* and primary group to *bin*. Verify the changes in the authentication files and explain which fields were modified. Finally, delete the user and verify the removal from all authentication files. (Hint: Local User Authentication Files, User Account Management, and The useradd/usermod/userdel Commands).

Chapter 06

Advanced User and Group Management

By the end of this chapter, you will be able to:

- Enforce Password Security Policies with Aging Attributes
- Lock and Unlock User Accounts to Control System Access
- Manage Group Memberships and Properties
- Switch User Identities
- Delegate Administrative Privileges
- Change File and Directory Owning User and Owning Group

RHCSA Objectives:

05. Log in and switch users in multi-user targets
52. Change passwords and adjust password aging for local user accounts (only the second part of this objective "adjust password aging for local user accounts" is covered in this chapter; the first part is in Chapter 05)
53. Create, delete, and modify local groups and group memberships
54. Configure superuser access

You can set password aging attributes on user accounts to enforce security policies regarding password changes and account validity. You can apply these settings to individual users or to all users on the system. Password aging information is stored in one of the authentication files that was discussed at length in the previous chapter. You can prevent individual user accounts from logging in to the system by locking their access for a period of time or permanently. You can lift this lock when required. Setting password aging and locking/unlocking accounts are administrative functions that you must perform with elevated privileges of the root user.

Users receive membership to a single group at the time you add them to the system. Later, you can assign them membership to additional groups. Members of the same group possess the same access rights on files and directories. You can optionally give other users and members of other groups access to those files. Group membership information is stored in user and group authentication files that were examined in the previous chapter.

Users may switch to other user accounts, including the root user, provided they know the target user's password. You can allow normal users access to privileged commands by defining them appropriately in a configuration file. Each file that exists on the system has an owning user and an owning group. Similarly, every file that a user creates is in the ownership of that user. As the root user, you can change the ownership and assign it to another user.

Password Aging and its Management

Password aging is a security mechanism for controlling user passwords in Linux. Key benefits include enforcing password expiration, account disablement, user locking and unlocking, and regulating password change frequency. These controls are applied to all user accounts at creation time and can be customized per user later. You can also disable aging completely for individual users.

Password aging information is stored in the */etc/shadow* file (fields 3 to 8) with default policies defined in the */etc/login.defs* file. These files were covered in Chapter 05 "Basic User and Group Management". This section explores the aging management tools—*chage* and *passwd*—and demonstrates how to apply password controls to user accounts. While the *usermod* command can also set some aging attributes (account and password expiration); this section focuses on its ability to lock and unlock user accounts.

The chage Command

The *chage* command sets or modifies password aging parameters for user accounts. It updates specific fields in the *shadow* file based on options provided. The command offers numerous switches in both short and long formats. Table 6-1 describes the most common ones.

Option	Description
-d (--lastday)	Sets the last password change date (YYYY-MM-DD) or the number of days since UNIX epoch. With -d 0, the user is forced to change the password at next login. It corresponds to field 3 in the shadow file.
-E (--expiredate)	Sets the account expiration date (YYYY-MM-DD) or the number of days since UNIX epoch. This feature can be disabled with -E -1. It corresponds to field 8 in the shadow file.
-I (--inactive)	Defines the number of days of inactivity after the password expiry and before the account is locked. The user may be able to log in during this period with their expired password. This feature can be disabled with -I -1. It corresponds to field 7 in the shadow file.
-l	Displays password aging attributes for a user account.
-m (--mindays)	Indicates the minimum number of days that must elapse before the password can be changed. A value of 0 allows the user to change their password at any time. It corresponds to field 4 in the shadow file.
-M (--maxdays)	Denotes the maximum number of days of password validity before the user password expires and it must be changed. This feature can be disabled with -M -1. It corresponds to field 5 in the shadow file.
-W (--warndays)	Designates the number of days for which the user gets alerts to change their password before it expires. It corresponds to field 6 in the shadow file.

Table 6-1 chage Command Options

You will use most of these flags in Exercise 6-1 and throughout this chapter.

Exercise 6-1: Set and Confirm Password Aging with chage

Perform this exercise on *server1* as *user1* with *sudo* where required. The use of *sudo* is discussed later in this chapter. In this exercise, you will:

- Create user *user100* with default attributes and assign a simple password
- Configure password aging for *user100* using the *chage* command
- Set mindays to 7, maxdays to 90, and warndays to 10
- Verify the new settings
- Rerun the command and set account expiry to December 31, 2027

- Confirm new account expiry

1. Create *user100* with default attributes, and assign a password:

```
[user1@server1 ~]$ sudo useradd user100
[user1@server1 ~]$ echo user123 | sudo passwd --stdin user100
```

2. Set password aging parameters for *user100*, and confirm:

```
[user1@server1 ~]$ sudo chage -m 7 -M 90 -W 10 user100
[user1@server1 ~]$ sudo chage -l user100
Last password change                                    : Nov 25, 2025
Password expires                                        : Feb 23, 2026
Password inactive                                       : never
Account expires                                         : never
Minimum number of days between password change          : 7
Maximum number of days between password change          : 90
Number of days of warning before password expires       : 10
```

The bottom three rows confirm the new settings. The current password expiry (February 23, 2026) reflects the 90-day duration from November 25, 2025 when this command was executed.

3. Set the account expiry to December 31, 2027, and confirm:

```
[user1@server1 ~]$ sudo chage -E 2027-12-31 user100
[user1@server1 ~]$ sudo chage -l user100
Last password change                                    : Nov 25, 2025
Password expires                                        : Feb 23, 2026
Password inactive                                       : never
Account expires                                         : Dec 31, 2027
Minimum number of days between password change          : 7
Maximum number of days between password change          : 90
Number of days of warning before password expires       : 10
```

The middle row reflects the new account expiry for *user100*. Likewise, you can also use the -d and -I options with the *chage* command as needed.

The passwd Command

While primarily used for settings passwords, the *passwd* command can also modify password aging attributes and lock or unlock user accounts. Table 6-2 describes some key options in both short and long formats.

Option	Description
-d (--delete)	Removes user password without expiring the account.
-e (--expire)	Forces password change at next login.
-i (--inactive)	Defines the number of days of inactivity after the password expiry and before the account is locked. It corresponds to field 7 in the shadow file.
-l (--lock)	Locks a user account.
-n (--minimum)	Specifies the number of days that must elapse before the password can be changed. It corresponds to field 4 in the shadow file.
-S (--status)	Displays the status information for a user.

Option	Description
-u (--unlock)	Unlocks a locked user account.
-w (--warning)	Designates the number of days for which the user gets alerts to change their password before it actually expires. It corresponds to field 6 in the shadow file.
-x (--maximum)	Denotes the maximum number of days of password validity before the user password expires and it must be changed. It corresponds to field 5 in the shadow file.

Table 6-2 passwd Command Options

You will use most of these flags in Exercise 6-2 and throughout this chapter.

Exercise 6-2: Set and Confirm Password Aging with passwd

Perform this exercise on *server1* as *user1* with *sudo* where required. The use of *sudo* is discussed later in this chapter. In this exercise, you will:

- Create user *user200* with default attributes and assign a simple password
- Configure password aging for *user200* using the *passwd* command
- Set mindays to 4, maxdays to 60, and warndays to 5
- Verify the new settings
- Set the number of inactivity days to 5
- Ensure that the user is forced to change their password upon next login
- Confirm the new settings

1. Create *user200* with default attributes and assign a password:

```
[user1@server1 ~]$ sudo useradd user100
[user1@server1 ~]$ echo user123 | sudo passwd --stdin user100
```

2. Set password aging attributes for *user200*, and confirm:

```
[user1@server1 ~]$ sudo passwd -n 4 -x 60 -w 5 user200
passwd: password changed.
[user1@server1 ~]$ sudo passwd -S user200
user200 P 2025-11-25 4 60 5 -1
```

The output confirms the three new settings (4, 60, and 5).

3. Set the number of inactivity days, and confirm:

```
[user1@server1 ~]$ sudo passwd -i5 user200
passwd: password changed.
[user1@server1 ~]$ sudo passwd -S user200
user200 P 2025-11-25 4 60 5 5
```

The output verifies the new setting (5) in the last column.

4. Configure the attribute to force the user to change their password at next login, and confirm:

```
[user1@server1 ~]$ sudo passwd -e user200
passwd: password changed.
[user1@server1 ~]$ sudo passwd -S user200
user200 P 1970-01-01 4 60 5 5
```

The date is set to the UNIX epoch. This user will be prompted to change their password the next time they attempt to log in.

5. Try logging in:

```
[user1@server1 ~]$ su - user200
Password:
You are required to change your password immediately (administrator enforced).
Current password:
```

As expected, the user is forced to change their password.

The usermod Command

The common use of the *usermod* command is to modify user attributes, but it can also lock or unlock their account. Table 6-3 explains the two options in both short and long formats.

Option	Description
-L (--lock)	Locks user account by prepending an exclamation mark (!) to the password hash in the /etc/shadow file.
-U (--unlock)	Unlocks user account by removing the exclamation mark (!) from the password hash in the /etc/shadow file.

Table 6-3 usermod Command Options for User Lock/Unlock

Let's apply these options in the next exercise.

Exercise 6-3: Lock and Unlock a User Account with usermod and passwd

Perform this exercise on *server1* as *user1* with *sudo* where required. The use of *sudo* is discussed later in this chapter. In this exercise, you will:

- Disable login capability for *user200* using the *usermod* command
- Verify the change
- Enable login capability for *user200* using the *passwd* command
- Confirm the reversal

1. Obtain the current password information for *user200* from the *shadow* file:

```
[user1@server1 ~]$ sudo grep user200 /etc/shadow
user200:$y$j9T$2SRk2ZAN.j4nmyO41W0XX0$BuTfbBZkpknZ07.uiLXF0uk.OA
C:0:4:60:5:5::
```

An unlocked user account never has its password field begin with an exclamation mark (!). The above output is indicative of the fact that the account is currently not locked.

2. Lock the account for *user200*, and confirm:

```
[user1@server1 ~]$ sudo usermod -L user200
[user1@server1 ~]$ sudo grep user200 /etc/shadow
user200:!$y$j9T$2SRk2ZAN.j4nmyO41W0XX0$BuTfbBZkpknZ07.uiLXF0uk.OAsWoZAmxKW7S8we
tC:0:4:60:5:5::
```

Notice that an exclamation mark (!) is prepended to the encrypted password, which indicates a locked account.

3. Unlock the account, and confirm:

```
[user1@server1 ~]$ sudo passwd -u user200
passwd: password changed.
[user1@server1 ~]$ sudo grep user200 /etc/shadow
user200:$y$j9T$2SRk2ZAN.j4nmyO41W0XX0$BuTfbBZkpknZ07.uiLXF0uk.OAsWoZAmxKW7S8we
C:0:4:60:5:5::
```

The account is now unlocked. You can try logging in to validate.

Linux Groups and their Management

Linux groups are collections of users with common permission requirements on files and directories. They allow group members to collaborate on files of common interest.

Group information is stored in */etc/group* with default policies in */etc/login.defs*. Furthermore, the */etc/gshadow* file stores group administrator information and group-level passwords. These files were thoroughly examined in Chapter 05 "Basic User and Group Management".

This section explores the group management tools—*groupadd*, *groupmod*, and *groupdel*—and looks at how to utilize them to create, alter, and erase groups. Additional group administration operations, such as adding and deleting group administrators, and setting and revoking group-level passwords, are beyond the scope.

The groupadd, groupmod, and groupdel Commands

This set of management commands is used to add, modify, and delete a group from the system. The *groupadd* command adds entries to the *group* and *gshadow* files for each group you add to the system. Table 6-4 lists and explains some of the *groupadd* command options in both short and long formats.

Option	Description
-g (--gid)	Assigns a specific GID to the new group
-n (--new-name)	Renames a group
-o (--non-unique)	Creates a group with a matching GID of an existing group. The system treats both groups as one.
-r	Creates a system group with GID between 1 and 999
groupname	Specifies a group name

Table 6-4 groupadd Command Options

The *groupadd* command picks up the default values from the *login.defs* file.

You can modify the attributes of a group with the *groupmod* command. The syntax of this command is similar to *groupadd* with several identical options. The additional option unique to this command is -n, which allows you to rename a group.

The *groupdel* command is straightforward. It removes entries for the specified group from both *group* and *gshadow* files.

Exercise 6-4: Create a Group and Add Members

Perform this exercise on *server1* as *user1* with *sudo* where required. The use of *sudo* is discussed later in this chapter. In this exercise, you will:

- Create a group called *linuxadm* with GID 5000
- Create another group called *dba* sharing the GID 5000 with *linuxadm* group
- Add *user1* as a secondary member to group *dba*
- Verify the updated group membership

1. Create the group *linuxadm* with GID 5000:

```
[user1@server1 ~]$ sudo groupadd -g 5000 linuxadm
```

2. Create a group called *dba* with the same GID as that of group *linuxadm*:

```
[user1@server1 ~]$ sudo groupadd -og 5000 dba
```

3. Confirm the creation of both groups:

```
[user1@server1 ~]$ grep linuxadm /etc/group
linuxadm:x:5000:
[user1@server1 ~]$ grep dba /etc/group
dba:x:5000:
```

The GID for both groups is identical.

4. Add *user1* as a secondary member of group *dba* using the *usermod* command. The existing membership for the user must remain intact.

```
[user1@server1 ~]$ sudo usermod -aG dba user1
```

5. Verify the updated group membership information for *user1* by extracting the relevant entry from the *group* file, and running the *id* and *groups* command for *user1*:

```
[user1@server1 ~]$ grep dba /etc/group
dba:x:5000:user1
[user1@server1 ~]$ sudo id user1
uid=1000(user1) gid=1000(user1) groups=1000(user1),10(wheel),5000(linuxadm)
[user1@server1 ~]$ sudo groups user1
user1 : user1 wheel linuxadm
```

The output confirms the primary (*user1*) and secondary (*dba*) group memberships for *user1*.

Exercise 6-5: Modify and Delete a Group Account

Perform this exercise on *server1* as *user1* with *sudo* where required. The use of *sudo* is discussed in the next section. In this exercise, you will:

- Rename the *linuxadm* group to *sysadm* and the GID to 6000
- Add *user200* to *sysadm* group as a secondary member
- Remove the *sysadm* group
- Verify the group removal

1. Alter the name of *linuxadm* to *sysadm*:

```
[user1@server1 ~]$ sudo groupmod -n sysadm linuxadm
```

2. Change the GID of *sysadm* to 6000:

```
[user1@server1 ~]$ sudo groupmod -g 6000 sysadm
```

3. Add *user200* to *sysadm* as a secondary member:

```
[user1@server1 ~]$ sudo usermod -aG sysadm user200
```

4. Confirm the above actions:

```
[user1@server1 ~]$ grep sysadm /etc/group
sysadm:x:6000:user200
[user1@server1 ~]$ grep linuxadm /etc/group
[user1@server1 ~]$
```

The outputs confirm both actions. The new group name is *sysadm* and the new GID is 6000. *user200* is a member of the *sysadm* group. Note that renaming *linuxadm* to *sysadm* removed the original group.

5. Delete the *sysadm* group and confirm:

```
[user1@server1 ~]$ sudo groupdel sysadm
[user1@server1 ~]$ grep sysadm /etc/group
[user1@server1 ~]$
```

The second command returns nothing, which confirms the group deletion.

Substituting Users and Doing as Substitute User

In real world Linux environments, you should always log in as a normal user, not as *root*. Normal users have limited rights on the system. Their profiles allow them to accomplish routine tasks efficiently. This practice enhances system security and prevents unexpected issues. There are times though when a normal user needs to assume the identity of a different user to carry out a task as that user or execute a command successfully that requires elevated privileges. Linux offers two fundamental tools to support users in both situations.

Substituting Users

Even though you can log in to the system directly as *root*, it is not a recommended practice. Instead, log in with a normal user account and then switch to *root* if necessary. This practice is a critical security measure. In addition to becoming *root*, you can also switch to other user accounts. In either case, you need the target user's password to switch successfully. The *su* command (*substitute user*, *super user*, or *switch user*) allows you to switch to other user accounts.

To switch from *user1* to *root* without running the target user's startup scripts (which define their environment, and are explained in Chapter "The Bash Shell"), run *su* and enter the *root* password:

```
[user1@server1 ~]$ su
```

Press `Ctrl+d` to return to the *user1* command prompt. Then rerun *su* with the hyphen character (-) to ensure that startup scripts for the *root* user are also executed to simulate a real login:

```
[user1@server1 ~]$ su -
```

To switch to a different user account, such as *user100*, specify the name of the user with the command. You must enter the password of the target user when prompted.

```
[user1@server1 ~]$ su - user100
```

RHEL offers two tools—*whoami* (*who am i*) and *logname* (*login name*)—that show a user's current identity (after *su*'ing into the target user) and the identity of the user who originally logged in. Let's see what they report after switching into *user100*:

```
[user100@server1 ~]$ whoami
user100
[user100@server1 ~]$ logname
user1
```

The *whoami* command returns the effective (current) username (*user100*), and the *logname* command reports the user's real (original) username (*user1*).

To issue a command as a different user without switching into that user, use the -c option with *su*. For example, the *firewall-cmd* command with the --list-services option requires superuser privileges. *user1* can use *su* as follows and execute this privileged command to obtain desired results:

```
[user1@server1 ~]$ su -c 'firewall-cmd --list-services'
```

The *root* user can switch to any user account that exists on the system without being prompted for that user's password.

The firewall-cmd command is used to manage the Linux firewall at the command line. It is discussed in detail in Chapter 21 "The Linux Firewall".

While *su* is a useful tool, routinely switching to the *root* account has significant drawbacks from an auditing and security perspective. It does not log which original user performed privileged actions in system logs, and it gives the user full *root* power for the entire session. The preferred, more secure method is to use *sudo*, which provides granular control, logs all actions under the original user's name, and limits the scope of privileges.

Doing as Substitute User

On production servers, users need appropriate privileges to perform their duties efficiently. In most cases, this requires privileged access to certain tools and functions, which the *root* user is normally allowed to run.

RHEL provides normal users the ability to run a set of privileged commands or to access non-owning files without the knowledge of the *root* password. This allows assigning specific privileged commands to individual users or groups of users based on their needs. These users can then precede one of those commands with a utility called *sudo* (*superuser do* or *substitute user do*) at the time of executing that command. Users are prompted for their own password, and if correct, the command is executed successfully for them. The *sudo* utility is designed to provide protected access to administrative functions as defined in the */etc/sudoers* file or files in the drop-in directory */etc/sudoers.d*. It can also be used to allow a user or a group of users to run scripts and applications owned by a different user.

You define any normal user that requires privileged access to administrative commands or non-owning files in the *sudoers* file. You should edit this file using the *visudo* command, which opens it in a safe editing environment with syntax validation. *visudo* creates a temporary copy named */etc/sudoers.tmp* during editing and validates the syntax before saving it. If errors are detected, it prevents saving and alerts you to fix them, avoiding a broken sudo configuration that could lock all users out of administrative access. After successful editing, the updated file overwrites the original *sudoers* file and deletes *sudoers.tmp*. This process also prevents multiple users from editing the file simultaneously.

The syntax for user and group entries in the file is similar to the following example entries for user *user1* and group *dba*:

```
user1     ALL=(ALL)     ALL
%dba      ALL=(ALL)     ALL
```

These entries can be added to the beginning of the file, and they are intended to provide full access to every administrative function to *user1* and members of the *dba* group (group is prefixed by the percentage sign (%)). In other words, *user1* and *dba* group members will have full *root* authority on the system.

When *user1* or a member of *dba* group attempts to access a privileged function, they will be required to enter their own password. For instance:

```
[user1@server1 ~]$ sudo head /etc/sudoers
[sudo] password for user1:
user1 ALL=(ALL) ALL
%dba ALL=(ALL) ALL
## Sudoers allows particular users to run various commands as
## the root user, without needing the root password.
##
## Examples are provided at the bottom of the file for collections
## of related commands, which can then be delegated out to particular
## users or groups.
##
## This file must be edited with the 'visudo' command.
```

If you want *user1* and *dba* group members not to be prompted for their passwords, modify the entries in the *sudoers* file to look like:

```
user1     ALL=(ALL)    NOPASSWD:ALL
%dba      ALL=(ALL)    NOPASSWD:ALL
```

Rather than granting full system access, you can restrict users to only the specific commands they require. For example, to limit their access to a single command */usr/bin/cat*, modify the directives as follows:

```
user1     ALL=/usr/bin/cat
%dba      ALL=/usr/bin/cat
```

These users should now be able to use the *cat* command to view the content of the */etc/sudoers* or any other file that requires the *root* privilege. Try **cat /etc/sudoers** as *user1* and then again as **sudo cat /etc/sudoers**. You will notice the difference.

Configuring sudo to work the way it has just been explained may result in a cluttered *sudoers* file with too many entries to fulfill diversified needs of users and groups. A preferred method is to use predefined aliases—User_Alias and Cmnd_Alias—to configure groups of users and commands, and assign access as required. For instance, you can define a Cmnd_Alias called PKGCMD containing *yum* and *rpm* package management commands, and a User_Alias called PKGADM for *user1*, *user100*, and *user200*. These users may or may not belong to the same Linux group.

Next, assign PKGCMD to PKGADM. This way one rule is set that allows a group of users access to a group of commands. You can add or remove commands and users anytime as needed, and the change will take effect right away. Here is what this configuration will look like:

```
Cmnd_Alias     PKGCMD = /usr/bin/yum, /usr/bin/rpm
User_Alias     PKGADM = user1, user100, user200
PKGADM         ALL = PKGCMD
```

Append the above to the bottom of the *sudoers* file and then run the *yum* or *rpm* command preceded by *sudo* as one of the users listed. You will be able to perform software management tasks just like the *root* user.

The *sudo* command logs successful authentication and command data to the */var/log/secure* file under the name of the actual user executing the command (and not *root*).

The *sudoers* file contains several examples with a brief explanation. It is a good idea to look at those examples for additional understanding.

Now that the normal user *user1* is added to the *sudoers* configuration file, you will be using this user account with *sudo* where appropriate in the examples and exercises in the remainder of the book.

Owning User and Owning Group

In Linux, every file and directory has an owner. By default, the creating user owns the file, but you can alter this and allocate it to a different user if required.

Similarly, every user is a member of one or more groups. A group is a collection of users with common permission requirements. By default, the creating user's primary group is assigned to a file or directory.

Create a file *file1* as *user1* in their home directory and exhibit the file's long listing:

```
[user1@server1 ~]$ touch file1
[user1@server1 ~]$ ls -l file1
-rw-r--r--. 1 user1 user1 0 Jan 29 18:53 file1
```

The output indicates that the owner of *file1* is *user1* who belongs to group *user1*. If you wish to view the corresponding UID and GID instead, you can specify the -n option with the command:

```
[user1@server1 ~]$ ls -ln file1
-rw-r--r--. 1 1000 1000 0 Jan 29 18:53 file1
```

Linux provides the *chown* and *chgrp* commands that can alter the owning user and owning group for files and directories; however, you must have the *root* user privilege to make these modifications.

Exercise 6-6: Modify File Owner and Owning Group

Perform this exercise on *server1* as *user1* with *sudo* where required. In this exercise, you will:

- Create a file */tmp/file10* and a directory */tmp/dir10* as *user1*
- Change the owning user for *file10* to *user100*
- Change the owning group to *dba*
- Apply owning user on *file10* to *user200* and owning group to *user100* in one shot
- Change the two attributes on the directory to *user200:dba* recursively

1. Change into the */tmp* directory and create *file10* and *dir10*:

```
[user1@server1 ~]$ cd /tmp
[user1@server1 tmp]$ touch file10
[user1@server1 tmp]$ mkdir dir10
```

2. Check and validate that both attributes are set to *user1*:

```
[user1@server1 tmp]$ ls -l file10
-rw-r--r--. 1 user1 user1 0 Jan 29 18:54 file10
[user1@server1 tmp]$ ls -ld dir10/
drwxr-xr-x. 2 user1 user1 6 Jan 29 18:54 dir10/
```

3. Set the owning user to *user100* and confirm:

```
[user1@server1 tmp]$ sudo chown user100 file10
[user1@server1 tmp]$ ls -l file10
-rw-r--r--. 1 user100 user1 0 Jan 29 18:54 file10
```

4. Alter the owning group to *dba* and verify:

```
[user1@server1 tmp]$ sudo chgrp dba file10
[user1@server1 tmp]$ ls -l file10
-rw-r--r--. 1 user100 dba 0 Jan 29 18:54 file10
```

5. Change the owning user to *user200* and owning group to *user100* and confirm:

```
[user1@server1 tmp]$ sudo chown user200:user100 file10
[user1@server1 tmp]$ ls -l file10
-rw-r--r--. 1 user200 user100 0 Jan 29 18:54 file10
```

6. Modify the owning to *user200* and owning group to *dba* recursively on *dir10* and validate:

```
[user1@server1 tmp]$ sudo chown -R user200:dba dir10/
[user1@server1 tmp]$ ls -ld dir10/
drwxr-xr-x. 2 user200 dba 6 Jan 29 18:54 dir10/
```

You can also use **ls -lR dir10** to view file and directory information under *dir10*; however, it will show nothing as the directory is currently empty.

Chapter Summary

This chapter delved into advanced user and group account management, beginning with an explanation of password aging attributes and the configuration files that define default settings for new users. We then practiced modifying these aging attributes for existing accounts and employed a tool to temporarily lock and unlock user access.

The chapter covered essential group management commands, using them in exercises to create, modify, and delete groups, as well as assign users to supplementary groups. We also explored tools for privilege escalation, including switching user identities and executing commands with administrative rights, with a specific recommendation for using sudo.

Finally, we analyzed file and directory ownership, explaining how user and group assignments are established. Hands-on exercises demonstrated the rules governing which users are authorized to modify these ownership attributes.

Review Questions

1. The *chown* command may be used to modify both owning user and owning group on a file. True or False?
2. What would the command *passwd -n 7 -x 15 -w 3 user5* do?
3. Write the two command names for managing all of the password aging attributes.
4. What would the command *chage -d 0 user60* do?
5. Which file has the default password aging settings defined?
6. What would the command *chage -E 2024-10-22 user10* do?
7. What would the command *chage -l user5* do?
8. Which two commands can be used to lock and unlock a user account?
9. When using *sudo*, log files record activities under the *root* user account. True or False?
10. What is the difference between running the *su* command with and without the hyphen sign?
11. What is the significance of the -o option with the *groupadd* and *groupmod* commands?
12. What would the entry user10 ALL=(ALL) NOPASSWD:ALL in the sudoers file imply?
13. Which command can be used to display the effective (current) username?
14. What is the recommended location to store custom *sudo* rules?
15. What would the command *passwd -l user10* do?
16. The *chgrp* command may be used to modify both owning user and owning group on a file. True or False?

Answers to Review Questions

1. True.
2. The command will set mindays to 7, maxdays to 15, and warndays to 3 for *user5*.
3. The *passwd* and *chage* commands.
4. The command provided will force *user60* to change their password at next login.
5. The */etc/login.defs* file has the defaults for password aging defined.
6. The command provided will set October 22, 2024, as the expiry date for *user10*.
7. The command provided will display password aging attributes for *user5*.
8. The *usermod* and *passwd* commands can be used to lock and unlock a user account.
9. False. The activities are registered under the username who invokes *sudo*.
10. The hyphen causes *su* to process the target user's startup files, creating a full login environment. Without it, the current shell environment remains unchanged.
11. The -o option allows creating or modifying a group with a non-unique GID.
12. It allows *user10* to run any command without being prompted for a password.
13. The *whoami* command reports the effective username of the user running this command.
14. The custom sudo rules should be stored in files under the */etc/sudoers.d* directory.
15. This command will lock *user10*.
16. False.

Do-It-Yourself Challenge Labs

The following labs are designed to reinforce most of the concepts and skills covered in this chapter. You are expected to complete these labs without external assistance. A step-by-step guide is not provided, as the required knowledge has already been presented in the chapter; however, each lab includes hints pointing to the relevant major topic(s).

Use the lab environment created specifically for the end-of-chapter labs. See the sub-section "Lab Environment for End-of-Chapter Labs" in Chapter 01 "Local Installation" for details.

Lab 6-1: Create User and Configure Password Aging

As *root* on *server3*, create group *lnxgrp* with GID 6000. Create user *user5000* with UID 5000 and GID 6000. Assign this user a password, and configure password aging so that this user cannot change their password within 4 days after setting it and with a password validity of 30 days. This user should start getting warning messages for changing password 10 days prior to password expiration. This user account needs to expire on the 20th of December 2026. (Hint1: Chapter 05: Local User Authentication Files, and User Account Management). (Hint2: Password Aging and its Management, and Linux Groups and their Management).

Lab 6-2: Lock and Unlock User

As *root* on *server3*, lock the user account for *user5000* using the *passwd* command, and confirm by examining the change in the */etc/shadow* file. Try logging in with *user5000* and observe what happens. Use the *usermod* command and unlock this account. Verify the unlocking by checking the entry for the user in the */etc/shadow* file. (Hint: Password Aging and its Management).

Lab 6-3: Modify Group

As *root* on *server3*, modify the GID from 6000 to 7000 for the *lnxgrp* group. Add users *user1000* and *user2000* as supplementary members (create users if needed). Change the group's name to *dbagrp*, and verify. (Hint: Linux Groups and their Management).

Lab 6-4: Configure sudo Access

As *root* on *server3*, use *visudo* to add a rule granting *user5000* full passwordless *root* access on the system. Switch to *user5000* and verify by running *sudo vgs*. (Hint: Substituting Users and Doing as Substitute User).

Lab 6-5: Modify Owning User and Group

As *user1* on *server3*, create a file *f6* and directory *d6* under */tmp*. Change owning user for *f6* to *user90* (create user) using *sudo chown*, and owning group to *dbagrp* with *sudo chgrp*. Recursively change both owning user and owning group on *d6* to *user90:g1* (create group) using *sudo chown*. (Hint: Owing User and Owning Group).

Chapter 07

The Bash Shell

By the end of this chapter, you will be able to:

- Navigate and Interact with the System Efficiently
- Manage Shell and Environment Variables
- Use Command and Variable Substitutions
- Leverage Shell Features such as Tab Completion, Command History, Quick Navigation and Editing at the Command Line, Tilde Substitution, and Alias Substitution
- Utilize Metacharacters in Redirections, Piping, and Quoting Mechanisms
- Perform Pattern Matching using Filename Globbing
- Implement Pattern Matching using Regular Expressions
- Configure System-Wide and Per-User Shell Environments

RHCSA Objectives:

02. Use input-output redirection (>, >>, |, 2>, etc.)
03. Use grep and regular expressions to analyze text

Shells allow you to interact with the operating system by executing programs, commands, and applications. RHEL supports a variety of shells, of which the bash shell is the most common. It is also the default shell in RHEL and many other Linux distributions. This shell offers a variety of features that help you perform your job with ease and flexibility. Key features include assigning the output of a command to a variable, recalling a command from history and editing it at the command line before running it, creating command shortcuts, sending output and error messages to non-default locations, sending output of one command as input to the next, using special characters to match filenames and text, treating a special character as a literal character, and so on.

At login, plenty of system and user startup scripts are processed to set up the user environment. The system startup scripts may be customized for all users by the Linux administrator, and the user startup scripts may be modified by individual users as per their need.

The Bourne-Again Shell

A *shell* functions as a command interpreter, serving as the interface between users and the Linux kernel. It accepts instructions (commands) from users or programs, interprets them, and passes them to the kernel for execution. The kernel utilizes hardware and software resources to process these instructions, then returns the results to the shell for display. The shell also displays any error messages generated during command execution. In addition, the shell provides a customizable environment to users.

The *bash* (*bourne-again shell*) is widely used by Linux users and administrators. Developed as an enhanced replacement for the original *Bourne* shell, bash incorporates numerous improvements and features from other shells. It serves as the default shell in most Linux distributions including RHEL 10. Bash offers extensive capabilities such as variable manipulation and substitution, command substitution, input/output redirection, tab completion, history expansion, tilde expansion, alias substitution, metacharacter handling, filename globbing, pattern matching, quoting mechanisms, conditional execution, flow control, and shell scripting. This section covers all these features except the last three.

The bash shell is identified by the $ sign for normal users and the # sign for the *root* user. The bash shell executable is located at */usr/bin/bash*.

Shell and Environment Variables

A *variable* stores data in the shell's memory space for the duration of the session. It retains information that you use to customize the shell environment and that programs reference to function properly. When assigning values containing one or more whitespace characters to variables, enclose the value in quotation marks.

There are two types of variables: *local* (or *shell*) and *environment*. A local variable is private to the shell in which it is created. Its value is not available to programs or processes started outside that shell. This leads to the concepts of the *current* shell and the *sub*-shell (or *child* shell). The current shell is where a program or command is executed, while a sub-shell (or child shell) is a new shell created within the current one to run a program. The value of a local variable exists only in the shell where it is defined and is not inherited by sub-shells.

Child shells inherit the environment variables from their parent shell. In other words, the value stored in an environment variable is accessible to the program, as well as any sub-programs that it spawns during its lifecycle. Any environment variable set in a sub-shell is lost when the sub-shell terminates.

There are multiple predefined environment variables that are set for each user during login. Use the **env** or **printenv** command to view their values. Run these commands on *server1* as *user1* and observe the output. There should be around 25 of them. Some of the common predefined environment variables are described in Table 7-1.

Variable	Description
DISPLAY	Stores the hostname or IP address for graphical terminal sessions
HISTFILE	Defines the file for storing the history of executed commands
HISTSIZE	Defines the maximum number of commands to be kept in memory during the session
HOME	Sets the home directory path
LOGNAME	Retains the login name
MAIL	Contains the path to the user mail directory
PATH	Defines a colon-separated list of directories to be searched when executing a command. A proper configuration of this variable allows command execution without specifying absolute paths.
PPID	Holds the identifier number for the parent program
PS1	Defines the primary command prompt
PS2	Defines the secondary command prompt
PWD	Stores the current directory location
SHELL	Holds the absolute path to the primary shell file
TERM	Holds the terminal type value
UID	Holds the logged-in user's UID
USER	Retains the name of the logged-in user

Table 7-1 Predefined Environment Variables

RHEL provides the *echo* command to view the values stored in variables. For instance, to view the value for the PATH variable, run the *echo* command and ensure to prepend the variable name (PATH) with the $ sign:

```
[user1@server1 ~]$ echo $PATH
/home/user1/.local/bin:/home/user1/bin:/usr/local/bin:/usr/bin:/usr/local/sbin:/
usr/sbin
```

Try running **echo $HOME**, **echo $SHELL**, **echo $TERM**, **echo $PPID**, **echo $PS1**, and **echo $USER** and see what values they store.

Setting and Unsetting Variables

You can set or unset shell and environment variables at the command prompt or via programs, and view and use their values as necessary. You define and undefine variables and view their values using built-in shell commands such as *export*, *unset*, and *echo*. Use uppercase letters for variable names to avoid potential conflicts with a command, program, file, or directory name. To understand how variables are defined, viewed, made environment, and undefined, a few examples are presented below. We run the commands as *user1*.

To define a local variable named VR1:

```
[user1@server1 ~]$ VR1=RHEL
```

To view the value stored in VR1:

```
[user1@server1 ~]$ echo $VR1
RHEL
```

Now, start a sub-shell by typing **bash**. Run **echo $VR1** to check if the variable is visible. It will not be, because it was defined as a local variable, not an environment variable. Exit the sub-shell by typing **exit**.

To make this variable an environment variable, use the *export* command:

```
[user1@server1 ~]$ export VR1
```

Repeat the previous test by running the **bash** command and then the **echo $VR1**. You should be able to see the variable in the sub-shell, as it is now an environment variable. Return to the parent shell by running the **exit** command.

To undefine this variable and erase it from the shell environment:

```
[user1@server1 ~]$ unset VR1
```

To define a local variable that contains a value with one or more white space characters:

```
[user1@server1 ~]$ VR2="I love RHEL"
```

To define and make the variable an environment variable at the same time:

```
[user1@server1 ~]$ export VR3="RHCSA exam is tough"
```

The *echo* command is restricted to showing the value of a specific variable and the *env* and *printenv* commands display environment variables only. If you want to view both local and environment variables, use the *set* command. Try running **set** and observe the output.

Command and Variable Substitutions

The primary command prompt displays # for the *root* user and $ for normal users. Customizing the prompt to display information such as who you are, the system you are logged in to, and your current location in the directory tree is a useful practice. By default, this setting is already in place through the PS1 environment variable, which defines the primary command prompt. You can validate this information by looking at the command prompt **[user1@server1 ~]$**.

You can also view the value stored in PS1 by issuing **echo $PS1**. The default value is \u@\h \W\$. The \u translates into the logged-in username, \h represents the system hostname, \W shows the current directory, and \$ indicates the end of the command prompt.

Exercise 7-1 demonstrates how to employ the command and variable substitution features to customize the primary command prompt for *user1*. You will use the *hostname* command and assign its output to the PS1 variable. This is an example of *command substitution*. Note that the command whose output you want assigned to a variable must be encapsulated within backticks `hostname` or the preferred parentheses $(hostname).

There are two instances of the *variable substitution* feature employed in Exercise 7-1. The LOGNAME and the PWD environment variables to display the username and to reflect the current directory location.

Exercise 7-1: Modify Primary Command Prompt

Perform this exercise on *server1* as *user1*. In this exercise, you will:

- Customize the primary shell prompt for *user1* to display the information enclosed within the quotes "< username on hostname in pwd >: " using the variable and command substitution features
- Open the *$HOME/.bash_profile* file and add the new value for persistence (see Shell Startup Files later in this chapter to understand the purpose of *.bash_profile*), otherwise, the value will be lost when *user1* closes the terminal window or logs off.

1. Change the value of PS1 to reflect the desired information:

```
[user1@server1 ~]$ export PS1="< $LOGNAME on $(hostname) in \$PWD > "
< user1 on server1.example.com in /home/user1 >
```

The new prompt shows the desired information.

2. Edit the *.bash_profile* file and define the value exactly as it was run in Step 1.
3. Test by logging off and logging back in as *user1*. The new command prompt will be displayed.

This concludes the exercise.

Tab Completion

Tab completion (a.k.a. *command-line completion*) allows automatic completion of filenames, directory names, or command names by pressing the `Tab` key once after typing initial characters. Pressing `Tab` twice shows all possible completions. You can then type one or more following characters and press `Tab` again to further narrow down the possibilities. When the desired name appears, press `Enter` to accept it. One of the major benefits of using this feature is the time saved on typing a long file, directory, or command name.

Try this feature out on your Linux terminal window and familiarize yourself with it.

History Expansion

History expansion (*command history* or *history substitution*) is a time-saving feature that keeps a chronological log of every command you run at the command prompt, with one command per line. This feature is enabled by default; however, you can disable and re-enable it if required. The bash shell stores command history in a file located in the user's home directory and in system memory. You may retrieve the commands from history, modify them at the command prompt, and rerun them.

There are three variables—HISTFILE, HISTSIZE, and HISTFILESIZE—that control the location and history storage. HISTFILE defines the name and location of the history file to be used to store command history, and the default is *.bash_history* in the user's home directory. HISTSIZE sets the number of commands kept in memory during the current session. HISTFILESIZE sets the maximum number of lines contained in HISTFILE. Usually, HISTSIZE and HISTFILESIZE are set to a common value. These variables and their values can be viewed with the *echo* command. The following shows the settings for *user1*:

```
[user1@server1 ~]$ echo $HISTFILE
/home/user1/.bash_history
[user1@server1 ~]$ echo $HISTSIZE
1000
[user1@server1 ~]$ echo $HISTFILESIZE
1000
```

The values of any of these variables may be altered for individual users by editing the *.bashrc* or *.bash_profile* file in the user's home directory. A discussion on these files is provided later in this chapter.

In RHEL, the *history* command displays or reruns previously executed commands. This command gets the history data from the system memory as well as from the *.bash_history* file. By default, it shows all entries. Run this command at the prompt without any options and it will display all entries:

```
[user1@server1 ~]$ history
```

The *history* command has some useful options. The following examples demonstrate these options.

To display this command and the ten preceding entries:

```
[user1@server1 ~]$ history 10
```

To re-execute a command by its line number (line 15 for example):

```
[user1@server1 ~]$ !15
```

To re-execute the most recent command starting with a specific string (for example, ch):

```
[user1@server1 ~]$ !ch
```

To issue the most recent command that contained "grep":

```
[user1@server1 ~]$ !?grep?
```

To remove entry 24 from history:

```
[user1@server1 ~]$ history -d 24
```

To repeat the last command executed:

```
[user1@server1 ~]$ !!
```

The second exclamation mark (!) in the above example is used to retrieve the last executed command.

You may disable the history expansion feature by issuing **set +o history** at the command prompt and re-enable it with **set -o history**. The *set* command is used in this way to enable or disable a bash shell feature.

Navigating and Editing at the Command Line

While typing a command with a multitude of options and arguments at the command prompt, you often need to move the cursor backward to add or modify something. For instance, if you are typing a long command as a normal user and then realize the command needs to have *sudo* added at the beginning, move the cursor quickly to the start of the command. This is a shortcut to save time. There are plenty of key combinations for rapid movement on the command line. Table 7-2 lists and explains several of these.

Key Combinations	Action
Ctrl+a / Home	Moves the cursor to the beginning of the command line
Ctrl+e / End	Moves the cursor to the end of the command line
Ctrl+u	Erases from the cursor to the start of the command line
Ctrl+k	Erases from the cursor to the end of the command line
Alt+f	Moves the cursor to the right one word at a time
Alt+b	Moves the cursor to the left one word at a time
Ctrl+f / Right arrow	Moves the cursor to the right one character at a time
Ctrl+b / Left arrow	Moves the cursor to the left one character at a time

Table 7-2 Command-Line Editing Shortcuts

For normal users and administrators who often work at the command line, these time-saving key combinations will be very helpful.

Tilde Expansion

Tilde expansion (or *tilde substitution*) is performed on words that begin with the tilde character (~). The rules to keep in mind when using the ~ are:

1. If ~ is used as a standalone character, the shell refers to the $HOME directory of the user running the command. The following example displays the $HOME directory of *user1*:

```
[user1@server1 ~]$ echo ~
/home/user1
```

2. If the plus sign (+) follows the ~, the shell refers to the current directory. For example, if *user1* is in the */usr/bin* directory, using ~+ exhibits the user's current directory location:

```
[user1@server1 bin]$ echo ~+
/usr/bin
```

3. If the hyphen character (-) follows the ~, the shell refers to the previous working directory. For example, if *user1* switches into the */usr/share/man* directory from */usr/bin* and does ~-, the output displays the user's last working directory:

```
[user1@server1 bin]$ cd /usr/share/man
[user1@server1 man]$ echo ~-
/usr/bin
```

4. If a username has the ~ prepended, the shell refers to the $HOME directory of that user:

```
[user1@server1 man]$ echo ~user200
/home/user200
```

You can use the tilde substitution directly with commands such as *cd* and *ls*. For instance, to *cd* into the home directory of *user1* (or any other user for that matter) from anywhere in the directory structure, specify the login name with the ~:

```
[user1@server1 man]$ cd ~user1
[user1@server1 ~]$ pwd
/home/user1
```

This command only succeeds if *user1* has the necessary permissions to navigate to the target user's home directory. Run the following example as the *root* user:

```
[root@server1 ~]# cd ~user100
[root@server1 user100]# pwd
/home/user100
```

The example above demonstrates navigating to *user100*'s home directory as *root*. By default, the *root* user has permission to *cd* into any user's home directory.

The next example exhibits how a user can navigate directly to one of their subdirectories (such as */home/user1/dir1*)from anywhere (*/etc/systemd/system*) in the directory structure (create *dir1* for this test):

```
[user1@server1 ~]$ cd
[user1@server1 ~]$ mkdir dir1
[user1@server1 ~]$ cd /etc/systemd/system/
[user1@server1 system]$ pwd
/etc/systemd/system
[user1@server1 system]$ cd ~/dir1
[user1@server1 dir1]$ pwd
/home/user1/dir1
```

Use the ~ with the *ls* command. For example, run **sudo ls -ld ~root/.cache** as *user1*.

Alias Substitution

Alias substitution (a.k.a. *command aliasing* or *alias*) allows you to define a shortcut for a lengthy and complex command or a set of commands. Defining and using aliases saves time and reduces typing. The shell executes the corresponding command or set of commands when an alias is run.

The bash shell includes several predefined aliases that are set during user login. These aliases may be viewed with the *alias* command. The following shows all the aliases that are currently set for *user1*:

```
[user1@server1 ~]$ alias
alias egrep='grep -E --color=auto'
alias fgrep='grep -F --color=auto'
alias grep='grep --color=auto'
alias l.='ls -d .* --color=auto'
alias ll='ls -l --color=auto'
alias ls='ls --color=auto'
alias which='(alias; declare -f) | /usr/bin/which --tty-only
--read-alias --read-functions --show-tilde --show-dot'
alias xzegrep='xzegrep --color=auto'
alias xzfgrep='xzfgrep --color=auto'
........
```

There are a few additional default aliases set for the *root* user. Run *alias* as *root*:

```
[root@server1 ~]# alias
alias cp='cp -i'
alias egrep='grep -E --color=auto'
alias fgrep='grep -F --color=auto'
alias grep='grep --color=auto'
alias l.='ls -d .* --color=auto'
alias ll='ls -l --color=auto'
alias ls='ls --color=auto'
alias mv='mv -i'
alias rm='rm -i'
alias which='(alias; declare -f) | /usr/bin/which --tty-only
--read-alias --read-functions --show-tilde --show-dot'
........
```

Many aliases have the option "color" set to auto, which implies that the output will highlight the file names and pattern matches in a color. Table 7-3 describes the common aliases from the previous two outputs.

Alias	Value	Definition
cp	cp -i	Issues the cp command in interactive mode
ll	ls -l	Shows the ls command output in long format
mv	mv -i	Executes the mv command in interactive mode
rm	rm -i	Runs the rm command in interactive mode

Table 7-3 Predefined Aliases

In addition to listing the set aliases, the *alias* command can also be used to define new aliases. The opposite function of unsetting an alias is performed with the *unalias* command. Both *alias* and *unalias* are internal shell commands. Consider the following examples.

Create an alias "search" to abbreviate the *find* command with several switches and arguments. Enclose the entire command within single quotation marks ('') to ensure white spaces are taken care of. Do not leave any spaces before and after the equal sign (=).

```
[user1@server1 ~]$ alias search='sudo find / -name core -exec ls -ld {} \;'
```

Now, when you type the string "search" at the command prompt and press `Enter`, the shell will substitute the alias "search" with its defined value and run it. Essentially, you have created a shortcut to that lengthy command.

Sometimes you define an alias with a name that matches an existing system command. In this case, the shell gives precedence to the alias, meaning it will execute the alias instead of the original command. For example, the *rm* command deletes files without warning when run by a normal user. To prevent accidental deletion, you can create an alias matching the command name but with the interactive option added, as shown below:

```
[user1@server1 ~]$ alias rm='rm -i'
```

Now when you execute *rm* to remove a file, the shell runs the alias instead of the original *rm* command. If you wish to run the original *rm* command, precede it with a backslash (\):

```
[user1@server1 ~]$ \rm file1
```

You can use the *unalias* command to unset one or more specified aliases if they are no longer in need. The following will undefine the two aliases that were defined for our examples:

```
[user1@server1 ~]$ unalias search rm
```

Metacharacters Overview

Metacharacters are characters with special meaning to the shell, affecting how commands and filenames are interpreted. Common metacharacters include the dollar sign ($), caret (^), period (.), asterisk (*), question mark (?), exclamation mark (!), square brackets ([]), angle brackets (< >), curly brackets ({}), parentheses (()), plus (+), pipe (|), semicolon (;), and backslash (\). Depending on the context, metacharacters are used for:

- Shell control and redirection: <, >, |, and ;
- Pattern matching using filename expansion (or filename globbing): *, ?, [], and !. These specific metacharacters are called wildcard characters, and they are used for shell-level pattern matching.
- Pattern matching using regular expressions. Regular expressions are used for text-level pattern matching.

The following sub-sections discuss the usage of many of these metacharacters.

Redirections

Programs read input from the keyboard and write output to the terminal window where they are initiated. Any errors, if encountered, are printed on the terminal window too. This is the default behavior. The Bash shell handles input, output, and errors as character streams. If you do not want input to come from the keyboard or output and error to go to the terminal screen, the shell gives you the flexibility to redirect input, output, and error messages to allow programs and commands to read input from a non-default source, and forward output and errors to one or more non-default destinations.

> **EXAM TIP:** You may be asked to run a command and redirect its output and/or error messages to a file.

The default (or the standard) locations for the three streams are referred to as *standard input* (or *stdin*), *standard output* (or *stdout*), and *standard error* (or *stderr*). These streams are also represented using the opening angle bracket symbol (<) for stdin, and the closing angle bracket symbol (>) for stdout and stderr. Alternatively, you may use the *file descriptors* (the digits 0, 1, and 2) to represent the three streams.

Redirecting Standard Input

Input redirection instructs a command to read input from an alternative source, such as a file, instead of the keyboard. The opening angle bracket (<) is used for input redirection. For example, run the following to have the *cat* command read the */etc/redhat-release* file and display its content on the standard output (terminal screen):

```
[user1@server1 ~]$ cat < /etc/redhat-release
Red Hat Enterprise Linux release 10.0 (Coughlan)
```

Redirecting Standard Output

Output redirection sends a command's output to an alternative destination, such as a file, instead of the terminal window. The closing angle bracket (>) is used for this purpose. For instance, the following directs the *ls* command output to a file called *ls.out*. This will overwrite any existing *ls.out* file if there is one; otherwise, a new file will be created.

```
[user1@server1 ~]$ ls > ls.out
```

The above can also be run as **ls 1> ls.out** where the digit "1" represents the standard output location.

If you want to prevent an inadvertent overwriting of the output file, you can enable the shell's noclobber feature with the *set* command and verify its activation by re-running the redirection example:

```
[user1@server1 ~]$ set -o noclobber
[user1@server1 ~]$ ls > ls.out
-bash: ls.out: cannot overwrite existing file
```

The shell prevents file overwriting.

You can disable the noclobber option by running **set +o noclobber** at the command prompt.

To direct the *ls* command to append the output to the *ls.out* file instead of overwriting it, use the two closing angle brackets (>>):

```
[user1@server1 ~]$ ls >> ls.out
```

Again, the equivalent for the above is **ls 1>> ls.out**.

Redirecting Standard Error

Error redirection forwards any error messages generated to an alternative destination rather than to the terminal window. An alternative destination could be a file. For example, the following directs the *find* command issued as a normal user to search for all occurrences of files by the name *core* in the entire directory tree and sends any error messages produced to */dev/null* (*/dev/null* is a special file that is used to discard data). This way only the useful output is exhibited on the screen and errors are thrown away.

```
[user1@server1 ~]$ find / -name core -print 2> /dev/null
```

Redirecting both Standard Output and Error

You may redirect both output and error to alternative locations as well. For instance, issue the following to forward them both to a file called *outerr.out*:

```
[user1@server1 ~]$ ls /usr /cdr &> outerr.out
```

This example produces a listing of the */usr* directory and saves the result in *outerr.out*. At the same time, it will generate an error message complaining about the non-existence of */cdr*, and it will send it to the same file as well.

Another method to run the above command is by typing **ls /usr /cdr 1> outerr.out 2>&1**, which essentially means to redirect errors to wherever the output is going.

You can use &>> instead of &> in the above example to append the output and errors to the file, rather than overwriting it.

Piping Output of One Command as Input to Another

The *pipe*, represented by the vertical bar (|) and normally resides with the backslash (\) on most keyboards, is used to send the output of one command as input to the next. This character is also used to define alternations in regular expressions. You can use the pipe operator multiple times in a single command line.

The */usr/lib/systemd* directory contains plenty of files, but they all do not fit on one terminal screen when you want to see its long listing. You can use the pipe operator to pipe the output to the *less* command to view the directory listing one screenful at a time:

```
[user1@server1 ~]$ ls -l /usr/lib/systemd | less
total 3936
drwxr-xr-x.  2 root root       6 Mar  9  2025 boot
drwxr-xr-x.  2 root root    4096 Oct 27 10:42 catalog
-rw-r--r--.  1 root root     986 Mar  9  2025 coredump.conf
-rw-r--r--.  1 root root    1425 Mar  9  2025 journald.conf
-rw-r--r--.  1 root root    1784 Mar  9  2025 logind.conf
drwxr-xr-x.  2 root root      61 Oct 27 10:42 network
drwxr-xr-x.  2 root root      29 Oct 27 10:49 ntp-units.d
```

In another example, the *last* command is run and its output is piped to the *nl* command to number each output line:

```
[user1@server1 ~]$ last | nl
     1  user1    pts/1        192.168.0.86     Wed Nov 26 11:00 - 11:01  (00:00)
     2  user1    pts/0        192.168.0.86     Wed Nov 26 11:00   still logged in
     3  reboot   system boot  6.12.0-55.9.1.el Wed Nov 26 10:53   still running
     4  user1    pts/0        192.168.0.86     Mon Nov 24 21:49 - 07:37 (1+09:48)
     5  user1    pts/0        192.168.0.86     Mon Nov 24 12:07 - 12:44  (00:36)
     6  user1    pts/0        192.168.0.86     Mon Nov 24 09:41 - 11:41  (02:00)
```

The nl command reveals numbering for each line in the output.

The following example sends the output of *ls* to *grep* for the lines that do not contain the pattern "root". The new output is further piped for a case-insensitive selection of all lines that exclude the pattern "dec". The filtered output is numbered, and the final result shows the last four lines on the display.

```
[user1@server1 ~]$ sudo ls -l /proc | grep -v root | grep -iv dec | nl | tail -4
    59  dr-xr-xr-x.  9 libstoragemgmt libstoragemgmt          0 Nov 26 10:53 842
    60  dr-xr-xr-x.  9 polkitd        polkitd                 0 Nov 26 10:53 844
    61  dr-xr-xr-x.  9 rtkit          rtkit                   0 Nov 26 10:53 845
    62  dr-xr-xr-x.  9 avahi          avahi                   0 Nov 26 11:00 855
```

A command chain with multiple pipes is called a *pipeline*.

Pattern Matching using Filename Expansion

The Bash shell supports several metacharacters for matching filenames or directory names. This is called *filename expansion* or *filename globbing*. When you issue a command containing certain metacharacters—*, ?, [], and !—the Bash shell expands these characters to match filenames before the command is executed. This group of metacharacters is called the *wildcard characters*. They allow you to work with groups of files efficiently without typing each name individually.

The * Character

The asterisk (*) matches any sequence of characters, but by default does not match leading dots (.) in hidden filenames unless explicitly specified (e.g., .*). See the following examples of its usage.

To list all files in the */etc* directory that begin with letters "ma" and followed by any characters:

```
[user1@server1 ~]$ ls /etc/ma*
/etc/machine-id  /etc/mailcap                    /etc/man_db.conf
/etc/magic       /etc/makedumpfile.conf.sample
```

To list all hidden files and directories in */home/user1*:

```
[user1@server1 ~]$ ls -d .*
.bash_history  .bash_profile  .cache   .local    .viminfo
.bash_logout   .bashrc        .config  .mozilla
```

To list all files in the */var/log* directory that end in ".log":

```
[user1@server1 ~]$ ls /var/log/*.log
/var/log/boot.log          /var/log/dnf.log
/var/log/dnf.librepo.log   /var/log/dnf.rpm.log
```

The * is the most common metacharacter that is used in pattern matching.

The ? Character

The question mark (?) matches exactly one character except for the leading period in a hidden filename. See the following example to understand its usage.

To list all files and directories under */var/log* with exactly four characters in their names:

```
[user1@server1 ~]$ ls -d /var/log/????
/var/log/btmp  /var/log/cups  /var/log/sssd
/var/log/cron  /var/log/rhsm  /var/log/wtmp
```

The ? is another metacharacter that is used widely in pattern matching.

The Square Brackets [] and the Exclamation Mark !

The square brackets ([]) can be used to match either a set of characters or a range of characters for a single character position.

For a set of characters specified in this enclosure, the order in which they are listed has no importance. This means the shell will interpret [xyz], [yxz], [xzy], and [zyx] alike during pattern matching. In the following example, two characters are enclosed within the square brackets. The output will include all files and directories that begin with either of the two characters and followed by any number of characters.

```
[user1@server1 ~]$ ls /usr/bin/[yw]*
/usr/bin/w              /usr/bin/which              /usr/bin/yelp-build
/usr/bin/wait           /usr/bin/whiptail           /usr/bin/yelp-build-ur
/usr/bin/waitpid        /usr/bin/who                /usr/bin/yelp-check
/usr/bin/wall           /usr/bin/whoami             /usr/bin/yelp-new
/usr/bin/watch          /usr/bin/wireplumber        /usr/bin/yes
```

A range of characters must be specified in a proper sequence such as [a-z] or [0-9]. The following example matches all directory names that begin with any letter between "m" and "o" in the */etc/systemd/system* directory:

```
[user1@server1 ~]$ ls -d /etc/systemd/system/[m-o]*
/etc/systemd/system/multi-user.target.wants
/etc/systemd/system/network-online.target.wants
```

The exclamation mark (!) within square brackets negates the match. For instance, [!a-d]* would exclude all filenames that begin with any of the first four alphabets. The following example produces the reverse of the previous example's result:

```
[user1@server1 ~]$ ls -d /etc/systemd/system/[!m-o]*
 /etc/systemd/system/basic.target.wants
 /etc/systemd/system/bluetooth.target.wants
 /etc/systemd/system/ctrl-alt-del.target
 /etc/systemd/system/dbus-org.bluez.service
 /etc/systemd/system/dbus-org.fedoraproject.FirewallD1.service
 /etc/systemd/system/dbus-org.freedesktop.Avahi.service
 /etc/systemd/system/dbus-org.freedesktop.ModemManager1.service
 /etc/systemd/system/dbus-org.freedesktop.nm-dispatcher.service
 /etc/systemd/system/dbus.service
 /etc/systemd/system/default.target
```

The output will display numerous filenames.

Pattern Matching using Regular Expressions

Regular expressions (a.k.a. *regex*) are patterns used to match character combinations in text files or other input. The pattern may include a single character, multiple random characters, a range of characters, word, phrase, or an entire sentence. Any pattern containing one or more white spaces must be surrounded by quotation marks.

RHEL provides a powerful tool called *grep* (*global regular expression print* or *get regular expression and print*) to work with pattern matching in regular expressions. This tool searches the contents of one or more text files or input supplied for a match. If the expression is matched, *grep* prints every line containing that expression on the screen without changing the source content. *grep* has plenty of options and supports various expression formats.

> **EXAM TIP:** The grep command is a handy tool to extract needed information from a file or command output. The extracted information can then be redirected to a file. The sequence of the grep'ed data remains unchanged.

Consider the following examples to comprehend the usage of the *grep* command.

To search for the pattern "operator" in the */etc/passwd* file:

```
[user1@server1 ~]$ grep operator /etc/passwd
operator:x:11:0:operator:/root:/usr/sbin/nologin
```

To search for the space-separated pattern "aliases and functions" in the $HOME/.bashrc file:

```
[user1@server1 ~]$ grep 'aliases and functions' .bashrc
# User specific aliases and functions
```

To search for the pattern "nologin" in the *passwd* file and exclude (-v) the lines in the output that contain this pattern. Add the -n switch to show the line numbers associated with the matched lines.

```
[user1@server1 ~]$ grep -nv nologin /etc/passwd
1:root:x:0:0:Super User:/root:/bin/bash
6:sync:x:5:0:sync:/sbin:/bin/sync
7:shutdown:x:6:0:shutdown:/sbin:/sbin/shutdown
8:halt:x:7:0:halt:/sbin:/sbin/halt
39:user1:x:1000:1000:user1:/home/user1:/bin/bash
40:user3:x:1010:1010::/usr/user3a:/bin/sh
42:user100:x:1012:1012::/home/user100:/bin/bash
43:user200:x:1013:1013::/home/user200:/bin/bash
```

To find any duplicate entries for the *root* user in the *passwd* file. Prepend the caret sign (^) to the pattern "root" to mark the beginning of a line.

```
[user1@server1 ~]$ grep ^root /etc/passwd
root:x:0:0:Super User:/root:/bin/bash
```

To identify all users in the *passwd* file with bash as their primary shell. Append the $ sign to the pattern "bash" to mark the end of a line.

```
[user1@server1 ~]$ grep bash$ /etc/passwd
root:x:0:0:Super User:/root:/bin/bash
user1:x:1000:1000:user1:/home/user1:/bin/bash
user100:x:1012:1012::/home/user100:/bin/bash
user200:x:1013:1013::/home/user200:/bin/bash
```

To show the entire *login.defs* file but exclude all the empty lines:

```
[user1@server1 ~]$ grep -v ^$ /etc/login.defs
```

To perform a case-insensitive search (-i) for all the lines in the */etc/bashrc* file that match the pattern "path."

```
[user1@server1 ~]$ grep -i path /etc/bashrc
    # Need to redefine pathmunge, it gets undefined at the end of /etc/profile
    pathmunge () {
        case ":${PATH}:" in
                    PATH=$PATH:$1
                    PATH=$1:$PATH
    unset -f pathmunge
```

To print all the lines from the */etc/lvm/lvm.conf* file that contain an exact match for a word (-w). You can use the period character (.) in the search string to match a single position. The following example searches for words in the *lvm.conf* file that begin with letters "acce" followed by exactly two characters:

```
[user1@server1 ~]$ grep -w acce.. /etc/lvm/lvm.conf
        # Commands also accept this as a prefix on volume group names.
        # This is a list of regular expressions used to accept or reject block
        # (or any character) and is preceded by 'a' to accept the path, or
        # device is rejected. Unmatching path names do not affect the accept
```

In addition to the caret (^), dollar ($), and period (.), the pipe (|), asterisk (*), question mark (?), square brackets ([]), and curly brackets ({}) are also used in regular expressions.

To print all lines from the output of the *ls* command that contain either (-E) the pattern "cron" or "ly", you can use *extended grep*. The pipe | character acts as a logical OR between the two patterns. Regex allows you to add more patterns to this set if desired. For instance, if you search for three patterns, use 'pattern1|pattern2|pattern3'. The patterns must be enclosed within single or double quotes. Here is what you will issue when you want to look for the patterns "cron" and "ly" in the */etc* directory listing:

```
[user1@server1 ~]$ ls -l /etc | grep -E 'cron|ly'
-rw-r--r--.  1 root root       541 Jul 11  2022 anacrontab
drwxr-xr-x.  2 root root        21 Jan 26 16:38 cron.d
drwxr-xr-x.  2 root root         6 Mar 23  2022 cron.daily
-rw-r--r--.  1 root root         0 Jul 11  2022 cron.deny
drwxr-xr-x.  2 root root        22 Mar 23  2022 cron.hourly
drwxr-xr-x.  2 root root         6 Mar 23  2022 cron.monthly
-rw-r--r--.  1 root root       451 Mar 23  2022 crontab
drwxr-xr-x.  2 root root         6 Mar 23  2022 cron.weekly
drwxr-xr-x.  2 root root        28 Jan 26 16:39 plymouth
```

To show all the lines from the */etc/ssh/sshd_config* file but exclude (-v) the empty lines and the rows that begin with the hash (#) character (commented lines). Using the -e flag multiple times as shown below is equivalent to how "-E 'pattern1|pattern2'" was used in the above example.

```
[user1@server1 ~]$ sudo grep -ve ^$ -ve ^# /etc/ssh/sshd_config
Include /etc/ssh/sshd_config.d/*.conf
AuthorizedKeysFile      .ssh/authorized_keys
Subsystem       sftp    /usr/libexec/openssh/sftp-server
```

You can combine options and employ diverse regular expression criteria to perform complex matches on input. Issue **man 7 regex** in a terminal window to learn more about regex. Also consult the manual pages for the *grep* command to view available options and other details.

Quoting Mechanisms

Metacharacters have special meaning to the shell. To use them as regular characters, the bash shell offers three *quoting mechanisms* to disable their special meaning and allow the shell to treat them as literal characters. These mechanisms are available through the use of the backslash (\), single quotation (‘’), and double quotation (“”) characters, and work by prepending a special character to the backslash, or enclosing it within single or double quotation marks.

Prefixing with a Backslash (\)

The backslash character (\), also called the *escape* character in shell terminology, directs the shell to suppress the special meaning of any character that follows it. For example, if a file exists by the name * and you want to remove it with the *rm* command, you will have to escape the * so that it is treated as a regular character, not as a wildcard character.

```
[user1@server1 ~]$ rm \*
```

In the above example, if you forget to escape the *, the *rm* command will remove all files from the directory.

Enclosing within Single Quotes (‘’)

The single quotation marks (‘’) instructs the shell to mask the meaning of all encapsulated special characters. For example, LOGNAME is a variable, and its value can be viewed with the *echo* command:

```
[user1@server1 ~]$ echo $LOGNAME
user1
```

If you encapsulate $LOGNAME within single quotes, the *echo* command will exhibit the entire string as is:

```
[user1@server1 ~]$ echo '$LOGNAME'
$LOGNAME
```

In the above example, the shell interprets the $ sign as a literal character, and that’s why the *echo* command displays what is inside the enclosure, including the $ rather than the value of the variable.

Enclosing within Double Quotes (“”)

The double quotation marks (“”) commands the shell to mask the meaning of all but the backslash (\), dollar sign ($), and single quotes (‘’). These three special characters retain their special meaning when they are enclosed within double quotes. Look at the following examples to understand its usage.

```
[user1@server1 ~]$ echo "$SHELL"
/bin/bash
[user1@server1 ~]$ echo "\$PWD"
$PWD
[user1@server1 ~]$ echo "'\'"
'\'
```

The above three instances confirm the use of the double quotes as a special character pair, as depicted in the outputs.

Shell Startup Files

Earlier in this chapter, you used local and environment variables and learned how to modify the primary command prompt to add useful information to it. In other words, you modified the default shell environment to suit your needs. You stored the PS1 value in a shell startup file to ensure the changes are always available after you log off and log back in.

Modifications to the default shell environment can be stored in *startup* (or *initialization*) files. These files are sourced by the shell following user authentication at the time of logging in and before the command prompt appears. In addition, aliases, functions, and scripts can be added to these files as well. There are two types of startup files: *system-wide* and *per-user*.

System-wide Shell Startup Files

System-wide startup files set the general environment for all users at the time of their login to the system. These files are located in the */etc* directory and are maintained by the Linux administrator. System-wide files can be modified to include general environment settings and customizations.

Table 7-4 lists and describes system-wide startup files for bash shell users.

File	Comments
/etc/bashrc	Defines functions and aliases, sets umask for user accounts with a non-login shell, establishes the command prompt, etc. It may include settings from the shell scripts located in the /etc/profile.d directory.
/etc/profile	Sets common environment variables such as PATH, USER, LOGNAME, MAIL, HOSTNAME, HISTSIZE, and HISTCONTROL for all users, establishes umask for user accounts with a login shell, processes the shell scripts located in the /etc/profile.d directory, and so on.
/etc/profile.d	Contains scripts for bash shell users that are executed by the /etc/profile file.

Table 7-4 System-wide Startup Files

Excerpts from the *bashrc* and *profile* files and a list of files in the *profile.d* directory are displayed below:

```
[user1@server1 ~]$ head /etc/bashrc
# /etc/bashrc

# System wide functions and aliases
# Environment stuff goes in /etc/profile

# It's NOT a good idea to change this file unless you know what you
# are doing. It's much better to create a custom.sh shell script in
# /etc/profile.d/ to make custom changes to your environment, as this
# will prevent the need for merging in future updates.
```

```
[user1@server1 ~]$ head /etc/profile
# /etc/profile

# System wide environment and startup programs, for login setup
# Functions and aliases go in /etc/bashrc

# It's NOT a good idea to change this file unless you know what you
# are doing. It's much better to create a custom.sh shell script in
# /etc/profile.d/ to make custom changes to your environment, as this
# will prevent the need for merging in future updates.

[user1@server1 ~]$ ls -l /etc/profile.d/
total 120
lrwxrwxrwx. 1 root root   57 Mar  9  2025 70-systemd-shell-ext
./../usr/lib/systemd/profile.d/70-systemd-shell-extra.sh
-rw-r--r--. 1 root root 1553 Oct 28  2024 bash-color-prompt.sh
-rw-r--r--. 1 root root  726 Oct 28  2024 bash_completion.sh
-rw-r--r--. 1 root root  200 Oct 28  2024 colorgrep.csh
-rw-r--r--. 1 root root  205 Oct 28  2024 colorgrep.sh
-rw-r--r--. 1 root root 1586 Nov 25  2024 colorls.csh
```

Any file in the *profile.d* directory can be edited and updated. Alternatively, you can create your own file and define any customization that you want.

Per-user Shell Startup Files

Per-user shell startup files override or modify system default definitions set by the system-wide startup files. These files may be customized by individual users to suit their needs. By default, two such files, in addition to the *.bash_logout* file, are located in the skeleton directory */etc/skel* and are copied into user home directories at the time of user creation.

You may create additional files in your home directories to set more environment variables or shell properties if required.

Table 7-5 lists and describes per-user startup files for bash shell users.

File	Comments
.bashrc	Defines functions and aliases. This file sources global definitions from the /etc/bashrc file.
.bash_profile	Sets environment variables and sources the .bashrc file to set functions and aliases.
.gnome2/	Directory that holds environment settings when GNOME desktop is started. Only available if GNOME is installed.

Table 7-5 Per-user Startup Files

Excerpts from the *.bashrc* and *.bash_profile* files are exhibited below:

```
[user1@server1 ~]$ cat .bashrc
# .bashrc

# Source global definitions
if [ -f /etc/bashrc ]; then
        . /etc/bashrc
fi

# User specific environment
if ! [[ "$PATH" =~ "$HOME/.local/bin:$HOME/bin:" ]]
then
    PATH="$HOME/.local/bin:$HOME/bin:$PATH"
fi
export PATH

[user1@server1 ~]$ cat .bash_profile
# .bash_profile

# Get the aliases and functions
if [ -f ~/.bashrc ]; then
        . ~/.bashrc
fi

# User specific environment and startup programs
```

The order in which the system-wide and per-user startup files are processed is important to grasp. The system runs the */etc/profile* file first, followed by *.bash_profile*, *.bashrc*, and finally the */etc/bashrc* file.

EXAM TIP: For persistence, per-user settings must be added to an appropriate file.

There is also a per-user file *.bash_logout* in the user's home directory. This file is executed when the user leaves the shell or logs off. This file may be customized as well.

Chapter Summary

This chapter explored the powerful features of the Bash shell, the default user interface in RHEL and many other Linux distributions. We examined essential capabilities including variable settings, command prompt customization, tab completion, command history expansion, and command-line editing. The chapter also covered practical techniques such as tilde substitution and command aliasing for improved efficiency.

We delved into the use of metacharacters, demonstrating their roles in input/output/error redirection, piping, filename globbing, and regular expressions. Quoting mechanisms were analyzed to illustrate how the shell interprets special characters. A practical example demonstrated how to construct a multi-stage command pipeline.

Finally, we analyzed the system-wide and user-specific initialization scripts that execute upon login to configure the user environment. This included understanding how these scripts can be customized globally or on a per-user basis to establish a tailored shell experience.

Review Questions

1. What would the command *ls /cdr /usr > output* do? Assume */cdr* does not exist.
2. What is the name of the command that allows a user to define shortcuts to lengthy commands?
3. Which file typically defines history variables for all users?
4. You have a command running that is tied to your terminal window. You want to get the command prompt back without terminating the running command. Which key combination would you press to return to the command prompt?
5. Name the three quoting mechanisms?
6. What would the command export *VAR1="I passed RHCSA"* do?
7. Name the default filename and location where user command history is stored?
8. What is the primary function of the shell in Linux?
9. What would the command *cd ~user20* do if executed as *user10*?
10. You want to change the command prompt for yourself. Where (the bash shell file) would you define it so that you get the custom command prompt whenever you log in?
11. What is the other name for the command-line completion feature?
12. What is a common use of the pipe symbol?
13. Which directory location stores most, if not all, privileged commands?
14. You have a file called "?" in your home directory along with other one-letter files. What would you run to delete the "?" file only?
15. Which command would you use to display all matching lines from a text file?
16. What would the command *ls > ls.out* do?

Answers to Review Questions

1. The command will redirect *ls /usr* output to the specified file and send *ls /cdr* (error) to the terminal since error redirection is not specified.
2. The *alias* command.
3. */etc/profile* typically sets history variables system-wide, though they can also be defined in */etc/bashrc*.
4. The `Ctrl+z` key combination will suspend the running program and give you access to the command prompt.
5. The three quoting mechanisms are backslash, single quotation mark, and double quotation mark.
6. The command provided will set an environment variable with the quoted string as its value.
7. The user command history is stored in *~/.bash_history* file.
8. The shell acts as an interface between a user and the system.
9. The command provided will allow *user10* to *cd* into *user20*'s home directory provided *user10* has proper access permissions.
10. You can define it in the *~/.bash_profile* file.
11. The other name for the command-line completion feature is tab completion.
12. A common use of the pipe character is to receive the output of one command and pass it along to the next command as an input.
13. Privileged commands are typically stored in the */usr/sbin* directory.
14. You can issue *rm \?* to remove the file.
15. The *grep* command.
16. The command provided will redirect the *ls* command output to the specified file.

Do-It-Yourself Challenge Labs

The following labs are designed to reinforce most of the concepts and skills covered in this chapter. You are expected to complete these labs without external assistance. A step-by-step guide is not provided, as the required knowledge has already been presented in the chapter; however, each lab includes hints pointing to the relevant major topic(s).

Use the lab environment created specifically for the end-of-chapter labs. See the sub-section "Lab Environment for End-of-Chapter Labs" in Chapter 01 "Local Installation" for details.

Lab 7-1: Create and Test Shell Variables and History

As *user1* on *server3*, create a local variable RHCSA with the value "RHCSA on RHEL10" and convert it to an environment variable. Verify the variable persists in a sub-shell. Add this as an environment variable to an appropriate per-user startup file for permanence. (Hint: Shell and Environment Variables).

Lab 7-2: Customize the Command Prompt

As *user1* on *server3*, customize the primary shell prompt to display the information enclosed within the quotes "<user1@server1 in /etc >: " when this user switches into the */etc* directory. The prompt should always reflect the current directory path. Add this to the appropriate per-user startup file for permanence. (Hint: Command and Variable Substitutions).

Lab 7-3: Redirect Standard Output and Error

As *user1* on *server3*, run the *ls* command on */etc*, */dvd*, and */var*. Have the output printed on the screen and the errors forwarded to file */tmp/ioerror*. Check both files after the command execution and analyze the results. (Hint: Redirections).

Chapter 08

Bash Shell Scripting

By the end of this chapter, you will be able to:

- Explain the Purpose of Scripts and How to Create them
- Build Your First Scripts: Display System Data, Use Variables, and Process Command-Line Arguments
- Execute Scripts and Implement Debugging Techniques
- Implement Logic with Exit Codes and Tests
- Control Script Flow with Conditional Statements
- Automate Repetitive Tasks with Looping Constructs

RHCSA Objectives:

16. Conditionally execute code (use of: if, test, [], etc.)
17. Use Looping constructs (for, etc.) to process file, command line input
18. Process script inputs ($1, $2, etc.)
19. Processing output of shell commands within a script

Shell scripts are text files containing a series of Linux commands, control structures, and optional comments. Their primary purpose is to automate lengthy and repetitive tasks. You can include any simple to complex command in scripts and execute them directly at the Linux command prompt. They do not need to be compiled as they are interpreted by the shell line by line.

I ♡ #/bin/bash

This chapter presents example scripts and analyzes them to solidify the learning. These scripts begin with simple programs and advance to more complicated ones. As with any other programming language, the scripting skill develops over time as more and more scripts are read, written, and examined. This chapter also discusses a debug technique that can be helpful in troubleshooting the code.

Shell Scripts

Shell scripts (a.k.a. *shell programs* or simply *scripts*) are text files that contain Linux commands and control structures to automate lengthy, complex, or repetitive tasks that you would otherwise perform manually. These tasks include managing packages and users, administering partitions and file systems, monitoring file system utilization, trimming log files, archiving and compressing files, finding and removing unnecessary files, starting and stopping database services and applications, and generating reports. The shell interprets and runs script commands sequentially, processing each line as if it were typed directly at the command prompt. Control structures enable conditional operations and looping constructs. Scripts typically include comments documenting information, such as the author name, creation date, previous modification dates, purpose, and usage. If the script encounters errors during execution, error messages are displayed on the screen.

Scripts presented in this chapter are written in the bash shell and may be used in other Linux shells with slight modifications.

You can use any text editor to write scripts. It is suggested that you use the *vim* editor as you learn both scripting and the editor. Store your scripts in the */usr/local/bin* directory so that other users can access them as well. This directory path is predefined in the PATH variable for all users by default. To quickly identify where things are in your scripts, you can use the *nl* command to enumerate the lines.

Script01: Displaying System Information

Create your first script called *sys_info.sh* on *server1* in the */usr/local/bin* directory and examine it line by line. Use the *vim* editor with *sudo* to write the script. Type what you see below. Do not enter the line numbers, as they are used for explanation and reference.

```
[user1@server1 ~]$ nl /usr/local/bin/sys_info.sh
     1  #!/bin/bash
     2  # The script name is sys_info.sh
     3  # The script is written by Asghar Ghori on November 27, 2025
     4  # The script should be located in /usr/local/bin
     5  # The script shows basic system information
     6  echo "Display Basic System Information"
     7  echo "================================="
     8  echo
     9  echo "The hostname, hardware, and OS information is:"
    10  /usr/bin/hostnamectl
    11  echo
    12  echo "The following users are currently logged in:"
    13  /usr/bin/who
```

Within vim, press the ESC key and then type :set nu to view line numbers associated with each line entry.

This script uses comments and commands as follows:

- **Line 1:** Specifies which shell will execute the script's commands. This line must start with the "#!" character combination (called a *shebang*), followed by the full path to the shell.
- **Line 2 to 5:** Contain comments describing the script's name, author, creation date, default storage location, and purpose. The number sign (#) marks a line as a comment. Anything following it on the same line is informational and is ignored during script execution. Note that while the first line also uses the number character (#),it is followed by an exclamation mark (!); this combination has a special meaning to the shell.
- **Line 6:** Contains the script's first command. The *echo* command prints the text that follows it ("Display Basic System Information") to the screen. It is commonly used for general comments, errors, or usage information.
- **Line 7:** Underlines the previous heading by printing a line of equal signs.
- **Line 8:** Uses the *echo* command without any text, which inserts a blank line into the output for better readability.
- **Line 9:** Prints the text "The hostname, hardware, and OS information is:".
- **Line 10:** Executes the *hostnamectl* command to display basic system information.
- **Line 11:** Inserts another blank line.
- **Line 12:** Prints "The following users are currently logged in:".
- **Line 13:** Executes the *who* command to list the currently logged-in users.

Here is the listing of the *sys_info.sh* file created in the */usr/local/bin* directory:

```
[user1@server1 ~]$ ls -l /usr/local/bin/sys_info.sh
-rw-r--r--. 1 root root 429 Nov 27 09:29 /usr/local/bin/sys_info.sh
```

Executing a Script

The script you created does not have the execute permission because the default umask for the *root* user is 0022. This umask allows read and write access for the owner, but only read access for everyone else. To make the script executable, you must run the *chmod* command to add execute permissions for all users:

```
[user1@server1 ~]$ sudo chmod +x /usr/local/bin/sys_info.sh
[user1@server1 ~]$ ls -l /usr/local/bin/sys_info.sh
-rwxr-xr-x. 1 root root 429 Nov 27 09:29 /usr/local/bin/sys_info.sh
```

Any user on the system can now run this script using either its name or the full path.

Run the script and see what the output will look like:

```
[user1@server1 ~]$ sys_info.sh
Display Basic System Information
================================

The hostname, hardware, and OS information is:
 Static hostname: server1.example.com
       Icon name: computer-vm
         Chassis: vm
      Machine ID: cde21919216441f8ab5a8ac30cdc4e38
         Boot ID: 60bc99e3400f455a87bec33615c4ee22
  Virtualization: oracle
Operating System: Red Hat Enterprise Linux 10.0 (Coughlan)
     CPE OS Name: cpe:/o:redhat:enterprise_linux:10::baseos
          Kernel: Linux 6.12.0-55.9.1.el10_0.x86_64
    Architecture: x86-64
 Hardware Vendor: innotek GmbH
  Hardware Model: VirtualBox
Firmware Version: VirtualBox
   Firmware Date: Fri 2006-12-01
    Firmware Age: 18y 11month 3w 6d

The following users are currently logged in:
user1    pts/0        2025-11-27 11:13 (192.168.0.86)
```

The output reflects the execution of the commands as scripted.

The *hostnamectl* command displays the hostname of the system, type of platform (physical, virtual) it is running on, hypervisor vendor name, operating system name and version, current kernel version, hardware architecture, and other information.

Debugging a Script

Scripts often require several rounds of testing and modification before they work correctly. You can use a debugging technique that will help identify where the script might have failed or did not function as expected. You can either append the -x option to the "#!/bin/bash" at the beginning of the script to look like "#!/bin/bash -x", or execute the script as follows:

```
[user1@server1 ~]$ bash -x sys_info.sh
+ echo 'Display Basic System Information'
Display Basic System Information
+ echo ================================
================================
+ echo

+ echo 'The hostname, hardware, and OS information is:'
The hostname, hardware, and OS information is:
+ /usr/bin/hostnamectl
 Static hostname: server1.example.com
........
```

The above output now also includes the actual lines from the script prefixed by the + sign and followed by the command execution result. It also shows the line number of the problem line in the output if there is any. This way you can identify any issues pertaining to the path, command name, use of special characters, etc., and address it quickly. Try changing any of the *echo* commands in the script to "iecho" and re-run the script in the debug mode to confirm what has just been said.

Script02: Using Local Variables

You had worked with variables earlier in the book and seen their usage. To recap, there are two types of variables: *local* (also called *private* or *shell*) and *environment*. Both can be defined and used in scripts and at the command line.

The following script called *use_var.sh* will define a local variable and display its value on the screen. You will re-check the value of this variable after the script execution has completed. The comments have been excluded for brevity.

```
[user1@server1 ~]$ cat /usr/local/bin/use_var.sh
#!/bin/bash
echo "Setting a Local Variable"
echo "========================="
SYSNAME=server1.example.com
echo "The hostname of this system is $SYSNAME"
```

Add the execute bit to the script. The following output will be generated when run:

```
[user1@server1 ~]$ use_var.sh
Setting a Local Variable
=========================
The hostname of this system is server1.example.com
```

If you run the *echo* command to see what is stored in the SYSNAME variable, you will get nothing:

```
[user1@server1 ~]$ echo $SYSNAME

[user1@server1 ~]$
```

The output is self-explanatory.

Script03: Using Pre-Defined Environment Variables

The following script called *pre_env.sh* will display the values of SHELL and LOGNAME environment variables:

```
[user1@server10 ~]$ cat /usr/local/bin/pre_env.sh
#!/bin/bash
echo "The location of my shell command is:"
echo $SHELL
echo "I am logged in as $LOGNAME"
```

Add the execute bit to the script, and run to view the result:

```
[user1@server1 ~]$ cat /usr/local/bin/pre_env.sh
#!/bin/bash
echo "The location of my shell command is:"
echo $SHELL
echo "I am logged in as $LOGNAME"
```

The output is self-explanatory.

Script04: Using Command Substitution

During the execution of a script, you can use the command substitution feature of the bash shell and store the output generated by the command into a variable. For example, the following script called *cmd_out.sh* will run the *hostname* and *uname* commands and save their outputs in variables. This script shows two different ways to use command substitution. Make sure to enclose the *uname* command in backticks (the backtick is located with the ~ character on the keyboard).

```
[user1@server1 ~]$ cat /usr/local/bin/cmd_out.sh
#!/bin/bash
SYSNAME=$(hostname)
KERNVER=$(uname -r)
echo "The hostname is $SYSNAME"
echo "The kernel version is $KERNVER"
```

Add the execute bit and run the script:

```
[user1@server1 ~]$ cmd_out.sh
The hostname is server1.example.com
The kernel version is 6.12.0-55.9.1.el10_0.x86_64
```

The output is self-explanatory.

Understanding Shell Parameters

A *shell parameter* is an entity that stores a value such as a name, special character, or number. The parameter that holds a name is called a variable; a special character is referred to as a *special parameter*; and one or more digits, except for 0, is known as a *positional parameter* (a.k.a. a *command-line argument*). A special parameter represents the command or script itself ($0), count of supplied arguments ($* or $@), all arguments ($#), and PID of the process ($$). A positional parameter ($1, $2, $3 . . .) is an argument supplied to a script at the time of its invocation, and its position is determined by the shell based on its location with respect to the calling script. Figure 8-1 gives a pictorial view of the special and positional parameters.

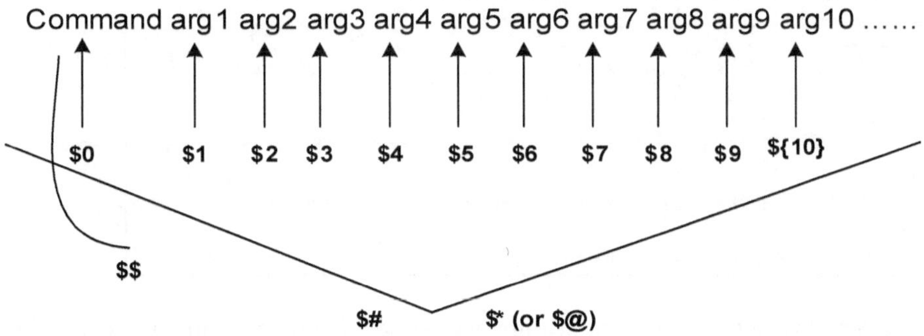

Figure 8-1 Shell Parameters

Figure 8-1 also shows that positional parameters beyond 9 are to be enclosed in curly brackets. Just like the variable and command substitutions, the shell uses the dollar ($) sign for special and positional parameter expansions as well.

Script05: Using Special and Positional Parameters

The script *com_line_arg.sh* below will show the supplied arguments, total count, value of the first argument, and PID of the script:

```
[user1@server1 ~]$ cat /usr/local/bin/com_line_arg.sh
#!/bin/bash
echo "There are $# arguments specified at the command line"
echo "The arguments supplied are: $*"
echo "The first argument is: $1"
echo "The Process ID of the script is: $$"
```

The result will be as follows when the script is executed with four arguments. Do not forget to add the execute bit prior to running it.

```
[user1@server1 ~]$ com_line_arg.sh Vancouver Hamilton Toronto Calgary
There are 4 arguments specified at the command line
The arguments supplied are: Vancouver Hamilton Toronto Calgary
The first argument is: Vancouver
The Process ID of the script is: 7910
```

The output is self-explanatory.

Script06: Shifting Command-Line Arguments

The *shift* command moves command-line arguments one position to the left. During this move, the value of the first argument is lost. The *com_line_arg_shift.sh* script below is an extension to the *com_line_arg.sh* script. It uses the *shift* command to show what happens when arguments are moved.

```
[user1@server1 ~]$ cat /usr/local/bin/com_line_arg_shift.sh
#!/bin/bash
echo "There are $# arguments specified at the command line"
echo "The arguments supplied are: $*"
echo "The first argument is: $1"
echo "The Process ID of the script is: $$"
shift
echo "The new first argument after the first shift is: $1"
shift
echo "The new first argument after the second shift is: $1"
```

Execute the script with the same four arguments. Notice that a new value is assigned to $1 after each shift.

```
[user1@server1 ~]$ com_line_arg_shift.sh Vancouver Hamilton Toronto Calgary
There are 4 arguments specified at the command line
The arguments supplied are: Vancouver Hamilton Toronto Calgary
The first argument is: Vancouver
The Process ID of the script is: 7949
The new first argument after the first shift is: Hamilton
The new first argument after the second shift is: Toronto
```

Multiple shifts in a single attempt may be performed by furnishing a count of desired shifts to the *shift* command as an argument. For example, "*shift* 2" will carry out two shifts, "*shift* 3" will make three shifts, and so on.

The *shift* command is particularly useful in scripts that process a series of arguments, allowing you to sequentially consume each one, as demonstrated by the above script.

Logical Constructs

So far, we have talked about simple scripts that run the code line by line. Logical constructs control a script's flow of execution. They use test conditions to decide the next action based on whether the condition evaluates to true or false.

The shell offers two logical constructs: the *if-then-fi* construct and the *case* construct. The if-then-fi construct has a few variations and they are covered as well. A discussion on the case construct is beyond the scope.

Before looking at the example scripts and view how logical constructs are used, let's discuss exit codes and various test conditions. They are used later in the example scripts.

Exit Codes

An exit code (or *exit value*) is a value returned by a command when it finishes execution. This value is based on the outcome of the command. If the command runs successfully, you typically get a zero exit code, otherwise you get a non-zero value. This code is also called a *return code,* and it is stored in a special shell parameter called *?* (question mark). Look at the following two examples to understand their usage:

```
[user1@server1 ~]$ pwd
/home/user1
[user1@server1 ~]$ echo $?
0
[user1@server1 ~]$ man
What manual page do you want?
For example, try 'man man'.
[user1@server1 ~]$ echo $?
1
```

In the first example, the *pwd* command ran successfully and it produced the desired result, hence a zero exit code was returned and stored in the ?. In the second example, the *man* command did not run successfully because of a missing argument, therefore a non-zero exit code was returned and stored in the ?.

You can define exit codes within a script at different locations to help debug the script by knowing where exactly it terminated.

Test Conditions

Test conditions determine the execution path within logical constructs. They can be set on integer values, string values, or files using the *test* command or by enclosing them within the square brackets []. Table 8-1 describes various test condition operators.

Operation on Integer Value	**Description**
integer1 -eq (-ne) integer2	Integer1 is equal (not equal) to integer2
integer1 -lt (-gt) integer2	Integer1 is less (greater) than integer2
integer1 -le (-ge) integer2	Integer1 is less (greater) than or equal to integer2
Operation on String Value	**Description**
string1=(!=)string2	Tests whether the two strings are identical (not identical)
-l string or -z string	Tests whether the string length is zero
string or -n string	Tests whether the string length is non-zero
Operation on File	**Description**
-b (-c) file	Tests whether the file is a block (character) device file
-d (-f) file	Tests whether the file is a directory (normal file)
-e (-s) file	Tests whether the file exists (non-empty)
-L file	Tests whether the file is a symlink
-r (-w) (-x) file	Tests whether the file is readable (writable) (executable)
file1 -nt (-ot) file2	Tests whether file1 is newer (older) than file2
Logical Operators	**Description**
!	The logical NOT operator
-a or && (two ampersand characters)	The logical AND operator. Both operands must be true for the condition to be true. Syntax: [-b file1 && -r file1]
-o or || (two pipe characters)	The logical OR operator. Either of the two or both operands must be true for the condition to be true. Syntax: [(x == 1 -o y == 2)]

Table 8-1 Test Conditions

The following example scripts demonstrate the use of exit codes and test conditions.

The if-then-fi Construct

The if-then-fi statement evaluates a condition as either true or false. It executes the specified action if the condition is true; otherwise, it exits the construct. The if-then-fi statement begins with an "if" and ends with a "fi", as depicted in the flow diagram in Figure 8-2:

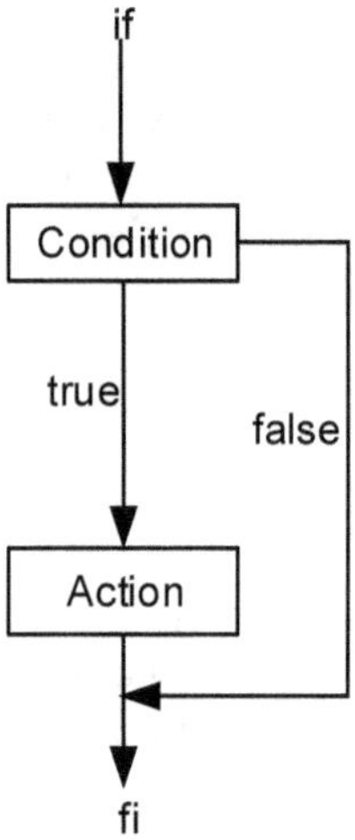

Figure 8-2 The if-then-fi Construct

The general syntax of this statement is as follows:

```
if    condition
then
      action
fi
```

This construct is used in the following script.

Script07: The if-then-fi Construct

You saw earlier how to check the number of arguments supplied at the command line. The following script called *if_then_fi.sh* determines the number of arguments and prints an error message if there are none provided:

```
[user1@server1 ~]$ cat /usr/local/bin/if_then_fi.sh
#!/bin/bash
if [ $# -ne 2 ]  # Ensure there is a space after [ and before ]
then
  echo "Error: Invalid number of arguments supplied"
  echo "Usage: $0 source_file destination_file"
  exit 2
fi
echo "Script terminated"
```

This script will display the following messages on the screen if it is executed without exactly two arguments specified at the command line:

```
[user1@server1 ~]$ if_then_fi.sh a
Error: Invalid number of arguments supplied
Usage: /usr/local/bin/if_then_fi.sh source_file destination_file
```

A value of 2 appears upon examining the return code as follows. This value reflects the exit code that you defined in the script on line 6.

```
[user1@server1 ~]$ echo $?
2
```

Conversely, the return code will be 0 and the message will be as follows if you supply a pair of arguments:

```
[user1@server1 ~]$ if_then_fi.sh a b
Script terminated
[user1@server1 ~]$ echo $?
0
```

The if-then-else-fi Construct

The if-then-fi construct has a limitation: it only executes actions if the condition is true. It quits the statement if the condition is untrue. The if-then-else-fi statement, in contrast, is more advanced in the sense that it can execute an action if the condition is true and another action if the condition is false. The flow diagram for this structure is shown in Figure 8-3:

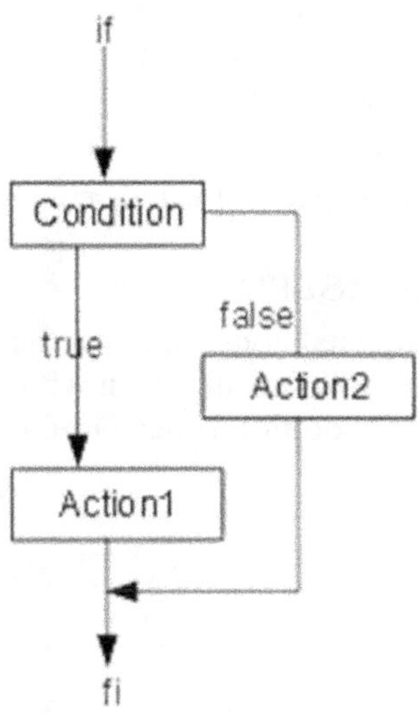

Figure 8-3 The if-then-else-fi Construct

The general syntax of this statement is as follows:

```
if    condition
then
      action1
else
      action2
fi
```

action1 or action2 is performed based on the true or false evaluation of the condition.

Script08: The if-then-else-fi Construct

The following script called *if_then_else_fi.sh* will accept an integer value as an argument and tell if the value is positive or negative:

```
[user1@server1 ~]$ cat /usr/local/bin/if_then_else_fi.sh
#!/bin/bash
if [ $1 -gt 0 ]
then
  echo "$1 is a positive integer value"
else
  echo "$1 is a negative integer value"
fi
```

Run this script one time with a positive integer value and the next time with a negative value:

```
[user1@server1 ~]$ if_then_else_fi.sh 10
10 is a positive integer value
[user1@server1 ~]$ if_then_else_fi.sh -10
-10 is a negative integer value
```

Try the script again but with a non-integer value and see what it does.

The if-then-elif-fi Construct

The if-then-elif-fi is a more sophisticated construct than the other two conditional statements. You can define multiple conditions and associate an action with each one of them. During the evaluation, the action corresponding to the true condition is performed. The flow diagram for this structure is shown in Figure 8-4:

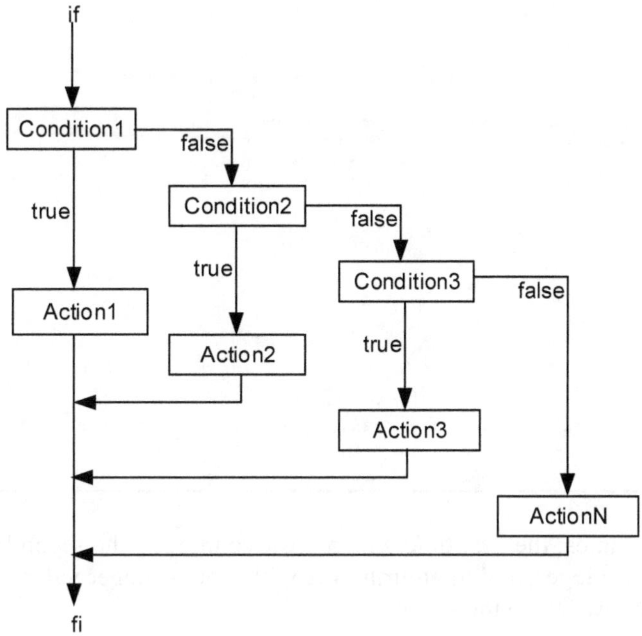

Figure 8-4 The if-then-elif-fi Construct

The general syntax of this statement is as follows:

```
if      condition1
then
        action1
elif    condition2
then
        action2
elif    condition3
then
        action3
............
else
        action(n)
fi
```

The following two scripts demonstrate the use of the if-then-elif-fi construct.

Script09: The if-then-elif-fi Construct (Example 1)

The *if_then_elif_fi.sh* script is an enhanced version of the *if_then_else_fi.sh* script. It accepts an integer value as an argument and tells if it is positive, negative, or zero. If a non-integer value or no argument is supplied, the script will complain. Notice that the script employs the *exit* command after each action to help you identify where it exited.

```
[user1@server1 ~]$ cat /usr/local/bin/if_then_elif_fi.sh
#!/bin/bash
if [ $1 -gt 0 ]
then
  echo "$1 is a positive integer value"
  exit 1
elif [ $1 -eq 0 ]
then
  echo "$1 is a zero integer value"
  exit 2
elif [ $1 -lt 0 ]
then
  echo "$1 is a negative integer value"
  exit 3
else
  echo "$1 is not an integer value. Please supply an integer."
  exit 4
fi
```

Run this script four times: the first time with a positive integer, the second time with 0, the third time with a negative integer, and the fourth time with a non-integer value. Check the exit code after each execution to know where the script exited.

```
[user1@server1 ~]$ if_then_elif_fi.sh 20
20 is a positive integer value
[user1@server1 ~]$ echo $?
1
[user1@server1 ~]$
[user1@server1 ~]$ if_then_elif_fi.sh 0
0 is a zero integer value
[user1@server1 ~]$ echo $?
2
[user1@server1 ~]$
[user1@server1 ~]$ if_then_elif_fi.sh -20
-20 is a negative integer value
[user1@server1 ~]$ echo $?
3
[user1@server1 ~]$
[user1@server1 ~]$ if_then_elif_fi.sh abcd
abcd is not an integer value. Please supply an integer.
[user1@server1 ~]$ echo $?
4
```

The outputs and exit values reflect the program code.

Script10: The if-then-elif-fi Construct (Example 2)

The script *ex200_ex294.sh* will display the name of the Red Hat exam RHCSA or RHCE in the output based on the input argument (ex200 or ex294). If a random or no argument is provided, it will print "Usage: Acceptable values are ex200 and ex294". Make sure to add white spaces in the conditions as shown.

```
[user1@server1 ~]$ cat /usr/local/bin/rhcsa_rhce.sh
#!/bin/bash
if [ "$1" = RHCSA ]
then
  echo "EX200"
elif [ "$1" = RHCE ]
then
  echo "EX294"
else
  echo "Usage: Acceptable values are RHCSA and RHCE (all uppercase)"
fi
```

Run this script three times: the first time with argument ex200, the second time with argument ex294, and the third time with something random as an argument:

```
[user1@server1 ~]$ rhcsa_rhce.sh RHCSA
EX200
[user1@server1 ~]$ rhcsa_rhce.sh RHCE
EX294
[user1@server1 ~]$ rhcsa_rhce.sh RHEL
Usage: Acceptable values are RHCSA and RHCE (all uppercase)
```

The results are as expected.

EXAM TIP: A good understanding of the usage of logical statements is important.

Looping Constructs

As a Linux user and administrator, you often want to perform certain task on given elements or repeatedly until a specified condition becomes true or false. For instance, if plenty of disks need to be initialized for use in LVM, you can either run the *pvcreate* command on each disk one at a time manually or employ a loop to do it for you. Likewise, based on a condition, you may want a program to continue to run until that condition becomes true or false.

There are three constructs—*for-do-done*, *while-do-done*, and *until-do-done*—that you can use to implement looping.

The for loop is also referred to as the foreach loop.

The for loop iterates on a list of given values until the list is exhausted. The while loop runs repeatedly until the specified condition becomes false. The until loop does just the opposite of the while loop; it performs an operation repeatedly until the specified condition becomes true. This chapter discusses the for loop only; the other two are out of scope.

Test Conditions

The *let* command is used in looping constructs to evaluate a condition at each iteration. It compares the value stored in a variable against a pre-defined value. Each time the loop does an iteration, the variable value is altered. You can enclose the condition for arithmetic evaluation within a pair of parentheses (( )) or quotation marks (“ ”) instead of using the *let* command explicitly.

Table 8-2 lists operators that can be used in test conditions.

Operator	Description
!	Negation
+ / – / * / /	Addition / subtraction / multiplication / division
%	Remainder
< / <=	Less than / less than or equal to
> / >=	Greater than / greater than or equal to
=	Assignment
== / !=	Comparison for equality / non-equality

Table 8-2 Arithmetic Operators

The following scripts demonstrate the for loop syntax and the use of test conditions.

The for Loop

The for loop iterates over a list of elements, processing each one until the list is exhausted. Each element is assigned to a variable one after the other for processing. The flow diagram for this construct is displayed in Figure 8-5:

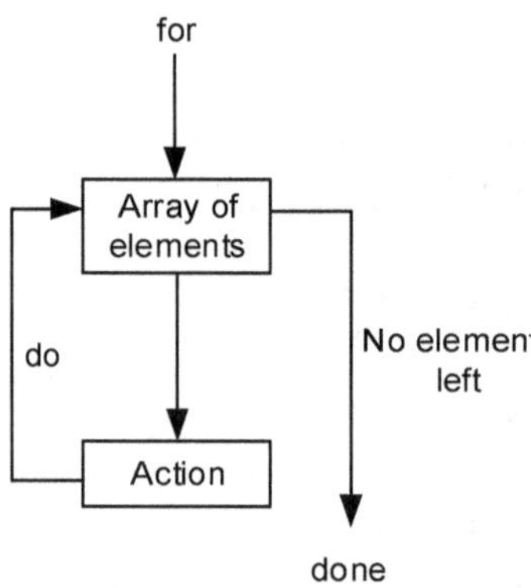

Figure 8-5 The for Loop

The general syntax of this construct is as follows:

```
for VAR in list
do
    action
done
```

Script11: Print Alphabets Using for Loop

The *for_do_done.sh* script initializes the variable COUNT to 0. The for loop will read each letter sequentially from the range placed within curly brackets (no spaces before the letter A and after the letter Z), assign it to another variable LETTER, and display the value on the screen. The *expr* (expression) command evaluates arithmetic and string expressions. In this script, it increments the COUNT variable by 1 at each loop iteration.

```
[user1@server1 ~]$ cat /usr/local/bin/for_do_done.sh
#!/bin/bash
COUNT=0
for LETTER in {A..Z}
do
  COUNT=`/usr/bin/expr $COUNT + 1`
  echo "Letter $COUNT is [$LETTER]"
done
```

The output of the script will be:

```
[user1@server1 ~]$ for_do_done.sh
Letter 1 is [A]
Letter 2 is [B]
Letter 3 is [C]
Letter 4 is [D]
Letter 5 is [E]
........
Letter 25 is [Y]
Letter 26 is [Z]
```

Script12: Create Users Using for Loop

The *create_user.sh* script can create several Linux user accounts. As each account is created, the value of the variable ? is checked. If the value is 0, a message saying the account is created successfully will be displayed, otherwise the script will terminate. In case of a successful account creation, the *passwd* command will be invoked to assign the user the same password as their username.

```
[user1@server1 ~]$ cat /usr/local/bin/create_user.sh
#!/bin/bash
for USER in user{10..12}
do
  echo "Creating account for user $USER"
  /usr/sbin/useradd $USER
  if [ $? = 0 ]
  then
    echo $USER | /usr/bin/passwd --stdin $USER
    echo "$USER is created successfully"
  else
    echo "Failed to create account $USER"
    exit
  fi
done
```

The result of the script execution below confirms the addition of three new user accounts:

```
[user1@server1 ~]$ sudo /usr/local/bin/create_user.sh
Creating account for user user10
BAD PASSWORD: The password is shorter than 8 characters
user10 is created successfully
Creating account for user user11
BAD PASSWORD: The password is shorter than 8 characters
user11 is created successfully
Creating account for user user12
BAD PASSWORD: The password is shorter than 8 characters
user12 is created successfully
```

If this script is re-executed without modifying the list of elements (usernames), the following appears:

```
[user1@server1 ~]$ sudo /usr/local/bin/create_user.sh
Creating account for user user10
useradd: user 'user10' already exists
Failed to create account user10
```

EXAM TIP: A good understanding of the looping construct will help on the exam.

Chapter Summary

This chapter introduced the fundamentals of bash shell scripting, a powerful tool for automating tasks in RHEL. We began with an overview of scripting concepts and progressed to writing and analyzing basic scripts. The chapter systematically built upon this foundation, advancing to more complex scripts that incorporated variables, conditional logic, and looping constructs.

A critical skill covered was debugging, where we learned techniques to identify and resolve errors in script execution. By the chapter's conclusion, you should possess the ability to write functional scripts for automation, effectively use variables and control structures, troubleshoot execution errors, and comprehend scripts written by others.

Review Questions

1. What are the two types of logical constructs mentioned in this chapter?
2. What would != imply in a looping condition?
3. What is the function of the *shift* command?
4. You can script the startup and shutdown of a database. True or False?
5. What is the difference between a line in a script starting with a "#" and a "#!"?
6. What comments may you want to include in a shell script? Write any six.
7. What is one benefit of writing shell scripts?
8. What are the three major components in a shell script?
9. Which looping construct can be used to perform an action on listed items?
10. What does the *echo* command do without any arguments?
11. What would the command *echo $?* do?
12. When would you want to use an exit code in your script?
13. What would you modify in a shell script to run it in the debug mode?
14. What would the command *bash -x /usr/local/bin/script1.sh* do?

Answers to Review Questions

1. The if and case constructs.
2. != would check a string or numeric value for inequality.
3. The *shift* command moves an argument to the left.
4. True.
5. The former is used to include general comments in the script and the latter combination dictates the full path to the shell file that is to be used to execute the script.
6. The author name, creation date, last modification date, location, purpose, and usage.
7. One major benefit of writing shell scripts is to automate lengthy and repetitive tasks.
8. The three major components in a shell script are commands, control structures, and comments.
9. The for loop.
10. The *echo* command inserts an empty line in the output when used without arguments.
11. This command will display the exit code of the last command executed.
12. The purpose of using an exit code is to determine exactly where the script quits.
13. We would specify -x as an argument to the shell path.
14. This command will execute *script1.sh* in debug mode.

Do-It-Yourself Challenge Labs

The following labs are designed to reinforce most of the concepts and skills covered in this and previous chapters. You are expected to complete these labs without external assistance. A step-by-step guide is not provided, as the required knowledge has already been presented; however, each lab includes hints pointing to the relevant major topic(s).

Use the lab environment created specifically for the end-of-chapter labs. See the sub-section "Lab Environment for End-of-Chapter Labs" in Chapter 01 "Local Installation" for details.

Lab 8-1: Write Script to Automate User and Directory Management

For this lab, as *user1* with *sudo* on *server4*, write a single bash script to create three users (*scriptuser1*, *scriptuser2*, and *scriptuser3*) and set up their directory structures. Create subdirectories *documents*, *projects*, and *archives* in each user's home directory. Create a group called *scriptgroup* and add all three users to it (supplementary group membership). Set up a shared directory */shared/teamfiles* with group ownership and configure permissions so that each user has full access to their home directories while all group members have read/write access to the shared area. The script should generate a summary report showing the created users, directory structure, and permission settings. (Hint1: *useradd*, *mkdir*, *groupadd*, *usermod*, *chown*, *chgrp*, and *chmod* commands). (Hint2: variables and looping construct).

Lab 8-2: Write Script for System Inventory and File Analysis

For this lab, as *user1* with *sudo* on *server4*, write a single bash script to gather basic system information and perform file analysis. The script should display the system hostname, current date and time, and OS version. It should list all users with UID 1000 or higher from */etc/passwd* and count the total number of files in the */etc* directory structure. The script should save all findings to a file in */tmp/system_report.txt* and display a summary on the screen. (Hint1: *uname*, *date*, *redirection*, *wc*, and *grep* commands). (Hint2: variables and conditional and looping constructs).

Lab 8-3: Write Script for Automated Backup and File Operations

For this lab, as *user1* with *sudo* on *server4*, write a single bash script to perform automated backup and file management tasks. The script should create a backup of */home/user1* to */home/user1/backups/user1_backup.tar.gz*, copy all *.conf* files from */etc* to */home/user1/config_backup/*, find and list all files larger than 10 MB in */usr*, clean up empty files and directories in */tmp*, and generate an operation summary report. (Hint1: *tar*, *mkdir*, and *find* commands).

Chapter 09

Process Management and Job Scheduling

By the end of this chapter, you will be able to:

- View and Identify Processes to Monitor System Activity
- Inspect Process States and Understand How Execution Priority is Determined
- Adjust Process Niceness to Influence CPU Scheduling
- Terminate, Pause, and Restart Programs with Signals
- Run Commands in the Future without Manual Intervention
- Control Which Users can Schedule Tasks
- Schedule and Manage One-Time Jobs
- Describe the Crontab Syntax to Automate Routine Tasks
- Schedule and Manage Recurring Jobs

RHCSA Objectives:

23. Identify CPU/memory intensive processes and kill processes
24. Adjust process scheduling
41. Schedule tasks using at and cron

A process is any program, command, or application running on the system. Every process has a unique numeric identifier, and the kernel manages it through its entire lifespan. You can view, list, and monitor processes, and launch them at non-default priorities based on requirements and available computing resources. A process is in one of several states at any given time during its lifecycle. A process may be tied to the terminal window where it is initiated, or it may run on the system as a service.

You can pass various signals to processes to accomplish different actions. These actions include hard killing a process, soft terminating it, and forcing it to restart with the same identifier.

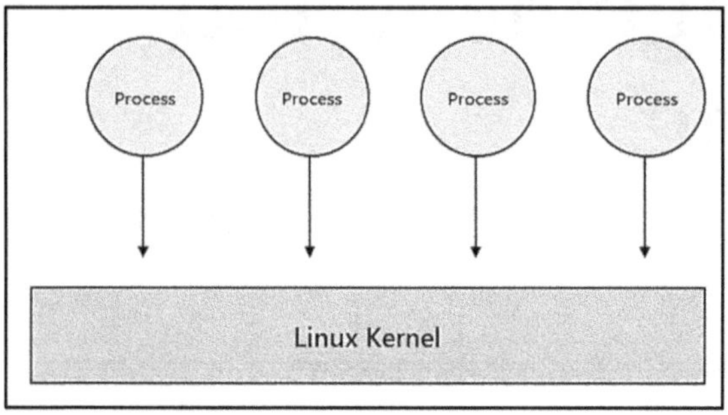

Job scheduling allows you to schedule commands for one-time or recurring execution in the future. You can submit and manage your submitted jobs if you are an authorized user. The system logs all executed jobs.

Processes and Priorities

A *process* is an instance of a running program that consumes system resources such as CPU and memory. Processes include programs, applications, services, or commands executing on the system. The system creates a process in memory when a program, application, or command is initiated. Processes are organized hierarchically. Each process has a *parent process* that spawns it. A single parent process may have one or many *child processes* and passes many of its attributes to them at the time of their creation. Each process receives a unique identification number called the *Process IDentifier* (PID), which is used by the kernel to manage and control the process through its lifecycle. When a process completes its lifespan or is terminated, this event is reported back to its parent process, and all the resources provisioned to it (cpu cycles, memory, etc.) are then freed and the PID is removed from the system.

Many processes start during system boot. These background processes, known as *daemons*, remain in memory awaiting service requests. Daemons perform critical system functions and typically remain active until the system shuts down.

Process States

A process transitions through multiple states during its lifecycle. Various factors—the processor load, available memory, process priority, and dependencies on other processes—influence these state changes. A process may remain in a non-running state while waiting for resources, user input, or data from other processes before it can resume execution.

There are five basic process states: *running* (or *runnable*), *interruptible sleep*, *uninterruptible sleep*, *stopped*, and *zombie*. Each process is in one state at any given time. See Figure 9-1.

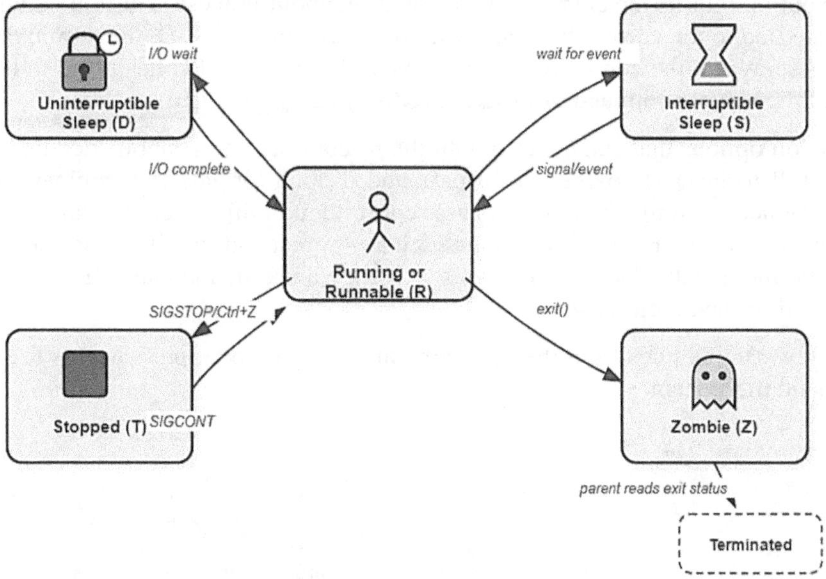

Figure 9-1 Process State Transition

Running or Runnable (R): The process is either currently executing on a CPU or is in the run queue waiting to be scheduled for execution.
Interruptible Sleep (S): The process is waiting for an event to complete, such as user input, data from a disk, or a resource to become available. It can be awakened by a signal.
Uninterruptible Sleep (D): The process is waiting for a hardware I/O operation to complete and cannot be terminated or interrupted by signals, even with *kill -9*. This state often indicates issues with storage hardware or drivers.
Stopped (T): The process has been suspended by a signal, such as SIGSTOP or `Ctrl+z`), and remains inactive until resumed by another signal, such as SIGCONT. (Signals are explained later in this chapter).
Zombie (Z): The process has completed execution but still has an entry in the process table. The zombie state persists until the parent process reads the child's exit status, at which point the system removes the process entry from the table. A zombie process is also called a *defunct* process.

Viewing and Monitoring Processes with ps

A system can have hundreds or thousands of processes running concurrently, depending on its purpose. You can view and monitor these processes using various native tools such as *ps* (*process status*) and *top* (*table of processes*). The *ps* command offers plentiful switches that influence its output, whereas *top* is used for real-time viewing and monitoring of processes and system resources.

Without options, the *ps* command lists only the processes associated with the current terminal session:

```
[user1@server1 ~]$ ps
    PID TTY          TIME CMD
   2762 pts/0    00:00:00 bash
   2908 pts/0    00:00:00 ps
```

The above output returns the elementary information about processes in four columns. These processes are tied to the current terminal window. It exhibits the PID, the terminal (TTY) where the process was spawned, the cumulative time (TIME) the system CPU has given to the process, and the name of the actual command or program (CMD) being executed.

Some common options that can be used with the *ps* command to generate detailed reports include -e (every), -f (full-format), -F (extra full-format), and -l (long format). A combination of -e, -F, and -l (**ps -eFl**) produces a comprehensive process report, though this level of detail may be unnecessary for most situations. Other common options such as --forest and -x will report the output in tree-like hierarchy and include the daemon processes as well. Check the manual pages for the command for additional options and their usage.

Here are a few sample lines from the beginning and end of the output when *ps* is executed with -e and -f flags on the system.

```
[user1@server1 ~]$ ps -ef
UID          PID    PPID  C STIME TTY          TIME CMD
root           1       0  0 12:28 ?        00:00:02 /usr/lib/systemd/systemd
root           2       0  0 12:28 ?        00:00:00 [kthreadd]
root           3       2  0 12:28 ?        00:00:00 [rcu_gp]
root           4       2  0 12:28 ?        00:00:00 [rcu_par_gp]
root           5       2  0 12:28 ?        00:00:00 [netns]
root           7       2  0 12:28 ?        00:00:00 [kworker/0:0H-events_high
root           9       2  0 12:28 ?        00:00:11 [kworker/0:1H-events_high
root          10       2  0 12:28 ?        00:00:00 [mm_percpu_wq]
root          12       2  0 12:28 ?        00:00:00 [rcu_tasks_kthre]
```

This output is displayed across eight columns showing details about every process running on the system. Table 9-1 describes the content type of each column.

Column	Description
UID	User ID or name of the process owner
PID	Process ID of the process
PPID	Process ID of the parent process
C	Processor utilization
STIME	Process start time (date if process started over 24 hours ago)
TTY	Controlling terminal. "pts" indicates pseudo terminal, "tty" indicates physical terminal, "?" represents no controlling terminal (daemon processes), and "Console" represents the graphical console.
TIME	Aggregated execution time for a process
CMD	The command or program name

Table 9-1 ps Command Output Description

The *ps* output above pinpoints several daemon processes running in the background. These processes are not associated with any terminal, which is why there is a ? in the TTY column. Notice the PID and PPID numbers. The smaller the number, the earlier it is started. The process with PID 0 is started first at system boot, followed by the process with PID 1, and so on. Each PID has an associated PPID in column 3. The owner of each process is exposed in the UID column along with the name of the command or program under CMD.

Information for each running process is recorded and maintained in the */proc* file system, which *ps* and many other commands reference to acquire desired data for viewing.

The *ps* command output may be customized to view only the desired columns. For instance, if you want to produce an output with the command name in column 1, PID in column 2, PPID in column 3, and owner name in column 4, run it as follows:

```
[user1@server1 ~]$ ps -o comm,pid,ppid,user
COMMAND              PID    PPID USER
bash                2762    2761 user1
ps                  2913    2762 user1
```

Make sure the -o option is specified for a user-defined format and there is no white space before or after the column names. You can add or remove columns and switch their positions as needed.

Another switch to look at with the *ps* command is -C (command list). This option is used to list only those processes that match the specified command name. For example, run it to check how many *sshd* processes are currently running on the system:

```
[user1@server1 ~]$ ps -C sshd
    PID TTY          TIME CMD
    873 ?        00:00:00 sshd
   1254 ?        00:00:00 sshd
   1668 ?        00:00:05 sshd
```

The output exhibits multiple background *sshd* processes.

Viewing and Monitoring Processes with top

The other popular tool for viewing process information is the *top* command. This command displays real time, continuously updated statistics, which can help identify performance issues on the system. A sample of a running *top* session is shown below:

```
[user1@server1 ~]$ top
top - 19:44:20 up  7:15,  1 user,  load average: 0.00, 0.01, 0.00
Tasks: 170 total,   1 running, 169 sleeping,   0 stopped,   0 zombie
%Cpu(s):  0.0 us,  0.0 sy,  0.0 ni, 99.8 id,  0.0 wa,  0.0 hi,  0.2 si,  0.0 st
MiB Mem :   1770.9 total,    755.9 free,    662.0 used,    516.4 buff/cache
MiB Swap:   2048.0 total,   2048.0 free,      0.0 used.   1108.9 avail Mem

    PID USER      PR  NI    VIRT    RES    SHR S  %CPU  %MEM     TIME+ COMMAND
    864 root      20   0  474112  20520  17796 S   0.3   1.1   0:07.78 NetworkMan
   1668 root      20   0   19352   7420   5144 S   0.3   0.4   0:05.39 sshd
   2911 root      20   0       0      0      0 I   0.3   0.0   0:00.05 kworker/0:
   2916 user1     20   0  225916   4176   3552 R   0.3   0.2   0:00.02 top
      1 root      20   0  106320  16052  10468 S   0.0   0.9   0:02.76 systemd
      2 root      20   0       0      0      0 S   0.0   0.0   0:00.14 kthreadd
      3 root       0 -20       0      0      0 I   0.0   0.0   0:00.00 rcu_gp
      4 root       0 -20       0      0      0 I   0.0   0.0   0:00.00 rcu_par_gp
      5 root       0 -20       0      0      0 I   0.0   0.0   0:00.00 netns
```

Press q to quit.

The *top* output may be divided into two major portions: the summary portion and the tasks portion. The summary area spreads over the first five lines of the output, and it shows the information as follows:

Line 1: Indicates the system uptime, number of users logged in, and system load averages over the period of 1, 5, and 15 minutes. See the description for the *uptime* command output in Chapter 02 "Initial System Interaction".
Line 2: Displays the task (or process) information, which includes the total number of tasks running on the system and how many of them are in running, sleeping, stopped, and zombie states.
Line 3: Shows CPU utilization percentages: us (user processes), sy (system processes), id (idle), wa (I/O wait), hi (hardware interrupts), si (software interrupts), and st (steal time).
Line 4: Shows memory usage: total physical memory, free memory, used memory, and memory used for buffers and cache.
Line 5: Exhibits swap (virtual memory) usage that includes the total amount of swap allocated to the system, and how much of it is free and in use. The "avail Mem" shows an estimate of the amount of memory available for starting new processes without using the swap.

The second major portion in the *top* command output showcases the details for each process in 12 columns as described below:

Columns 1 and 2: Pinpoint the process identifier (PID) and owner (USER)
Columns 3 and 4: Display the process priority (PR) and nice value (NI)
Columns 5 and 6: Depict amounts of virtual memory (VIRT) and non-swapped resident memory (RES) in use
Column 7: Shows the amount of shared memory used by the process (SHR)
Column 8: Represents the process status (S)
Columns 9 and 10: Express the CPU (%CPU) and memory (%MEM) utilization
Column 11: Exhibits total CPU time used by the process (TIME+)
Column 12: Identifies the process name (COMMAND)

While in *top*, you can press "o" to re-sequence the process list, "f" to add or remove fields, "F" to select the field to sort on, and "h" to obtain help. *top* is highly customizable. See the command's manual pages for details.

Listing a Specific Process

While *ps* and *top* show detailed process information, the *pidof* and *pgrep* commands are used to quickly find the PID of a specific process. These commands have switches to modify their behavior; however, their most elementary use is to pass a process name as an argument to view its PID. For instance, to list the PID of the *rsyslogd* daemon, use either of the following:

```
[user1@server1 ~]$ pidof rsyslogd
744
[user1@server1 ~]$ pgrep rsyslogd
744
```

Both commands produce an identical result if used without an option.

Listing Processes by Ownership

A process can be listed by its owning user or owning group. You can use the *ps* command for this purpose. For example, to list all processes owned by *user1*, specify the -U (or -u) option with the command and then the username:

```
[user1@server1 ~]$ ps -U user1
    PID TTY          TIME CMD
   2762 pts/0    00:00:00 bash
   2922 pts/0    00:00:00 ps
```

The command lists the PID, TTY, TIME, and CMD name for all the processes owned by *user1*. You can specify the -G (or -g) option instead and the name of an owning group to print processes associated with that group only:

```
[user1@server1 ~]$ ps -G root
    PID TTY          TIME CMD
      1 ?        00:00:02 systemd
      2 ?        00:00:00 kthreadd
      3 ?        00:00:00 rcu_gp
      4 ?        00:00:00 rcu_par_gp
      5 ?        00:00:00 netns
```

The above output reveals all the running processes with *root* as their owning group.

Understanding Process Niceness and Priority

Linux is a multitasking operating system. It creates the illusion of simultaneous execution on a single CPU core by rapidly switching between processes, giving each a small slice of time. The process scheduler performs rapid switching of processes, giving the notion of concurrent execution of multiple processes.

Every process starts with a priority based on a numeric value called its *niceness* (or *nice* value). There are 40 niceness values, ranging from -20 (highest priority, most favorable) to +19 (lowest priority, least favorable). Most system-started processes run at the default niceness of 0. A higher niceness lowers the execution priority of a process, and a lower niceness increases it. Consequently, a process with a higher priority (lower niceness) receives more CPU time. A child process inherits the niceness of its calling process in its priority calculation. Though programs are normally run at the default niceness, you can choose to initiate them at a different niceness to adjust their priority based on urgency, importance, or system load. Normal users can only lower a process's priority (increase its niceness), but the *root* user can either increase or decrease the priority (change niceness in either direction).

RHEL provides the *nice* command to launch a program at a non-default priority.

The default niceness can be viewed with the *nice* command as follows:

```
[user1@server1 ~]$ nice
0
```

The *ps* command with the -l option along with the -ef options can be used to list priority (PRI, column 7) and niceness (NI, column 8) for all processes:

```
[user1@server1 ~]$ ps -efl
F S UID         PID   PPID  C PRI  NI ADDR SZ WCHAN  STIME TTY          TIME CMD
4 S root          1      0  0  80   0 - 26580 -      12:28 ?        00:00:02 /usr/lib
1 S root          2      0  0  80   0 -     0 -      12:28 ?        00:00:00 [kthread
1 I root          3      2  0  60 -20 -     0 -      12:28 ?        00:00:00 [rcu_gp]
1 I root          4      2  0  60 -20 -     0 -      12:28 ?        00:00:00 [rcu_par
1 I root          5      2  0  60 -20 -     0 -      12:28 ?        00:00:00 [netns]
```

The output indicates that the first two processes are running at the default niceness of 0 and the next three at the highest niceness of -20. These values are used by the process scheduler to adjust the execution time of the processes on the CPU. The *ps* command displays priority (PRI) and niceness (NI) values. The priority is dynamically adjusted by the kernel, while niceness influences this adjustment. Lower PRI values indicate higher scheduling priority. For example, a niceness of 0 typically corresponds to priority 80, whereas a niceness of -20 corresponds to priority 60.

Exercise 9-1: Start Processes at Non-Default Priorities

Perform this exercise on *server1* as *user1* with *sudo* where required.

You will need two terminal sessions to perform this exercise. Call them Terminal 1 and Terminal 2.

In this exercise, you will:

- Launch the *top* program three times and observe how the *ps* command reports the priority and niceness values
- Execute the program the first time at the default priority, the second time at a lower priority, and the third time at a higher priority
- Control which priority to run the program at by specifying a niceness value with the *nice* command
- Verify the new niceness and priority after each execution of the *top* session

1. Run the *top* command at the default priority/niceness in Terminal 1:

```
[user1@server1 ~]$ top
```

2. Check the priority and niceness for the *top* command in Terminal 2 using the *ps* command:

```
[user1@server1 ~]$ ps -efl | grep top
0 S user1        3051     2762  0  80    0 - 56479 do_sel 20:32 pts/0     00:00:00 top
```

The command reports the values as 80 and 0, which are the defaults.

3. Terminate the *top* session in Terminal 1 by pressing *q* and relaunch it at a lower priority (higher niceness) with a nice value of +2:

```
[user1@server1 ~]$ nice -n 2 top
```

4. Check the priority and niceness for the *top* command in Terminal 2 using the *ps* command:

```
[user1@server1 ~]$ ps -efl | grep top
0 S user1        3056     2762  0  82    2 - 56479 do_sel 20:33 pts/0     00:00:00 top
```

The command reports the new values as 82 and 2.

5. Terminate the *top* session in Terminal 1 by pressing *q* and relaunch it at a higher priority (lower niceness) with a nice value of -10. Use *sudo* for *root* privileges.

```
[user1@server1 ~]$ sudo nice -n -10 top
```

6. Check the priority and niceness for the *top* command in Terminal 2 using the *ps* command:

```
[user1@server1 ~]$ ps -efl | grep top
4 S root        3064    3062  0  70 -10 - 56479 -      20:34 pts/0    00:00:00 top
```

As you can see, the process is running at a higher priority (70) with a nice value of -10. Terminate the *top* session by pressing *q*.

This concludes the exercise.

Controlling Processes with Signals

A system may have hundreds or thousands of processes running. Sometimes you need to alert a process of an event. You do this by sending a control signal to the process. Processes may use signals to alert each other as well. Upon receiving a signal, a process interrupts its current activity and performs the action associated with that signal. The instructions may include terminating the process gracefully, killing it abruptly, or forcing it to re-read its configuration.

There are plentiful signals available for use, but only a few are common. Each signal is associated with a unique numeric identifier, a name, and an action. A list of available signals can be viewed with the *kill* command using the -l option:

```
[user1@server1 ~]$ kill -l
 1) SIGHUP       2) SIGINT       3) SIGQUIT      4) SIGILL       5) SIGTRAP
 6) SIGABRT      7) SIGBUS       8) SIGFPE       9) SIGKILL     10) SIGUSR1
11) SIGSEGV     12) SIGUSR2     13) SIGPIPE     14) SIGALRM     15) SIGTERM
16) SIGSTKFLT   17) SIGCHLD     18) SIGCONT     19) SIGSTOP     20) SIGTSTP
21) SIGTTIN     22) SIGTTOU     23) SIGURG      24) SIGXCPU     25) SIGXFSZ
26) SIGVTALRM   27) SIGPROF     28) SIGWINCH    29) SIGIO       30) SIGPWR
31) SIGSYS      34) SIGRTMIN    35) SIGRTMIN+1  36) SIGRTMIN+2  37) SIGRTMIN+3
38) SIGRTMIN+4  39) SIGRTMIN+5  40) SIGRTMIN+6  41) SIGRTMIN+7  42) SIGRTMIN+8
43) SIGRTMIN+9  44) SIGRTMIN+10 45) SIGRTMIN+11 46) SIGRTMIN+12 47) SIGRTMIN+13
48) SIGRTMIN+14 49) SIGRTMIN+15 50) SIGRTMAX-14 51) SIGRTMAX-13 52) SIGRTMAX-12
53) SIGRTMAX-11 54) SIGRTMAX-10 55) SIGRTMAX-9  56) SIGRTMAX-8  57) SIGRTMAX-7
58) SIGRTMAX-6  59) SIGRTMAX-5  60) SIGRTMAX-4  61) SIGRTMAX-3  62) SIGRTMAX-2
63) SIGRTMAX-1  64) SIGRTMAX
```

The output returns 64 signals available for process-to-process and user-to-process communication. Table 9-2 describes the control signals that are most often used.

Signal Number	Signal Name	Action
1	SIGHUP	Hang up signal causes a process to disconnect itself from a closed terminal that it was tied to. Also used to instruct a running daemon to re-read its configuration without a restart.
2	SIGINT	The ^c (Ctrl+c) signal issued on the controlling terminal to interrupt the execution of a process.
9	SIGKILL	Terminates a process abruptly
15	SIGTERM	Soft termination signal to stop a process in an orderly fashion. This is the default signal if none is specified with the command.
18	SIGCONT	Same as using the bg command to resume
19	SIGSTOP	Same as using Ctrl+z to suspend a job
20	SIGTSTP	Same as the fg command

Table 9-2 Control Signals

The commands used to pass a signal to a process are *kill* and *pkill*. These commands are usually used to terminate a process. Ordinary users can kill processes that they own, while the *root* user privilege is needed to kill any process on the system.

The *kill* command requires one or more PIDs, and the *pkill* command requires one or more process names to send a signal to. You can specify a non-default signal name or number with either utility.

Consider the following examples to understand the usage of these tools.

To pass the soft termination signal to the *crond* daemon, use either of the following:

```
[user1@server1 ~]$ sudo pkill crond
[user1@server1 ~]$ sudo kill $(pidof crond)
```

The *pidof* command in the above example discovers the PID of the *crond* process using command substitution, which is then passed to the *kill* command for termination. You may also use the *pgrep* command to determine the PID of a process, as demonstrated in the next example. Use **ps -ef | grep crond** to confirm the process termination.

Using the *pkill* or *kill* command without specifying a signal name or number sends the default signal of 15 to the process. This signal may or not terminate the process. Some processes ignore the soft termination signal as they could be in a waiting state. These processes may be ended forcefully using signal 9 in any of the following ways:

```
[user1@server1 ~]$ sudo pkill -9 crond
[user1@server1 ~]$ sudo pkill -s SIGKILL crond
[user1@server1 ~]$ sudo kill -9 $(pgrep crond)
```

Always try to terminate a process gracefully first by sending the default signal. This allows the process to clean up resources (like closing files) before exiting. Use the SIGKILL signal only as a last resort, as it immediately terminates the process without any cleanup, which can potentially lead to data loss or corruption.

You may run the *killall* command to terminate all processes that match a criterion. Here is how you can use this command to kill all *crond* processes (assuming many of them running):

```
[user1@server1 ~]$ sudo killall crond
```

There are plenty of options available with the *kill*, *killall*, *pkill*, *pgrep*, and *pidof* commands. Consult respective manual pages for more details.

Job Scheduling

Job scheduling lets you execute commands at a specified time in the future. The execution of the command could be one time or periodic based on a pre-determined time schedule. A one-time execution may be scheduled for an activity that needs to be performed at a time of low system usage. One example of such an activity would be the execution of a lengthy shell program. In contrast, a recurring activity could include creating a compressed archive, trimming log files, monitoring the system, running a custom script, or removing unwanted files from the system.

Job scheduling and execution is taken care of by two service daemons: *atd* and *crond*. While *atd* manages the jobs scheduled to run one time in the future, *crond* is responsible for running jobs repetitively at pre-specified times. At startup, this daemon reads the schedules in files located in the */var/spool/cron* and */etc/cron.d* directories, and loads them in the memory for on-time execution. It scans these files at short intervals and updates the in-memory schedules to reflect any modifications. This daemon runs a job at its scheduled time only and does not entertain any missed jobs. In contrast, if a system is offline during a scheduled *at* job, the *atd* daemon will attempt to run it when the system starts. For any additions or changes, however, neither daemon needs a restart.

Controlling User Access

By default, all users can schedule at and cron jobs. However, you can control and restrict this access to specific users. You do this by listing users in the allow or deny file located in the */etc* directory for either service. These files are named *at.allow* and *at.deny* for the at service and *cron.allow* and *cron.deny* for the cron service.

The syntax for the four files is identical. You only need to list usernames that are to be allowed or denied access to these scheduling tools. Each file contains one username per line. The *root* user is always permitted; it is affected neither by the existence or non-existence of these files nor by the inclusion or exclusion of its entry in these files.

Table 9-3 shows various combinations and their impact on user access.

at.allow / cron.allow	at.deny / cron.deny	Impact
Exists, and contains user entries	Existence does not matter	All users listed in allow files are permitted
Exists, but is empty	Existence does not matter	No users are permitted
Does not exist	Exists, and contains user entries	All users, other than those listed in deny files, are permitted
Does not exist	Exists, but is empty	All users are permitted
Does not exist	Does not exist	No users are permitted

Table 9-3 User Access Restrictions to Scheduling Tools

By default, the *deny* files exist and are empty, and the *allow* files are non-existent. This opens up full access to using both tools for all users.

The existence of an allow file overrides any deny file settings.

EXAM TIP: One username is entered per line entry in an appropriate allow or deny file.

The following message appears if an unauthorized user attempts to execute *at*:

```
You do not have permission to use at.
```

And the following warning is displayed for unauthorized access attempt to the cron service:

```
You (user1) are not allowed to use this program (crontab)
See crontab(1) for more information
```

To generate the denial messages, you need to place entries for *user1* in the *deny* files.

Scheduler Log File

All activities for *atd* and *crond* services are logged to the */var/log/cron* file. Information such as the time of activity, hostname, process name and PID, owner, and a message for each invocation is captured. The file also keeps track of other events for the *crond* service such as the service start time and any delays. A few sample entries from the log file are shown below:

```
[user1@server1 ~]$ sudo cat /var/log/cron
Jan 29 12:29:12 server1 crond[950]: (CRON) STARTUP (1.5.7)
Jan 29 12:29:12 server1 crond[950]: (CRON) INFO (Syslog will be used inste
.)
Jan 29 12:29:12 server1 crond[950]: (CRON) INFO (RANDOM_DELAY will be scal
 10% if used.)
Jan 29 12:29:12 server1 crond[950]: (CRON) INFO (running with inotify supp
Jan 29 13:01:01 server1 CROND[1859]: (root) CMD (run-parts /etc/cron.hourl
Jan 29 13:01:01 server1 run-parts[1859]: (/etc/cron.hourly) starting 0anac
Jan 29 13:01:01 server1 anacron[1872]: Anacron started on 2023-01-29
```

The truncated output shows some past entries from the file. You need the *root* user privilege to be able to read the file content.

Using at

The *at* command is used to schedule a one-time execution of a program in the future. All submitted jobs are spooled in the */var/spool/at* directory and executed by the *atd* daemon at their scheduled times. Each submitted job will have a file created containing the settings for establishing the user's shell environment to ensure a successful execution. This file also includes the name of the command or program to be run. You do not need to restart the *atd* or *crond* daemon after submitting a job.

There are multiple ways and formats for expressing time with *at*. Some examples are:

at 1:15am	(next 1:15 a.m.)
at noon	(12:00 p.m.)
at 23:45	(11:45 p.m.)
at midnight	(12:00 a.m.)
at 17:05 tomorrow	(5:05 p.m. on the next day)
at now + 5 hours	(5 hours from now. You can specify minutes, days, or weeks instead of hours)
at 3:00 10/15/26	(3:00 a.m. on October 15, 2026)

at assumes the current year and today's date if the year and date are not mentioned.

You may supply a filename with the *at* command using the -f option. The command will execute that file at the specified time. For instance, the following will run */home/user1/.bash_profile* file for *user1* 2 hours from now:

```
[user1@server1 ~]$ at -f ~/.bash_profile now + 2 hours
warning: commands will be executed using /bin/sh
job 1 at Sat Nov 29 03:28:00 2025
```

The above will be executed as scheduled and will have an entry placed for it in the log file.

Exercise 9-2: Submit, View, List, and Erase an at Job

Perform this exercise on *server1* as *user1*. In this exercise, you will

- Submit an at job to run the *date* command at 11:30 p.m. on March 31, 2026, and have the output and any error messages generated redirected to the */tmp/date.out* file.
- List the submitted job
- Exhibit the job's content for verification
- Remove the job

1. Run the *at* command and specify the correct execution time and date for the job. Type the entire command at the first at> prompt and press `Enter`. Press `Ctrl+d` at the second at> prompt to complete the job submission and return to the shell prompt.

```
[user1@server1 ~]$ at 11:30pm 3/31/26
warning: commands will be executed using /bin/sh
at Tue Mar 31 23:30:00 2026
at> date &> /tmp/date.out
at> <EOT>
job 2 at Tue Mar 31 23:30:00 2026
```

The system assigned job ID 2 to it, and the output also pinpoints the job's execution time.

2. List the job file created in the */var/spool/at* directory:

```
[user1@server1 ~]$ sudo ls -l /var/spool/at/
total 4
-rwx------. 1 user1 user1 3877 Nov 29 01:31 a0000201c368d2
```

3. List the spooled job with the *at* (or *atq*) command:

```
[user1@server1 ~]$ at -l
2       Tue Mar 31 23:30:00 2026 a user1
```

4. Display the content of this file with the *at* command and specify the job ID:

```
[user1@server1 ~]$ at -c 2
#!/bin/sh
# atrun uid=1000 gid=1000
# mail root 0
umask 22
SHELL=/bin/bash; export SHELL
HISTCONTROL=ignoredups; export HISTCONTROL
HISTSIZE=1000; export HISTSIZE
HOSTNAME=server1.example.com; export HOSTNAME
PWD=/home/user1; export PWD
LOGNAME=user1; export LOGNAME
```

5. Remove the spooled job with the *at* command by specifying its job ID. You can also run **atrm 2** to delete it.

```
[user1@server1 ~]$ at -d 2
```

This should erase the job file from the */var/spool/at* directory. You can confirm the deletion by running **atq** or **at -l**.

Using crontab

The *crontab* command is the other method you can use to schedule tasks to run in the future. Unlike *atd*, *crond* executes cron jobs on a regular basis if they comply with the format defined in the */etc/crontab* file. Crontab files (or Crontables) are stored in the */var/spool/cron* directory. Each authorized user with a scheduled job has a file matching their login name in this directory.

For example, the crontable for *user1* would be */var/spool/cron/user1*. The other two locations where system crontables can be stored are the */etc/crontab* file and the */etc/cron.d* directory; however, only the *root* user is allowed to create, modify, and delete them. The *crond* daemon checks the crontab files in the three locations to determine which jobs to run and when. The daemon runs the commands or programs at specified times and adds a log entry to the */var/log/cron* file for each invocation. There is no need to restart the daemon after submitting a new or modifying an existing cron job.

The *crontab* command is used to edit (-e), list (-l), and remove (-r) crontables. The -u option is also available for users who wish to modify a different user's crontable, provided they are allowed to do so and the other user is listed in the *cron.allow* file. The *root* user can also use the -u flag to alter other users' crontables even if the affected users are not listed in the *allow* file. By default, crontab files are opened in the *vim* editor when the *crontab* command is issued to edit them.

Syntax of User Crontables

The */etc/crontab* file specifies the syntax that each user cron job must comply with in order for *crond* to interpret and execute it successfully. Based on this structure, each line in a user crontable with an entry for a scheduled job is comprised of six fields. Fields 1 to 5 are for the schedule, field 6 may contain the login name of the executing user, and the rest for the command or program to be executed. See Figure 9-2 for the syntax.

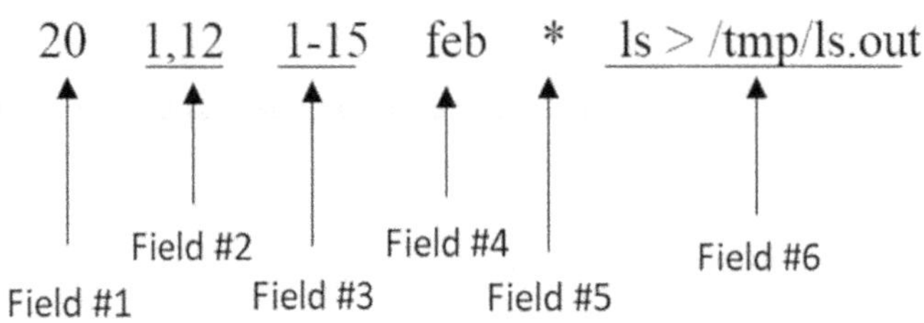

Figure 9-2 Syntax of Crontables

A description of each field is provided in Table 9-4.

Field	Field Content	Description
1	Minute of the hour	Valid values are 0 (the exact hour) to 59. This field can have one specific value as in field 1, multiple comma-separated values as in field 2, a range of values as in field 3, a mix of fields 2 and 3 (1-5,6-19), or an * representing every minute of the hour as in field 5.
2	Hour of the day	Valid values are 0 (midnight) to 23. Same usage applies as described for field 1.
3	Day of the month	Valid values are 1 to 31. Same usage applies as described for field 1.
4	Month of the year	Valid values are 1 to 12 or jan to dec. Same usage applies as described for field 1.
5	Day of the week	Valid values are 0 to 7 or sun to sat, with 0 and 7 representing Sunday, 1 representing Monday, and so on. Same usage applies as described for field 1.
6	Command or program to execute	Specifies the full path name of the command or program to be executed, along with any options or arguments that it requires.

Table 9-4 Crontable Syntax Explained

Furthermore, step values may be used with * and ranges in the crontables using the forward slash character (/). Step values allow the number of skips for a given value. For example, */2 in the minute field would mean every second minute, */3 would mean every third minute, 0-59/4 would mean every fourth minute, and so on. Step values are also supported in the same format in fields 2 to 5.

EXAM TIP: Make sure you understand and memorize the order of the fields defined in crontables.

Consult the manual pages for the *crontab* configuration file (**man 5 crontab**) for more details on the syntax.

Exercise 9-3: Add, List, and Erase a Cron Job

Perform this exercise on *server1* as *user1* with *sudo* where required.

For this exercise, assume that all users are currently denied access to cron. In this exercise, you will:

- Submit a cron job as *user1* to echo "Hello, this is a cron test."
- Schedule this command to execute at every fifth minute past the hour between 10:00 a.m. and 11:00 a.m. on the fifth and twentieth of every month
- Redirect the output to the */tmp/hello.out* file
- List the cron entry
- Remove the job

1. Create or edit the */etc/cron.allow* file and add *user1* to it:

```
[user1@server1 ~]$ sudo vim /etc/cron.allow
user1
```

2. Open the crontable and append the following schedule to it. Save the file when done and exit out of the editor.

```
[user1@server1 ~]$ crontab -e
*/5 10-11 5,20 * * echo "Hello, this is a cron test." > /tmp/hello.out
```

3. Check for the presence of a new file by the name *user1* under the */var/spool/cron* directory:

```
[user1@server1 ~]$ sudo ls -l /var/spool/cron/
```

4. List the contents of the crontable:

```
[user1@server1 ~]$ crontab -l
*/5 10-11 5,20 * * echo "Hello, this is a cron test." > /tmp/hello.out
```

5. Remove the crontable and confirm the deletion:

```
[user1@server1 ~]$ crontab -r
[user1@server1 ~]$ crontab -l
no crontab for user1
```

Note that the command **crontab -r** removes the entire crontab file. To delete only specific jobs, use **crontab -e** to edit the file and remove the corresponding lines.

Chapter Summary

This chapter covered two essential system administration areas: process management and job scheduling. A firm understanding of these topics is critical for monitoring system health and automating tasks.

The first half focused on processes. We learned to list and analyze running processes, their resource consumption, ownership, and states. We examined process execution priorities and practiced adjusting them using the niceness value. The chapter also covered process signaling, analyzing various signals, and demonstrating how to send signals to processes to alter their behavior.

The second half was dedicated to automating future tasks. We explored the at and cron services, their controlling daemons, and the configuration files that manage user access. We analyzed the dedicated log file for job execution records and reviewed the syntax for both crontab entries and at job time formats. Practical exercises provided hands-on experience in scheduling one-time and recurring jobs.

Review Questions

1. The default location to send application error messages is the system log file. True or False?
2. What are the five process states?
3. Signal 9 is used for a hard termination of a process. True or False?
4. You must restart the *crond* service after modifying the */etc/crontab* file. True or False?
5. What are the background service processes normally referred to in Linux?
6. What is the default nice value?
7. The parent process gets the nice value of its child process. True or False?

8. When would the *cron* daemon execute a job submitted as */10 * 2-6 6 * /home/user1/script1.sh*?
9. What is the other command besides *ps* to view running processes?
10. Every process that runs on the system has a unique identifier called UID. True or False?
11. What are the two commands to list the PID of a specific process?
12. By default the **.allow* files exist. True or False?
13. Where do the scheduling daemons store log information of executed jobs?
14. Which user does not have to be explicitly defined in either **.allow* or **.deny* file to run the at and cron jobs?
15. When would the *at* command execute a job that is submitted as at 01:00 12/12/2026?
16. What are the two commands that you can use to terminate a process?
17. What is the directory location where user crontab files are stored?
18. What would the *nice* command display without any options or arguments?
19. Which command can be used to edit crontables?

Answers to Review Questions

1. False. The default location is the user's terminal where the program was launched.
2. The five process states are Running/Runnable (R), Interruptible Sleep (S), Uninterruptible Sleep (D), Stopped (T), and Zombie (Z).
3. True.
4. False. The *crond* service automatically detects changes to crontables and does not require a restart.
5. The background service processes are referred to as daemons.
6. The default nice value is zero.
7. False. Child processes inherit the niceness value from their parent process.
8. The *cron* daemon will run the script every tenth minute past the hour on the 2nd, 3rd, 4th, 5th, and 6th day of June.
9. The *top* command.
10. False. It is called the PID.
11. The *pidof* and *pgrep* commands.
12. False. By default, the **.deny* files exist.
13. The scheduling daemons store log information of executed jobs in the */var/log/cron* file.
14. The *root* user.
15. The *at* command will run it at 1am on December 12, 2026.
16. The *kill* and *pkill* commands.
17. The user crontab files are stored in the */var/spool/cron* directory.
18. The *nice* command displays the current niceness value when executed without any options.
19. The *crontab* command with the -e option is used to edit crontab entries.

Do-It-Yourself Challenge Labs

The following labs are designed to reinforce most of the concepts and skills covered in this chapter. You are expected to complete these labs without external assistance. A step-by-step guide is not provided, as the required knowledge has already been presented in the chapter; however, each lab includes hints pointing to the relevant major topic(s).

Use the lab environment created specifically for the end-of-chapter labs. See the sub-section "Lab Environment for End-of-Chapter Labs" in Chapter 01 "Local Installation" for details.

Lab 9-1: Manage Processes and Use Signals

As *user1* on *server3*, start a long-running process (sleep 300). Use *ps* to identify its PID and monitor its state. Send a SIGSTOP signal to suspend the process, verify it has stopped using *ps*, then resume it with SIGCONT. Finally, terminate the process using both SIGTERM and if needed, SIGKILL. Record each state change observed. (Hint: Process States and Signals).

Lab 9-2: Manage Process Priority and Niceness Values

As *user1* on *server3*, launch three instances of the *top* command: one at default priority, one with lowered priority (*nice +5 top*), and one with elevated priority (*sudo nice -5 top*). Use *ps -l* to compare their NI and PRI values. Record how niceness affects process scheduling. (Hint: Process Priorities and nice command).

Lab 9-3: Configure a User Crontab File

As *user1* on *server3*, run the *tty* and *date* commands to determine the terminal file (assume */dev/pts/1*) and current system time. Create a cron entry to display "Hello World" on the terminal. Schedule *echo "Hello World" > /dev/pts/1* to run 3 minutes from the current system time. As *root*, ensure *user1* can schedule cron jobs. (Hint: Job Scheduling).

Chapter 10

Basic Package Management

By the end of this chapter, you will be able to:

- Explain the Structure, Naming Conventions, and Management Tools for Red Hat Packages
- Describe the Concepts of Package Dependencies and the RPM Database
- Query, Install, Upgrade, Freshen, Overwrite, and Remove Packages
- Extract Files from Installable Packages
- Validate Package Integrity and Authenticity
- View GPG Keys and Verify Package and File Attributes
- Perform Comprehensive Package Management Using the rpm Command

RHCSA Objectives:

13. Install and remove RPM software packages
45. Install and update software packages from Red Hat Network, a remote repository, or from the local file system (part of this objective is also covered in Chapter 11)

The Red Hat software management system is known as RPM Package Manager (RPM). RPM also refers to the package files themselves, which are stored in a special file format with the .rpm extension. You manipulate these rpm files (also called rpms, rpm packages, or packages) using the RPM package management system. Each package included in and available for RHEL is in this file format. Packages have meaningful names and contain necessary files alongside metadata, such as file ownership, permissions, and installation paths. You can download and save packages locally or on a network share for quick access, and they may have dependencies over files or other packages. In other words, a package may require the presence of additional files, another package, or a group of packages to be installed successfully and operate properly. Once a package has been installed and its metadata information stored in a package database, future attempts to update the package are reflected in the metadata as well.

RHEL provides a powerful tool for the installation and administration of RPM packages. The rpm command is flexible and offers multitude of options and subcommands to perform functions such as querying, installing, upgrading, freshening, removing, and decompressing packages, and validating package integrity and authenticity.

Package Overview

RHEL consists of packages grouped together to form a complete operating system. They are prepackaged for installation and assembled for various intended use cases. These packages are built around the Linux kernel and include thousands of digitally signed, tested, and certified software components. There are several basic and advanced concepts associated with packages, packaging, and their management that are touched upon in this and the next chapter.

Packages and Packaging

A software *package* contains files organized in a specific directory structure, along with metadata and installation scripts that comprise a software application. They are available in two types: *binary* (or *installable*) and *source*. Binary packages are installation-ready and are bundled for distribution.

They have .rpm extension and contain install scripts, pre- and post-installation scripts, executables, configuration files, library files, dependency information, where to install files, and documentation. The documentation includes detailed instructions on how to install and uninstall the package, manual pages for the configuration files and commands, and other necessary information pertaining to the installation and usage of the package.

All metadata related to packages is stored at a central location and includes information such as package version, installation location, checksum values, and a list of included files with their attributes. This allows the package management toolset to handle package administration tasks efficiently by referencing this metadata.

Package installation scripts are used by package administration tools for a successful completion of the package installation process. It may include information on prerequisites, user account setup (if required), and any directories and soft links that need to be created. The scripts also include the reverse of this process for uninstallation.

Source packages come with the original unmodified version of the software that may be unpacked, modified as desired, and repackaged in the binary format for installation or redistribution. They are identified with the .src extension.

Package Naming

Red Hat software packages follow a standard naming convention. Typically, there are five parts to a package name: (1) the package name, (2) its version, (3) its release (revision or build), (4) created for, and (5) the processor architecture it is built for. An installable package name always has the .rpm extension; however, this extension is removed from the installed package name.

For example, if the name of an installable package is openssl-3.2.2-16.el10.x86_64.rpm, its installed name would be openssl-3.2.2-16.el10.x86_64. Here is a description of each part of the package name:

openssl: package name
3.2.2: version
16: release
El10: indicates compatibility with *Enterprise Linux* 10 (not all packages include this designation)
x86_64: the processor architecture. Other common values include "noarch" for architecture-independent packages, and "src" for source packages.
.rpm: the extension

Package Dependency

An installable package may require the presence of one or more additional packages to be installed successfully. Likewise, a software package component may require the functionality provided by one or more packages to exist to operate as expected. This is referred to as *package dependency*, where one package depends on one or more other packages for installation or execution. Package dependency information is recorded in each package's metadata from where it is read by package handling utilities.

Package Database

Metadata for installed packages and package files is stored and maintained in the */var/lib/rpm* directory. This directory location is referred to as the *package database*, and it is referenced by package manipulation utilities to obtain package name and version data and information about ownerships, permissions, timestamps, and sizes for every file that is part of the package. The package database also contains information on dependencies. All this data aids management commands in listing and querying packages, verifying dependencies and file attributes, installing new packages, upgrading and uninstalling existing packages, and carrying out other package handling tasks.

The package database replaces package metadata entirely during package upgrades rather than incrementally updating existing information.

Management Tools

The primary tool you will use for package management in RHEL is called *rpm* (*redhat package manager*). This tool provides comprehensive package management capabilities; however, it does not automatically resolve package dependencies. To overcome this gap, a more innovative tool called *yum* (*yellowdog update, modified*) was introduced, which offered an easier method for package management that can find, get, and install all required dependent packages automatically.

Beginning with RHEL 8, DNF (*Dandified YUM*) replaced YUM as the default package manager. The *yum* command remains available in RHEL 10 as a symbolic link to *dnf* for compatibility. Both *dnf* and *yum* are located in the */usr/bin* directory.

This chapter focuses on the use of the *rpm* command. Chapter 11 "Advanced Package and Repository Management" details the *dnf* command.

Package Management with rpm

The *rpm* command handles package management tasks including querying, installing, upgrading, freshening, overwriting, removing, extracting, validating, and verifying packages. As mentioned, this command has a major drawback as it does not have the ability to automatically satisfy package dependencies, which can be frustrating during software installation and upgrade. The *rpm* command works with both installed and installable packages.

The rpm Command

Before getting into the details, let's look at some common *rpm* command options. Table 10-1 describes query options in both short and long option formats. You may use either format.

Query Options	Description
-q (--query)	Queries and displays packages
-qa (--query --all)	Lists all installed packages
-qc (--query --configfiles)	Lists configuration files in a package
-qd (--query --docfiles)	Lists documentation files in a package
-qf (--query --file)	Shows which package provides a specific file
-qi (--query --info)	Shows installed package information including version, size, installation status and date, signature, and description
-qip (--query --info --package)	Shows installable package information including version, size, installation status and date, signature, and description

Query Options	Description
-ql (--query --list)	Lists all files in a package
-qR (--query --requires)	Lists package dependencies (required packages)
-q --whatprovides	Lists packages that provide the specified package or file
-q --whatrequires	Lists packages that require the specified package or file

Table 10-1 rpm Command Query Options

Query options work on installed packages unless the -p option is used to query installable packages.

Table 10-2 describes options related to package installation, removal, and verification. These options are also available in both short and long formats. You may use either format.

Install/Remove Options	Description
-e (--erase)	Removes a package
--force	Installs and replaces a package or files of the same version
-F (--freshen)	Upgrades a package only if an older version is installed
-h (--hash)	Shows installation progress with hash marks
-i (--install)	Installs a package
--import	Imports a public key
-K	Validates the package's integrity (checksum) and authenticity (GPG signature)
-U (--upgrade)	Upgrades a package if installed, otherwise installs it
-v (--verbose) or -vv	Displays detailed information
-V (--verify)	Verifies the integrity of a package or package files

Table 10-2 rpm Command Install/Remove/Verify Options

The examples in this chapter employ most of these options in short format to understand how they are used to achieve desired results.

Exercise 10-1: Mount RHEL 10 ISO Persistently

Perform this exercise on *server1* as *user1* with *sudo* where required. In this exercise, you will:

- Attach the RHEL 10 ISO image to the *RHEL10-VM1* in VirtualBox
- Mount the image to */mnt* directory to access and manipulate the software packages with the *rpm* command
- Ensure that the image is automatically mounted on each system reboot
- Confirm access to the packages by listing the subdirectories that store them

1. Go to VirtualBox and make sure that the RHEL 10 image is attached to *RHEL10-VM1* as depicted below:

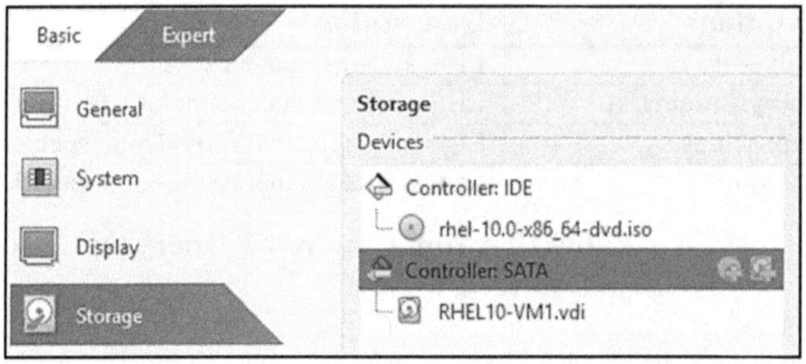

2. Open the */etc/fstab* file in the *vim* editor (or another editor of your choice) and add the following line entry at the end of the file to mount the DVD image (*/dev/sr0*) in read-only (ro) mode on the */mnt* directory.

```
/dev/sr0  /mnt  iso9660  ro  0 0
```

/dev/sr0 represents the first optical drive device, and iso9660 is the standard file system format for optical media.

3. Mount the file system as per the configuration defined in the */etc/fstab* file using the *mount* command with the -a (all) option:

```
[user1@server1 ~]$ sudo mount -a
[user1@server1 ~]$
```

The command should return without displaying anything in the output. This will confirm that the new entry was placed correctly in the file. See Chapter 16 “Local File Systems and Swap Space” for details on mount and mount point concepts.

4. Verify the mount using the *df* command:

```
[user1@server1 ~]$ df -h | grep mnt
/dev/sr0                 7.9G  7.9G     0 100% /mnt
```

The image and the packages therein can now be accessed via the */mnt* directory just like any other local directory on the system.

5. List the two directories—*/mnt/BaseOS/Packages* and */mnt/AppStream/Packages*—that contain all the software packages (directory names are case sensitive):

```
[user1@server1 ~]$ ls -l /mnt/BaseOS/Packages/ | more
total 1281948
-r--r--r--. 1 root root    88576 Dec  6  2024 accel-config-4.1.8-2.el10.x86_6
pm
-r--r--r--. 1 root root    56427 Dec  6  2024 accel-config-libs-4.1.8-2.el10.:
_64.rpm
-r--r--r--. 1 root root    83041 Oct 30  2024 acl-2.3.2-4.el10.x86_64.rpm
-r--r--r--. 1 root root   131693 Mar  3  2025 adcli-0.9.2-9.el10.x86_64.rpm
-r--r--r--. 1 root root    45867 Oct 31  2024 alternatives-1.30-2.el10.x86_64
m
-r--r--r--. 1 root root   396841 Mar 17  2025 amd-ucode-firmware-20250314-15.
0.noarch.rpm
........
```

```
[user1@server1 ~]$ ls -l /mnt/AppStream/Packages/ | more
total 5358698
-r--r--r--. 1 root root   2903275 Feb 19  2025 389-ds-base-3.0.6-3.el10_0.x86_
.rpm
-r--r--r--. 1 root root   1548659 Feb 19  2025 389-ds-base-libs-3.0.6-3.el10_(
86_64.rpm
-r--r--r--. 1 root root     42908 Feb 19  2025 389-ds-base-snmp-3.0.6-3.el10_(
86_64.rpm
-r--r--r--. 1 root root     38476 Oct 30  2024 a52dec-0.7.4-50.el10.x86_64.rpn
-r--r--r--. 1 root root    928671 Feb 10  2025 aardvark-dns-1.14.0-1.el10.x86_
.rpm
........
```

There are thousands of files in the two locations, each representing a single rpm package.

This concludes the exercise.

Querying Packages

You can query for packages in the package database or at the specified location. The following are some examples.

To query all installed packages:

```
[user1@server1 ~]$ rpm -qa
libgcc-14.2.1-7.el10.x86_64
fonts-filesystem-2.0.5-18.el10.noarch
google-noto-fonts-common-20240401-5.el10.noarch
google-noto-sans-vf-fonts-20240401-5.el10.noarch
........
```

To query whether the specified package is installed:

```
[user1@server1 ~]$ rpm -q perl
package perl is not installed
```

To list all files in a package:

```
[user1@server1 ~]$ rpm -ql iproute
/usr/lib/.build-id
/usr/lib/.build-id/19
/usr/lib/.build-id/19/177a9628559e5ec4c0f011da57cd6fe0f4ed1f
/usr/lib/.build-id/23
/usr/lib/.build-id/23/8815544680a92e66be24e219b3f4e05804ba96
/usr/lib/.build-id/34
........
```

To list only the documentation files in a package:

```
[user1@server1 ~]$ rpm -qd audit
/usr/share/doc/audit/ChangeLog
/usr/share/doc/audit/README
/usr/share/doc/audit/auditd.cron
........
```

To list only the configuration files in a package:

```
[user1@server1 ~]$ rpm -qc cups
/etc/cups/classes.conf
/etc/cups/client.conf
/etc/cups/cups-files.conf
/etc/cups/cupsd.conf
/etc/cups/lpoptions
........
```

To identify which package owns the specified file:

```
[user1@server1 ~]$ rpm -qf /etc/passwd
setup-2.14.5-4.el10.noarch
```

To display information about an installed package including version, release, installation status, installation date, size, signatures, description, and so on:

```
[user1@server1 ~]$ rpm -qi setup
Name        : setup
Version     : 2.14.5
Release     : 4.el10
Architecture: noarch
Install Date: Mon 27 Oct 2025 10:40:15 AM
Group       : System Environment/Base
Size        : 737724
License     : LicenseRef-Fedora-Public-Domain
Signature   : RSA/SHA256, Mon 11 Nov 2024 07:12:09 AM, Key ID 199e2f91fd431
Source RPM  : setup-2.14.5-4.el10.src.rpm
Build Date  : Tue 29 Oct 2024 04:51:47 PM
Build Host  : ppc-015.brew-001.prod.nsh.tph.redhat.com
Packager    : Red Hat, Inc. <http://bugzilla.redhat.com/bugzilla>
Vendor      : Red Hat, Inc.
URL         : https://pagure.io/setup/
Summary     : A set of system configuration and setup files
Description :
The setup package contains a set of important system configuration and
setup files, such as passwd, group, and profile.
```

To list all file and package dependencies for a given package:

```
[user1@server1 ~]$ rpm -qR chrony
/bin/sh
/bin/sh
/bin/sh
/bin/sh
/usr/bin/bash
/usr/bin/sh
config(chrony) = 4.6.1-1.el10
libc.so.6()(64bit)
........
```

To query an installable package for metadata information (version, release, architecture, description, size, signatures, etc.), use the -p option:

```
[user1@server1 ~]$ rpm -qip /mnt/BaseOS/Packages/zsh-5.9-15.el10.x86_64.rpm
warning: /mnt/BaseOS/Packages/zsh-5.9-15.el10.x86_64.rpm: Header V4 RSA/SHA
ignature, key ID fd431d51: NOKEY
Name         : zsh
Version      : 5.9
Release      : 15.el10
Architecture: x86_64
Install Date: (not installed)
Group        : Unspecified
Size         : 8307257
License      : MIT-Modern-Variant AND ISC AND GPL-2.0-only
Signature    : RSA/SHA256, Thu 21 Nov 2024 11:19:14 AM, Key ID 199e2f91fd431
Source RPM   : zsh-5.9-15.el10.src.rpm
Build Date   : Tue 29 Oct 2024 07:06:27 PM
........
```

To determine what packages require the specified package to operate properly:

```
[user1@server1 ~]$ rpm -q --whatrequires lvm2
libblockdev-lvm-3.2.0-3.el10_0.x86_64
udisks2-lvm2-2.10.90-5.el10.x86_64
```

The above output lists all the packages that will require the specified package "lvm2" to work fully and properly.

Installing a Package

Installing a package creates the necessary directory structure for the package, installs the required files, and runs any post-installation steps. The following command installs a package called *zsh* on the system:

```
[user1@server1 ~]$ sudo rpm -ivh /mnt/BaseOS/Packages/zsh-5.9-15.el10.x86_64.rpm
warning: /mnt/BaseOS/Packages/zsh-5.9-15.el10.x86_64.rpm: Header V4 RSA/SHA256 Si
y ID fd431d51: NOKEY
Verifying...                          ################################# [100%]
Preparing...                          ################################# [100%]
Updating / installing...
   1:zsh-5.9-15.el10                  ################################# [100%]
```

If required dependencies are missing, *rpm* displays an error and aborts the installation. For example, if *zsh* required a library package called *libzsh*, the command would fail with an error like "error: Failed dependencies: libzsh is needed by zsh". To resolve this, you would first need to locate and install the *libzsh* package using the *rpm* command, dealing with each dependency manually—a process that can become complex. This highlights the primary motivation for using higher-level tools like *dnf*.

Upgrading a Package

Upgrading a package upgrades an installed version of the package. In the absence of an existing version, the upgrade simply installs the package.

To upgrade a package called *yara*, use the -U option with the *rpm* command. This package is located in the *AppStream* directory.

```
[user1@server1 ~]$ sudo rpm -Uvh /mnt/AppStream/Packages/yara-4.5.2-2.el10.x86_64.rpm
warning: /mnt/AppStream/Packages/yara-4.5.2-2.el10.x86_64.rpm: Header V4 RSA/SHA256 Sign
e, key ID fd431d51: NOKEY
Verifying...                          ################################# [100%]
Preparing...                          ################################# [100%]
Updating / installing...
   1:yara-4.5.2-2.el10                ################################# [100%]
```

The command makes a backup of all the affected configuration files during the upgrade process (if there are any) and adds the extension *.rpmsave* to them. In the above example, the *yara* package was installed, as it was not already on the system.

Freshening a Package

Freshening a package upgrades only the older version of an installed package, unlike upgrading (-U) which installs if not present.

To freshen the *yara* package, use the -F option:

```
[user1@server1 ~]$ sudo rpm -Uvh /mnt/AppStream/Packages/yara-4.5.2-2.el10.x86_64.rpm
warning: /mnt/AppStream/Packages/yara-4.5.2-2.el10.x86_64.rpm: Header V4 RSA/SHA256 S
e, key ID fd431d51: NOKEY
Verifying...                          ################################# [100%]
Preparing...                          ################################# [100%]
        package yara-4.5.2-2.el10.x86_64 is already installed
```

The above command did nothing because the specified package version is already installed on the system.

Overwriting a Package

Overwriting a package replaces the existing files associated with the package of the same version.

To overwrite the package *zsh* that was installed earlier, use the --replacepkgs option:

```
[user1@server1 ~]$ sudo rpm -ivh --replacepkgs /mnt/BaseOS/Packages/zsh-5.9-15.el10.x86_64.
pm
warning: /mnt/BaseOS/Packages/zsh-5.9-15.el10.x86_64.rpm: Header V4 RSA/SHA256 Signature, k
y ID fd431d51: NOKEY
Verifying...                          ################################# [100%]
Preparing...                          ################################# [100%]
Updating / installing...
   1:zsh-5.9-15.el10                  ################################# [100%]
```

The installation progress indicates that the *zsh* package was replaced successfully. This action is particularly useful when you suspect corruption in one or more installed package files, and you want to start afresh.

Removing a Package

Removing a package uninstalls the package and all its associated files and the directory structure.

To remove the package *yara*, use the -e option and specify -v for verbosity:

```
[user1@server1 ~]$ sudo rpm yara -ve
Preparing packages...
yara-4.5.2-2.el10.x86_64
```

This command performs a dependency inspection to check whether there are any packages that require the existence of the package being weeded out and fails the removal if it detects a dependency.

Extracting Files from an Installable Package

Files in an installable package can be extracted using the *rpm2cpio* command for reasons such as examining the contents of the package, replacing a corrupted or lost command, or replacing a critical configuration file of an installed package to its original state.

Assuming you have lost the */etc/chrony.conf* configuration file, which is part of a package called *chrony*, and want to retrieve it from its installable package and put it back, you will first need to determine what package this file comes from:

```
[user1@server1 ~]$ rpm -qf /etc/chrony.conf
chrony-4.6.1-1.el10.x86_64
```

Now use the *rpm2cpio* command to extract (-i) all files from the *chrony* package (located under */mnt/BaseOS/Packages*) and create (-d) the necessary directory structure during the retrieval. Extract the files in a temporary location such as the */tmp* directory before you proceed with overwriting the destination under */etc*.

```
[user1@server1 tmp]$ sudo rpm2cpio /mnt/BaseOS/Packages/chrony-4.6.1-1.el10.x86_64.rpm | cpio -imd
1347 blocks
```

Run *find* to locate the *chrony.conf* file:

```
[user1@server1 tmp]$ sudo find . -name chrony.conf
./etc/chrony.conf
./usr/lib/sysusers.d/chrony.conf
```

The above output shows that the file is under */tmp/etc*. You can copy it to the */etc* directory now, and you are back in business.

Validating Package Integrity and Credibility

Before it is installed, a package may be checked for integrity (completeness and error-free state) and credibility (authenticity) after it has been copied to another location, downloaded from the web, or obtained elsewhere. RPM uses embedded checksums for integrity verification and GPG signatures for authenticity validation. This will ensure an uncorrupted and genuine piece of software.

The commercial version of GPG is referred to as PGP (Pretty Good Privacy).

To check the integrity of a package such as *chrony* located in */mnt/BaseOS/Packages*:

```
[user1@server1 ~]$ rpm -K /mnt/BaseOS/Packages/chrony-4.6.1-1.el10.x86_64.rpm --nosignature
/mnt/BaseOS/Packages/chrony-4.6.1-1.el10.x86_64.rpm: digests OK
```

The OK in the output confirms that the package is free of corruption.

Red Hat signs their products and updates with a GPG key and includes necessary public keys in the products for verification. For RHEL, the keys are in files on the installation media and are copied to the */etc/pki/rpm-gpg/* directory during the OS installation. Refer to Table 10-3 for a list of files in that directory and a short explanation.

GPG File	Description
RPM-GPG-KEY-redhat-release	Primary GPG key for all RHEL 10 packages and updates
RPM-GPG-KEY-redhat-beta	Beta/development packages (if applicable)

Table 10-3 Red Hat GPG Key Files

To check the credibility of a package, import the relevant GPG key and then verify the package. The table above shows that the GPG file for the recent packages is *RPM-GPG-KEY-redhat-release*. In the following example, run the *rpm* command to import the GPG key from this file and verify the signature for the *chrony* package using the -K option with the command:

```
[user1@server1 ~]$ sudo rpmkeys --import /etc/pki/rpm-gpg/RPM-GPG-KEY-redhat-release
[user1@server1 ~]$ sudo rpmkeys -K /mnt/BaseOS/Packages/chrony-4.6.1-1.el10.x86_64.rpm
/mnt/BaseOS/Packages/chrony-4.6.1-1.el10.x86_64.rpm: digests signatures OK
```

The OK validates the package signature and certifies the authenticity and integrity of the package.

Viewing GPG Keys

The GPG key imported in the previous subsection can be viewed with the *rpm* command. You can list the key and display its details as well. Run the command as follows to list the imported key:

```
[user1@server1 ~]$ rpm -q gpg-pubkey
gpg-pubkey-fd431d51-4ae0493b
gpg-pubkey-5a6340b3-6229229e
```

The output suggests that there are two GPG public keys currently imported on the system. View the details for the second one:

```
[user1@server1 ~]$ rpm -qi gpg-pubkey-5a6340b3-6229229e
Name        : gpg-pubkey
Version     : 5a6340b3
Release     : 6229229e
Architecture: (none)
Install Date: Sat 29 Nov 2025 05:36:05 AM
Group       : Public Keys
Size        : 0
License     : pubkey
Signature   : (none)
Source RPM  : (none)
Build Date  : Wed 09 Mar 2022 04:56:46 PM
Build Host  : localhost
Packager    : Red Hat, Inc. (auxiliary key 3) <security@redhat.com>
Summary     : Red Hat, Inc. (auxiliary key 3) <security@redhat.com>
Description :
-----BEGIN PGP PUBLIC KEY BLOCK-----

mQINBGIpIp4BEAC/o5e1WzLIsS6/JOQCs4XYATYTcf6B6ALzcP05G0W3uRpUQSrL
........
```

The output returns both the metadata and the key data for the specified GPG public key.

Verifying Package Attributes

Verifying the integrity of an installed package compares the attributes of files in the package with the original file attributes saved and stored in the package database at the time of package installation. The verification process uses the *rpm* command with the -V option to compare the owner, group, permission mode, size, modification time, digest, and type among other attributes. The command returns to the prompt without exhibiting anything if it detects no changes in the attributes. You can use the -v or -vv option with the command for increased verbosity.

Run this check on the *at* package:

```
[user1@server1 ~]$ sudo rpm -V at
```

The command returned nothing, which implies that the file attributes are intact. Now change the permissions on one of the files, */etc/sysconfig/atd*, in this package to 770 from the current value of 644, and then re-execute the verification test:

```
[user1@server1 ~]$ ls -l /etc/sysconfig/atd
-rw-r--r--. 1 root root 403 Nov  5  2024 /etc/sysconfig/atd
[user1@server1 ~]$ sudo chmod -v 770 /etc/sysconfig/atd
mode of '/etc/sysconfig/atd' changed from 0644 (rw-r--r--) to 0770 (rwxrwx---)
[user1@server1 ~]$ sudo rpm -V at
.M.......  c /etc/sysconfig/atd
```

The output is indicative of a change in the permission mode on the *atd* file in the *at* package. You may alternatively run the verification check directly on the file by adding the -f option to the command and passing the filename as an argument:

```
[user1@server1 ~]$ sudo rpm -Vf /etc/sysconfig/atd
.M.......  c /etc/sysconfig/atd
```

The output returns three columns: column 1 contains nine fields, column 2 shows the file type, and column 3 expresses the full path of the file. The command performs nine checks, as illustrated by the codes in column 1, and displays any changes that have occurred since the package that contains the file was installed. Each of these codes has a meaning. Table 10-4 describes the codes as they appear from left to right. A period (.) appears for an attribute that is not in an altered state.

Code	Description
S	Appears if the file size is different
M	Appears if the (mode) permission or file type is altered
5	Appears if MD5 checksum does not match
D	Appears if the file is a device file and its major or minor number has changed
L	Appears if the file is a symlink and its path has altered
U	Appears if the owning user is changed
G	Appears if the group membership is changed
T	Appears if timestamp has changed
P	Appears if capabilities have altered
.	Appears if no modification is detected

Table 10-4 Package Verification Codes

Column 2 in the output above exposes a code that represents the type of file. Table 10-5 lists them.

File Type	Description
c	Configuration file
d	Documentation file
g	Ghost file
l	License file
r	Readme file

Table 10-5 File Type Codes

Based on the information in the tables, the */etc/sysconfig/atd* is a configuration file with a modified permission mode. Reset the attribute to its previous value and rerun the check to ensure the file is back to its original state.

```
[user1@server1 ~]$ sudo chmod -v 644 /etc/sysconfig/atd
mode of '/etc/sysconfig/atd' changed from 0770 (rwxrwx---) to 0644 (rw-r--r--)
[user1@server1 ~]$ sudo rpm -V at
```

The command produced no output, which confirms the integrity of the file as well as the package.

Exercise 10-2: Perform Package Management Using rpm

Perform this exercise on *server1* as *user1* with *sudo* where required. In this exercise, you will:

- Verify the integrity and authenticity of a package called *rmt* located in the */mnt/BaseOS/Packages* directory on the installation image
- Install this package
- Display basic information about the package
- Show files it contains
- List only documentation files
- Verify package attributes
- Erase the package

1. Run *find* on */mnt/BaseOS/Packages* to confirm that the *rmt* package is available:

```
[user1@server1 ~]$ sudo find /mnt -name rmt*
/mnt/BaseOS/Packages/rmt-1.6-18.el10_0.x86_64.rpm
```

2. Verify the integrity and credibility of the package:

```
[user1@server1 ~]$ rpmkeys -K /mnt/BaseOS/Packages/rmt-1.6-18.el10_0.x86_64.rpm
/mnt/BaseOS/Packages/rmt-1.6-18.el10_0.x86_64.rpm: digests signatures OK
```

3. Install the package:

```
[user1@server1 ~]$ sudo rpm -ivh /mnt/BaseOS/Packages/rmt-1.6-18.el10_0.x86_64.rpm
Verifying...                          ################################# [100%]
Preparing...                          ################################# [100%]
Updating / installing...
   1:rmt-2:1.6-18.el10_0              ################################# [100%]
```

4. Show basic information about the package:

```
[user1@server1 ~]$ rpm -qi rmt
Name         : rmt
Epoch        : 2
Version      : 1.6
Release      : 18.el10_0
Architecture: x86_64
Install Date: Sat 29 Nov 2025 05:46:06 AM
Group        : Unspecified
Size         : 92562
License      : CDDL-1.0 AND GPL-2.0-only
Signature    : RSA/SHA256, Tue 01 Apr 2025 02:47:43 AM, Key ID 199e2f!
Source RPM   : star-1.6-18.el10_0.src.rpm
Build Date   : Mon 31 Mar 2025 06:24:34 AM
Build Host   : konflux.redhat.com
........
```

5. Show all the files the package contains:

```
[user1@server1 ~]$ rpm -ql rmt
/etc/default/rmt
/etc/rmt
/usr/lib/.build-id
........
```

6. List only the documentation files the package has:

```
[user1@server1 ~]$ rpm -qd rmt
/usr/share/doc/star/CDDL.Schily.txt
/usr/share/doc/star/COPYING
/usr/share/man/man1/rmt.1.gz
```

7. Verify the attributes of each file in the package. Use verbose mode.

```
[user1@server1 ~]$ rpm -Vv rmt
.........  c /etc/default/rmt
.........    /etc/rmt
.........  a /usr/lib/.build-id
.........  a /usr/lib/.build-id/8b
.........  a /usr/lib/.build-id/8b/5cc773e70f70e8b5aac
.........    /usr/sbin/rmt
.........    /usr/share/doc/star
.........  d /usr/share/doc/star/CDDL.Schily.txt
.........  d /usr/share/doc/star/COPYING
.........  d /usr/share/man/man1/rmt.1.gz
```

8. Remove the package:

```
[user1@server1 ~]$ sudo rpm -ve rmt
Preparing packages...
rmt-2:1.6-18.el10_0.x86_64
```

This concludes the exercise.

Chapter Summary

This chapter introduced the foundational principles of software management in RHEL, establishing the core concepts necessary for advanced package administration. We began by defining essential elements such as software packages, the packaging process, standard naming conventions, and dependency relationships. The role of the RPM package manager and its patch database was also explained.

The core of the chapter focused on the versatile rpm command-line utility. We explored a wide range of its options and put them into practice, demonstrating how to install, upgrade, verify, and remove software packages. Furthermore, we utilized the tool to query detailed metadata, validate package integrity and authenticity using GPG keys, and inspect various package attributes.

Review Questions

1. What would the *rpm -ql zsh* command do?
2. What is the difference between installing and upgrading a package?
3. Package database is located in the */var/lib/rpm* directory. True or False?
4. What would the *rpm -qf /bin/bash* command do?
5. Name the directory where RHEL 10 stores GPG signatures.
6. What would the options ivh cause the *rpm* command to do?
7. State the purpose of the *rpm2cpio* command.
8. What is the difference between freshening and upgrading a package?
9. The *rpm* command automatically takes care of package dependencies. True or False?
10. What would the *rpm -qa* command do?

Answers to Review Questions

1. The command provided will list all the files that are included in the installed *zsh* package.
2. Installing adds a new package to the system. Upgrading replaces an existing package with a newer version, or installs it if not present.
3. True.
4. The command will identify which package owns the */bin/bash* file.
5. RHEL 10 stores GPG signatures in the */etc/pki/rpm-gpg* directory.
6. The *rpm* command will install the specified package (-i) and show installation details (-v) and hash signs for progress (-h).
7. The *rpm2cpio* command is used to extract files from the specified package.
8. Upgrading (-U) installs or upgrades a package. Freshening (-F) only upgrades packages that are already installed; it does not install new packages.
9. False.
10. The command provided will list all installed packages.

Do-It-Yourself Challenge Labs

The following labs are designed to reinforce most of the concepts and skills covered in this chapter. You are expected to complete these labs without external assistance. A step-by-step guide is not provided, as the required knowledge has already been presented in the chapter; however, each lab includes hints pointing to the relevant major topic(s).

Use the lab environment created specifically for the end-of-chapter labs. See the sub-section "Lab Environment for End-of-Chapter Labs" in Chapter 01 "Local Installation" for details.

Lab 10-1: Install and Verify Packages

As *user1* with *sudo* on *server3*, make sure the RHEL 10 ISO image is attached to the VM and mounted. Use the *rpm* command and install the *zsh* package by specifying its full path. Run the *rpm* command again and perform the following on the *zsh* package: (1) show information, (2) verify package integrity and authenticity, and (3) display attributes. (Hint: Package Management with rpm).

Lab 10-2: Query and Erase Packages

As *user1* with *sudo* on *server3*, make sure the RHEL 10 ISO image is attached to the VM and mounted. Use the *rpm* command to perform the following: (1) check whether the *setup* package is installed, (2) list configuration files in the *setup* package, (3) show information for the *zlib-devel* package file on the ISO image (use -p option), (4) reinstall the *zsh* package (--reinstall -vh), and (5) remove the *zsh* package. (Hint: Package Management with rpm).

Lab 10-3: Manage Package Dependencies

As *user1* with *sudo* on *server3*, use the *rpm* command to determine what package provides the */bin/ls* command. List all files in the *coreutils* package. Check what packages require the *zlib* package to function. Extract the */etc/passwd* file from the *setup* package to the */tmp* directory using *rpm2cpio*. Verify the integrity of all files in the *setup* package and document any changes found. (Hint: Package Management with rpm).

Chapter 11

Advanced Package and Repository Management

By the end of this chapter, you will be able to:

- Describe Package Groups
- Configure and Access Software Repositories
- Perform Software Management Operations using dnf
- List, Install, Update, and Remove Individual Packages and Package Groups
- Display Detailed Package Information and Search Metadata
- Examine the Contents and Details of Available Package Groups

RHCSA Objectives:

12. Configure access to RPM repositories
13. Install and remove RPM software packages
45. Install and update software packages from Red Hat Network, a remote repository, or from the local file system (part of this objective is covered in Chapter 10)

This is the second of the three chapters that discuss software administration in RHEL. While the first chapter (Chapter 10) explained the basic concepts of rpm package management and demonstrated a basic command to manipulate individual packages, this chapter elaborates on the concepts and handling of package groups. You will also learn about software repositories and how to configure them.

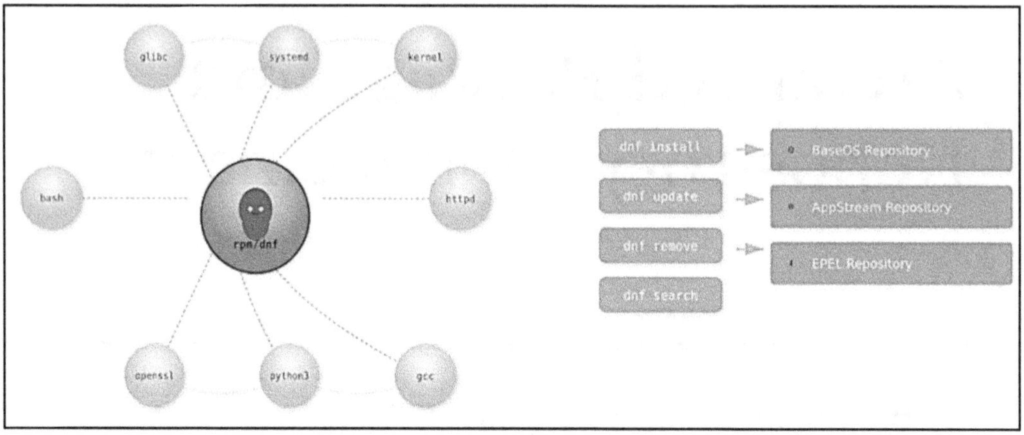

The dnf command is superior to the rpm tool in the sense that it performs automatic dependency checks and marks any extra packages for installation. You will use numerous options and subcommands available with this advanced tool to interact with software repositories.

Advanced Package Management Concepts

The previous chapter covered basic package management concepts using the *rpm* utility for individual package operations. The focus of this chapter is on understanding advanced software packaging and distribution techniques, and using DNF, a tool that efficiently manages individual packages and package groups.

RHEL 10 is shipped with two core repositories called *BaseOS* and *Application Stream* (AppStream).

Package Groups

A *package group* is a collection of related packages that serve a common purpose. It provides the convenience of querying, installing, and deleting as a single unit rather than dealing with packages individually. There are two types of package groups: *environment groups* and *package groups*. The environment groups available in RHEL 10 are *server*, *server with GUI*, *minimal install*, *workstation*, *virtualization host*, and *custom operating system*. These are listed on the software selection window during RHEL 10 installation. The package groups include container management, smart card support, security tools, system tools, network servers, etc.

BaseOS Repository

The BaseOS repository includes the core set of RHEL 10 components including the kernel, modules, bootloader, and other foundational software packages. These components lay the foundation to install and run software applications and programs. BaseOS repository contains core operating system components delivered in traditional rpm format.

AppStream Repository

The AppStream repository contains applications, development tools, and runtime languages, available in both traditional rpm format and as modular content. These add-ons include web server software, development languages, database software, etc. and are shipped to support a variety of use cases and deployments.

Benefits of Segregation

Separating BaseOS from AppStream provides two key benefits: (1) it separates the application components from the core operating system elements, and (2) it allows publishers to deliver and administrators to apply application updates more frequently. In RHEL version 7 and older, an OS update would update all installed components including the kernel, service, and application components to the latest versions by default. This could cause system instability or application issues due to incompatible package versions. By detaching the base OS components from the applications, either of the two can be updated independent of the other. This provides enhanced flexibility in tailoring the system components and application workloads without impacting the underlying stability of the system.

dnf Repository

A *dnf repository* (*yum repository* or simply a *repo*) is a digital library for storing software packages and metadata. You access repositories for package retrieval, query, update, and installation, and they may be free or for a fee. BaseOS and AppStream repositories are included on the RHEL ISO image. Red Hat maintains additional repositories accessible via subscription management. Furthermore, you can build private custom repositories for internal IT use for stocking and delivering software. This may prove to be a good practice for organizations with a large Linux server base, as it manages dependencies automatically and aids in maintaining software consistency across the board. These repositories can also be used to store in-house developed packages.

It is important to obtain software packages from authentic and reliable sources such as Red Hat to prevent potential damage to your system and to circumvent possible software corruption.

There is a process to create repositories and to access preconfigured repositories. While creating custom repositories is an advanced topic, you will now configure access to the pre-existing BaseOS and AppStream repositories via a definition file to support the exercises and lab environment.

A sample repo definition file is shown below with some key directives:

```
[BaseOS_RHEL_10]
name= RHEL 10 base operating system
baseurl=file:///mnt/BaseOS
enabled=1
gpgcheck=0
```

> **EXAM TIP:** Knowing how to configure a dnf repository using a URL plays an important role in completing some of the RHCSA exam tasks successfully. Use two forward slash characters (//) with the baseurl directive for an FTP, HTTP, or HTTPS source.

The above example shows five lines from a sample repo file. Line 1 defines an exclusive ID within the square brackets. Line 2 is a brief description of the repo with the "name" directive. Line 3 specifies the repository location with the "baseurl" directive. Line 4 shows whether this repository is active. Line 5 shows if packages are to be GPG-checked for authenticity.

Each repository definition file must have a unique ID, a description, and a baseurl directive defined at a minimum; other directives are set as required. The baseurl directive specifies the repository's location. For local directories, use *file:///local_path* (note: file:// indicates the URL scheme, followed by the absolute path starting from root). For example, *file:///mnt/BaseOS* points to the */mnt/BaseOS* directory on your local system. For FTP and HTTP(S), the URLs will be *ftp://hostname/network_path* and *http(s)://hostname/network_path*, respectively. The network path must include a resolvable hostname or an IP address.

Software Management with dnf

Software for enterprise Linux distributions such as Red Hat and CentOS is available in the rpm format. These distributions offer tools to work with individual packages as well as package groups. The *rpm* command was used in the previous chapter to query, list, install, and erase packages, in addition to a few other tasks that it can perform. This command is limited to managing one package at a time.

dnf is the primary package manager for handling individual packages and package groups. This tool has an associated configuration file that can define settings to control its behavior.

dnf Configuration File

The key configuration file for *dnf* is *dnf.conf* that resides in the */etc/dnf* directory. The "main" section in the file sets directives that have a global effect on dnf operations. You can define separate sections for each custom repository that you plan to set up on the system. Repository definitions are stored as individual *.repo* files in the */etc/yum.repos.d* directory, which is the default location created for this purpose. The default content of the *dnf* configuration file is listed below:

```
[user1@server1 ~]$ cat /etc/dnf/dnf.conf
[main]
gpgcheck=1
installonly_limit=3
clean_requirements_on_remove=True
best=True
skip_if_unavailable=False
```

Table 11-1 explains the above and a few other directives that you may define in the file. The directives in Table 11-1 are listed in an alphabetical order.

Directive	Description
best	Specifies whether to install the latest available version
clean_requirements_on_remove	Defines whether to remove dependencies during a package removal process that are no longer in use
debuglevel	Sets the level between 1 (minimum) and 10 (maximum) at which the debug is to be recorded in the logfile. Default is 2. A value of 0 disables this feature.

Directive	Description
gpgcheck	Indicates whether to check the GPG signature for package authenticity. Default is 1 (enabled).
installonly_limit	Specifies a count of packages that can be installed concurrently. Default is 3.
keepcache	Defines whether to store the package and header cache following a successful installation. Default is 0 (disabled).
logdir	Sets the directory location to store the log files. Default is */var/log*.
obsoletes	Checks and removes any obsolete dependent packages during installs and updates. Default is 1 (enabled).
skip_if_unavailable	DNF will continue to run and disable any repositories that could not be synchronized.

Table 11-1 Directive Settings in dnf.conf File

There are a multitude of additional directives available that you may want to set in the main section of this file or in custom repository definition files. Run **man 5 dnf.conf** for details.

The dnf Command

The *dnf* command is the advanced package management tool in RHEL. This utility requires the system to have access to a local or remote software repository or to a local installable package file. The *Red Hat Subscription Management* (RHSM) service available in the Red Hat Customer Portal offers access to official Red Hat software repositories. There are other web-based repositories that host packages that you may want to install and use. Alternatively, you can set up a local, custom repository on your RHEL system and add packages of your choice to it.

The primary benefit of using *dnf* over *rpm* is the former's ability to resolve dependencies automatically by identifying and installing any packages required for a successful installation of the specified software. With multiple repositories in place, *dnf* extracts the software from wherever it finds it.

dnf invokes the *rpm* utility in the background and can perform numerous operations on individual packages or package groups such as listing, querying, installing, and removing them.

Table 11-2 summarizes the software handling tasks that *dnf* can perform on packages. It also lists two subcommands (clean and repolist) that are for repository operations. The subcommands are sequenced alphabetically. Refer to the *dnf* command manual pages for additional subcommands, operators, options, and examples.

Subcommand	Description
check-update	Checks if updates are available for installed packages
clean	Removes cached data
history	Displays previous dnf activities as recorded in the /var/lib/dnf/history directory
info	Shows details for a package
install	Installs or updates a package
list	Lists installed and available packages
provides	Searches for packages that contain the specified file or feature
reinstall	Reinstalls the exact version of an installed package

Subcommand	Description
remove	Removes a package and its dependencies
repolist	Lists enabled repositories
repoquery	Runs queries on available packages
search	Searches package metadata for the specified string
upgrade	Updates all installed packages to latest available versions

Table 11-2 dnf Subcommands for Package and Repository Manipulation

Table 11-3 lists and describes *dnf* subcommands that are intended for operations on package groups.

Subcommand	Description
group install	Installs or updates a package group
group info	Returns details for a package group
group list	Lists available package groups
group remove	Removes a package group

Table 11-3 dnf Subcommands for Package Group Manipulation

You will use most of the subcommands from the two Tables in the examples and exercises that follow, but first you will need to create a definition file and configure access to the two repositories available on the RHEL 10 ISO image.

Exercise 11-1: Configure Access to dnf Repositories

Perform this exercise on *server1* as *user1* with *sudo* where required. In this exercise, you will:

- Set up access to the two dnf repositories that are available on RHEL 10 image. You have already configured an automatic mounting of RHEL 10 image on */mnt* in Chapter 10 "Basic Package Management".
- Create a definition file for the repositories and confirm

1. Verify that the image is currently mounted:

```
[user1@server1 ~]$ df -h | grep mnt
/dev/sr0                7.9G  7.9G     0 100% /mnt
```

2. Create a file called *local.repo* in the */etc/yum.repos.d* directory using the *vim* editor and add the following definitions for both repositories:

```
[BaseOS]
name=Base OS software
baseurl=file:///mnt/BaseOS
enabled=1
gpgcheck=0

[AppStream]
name=Application software
baseurl=file:///mnt/AppStream
enabled=1
gpgcheck=0
```

3. Confirm access to the repositories:

```
[user1@server1 ~]$ sudo dnf repolist -v
DNF version: 4.20.0
cachedir: /var/cache/dnf
Last metadata expiration check: 0:26:19 ago on Sat 29 Nov 2025 12:26:34 PM.
Repo-id            : AppStream
Repo-name          : AppStream
Repo-revision      : 1744312217
Repo-updated       : Thu 10 Apr 2025 03:10:17 PM
Repo-pkgs          : 4,425
Repo-available-pkgs: 4,425
Repo-size          : 5.1 G
Repo-baseurl       : file:///mnt/AppStream
Repo-expire        : 172,800 second(s) (last: Sat 29 Nov 2025 12:26:34 PM)
Repo-filename      : /etc/yum.repos.d/local.repo

Repo-id            : BaseOS
Repo-name          : BaseOS
Repo-revision      : 1744312234
Repo-updated       : Thu 10 Apr 2025 03:10:34 PM
Repo-pkgs          : 945
Repo-available-pkgs: 945
Repo-size          : 1.2 G
Repo-baseurl       : file:///mnt/BaseOS
Repo-expire        : 172,800 second(s) (last: Sat 29 Nov 2025 12:26:34 PM)
Repo-filename      : /etc/yum.repos.d/local.repo
Total packages: 5,370
```

Ignore any lines that are related to subscription and system registration (not shown in the above output). The output provides details for the two repositories. It shows general cache information (line 2) followed by separate metadata sections for each repository. The output also shows the repository ID, name, revision, last update timestamp, package count, total size of all packages, mount location, and the filename holding the repo information. As depicted, the AppStream repo consists of 4,425 packages and the BaseOS repo contains 945 packages. Both repos are enabled and are ready for use.

We have divided software administration operations into two sections below to focus on individual packages and package groups.

Individual Package Management

The *dnf* command can be used to perform a variety of operations on individual packages, just like the *rpm* command. The following subsections elaborate with examples on using this tool to list, install, query, and remove packages.

Listing Available and Installed Packages

Listing the packages that are available for installation from one or more enabled repositories helps you understand what is in the current software inventory and what is needed. Likewise, listing the packages that are already installed on the system enables you to make important decisions as to whether they should be retained, upgraded, downgraded, or erased. The *dnf* command lists available packages as well as installed packages.

To list all packages available for installation from all enabled repos, run a query against the two repositories that we configured earlier, as those are the only ones you currently have access to. The following command will result in a long output.

```
[user1@server1 ~]$ sudo dnf repoquery
Last metadata expiration check: 0:28:43 ago on Sat 29 Nov 2025 12:26:34 PM
389-ds-base-0:3.0.6-3.el10_0.x86_64
389-ds-base-libs-0:3.0.6-3.el10_0.x86_64
389-ds-base-snmp-0:3.0.6-3.el10_0.x86_64
CUnit-0:2.1.3-34.el10.x86_64
HdrHistogram_c-0:0.11.8-7.el10.x86_64
Judy-0:1.0.5-38.el10.x86_64
ModemManager-0:1.22.0-7.el10.x86_64
ModemManager-glib-0:1.22.0-7.el10.x86_64
NetworkManager-1:1.52.0-1.el10_0.x86_64
........
```

To limit the above to the list of packages that are available only from a specific repo:

```
[user1@server1 ~]$ sudo dnf repoquery --repo "BaseOS"
Last metadata expiration check: 0:31:10 ago on Sat 29 Nov 2025 12:26:34 PM.
ModemManager-0:1.22.0-7.el10.x86_64
ModemManager-glib-0:1.22.0-7.el10.x86_64
NetworkManager-1:1.52.0-1.el10_0.x86_64
NetworkManager-adsl-1:1.52.0-1.el10_0.x86_64
NetworkManager-bluetooth-1:1.52.0-1.el10_0.x86_64
NetworkManager-config-server-1:1.52.0-1.el10_0.noarch
NetworkManager-libnm-1:1.52.0-1.el10_0.x86_64
........
```

You can *grep* for an expression to narrow down your search. For example, to find whether the BaseOS repo includes the *zsh* package, run the following:

```
[user1@server1 ~]$ sudo dnf repoquery --repo BaseOS | grep zsh
Last metadata expiration check: 0:33:58 ago on Sat 29 Nov 2025 12:26:34 PM.
zsh-0:5.9-15.el10.x86_64
```

To list all installed packages on the system:

```
[user1@server1 ~]$ sudo dnf list installed
Installed Packages
ModemManager.x86_64                          1.22.0-7.el10             @anaconda
ModemManager-glib.x86_64                     1.22.0-7.el10             @anaconda
NetworkManager.x86_64                        1:1.52.0-1.el10_0         @anaconda
NetworkManager-adsl.x86_64                   1:1.52.0-1.el10_0         @anaconda
NetworkManager-bluetooth.x86_64              1:1.52.0-1.el10_0         @anaconda
NetworkManager-config-server.noarch          1:1.52.0-1.el10_0         @anaconda
NetworkManager-libnm.x86_64                  1:1.52.0-1.el10_0         @anaconda
NetworkManager-tui.x86_64                    1:1.52.0-1.el10_0         @anaconda
NetworkManager-wifi.x86_64                   1:1.52.0-1.el10_0         @anaconda
NetworkManager-wwan.x86_64                   1:1.52.0-1.el10_0         @anaconda
PackageKit.x86_64                            1.2.8-8.el10              @AppStream
PackageKit-command-not-found.x86_64          1.2.8-8.el10              @AppStream
........
```

The graphic above shows the output in three columns: package name, package version, and the repo it was installed from. @anaconda means the package was installed at the time of RHEL installation.

To list all installed packages and all packages available for installation from all enabled repositories:

```
[user1@server1 ~]$ sudo dnf list
Installed Packages
ModemManager.x86_64                          1.22.0-7.el10          @anaconda
ModemManager-glib.x86_64                     1.22.0-7.el10          @anaconda
NetworkManager.x86_64                        1:1.52.0-1.el10_0      @anaconda
NetworkManager-adsl.x86_64                   1:1.52.0-1.el10_0      @anaconda
NetworkManager-bluetooth.x86_64              1:1.52.0-1.el10_0      @anaconda
........
Available Packages
389-ds-base.x86_64                           3.0.6-3.el10_0         AppStream
389-ds-base-libs.x86_64                      3.0.6-3.el10_0         AppStream
389-ds-base-snmp.x86_64                      3.0.6-3.el10_0         AppStream
CUnit.x86_64                                 2.1.3-34.el10          AppStream
........
```

The @ sign that precedes a repository name in column 3 identifies the package as installed.

To list available updates for installed packages from all enabled repositories:

```
[user1@server1 ~]$ sudo dnf list updates
```

To list whether a package (*bc*, for instance) is installed or available for installation from any enabled repository:

```
[user1@server1 ~]$ sudo dnf list bc
```

To list all installed packages whose names begin with the string "gnome" followed by any number of characters:

```
[user1@server1 ~]$ sudo dnf list installed gnome*
```

To list recently added packages:

```
[user1@server1 ~]$ sudo dnf list recent
```

Refer to the *repoquery* and *list* subsections of the *dnf* command manual pages for more options and examples.

Installing and Updating Packages

Installing a package creates the necessary directory tree for the specified and dependent packages, installs the required files, and run

s any post-installation steps. If a package is already installed, *dnf* upgrades it to the latest available version from enabled repositories. By default, *dnf* prompts for a yes or no confirmation unless the -y flag is entered with the command.

The following attempts to install a package called *ant*, but proceeds with an update if it detects the presence of an older version:

```
[user1@server1 ~]$ sudo dnf install ant

Dependencies resolved.
================================================================================
 Package                  Arch       Version              Repository      Size
================================================================================
Installing:
 ant                      noarch     1.10.15-1.el10       AppStream      176 k
Installing dependencies:
 ant-lib                  noarch     1.10.15-1.el10       AppStream      2.1 M
 ant-unbound              noarch     1.10.15-1.el10       AppStream       10 k
 javapackages-filesystem  noarch     6.4.0-1.el10         AppStream       19 k
 javapackages-tools       noarch     6.4.0-1.el10         AppStream       40 k

Transaction Summary
================================================================================
Install  5 Packages

Total size: 2.3 M
Installed size: 2.8 M
Is this ok [y/N]: y
........
Installed:
  ant-1.10.15-1.el10.noarch
  ant-lib-1.10.15-1.el10.noarch
  ant-unbound-1.10.15-1.el10.noarch
  javapackages-filesystem-6.4.0-1.el10.noarch
  javapackages-tools-6.4.0-1.el10.noarch

Complete!
```

The above *dnf* command example resolved dependencies and showed a list of the packages that it would install. It exhibited the size of the packages and the amount of disk space that the installation would consume. It downloaded the packages after confirmation to proceed and installed them. It completed the installation after every package was verified. A list of the installed packages was displayed at the bottom of the output.

To install or update a package called *dcraw* located locally at */mnt/AppStream/Packages*:

```
[user1@server1 ~]$ sudo dnf localinstall /mnt/AppStream/Packages/dcraw-9.28.0-25
.el10.x86 64.rpm
```

To update a specific installed package (*autofs*, for example). If the package is not installed, *dnf* will report it as not found.

```
[user1@server1 ~]$ sudo dnf update autofs
Package autofs available, but not installed.
No match for argument: autofs
Error: No packages marked for upgrade.
```

To update all installed packages to the latest available versions:

```
[user1@server1 ~]$ sudo dnf -y update
```

Refer to the *install* and *update* subsections of the *dnf* command manual pages for more options and examples.

Displaying Package Information

Displaying information for a package shows its name, architecture it is built for, version, release, size, whether it is installed or available for installation, repo name it was installed or is available from, short and long descriptions, license, and so on. Use the *info* subcommand to display detailed package metadata.

To view information about a package called *autofs*:

```
[user1@server1 ~]$ dnf info autofs
BaseOS                                                  30 MB/s | 1.5 MB     00:00
AppStream                                               24 MB/s | 1.5 MB     00:00
Available Packages
Name         : autofs
Epoch        : 1
Version      : 5.1.9
Release      : 11.el10
Architecture : x86_64
Size         : 395 k
Source       : autofs-5.1.9-11.el10.src.rpm
Repository   : BaseOS
Summary      : A tool for automatically mounting and unmounting filesystems
```

The output shows that *autofs* is not currently installed, but it is available for installation from the BaseOS repo. The *info* subcommand automatically determines whether the specified package is installed.

Refer to the *info* subsection of the *dnf* command's manual pages for more options available for viewing package information.

Removing Packages

Removing a package uninstalls it and removes all associated files and directory structure. It also erases any dependencies as part of the deletion process. By default, *dnf* prompts for a yes or no confirmation unless the -y flag is specified at the command line.

To remove a package called *ant*:

```
[user1@server1 ~]$ sudo dnf remove ant
........
Removing:
 ant                         noarch     1.10.15-1.el10      @AppStream     478 k
Removing unused dependencies:
 ant-lib                     noarch     1.10.15-1.el10      @AppStream     2.3 M
 ant-unbound                 noarch     1.10.15-1.el10      @AppStream      26
 javapackages-filesystem     noarch     6.4.0-1.el10        @AppStream     2.0 k
 javapackages-tools          noarch     6.4.0-1.el10        @AppStream      72 k

Transaction Summary
================================================================================
Remove  5 Packages

Freed space: 2.8 M
Is this ok [y/N]: y
........
```

```
Removed:
  ant-1.10.15-1.el10.noarch
  ant-lib-1.10.15-1.el10.noarch
  ant-unbound-1.10.15-1.el10.noarch
  javapackages-filesystem-6.4.0-1.el10.noarch
  javapackages-tools-6.4.0-1.el10.noarch

Complete!
```

The above output resolved dependencies and showed a list of the packages that it would remove. It displayed the amount of disk space that their removal would free up. After confirmation, it erased the identified packages and verified their removal. A list of the removed packages was exhibited at the bottom of the output.

Refer to the *remove* subsection of the *dnf* command's manual pages for more options and examples available for removing packages.

Exercise 11-2: Manipulate Individual Packages

Perform this exercise on *server1* as *user1* with *sudo* where required. In this exercise, you will:

- Determine if the *cifs-utils* package is already installed and if it is available for installation
- Display its information before installing it
- Install the package and exhibit its information
- Erase the package along with its dependencies
- Confirm the removal

1. Check whether the *cifs-utils* package is already installed:

```
[user1@server1 ~]$ dnf list installed |grep cifs-utils
[user1@server1 ~]$
```

The command returned to the prompt without any output, which implies that the specified package is not installed.

2. Determine if the *cifs-utils* package is available for installation:

```
[user1@server1 ~]$ dnf repoquery cifs-utils
cifs-utils-0:7.1-2.el10.x86_64
```

The package is available for installation. The output shows its version as well.

3. Display detailed information about the package:

```
[user1@server1 ~]$ dnf info cifs-utils
Available Packages
Name         : cifs-utils
Version      : 7.1
Release      : 2.el10
Architecture : x86_64
Size         : 121 k
Source       : cifs-utils-7.1-2.el10.src.rpm
Repository   : BaseOS
Summary      : Utilities for mounting and managing CIFS mounts
```

The output indicates that the package is available for installation from the BaseOS repo.

4. Install the package:

```
[user1@server1 ~]$ sudo dnf install -y cifs-utils
```

5. Display the package information again:

```
[user1@server1 ~]$ dnf info cifs-utils
Installed Packages
Name         : cifs-utils
Version      : 7.1
Release      : 2.el10
Architecture : x86_64
Size         : 268 k
Source       : cifs-utils-7.1-2.el10.src.rpm
Repository   : @System
From repo    : BaseOS
```

The output reveals that the package is now installed.

6. Remove the package:

```
[user1@server1 ~]$ sudo dnf remove -y cifs-utils
```

7. Confirm the removal:

```
[user1@server1 ~]$ dnf list installed | grep cifs-utils
[user1@server1 ~]$
```

The absence of output confirms the package is not installed.

Determining Provider and Searching Package Metadata

Determining package contents involves operations on both installed and available packages. For instance, you can determine which package a specific file belongs to or which package contains a certain string. The following examples demonstrate how to carry out these tasks.

To search for packages that contain a specific file such as */etc/passwd*, use the *provides* or the *whatprovides* subcommand with *dnf*:

```
[user1@server1 ~]$ dnf provides /etc/passwd
setup-2.14.5-4.el10.noarch : A set of system configuration and setup files
Repo         : @System
Matched from:
Filename     : /etc/passwd

setup-2.14.5-4.el10.noarch : A set of system configuration and setup files
Repo         : BaseOS
Matched from:
Filename     : /etc/passwd
```

The output shows the file is provided by the *setup* package, with both installed and available versions listed.

With the *provides* (*whatprovides*) subcommand, you can also use a wildcard character for filename expansion. For example, the following command will list all packages that contain filenames beginning with "system-config" followed by any number of characters:

```
[user1@server1 ~]$ dnf whatprovides /usr/bin/system-config*
```

To search for all the packages that match the specified string in their name or summary:

```
[user1@server1 ~]$ dnf search system-config
================================ Name Matched: system-config ==========
system-config-printer-libs.noarch : Libraries and shared code for prir
                                  : tool
system-config-printer-udev.x86_64 : Rules for udev for automatic confi
                                  : printers
============================== Summary Matched: system-config =========
cups-pk-helper.x86_64 : A helper that makes system-config-printer use
```

The above outcome depicts three matches, two in package names and one in summary.

Package Group Management

The *dnf* command can be used to perform ample operations on package groups by specifying the *group* subcommand with it. The following subsections elaborate with examples on using this tool to list, install, query, and remove groups of packages.

Listing Available and Installed Package Groups

The *group list* subcommand can be used with *dnf* to list the package groups available for installation from either or both repos, as well as to list the package groups that are already installed.

To list all available and installed package groups from all repositories:

```
[user1@server1 ~]$ dnf group list
Available Environment Groups:
   Server
   Minimal Install
   Workstation
   Custom Operating System
   Virtualization Host
Installed Environment Groups:
   Server with GUI
Installed Groups:
   Container Management
   Headless Management
Available Groups:
   Legacy UNIX Compatibility
   Console Internet Tools
   Development Tools
   .NET Development
   Graphical Administration Tools
   Network Servers
   RPM Development Tools
   Scientific Support
   Security Tools
   Smart Card Support
   System Tools
```

The output reveals two categories of package groups: an *environment group* and a *group*. An environment group is a larger collection of RHEL packages that provides all necessary software to build the operating system foundation for a desired purpose. The Server with GUI environment group is an example that was selected at the time of installing *server1*, which installed a multitude of packages as well as the GNOME desktop. See Table 1-2 in Chapter 01 "Local Installation" for a description of other environment groups.

A regular group, on the other hand, is a smaller, thematic collection of RHEL packages that serve a common purpose. It also saves time on the deployment of individual and dependent packages. The above output shows two installed and several available package groups.

To display the number of installed and available package groups:

```
[user1@server1 ~]$ dnf group summary
Installed Groups: 2
Available Groups: 11
```

To list all installed and available package groups including those that are hidden:

```
[user1@server1 ~]$ dnf group list hidden
Available Environment Groups:
   Server
   Minimal Install
   Workstation
   Custom Operating System
   Virtualization Host
Installed Environment Groups:
   Server with GUI
Installed Groups:
   Hardware Support
   Server product core
   base-x
   Container Management
   Core
........
```

Try *group list* with --installed and --available options to narrow down the output list.

To list all packages that a specific package group such as *Base* (not shown in the above output) contains:

```
[user1@server1 ~]$ dnf group info Base
Group: Base
 Description: The standard install.
 Mandatory Packages:
   acl
   at
   attr
   bc
   cpio
   crontabs
   cyrus-sasl-plain
   dbus
   ed
   file
........
```

You may use the -v option with *group info* for more information. Refer to the *group list* and *group info* subsections of the *dnf* command's manual pages for more details.

Installing and Updating Package Groups

Installing a package group creates the necessary directory structure for all the packages included in the group and all dependent packages, installs the required files, and runs any post-installation steps. If the package group is being loaded or part of it is already present, the command attempts to update all the packages included in the group to the latest available versions. By default, *dnf* prompts for a yes or no confirmation unless the -y flag is entered with the command.

The following example attempts to install a package group called *smart card support*, but proceeds with an update if it detects the presence of an older version. You may enclose the group name within either single or double quotation marks. Add the -v option for verbose output.

```
[user1@server1 ~]$ sudo dnf -y groupinstall "smart card support"
```

To update the *smart card support* group to the latest version:

```
[user1@server1 ~]$ sudo dnf groupupdate "smart card support" -y
```

The above command will update all the packages within the package group to their latest versions if it has access to them. Refer to the *group install* and *group update* subsections of the *dnf* command's manual pages for more details.

Removing Package Groups

Removing a package group uninstalls all the included packages and deletes all associated files and directory structure. It also erases any dependencies as part of the deletion process. By default, *dnf* prompts for a yes or no confirmation unless the -y flag is specified at the command line.

To erase the *smart card support* package group that was installed earlier:

```
[user1@server1 ~]$ sudo dnf -y groupremove 'smart card support'
```

The above command will remove the specified package group without showing details in the output. Add the -v option for verbosity.

Refer to the *group remove* subsection of the *dnf* command's manual pages for more details.

Exercise 11-3: Manipulate Package Groups

Perform this exercise on *server1* as *user1* with *sudo* where required. In this exercise, you will:

- Find out if the *system tools* package group is installed
- Check if this package group is available for installation
- List the packages it contains and install it
- Remove this group along with dependencies
- Confirm the removal

1. Check whether the *system tools* package group is already installed:

```
[user1@server1 ~]$ dnf group list installed 'system tools'
```

The output does not show it installed.

2. Determine if this package group is available for installation:

```
[user1@server1 ~]$ dnf group list available 'system tools'
Available Groups:
   System Tools
```

The group is available for installation.

3. Display the list of packages this group contains:

```
[user1@server1 ~]$ dnf group info 'system tools'
Group: System Tools
 Description: This group is a collection of various tools for
 the system, such as the client for connecting to SMB shares
and tools to monitor network traffic.
 Default Packages:
   NetworkManager-libreswan
   chrony
   cifs-utils
   libreswan
   nmap
   openldap-clients
   samba-client
   setserial
   tmux
   zsh
 Optional Packages:
   PackageKit-command-not-found
   aide
   autofs
   chrpath
   convmv
   createrepo_c
   environment-modules
   freerdp
........
```

The output returns a list of packages that this group contains. All mandatory and default packages will be installed as part of the group installation.

4. Install the group:

```
[user1@server1 ~]$ sudo dnf group install 'system tools'
```

```
Dependencies resolved.
================================================================================
 Package                  Arch    Version                       Repo       Size
================================================================================
Installing group/module packages:
 NetworkManager-libreswan
                          x86_64 1.2.24-2.el10                  AppStream 171 k
 cifs-utils               x86_64 7.1-2.el10                     BaseOS    121 k
 libreswan                x86_64 5.2-1.el10_0                   AppStream 1.4 M
 nmap                     x86_64 4:7.92-3.el10                  AppStream 5.6 M
 openldap-clients         x86_64 2.6.8-3.el10                   BaseOS    188 k
 samba-client             x86_64 4.21.3-102.el10                AppStream 752 k
 setserial                x86_64 2.17-63.el10                   BaseOS     29 k
 tmux                     x86_64 3.3a-13.20230918gitb202a2f.el10 BaseOS    521 k
Installing dependencies:
 ldns                     x86_64 1.8.3-18.el10                  AppStream 177 k
 nss-tools                x86_64 3.101.0-13.el10                AppStream 456 k
 unbound-libs             x86_64 1.20.0-9.el10                  AppStream 551 k
Installing weak dependencies:
 unbound-anchor           x86_64 1.20.0-9.el10                  AppStream  37 k
Installing Groups:
 System Tools

Transaction Summary
================================================================================
Install  12 Packages

..........
Installed:
  NetworkManager-libreswan-1.2.24-2.el10.x86_64
  cifs-utils-7.1-2.el10.x86_64
  ldns-1.8.3-18.el10.x86_64
  libreswan-5.2-1.el10_0.x86_64
  nmap-4:7.92-3.el10.x86_64
  nss-tools-3.101.0-13.el10.x86_64
  openldap-clients-2.6.8-3.el10.x86_64
  samba-client-4.21.3-102.el10.x86_64
  setserial-2.17-63.el10.x86_64
  tmux-3.3a-13.20230918gitb202a2f.el10.x86_64
  unbound-anchor-1.20.0-9.el10.x86_64
  unbound-libs-1.20.0-9.el10.x86_64

Complete!
```

5. Remove the group:

```
[user1@server1 ~]$ sudo dnf group remove 'system tools' -y
```

6. Confirm the removal:

```
[user1@server1 ~]$ dnf group list installed
Installed Environment Groups:
   Server with GUI
Installed Groups:
   Container Management
   Headless Management
```

The group no longer appears in the installed groups list, confirming its removal.

Chapter Summary

This chapter, the second installment on software management, delved into advanced administration topics: repositories and package groups. We explored the role of repositories in simplifying software management, demonstrating how to configure access to a local repository. This approach automates dependency resolution, offering a significant advantage over manual package handling with the rpm command.

We then examined package groups, highlighting their efficiency for installing cohesive software sets compared to managing individual packages. The chapter focused extensively on the dnf command, detailing its superior functionality over rpm. Through practical examples, we utilized key dnf subcommands for installing, querying, updating, and removing both individual packages and entire package groups. Additional operations, such as displaying detailed package information, identifying which package provides a specific file, and searching repository metadata, were also covered.

Review Questions

1. What *dnf* subcommand would we use to check available updates for installed packages?
2. What command shows transaction history?
3. What must be the extension of a yum repository file?
4. What would the *dnf list zsh* command do?
5. What would the *dnf list installed *gnome** command do?
6. What is the difference between *dnf install* and *dnf reinstall*?
7. How many package names can be specified at a time with the *dnf install* command?
8. Name the two default dnf repositories that contain all the packages for RHEL 10?
9. What would the *dnf group info Base* command do?
10. Which *dnf* subcommand can be used to list all available repositories?
11. What is the use of the -y option with the *dnf group install* command?
12. What is the main advantage of using *dnf* over *rpm*?
13. We can update all the packages within a package group using the *groupupdate* subcommand with *dnf*. True or False?
14. What would the *dnf info zsh* command do?

Answers to Review Questions

1. The *check-update* subcommand.
2. The *dnf history* command.
3. The extension of a dnf repository configuration file must be *.repo* to be recognized as a valid repo file.
4. The command provided will display installed and available *zsh* package.
5. The command provided will display all installed packages that contain gnome in their names.
6. *dnf install* installs a package if not present or updates it if older. *dnf reinstall* reinstalls the exact same version of an already installed package, useful for recovering corrupted files.
7. There is no limit.
8. The two dnf repositories are BaseOS and AppStream.
9. The command displays package group metadata, including mandatory, default, and optional packages.
10. The *repolist* subcommand.
11. *dnf* will not prompt for user confirmation if the -y option is used with it.

12. *dnf* resolves and installs dependent packages automatically.
13. True.
14. The command provided will display detailed metadata for the *zsh* package.

Do-It-Yourself Challenge Labs

The following labs are designed to reinforce most of the concepts and skills covered in this chapter. You are expected to complete these labs without external assistance. A step-by-step guide is not provided, as the required knowledge has already been presented in the chapter; however, each lab includes hints pointing to the relevant major topic(s).

Use the lab environment created specifically for the end-of-chapter labs. See the sub-section "Lab Environment for End-of-Chapter Labs" in Chapter 01 "Local Installation" for details.

Lab 11-1: Configure Access to RHEL 10 Repositories

As *user1* with *sudo* on *server3*, make sure the RHEL 10 ISO image is attached to the VM and mounted. Create a definition file under */etc/yum.repos.d*, and define two blocks (one for BaseOS and another for AppStream). Verify the configuration with *dnf repolist*. You should see numbers in thousands under the Status column for both repositories. (Hint1: Chapter 10: Package Management with rpm). (Hint2: Chapter 11: Software Management with dnf).

Lab 11-2: Install and Manage Individual Packages

As *user1* with *sudo* on *server3* and using the *dnf* command, list all installed and available packages separately. Show which package owns the */etc/group* file. Install the package *httpd*. Review */var/log/dnf.log* for confirmation. Perform the following on the *httpd* package: (1) show metadata, (2) list dependencies, and (3) remove it. (Hint: Individual Package Management).

Lab 11-3: Install and Manage Package Groups

As *user1* with *sudo* on *server3* and using the *dnf* command, list all installed and available package groups separately. Install the package groups *security tools* and *scientific support*. Review */var/log/dnf.log* for confirmation. Show the metadata for the *scientific support* package group and then delete this group. (Hint: Package Group Management).

Chapter 12

Flatpak Application Management

By the end of this chapter, you will be able to:

- Explore the Flatpak Application Framework and its Containerized Approach
- Explain the Core Architecture, including Sandboxing and OSTree Storage
- Compare and Contrast Flatpak Applications with Traditional RPM Packages
- Configure and Manage Flatpak Remotes (Repositories)
- Search for, Install, Run, Update, and Remove Flatpak Applications and Runtimes
- Manage Application Permissions

RHCSA Objectives:

14. Configure access to Flatpak repositories
15. Install and remove Flatpak software packages

THIS is the third and final chapter on software administration in RHEL. While the previous two chapters (Chapters 10 and 11) focused on managing system software using RPM and DNF, this chapter introduces Flatpak—a modern framework designed specifically for desktop applications.

Unlike traditional package managers such as rpm and dnf, the flatpak command deploys desktop applications in isolated, containerized environments.

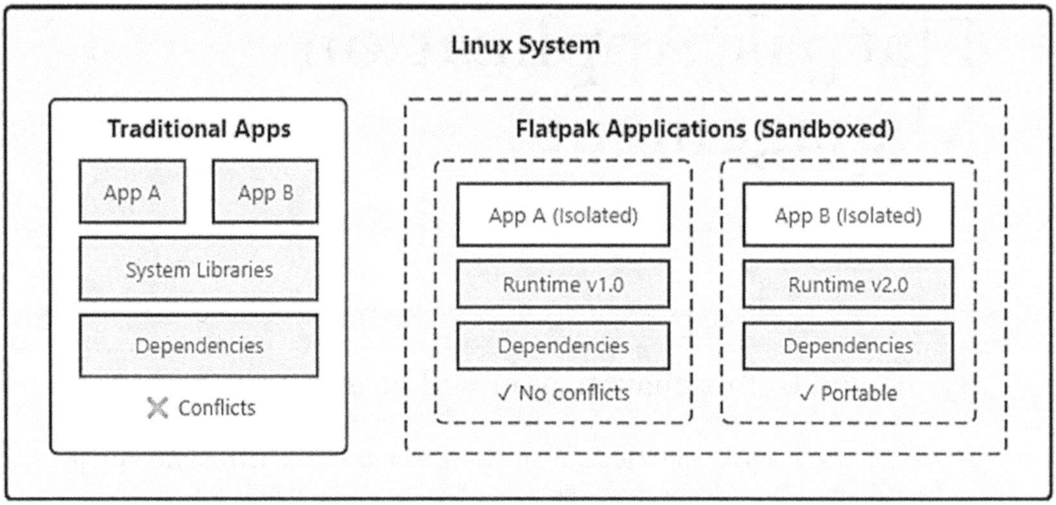

This approach eliminates version conflicts, allows multiple application versions to coexist, and enhances system security through controlled permissions. In this chapter, you will learn about Flatpak's architecture, repository/remote configuration, and sandboxing mechanisms, along with practical usage of the flatpak command for managing desktop applications on RHEL.

Overview

Flatpak is an application packaging and distribution framework designed to provide secure, portable, and version-flexible software deployment across Linux distributions. Introduced as a fully supported feature in RHEL 10, Flatpak solves key limitations of traditional package management systems. It runs each application in an isolated container, along with all its necessary dependencies.

The framework was developed to solve several longstanding challenges in Linux software distribution. Traditional package managers like RPM require deep system integration and can create dependency conflicts when different applications need different versions of the same library. Flatpak eliminates these conflicts by allowing each application to bundle its specific dependencies, running them in isolation from the underlying host system.

Flatpak applications are distributed as single files or through remote repositories, making them portable across different Linux distributions. This distribution-agnostic approach means developers can package their applications once and have them run on any Linux system with Flatpak support, significantly reducing the maintenance burden of supporting multiple distributions.

Security is enhanced through Flatpak's sandbox architecture, which runs applications with restricted permissions by default. Applications must explicitly request access to system resources such as the network, filesystem, or hardware devices, and users can review and modify these permissions. This granular permission model provides better control over what applications can access compared to traditional packages that run with the user's full privileges.

Terminology

There are several key terms that you need to grasp to effectively administer Flatpak applications. Table 12-1 describes them.

Term	Description
BaseApp	Application that provides shared functionality for other applications
Bundle	Single file that contains a complete Flatpak application or runtime
Commit	Specific version of an application or runtime in OSTree
Deploy	Active version of an installed application or runtime
Extension Point	Location where extensions can be mounted
Installation	Location where Flatpak stores applications (system or user)
Override	Permission modification from default sandbox settings
Portal	Provides controlled, permission-based communication between a sandboxed application and the host system resources.
Ref	Unique identifier for a Flatpak component (name/arch/branch)
Remote (Repository)	It contains Flatpak applications, runtimes, and extensions
Runtime	Base platform that provides libraries and dependencies for applications
Sandbox	Isolated environment where applications run

Table 12-1 Flatpak Terminology

Most of these terms will be used in the remainder of this chapter.

RPM vs. Flatpak Packages

Understanding the differences between RPM packages and Flatpak applications is crucial for Linux administrators to make informed decisions about software deployment. Table 12-2 provides a comparison between the two.

Aspect	RPM Package	Flatpak Applications
Installation scope	System-wide	System-wide or per-user
Dependency model	Shared system libraries	Bundled or runtime-provided
Version management	Single version per system	Multiple versions coexist
System integration	Deep integration with OS	Sandboxed isolation
Update Mechanism	dnf/yum commands	flatpak command
Storage Efficiency	Shared libraries minimize space	Larger due to bundled dependencies
Security Model	Runs with user permissions	Sandboxed with controlled permissions
Distribution Compatibility	Distribution-specific	Cross-distribution
Rollback Support	Limited	Built-in
File Access	Full filesystem access	Restricted by default
Suitable For	System services, drivers, tools	Desktop applications
Developer Burden	Per-distribution packaging	Single application for all distributions
Repository Format	Dnf repos	OSTree-based remotes
Package Format	.rpm files	.flatpak or .flatpakref files

Table 12-2 Comparison of RPM and Flatpak Software Management Systems

This comparison highlights that RPM and Flatpak are designed for different purposes. RPM packages remain essential for system components, drivers, and services that require deep OS integration. Flatpak is for desktop applications where isolation, portability, and version flexibility are priorities. Remember that Flatpak complements, not replaces, traditional package management.

Architecture and Core Components

Flatpak's architecture consists of several interconnected components that work together to provide application isolation and distribution. The primary components include:

- **Applications:** Software programs that users run. Each application is identified by a unique three-part identifier following reverse-DNS notation, such as org.mozilla.firefox. Applications contain the executable code, assets, and metadata describing permissions and dependencies.
- **Runtimes:** Collections of base libraries and dependencies that applications require to run successfully. Instead of each application bundling its own copy of common libraries, multiple applications can share a single runtime. This shared approach provides shared dependencies, reducing disk space usage and bandwidth consumption for applications that rely on the same platform. Examples include *org.freedesktop.Platform* for general applications and *org.gnome.Platform* for GNOME-based applications. Runtimes are versioned independently, allowing multiple versions to coexist on the same system.
- **Extensions:** Additional functionality provided to applications or runtimes without modifying their core files. Examples include language packs, hardware drivers, and additional fonts.
- **Remotes (a.k.a. Repositories):** Remotes that host Flatpak applications, runtimes, and extensions. The most prominent public remote is *Flathub*, though organizations can host private remotes for internal software distribution.

Remote Types and Sources

Flatpak remotes can be categorized into four main types, based on scope and trust level:

- **System remotes:** configured globally in the */etc/flatpak/remotes.d/* directory and require administrative privileges to modify. Applications installed from system remotes are available to all users.
- **User remotes:** configured per-user in the *~/.local/share/flatpak/repo/* directory and can be managed without administrative privileges. Applications installed from user remotes are only available to that user.
- **Official remotes:** maintained by trusted organizations with vetted applications. An example is Flathub.
- **Third-party remotes:** provided by independent developers or organizations. These remotes should be carefully evaluated before being added.

Flatpak remotes come from different sources. The most common are:

- **Flathub** (https://flathub.org): The primary public remote containing thousands of apps.
- **RHEL remotes:** Red Hat-provided and maintained applications with versions of certain applications commercially supported.
- **Private remotes:** Hosted internally by organizations to distribute custom or proprietary software. These use OSTree technology and are accessed via internal URLs.

OSTree and Content Deduplication

OSTree is the underlying technology that Flatpak uses for content storage and distribution. When multiple applications use the same files, OSTree stores only one copy and creates hard links to share the content. This deduplication occurs at the file level, meaning identical files across different applications or runtimes consume disk space only once. For example, if five applications use the same version of a library, that library is stored only once on disk, reducing storage requirements.

Sandbox Technology

Flatpak uses *Bubblewrap* as its core sandboxing technology to run each Flatpak application in isolation. It utilizes Linux features to control filesystem visibility, isolate process trees, restrict network access, control inter-process communication, and map user/group IDs for privilege separation.

By default, sandboxed applications have minimal access to the host system. They cannot see other processes, access arbitrary files, or modify system configuration. This isolation reduces the potential impact of security vulnerabilities.

Portal System for Resource Access

If applications are completely isolated in a sandbox, how can they open a file from your home directory or print a document? The answer is *Portals*. Portals provide a secure mechanism for sandboxed applications to access system resources and services. Instead of granting full permissions, portals allow applications to request specific actions that require user consent or system mediation. XDG Desktop Portals, for instance, implement standard interfaces for common desktop operations, such as opening/saving files, printing, taking screenshots, sending notifications, and accessing system preferences.

When an application needs to open a file, it calls the relevant portal. The portal presents a dialog to the user and provides access to the specific file the user selects. This approach maintains security while preserving functionality.

Putting It All Together

Figure 11-1 illustrates how Flatpak's core components work together to provide secure application deployment. Applications are distributed from remotes and stored locally in OSTree storage, which uses deduplication to conserve disk space. The downloaded application is mounted into a sandbox, where it runs in isolation with restricted permissions alongside its runtime that provides necessary libraries and dependencies.

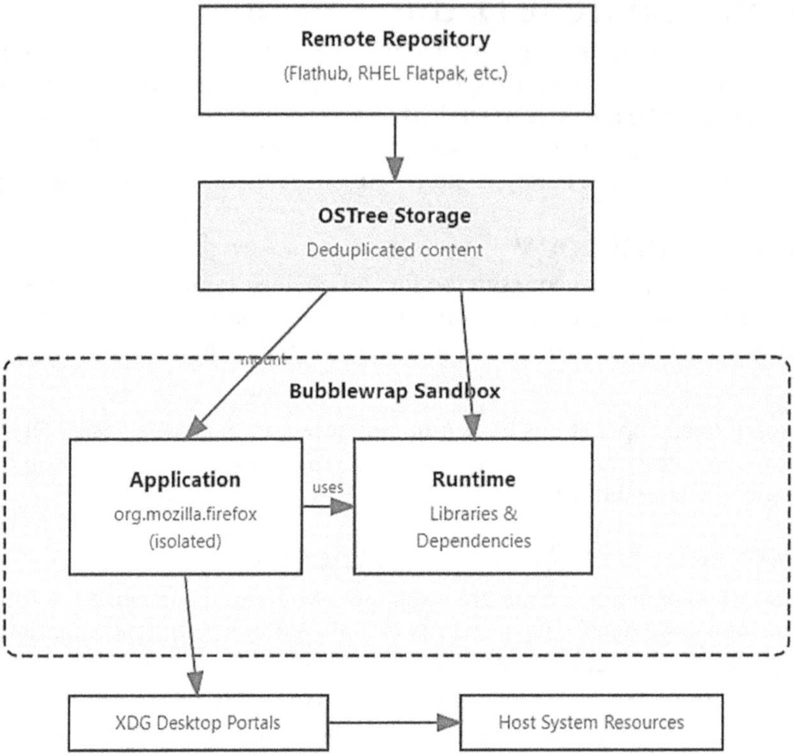

Figure 12-1 Flatpak Components Interaction

When the sandboxed application needs to access system resources like files or printers, it goes through the relevant portal, which acts as an intermediary between the isolated application and the system resources, ensuring that applications only get access to what is explicitly allowed to them.

Remote and Application Management

Flatpak allows you as an administrator to manage desktop applications independently from the system package managers. It uses *remotes*, which you can configure system-wide or per-user. Understanding how to add, list, and manage remotes, and how to install and update applications with the *flatpak* command, is important for your administrative tasks.

Flatpak Configuration and Remotes

Flatpak configuration is stored under */etc/flatpak/* for system-wide settings and *~/.local/share/flatpak/* for per-user installations. Two subdirectories are especially important:

- **/etc/flatpak/remotes.d/:** defines system remotes available to all users
- **/etc/flatpak/installations.d/:** lists system installation paths

User-specific remotes and installations follow the same structure within the user's home directory. The optional system-wide configuration file, */etc/flatpak/flatpak.conf*, can define global settings such as the default installation scope. RHEL 10 includes a sample repository definition file named *rhel.flatpakrepo*, which can be used to enable access to Red Hat-maintained Flatpak applications.

You can add as many remotes as needed, and then search, install, and update applications from them. Flatpak remotes are cryptographically signed using GPG keys to ensure the integrity and authenticity of downloaded applications. Each remote contains metadata, remote URLs, and GPG key information.

Applications and runtimes are downloaded and installed under */var/lib/flatpak/* in the *app* and *runtime* subdirectories, respectively. Information about all added remotes is stored in the *repo* subdirectory within the same installation path.

```
[user1@server1 flatpak]$ pwd
/var/lib/flatpak
[user1@server1 flatpak]$ ls -l
total 0
drwxr-xr-x. 3 root root 18 Oct 27 12:19 appstream
drwxr-xr-x. 2 root root  6 Oct 27 12:11 oci
drwxr-xr-x. 7 root root 89 Oct 27 12:10 repo
```

You will practice operations on remotes in the upcoming exercises.

Run **man 5 flatpakrepo** for details.

The flatpak Command

The *flatpak* command is the primary tool for managing Flatpak remotes, applications, and permissions. There are several subcommands described in Table 12-3.

Subcommand	Description
history	Shows update history
info	Shows details about installed items
install	Installs applications or runtimes
list	Displays installed applications and runtimes
override	Modifies application permissions
remote-add	Adds a repository
remote-delete	Removes a repository
remote-list	Displays configured repositories
repair	Repairs an application
run	Launches an application
search	Searches for applications in remotes
uninstall	Removes an application or runtime
update	Updates installed applications

Table 12-3 flatpak Subcommands

You will practice many of these subcommands in the upcoming examples and exercises. Refer to the manual pages for the *flatpak* command for more details.

Exercise 12-1: Install Flatpak and Configure Flathub Remote

Perform this exercise on *server1* as *user1* with *sudo* where required. In this exercise, you will:

- Install and verify Flatpak
- Check and add the Flathub remote
- Display a count and list of applications and runtimes
- Show metadata for an application.

1. Install the Flatpak package:

```
..........
[user1@server1 ~]$ sudo dnf install -y flatpak
Package flatpak-1.16.0-5.el10.x86_64 is already installed.
Dependencies resolved.
Nothing to do.
Complete!
```

The output indicates that the package is already installed.

2. List existing remotes:

```
[user1@server1 ~]$ flatpak remotes
Name Options
rhel system,oci,no-gpg-verify
```

A remote called *rhel* is already added by default using the configuration defined in the */etc/flatpak/remotes.d/rhel.flatpakrepo* file.

3. Add the Flathub remote:

```
[user1@server1 ~]$ sudo flatpak remote-add flathub \
> https://flathub.org/repo/flathub.flatpakrepo
```

4. Verify the remote was added. Run the command with the -d option for expanded information:

```
[user1@server1 ~]$ flatpak remotes -d
Name    Title                   URL                                   Collection ID     Subset F
ilter Priority Options                    … … Homepage
   Icon
flathub Flathub                 https://dl.flathub.org/repo/          -                 -      -
      1        system                     … … https://flathub.org/
   https://dl.flathub.org/repo/logo.svg
rhel    Red Hat Enterprise Linux oci+https://flatpaks.redhat.io/rhel/ com.redhat.Stable -      -
      1        system,oci,no-gpg-verify … … https://catalog.redhat.com/software/containers/explo
re https://www.redhat.com/misc/favicon.ico
```

The output shows that there are two remotes—*rhel* and *flathub*. It also displays the title and URL of the remotes along with additional information.

5. Update appstream data (both applications and their metadata) in all remotes:

```
[user1@server1 ~]$ sudo flatpak update --appstream
Updating appstream data for remote flathub
Updating appstream data for remote rhel
```

By specifying a remote name, you can restrict updates to that specific remote.

6. Count available applications (--app) in Flathub and list a few of them:

```
[user1@server1 ~]$ flatpak remote-ls flathub --app | wc -l
3248
[user1@server1 ~]$ flatpak remote-ls flathub --app | more
AuthPass          app.authpass.AuthPass    1.9.6_1904       stable
Blackboard Sync app.bbsync.BlackboardSync         0.18.0  stable
BlueBubbles       app.bluebubbles.BlueBubbles     1.15.4.0
Cantara app.cantara.Cantara       2.6.0    stable
Curo Calculator app.curocalc.calculator 2.0.0   stable
..........
```

Run the commands above and below against the *rhel* remote.

7. Count available runtimes (--runtime) in Flathub and list a few of them:

```
[user1@server1 ~]$ flatpak remote-ls flathub --runtime | wc -l
2226
[user1@server1 ~]$ flatpak remote-ls flathub --runtime | more
HEIC     app.fotema.Fotema.HEIC              stable
Fightcade SteamOS Addon com.fightcade.Fightcade.Steamos
Wine     com.fightcade.Fightcade.Wine               stable
Clapper Enhancers        com.github.rafostar.Clapper.Enhancers
OCR Afrikaans    com.github.unrud.djpdf.OCR.Afr            stable
OCR Amharic      com.github.unrud.djpdf.OCR.Amh            stable
OCR Arabic       com.github.unrud.djpdf.OCR.Ara            stable
..........
```

8. View metadata for application ID app.authpass.AuthPass:

```
[user1@server1 ~]$ flatpak remote-info flathub app.authpass.AuthPass

AuthPass - Password Manager: Keep your passwords safe across all platforms and
devices

        ID: app.authpass.AuthPass
       Ref: app/app.authpass.AuthPass/x86_64/stable
      Arch: x86_64
    Branch: stable
   Version: 1.9.6_1904
   License: GPL-3.0-or-later
Collection: org.flathub.Stable
  Download: 14.8 MB
 Installed: 35.9 MB
   Runtime: org.freedesktop.Platform/x86_64/23.08
       Sdk: org.freedesktop.Sdk/x86_64/23.08
..........
```

Application IDs are written in reverse-DNS notation to uniquely identify them.

Exercise 12-2: Search, Install, Launch, and Close Applications

Perform this exercise on *server1* as *user1* with sudo where required. In this exercise, you will:

- Search, query, install, verify, launch, and terminate applications inside the RHEL desktop.

1. Search for text editing applications and show only the first five:

```
[user1@server1 ~]$ sudo flatpak search editor | head -5
Micro Text Editor       A modern and intuitive terminal-based text editor       io.github.zyedid
ia.micro        2.0.14  stable  flathub
NTag (audio file tag editor)    NTag is a cross platform-graphical tag editor focused on everyda
y life use cases.       com.github.nrittsti.NTag        1.2.16  stable  flathub
Translation Editor      Translate apps in your language org.gnome.Gtranslator   49.0    stable f
lathub
Titania X3D Editor      Edit, view, and navigate in X3D and VRML worlds de.create3000.titania  4
.6.12   stable  flathub
Crossword Editor        Create crossword puzzles        org.gnome.Crosswords.Editor     0.3.16 s
table   flathub
```

2. Get detailed information about the *gedit* editor:

```
[user1@server1 ~]$ flatpak remote-info flathub org.gnome.gedit

gedit - Text editor

        ID: org.gnome.gedit
       Ref: app/org.gnome.gedit/x86_64/stable
      Arch: x86_64
    Branch: stable
   Version: 48.1.1
   License: GPL-2.0+
Collection: org.flathub.Stable
  Download: 5.2 MB
 Installed: 14.5 MB
   Runtime: org.gnome.Platform/x86_64/49
       Sdk: org.gnome.Sdk/x86_64/49

    Commit: 90ccbb6251f6108660b579a298ce7c6e341e485efa8790ad69ea12531f67f5a0
    Parent: 98b62b3cac915c1731881aa5a4bc6eaac3e6c47c25f99e5c9b80df760fa0744f
   Subject: vte: Update vte-0.82.0.tar.xz to 0.82.1 (ebe6cb7cc2dc)
      Date: 2025-10-13 10:09:35 +0000
```

3. Install *gedit* for all users:

```
[user1@server1 ~]$ sudo flatpak install -y flathub org.gnome.gedit
Looking for matches…
Required runtime for org.gnome.gedit/x86_64/stable (runtime/org.gnome.Platform/x86_64/49) foun
in remote flathub

org.gnome.gedit permissions:
    ipc                  fallback-x11       wayland       x11       file access [1]
    dbus access [2]

    [1] host, xdg-run/gvfsd
    [2] org.gtk.vfs.*


        ID                                        Branch          Op  Remote   Download
 1. [✓] org.freedesktop.Platform.GL.default       25.08           i   flathub  139.4 MB / 140.0 MB
 2. [✓] org.freedesktop.Platform.GL.default       25.08-extra     i   flathub   24.5 MB / 140.1 MB
 3. [✓] org.freedesktop.Platform.codecs-extra     25.08-extra     i   flathub   14.2 MB / 14.4 MB
 4. [✓] org.gnome.Platform.Locale                 49              i   flathub   18.6 kB / 384.9 MB
 5. [✓] org.gnome.Platform                        49              i   flathub  347.1 MB / 403.7 MB
 6. [✓] org.gnome.gedit.Locale                    stable          i   flathub    9.0 kB / 3.5 MB
 7. [✓] org.gnome.gedit                           stable          i   flathub    3.4 MB / 5.2 MB

Installation complete.
```

The download might take a few minutes depending on your Internet speed.

4. Search for *calculator* applications:

```
[user1@server1 ~]$ flatpak search calculator
```

You will see numerous calculator applications in the output. One of them is called *Calculator*.

5. Install the *Calculator* application:

```
[user1@server1 ~]$ sudo flatpak -y install flathub org.gnome.Calculator
```

6. View all installed applications and show only specific columns:

```
[user1@server1 ~]$ flatpak list --columns=application,version,installation,size
Application ID                              Version      Installation       Installed size
org.freedesktop.Platform.GL.default         25.2.4       system             428.3 MB
org.freedesktop.Platform.GL.default         25.2.4       system             428.3 MB
org.freedesktop.Platform.codecs-extra                    system              43.6 MB
org.gnome.Calculator                        49.1.1       system               5.4 MB
org.gnome.Platform                                       system               1.1 GB
org.gnome.gedit                             48.1.1       system              14.5 MB
```

gedit and *Calculator* are installed applications; the rest are runtime dependencies. You can also verify the installed applications and runtimes by re-running the command separately with --app and --runtime options.

7. Log in to the RHEL desktop.
8. Open a terminal session on the desktop and launch *gedit* in the background:

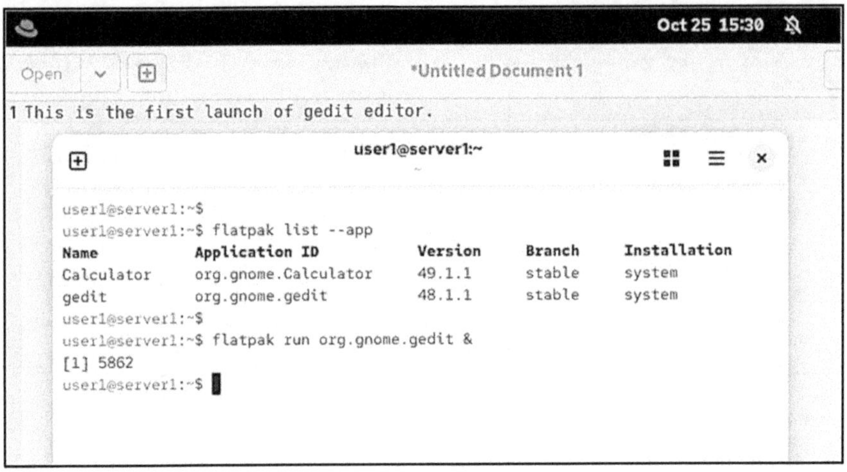

The *flatpak list* command confirms two applications installed and the *flatpak run* command launches the editor.

9. View the application process:

```
user1@server1:~$ flatpak ps
Instance   PID  Application     Runtime
2593688514 5862 org.gnome.gedit org.gnome.Platform
```

The application shown in the output has a unique instance ID, a process ID, the application name, and the runtime it uses.

10. Terminate the *gedit* process:

```
user1@server1:~$ flatpak kill org.gnome.gedit
[1]+  Exit 137                flatpak run org.gnome.gedit
user1@server1:~$
user1@server1:~$ flatpak ps
user1@server1:~$
```

The process was terminated successfully, as confirmed by the last command.

For additional practice, launch and manage the *Calculator* application.

Exercise 12-3: Configure Application Permissions

Perform this exercise on *server1* as *user1* with *sudo* where required In this exercise, you will:

- Examine default permissions
- Modify permissions using overrides
- Test the changes
- Reset permissions to defaults

1. View current sandbox permissions for the *gedit* application:

```
[user1@server1 ~]$ flatpak info --show-permissions org.gnome.gedit
[Context]
shared=ipc;
sockets=x11;wayland;fallback-x11;
filesystems=xdg-run/gvfsd;host;

[Session Bus Policy]
org.gtk.vfs.*=talk
```

The output shows that *gedit* is allowed (shared) to use inter-process communication within the sandbox, open (sockets) graphical windows via the Wayland display system, communicate (filesystems) with GVFS (*GNOME Virtual File System*) for file access, access limited parts of the host filesystem (filesystems), and communicate with all D-Bus services under the org.gtk.vfs namespace.

2. Grant *gedit* access to *~/Documents* folder:

```
[user1@server1 ~]$ sudo flatpak override org.gnome.gedit \
> --filesystem=~/Documents
```

The application can now create and access files under the *$HOME/Documents* directory.

3. Add network access:

```
[user1@server1 ~]$ sudo flatpak override org.gnome.gedit --share=network
```

With network access allowed, the *gedit* application will now be able to make or receive network connections such as opening remote network files, if supported. This change persists across system reboots.

4. Verify the updated permissions:

```
[user1@server1 ~]$ sudo flatpak override --show org.gnome.gedit
[Context]
filesystems=~/Documents;
shared=network;
```

5. Create a test file called *test.out* under *$HOME/Documents* folder:

```
[user1@server1 ~]$ echo "Testing access" > ~/Documents/test.out
```

6. Test access to the file by listing the content of the *$HOME/Documents* directory:

```
[user1@server1 ~]$ flatpak run --command=ls org.gnome.gedit ~/Documents
test.out
```

The *ls* command confirms the existence of and access to the *test.out* file.

7. Add read-only access to */etc*:

```
[user1@server1 ~]$ sudo flatpak override org.gnome.gedit \
> --filesystem=/etc:ro
```

8. Revoke network access:

```
[user1@server1 ~]$ sudo flatpak override org.gnome.gedit --unshare=network
```

9. Reset all permissions to defaults:

```
[user1@server1 ~]$ sudo flatpak override --reset org.gnome.gedit
```

10. Confirm permissions are reset:

```
[user1@server1 ~]$ sudo flatpak override --show org.gnome.gedit
```

11. Delete the *test.out* file:

```
[user1@server1 ~]$ rm ~/Documents/test.out
```

Exercise 12-4: Update and Remove Applications and Runtimes

Perform this exercise on *server1* as *user1* with *sudo* where required. In this exercise, you will:

- Check and apply updates to all applications
- View update history
- Remove both applications and all runtimes
- Verify the removal

1. Check for available updates:

```
[user1@server1 ~]$ sudo flatpak update
Looking for updates…

Nothing to do.
```

There are no updates available for any of the installed Flatpak applications.

2. View update history:

```
[user1@server1 ~]$ flatpak history

[user1@server1 ~]$
```

The updates were never applied, which is why the output shows nothing.

3. Remove both *gedit* and *Calculator*:

```
[user1@server1 ~]$ sudo flatpak uninstall org.gnome.gedit org.gnome.Calculator

        ID                                   Branch          Op
 1. [-] org.gnome.Calculator                 stable          r
 2. [-] org.gnome.Calculator.Locale          stable          r
 3. [-] org.gnome.gedit                      stable          r
 4. [-] org.gnome.gedit.Locale               stable          r

Uninstall complete.
```

You could specify the -y option after the *uninstall* subcommand for non-interactive removal.

4. Remove application data for both applications:

```
[user1@server1 ~]$ rm -rf ~/.var/app/org.gnome.*
```

This will remove any data stored by the applications in the user home directory.

5. Remove unused runtimes:

```
[user1@server1 ~]$ sudo flatpak uninstall -y --unused

        ID                                            Branch            Op
 1. [-] org.freedesktop.Platform.GL.default           25.08             r
 2. [-] org.freedesktop.Platform.GL.default           25.08-extra       r
 3. [-] org.gnome.Platform                            49                r
 4. [-] org.gnome.Platform.Locale                     49                r
 5. [-] org.freedesktop.Platform.codecs-extra         25.08-extra       r

Uninstall complete.
```

Over time, your system may have accumulated many runtimes that are no longer needed. This command ensure that they are deleted.

6. Verify that the applications and runtimes have been removed:

```
[user1@server1 ~]$ flatpak list
[user1@server1 ~]$
```

The output lists nothing, which confirms the deletion.

Chapter Summary

This chapter concluded the software management series with an in-depth exploration of Flatpak, a modern application packaging and distribution framework. We examined its architecture, which addresses traditional package management limitations through application isolation, dependency bundling, and a robust security model.

The discussion covered core components, including remote repositories, the OSTree-based storage system with deduplication, and the Bubblewrap sandbox that provides application isolation. We detailed how the portal system enables controlled resource access, allowing applications to request specific permissions. The chapter also explained key elements such as applications (identified by reverse-DNS notation), runtimes that provide foundational libraries, and extensions that add supplementary functionality.

Finally, we performed essential management operations, including adding remotes, searching for applications, and installing, running, and updating applications. We also covered viewing application details, managing permissions, and removing unused runtimes to free up disk space.

Review Questions

1. How would you install the application org.gimp.GIMP from Flathub?
2. Flatpak applications require root privileges to install when using user-level installations. True or False?
3. What command lists all installed Flatpak applications on your system?
4. Flatpak applications use reverse-DNS notation for their identifiers. True or False?
5. How would you run the installed application org.gnome.gedit at the command line?
6. What are the three main components that can be distributed through Flatpak repositories?
7. A single runtime can be shared by multiple Flatpak applications. True or False?
8. What command would you use to add Flathub as a remote repository?
9. What is the primary purpose of the Bubblewrap sandbox in Flatpak?
10. What is the difference between system and user remote installations?
11. What role do XDG Desktop Portals play in Flatpak's security model?
12. Applications running in a Flatpak sandbox can directly access all system files by default. True or False?
13. What command would you use to search for Firefox in Flatpak repositories?
14. An application, org.example.App, needs access to your home directory but currently does not have permission. What command would you use to grant this access?
15. Explain how OSTree deduplication helps save disk space.
16. OSTree stores identical files multiple times when they appear in different applications. True or False?
17. You notice that old unused runtimes are taking up disk space. What command would remove them?

Answers to Review Questions

1. *flatpak install flathub org.gimp.GIMP*
2. False, user installations do not require root privileges.
3. *flatpak list --app*
4. True
5. *flatpak run org.gnome.gedit*
6. Applications (the actual programs), Runtimes (base libraries and dependencies), and Extensions (additional functionality such as language packs, drivers, and fonts).
7. True
8. *flatpak remote-add flathub https://flathub.org/repo/flathub.flatpakrepo*
9. To provide application isolation by running applications with restricted permissions.
10. System remotes are configured globally in */etc/flatpak/remotes.d/*, require root privileges, and applications are available to all users. User remotes are configured per-user in *~/.local/share/flatpak/repo/*, do not require root, and applications are only available to that user.

11. Portals act as secure intermediaries between sandboxed applications and system resources. They allow applications to request specific actions (such as file access) that require user consent. This helps maintain security while preserving functionality.
12. False, sandboxed applications have minimal access by default and must request permissions.
13. *flatpak search firefox*
14. *flatpak override --user --filesystem=home org.example.App*
15. OSTree stores identical files only once and creates hard links to share content between applications. If multiple applications use the same file, it is stored once and referenced multiple times.
16. False, OSTree uses deduplication and stores identical files only once using hard links.
17. *flatpak uninstall --unused*

Do-It-Yourself Challenge Labs

The following labs are designed to reinforce most of the concepts and skills covered in this chapter. You are expected to complete these labs without external assistance. A step-by-step guide is not provided, as the required knowledge has already been presented in the chapter; however, each lab includes hints pointing to the relevant major topic(s).

Use the lab environment created specifically for the end-of-chapter labs. See the sub-section "Lab Environment for End-of-Chapter Labs" in Chapter 01 "Local Installation" for details.

Lab 12-1: Configure Flatpak and Add Remotes

As *user1* with *sudo* on *server3*, install the flatpak package if not already installed. Add Flathub as a system-wide remote repository. Add the Fedora Flatpak repository as a user remote (without sudo). Verify that both remotes are configured correctly, and list the number of applications available in each. Display metadata for both remotes to confirm they are accessible. (Hint1: Remote Types and Sources). (Hint2: The Flathub URL is *https://flathub.org/repo/flathub.flatpakrepo*). (Hint3: The Fedora URL is *oci+https://registry.fedoraproject.org*).

Lab 12-2: Install and Manage Applications

As *user1* on *server3*, search for the *gedit* text editor in the configured repositories. Install org.gnome.gedit from Flathub as a user installation (no sudo). List all installed applications and verify *gedit* appears. Run the application to confirm it works, then display detailed information about the application including its size and runtime dependencies. Finally, uninstall the application. (Hint: Application identifiers use reverse-DNS notation).

Lab 12-3: Work with Runtimes and Application Permissions

As *user1* with *sudo* on *server3*, install *org.mozilla.firefox* as a system-wide application from Flathub. List all installed runtimes and note which runtime Firefox uses. Display the current permissions for Firefox. Override Firefox's permissions to grant access to the *~/Documents* directory only (not the entire home directory). Verify the override is in place, then reset Firefox permissions back to defaults. (Hint1: Sandbox Technology). (Hint2: Use *flatpak override* with --filesystem option).

Lab 12-4: Manage Multiple Applications and Storage

As *user1* on *server3*, install at least two applications that share the same runtime (e.g., *org.gnome.Calculator* and *org.gnome.Calendar* from Flathub). List all installed applications and runtimes and note the shared runtime. Check the disk usage for Flatpak installations. Update all installed Flatpak applications and runtimes to their latest versions. Remove any unused runtimes to free up disk space and verify the space has been reclaimed. (Hint1: OSTree and Content Deduplication). (Hint2: The --unused option helps with cleanup).

Chapter 13

Boot Process, GRUB2, and the Linux Kernel

By the end of this chapter, you will be able to:

- Explain the Linux Boot Process: Firmware, Bootloader, Kernel, and Initialization
- Interact with GRUB2 to Interrupt the Boot Process and Modify Boot Parameters
- Manage GRUB2 Configuration to Persistently Change Boot Settings
- Boot the System Into Specific Targets for Troubleshooting or Testing
- Recover System Access by Resetting a Lost or Forgotten root Password
- Analyze the Linux Kernel, including its Package Composition, Version Anatomy, and Critical Directories
- Update the Kernel by Downloading and Installing a New Version without Removing the Old One

RHCSA Objectives:

22. Interrupt the boot process in order to gain access to a system
46. Modify the system bootloader

RHEL goes through multiple phases during the boot process. It starts selective services during its transition from one phase into another. You have the opportunity to interact with a preboot program to boot the system into a non-default target, pass an option to the kernel, or reset the lost or forgotten root user password. The system launches numerous services during its transition to the default or specified target.

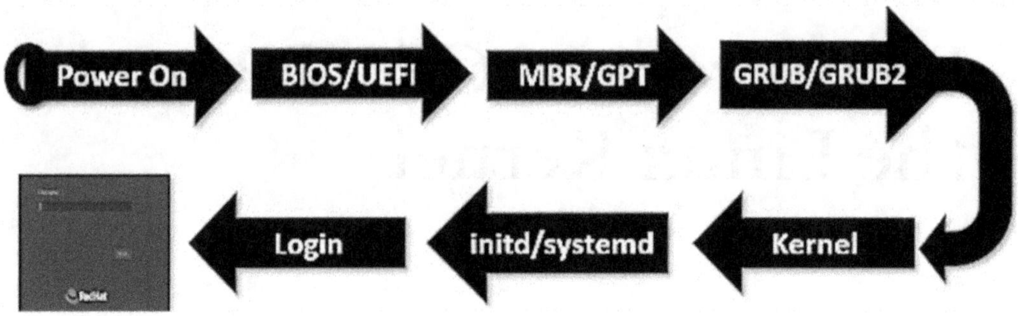

The kernel controls everything on the system. It controls the system hardware, enforces security and access controls, and runs, schedules, and manages processes and service daemons. The kernel is comprised of several modules. You must install a new kernel or upgrade an existing kernel when the need arises from an application or functionality standpoint.

Linux Boot Process

RHEL goes through a defined *boot* process after the system has been powered on or restarted. The boot process lasts until all enabled services are started and a login prompt appears. Although the process is automatic, you may need to interact with it to take a non-default action, such as booting an alternative kernel, booting into a different operational state, repairing the system, or recovering from an unbootable condition. The boot process on an x86-64 system comprises four major phases: (1) the firmware phase, (2) the bootloader phase, (3) the kernel phase, and (4) the initialization phase. The system proceeds through these phases in sequence while performing and completing the tasks identified for each.

The Firmware Phase (BIOS and UEFI)

The system *firmware*—either BIOS (*Basic Input/Output System*) or UEFI (*Unified Extensible Firmware Interface*)—is code stored in non-volatile flash memory on the motherboard. It runs the *Power-On Self-Test* (POST) to detect, test, and initialize hardware. During POST, it loads drivers for the video hardware and displays system messages. The firmware then scans storage devices to locate a bootable device. On BIOS systems, it looks for a 512-byte *Master Boot Record* (MBR) in the first sector of the disk. The MBR contains a 446-byte bootloader stub, a 64-byte partition table, and a 2-byte boot signature. Once a usable boot device is found, the firmware loads the bootloader into memory and transfers control to it.

BIOS firmware stores configurable hardware settings such as date and time, boot order, and I/O parameters. Depending on the system, pressing a key such as `F2` or `Del` opens the BIOS setup utility. The firmware initializes hardware, runs POST on discovered devices, loads video drivers, and displays status messages. Supported boot sources typically include disk drives, optical media, USB flash devices, and network interfaces.

UEFI is a modern, architecture-independent replacement for legacy BIOS. It provides enhanced boot and runtime services, supports its own device drivers, can mount and read FAT-formatted partitions, and includes tools and utilities for system management. UEFI supports multiple bootloaders and includes a built-in boot manager that allows selecting an alternate boot source. Although UEFI features vary by vendor, most systems follow the same basic UEFI specification.

The Bootloader Phase

After the firmware phase, the system loads the *bootloader* software from the selected boot device. RHEL uses GRUB2 (*GRand Unified Bootloader*) version 2 as the bootloader program, which supports both BIOS and UEFI systems.

The primary responsibility of GRUB2 is to locate the Linux kernel in the */boot* file system, load it into memory as configured in the */boot/grub2/grub.cfg* file, and transfer control to it. On UEFI systems, GRUB2 runs as a UEFI application stored in the *EFI System Partition* (ESP) at */boot/efi/EFI/redhat/grub.efi* and uses */boot/grub2/grub.cfg* for its configuration. The next section discusses interacting with the bootloader.

The Kernel Phase

The *kernel* is the central program of Linux, providing access to hardware and system services. After gaining control from the bootloader, the kernel loads the *initial RAM filesystem* (*initramfs*) image from */boot*, unpacks it into memory, and uses it as a temporary root filesystem.

The kernel then executes the */init* program inside the initramfs. This program is a minimal systemd-based environment that performs essential early boot tasks, including:

- Loading required kernel drivers called *modules*
- Discovering and activating storage devices
- Assembling storage configurations (such as LVM or encrypted volumes)
- Identifying and preparing the real root filesystem

Once the real root filesystem becomes available, initramfs mounts it at */sysroot* and performs a switch-root, transitioning the system to use the real root file system. The initramfs environment is then discarded from memory.

After the switch-root, *systemd* is executed as PID 1 from the real root filesystem and continues the normal boot process—launching services, initializing targets, and completing system startup.

The Initialization Phase

This is the fourth and final phase of the boot process. During this phase, *systemd*—the default system initialization framework in RHEL 10—takes control from the kernel and continues system startup. *systemd* starts all enabled userspace system and network services and brings the system to the configured boot target.

A *boot target* is an operational state defined by a set of *systemd* units. A target is reached after the required services and dependencies have been started. A detailed discussion of *systemd*, units, and targets is provided in Chapter 14 “System Initialization, Message Logging, and System Tuning”.

The system boot process is considered complete when all enabled services for the boot target are active and users are able to log in.

The GRUB2 Bootloader

After the firmware phase concludes, the bootloader presents a menu with a list of bootable kernel entries and waits for a predefined amount of time before booting the default kernel entry. You can interrupt this timeout to select a different kernel, boot into a different target, or customize the kernel boot string.

Pressing any key before the timeout interrupts the autoboot process and allows interaction with GRUB2. If you want the system to boot using the default settings on the default boot device, do not press any key, as shown in Figure 13-1, and let the system continue through the autoboot process.

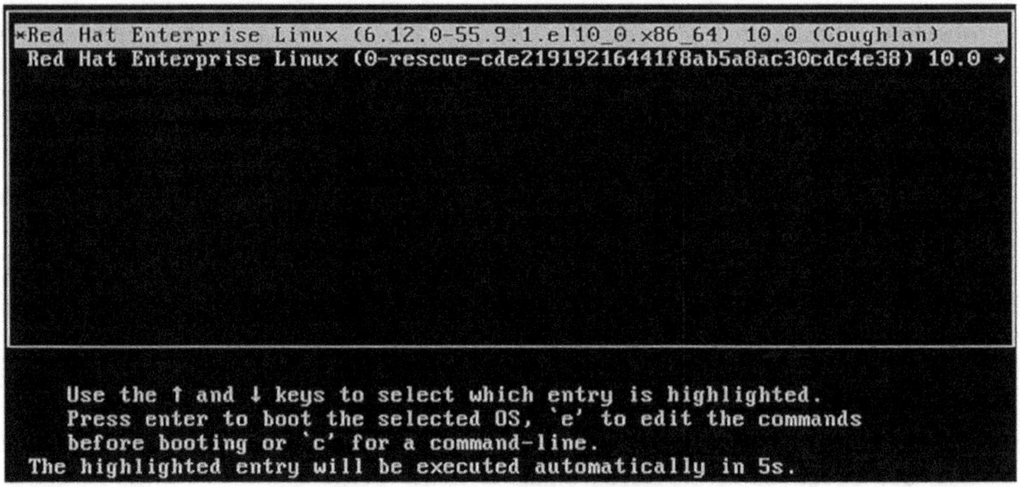

Figure 13-1 GRUB2 Menu

The line at the bottom of Figure 13-1 shows the countdown timer in seconds. The default value is 5 seconds. If no key is pressed within those 5 seconds, the highlighted kernel boots automatically.

Interacting with GRUB2

The GRUB2 main menu displays a list of bootable kernel entries at the top. You can change the active selection using the `Up` or `Down` arrow key. You can edit the selected entry by pressing *e*, or access the grub> command prompt by pressing *c*.

In edit mode, GRUB2 loads the configuration for the selected kernel entry from the */boot/grub2/grub.cfg* file into a temporary editor, enabling you to make modifications before booting. For instance, you can boot the system into a less capable operating target by adding "rescue", "emergency", or "3" to the end of the line beginning with the keyword "linux", as depicted in Figure 13-2. Press `Ctrl+x` when done to boot. Remember that this is a one-time, temporary change and does not modify the *grub.cfg* file.

```
load_video
set gfxpayload=keep
insmod gzio
linux ($root)/vmlinuz-6.12.0-55.9.1.el10_0.x86_64 root=/dev/mapper/rhel-roo\
t ro crashkernel=2G-64G:256M,64G-:512M resume=UUID=b1103e6a-18ac-407b-815f-\
cf03d3096091 rd.lvm.lv=rhel/root rd.lvm.lv=rhel/swap rhgb quiet
initrd ($root)/initramfs-6.12.0-55.9.1.el10_0.x86_64.img $tuned_initrd

   Minimum Emacs-like screen editing is supported. TAB lists
   completions. Press Ctrl-x or F10 to boot, Ctrl-c or F2 for
   a command-line or ESC to discard edits and return to the GRUB menu.
```

Figure 13-2 GRUB2 Kernel Entry Edit

If you do not wish to boot the system after making changes, press `ESC` to discard them, and return to the main menu.

The grub> command prompt appears when you press `Ctrl+c` while in the edit window or *c* from the main menu. Command mode allows you to perform debugging, recovery, and other advanced tasks. Press `TAB` to view the list of available commands, as shown in Figure 13-3.

```
grub>
Possible commands are:

 . [ acpi all_functional_test authenticate background_color background_image
backtrace badram blocklist bls_import blscfg boot break
btrfs-get-default-subvol btrfs-info btrfs-list-subvols btrfs-mount-subvol cat
cbmemc chainloader clear cmosclean cmosdump cmosset cmostest cmp configfile
continue coreboot_boottime cpuid crc cryptomount cutmem date decrement distrust
distrust_certificate drivemap dump echo efiemu_loadcore efiemu_prepare
efiemu_unload eval exit export extract_entries_configfile
extract_entries_source extract_legacy_entries_configfile
extract_legacy_entries_source extract_syslinux_entries_configfile
extract_syslinux_entries_source false file freedos functional_test gdbstub
```

Figure 13-3 GRUB2 Commands

There are numerous commands available for performing a variety of tasks at the GRUB2 level.

> **EXAM TIP:** Although GRUB2 provides many advanced capabilities, for the RHCSA exam the essential skills are interrupting the boot process, editing kernel parameters, and understanding the configuration files involved.

Understanding GRUB2 Configuration and Source Files

GRUB2's behavior is defined by multiple source files that are compiled into a single boot configuration file called *grub.cfg*. This file is auto-generated and should not be edited manually, as it is built from several sources.

Let's analyze these files.

The /boot/grub2/grub.cfg Configuration File

The *grub.cfg* file is the main GRUB2 configuration file that supplies boot-time configuration. This file is located in the */boot/grub2* directory on BIOS systems. On UEFI systems, this file is also stored in */boot/grub2*. The UEFI firmware loads the GRUB2 bootloader executable (*grubx64.efi* or *shimx64.efi*) from the *EFI System Partition* (ESP), which then reads the configuration from this file. This file can be recreated manually with the *grub2-mkconfig* utility. It is also regenerated automatically when additional kernel versions are installed, in which case any previous manual edits to this file are lost.

When new kernel versions are installed, existing kernel entries remain intact. All bootable kernels appear in the GRUB2 menu and can be selected manually.

The /etc/default/grub Source File

This file provides variable definitions that are used by the scripts under */etc/grub.d* during regeneration. This file defines several key directives. The enumerated list of the default settings in the file is provided below, along with their explanations in Table 13-1:

```
[user1@server1 ~]$ nl /etc/default/grub
     1  GRUB_TIMEOUT=5
     2  GRUB_DISTRIBUTOR="$(sed 's, release .*$,,g' /etc/system-release)"
     3  GRUB_DEFAULT=saved
     4  GRUB_DISABLE_SUBMENU=true
     5  GRUB_TERMINAL_OUTPUT="console"
     6  GRUB_CMDLINE_LINUX="crashkernel=2G-64G:256M,64G-:512M resume=UUID=b110
c-407b-815f-cf03d3096091 rd.lvm.lv=rhel/root rd.lvm.lv=rhel/swap rhgb quiet"
     7  GRUB_DISABLE_RECOVERY="true"
     8  GRUB_ENABLE_BLSCFG=true
```

Directive	Description
GRUB_TIMEOUT	Defines the wait time, in seconds, before booting the default kernel. Default value is 5.
GRUB_DISTRIBUTOR	Sets the name of the Linux distribution
GRUB_DEFAULT	Sets the default boot entry. "saved" boots the last-selected entry; "0" boots the first entry.
GRUB_DISABLE_SUBMENU	Enables/disables GRUB2 submenu display
GRUB_TERMINAL_OUTPUT	Sets the default terminal
GRUB_CMDLINE_LINUX	Specifies command-line options to pass to the kernel
GRUB_DISABLE_RECOVERY	Shows/hides system recovery menu entries
GRUB_ENABLE_BLSCFG	Enables/disables the BootLoader Specification (BLS) format. When enabled, each kernel has a separate .conf file under the /boot/loader/entries directory.

Table 13-1 GRUB2 Default Settings

The default settings are generally appropriate for normal operations.

The /etc/grub.d Source Directory

This directory contains executable shell scripts that the grub2-mkconfig command runs in sort-order to generate sections of *grub.cfg*. The following shows a listing of the directory, followed by a brief description of a few of them:

```
[user1@server1 ~]$ sudo ls -l /etc/grub.d/
total 112
-rwxr-xr-x. 1 root root  9380 Mar 24  2025 00_header
-rwxr-xr-x. 1 root root  1100 Feb  3  2025 00_tuned
-rwxr-xr-x. 1 root root   236 Mar 24  2025 01_users
-rwxr-xr-x. 1 root root   835 Mar 24  2025 08_fallback_counting
-rwxr-xr-x. 1 root root 20334 Mar 24  2025 10_linux
-rwxr-xr-x. 1 root root   833 Mar 24  2025 10_reset_boot_success
-rwxr-xr-x. 1 root root   892 Mar 24  2025 12_menu_auto_hide
-rwxr-xr-x. 1 root root   410 Mar 24  2025 14_menu_show_once
-rwxr-xr-x. 1 root root 14627 Mar 24  2025 20_linux_xen
-rwxr-xr-x. 1 root root  2562 Mar 24  2025 20_ppc_terminfo
-rwxr-xr-x. 1 root root   869 Mar 24  2025 25_bli
-rwxr-xr-x. 1 root root 11006 Mar 24  2025 30_os-prober
-rwxr-xr-x. 1 root root  1166 Mar 24  2025 30_uefi-firmware
-rwxr-xr-x. 1 root root   725 Dec 15  2024 35_fwupd
-rwxr-xr-x. 1 root root   218 Mar 24  2025 40_custom
-rwxr-xr-x. 1 root root   219 Mar 24  2025 41_custom
-rw-r--r--. 1 root root   483 Mar 24  2025 README
```

Key scripts include:

- **00_header:** sets the GRUB2 environment and loads settings from */etc/default/grub*
- **10_linux:** detects installed kernels on the root file system
- **30_os-prober:** scans for the presence of other operating systems
- **40_custom** and **41_custom:** templates for adding custom menu entries

The /boot/grub2/grubenv Source File

The *grubenv* file stores persistent GRUB2 environment variables. For example, the saved_entry variable is used by the GRUB_DEFAULT=saved setting to remember the last-booted menu entry across reboots. Here is what this file contains by default:

```
[user1@server1 ~]$ sudo cat /boot/grub2/grubenv
# GRUB Environment Block
# WARNING: Do not edit this file by tools other than grub-editenv!!!
saved_entry=cde21919216441f8ab5a8ac30cdc4e38-6.12.0-55.9.1.el10_0.x86_64
menu_auto_hide=1
boot_success=1
boot_indeterminate=0
##########################################################################
```

Exercise 13-1: Change Default System Boot Timeout

Perform this exercise on *server1* as *user1* with *sudo* where required. In this exercise, you will:

- Change the default system boot timeout value to 8 seconds persistently
- Validate the change

1. Edit the */etc/default/grub* file and change the setting as follows:

```
GRUB_TIMEOUT=8
```

2. Execute the *grub2-mkconfig* command to reproduce *grub.cfg*:

```
[user1@server1 ~]$ sudo grub2-mkconfig -o /boot/grub2/grub.cfg
Generating grub configuration file ...
Adding boot menu entry for UEFI Firmware Settings ...
done
```

3. Restart the system with **sudo reboot** and confirm the new timeout value when GRUB2 menu appears.

This concludes the exercise.

Booting into Specific Targets

RHEL boots into the graphical target by default if the "Server with GUI" environment group was selected during installation; otherwise, it boots into the multi-user target. You can also boot into less capable targets directly from the GRUB2 menu. Additionally, for full administrative access or for system recovery, RHEL offers *emergency* and *rescue* boot targets. To invoke them, select a kernel in the GRUB2 menu, press *e* to edit, and append the desired target name to the line beginning with "linux".

> **EXAM TIP:** You must know how to boot a RHEL 10 system into a specific target from the GRUB2 menu to repair the /etc/fstab file or reset an unknown root user password.

The following shows how you would append "emergency" to the kernel line entry:

```
load_video
set gfxpayload=keep
insmod gzio
linux ($root)/vmlinuz-5.14.0-162.6.1.el9_1.x86_64 root=/dev/mapper/rhel-root r\
o crashkernel=1G-4G:192M,4G-64G:256M,64G-:512M resume=/dev/mapper/rhel-swap rd\
.lvm.lv=rhel/root rd.lvm.lv=rhel/swap rhgb quiet emergency_
initrd ($root)/initramfs-5.14.0-162.6.1.el9_1.x86_64.img $tuned_initrd
```

After editing, press `Ctrl+x` to boot into the supplied target. You will be prompted for the *root* user password to log in. Run *reboot* when finished to reboot the system.

```
You are in emergency mode. After logging in, type "journalctl -xb" to view
system logs, "systemctl reboot" to reboot, "systemctl default" or "exit"
to boot into default mode.
Give root password for maintenance
(or press Control-D to continue): _
```

Similarly, appending "rescue" (or the legacy designations "1", "s", or "single") to the "linux" line and pressing `Ctrl+x` will boot into the rescue target.

Exercise 13-2: Reset the root User Password

Perform this exercise on *server1*.

For this exercise, assume that the *root* user password is lost or forgotten, and it must be reset.

In this exercise, you will:

- Terminate the boot process at an early stage and reset the *root* password.

1. Reboot or reset *server1*, and interact with GRUB2 by pressing a key before the autoboot times out. Highlight the rescue kernel entry in the GRUB2 menu and press *e* to enter edit mode. Scroll down to the line entry that begins with the keyword "linux" and press the `End` key to go to the end of that line:

```
load_video
set gfxpayload=keep
insmod gzio
linux ($root)/vmlinuz-0-rescue-cde21919216441f8ab5a8ac30cdc4e38 root=/dev/m\
apper/rhel-root ro crashkernel=2G-64G:256M,64G-:512M resume=UUID=b1103e6a-1\
8ac-407b-815f-cf03d3096091 rd.lvm.lv=rhel/root rd.lvm.lv=rhel/swap rhgb qui\
et
initrd ($root)/initramfs-0-rescue-cde21919216441f8ab5a8ac30cdc4e38.img
```

2. Modify the kernel string and append "init=/bin/bash" to the end of the line. It should look like:

```
load_video
set gfxpayload=keep
insmod gzio
linux ($root)/vmlinuz-0-rescue-cde21919216441f8ab5a8ac30cdc4e38 root=/dev/m\
apper/rhel-root ro crashkernel=2G-64G:256M,64G-:512M resume=UUID=b1103e6a-1\
8ac-407b-815f-cf03d3096091 rd.lvm.lv=rhel/root rd.lvm.lv=rhel/swap rhgb qui\
et init=/bin/bash
initrd ($root)/initramfs-0-rescue-cde21919216441f8ab5a8ac30cdc4e38.img
```

3. Press `Ctrl+x` when done. The system mounts the root file system read-only on the / directory, and provide you direct access to the root shell without starting the *systemd* service. You can verify the mount point by running the *pwd* command:

```
 Booting a command list

[    7.026395] Warning: Unmaintained driver is detected: cnic
[    7.047601] Warning: Unmaintained driver is detected: bnx2i
[    8.537371] Warning: Unmaintained driver is detected: e1000
[    9.055756] vmwgfx 0000:00:02.0: [drm] *ERROR* vmwgfx seems to be running
an unsupported hypervisor.
[    9.055766] vmwgfx 0000:00:02.0: [drm] *ERROR* This configuration is like
roken.
[    9.055771] vmwgfx 0000:00:02.0: [drm] *ERROR* Please switch to a support
raphics device to avoid problems.
bash-5.2# pwd
/
```

4. Remount the root file system in read/write mode to allow the *passwd* command to modify the */etc/shadow* file and replace the password:

```
bash-5.2# mount -o remount,rw /
```

5. Enter a new password for *root* using the *passwd* command:

```
bash-5.2# passwd
New password:
BAD PASSWORD: The password is shorter than 8 characters
Retype new password:
passwd: password updated successfully
```

6. Create a hidden file named *.autorelabel* to instruct the operating system to run SELinux relabeling on all files, including the */etc/shadow* file, before the next reboot. This is to ensure compliance with SELinux policy.

```
bash-5.2# touch .autorelabel
```

SELinux is discussed in detail in Chapter 22 “Security Enhanced Linux”.

7. Issue the *exec /sbin/init* command to initiate the relabeling process followed by restarting the system using the default kernel:

```
bash-5.2# exec /sbin/init
[  598.212998] selinux-autorelabel[992]: *** Warning -- SELinux targeted policy relabel is required.
[  598.218903] selinux-autorelabel[992]: *** Relabeling could take a very long time, depending on file
[  598.219431] selinux-autorelabel[992]: *** system size and speed of hard drives.
[  598.247464] selinux-autorelabel[992]: Running: /sbin/fixfiles -T 0  restore
```

Depending on the disk size and speed, it might take a few minutes for the system to complete the relabeling process and return to a fully functional state.

The Linux Kernel

The Linux *kernel* is the core component of the operating system. It manages hardware, enforces security, regulates system access, and handles processes, services, and application workloads. It consists of a monolithic core along with numerous software components called *modules* that work together to provide a stable and controlled platform. Modules primarily function as *device drivers* that control hardware devices—processors, memory, storage, controller cards, and peripheral equipment—and also implement software subsystems for storage, file systems, networking, and virtualization.

If the hardware is the body of the computer, the kernel is its brain and central nervous system. It maintains complete oversight and control of the system.

Some modules are built directly into the kernel (static), while others are loaded dynamically during runtime. Dynamic loading and unloading improves efficiency, reduces memory usage, and minimizes the likelihood of kernel crashes. RHEL 10 ships with kernel version 6.12.0 for x86_64 Intel/AMD systems, supporting single-core, multi-core, and multi-processor configurations. The system architecture can be verified using the **uname -m** command.

The kernel installed during the installation is generally adequate for most needs; however, kernel changes may be required when adding or removing functionality. Examples include installing new hardware, updating the kernel package, or changing system components that depend on kernel support. Removing unnecessary features can also reduce the kernel's footprint, improving performance and lowering memory usage.

Kernel behavior—including modules and system limits—is influenced by a set of tunable parameters. Some applications and database platforms require specific kernel parameters to be adjusted for proper installation and performance.

RHEL allows you to generate and store several custom kernels with varied configuration and required modules, but only one of them can be active at a time. A different kernel may be loaded by interacting with GRUB2.

Kernel Packages

Like other RHEL software packages, the kernel packages are also distributed as rpm packages. A minimum set of core packages must be present for the kernel to function, and additional packages provide optional capabilities. Table 13-2 lists and describes the core and some add-on kernel packages.

Kernel Package	Description
kernel	Contains no files, but ensures other kernel packages are accurately installed
kernel-core	Includes essential modules to provide core functionality
kernel-devel	Includes support for building kernel modules for external products
kernel-headers	Includes files to support the interface between the kernel and userspace libraries and programs
kernel-modules	Contains modules for common hardware devices
kernel-modules-core	Contains modules for core hardware devices
kernel-modules-extra	Contains modules for not-so-common hardware devices
kernel-tools	Includes tools to manipulate the kernel
kernel-tools-libs	Includes the libraries to support the kernel tools

Table 13-2 Kernel Packages

Moreover, packages containing RHEL 10 source code are also available for those who wish to customize or recompile the kernel for their precise needs.

Currently, the following kernel packages are installed on *server1*:

```
[user1@server1 ~]$ rpm -qa |grep ^kernel
kernel-tools-libs-6.12.0-55.9.1.el10_0.x86_64
kernel-modules-core-6.12.0-55.9.1.el10_0.x86_64
kernel-core-6.12.0-55.9.1.el10_0.x86_64
kernel-modules-6.12.0-55.9.1.el10_0.x86_64
kernel-modules-extra-6.12.0-55.9.1.el10_0.x86_64
kernel-tools-6.12.0-55.9.1.el10_0.x86_64
kernel-6.12.0-55.9.1.el10_0.x86_64
```

The output indicates that seven kernel-related packages were installed during the OS installation.

Analyzing Kernel Version

Determining the running kernel version is often required to validate compatibility with certain applications or hardware. The **uname -r** command displays the current kernel version:

```
[user1@server1 ~]$ uname -r
6.12.0-55.9.1.el10_0.x86_64
```

The output shows the running kernel version. An anatomy of the version is illustrated in Figure 13-4 and explained subsequently.

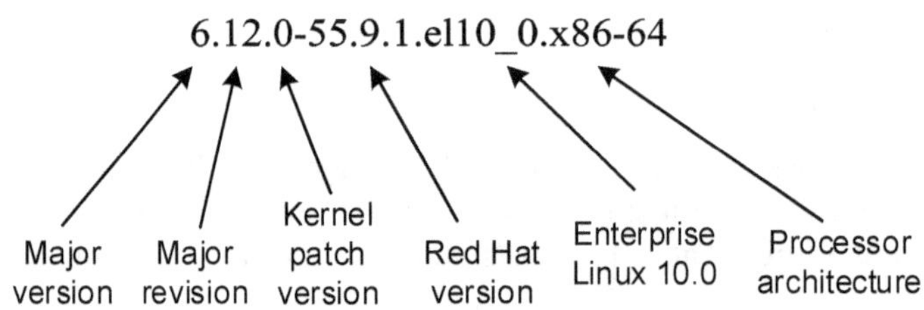

Figure 13-4 Anatomy of a Kernel Version

From left to right:

- ✓ (6) major kernel version. It changes when significant alterations, enhancements, and updates to the previous major version are made.
- ✓ (12) major revision of the 6th major version
- ✓ (0) represents patched version of 6.12 with minor bug and security hole fixes, minor enhancements, and so on.
- ✓ (55.9.1) Red Hat customized version of 6.12.0
- ✓ (el10_0) Enterprise Linux this kernel is built for
- ✓ (x86_64) hardware architecture this kernel is built for

A further analysis designates that 6.12.0 holds the general Linux kernel version information, the numbers and letters (55.9.1.el10_0) represent the Red Hat specific information, and x86_64 identifies the hardware architecture type.

Understanding Kernel Directory Structure

Kernel and its support files are stored across several locations in the directory hierarchy, of which three locations—*/boot*, */proc*, and */usr/lib/modules*—are noteworthy.

The /boot Location

/boot is a file system that is created during installation. It houses the Linux kernel, GRUB2 configuration, and other kernel and boot support files. A directory listing of this file system shows files for both the active kernel and the rescue kernel:

```
[user1@server1 ~]$ ls -l /boot
total 278796
-rw-r--r--. 1 root root    249779 Mar 24  2025 config-6.12.0-55.9.1.el10_0.x86_6
4
drwxr-xr-x. 3 root root        17 Oct 27 10:40 efi
drwx------. 5 root root        97 Dec  4 08:51 grub2
-rw-------. 1 root root 162323564 Oct 27 10:57 initramfs-0-rescue-cde21919216441
f8ab5a8ac30cdc4e38.img
-rw-------. 1 root root  33527332 Oct 27 11:05 initramfs-6.12.0-55.9.1.el10_0.x8
6_64.img
-rw-------. 1 root root  48433152 Nov 30 22:33 initramfs-6.12.0-55.9.1.el10_0.x8
6_64kdump.img
drwxr-xr-x. 3 root root        21 Oct 27 10:49 loader
-rw-r--r--. 1 root root    275084 Oct 27 10:57 symvers-6.12.0-55.9.1.el10_0.x86_
64.xz
-rw-r--r--. 1 root root   8932873 Mar 24  2025 System.map-6.12.0-55.9.1.el10_0.x
86_64
-rwxr-xr-x. 1 root root  15865976 Oct 27 10:53 vmlinuz-0-rescue-cde21919216441f8
ab5a8ac30cdc4e38
-rwxr-xr-x. 1 root root  15865976 Mar 24  2025 vmlinuz-6.12.0-55.9.1.el10_0.x86_
64
```

Key files in this directory are:

- **vmlinuz-6*:** compressed kernel executable
- **config-6*:** kernel build configuration
- **initramfs-6*:** initial RAM file system used for early boot
- **symvers-6*:** symbol versioning information for module compatibility
- **system.map-6*:** memory address mapping for kernel symbols

The files for the rescue version have the string "rescue" embedded in their names, as indicated in the above output.

The *efi* and *grub2* subdirectories under */boot* hold bootloader information specific to firmware type used on the system: UEFI or BIOS.

The subdirectory *loader* under */boot* is the storage location for configuration of the running and rescue kernels. The configuration is stored in files under the *entries* subdirectory, as shown below:

```
[user1@server1 ~]$ sudo ls -l /boot/loader/entries/
total 8
-rw-r--r--. 1 root root 498 Oct 27 11:00 cde21919216441f8ab5a8ac30cdc4e38-0-resc
ue.conf
-rw-r--r--. 1 root root 456 Oct 27 11:00 cde21919216441f8ab5a8ac30cdc4e38-6.12.(
-55.9.1.el10_0.x86_64.conf
```

The files are named using the machine id of the system as stored in the */etc/machine-id* file and the kernel version they are associated with. The content of the kernel file is presented below:

```
[user1@server1 ~]$ sudo cat /boot/loader/entries/cde21919216441f8ab5a8ac30cdc4e3
8-6.12.0-55.9.1.el10_0.x86_64.conf
title Red Hat Enterprise Linux (6.12.0-55.9.1.el10_0.x86_64) 10.0 (Coughlan)
version 6.12.0-55.9.1.el10_0.x86_64
linux /vmlinuz-6.12.0-55.9.1.el10_0.x86_64
initrd /initramfs-6.12.0-55.9.1.el10_0.x86_64.img $tuned_initrd
options root=/dev/mapper/rhel-root ro crashkernel=2G-64G:256M,64G-:512M resume=U
UID=b1103e6a-18ac-407b-815f-cf03d3096091 rd.lvm.lv=rhel/root rd.lvm.lv=rhel/swap
 rhgb quiet
grub_users $grub_users
grub_arg --unrestricted
grub_class rhel
```

The "title" is displayed on the bootloader screen where the countdown to autoboot a selected kernel entry runs. Other than the kernel version, and the default kernel and boot image filenames, the environment variables "kernelopts" and "tuned_params" supply various values to the booting kernel to control its behavior.

The /proc Location

/proc is a virtual file system. Its contents are generated in memory at system boot, updated dynamically during runtime, and destroyed at system shutdown. It maintains information about the current state of the kernel, which includes hardware configuration and status information about CPU, memory, storage, file systems, swap, processes, network interfaces and connections, routing, etc. This data is kept in tens of thousands of zero-byte files organized in a hierarchy of hundreds of subdirectories. A long directory listing of */proc* is provided below:

```
[user1@server1 ~]$ ls -l /proc/
total 0
dr-xr-xr-x.  9 root            root                             0 Dec  4 08:08 1
dr-xr-xr-x.  9 root            root                             0 Dec  4 08:08 10
dr-xr-xr-x.  9 root            root                             0 Dec  4 08:09 1022
dr-xr-xr-x.  9 gdm             gdm                              0 Dec  4 08:09 1033
dr-xr-xr-x.  9 gdm             gdm                              0 Dec  4 08:09 1036
dr-xr-xr-x.  9 gdm             gdm                              0 Dec  4 09:03 1041
........
```

Numerically named subdirectories (e.g., /proc/1) correspond to running processes, where the directory name matches the process ID (PID). Within each subdirectory are other files and subdirectories containing a plethora of information, such as memory segments for processes and configuration data for system components. You can view the configuration of a particular item using any text-file viewing tool. The following show selections from the *cpuinfo* and *meminfo* files that hold processor and memory information:

```
[user1@server1 ~]$ cat /proc/cpuinfo
processor       : 0
vendor_id       : GenuineIntel
cpu family      : 6
model           : 142
model name      : Intel(R) Core(TM) i7-10510U CPU @ 1.80GHz
stepping        : 12
microcode       : 0xffffffff
cpu MHz         : 2304.004
cache size      : 8192 KB
physical id     : 0
siblings        : 2
core id         : 0
cpu cores       : 2
........
[user1@server1 ~]$ cat /proc/meminfo
MemTotal:        1746220 kB
MemFree:          646944 kB
MemAvailable:    1020072 kB
Buffers:            4240 kB
Cached:           496408 kB
SwapCached:            0 kB
Active:           693336 kB
Inactive:         206692 kB
........
```

The data stored under */proc* is referenced by many system utilities, including *top*, *ps*, *uname*, *free*, *uptime*, and *w* to produce their output.

The /usr/lib/modules Location

This directory holds information about kernel modules. Underneath it are subdirectories specific to the kernels installed on the system. For example, the long listing of */usr/lib/modules* below shows that there is only one kernel installed. The name of the subdirectory corresponds with the installed kernel version.

```
[user1@server1 ~]$ ls -l /usr/lib/modules
total 4
drwxr-xr-x. 7 root root 4096 Oct 27 11:01 6.12.0-55.9.1.el10_0.x86_64
```

And this subdirectory contains:

```
[user1@server1 ~]$ ls -l /usr/lib/modules/6.12.0-55.9.1.el10_0.x86_64/
total 28476
lrwxrwxrwx.  1 root root       44 Mar 24  2025 build -> /usr/src/kernels/6.12.0-
55.9.1.el10_0.x86_64
-rw-r--r--.  1 root root   249779 Mar 24  2025 config
drwxr-xr-x. 12 root root      131 Oct 27 10:42 kernel
-rw-r--r--.  1 root root   893620 Oct 27 11:01 modules.alias
-rw-r--r--.  1 root root   846315 Oct 27 11:01 modules.alias.bin
........
```

There are several files and a few subdirectories here; they hold module-specific information for the kernel version.

One of the key subdirectories is */usr/lib/modules/6.12.0-55.6.1.el10_0.x86_64/kernel/drivers*, which stores modules for a variety of hardware and software components in various subdirectories, as shown in the listing below:

```
[user1@server1 ~]$ ls -l /usr/lib/modules/6.12.0-55.9.1.el10_0.x86_64/kernel/dri
vers/
total 68
drwxr-xr-x.  3 root root   18 Oct 27 10:42 accel
drwxr-xr-x.  3 root root   21 Oct 27 10:42 accessibility
drwxr-xr-x.  5 root root 4096 Oct 27 10:42 acpi
drwxr-xr-x.  2 root root  169 Oct 27 10:42 ata
........
```

Additional modules may be installed on the system to support more components.

Installing the Kernel

Installing kernel packages requires extra care because it could leave your system in an unbootable or undesirable state. It is advisable to have the bootable medium handy prior to starting the kernel install process. By default, the *dnf* command adds a new kernel to the system, leaving the existing kernel(s) intact. It does not replace or overwrite any existing kernel files.

A newer kernel version may be required for specific hardware support, security updates, or features needed by an application. Kernel updates address security vulnerabilities, fix bugs, add hardware support, and occasionally introduce new features while maintaining stability.

The *dnf* command is the preferred tool to install a kernel, as it resolves and installs any required dependencies automatically. The *rpm* command may alternatively be used; however, you must install any reported dependencies manually.

The kernel packages for RHEL 10 are available to subscribers for download on Red Hat's Customer Portal. You need a user account to log in.

Exercise 13-3: Download and Install a New Kernel

Perform this exercise on *server1* as *user1* with *sudo* where required. In this exercise, you will:

- Download the latest available kernel packages from the Red Hat Customer Portal
- Install kernel packages
- Ensure that the existing kernel and its configuration remain intact

1. Check the version of the running kernel:

```
[user1@server1 ~]$ uname -r
6.12.0-55.9.1.el10_0.x86_64
```

The output discloses the current active kernel version.

2. List the kernel packages currently installed:

```
[user1@server1 ~]$ rpm -qa |grep ^kernel
kernel-tools-libs-6.12.0-55.9.1.el10_0.x86_64
kernel-modules-core-6.12.0-55.9.1.el10_0.x86_64
kernel-core-6.12.0-55.9.1.el10_0.x86_64
kernel-modules-6.12.0-55.9.1.el10_0.x86_64
kernel-modules-extra-6.12.0-55.9.1.el10_0.x86_64
kernel-tools-6.12.0-55.9.1.el10_0.x86_64
kernel-6.12.0-55.9.1.el10_0.x86_64
```

There are seven kernel packages on the system as reported.

3. Access the Red Hat Customer Portal webpage at *access.redhat.com* and click Log In to sign in to the portal using the credentials you used/created in Chapter 01 "Local Installation" for the developer account:
4. Click Downloads at the top:

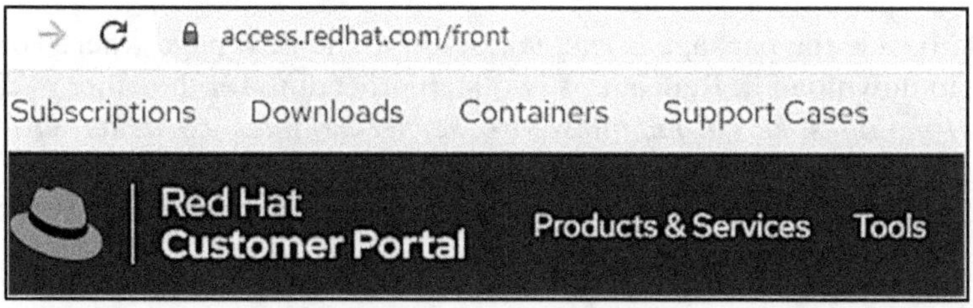

5. Click "Red Hat Enterprise Linux" under "By Category" on the next screen:

6. Scroll down and click "Red Hat Packages Search" under "Software Components".
7. Enter "kernel" in the Search bar and select "Red Hat Enterprise Linux for x86_64" from the dropdown on the right to narrow the list of available packages:

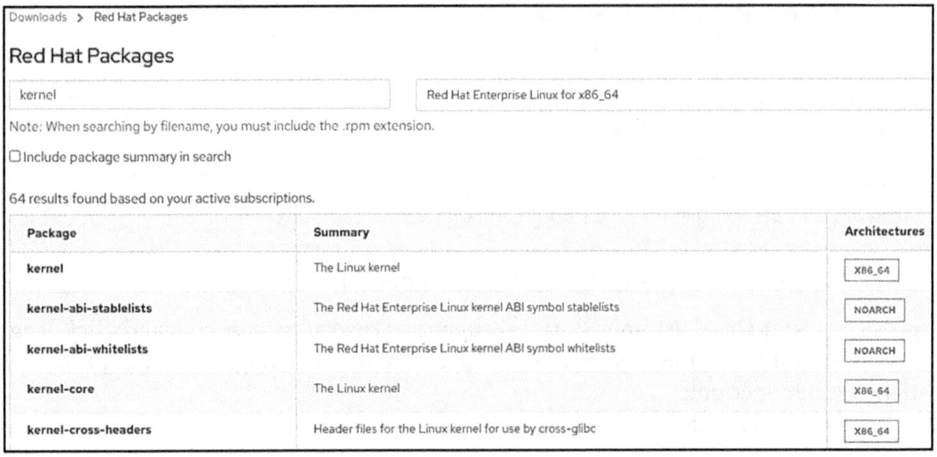

8. Clicking "x86_64" beside the package *kernel* takes you to the next page where you can click "Download now" to download it. Repeat this two-step procedure for the other packages: *kernel-core*, *kernel-modules*, *kernel-modules-core*, *kernel-modules-extra*, *kernel-tools*, and *kernel-tools-libs*.
9. Once downloaded, move the packages to the */tmp* directory using the *mv* command.
10. List the packages after moving them:

```
[user1@server1 ~]$ ls /tmp/kernel*
/tmp/kernel-6.12.0-124.16.1.el10_1.x86_64.rpm
/tmp/kernel-core-6.12.0-124.16.1.el10_1.x86_64.rpm
/tmp/kernel-modules-6.12.0-124.16.1.el10_1.x86_64.rpm
/tmp/kernel-modules-core-6.12.0-124.16.1.el10_1.x86_64.rpm
/tmp/kernel-modules-extra-6.12.0-124.16.1.el10_1.x86_64.rpm
/tmp/kernel-tools-6.12.0-124.16.1.el10_1.x86_64.rpm
/tmp/kernel-tools-libs-6.12.0-124.16.1.el10_1.x86_64.rpm
```

11. Install all the packages at once using the *dnf* command:

```
    [user1@server1 ~]$ sudo dnf install /tmp/kernel* -y
Dependencies resolved.
==========================================================================
 Package                 Arch     Version                 Repository    Size
==========================================================================
Installing:
 kernel                  x86_64   6.12.0-124.16.1.el10_1  @commandline  1.4 M
Upgrading:
 kernel-tools            x86_64   6.12.0-124.16.1.el10_1  @commandline  1.9 M
 kernel-tools-libs       x86_64   6.12.0-124.16.1.el10_1  @commandline  1.4 M
Installing dependencies:
 kernel-core             x86_64   6.12.0-124.16.1.el10_1  @commandline   18 M
 kernel-modules          x86_64   6.12.0-124.16.1.el10_1  @commandline   41 M
 kernel-modules-core     x86_64   6.12.0-124.16.1.el10_1  @commandline   30 M
 kernel-modules-extra    x86_64   6.12.0-124.16.1.el10_1  @commandline  2.8 M

Transaction Summary
==========================================================================
Install  5 Packages
Upgrade  2 Packages

Total size: 96 M
Downloading Packages:
```

```
........
Generating grub configuration file ...
Adding boot menu entry for UEFI Firmware Settings ...
done

  Running scriptlet: kernel-modules-6.12.0-124.16.1.el10_1.x86_64                    9/9
  Running scriptlet: kernel-tools-libs-6.12.0-55.9.1.el10_0.x86_64                   9/9
Installed products updated.

Upgraded:
  kernel-tools-6.12.0-124.16.1.el10_1.x86_64
  kernel-tools-libs-6.12.0-124.16.1.el10_1.x86_64
Installed:
  kernel-6.12.0-124.16.1.el10_1.x86_64
  kernel-core-6.12.0-124.16.1.el10_1.x86_64
  kernel-modules-6.12.0-124.16.1.el10_1.x86_64
  kernel-modules-core-6.12.0-124.16.1.el10_1.x86_64
  kernel-modules-extra-6.12.0-124.16.1.el10_1.x86_64

Complete!
```

12. Confirm the installation:

```
[user1@server1 ~]$ sudo dnf list installed kernel*
Installed Packages
kernel.x86_64                       6.12.0-55.9.1.el10_0           @anaconda
kernel.x86_64                       6.12.0-124.16.1.el10_1         @@commandline
kernel-core.x86_64                  6.12.0-55.9.1.el10_0           @anaconda
kernel-core.x86_64                  6.12.0-124.16.1.el10_1         @@commandline
kernel-modules.x86_64               6.12.0-55.9.1.el10_0           @anaconda
kernel-modules.x86_64               6.12.0-124.16.1.el10_1         @@commandline
kernel-modules-core.x86_64          6.12.0-55.9.1.el10_0           @anaconda
kernel-modules-core.x86_64          6.12.0-124.16.1.el10_1         @@commandline
kernel-modules-extra.x86_64         6.12.0-55.9.1.el10_0           @anaconda
kernel-modules-extra.x86_64         6.12.0-124.16.1.el10_1         @@commandline
kernel-tools.x86_64                 6.12.0-124.16.1.el10_1         @@commandline
kernel-tools-libs.x86_64            6.12.0-124.16.1.el10_1         @@commandline
```

The output indicates packages for both kernel versions.

13. The */boot/grub2/grubenv* file now has the directive "saved_entry" set to the new kernel, which implies that this new kernel will boot on the next system restart:

```
[user1@server1 ~]$ sudo cat /boot/grub2/grubenv
# GRUB Environment Block
# WARNING: Do not edit this file by tools other than grub-editenv!!!
saved_entry=cde21919216441f8ab5a8ac30cdc4e38-6.12.0-124.16.1.el10_1.x86_64
menu_auto_hide=1
boot_success=1
boot_indeterminate=2
```

14. Reboot the system. You will see the new kernel entry in the GRUB2 boot list at the top. The system will autoboot this new default kernel.

```
*Red Hat Enterprise Linux (6.12.0-124.16.1.el10_1.x86_64) 10.0 (Coughlan)
 Red Hat Enterprise Linux (6.12.0-55.9.1.el10_0.x86_64) 10.0 (Coughlan)
 Red Hat Enterprise Linux (0-rescue-cde21919216441f8ab5a8ac30cdc4e38) 10.0 →
```

15. Run the *uname* command after the system has been booted up to confirm the loading of the new kernel:

```
[user1@server1 ~]$ uname -r
6.12.0-124.16.1.el10_1.x86_64
```

The new kernel is active.

16. You can also view the contents of the *version* and *cmdline* files under */proc* to verify the active kernel:

```
[user1@server1 ~]$ cat /proc/version
Linux version 6.12.0-124.16.1.el10_1.x86_64 (mockbuild@b778f2918cbe46deaabe803f1
d54ba8e) (gcc (GCC) 14.3.1 20250617 (Red Hat 14.3.1-2), GNU ld version 2.41-58.e
l10) #1 SMP PREEMPT_DYNAMIC Sat Nov 22 19:23:12 EST 2025
[user1@server1 ~]$
[user1@server1 ~]$ cat /proc/cmdline
BOOT_IMAGE=(hd0,gpt2)/vmlinuz-6.12.0-124.16.1.el10_1.x86_64 root=/dev/mapper/rhe
l-root ro crashkernel=2G-64G:256M,64G-:512M resume=UUID=b1103e6a-18ac-407b-815f-
cf03d3096091 rd.lvm.lv=rhel/root rd.lvm.lv=rhel/swap rhgb quiet
```

This concludes the process of downloading and installing a new kernel on RHEL 10.

Chapter Summary

This chapter provided a detailed examination of the Linux boot process and kernel management. We began by tracing the four key phases of system startup, from firmware initialization to loading the bootloader. This included an analysis of bootloader configuration files and practical administration tasks, such as booting into specific targets and performing a critical exercise to reset a lost root password.

The second half focused on the Linux kernel. We dissected its components, versioning scheme, and the key directories hosting its information. The chapter concluded with a demonstration of downloading and installing a new kernel version alongside the existing one.

Review Questions

1. What is the purpose of the initramfs image?
2. You want to view the parameters passed to the kernel at boot time. Which virtual file would you look at?
3. Where are kernel module files stored on the system?
4. UEFI is replacing BIOS on new computers. True or False?
5. You have changed the timeout value in the *grub* configuration file located in the */etc/default* directory. Which command would you run now to ensure the change takes effect on next system reboots?
6. What is the name of the default bootloader program in RHEL 10?
7. Which file stores the location of the boot partition on BIOS systems?

8. You have lost the *root* user password and you need to reset it. What would you add to the default kernel boot string to break the boot process at an early stage?
9. After resetting the *root* user password, why is creating the */.autorelabel* file necessary before rebooting?
10. The *systemd* command may be used to rebuild a new kernel. True or False?
11. At what stage should you interrupt the boot sequence to boot the system into a non-default target?
12. Which two files would you view to obtain processor and memory information?
13. By default, GRUB2 is stored in the MBR on a BIOS-based system. True or False?
14. You have installed a new version of the kernel. What would you now have to do to make it the default boot kernel?
15. What is the system initialization and service management scheme called?

Answers to Review Questions

1. The initramfs provides a temporary root filesystem containing tools and drivers needed to mount the real root filesystem.
2. The */proc/cmdline* file.
3. In the */usr/lib/modules/$(uname -r)/kernel* directory.
4. True.
5. You must run the *grub2-mkconfig* command.
6. GRUB2.
7. The bootloader location is stored in the Master Boot Record (MBR) on BIOS systems. The *grub.cfg* file contains the kernel location within the */boot* filesystem.
8. You would add init=/sbin/bash or rd.break to the kernel boot string.
9. To trigger a full SELinux security context relabel on the next boot to ensure file contexts (including */etc/shadow*) match SELinux policy.
10. False.
11. At the GRUB2 stage.
12. The *cpuinfo* and *meminfo* files in the */proc* file system.
13. True.
14. Nothing, the new kernel becomes the default boot option automatically.
15. It is called *systemd.*

Do-It-Yourself Challenge Labs

The following labs are designed to reinforce most of the concepts and skills covered in this chapter. You are expected to complete these labs without external assistance. A step-by-step guide is not provided, as the required knowledge has already been presented in the chapter; however, each lab includes hints pointing to the relevant major topic(s).

Use the lab environment created specifically for the end-of-chapter labs. See the sub-section "Lab Environment for End-of-Chapter Labs" in Chapter 01 "Local Installation" for details.

Lab 13-1: Enable Verbose System Boot

As *user1* with *sudo* on *server3*, remove the "quiet" parameter from the GRUB_CMDLINE_LINUX variable in the */etc/default/grub* file, and run *grub2-mkconfig* to apply the update. Reboot the system and observe that the system now displays verbose information during the boot process. (Hint: The GRUB2 Bootloader and Exercise 13-1).

Lab 13-2: Reset the root Password

As *root* on *server4*, reset the *root* password by booting the system into the special shell environment with SELinux temporarily disabled. Log in as *root* and enter the new password after the reboot for validation. (Hint: The GRUB2 Bootloader and Exercise 13-2).

Lab 13-3: Install a New Kernel

As *user1* with *sudo* on *server3*, check the current version of the kernel using the *uname* or *rpm* command. Download a higher version from the Red Hat Customer Portal and install it. Reboot the system and ensure the new kernel is listed and is the default boot option on the bootloader menu. (Hint: The Linux Kernel and Exercise 13-3).

Chapter 14

System Initialization, Message Logging, and System Tuning

By the end of this chapter, you will be able to:

- Explain the Concepts of systemd Units and Targets
- Manage systemd Services and Targets
- Display and Configure Default System Boot Target
- Switch to Non-Default Targets for Testing or Troubleshooting
- Analyze System Log Configuration File
- Examine Log Rotation Settings
- Record Custom Messages in System Log File
- Retrieve, Filter, and Scrutinize Log Messages from systemd Journal
- Configure Persistent Journal Storage to Maintain Log Data Across System Reboots
- Apply and Manage Tuning Profiles to Enhance System Performance

RHCSA Objectives:

20. Boot, reboot, and shut down a system normally
21. Boot systems into different targets manually
28. Start, stop, and check the status of network services
42. Start and stop services and configure services to start automatically at boot
43. Configure systems to boot into a specific target automatically
49. Configure network services to start automatically at boot
26. Locate and interpret system log files and journals
27. Preserve system journals
25. Manage tuning profiles

After the kernel loads, the mantle of system control is passed to systemd, which is the modern system initialization and service management scheme used in RHEL. It can boot the system into one of several predefined targets and you use it to handle operational states of services. It employs the concepts of units and targets for initialization, service administration, and state changes. Your grasp of what unit and target configuration files store is key to understanding how systemd operates.

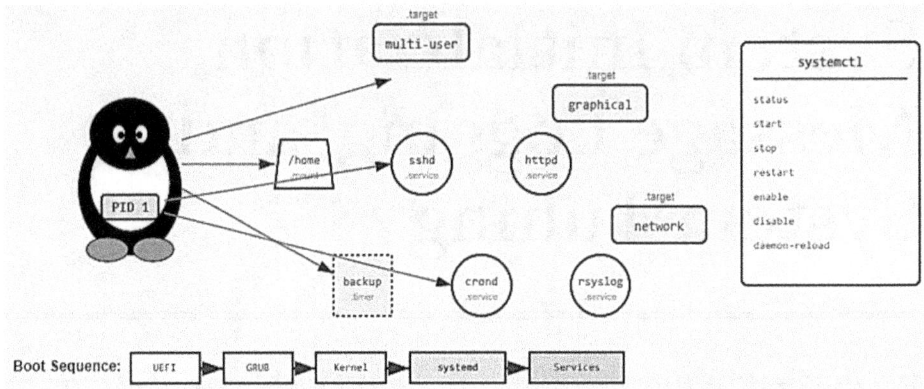

Alerts and messages generated by system services and user activities are forwarded to predefined locations for storage. These alerts and messages include those that are produced during system boot time. You can analyze the log data for debugging or auditing purposes. Log files grow over time and need to be rotated periodically to prevent the file system space from filling up. Configuration files define the default and custom locations to direct the log messages to and configure rotation settings. The system log file records custom messages sent to it. systemd includes a service for viewing and managing system logs in addition to the traditional logging service. This service maintains a log of runtime activities for faster retrieval, and you can configure it to store the information permanently.

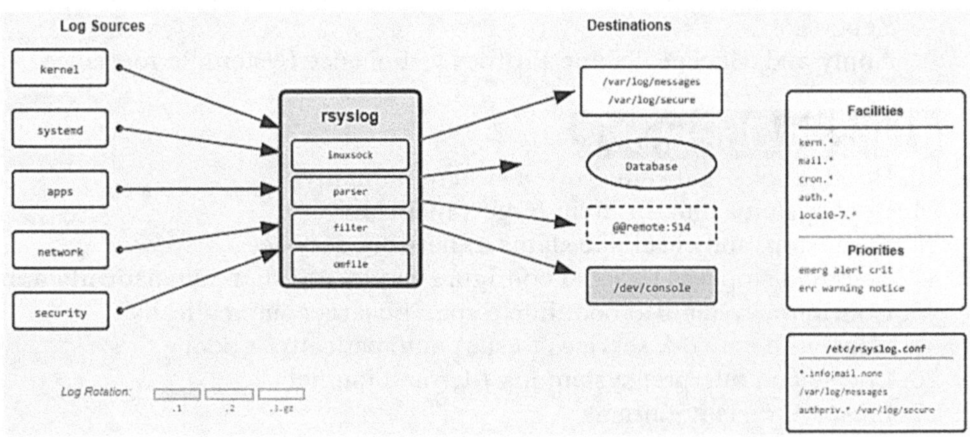

You empty the system tuning service to monitor connected devices and to tweak their parameters to improve performance or conserve power. You can identify and activate a recommended tuning profile for optimal performance and power saving.

System Initialization and Service Management

systemd (*system daemon*) is the system and service manager, responsible for system initialization, service management, and process tracking. It has fast-tracked system initialization and state transitioning by introducing features such as parallel processing of startup scripts, improved handling of service dependencies, and on-demand activation of services. Moreover, it supports snapshotting of system states, tracks processes using control groups, and automatically maintains mount points. *systemd* is started by the kernel as PID 1 and remains active until system shutdown.

systemd spawns several processes during service startup. It places the processes in a private hierarchy composed of *control groups* (or *cgroups*) to organize processes for monitoring and controlling system resources such as processors, memory, network bandwidth, and disk I/O. This includes limiting, isolating, and prioritizing their usage of resources. This way resources can be distributed among users, databases, and applications based on need and priority, resulting in overall improved system performance.

To benefit from parallelism, systemd initiates distinct services concurrently, taking advantage of multiple CPU cores and other computing resources. To that end, systemd creates listening sockets for services configured for socket-based activation early in the boot process. It passes them on to service daemon processes as they attempt to start in parallel. This approach lets systemd handle inter-service order dependencies and allows services to start without any delays. With systemd, dependent daemons need not be running; they only need the correct socket to be available. systemd creates sockets first, starts daemons next, and caches any client requests to daemons that have not yet started in the socket buffer. It fills the pending client requests when the daemons they were awaiting come online.

A socket is a communication endpoint that allows two processes on the same or different systems to exchange data.

systemd maintains sockets to allow client reconnection when services restart to preserve established connections where possible. Likewise, services that use activation based on D-Bus (*Desktop Bus*) are started when a client application attempts to communicate with them for the first time. Additional methods used by systemd for activation are device-based and path-based, with the former starting the service when a specific hardware type such as USB is plugged in, and the latter starting the service when a particular file or directory alters its state.

D-Bus is a message bus system that allows multiple services running on the same system to communicate with one another.

With on-demand activation, systemd defers the startup of services—Bluetooth and printing—until they are actually needed during the boot process or during runtime. Together, parallelization and on-demand activation save time and computing resources, and contribute to expediting the boot process considerably.

Another major benefit of parallelism witnessed at system boot is when systemd uses the autofs service to temporarily mount the configured file systems. During the boot process, the file systems are checked that may result in unnecessary delays. With autofs, the file systems are temporarily mounted on their normal mount points, and as soon as the checks on the file systems are finished, systemd remounts them using their standard devices. Parallelism in file system mounts does not affect the root and virtual file systems.

Units

Units are configuration files that describe a service, socket, mount point, or other system resource managed by *systemd*. The unit files are auto-generated from other configurations, created dynamically from the system state, produced at runtime, or user-developed. Units are in one of several operational states, including active, inactive, in the process of being activated or deactivated, and failed. Units can be enabled or disabled. An enabled unit can be started to an active state; a disabled unit cannot be started.

Units have a name and a type, and they are encoded in files with names in the form unitname.type. Some examples are *tmp.mount*, *sshd.service*, *syslog.socket*, and *umount.target*. Unit files are stored in three directory locations with the following precedence (highest to lowest):

- */etc/systemd/user/*: system administrator customizations
- */run/systemd/system/*: created at runtime and destroyed when no longer needed
- */usr/lib/systemd/system/*: default files distributed with installed packages

Unit files replace the System V init scripts (*/etc/rc.d/init.d/*) used in RHEL 6 and earlier.

systemd includes several unit types, which are described in Table 14-1.

Unit Type	Description
Automount	Offers automount capabilities for on-demand mounting of file systems
Device	Exposes kernel devices in systemd and may be used to implement device-based activation
Mount	Controls when and how to mount or unmount file systems
Path	Activates a service when monitored files or directories are accessed
Scope	Manages externally started processes (e.g., user sessions)
Service	Starts, stops, restarts, or reloads service daemons and the processes they are made up of
Slice	Used for resource allocation via cgroups
Socket	Encapsulates local inter-process communication or network sockets for use by matching service units
Swap	Encapsulates swap partitions
Target	Defines logical grouping of units
Timer	Useful for triggering activation of other units based on timers

Table 14-1 systemd Unit Types

Unit files contain common and specific configuration elements. Common elements fall under the [Unit] and [Install] sections, and comprise the description, documentation location, dependency information, conflict information, and other options that are independent of the type of unit. The unit-specific configuration data is located under the unit type section: [Service] for the service unit type, [Socket] for the socket unit type, and so forth. A sample unit file for *sshd.service* is shown below from the */usr/lib/systemd/system* directory:

```
[user1@server1 ~]$ cat /usr/lib/systemd/system/sshd.service
[Unit]
Description=OpenSSH server daemon
Documentation=man:sshd(8) man:sshd_config(5)
After=network.target sshd-keygen.target
Wants=sshd-keygen.target

[Service]
Type=notify
EnvironmentFile=-/etc/sysconfig/sshd
ExecStart=/usr/sbin/sshd -D $OPTIONS
ExecReload=/bin/kill -HUP $MAINPID
KillMode=process
Restart=on-failure
RestartSec=42s

[Install]
WantedBy=multi-user.target
```

Units can have dependency relationships among themselves based on a sequence (ordering) or a requirement. A sequence outlines one or more actions that need to be taken before or after the activation of a unit (the Before and After directives). A requirement specifies what must already be running (the Requires directive) or not running (the Conflicts directive) in order for the successful launch of a unit. For instance, the *graphical.target* unit file tells us that the system must already be operating in the multi-user mode and not in rescue mode in order for it to boot successfully into the graphical mode. Another option, Wants, may be used instead of Requires in the [Unit] or [Install] section so that the unit is not forced to fail activation if a required unit fails to start. Run **man systemd.unit** for details on systemd unit files.

There are a few other types of dependencies that you may see in other unit configuration files. systemd generally sets and maintains inter-service dependencies automatically; however, this can be done manually if needed.

Targets

Targets are simply logical collections of units. They are a special unit type with the .target file extension. They share the directory locations with other unit files. Targets are used to execute a series of units. This is typically true for booting the system to a desired operational state with all the required services up and running. Some targets inherit services from other targets and add their own to them. systemd includes several predefined targets that are described in Table 14-2.

Target	Description
default	A soft link that points to the default boot target (multi-user.target or graphical.target)
emergency	Runs an emergency shell. The root file system is mounted in read-only mode; other file systems are not mounted. Networking and other services remain disabled. It requires root password for access.
graphical	Multi-user target with full network support and GUI
halt	Shuts down and halts the system
hibernate	Puts the system into hibernation by saving the running state of the system on the hard disk and powering it off. When powered up, the system restores from its saved state rather than booting up.

Target	Description
multi-user	Multi-user target with full network support, but without GUI
poweroff	Shuts down and powers off the system
reboot	Shuts down and reboots the system
rescue	Single-user mode with networking disabled and local file systems mounted. This target is for administrators to perform any critical administrative or recovery function.
shutdown	Shuts down the system

Table 14-2 systemd Targets

Target unit files contain all information under the [Unit] section, and it comprises the description, documentation location, and dependency and conflict information. A sample file for the *graphical.target* target is shown below from the */usr/lib/systemd/system* directory:

```
[user1@server1 ~]$ cat /usr/lib/systemd/system/graphical.target
[Unit]
Description=Graphical Interface
Documentation=man:systemd.special(7)
Requires=multi-user.target
Wants=display-manager.service
Conflicts=rescue.service rescue.target
After=multi-user.target rescue.service rescue.target display-manager.service
AllowIsolate=yes
```

The file specifies dependencies: Requires (mandatory), Wants (optional), Conflicts (mutually exclusive), and After (ordering). It suggests that the system must have already accomplished the rescue.service, rescue.target, multi-user.target, and display-manager.service levels to be declared running in the graphical target. Run **man systemd.target** for details on systemd targets.

The systemctl Command

systemd comes with a set of management tools for querying and controlling operations. The primary tool you will use for interaction in this command suite is *systemctl*. The *systemctl* command performs administrative functions and supports plentiful subcommands and flags. Table 14-3 lists and describes some common operations.

Subcommand	Description
daemon-reload	Re-reads and reloads all unit files and recreates the entire user dependency tree.
enable (disable)	Activates (deactivates) a unit for autostart at system boot
get-default (set-default)	Shows (sets) the default boot target
get-property (set-property)	Returns (sets) the value of a property
is-active	Checks whether a unit is running
is-enabled	Displays whether a unit is set to autostart at system boot
is-failed	Checks whether a unit is in the failed state
isolate	Switches the running state of a system to the specified target
kill	Terminates all processes for a unit

Subcommand	Description
list-dependencies	Lists dependency tree for a unit
list-sockets	Lists units of type socket
list-unit-files	Lists installed unit files
list-units	Lists known units. This is the default behavior when systemctl is executed without any arguments.
mask (unmask)	Prevents (allows) a unit from being started by creating a symbolic link to */dev/null* to avoid potential conflicts. This has stronger impact than the disable subcommand.
reload	Forces a running unit to re-read its configuration file. This action does not change the PID of the running unit.
restart	Stop and start a unit
show	Shows unit properties
start (stop)	Starts (stops) a unit
status	Presents the unit status information

Table 14-3 systemctl Subcommands

You will use a majority of these subcommands with *systemctl* going forward. Refer to the manual pages for the command for more details.

Listing and Viewing Units

The *systemctl* command is used to view and manage all types of units. The following examples demonstrate common operations pertaining to viewing and querying units.

To list all units loaded in memory along with their status and description, run the *systemctl* command without any options or subcommands. A long output is generated. The graphic below shows a few starting and concluding lines followed by a brief explanation.

```
[user1@server1 ~]$ systemctl
  UNIT
  proc-sys-fs-binfmt_misc.automount
  sys-devices-pci0000:00-0000:00:01.1-ata1-host0-target0:0:0-0:0:0:0-bl
  sys-devices-pci0000:00-0000:00:03.0-net-enp0s3.device
  sys-devices-pci0000:00-0000:00:05.0-sound-card0-controlC0.device
  sys-devices-pci0000:00-0000:00:0d.0-ata3-host2-target2:0:0-2:0:0:0-bl
  sys-devices-pci0000:00-0000:00:0d.0-ata3-host2-target2:0:0-2:0:0:0-bl
  sys-devices-pci0000:00-0000:00:0d.0-ata3-host2-target2:0:0-2:0:0:0-bl
  sys-devices-pci0000:00-0000:00:0d.0-ata3-host2-target2:0:0-2:0:0:0-bl
  sys-devices-platform-serial8250-serial8250:0-serial8250:0.0-tty-ttyS0
  sys-devices-platform-serial8250-serial8250:0-serial8250:0.1-tty-ttyS1
  sys-devices-platform-serial8250-serial8250:0-serial8250:0.2-tty-ttyS2
  sys-devices-platform-serial8250-serial8250:0-serial8250:0.3-tty-ttyS3
  sys-devices-virtual-block-dm\x2d0.device

........
Legend: LOAD   → Reflects whether the unit definition was properly load
        ACTIVE → The high-level unit activation state, i.e. generalizat
        SUB    → The low-level unit activation state, values depend on

159 loaded units listed. Pass --all to see loaded but inactive units, t
To show all installed unit files use 'systemctl list-unit-files'.
lines 114-167/167 (END)
```

Here is a breakdown of the output:

- **UNIT:** the unit name and its location in the tree
- **LOAD:** whether the unit was properly loaded (other possibilities are not found, bad setting, error, and masked)
- **ACTIVE:** high-level activation state (other possible states are active, reloading, inactive, failed, activating, and deactivating)
- **SUB:** low-level unit activation state (reports unit-specific information)
- **DESCRIPTION:** brief description of the unit

By default, the *systemctl* command lists only the active units. You can use the --all option to include the inactive units too.

To list all (--all) active and inactive units of type (-t) socket:

```
[user1@server1 ~]$ systemctl -t socket --all
  UNIT                                        LOAD   ACTIVE   SUB       DESCRIPTION
  avahi-daemon.socket                         loaded active   running   Avahi mDNS/DNS-SD Stack Activati
  cockpit-session.socket                      loaded inactive dead      Initiator socket for Cockpit ses
  cockpit-wsinstance-http.socket              loaded inactive dead      Socket for Cockpit Web Service h
  cockpit-wsinstance-https-factory.socket loaded inactive dead      Socket for Cockpit Web Service h
  cockpit.socket                              loaded active   listening Cockpit Web Service Socket
  cups.socket                                 loaded active   running   CUPS Scheduler
  dbus.socket                                 loaded active   running   D-Bus System Message Bus Socket
  dm-event.socket                             loaded active   listening Device-mapper event daemon FIFOs
  iscsid.socket                               loaded active   listening Open-iSCSI iscsid Socket
  iscsiuio.socket                             loaded active   listening Open-iSCSI iscsiuio Socket
........
```

To list all units of type socket (column 2) loaded in memory and the service they activate (column 3), sorted by the listening address (column 1):

```
[user1@server1 ~]$ systemctl list-sockets
LISTEN                               UNIT                          ACTIVATE
@ISCSIADM_ABSTRACT_NAMESPACE         iscsid.socket                 iscsid.s
@ISCSID_UIP_ABSTRACT_NAMESPACE       iscsiuio.socket               iscsiuio
[::]:9090                            cockpit.socket                cockpit.
kobject-uevent 1                     systemd-udevd-kernel.socket   systemd-
vsock::22                            sshd-vsock.socket             -
/dev/rfkill                          systemd-rfkill.socket         systemd-
/run/.heim_org.h5l.kcm-socket        sssd-kcm.socket               sssd-kcm
/run/avahi-daemon/socket             avahi-daemon.socket           avahi-da
........
```

To list all unit files (column 1) installed on the system and their current state (column 2). This will generate a long list of units in the output. The following only shows a selection.

```
[user1@server1 ~]$ systemctl list-unit-files
UNIT FILE                                  STATE          VENDOR PR
proc-sys-fs-binfmt_misc.automount          static         -
-.mount                                    generated      -
boot.mount                                 generated      -
dev-hugepages.mount                        static         -
dev-mqueue.mount                           static         -
mnt.mount                                  generated      -
proc-sys-fs-binfmt_misc.mount              disabled       disabled
run-vmblock\x2dfuse.mount                  disabled       disabled
sys-fs-fuse-connections.mount              static         -
sys-kernel-config.mount                    static         -
sys-kernel-debug.mount                     static         -
sys-kernel-tracing.mount                   static         -
tmp.mount                                  disabled       disabled
........
```

To list all units that failed to start at the last system boot:

```
[user1@server1 ~]$ systemctl --failed
  UNIT LOAD ACTIVE SUB DESCRIPTION
0 loaded units listed.
```

To list the hierarchy of all dependencies (required and wanted units) for the current default target:

```
[user1@server1 ~]$ systemctl list-dependencies
default.target
● ├─accounts-daemon.service
● ├─gdm.service
○ ├─nvmefc-boot-connections.service
● ├─power-profiles-daemon.service
● ├─rtkit-daemon.service
● ├─switcheroo-control.service
○ ├─systemd-update-utmp-runlevel.service
● ├─udisks2.service
● ├─upower.service
● └─multi-user.target
●   ├─atd.service
........
```

To list the hierarchy of all dependencies (required and wanted units) for a specific unit such as *atd.service*:

```
[user1@server1 ~]$ systemctl list-dependencies atd.service
atd.service
● ├─system.slice
● └─sysinit.target
●   ├─dev-hugepages.mount
●   ├─dev-mqueue.mount
●   ├─dracut-shutdown.service
........
```

There are other listing subcommands and additional flags available that can be used to produce a variety of reports.

Managing Service Units

The *systemctl* command offers several subcommands to manage service units, including starting, stopping, restarting, and checking their status. These and other management operations are summarized in Table 12-3 earlier. The following examples demonstrate their use on a service unit called *atd.*

To check the current operational status and other details for the *atd* service:

```
[user1@server1 ~]$ systemctl status atd
● atd.service - Deferred execution scheduler
     Loaded: loaded (/usr/lib/systemd/system/atd.service; enabled; preset: enabled)
     Active: active (running) since Thu 2025-12-04 21:26:49 EST; 1 day 22h ago
 Invocation: 9b6678bab0f3476297b86110fce8cd71
       Docs: man:atd(8)
   Main PID: 948 (atd)
      Tasks: 1 (limit: 10665)
     Memory: 324K (peak: 1.1M)
        CPU: 43ms
     CGroup: /system.slice/atd.service
             └─948 /usr/sbin/atd -f
```

The above output reveals information about the *atd* service. On line 1, it shows the service description (read from the */usr/lib/systemd/system/atd.service* file). Line 2 illustrates the load status, which reveals the current load status of the unit configuration file in memory. Other possibilities for “Loaded” include “error” (if there was a problem loading the file), "not-found" (if no file associated with this unit was found), "bad-setting" (if a key setting was missing), and "masked" (if the unit configuration file is masked). Line 2 also shows us the unit load path and whether it is set (enabled or disabled) for autostart at system boot.

Line 3 exhibits the current activation status and the time the service was started. An activation status designates the current state of the service. Possible states include:

- **Active (running)**: The service is running with one or more processes
- **Active (exited):** Completed a one-time configuration
- **Active (waiting)**: Running but waiting for an event
- **Inactive:** Not running
- **Activating:** In the process of being activated
- **Deactivating**: In the process of being deactivated
- **Failed:** Service crashed or could not be started

The output also depicts the PID of the service process and other information.

To disable the *atd* service from autostarting at the next system reboot:

```
[user1@server1 ~]$ sudo systemctl disable atd
Removed /etc/systemd/system/multi-user.target.wants/atd.service.
```

To re-enable *atd* to autostart at the next system reboot:

```
[user1@server1 ~]$ sudo systemctl enable atd
Created symlink /etc/systemd/system/multi-user.target.wants/atd.service → /usr/lib/systemd/system/
atd.service.
```

To check whether *atd* is set to autostart at the next system reboot:

```
[user1@server1 ~]$ systemctl is-enabled atd
enabled
```

To check whether the *atd* service is running:

```
[user1@server1 ~]$ systemctl is-active atd
active
```

To stop and restart *atd*, run either of the following:

```
[user1@server1 ~]$ sudo systemctl stop atd ; sudo systemctl start atd
[user1@server1 ~]$ sudo systemctl restart atd
```

To show the details of the *atd* service:

```
[user1@server1 ~]$ systemctl show atd
Type=simple
ExitType=main
Restart=no
RestartMode=normal
........
```

To prohibit *atd* from being enabled or disabled:

```
[user1@server1 ~]$ sudo systemctl mask atd
Created symlink /etc/systemd/system/atd.service → /dev/null.
```

Try disabling or enabling *atd* and observe the effect of the previous command:

```
[user1@server1 ~]$ sudo systemctl disable atd
Unit /etc/systemd/system/atd.service is masked, ignoring.
[user1@server1 ~]$ sudo systemctl enable atd
Failed to enable unit: Unit file /etc/systemd/system/atd.service is masked.
```

Reverse the effect of the *mask* subcommand and try disable and enable operations:

```
[user1@server1 ~]$ sudo systemctl unmask atd
Removed /etc/systemd/system/atd.service.
[user1@server1 ~]$
[user1@server1 ~]$ sudo systemctl disable atd
Removed /etc/systemd/system/multi-user.target.wants/atd.service.
[user1@server1 ~]$ sudo systemctl enable atd
Created symlink /etc/systemd/system/multi-user.target.wants/atd.service → /usr/lib/systemd/system/
atd.service.
```

Notice that the *unmask* subcommand has removed the restriction that was placed on the *atd* service.

Managing Target Units

The *systemctl* command is also used to manage the target units. It can be used to view or change the default boot target, switch from one running target into another, and so on. These operations are briefed in Table 12-3 earlier. Consider the following examples.

To view what units of type (-t) target are currently loaded and active:

```
[user1@server1 ~]$ systemctl -t target
  UNIT                     LOAD   ACTIVE SUB    DESCRIPTION
  basic.target             loaded active active Basic System
  cryptsetup.target        loaded active active Local Encrypted Volume
  getty.target             loaded active active Login Prompts
  graphical.target         loaded active active Graphical Interface
  integritysetup.target    loaded active active Local Integrity Protec
  local-fs-pre.target      loaded active active Preparation for Local
  local-fs.target          loaded active active Local File Systems
  multi-user.target        loaded active active Multi-User System
  network-online.target    loaded active active Network is Online
  network-pre.target       loaded active active Preparation for Networ
  network.target           loaded active active Network
  nss-user-lookup.target   loaded active active User and Group Name Lo
  paths.target             loaded active active Path Units
  remote-fs-pre.target     loaded active active Preparation for Remote
  remote-fs.target         loaded active active Remote File Systems
  slices.target            loaded active active Slice Units
  sockets.target           loaded active active Socket Units
........
```

For each target unit, the above output returns the target unit's name, load state, high-level and low-level activation states, and a short description. Add the --all option to the above to see all loaded targets in either active or inactive state.

Viewing and Setting Default Boot Target

The *systemctl* command is used to view the current default boot target and to set it. Use the *get-default* and *set-default* subcommands with *systemctl* to perform these operations.

To check the current default boot target:

```
[user1@server1 ~]$ systemctl get-default
graphical.target
```

EXAM TIP: You may have to modify the default boot target persistently.

To persistently change the current default boot target from graphical.target to multi-user.target:

```
[user1@server1 ~]$ sudo systemctl set-default multi-user
Removed /etc/systemd/system/default.target.
Created symlink /etc/systemd/system/default.target → /usr/lib/systemd/system/multi-user.target.
```

The command simply removes the existing symlink (*default.target*) pointing to the old boot target and replaces it with the new target file path.

Execute **sudo systemctl set-default graphical** to revert the default boot target to graphical.

Switching into Specific Targets

The *systemctl* command can be used to transition the running system from one target state into another. There are a variety of potential targets available to switch to as listed in Table 12-2 earlier; however, only a few of them—graphical, multi-user, reboot, shutdown—are typically used. The rescue and emergency targets are for troubleshooting and system recovery purposes, poweroff and halt are similar to shutdown, and hibernate is suitable for mobile devices. Consider the following examples that demonstrate switching targets.

The current default target on *server1* is graphical. To switch to multi-user, use the *isolate* subcommand with *systemctl*:

```
[user1@server1 ~]$ sudo systemctl isolate multi-user
```

This should stop the graphical service on the system and display the text-based console login screen, as shown below:

```
Red Hat Enterprise Linux 10.0 (Coughlan)
Kernel 6.12.0-124.16.1.el10_1.x86_64 on x86_64

Web console: https://server1.example.com:9090/ or https://192.168.0.110:9090/

server1 login:
```

Type in a username such as *user1* and enter the password to log in:

```
server1 login: user1
Password:
Last login: Fri Dec  5 07:24:10 from 192.168.0.81
user1@server1:~$
```

To return to the graphical target:

```
[user1@server1 ~]$ sudo systemctl isolate graphical
```

The graphical login screen should appear shortly and you should be able to log back in.

To shut down the system and power it off, use the following or simply run the *poweroff* command:

```
[user1@server1 ~]$ sudo systemctl poweroff
```

To shut down and reboot the system, use the following or simply run the *reboot* command:

```
[user1@server1 ~]$ sudo systemctl reboot
```

The *halt*, *poweroff*, and *reboot* commands are mere symbolic links to the *systemctl* command, as the following long listing suggests:

```
[user1@server1 ~]$ ls -l /usr/sbin/halt /usr/sbin/poweroff /usr/sbin/reboot
lrwxrwxrwx. 1 root root 16 Mar  9  2025 /usr/sbin/halt -> ../bin/systemctl
lrwxrwxrwx. 1 root root 16 Mar  9  2025 /usr/sbin/poweroff -> ../bin/systemctl
lrwxrwxrwx. 1 root root 16 Mar  9  2025 /usr/sbin/reboot -> ../bin/systemctl
```

These classic commands are still maintained in RHEL 10 for compatibility and can be used for brevity. It is recommended to use the *systemctl* command instead when switching system states.

The three commands, without any arguments, perform the same action that the *shutdown* command would with the "-H now", "-P now", and "-r now" arguments, respectively. In addition, it also broadcasts a warning message to all logged-in users, blocks new user login attempts, waits for the specified amount of time for users to save their work and log off, stops the services, and eventually shut the system down to the specified target state.

System Logging

System logging (*syslog*) is a fundamental component of any operating system. It captures messages generated by the kernel, services, commands, applications, and system events, and forwards them to log files for security auditing, troubleshooting, and monitoring.

The daemon responsible for system logging is called *rsyslogd* (*rocket-fast system for log processing*). This service daemon is multi-threaded, with support for enhanced filtering, encryption-protected message relaying, and a variety of configuration options. The *rsyslogd* daemon reads its configuration file */etc/rsyslog.conf* and the configuration files located in the */etc/rsyslog.d* directory at startup. The default depository for most system log files is the */var/log* directory. Other services such as audit, Apache, and GNOME desktop manager have subdirectories under */var/log* for storing their respective log files.

The *rsyslog* service is modular, allowing the modules to be dynamically loaded into the service as and when needed. Each module brings a new functionality to the system upon loading.

The *rsyslogd* daemon can be stopped manually using **systemctl stop rsyslog**. Replace stop with start, restart, reload, and status as appropriate.

A PID is assigned to the daemon at startup and a file named */run/rsyslogd.pid* is created to save this PID. The reason for having this file is to prevent multiple instances of this daemon from running.

The Syslog Configuration File

The */etc/rsyslog.conf* is the primary syslog configuration file. The file is organized into three main sections: Global Directives, Modules, and Rules. The default uncommented line entries from the file are shown below and explained thereafter:

```
[user1@server1 ~]$ sudo grep -Ev '^#|^$' /etc/rsyslog.conf
#### GLOBAL DIRECTIVES ####
global(workDirectory="/var/lib/rsyslog")
```

```
#### MODULES ####
module(load="builtin:omfile" Template="RSYSLOG_TraditionalFileFormat")
module(load="imuxsock"    # provides support for local system logging (e.g. via
logger command)
       SysSock.Use="off") # Turn off message reception via local log socket;
                          # local messages are retrieved through imjournal now.
module(load="imjournal"             # provides access to the systemd journal
       UsePid="system" # PID nummber is retrieved as the ID of the process the j
ournal entry originates from
       FileCreateMode="0644" # Set the access permissions for the state file
       StateFile="imjournal.state") # File to store the position in the journal
include(file="/etc/rsyslog.d/*.conf" mode="optional")

#### RULES ####
*.info;mail.none;authpriv.none;cron.none                /var/log/messages
authpriv.*                                              /var/log/secure
mail.*                                                  -/var/log/maillog
cron.*                                                  /var/log/cron
*.emerg                                                 :omusrmsg:*
uucp,news.crit                                          /var/log/spooler
local7.*                                                /var/log/boot.log
```

Global Directives

The Global Directives section contains settings that affect overall rsyslog behavior. The workDirectory directive sets the location for storing auxiliary files such as queue, files, state files, and spool files. This is essential for reliable message delivery and queue persistence during system restarts.

Modules

The Modules section loads input and output modules. The *omfile* is an output module that writes to files using the traditional timestamp format. The *imuxsock* and *imjournal* are input modules. The *imuxsock* module furnishes support for local system logging via the *logger* command, and the *imjournal* module allows access to the systemd journal.

The include directive loads additional configurations from the */etc/rsyslog.d/*.conf* files if there are any.

Rules

The Rules section has multiple two-field line entries. The left field is called *selector*, and the right field is referred to as *action*. The selector field is further divided into two period-separated sub-fields called *facility* (left) and *priority* (right), with the former representing one or more system process categories that generate messages, and the latter identifying the severity associated with the messages. The semicolon (;) character is used as a distinction mark if multiple facility.priority groups are present. The action field determines the destination to send the messages to.

There are numerous supported facilities such as auth (security), authpriv (authentication), cron, daemon, kern, lpr, mail, news, syslog, user, uucp, and local0 through local7. The asterisk (*) character represents all of them.

Table 14-4 describes various priorities in descending criticality order:

Priority	Description
Emerg	System is unusable
Alert	Immediate action is required
Crit	Critical condition
Err	Error condition
Warning	Warning condition
Notice	Normal but significant
Info	Informational
Debug	Debug-level messages
None	No priority
*	Represents all priorities

Table 14-4 Log Message Priorities

When a priority is specified for a facility, *rsyslogd* logs all messages at that level and all higher severity levels.

The line entries from the rules section shown earlier are described below:

- **Line 1:** Logs all messages of info priority and higher to */var/log/messages*, excluding mail, authpriv, and cron facilities
- **Line 2:** Directs all authentication messages to */var/log/secure*
- **Line 3:** Routes all mail messages to */var/log/maillog*
- **Line 4:** Sends cron messages to */var/log/cron*
- **Line 5:** Broadcasts emergency messages to all logged-in users using the omusrmsg (*output module user message*)
- **Line 6:** Logs critical messages from uucp and news facilities to */var/log/spooler*
- **Line 7:** Records boot messages (local7 facility) to */var/log/boot.log*

Configuration Validation

If you modify this configuration file, you need to run the *rsyslogd* command with the -N switch and specify a numeric verbosity level to inspect the file for any syntax or typing issues:

```
[user1@server1 ~]$ sudo rsyslogd -N 1
rsyslogd: version 8.2412.0-1.el10, config validation run (level 1), mast
er config /etc/rsyslog.conf
rsyslogd: End of config validation run. Bye.
```

The validation returns the version of the command, verbosity level used, and the file path. With no issues reported, the *rsyslog* service can be restarted (or reloaded) for the changes to take effect.

Rotating Log Files

RHEL records all system activities in log files that are stored in a central location under the */var/log* directory, as defined in the rsyslog configuration file. A long listing of this directory reveals the files along with subdirectories that may have multiple service-specific logs. Here is a listing from *server1*:

```
[user1@server1 ~]$ ls -l /var/log/
total 5632
drwxr-xr-x. 2 root   root      4096 Nov 22 12:23 anaconda
drwx------. 2 root   root        43 Nov 26 10:53 audit
-rw-------. 1 root   root         0 Dec  5 00:55 boot.log
-rw-------. 1 root   root     26939 Nov 12 10:59 boot.log-20251112
-rw-------. 1 root   root     26749 Nov 16 09:55 boot.log-20251116
-rw-------. 1 root   root     26768 Nov 19 00:14 boot.log-20251119
-rw-------. 1 root   root     27705 Nov 27 00:22 boot.log-20251127
-rw-------. 1 root   root     26180 Dec  1 00:44 boot.log-20251201
-rw-------. 1 root   root    161136 Dec  4 00:14 boot.log-20251204
-rw-------. 1 root   root     83824 Dec  5 00:55 boot.log-20251205
-rw-rw----. 1 root   utmp         0 Dec  1 00:44 btmp
-rw-rw----. 1 root   utmp       384 Nov 25 09:33 btmp-20251201
drwxr-x---. 2 chrony chrony       6 Nov  5  2024 chrony
-rw-------. 1 root   root     57505 Dec  6 20:01 cron
```

The output shows log files for various services. Depending on the usage and the number of events generated and captured, log files may quickly fill up the */var* file system, potentially causing system issues. Also, they may grow to an extent that would make it difficult to load, read, send, or analyze them. To avoid getting into any unwanted situation, it is essential to ensure that they're rotated on a regular basis, and their archives are removed automatically.

To that end, a systemd unit file */usr/lib/systemd/system/logrotate.timer* invokes the *logrotate* service from */usr/lib/systemd/system/logrotate.service* on a daily basis. Here is what this file contains:

```
[user1@server1 ~]$ systemctl cat logrotate.timer
# /usr/lib/systemd/system/logrotate.timer
[Unit]
Description=Daily rotation of log files
Documentation=man:logrotate(8) man:logrotate.conf(5)

[Timer]
OnCalendar=daily
AccuracySec=1h
Persistent=true

[Install]
WantedBy=timers.target
```

The *logrotate* service runs rotations as per the schedule and other parameters defined in the */etc/logrotate.conf* and additional log configuration files located in the */etc/logrotate.d* directory. The following shows the content of */etc/logrotate.conf*:

```
[user1@server1 ~]$ grep -v ^$ /etc/logrotate.conf
# see "man logrotate" for details
# global options do not affect preceding include directives
# rotate log files weekly
weekly
# keep 4 weeks worth of backlogs
rotate 4
# create new (empty) log files after rotating old ones
create
# use date as a suffix of the rotated file
dateext
# uncomment this if you want your log files compressed
#compress
# packages drop log rotation information into this directory
include /etc/logrotate.d
```

The file content includes the default log rotation frequency (weekly). It indicates the period of time (4 weeks) to retain the rotated logs before deleting them. During rotation, the current log file is renamed (typically with a date suffix) and a new empty log file is created matching the original file name. The *rsyslog* service is reloaded to re-open the new log file to ensure continuous logging without interruption. The script presents the option of compressing the rotated files using the *gzip* utility. During the script execution, the *logrotate* command checks for the presence of files in the */etc/logrotate.d* directory and includes them as necessary. The directives defined in the *logrotate.conf* file have a global effect on all log files. You can define custom settings for a specific log file in *logrotate.conf* or create a separate file under */etc/logrotate.d*. Any settings defined in user-defined files overrides the global settings.

Here is the default list of additional log configuration files that reside in the */etc/logrotate.d* directory:

```
[user1@server1 ~]$ ls -l /etc/logrotate.d/
total 60
-rw-r--r--. 1 root root  91 Oct 28  2024 bootlog
-rw-r--r--. 1 root root 130 Jun 22  2020 btmp
-rw-r--r--. 1 root root 160 Oct  8  2024 chrony
-rw-r--r--. 1 root root  88 Apr 24  2024 dnf
-rw-r--r--. 1 root root  93 Jan 14  2025 firewalld
-rw-r--r--. 1 root root 105 Jan 23  2025 insights-client
-rw-r--r--. 1 root root 172 Oct 25  2023 iscsiuiolog
-rw-r--r--. 1 root root 162 Nov 21 19:00 kvm_stat
-rw-r--r--. 1 root root 408 Oct 28  2024 psacct
-rw-r--r--. 1 root root 221 Dec  4  2024 rsyslog
-rw-r--r--. 1 root root 155 Feb 16  2025 samba
-rw-r--r--. 1 root root 307 Feb 11  2025 sssd
-rw-r--r--. 1 root root  88 Mar  5  2025 subscription-manager
-rw-r--r--. 1 root root 100 Feb 12  2025 wpa_supplicant
-rw-r--r--. 1 root root 145 Jul 26  2021 wtmp
```

The above file listing shows files for services—*chrony*, *dnf*, *rsyslog*, *samba, etc.*—all with their own rules defined. The following shows the file content for *btmp* (records of failed user login attempts) that is used to control the rotation behavior for the */var/log/btmp* file:

```
[user1@server1 ~]$ cat /etc/logrotate.d/btmp
# no packages own btmp -- we'll rotate it here
/var/log/btmp {
    missingok
    monthly
    create 0660 root utmp
    rotate 1
}
```

The rotation is once a month. The replacement file will get read/write permission bits for the owner (*root*) and the owning group (*utmp*), and the *rsyslog* service will maintain only one rotated copy of the *btmp* file.

The Boot Log File

Logs generated during system startup display the service startup sequence with a status showing whether the service was started successfully. This information may help in any post-boot troubleshooting if required. Boot logs are stored in the *boot.log* file under */var/log*. Here are a few lines from the beginning of the file:

```
[user1@server1 ~]$ sudo head /var/log/boot.log
------------ Wed Nov 12 10:37:26 EST 2025 ------------
[  OK  ] Mounted sys-kernel-config.mount - Kernel Configuration File System.
[  OK  ] Started plymouth-start.service - Show Plymouth Boot Screen.
[  OK  ] Started systemd-ask-password-plymo…quests to Plymouth Directory Watch
[  OK  ] Reached target paths.target - Path Units.
[  OK  ] Stopped systemd-vconsole-setup.service - Virtual Console Setup.
         Stopping systemd-vconsole-setup.service - Virtual Console Setup...
         Starting systemd-vconsole-setup.service - Virtual Console Setup...
[  OK  ] Stopped systemd-vconsole-setup.service - Virtual Console Setup.
         Starting systemd-vconsole-setup.service - Virtual Console Setup...
```

OK or FAILED within the square brackets indicates whether or not a service was started.

The System Log File

The default location for storing most system activities, as defined in the *rsyslog.conf* file, is the */var/log/messages* file. This file saves log information in plain text format and may be viewed with any file display utility, such as *cat*, *more*, *pg*, *less*, *head*, or *tail*. This file may be observed in real time using the *tail* command with the -f switch. The *messages* file captures the date and time of the activity, hostname of the system, name and PID of the service, and a short description of the event being logged.

> **EXAM TIP:** It is helpful to "tail" the messages file when starting or restarting a system service or during testing to identify any issues encountered.

The following illustrates some recent entries from this file:

```
[user1@server1 ~]$ sudo tail /var/log/messages
Dec  6 20:01:58 server1 systemd[1]: Started fprintd.service - Fingerprint Authentic
Dec  6 20:02:08 server1 systemd-logind[836]: New session 4 of user user1.
Dec  6 20:02:08 server1 systemd[1]: Started session-4.scope - Session 4 of User use
Dec  6 20:02:08 server1 systemd[1]: Starting systemd-hostnamed.service - Hostname S
Dec  6 20:02:08 server1 systemd[1]: Started systemd-hostnamed.service - Hostname Se
Dec  6 20:02:28 server1 systemd[1]: fprintd.service: Deactivated successfully.
Dec  6 20:02:38 server1 systemd[1]: systemd-hostnamed.service: Deactivated successf
Dec  6 20:07:49 server1 systemd[1]: Starting packagekit.service - PackageKit Daemon
Dec  6 20:08:30 server1 packagekitd[9058]: g_path_get_basename: assertion 'file_nam
d
Dec  6 20:08:30 server1 systemd[1]: Started packagekit.service - PackageKit Daemon.
```

Each line entry represents the detail for a single event.

Logging Custom Messages

Many times, it is worthwhile to add a manual note to the system log file to mark the start or end of an activity for future reference. This is especially important when you run a script to carry out certain tasks and you want to record the status or add comments at various stages throughout its execution. This is also beneficial in debugging the startup of an application to know where exactly it is failing.

The Modules section in the *rsyslog.conf* file provides the support via the imuxsock module to record custom messages to the *messages* file using the *logger* command. This command can be run by normal users or the *root* user. The following example shows how to add a note indicating the calling user has rebooted the system:

```
[user1@server1 ~]$ logger -i "System rebooted by $USER"
```

tail the last line from the *messages* file and you will observe the message recorded along with the timestamp, hostname, and PID:

```
[user1@server1 ~]$ sudo tail -1 /var/log/messages
Dec  6 20:13:29 server1 user1[9156]: System rebooted by user1
```

You may add the -p option and specify a priority level either as a numerical value or in the facility.priority format. The default priority at which the events are recorded is user.notice. See the manual pages for the *logger* command for more details.

The systemd Journal

In addition to the *rsyslog* service, RHEL offers a systemd-based logging service for the collection and storage of logging data. This service is implemented via the *systemd-journald* daemon. The function of this service is to gather, store, and display logging events from a variety of sources such as the kernel, *rsyslog* and other services, initial RAM file system, and alerts generated during the early boot stage. It stores these messages in files called *journals* that are located in the */run/log/journal* directory. These files are structured and indexed for faster, easier searches, and may be viewed and managed using the *journalctl* command. As you know, */run* is a virtual file system that is created in memory at system boot, maintained during system runtime, and destroyed at shutdown. Therefore, the data stored therein is non-persistent, but you can enable persistent storage for the logs if desired.

RHEL runs both *rsyslogd* and *systemd-journald* concurrently. In fact, the data gathered by *systemd-journald* may be forwarded to *rsyslogd* for further processing and for persistent storage in text log files.

The main configuration file for this service is */etc/systemd/journald.conf*, which contains several default settings that affect the overall functionality of the service. These settings may be modified as required.

Retrieving and Viewing Messages

RHEL provides the *journalctl* command to retrieve messages from the journal for viewing in a variety of ways using different options. One common usage is to run the command without any options to see all available messages. The following shows a few initial entries from the journal:

```
[user1@server1 ~]$ sudo journalctl
Dec 04 21:26:21 server1.example.com kernel: Linux version 6.12.0-124.16.1.el10_1.x86_64 (mc
Dec 04 21:26:21 server1.example.com kernel: Command line: BOOT_IMAGE=(hd0,gpt2)/vmlinuz-6.1
Dec 04 21:26:21 server1.example.com kernel: BIOS-provided physical RAM map:
Dec 04 21:26:21 server1.example.com kernel: BIOS-e820: [mem 0x0000000000000000-0x000000000(
Dec 04 21:26:21 server1.example.com kernel: BIOS-e820: [mem 0x000000000009fc00-0x000000000(
Dec 04 21:26:21 server1.example.com kernel: BIOS-e820: [mem 0x00000000000f0000-0x000000000(
Dec 04 21:26:21 server1.example.com kernel: BIOS-e820: [mem 0x0000000000100000-0x000000007:
........
```

Notice that the format of the messages is similar to that of the events logged to the */var/log/messages* file that you saw earlier. Each line begins with a timestamp followed by the system hostname, process name with or without a PID, and the actual message.

Run the *journalctl* command with different options to produce various reports.

To display detailed output for each entry, use the -o verbose option:

```
[user1@server1 ~]$ sudo journalctl -o verbose
Thu 2025-12-04 21:26:21.934882 EST [s=312e3950209540559005b4e04cd7f2f3;i=1;b=a1b9:
    _SOURCE_BOOTTIME_TIMESTAMP=0
    _SOURCE_MONOTONIC_TIMESTAMP=0
    _TRANSPORT=kernel
    PRIORITY=5
    SYSLOG_FACILITY=0
    SYSLOG_IDENTIFIER=kernel
    MESSAGE=Linux version 6.12.0-124.16.1.el10_1.x86_64 (mockbuild@b778f2918cbe46c
    _BOOT_ID=a1b93710b4014dc0886c0f7e6c92861d
    _MACHINE_ID=cde21919216441f8ab5a8ac30cdc4e38
    _HOSTNAME=server1.example.com
    _RUNTIME_SCOPE=initrd
Thu 2025-12-04 21:26:21.934930 EST [s=312e3950209540559005b4e04cd7f2f3;i=2;b=a1b9:
    _SOURCE_BOOTTIME_TIMESTAMP=0
    _SOURCE_MONOTONIC_TIMESTAMP=0
    _TRANSPORT=kernel
    SYSLOG FACILITY=0
  ........
```

To view all events since the last system reboot, use the -b option:

```
[user1@server1 ~]$ sudo journalctl -b
```

You may specify -0 (default, since the last system reboot), -1 (the previous system reboot), -2 (two reboots before), and so on to view messages from previous system reboots.

To view only kernel-generated alerts since the last system reboot:

```
[user1@server1 ~]$ sudo journalctl -kb0
```

To limit the output to view a specific number of entries only (3 in the example below), use the -n option:

```
[user1@server1 ~]$ sudo journalctl -n3
Dec 06 20:24:06 server1.example.com systemd[1]: Finished fwupd-refresh.service - Refr
Dec 06 20:24:11 server1.example.com sudo[9258]:    user1 : TTY=pts/0 ; PWD=/home/user
Dec 06 20:24:11 server1.example.com sudo[9258]: pam unix(sudo:session): session opene
```

To show all alerts generated by a particular service, such as *crond*:

```
[user1@server1 ~]$ sudo journalctl /usr/sbin/crond
Dec 04 21:26:49 server1.example.com crond[949]: (CRON) STARTUP (1.7.0)
Dec 04 21:26:49 server1.example.com crond[949]: (CRON) INFO (Syslog will be used instead o
Dec 04 21:26:49 server1.example.com crond[949]: (CRON) INFO (RANDOM_DELAY will be scaled w
Dec 04 21:26:49 server1.example.com crond[949]: (CRON) INFO (running with inotify support)
Dec 04 22:01:01 server1.example.com CROND[2142]: (root) CMD (run-parts /etc/cron.hourly)
```

To retrieve all messages logged for a certain process, such as the PID associated with the *chronyd* service:

```
[user1@server1 ~]$ sudo journalctl  PID=$(pgrep chronyd)
```

To reveal all messages for a particular system unit, such as sshd.service:

```
[user1@server1 ~]$ sudo journalctl _SYSTEMD_UNIT=sshd.service
```

To get all warning messages that have appeared today, and display them in reverse chronological order:

```
[user1@server1 ~]$ sudo journalctl --since today -p warning -r
```

You can specify the time range in hh:mm:ss format, or yesterday, today, or tomorrow instead.

Similar to the -f (follow) option that is used with the *tail* command for real-time viewing of a log file, you can use the same switch with *journalctl* as well. Press `Ctrl+c` to terminate.

```
[user1@server1 ~]$ sudo journalctl -f
```

Check the manual pages for the *journalctl* command and the *systemd-journald* service for more details.

Preserving Journal Information

By default, journals are stored in the */run/log/journal* directory for the duration of system runtime. This data is transient and it does not survive across reboots. The *journalctl* command examples demonstrated earlier retrieve journal information from this temporary location. The *rsyslogd* daemon, by default, reads the temporary journals and stores messages in the */var/log/messages* file. You can enable a separate storage location for the journal to save all its messages there persistently. The default is under the */var/log/journal* directory. This will make the journal information available for future reference.

The *systemd-journald* service supports four options with the Storage directive in its configuration file *journald.conf* to control how the logging data is handled. These options are described in Table 14-5.

Option	Description
volatile	Stores data in memory only
persistent	Stores data permanently under /var/log/journal and falls back to the volatile (memory-only) option if this directory does not exist or has a permission or other issue. The service creates /var/log/journal in case of its non-existence.
auto	Similar to "persistent" but does not create /var/log/journal if it does not exist. This is the default option.
none	Disables both volatile and persistent storage options. Not recommended.

Table 14-5 Journal Data Storage Options

The default (auto) option appears more suitable as it stores data in both volatile and on-disk storage; however, you need to create the */var/log/journal* directory manually. This option provides two fundamental benefits: faster query responses from in-memory storage and access to historical log data from on-disk storage.

Exercise 14-1: Configure Persistent Storage for Journal Information

Perform this exercise on *server1* as *user1* with *sudo* where required. In this exercise, you will:

- Enable persistent storage for the journals
- Confirm persistent storage

1. Create a subdirectory called *journal* under the */var/log* directory and confirm:

```
[user1@server1 ~]$ sudo mkdir /var/log/journal
[user1@server1 ~]$ ls -ld /var/log/journal/
drwxr-xr-x. 2 root root 6 Dec  6 20:33 /var/log/journal/
```

2. Restart the *systemd-journald* service and confirm:

```
[user1@server1 ~]$ sudo systemctl status systemd-journald
● systemd-journald.service - Journal Service
     Loaded: loaded (/usr/lib/systemd/system/systemd-journald.service; static)
     Active: active (running) since Sat 2025-12-06 20:34:12 EST; 7s ago
 Invocation: 43abbd661d8b4cc9ae7cabed7c990e5a
TriggeredBy: ● systemd-journald-dev-log.socket
             ● systemd-journald.socket
             ○ systemd-journald-audit.socket
       Docs: man:systemd-journald.service(8)
             man:journald.conf(5)
   Main PID: 9360 (systemd-journal)
........
```

3. List the new directory and observe a subdirectory matching the machine ID of the system as defined in the */etc/machine-id* file is created:

```
[user1@server1 ~]$ sudo ls -l /var/log/journal/
total 0
drwxr-sr-x+ 2 root systemd-journal 53 Dec  6 20:46 cde21919216441f8ab5a8ac30cdc4e38
```

Compare the name of the subdirectory with the machine ID stored in the */etc/machine-id* file. They are identical.

The journal files are rotated automatically once a month based on the settings in the *journald.conf* file. Check the manual pages for the configuration file for details and relevant directives.

This concludes the exercise.

System Tuning

RHEL uses a system tuning service called *tuned* to monitor storage, networking, processors, audio, video, and various other connected devices, and adjust their parameters for better performance or power saving based on a chosen profile. There are several predefined tuning profiles for common use cases shipped with RHEL that may be activated either statically or dynamically.

The *tuned* service loads the selected profile at service startup and continues to use it until it is switched to a different profile. This is the static behavior, and it is enabled by default.

The dynamic mode adjusts system settings based on live activity data from monitored components to ensure optimal performance. In most cases, the utilization of system components varies throughout the day. For example, the disk and processor utilization increases during a program startup, and the network connection use goes up during a large file transfer. A surge in a component's activity results in heightened power consumption.

Tuning Profiles

tuned provides several predefined profiles to support a variety of use cases. In addition, you can create custom profiles from nothing or by using one of the existing profiles as a template. In either case, you need to store the custom profile under the */etc/tuned* directory to be recognized by the *tuned* service.

Tuning profiles may be separated into three groups: (1) optimized for better performance, (2) geared towards power consumption, and (3) those that offer a balance between the first two and the maximum performance/power combination. Table 14-6 lists and describes common profiles.

Profile	Description
Optimized for Better Performance	
Desktop	Based on the balanced profile for desktop systems. Offers improved throughput for interactive applications.
Latency-performance	For low-latency requirements
Network-latency	Based on the latency-performance for faster network throughput
Network-throughput	Based on the throughput-performance profile for maximum network throughput
Virtual-guest	Optimized for virtual machines
Virtual-host	Optimized for virtualized hosts
Optimized for Power Saving	
Balanced-battery	Saves maximum power at the cost of performance for battery-operated devices

Profile	Description
Optimized for Better Performance	
Powersave	Saves maximum power at the cost of performance for non-battery-operated devices
Balanced/Maximum	
Balanced	Preferred choice for systems that require a balance between performance and power saving
Throughput-performance	Provides maximum performance and consumes maximum power

Table 14-6 Tuning Profiles

Predefined profiles are located in */usr/lib/tuned/profiles* in subdirectories named after each profile. The following shows a long listing of the directory:

```
[user1@server1 ~]$ ls -l /usr/lib/tuned/profiles/
total 0
drwxr-xr-x. 2 root root 24 Oct 27 10:47 accelerator-performance
drwxr-xr-x. 2 root root 24 Oct 27 10:47 aws
drwxr-xr-x. 2 root root 24 Oct 27 10:47 balanced
drwxr-xr-x. 2 root root 24 Oct 27 10:47 balanced-battery
drwxr-xr-x. 2 root root 24 Oct 27 10:47 desktop
drwxr-xr-x. 2 root root 24 Oct 27 10:47 hpc-compute
drwxr-xr-x. 2 root root 24 Oct 27 10:47 intel-sst
drwxr-xr-x. 2 root root 24 Oct 27 10:47 latency-performance
drwxr-xr-x. 2 root root 24 Oct 27 10:47 network-latency
drwxr-xr-x. 2 root root 24 Oct 27 10:47 network-throughput
drwxr-xr-x. 2 root root 24 Oct 27 10:47 optimize-serial-console
drwxr-xr-x. 2 root root 41 Oct 27 10:47 powersave
drwxr-xr-x. 2 root root 24 Oct 27 10:47 throughput-performance
drwxr-xr-x. 2 root root 24 Oct 27 10:47 virtual-guest
drwxr-xr-x. 2 root root 24 Oct 27 10:47 virtual-host
```

The default active profile on *server1* and *server2* is *balanced.*

The tuned-adm Command

tuned comes with a single profile management command called *tuned-adm*. This tool can list active and available profiles, query current settings, switch between profiles, and disable tuning. This command can also recommend the best profile for the system based on many system attributes. Refer to the manual pages for more details.

The following exercise demonstrates the use of most of the management operations listed above.

Exercise 14-2: Manage Tuning Profiles

Perform this exercise on *server1* as *user1* with *sudo* where required. In this exercise, you will:

- Install and start the *tuned* service and enable it for auto-restart on future reboots
- Display all available profiles and the current active profile
- Switch to one of the available profiles and confirm
- Determine the recommended profile for the system and switch to it
- Deactivate tuning and reactivate it
- Confirm the activation to conclude the exercise.

1. Install the *tuned* package if it is not already installed:

```
[user1@server1 ~]$ sudo dnf install -y tuned
Package tuned-2.25.1-1.el10.noarch is already installed.
Dependencies resolved.
Nothing to do.
Complete!
```

The output shows that the package is already installed.

2. Start the *tuned* service and set it to autostart at reboots:

```
[user1@server1 ~]$ sudo systemctl --now enable tuned
```

3. Confirm the startup:

```
[user1@server1 ~]$ sudo systemctl status tuned
● tuned.service - Dynamic System Tuning Daemon
     Loaded: loaded (/usr/lib/systemd/system/tuned.service; enabled; preset: enabled)
     Active: active (running) since Sat 2025-12-06 20:46:41 EST; 29min ago
 Invocation: 7ca743c57c2b4d6cba2a2caf8165a1d0
       Docs: man:tuned(8)
             man:tuned.conf(5)
             man:tuned-adm(8)
   Main PID: 942 (tuned)
      Tasks: 4 (limit: 10665)
     Memory: 18.6M (peak: 20.1M)
        CPU: 1.275s
     CGroup: /system.slice/tuned.service
             └─942 /usr/bin/python3 -Es /usr/sbin/tuned -l -P
```

4. Display the list of available tuning profiles:

```
[user1@server1 ~]$ sudo tuned-adm list
Available profiles:
- accelerator-performance     - Throughput performance based tuning with
OP states
- aws                         - Optimize for aws ec2 instances
- balanced                    - General non-specialized tuned profile
- balanced-battery            - Balanced profile biased towards power sa\
- desktop                     - Optimize for the desktop use-case
- hpc-compute                 - Optimize for HPC compute workloads
- intel-sst                   - Configure for Intel Speed Select Base Fre
- latency-performance         - Optimize for deterministic performance at
er consumption
- network-latency             - Optimize for deterministic performance at
er consumption, focused on low latency network performance
- network-throughput          - Optimize for streaming network throughput
 on older CPUs or 40G+ networks
- optimize-serial-console     - Optimize for serial console use.
- powersave                   - Optimize for low power consumption
- throughput-performance      - Broadly applicable tuning that provides e
s a variety of common server workloads
- virtual-guest               - Optimize for running inside a virtual gue
- virtual-host                - Optimize for running KVM guests
Current active profile: balanced
```

The output shows several predefined profiles as well as the current active profile.

5. List only the current active profile:

```
[user1@server1 ~]$ sudo tuned-adm active
Current active profile: balanced
```

6. Switch to the *powersave* profile and confirm:

```
[user1@server1 ~]$ sudo tuned-adm profile powersave
[user1@server1 ~]$ sudo tuned-adm active
Current active profile: powersave
```

The active profile is now *powersave.*

7. Determine the recommended profile for *server1* and activate it:

```
[user1@server1 ~]$ sudo tuned-adm recommend
virtual-guest
[user1@server1 ~]$ sudo tuned-adm profile virtual-guest
[user1@server1 ~]$ sudo tuned-adm active
Current active profile: virtual-guest
```

The first instance of the command shows the best recommended profile for *server1* based on its characteristics, the second command activated the recommended profile, and the third instance confirmed the switching.

8. Disable tuning:

```
[user1@server1 ~]$ sudo tuned-adm off
[user1@server1 ~]$ sudo tuned-adm active
No current active profile.
```

The service will not perform any tuning until it is reactivated.

9. Enable tuning and confirm:

```
[user1@server1 ~]$ sudo tuned-adm profile virtual-guest
[user1@server1 ~]$ sudo tuned-adm active
Current active profile: virtual-guest
```

The tuning is re-enabled and the *virtual-guest* profile is in effect. This concludes the exercise.

Chapter Summary

This chapter covered three core system management areas in RHEL. We began with systemd, the central service manager and initialization system, exploring its architecture, unit files, target files, and the systemctl command for controlling services, targets, and the system state.

We then compared the traditional rsyslog service with the systemd journal, detailing their distinct logging mechanisms and configuration files for data capture, storage, and rotation. Finally, we explored the tuned daemon for performance optimization, analyzing preconfigured profiles and demonstrating how to select, activate, and apply a tuning profile tailored to the system's role.

Review Questions

1. What is the PID of the *systemd* process?
2. What is the effect of specifying mail.error in *rsyslog.conf*?
3. What is a target in *systemd*?
4. You need to append a text string "Hello world" to the system log file. What would be the command to achieve this?
5. The *systemd* command may be used to rebuild a new kernel. True or False?
6. Which command is used to manage system services?
7. Which configuration file must be modified to ensure journal log entries are stored persistently?
8. What is the recommended location to store custom log configuration files for *rsyslog*?
9. What would the command *systemctl list-dependencies crond* do?
10. What would the command *systemctl restart rsyslog* do?
11. What are the two common *systemd* targets production RHEL servers are typically configured to run at?
12. What is the difference between *systemctl disable* and *systemctl mask*?
13. By default, log files are rotated automatically every week. True or False?
14. Name the three directory paths where *systemd* unit files are stored.
15. What would you run to identify the recommended tuning profile for the system?
16. What would the command *systemctl get-default* do?
17. *systemd* starts multiple services concurrently during system boot. True or False?
18. What is the name of the boot log file?
19. Which *systemctl* subcommand is executed after a unit configuration file has been modified to apply the changes?
20. Which other logging service complements the *rsyslog* service?
21. You want to view all messages generated during the system boot process. Which log file would you look at?

Answers to Review Questions

1. The PID of the *systemd* process is 1.
2. Logs all mail facility messages at error priority and higher.
3. A target is a collection of units.
4. The command to accomplish the desired result would be *logger -i "Hello world"*.
5. False.
6. The *systemctl* command.
7. The */etc/systemd/journald.conf* file.
8. The recommended location to store custom log configuration files is */etc/rsyslog.d* directory.
9. The command provided will display all dependent units associated with the specified service.
10. The command provided will restart the *rsyslog* service.
11. The two common *systemd* boot targets are multi-user and graphical.
12. Disable prevents autostart but allows manual start. Mask prevents any start by linking to */dev/null*.
13. True.

14. The directory locations are */etc/systemd/system*, */usr/lib/systemd/system*, and */run/systemd/system*.
15. The *tuned-adm recommend* command.
16. The command provided will reveal the current default boot target.
17. True.
18. The *boot.log* file in the */var/log* directory.
19. The *daemon-reload* subcommand.
20. The *systemd-journald* service complements *rsyslog* by providing structured, binary logging with metadata.
21. The */var/log/boot.log* file.

Do-It-Yourself Challenge Labs

The following labs are designed to reinforce most of the concepts and skills covered in this chapter. You are expected to complete these labs without external assistance. A step-by-step guide is not provided, as the required knowledge has already been presented in the chapter; however, each lab includes hints pointing to the relevant major topic(s).

Use the lab environment created specifically for the end-of-chapter labs. See the sub-section "Lab Environment for End-of-Chapter Labs" in Chapter 01 "Local Installation" for details.

Lab 14-1: Modify Default Boot Target

As *user1* with *sudo* on *server3*, change the default boot target from graphical to multi-user, and reboot the system to test the change. After the reboot, verify the system is in multi-user mode using the *systemctl* and *who* commands. Restore the default boot target to graphical, reboot, and confirm the graphical login appears. (Hint: System Initialization and Service Management).

Lab 14-2: Manage System Services

As *user1* with *sudo* on *server3*, examine the status of the *sshd* service. Stop the service and verify it is no longer running. Attempt to connect to *server3* using SSH (e.g., with PuTTY or *ssh*). The connection should fail. Restart the *sshd* service and attempt to connect again; the connection should now succeed. (Hint: System Initialization and Service Management).

Lab 14-3: Record Custom Alerts

As *user1* with *sudo* on *server3*, write the message "This is $LOGNAME adding this marker on $(date)" to the */var/log/messages* file. Ensure that variable and command expansions work correctly. Verify the entry appears in the file. (Hint: System Logging).

Lab 14-4: Apply Tuning Profile

As *user1* with *sudo* on *server3*, identify the current tuning profile. List all available profiles, then show the recommended profile for the system. Apply the "virtual-guest" profile and verify the active profile with *tuned-adm*. (Hint: System Tuning).

Chapter 15

Storage Management

By the end of this chapter, you will be able to:

- Compare and Contrast Partition Tables: Master Boot Record (MBR) vs. GUID Partition Table (GPT)
- Identify Disks and Disk Partitions
- Create and Delete Partitions on MBR and GPT Disks
- Implement Thin Provisioning to Optimize Storage Allocation
- Describe Logical Volume Manager (LVM) and its Core Components
- Perform LVM Administration: Creating, Extending, Reducing, Renaming, and Removing all LVM Components
- Deconstruct LVM Configuration Non-Destructively and Return Disks to their Raw State

RHCSA Objectives:

30. List, create, and delete partitions on MBR and GPT disks
31. Create and remove physical volumes
32. Assign physical volumes to volume groups
33. Create and delete logical volumes
35. Add new partitions and logical volumes, and swap to a system non-destructively (the swap portion is covered in Chapter 16)
39. Extend existing logical volumes (additional coverage is in Chapter 16)

A raw disk is a blank slate. Before you can store data, you must initialize and partition it. You can create a partition on a portion of a disk, on an entire disk, or span it across multiple disks. You access and manage each partition independent of other partitions, and each can contain a file system or swap space. The system stores partition information at special disk locations that it references at boot time. RHEL offers you tools for partition management. Partitions you create with a combination of most of these tools can coexist on a single disk.

Thin provisioning is a powerful feature that guarantees an efficient use of storage space by allocating only what is needed and by storing data at adjacent locations. Many storage management solutions such as those we discuss later in this chapter and in the next incorporate thin provisioning technology in their core configuration.

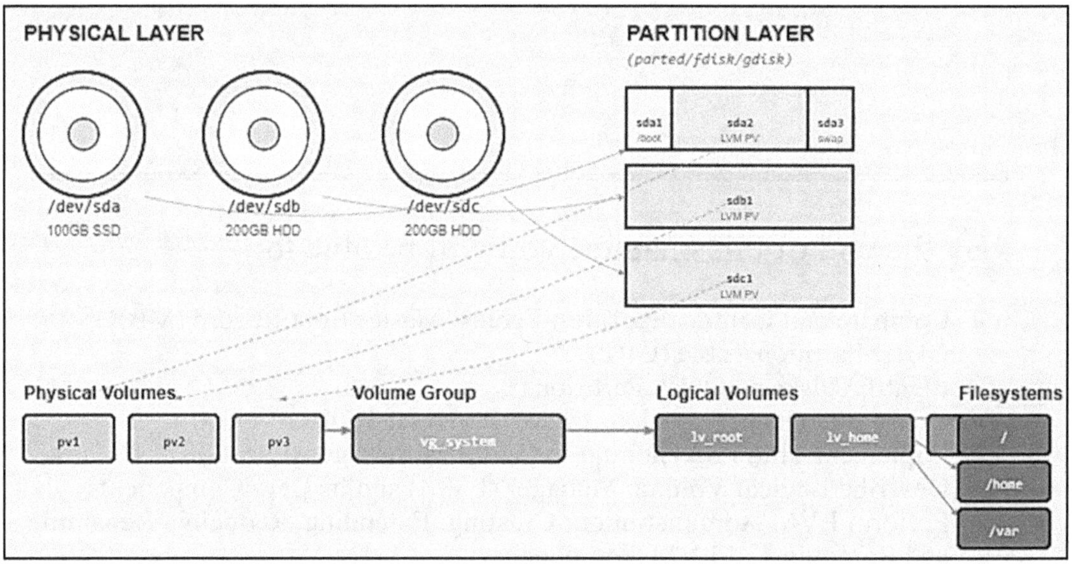

The Logical Volume Manager solution sets up an abstraction layer between the operating system and the storage hardware. It utilizes virtual objects for storage pooling and allocation, and offers a slew of commands to carry out management operations.

Storage Management Overview

Disks in RHEL can be divided into partitions. Partition information is stored in a small disk region that the operating system reads at boot. This region is called the *Master Boot Record* (MBR) on the BIOS-based systems, and *GUID Partition Table* (GPT) on the UEFI-based systems. At boot, the firmware (BIOS or UEFI) scans storage devices, detects MBR/GPT structures, identifies bootable disks, loads the bootloader into memory, executes boot code to read the partition table, locates the */boot* partition, loads the kernel, and transfers control to it. Though designed for different firmware types, both MBR and GPT serve the same purpose: storing partition information and boot code.

Master Boot Record (MBR)

The MBR occupies the first sector of the boot disk. It was the standard partitioning scheme for x86 systems. However, with the arrival of bigger and larger hard drives, a new firmware specification (UEFI) was introduced. MBR is still widely used, but its use is diminishing in favor of UEFI.

MBR supports three partition types: *primary*, *extended*, and *logical*. Only primary and logical partitions store data; extended partitions are containers for logical partitions and cannot store data directly. MBR allows up to four primary partitions numbered 1 through 4. For additional partitions, one of the primary partitions must be deleted and replaced with an extended partition, which can then contain up to 11 logical partitions. Logical partitions are numbered starting at 5. The maximum usable partitions under MBR is 14 (3 primary and 11 logical).

MBR cannot address storage beyond 2TB due to 32-bit addressing and 512-byte sector size limitations. MBR lacks redundancy; corruption renders the system unbootable. If your disk is smaller than 2TB and you don't intend to build more than 14 usable partitions, you can use MBR. For more information on MBR, refer to Chapter 13 "Boot Process, GRUB2, and the Linux Kernel".

GUID Partition Table (GPT)

For disks larger than 2TB, the 64-bit *Globally Unique IDentifier* (GUID) *Partition Table* (GPT) standard was developed and integrated with UEFI firmware. GPT offers significant improvements including support for up to 128 partitions (no extended and logical distinction), disks larger than 2TB, 4KB sector sizes, and redundant partition table storage.

GPT includes a *protective MBR* in the first sector, allowing BIOS systems to boot from GPT disks. UEFI firmware also supports *secure* boot, which requires digitally signed binaries to boot. For more information on UEFI and GPT, refer to Chapter 13 "Boot Process, GRUB2, and the Linux Kernel".

Disk Partitions

You can slice the space on a storage device into distinct partitions. You must take care to avoid overlapping existing partitions or leaving unusable gaps between partitions. On *server2*, the disk allocated during installation is recognized as *sda* (**s** for **S**ATA, SAS, or SCSI device) **d**isk **a**, with the first partition identified as *sda1* and the second partition as *sda2*. Additional disks appear as *sdb*, *sdc*, *sdd*, etc. with partitions numbered similarly.

RHEL offers a command called *lsblk* to list disk and partition information. The following graphic illustrates the current storage status on *server2*:

```
[user1@server2 ~]$ lsblk
NAME            MAJ:MIN RM  SIZE RO TYPE MOUNTPOINTS
sda               8:0    0   20G  0 disk
├─sda1            8:1    0    1M  0 part
├─sda2            8:2    0    1G  0 part /boot
└─sda3            8:3    0   19G  0 part
  ├─rhel-root   253:0    0   17G  0 lvm  /
  └─rhel-swap   253:1    0    2G  0 lvm  [SWAP]
sr0              11:0    1  7.9G  0 rom
```

The output shows a single 20 GB disk (*sda*) containing three partitions: *sda1*, *sda2*, and *sda3*. The first partition is a small 1 MB BIOS boot partition required when using GRUB2 on GPT disks. The second partition is a 1 GB standard partition mounted at */boot*, which contains the kernel, initramfs, and bootloader files. The third partition is a 19 GB LVM physical volume that encapsulates two logical volumes—*rhel-root* (17 GB) and *rhel-swap* (2 GB). Together, these three partitions span the entire disk. The entry *sr0* represents the virtual optical drive with an attached ISO image.

LVM is discussed at length later in this chapter.

Additional tools such as *fdisk* and *parted* can also be used to display disk and partition information. Run *fdisk* with -l and see what it reveals:

```
[user1@server2 ~]$ sudo fdisk -l
Disk /dev/sda: 20 GiB, 21474836480 bytes, 41943040 sectors
Disk model: VBOX HARDDISK
Units: sectors of 1 * 512 = 512 bytes
Sector size (logical/physical): 512 bytes / 512 bytes
I/O size (minimum/optimal): 512 bytes / 512 bytes
Disklabel type: gpt
Disk identifier: 7325135A-5287-4C03-A6B2-A94761D8298B

Device        Start      End  Sectors Size Type
/dev/sda1      2048     4095     2048   1M BIOS boot
/dev/sda2      4096  2101247  2097152   1G Linux extended boot
/dev/sda3   2101248 41940991 39839744  19G Linux LVM
Disk /dev/mapper/rhel-root: 17 GiB, 18249416704 bytes, 35643392 sectors
Units: sectors of 1 * 512 = 512 bytes
Sector size (logical/physical): 512 bytes / 512 bytes
I/O size (minimum/optimal): 512 bytes / 512 bytes


Disk /dev/mapper/rhel-swap: 2 GiB, 2147483648 bytes, 4194304 sectors
Units: sectors of 1 * 512 = 512 bytes
Sector size (logical/physical): 512 bytes / 512 bytes
I/O size (minimum/optimal): 512 bytes / 512 bytes
```

The first block of the output shows the overall properties of the disk */dev/sda*: its size in GB, bytes, and sectors; the disk model reported by the hypervisor (VBOX HARDDISK); the sector size; the I/O size; and the disk label type (GPT) along with its unique disk identifier.

The second block lists the three partitions on the disk. */dev/sda1* is a 1 MB BIOS boot partition required by GRUB2 when using a GPT label on BIOS-based systems; it does not contain a filesystem and is not marked with an asterisk in GPT layouts. */dev/sda2* is a 1 GB Linux extended boot partition, which RHEL uses to hold */boot* when installed on GPT systems (replacing older "Linux filesystem" type codes). */dev/sda3* is a 19 GB Linux LVM partition that serves as the physical volume (PV) for LVM.

The partition table displays each partition's starting and ending sector numbers, its total sector count, size, and partition type.

Storage Management Tools

RHEL provides *parted* and LVM as the primary storage management tools in RHEL 10. Partitions created with different tools can coexist on the same disk.

parted supports both MBR and GPT formats. LVM is a feature-rich logical volume management solution that gives flexibility in storage management.

Thin Provisioning

Thin provisioning technology allows for an economical allocation and utilization of storage space by moving arbitrary data blocks to contiguous locations, which results in eliminating empty blocks. With thin provisioning support in LVM, you create a *thin pool* and allocate thin volumes that appear much larger than the physical capacity of the pool. Volumes consume physical space only as data is written. When consumption reaches a threshold (80%, for instance), you can expand the pool dynamically by adding more physical storage. The volumes will automatically start using the new space right away. The thin provisioning technique helps prevent spending more money upfront.

Adding Storage for Practice

This and the next chapter include several exercises that require additional block storage. As noted in Chapter 01 "Local Installation" under "Lab Environment for Practice", *server2* requires 4 x 400 MB virtual disks for storage exercises. We assume *server2* was created in Lab 1-1 and is available.

Exercise 15-1: Add Required Storage to server2

This exercise will add the required storage to *server2* (*RHEL10-VM2*) using VirtualBox. In this exercise, you will:

- Start VirtualBox and add 4 x 400 MB disks to *server2* in preparation for exercises in this and the next chapter.

1. Start VirtualBox and highlight the *RHEL10-VM2* virtual machine you created in Lab 1-1. See Figure 15-1.

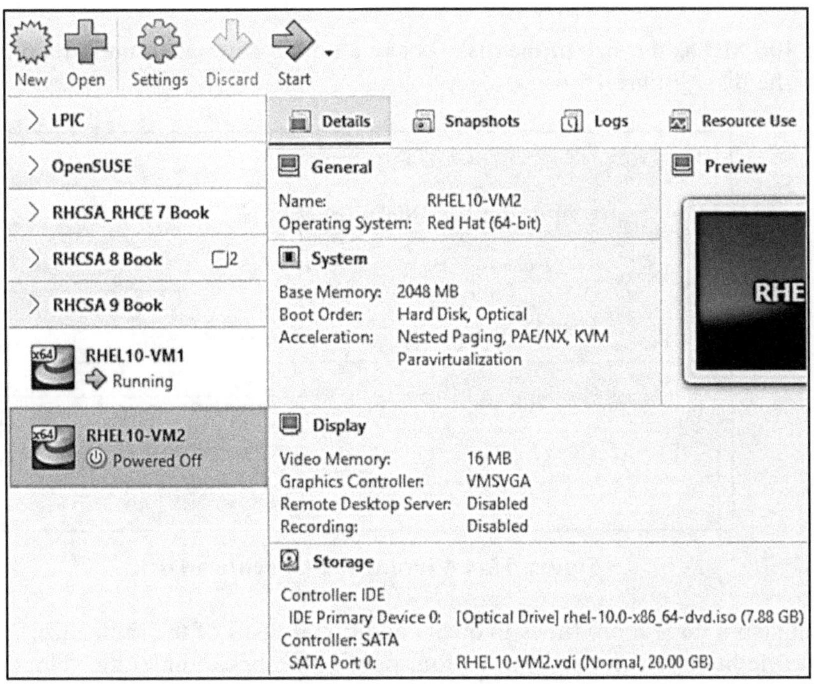

Figure 15-1 VirtualBox | RHEL10-VM2 Selected

2. Click Settings at the top and then Storage on the window that pops up. Click on "Controller: SATA" to select it. Figure 15-2.

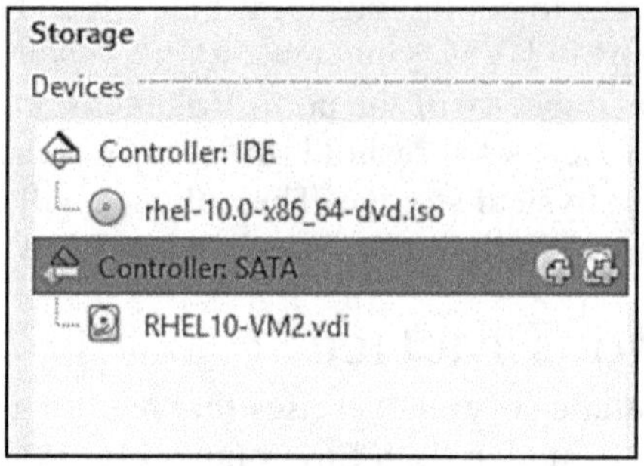

Figure 15-2 VirtualBox | Add Storage

3. Click on the right-side icon next to "Controller: SATA" to add a hard disk and then click Create (on the Medium Selector screen). Figure 15-3.

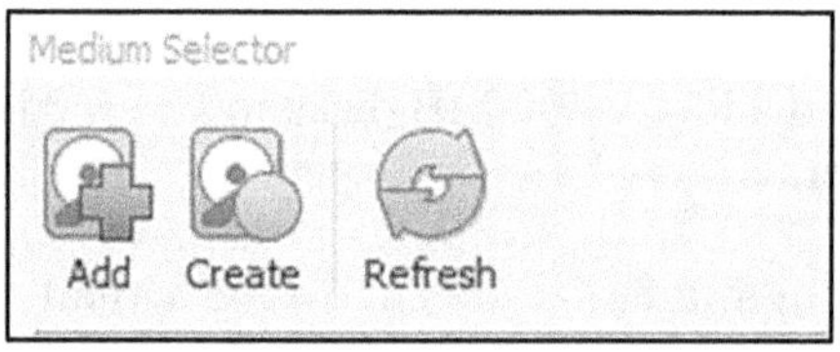

Figure 15-3 VirtualBox | Medium Selector Screen

4. Enter 400 MB as the size of the disk. Leave all other settings to their defaults. Click Finish to create the disk. Figure 15-4.

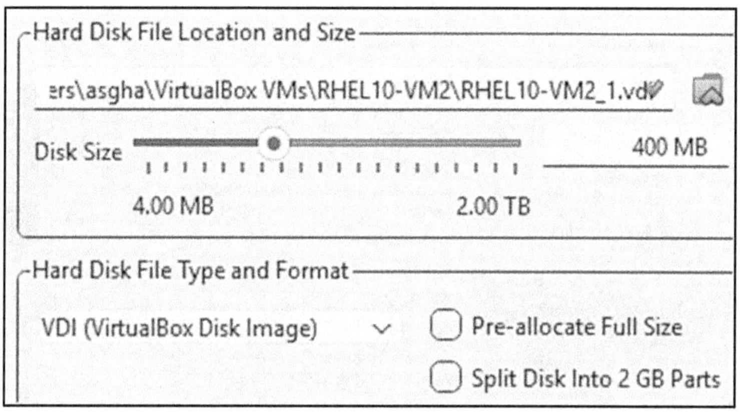

Figure 15-4 VirtualBox | Create a Disk

5. Repeat step 4 three more times to create additional disks of the same size.
6. On the Medium Selector screen, the four new disks appear under the "Not Attached" list of disks. Double-click on each one of them to add to RHEL10-VM2.

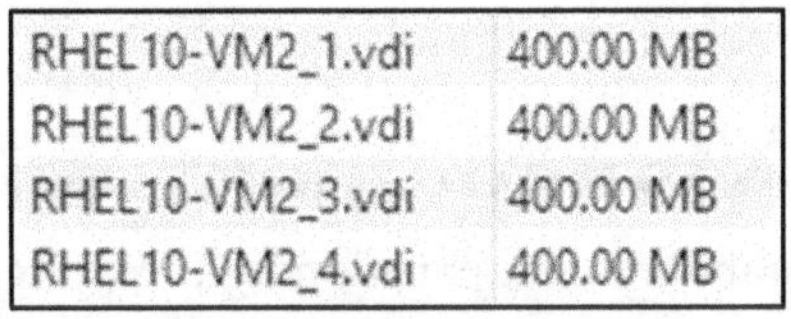

Figure 15-5 VirtualBox | 4 Disks Created

7. The final list of disks should look similar to what is shown in Figure 15-6 after the addition of all four disks (RHEL10-VM2_1 to RHEL10-VM2_4). Disk names may vary.

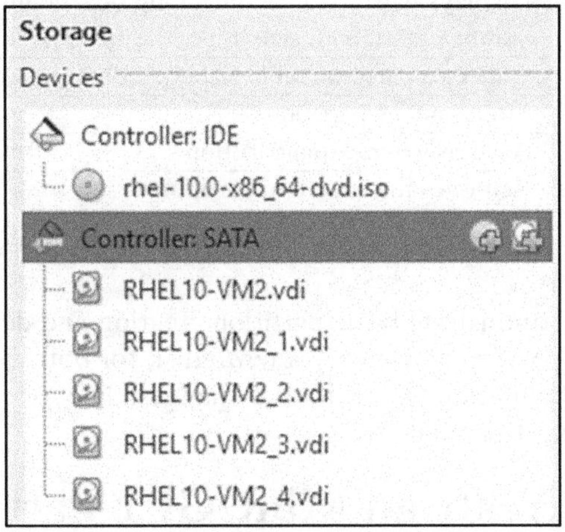

Figure 15-6 VirtualBox | 4 New Disks Added to VM

8. Click OK to return to the main VirtualBox interface.
9. Power on *RHEL10-VM2*.
10. When the server is booted up, log on as *user1* and run the *lsblk* command to verify the new storage:

```
[user1@server2 ~]$ lsblk
NAME              MAJ:MIN RM  SIZE RO TYPE MOUNTPOINTS
sda                 8:0    0   20G  0 disk
├─sda1              8:1    0    1M  0 part
├─sda2              8:2    0    1G  0 part /boot
└─sda3              8:3    0   19G  0 part
  ├─rhel-root     253:0    0   17G  0 lvm  /
  └─rhel-swap     253:1    0    2G  0 lvm  [SWAP]
sdb                 8:16   0  400M  0 disk
sdc                 8:32   0  400M  0 disk
sdd                 8:48   0  400M  0 disk
sde                 8:64   0  400M  0 disk
sr0                11:0    1  7.9G  0 rom  /mnt
```

11. The four new disks added to *server2* are *sdb*, *sdc*, *sdd*, and *sde*.

Ensure *server2* has these four disks before proceeding, as subsequent exercises depend on this configuration.

This concludes the exercise for storage addition to *server2*.

MBR Storage Management with parted

parted (*partition editor*) is a standard disk partitioning tool in RHEL. It can be used interactively or via command-line arguments. It supports both MBR and GPT schemes, and can create up to 128 partitions on a single GPT disk. *parted* provides subcommands for viewing, labeling, adding, naming, and deleting partitions. Table 15-1 describes these subcommands in that sequence.

Subcommand	Description
print	Displays partition table including disk geometry, partition details—number, start, end, size, type, file system—and flags.
mklabel	Creates a partition table (label). Common labels are gpt and msdos.
mkpart	Makes a new partition
name	Assigns a name to a partition
rm	Removes the specified partition

Table 15-1 Common parted Subcommands

Exercises 15-2 and 15-3 demonstrate basic partition creation and deletion using *parted* via command-line arguments. You will use the */dev/sdb* disk for both exercises. After making a partition, use the *print* subcommand to verify the changes. The */proc/partitions* file is updated automatically to reflect partition changes.

Exercise 15-2: Create an MBR/GPT Partition

Perform this exercise on *server2* as *user1* with *sudo* where required. In this exercise, you will:

- Assign partition type "msdos" to */dev/sdb* for using it as an MBR disk
- Create and confirm a 100 MB primary partition on the disk

1. Execute *parted* on */dev/sdb* to view the partition information:

```
[user1@server2 ~]$ sudo parted /dev/sdb print
Error: /dev/sdb: unrecognised disk label
Model: ATA VBOX HARDDISK (scsi)
Disk /dev/sdb: 419MB
Sector size (logical/physical): 512B/512B
Partition Table: unknown
Disk Flags:
```

There is an error on line 1 of the output. The error indicates no partition table exists. The disk must be labeled before it can be partitioned.

2. Create an "msdos" (MBR) partition table using *mklabel.* This operation needs to be performed only once on a disk.

```
[user1@server2 ~]$ sudo parted /dev/sdb mklabel msdos
Information: You may need to update /etc/fstab.

[user1@server2 ~]$
[user1@server2 ~]$ sudo parted /dev/sdb print
Model: ATA VBOX HARDDISK (scsi)
Disk /dev/sdb: 419MB
Sector size (logical/physical): 512B/512B
Partition Table: msdos
Disk Flags:

Number  Start  End  Size  Type  File system  Flags
```

The *print* subcommand confirms the successful application of the label.

For GPT, use "**sudo parted /dev/sdb mklabel gpt**".

3. Create a 100 MB primary partition starting at 1 MB (beginning of the disk) using *mkpart*:

```
[user1@server2 ~]$ sudo parted /dev/sdb mkpart primary 1 101m
```

4. Verify the new partition with *print*:

```
[user1@server2 ~]$ sudo parted /dev/sdb print
Number  Start   End    Size    Type     File system  Flags
 1      1049kB  101MB  99.6MB  primary
```

Partition numbering starts at 1.

5. Confirm the new partition with the *lsblk* command:

```
[user1@server2 ~]$ lsblk /dev/sdb
NAME   MAJ:MIN RM  SIZE RO TYPE MOUNTPOINTS
sdb      8:16   0  400M  0 disk
└─sdb1   8:17   0   95M  0 part
```

The device file for the first partition on the *sdb* disk is *sdb1* as identified on the bottom line. The partition size is 95 MB.

Different tools may report slightly different sizes due to rounding or unit conversion.

6. Check the */proc/partitions* file also:

```
[user1@server2 ~]$ cat /proc/partitions | grep sdb
   8        16     409600 sdb
   8        17      97280 sdb1
```

The virtual file is also updated with the new partition information. This completes the steps for creating and verifying an MBR partition using the *parted* command.

The *parted* command manages both MBR and GPT partitions with nearly identical syntax. The only difference is specifying "msdos" or "gpt" when creating the partition table with *mklabel*. Subsequent operations like *mkpart* and *rm* work identically for both schemes.

Exercise 15-3: Delete an MBR/GPT Partition

Perform this exercise on *server2* as *user1* with *sudo* where required. In this exercise, you will:

- Delete the *sdb1* partition created in Exercise 15-2
- Confirm the deletion

1. Execute *parted* on */dev/sdb* with the *rm* subcommand to remove partition 1:

```
[user1@server2 ~]$ sudo parted /dev/sdb rm 1
```

2. Confirm the partition deletion with *print*:

```
[user1@server2 ~]$ sudo parted /dev/sdb print
Number  Start  End  Size  Type  File system  Flags
```

The partition no longer exists.

3. Check the */proc/partitions* file:

```
[user1@server2 ~]$ cat /proc/partitions | grep sdb
   8       16     409600 sdb
```

The virtual file has the partition entry deleted as well. Run the *lsblk* command for additional verification. The partition is now removed.

The procedure for deleting MBR and GPT partitions is identical using the *parted* command.

EXAM TIP: Proficiency with parted is sufficient for performing partitioning tasks on the exam.

We will recreate partitions for use in LVM later in this chapter and then again in the next chapter to construct file system and swap structures.

Logical Volume Manager (LVM)

Logical Volume Manager (LVM) is widely used for managing block storage in Linux. It provides an abstraction layer between physical storage and file systems, enabling file systems to be resized, span multiple disks, and use arbitrary amounts of disk space. LVM aggregates space from partitions or entire disks called *Physical Volumes* into a logical container called *Volume Group*, which is then divided into logical partitions known as *Logical Volumes*. Additional key benefits of LVM include:

- Online resizing of volume groups and logical volumes
- Online data migration between logical volumes and between physical volumes
- User-defined naming for volume groups and logical volumes

- Mirroring and striping across multiple disks
- Snapshotting of logical volumes

Figure 15-7 depicts the LVM components.

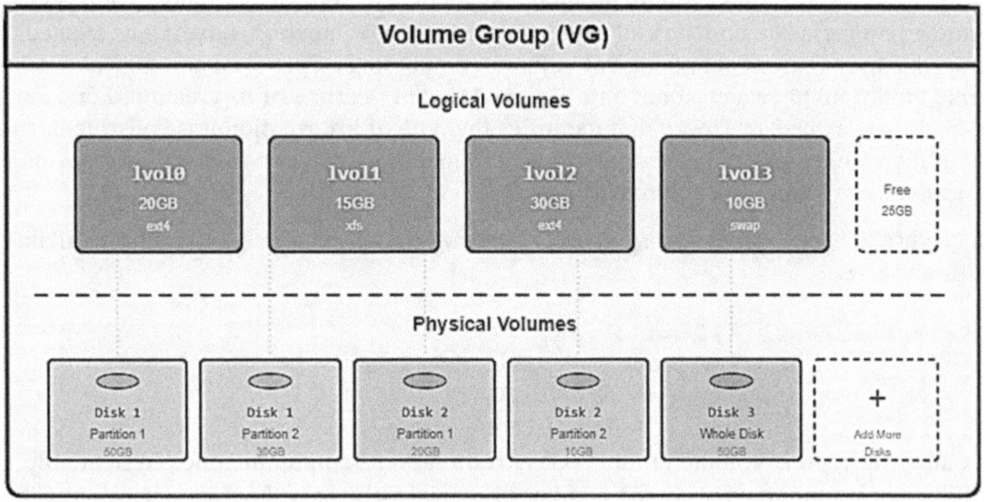

Figure 15-7 LVM Structure

As noted above, the LVM structure consists of three key objects—physical volume, volume group, and logical volume. These objects are subdivided into *Physical Extents* (PEs) and *Logical Extents* (LEs). The LVM components are explained in the following subsections.

Physical Volume

A *Physical Volume* (PV) is created by initializing a block device, such as a partition or an entire disk, for LVM use. This process writes LVM metadata structures to the device. The metadata includes the UUID, size, and pointers to the locations of data. Given the criticality of metadata, LVM stores a copy of it at the end of the physical volume as well. The rest of the device space is available for allocation.

You can use the *pvs* (*physical volume scan* or *summary*) command to scan and list available physical volumes on *server2*:

```
[user1@server2 ~]$ sudo pvs
  PV         VG   Fmt  Attr PSize   PFree
  /dev/sda3  rhel lvm2 a--  <19.00g    0
```

The output shows one physical volume (PV) */dev/sda3* of size 19 GB in *rhel* volume group (VG). Additional information displays the metadata format (Fmt) used, status of the physical volume under the Attr column (a for allocatable), and the amount of free space available on the physical volume (PFree).

Volume Group

A *Volume Group* (VG) is created when at least one physical volume is added to it. The space from all physical volumes in a volume group is aggregated to form one large pool of storage, which is then used to build logical volumes. The physical volumes added to a volume group may be of varying sizes. LVM writes volume group metadata on each physical volume that is added to it. The volume group metadata contains its name, date and time of creation, how it was created, the extent size used, a list of physical and logical volumes, a mapping of physical and logical extents, etc. A volume group can have a custom name assigned to it at the time of its creation. For example, it may be called *vg01*, *vgora*, or *vgweb* that identifies the type of information it is constructed to store. A copy of the volume group metadata is stored and maintained at two distinct locations on each physical volume within the volume group.

You can use the *vgs* (*volume group scan* or *summary*) command to scan and list available volume groups on *server2*:

```
[user1@server2 ~]$ sudo vgs
  VG    #PV #LV #SN Attr    VSize    VFree
  rhel    1   2   0 wz--n- <19.00g      0
```

The output shows one volume group (VG) *rhel* on *server2* containing one physical volume (#PV). Additional information displays the number of logical volumes (#LV) and snapshots (#SN) in the volume group, status of the volume group under the Attr column (w for writeable, z for resizable, and n for normal), size of the volume group (VSize), and the amount of free space available in the volume group (VFree).

Physical Extent

A physical volume is divided into several smaller logical pieces called *Physical Extents* (PE) when it is added to a volume group. An physical extent is the smallest allocatable unit in LVM. The default PE size is 4 MB, but you can specify a different size during VG creation. This implies that a 20 GB physical volume would have approximately 5,000 PEs. Any physical volumes added to this volume group thereafter will use the same PE size.

You can use the *vgdisplay* (*volume group display*) command on *server2* and *grep* for "PE Size" to view the PE size used in the *rhel* volume group:

```
[user1@server2 ~]$ sudo vgdisplay rhel | grep 'PE Size'
  PE Size               4.00 MiB
```

The output reveals the PE size used for the *rhel* VG.

Logical Volume

A volume group consists of a pool of storage taken from one or more physical volumes. This volume group space is used to create *Logical Volumes* (LVs). A logical volume can be created or removed online, expanded or shrunk online, and can use space taken from one or multiple physical volumes inside the volume group.

The default naming convention used for logical volumes is *lvol0, lvol1, lvol2*, and so on; however, you can assign custom names to them. For example, a logical volume can be called *system*, *undo*, or *webdata1* so as to establish the type of information it is constructed to store.

You can use an LVM command called *lvs* (*logical volume scan* or *summary*) to scan and list available logical volumes on *server2*:

```
[user1@server2 ~]$ sudo lvs
  LV   VG   Attr       LSize   Pool Origin
  root rhel -wi-ao---- <17.00g
  swap rhel -wi-ao----   2.00g
```

The output shows two logical volumes *root* and *swap* in *rhel* volume group. Additional information displays the status of the logical volumes under the Attr column (w for writeable, i for inherited allocation policy, a for active, and o for open) and their sizes.

Logical Extent

A logical volume is made up of *Logical Extents* (LE). Logical extents point to physical extents, and they may be random or contiguous. The larger a logical volume is, the more logical extents it will have. Logical extents are a set of physical extents allocated to a logical volume.

The LE size is always the same as the PE size in a volume group. The default LE size is 4 MB, which corresponds to the default PE size of 4 MB.

You can use the *lvdisplay* (*logical volume display*) command on *server2* to view information about the *root* logical volume in the *rhel* volume group.

```
[user1@server2 ~]$ sudo lvdisplay /dev/rhel/root
  --- Logical volume ---
  LV Path                /dev/rhel/root
  LV Name                root
  VG Name                rhel
  LV UUID                csuZvh-CAo8-pc06-rSwy-avrX-f39V-BiFiSF
  LV Write Access        read/write
  LV Creation host, time server2.example.com, 2025-10-27 12:21:48 -0400
  LV Status              available
  # open                 1
  LV Size                <17.00 GiB
  Current LE             4351
  Segments               1
  Allocation             inherit
  Read ahead sectors     auto
  - currently set to     256
  Block device           253:0
```

The output does not disclose the LE size; however, you can convert the LV size in MBs (17,000) and then divide the result by the Current LE count (4,351) to get the LE size (which comes close to 4 MB).

LVM Operations and Commands

LVM provides a comprehensive set of commands for storage management operations including creating and removing physical volumes, volume groups, and logical volumes; extending and reducing volume groups and logical volumes; renaming volume groups and logical volumes; and listing and displaying physical volume, volume group, and logical volume information.

Table 15-2 summarizes the common LVM tasks and the commands employed to accomplish them.

Command	Description
	Create and Remove Operations
pvcreate/pvremove	Initializes/uninitializes a disk or partition for LVM use
vgcreate/vgremove	Creates/removes a volume group
lvcreate/lvremove	Creates/removes a logical volume
	Extend and Reduce Operations
vgextend/vgreduce	Adds/removes a physical volume to/from a volume group
lvextend/lvreduce	Extends/reduces the size of a logical volume
lvresize	Resizes a logical volume. With the -r option, this command calls the fsadm command to resize the underlying file system as well.
	Rename Operations
vgrename	Renames a volume group
lvrename	Renames a logical volume
	List and Display Operations
pvs/pvdisplay	Lists/displays physical volume information
vgs/vgdisplay	Lists/displays volume group information
lvs/lvdisplay	Lists/displays logical volume information

Table 15-2 Common LVM Operations and Commands

All the commands accept the -v switch for verbose output. Refer to the manual pages for the commands for usage and additional details.

As noted earlier, there are four disks available on *server2* for practice. Issue the *lsblk* command to confirm:

```
sdb                    8:16   0   400M   0 disk
sdc                    8:32   0   400M   0 disk
sdd                    8:48   0   400M   0 disk
sde                    8:64   0   400M   0 disk
```

You will use the *sdc* and *sdd* disks for LVM activities in the following exercises.

Exercise 15-4: Create Physical Volume and Volume Group

Perform this exercise on *server2* as *user1* with *sudo* where required. In this exercise, you will:

- Initialize one partition *sdc1* (90 MB) and one disk *sdd* for use in LVM
- Create a volume group called *vgbook* with PE size 16 MB, and add both physical volumes to it
- List and display the volume group and the physical volumes

1. Create a partition of size 90 MB on *sdc* using the *parted* command and confirm. You need to label the disk first, as it is a new disk.

```
[user1@server2 ~]$ sudo parted /dev/sdc mklabel msdos
[user1@server2 ~]$ sudo parted /dev/sdc mkpart primary 1 91m
```

```
[user1@server2 ~]$ sudo parted /dev/sdc print
Model: ATA VBOX HARDDISK (scsi)
Disk /dev/sdc: 419MB
Sector size (logical/physical): 512B/512B
Partition Table: msdos
Disk Flags:

Number  Start   End     Size    Type     File system  Flags
 1      1049kB  91.2MB  90.2MB  primary
```

The *print* subcommand confirms the creation of the partition. It is the first partition on the disk.

2. Initialize the *sdc1* partition and the *sdd* disk using the *pvcreate* command. Note that there is no need to apply a disk label on *sdd* with *parted* as LVM does not require it.

```
[user1@server2 ~]$ sudo pvcreate /dev/sdc1 /dev/sdd -v
  Wiping signatures on new PV /dev/sdc1.
  Wiping signatures on new PV /dev/sdd.
  Set up physical volume for "/dev/sdc1" with 176128 available sectors
  Zeroing start of device /dev/sdc1.
  Writing physical volume data to disk "/dev/sdc1".
  Physical volume "/dev/sdc1" successfully created.
  Set up physical volume for "/dev/sdd" with 819200 available sectors.
  Zeroing start of device /dev/sdd.
  Writing physical volume data to disk "/dev/sdd".
  Physical volume "/dev/sdd" successfully created.
```

The command generated a verbose output. You now have two physical volumes available for use.

3. Create *vgbook* volume group using the *vgcreate* command and add the two physical volumes to it. Use the -s option to specify the PE size in MBs.

```
[user1@server2 ~]$ sudo vgcreate -vs 16 vgbook /dev/sdc1 /dev/sdd
  Wiping signatures on new PV /dev/sdc1.
  Wiping signatures on new PV /dev/sdd.
  Adding physical volume '/dev/sdc1' to volume group 'vgbook'
  Adding physical volume '/dev/sdd' to volume group 'vgbook'
  Creating volume group backup "/etc/lvm/backup/vgbook" (seqno 1).
  Volume group "vgbook" successfully created
```

The above command combines the two options with a single hyphen.

4. List the volume group information:

```
[user1@server2 ~]$ sudo vgs vgbook
  VG     #PV #LV #SN Attr   VSize   VFree
  vgbook   2   0   0 wz--n- 464.00m 464.00m
```

The total capacity available in the *vgbook* volume group is 464 MB.

5. Display detailed information about the volume group and the physical volumes it contains:

```
[user1@server2 ~]$ sudo vgdisplay -v vgbook
  --- Volume group ---
  VG Name               vgbook
  System ID
  Format                lvm2
  Metadata Areas        2
  Metadata Sequence No  1
  VG Access             read/write
  VG Status             resizable
  MAX LV                0
  Cur LV                0
  Open LV               0
  Max PV                0
  Cur PV                2
  Act PV                2
  VG Size               464.00 MiB
  PE Size               16.00 MiB
  Total PE              29
  Alloc PE / Size       0 / 0
  Free  PE / Size       29 / 464.00 MiB
  VG UUID               JsogJm-ut2f-5uEZ-MFI5-0x5u-pm29-cOMuHf

  --- Physical volumes ---
  PV Name               /dev/sdc1
  PV UUID               aVF9ea-sy4h-A75o-LTBj-iz2b-9O3U-Z8MLg3
  PV Status             allocatable
  Total PE / Free PE    5 / 5

  PV Name               /dev/sdd
  PV UUID               rjS4HH-KsE1-s6OQ-g7kv-sY94-6pRe-KJOmBv
  PV Status             allocatable
  Total PE / Free PE    24 / 24
```

The verbose output includes the physical volume attributes as well. There are 29 PEs in the volume group (5 in *sdc1* and 24 in *sdd*), and each PE is 16 MB in size. The collective size of all the physical volumes represents the total size of the volume group, which is 29 x 16 = 464 MB.

6. List the physical volume information:

```
[user1@server2 ~]$ sudo pvs
  PV         VG     Fmt  Attr PSize   PFree
  /dev/sda3  rhel   lvm2 a--  <19.00g       0
  /dev/sdc1  vgbook lvm2 a--   80.00m  80.00m
  /dev/sdd   vgbook lvm2 a--  384.00m 384.00m
```

The output shows the physical volumes in *vgbook*, along with their utilization status.

7. Display detailed information about the physical volumes:

```
[user1@server2 ~]$ sudo pvdisplay /dev/sdc1
  --- Physical volume ---
  PV Name               /dev/sdc1
  VG Name               vgbook
  PV Size               86.00 MiB / not usable 6.00 MiB
  Allocatable           yes
  PE Size               16.00 MiB
  Total PE              5
  Free PE               5
  Allocated PE          0
  PV UUID               aVF9ea-sy4h-A75o-LTBj-iz2b-9O3U-Z8MLg3

[user1@server2 ~]$ sudo pvdisplay /dev/sdd
  --- Physical volume ---
  PV Name               /dev/sdd
  VG Name               vgbook
  PV Size               400.00 MiB / not usable 16.00 MiB
  Allocatable           yes
  PE Size               16.00 MiB
  Total PE              24
  Free PE               24
  Allocated PE          0
  PV UUID               rjS4HH-KsE1-s6OQ-g7kv-sY94-6pRe-KJOmBv
```

Once a partition or disk is initialized and added to a volume group, they are treated identically within the volume group. LVM does not prefer one over the other.

Exercise 15-5: Create Logical Volumes

Perform this exercise on *server2* as *user1* with *sudo* where required In this exercise, you will:

- Create two logical volumes, *lvol0* and *lvbook1*, in the *vgbook* volume group
- Use 200 MB for *lvol0* and 260 MB for *lvbook1* from the available pool of space
- Display the details of the volume group and the logical volumes

1. Create a logical volume with the default name *lvol0* using the *lvcreate* command. Use the -L option to specify the logical volume size, 200 MB. You may use the -v, -vv, or -vvv option with the command for verbosity.

```
[user1@server2 ~]$ sudo lvcreate -vL 200 vgbook
  Rounding up size to full physical extent 208.00 MiB
  Creating logical volume lvol1
  Archiving volume group "vgbook" metadata (seqno 2).
  Activating logical volume vgbook/lvol1.
  activation/volume_list configuration setting not defined: Checking
ags for vgbook/lvol1.
  Creating vgbook-lvol1
  Loading table for vgbook-lvol1 (253:3).
  Resuming vgbook-lvol1 (253:3).
  Wiping known signatures on logical volume vgbook/lvol1.
  Initializing 4.00 KiB of logical volume vgbook/lvol1 with value 0.
  Logical volume "lvol1" created.
  Creating volume group backup "/etc/lvm/backup/vgbook" (seqno 3).
```

The size for the logical volume can be specified in units such as MBs, GBs, TBs, or as a count of LEs; however, MB is the default if no unit is specified (see the previous command). The size of a logical volume is always in multiples of the PE size. For instance, logical volumes created in *vgbook* with the PE size set at 16 MB can be 16 MB, 32 MB, 48 MB, 64 MB, and so on. The output above indicates that the logical volume is 208 MB (16 x 13), and not 200 MB as specified.

2. Create *lvbook1* of size 260 MB (16 x 16) using the *lvcreate* command. Use the -l switch to specify the size in logical extents and -n for the custom name. You may use -v for verbose information.

```
[user1@server2 ~]$ sudo lvcreate -l 16 -n lvbook1 vgbook
  Logical volume "lvbook1" created.
```

3. List the logical volume information:

```
[user1@server2 ~]$ sudo lvs
  LV      VG     Attr       LSize   Pool
  root    rhel   -wi-ao---- <17.00g
  swap    rhel   -wi-ao----   2.00g
  lvbook1 vgbook -wi-a----- 256.00m
  lvol0   vgbook -wi-a----- 208.00m
```

Both logical volumes are listed in the output with their attributes and sizes.

4. Display detailed information about the volume group including the logical volumes:

```
[user1@server2 ~]$ sudo vgdisplay -v vgbook

........
  --- Logical volume ---
  LV Path                /dev/vgbook/lvol0
  LV Name                lvol0
  VG Name                vgbook
  LV UUID                C7AMh8-2yks-sbVw-Yo9I-rGH6-yQxP-5jBAln
  LV Write Access        read/write
  LV Creation host, time server2.example.com, 2025-12-11 09:47:02 -0500
  LV Status              available
  # open                 0
  LV Size                208.00 MiB
  Current LE             13
  Segments               1
  Allocation             inherit
  Read ahead sectors     auto
  - currently set to     256
  Block device           253:2

  --- Logical volume ---
  LV Path                /dev/vgbook/lvbook1
  LV Name                lvbook1
  VG Name                vgbook
  LV UUID                fKmg3Z-iwdc-Zaru-aJK3-ruA3-xOwW-EhXpEN
  LV Write Access        read/write
  LV Creation host, time server2.example.com, 2025-12-11 09:48:04 -0500
  LV Status              available
  # open                 0
  LV Size                256.00 MiB
  Current LE             16
  Segments               2
  Allocation             inherit
  Read ahead sectors     auto
  - currently set to     256
  Block device           253:3
........
```

Alternatively, you can run the following to view only the logical volume details:

```
[user1@server2 ~]$ sudo lvdisplay /dev/vgbook/lvol0
[user1@server2 ~]$ sudo lvdisplay /dev/vgbook/lvbook1
```

Review the attributes of the logical volumes as detailed above.

Exercise 15-6: Extend a Volume Group and a Logical Volume

Perform this exercise on *server2* as *user1* with *sudo* where required. In this exercise, you will:

- Add another partition *sdc2* of size 158 MB to *vgbook* to increase allocatable space in the volume group
- Initialize the new partition prior to adding it to the volume group
- Increase the size of *lvbook1* to 400 MB from 256 MB
- Display basic information for the physical volumes, volume group, and logical volume

1. Create a partition of size 158 MB on *sdc* using the *parted* command. Display the new partition to confirm the partition number and size.

```
[user1@server2 ~]$ sudo parted /dev/sdc mkpart pri 92 250
[user1@server2 ~]$ sudo parted /dev/sdc set 2 lvm on
[user1@server2 ~]$ sudo parted /dev/sdc pr
........
2       92.3MB  250MB   157MB   primary
```

2. Initialize *sdc2* using the *pvcreate* command:

```
[user1@server2 ~]$ sudo pvcreate /dev/sdc2
  Physical volume "/dev/sdc2" successfully created.
```

3. Extend *vgbook* by adding the new physical volume to it:

```
[user1@server2 ~]$ sudo vgextend vgbook /dev/sdc2
  Volume group "vgbook" successfully extended
```

4. List the volume group:

```
[user1@server2 ~]$ sudo vgs
  VG       #PV #LV #SN Attr   VSize    VFree
  rhel       1   2   0 wz--n- <19.00g        0
  vgbook     3   2   0 wz--n- 608.00m 144.00m
```

The output reflects the addition of a third physical volume to *vgbook*. The total capacity of the volume group has now increased to 608 MB with 144 MB free.

5. Extend *lvbook1* to 400 MB by adding 144 MB using the *lvextend* command:

```
[user1@server2 ~]$ sudo lvextend -L +144 /dev/vgbook/lvbook1
  Size of logical volume vgbook/lvbook1 changed from 256.00 MiB (16 extents) to 400.00 MiB (25
extents).
  Logical volume vgbook/lvbook1 successfully resized.
```

EXAM TIP: Make sure the expansion of a logical volume does not affect the file system and the data it contains. More details in Chapter 16.

6. Issue *vgdisplay* on *vgbook* with the -v switch for the updated details:

```
[user1@server2 ~]$ sudo vgdisplay -v vgbook
```

<output truncated>

The output will show information about the volume group and the logical and physical volumes it contains. It will reflect the updates made in this exercise. In fact, each time a volume group or a logical volume is resized, *vgdisplay* will reflect those changes. The above output will display three physical volumes with the combined allocatable space grown to 608 MB. The number of PEs will have increased to 38, with all of them allocated to logical volumes and 0 unused. The Logical Volume sections will display the updated information for the logical volumes. And at the very bottom, the three physical volumes will show with their device names, and total and available PEs in each.

7. View a summary of the physical volumes:

```
[user1@server2 ~]$ sudo pvs
  PV         VG     Fmt  Attr PSize   PFree
  /dev/sda3  rhel   lvm2 a--  <19.00g    0
  /dev/sdc1  vgbook lvm2 a--   80.00m    0
  /dev/sdc2  vgbook lvm2 a--  144.00m    0
  /dev/sdd   vgbook lvm2 a--  384.00m    0
```

8. View a summary of the logical volumes:

```
[user1@server2 ~]$ sudo lvs
  LV      VG     Attr       LSize   Pool
  root    rhel   -wi-ao---- <17.00g
  swap    rhel   -wi-ao----   2.00g
  lvbook1 vgbook -wi-a----- 400.00m
  lvol0   vgbook -wi-a----- 208.00m
```

This brings the exercise to an end.

Exercise 15-7: Rename, Reduce, Extend, and Remove Logical Volumes

Perform this exercise on *server2* as *user1* with *sudo* where required. In this exercise, you will:

- Rename *lvol0* to *lvbook2*
- Decrease the size of *lvbook2* to 50 MB
- Add 32 MB to *lvbook2*

- Remove both logical volumes
- Display the summary for the volume groups, logical volumes, and physical volumes

1. Rename *lvol0* to *lvbook2* using the *lvrename* command and confirm with *lvs*:

```
[user1@server2 ~]$ sudo lvrename vgbook lvol0 lvbook2
  Renamed "lvol0" to "lvbook2" in volume group "vgbook"
[user1@server2 ~]$ sudo lvs
  LV      VG     Attr       LSize   Pool Origin Data%
  root    rhel   -wi-ao---- <17.00g
  swap    rhel   -wi-ao----   2.00g
  lvbook1 vgbook -wi-a----- 400.00m
  lvbook2 vgbook -wi-a----- 208.00m
```

2. Reduce the size of *lvbook2* to 50 MB with the *lvreduce* command. Specify the absolute desired size for the logical volume.

```
[user1@server2 ~]$ sudo lvreduce -L 50 /dev/vgbook/lvbook2
  Rounding size to boundary between physical extents: 64.00 MiB.
  No file system found on /dev/vgbook/lvbook2.
  Size of logical volume vgbook/lvbook2 changed from 208.00 MiB (13 ext
nts) to 64.00 MiB (4 extents).
  Logical volume vgbook/lvbook2 successfully resized.
```

3. Add 32 MB to *lvbook2* with the *lvresize* command:

```
[user1@server2 ~]$ sudo lvresize -L +32 /dev/vgbook/lvbook2
  Size of logical volume vgbook/lvbook2 changed from 64.00 MiB (4 extents) to
 96.00 MiB (6 extents).
  Logical volume vgbook/lvbook2 successfully resized.
```

4. Use the *pvs*, *lvs*, *vgs*, and *vgdisplay* commands to view the updated allocation.
5. Remove both *lvbook1* and *lvbook2* logical volumes using the *lvremove* command. Use the -f option to suppress the "Do you really want to remove active logical volume" message.

```
[user1@server2 ~]$ sudo lvremove /dev/vgbook/lvbook1 -f
  Logical volume "lvbook1" successfully removed
[user1@server2 ~]$ sudo lvremove /dev/vgbook/lvbook2 -f
  Logical volume "lvbook2" successfully removed
```

Removing a logical volume is a destructive task. Ensure that you perform a backup of any data in the target logical volume prior to deleting it. You must unmount the file system or disable swap in the logical volume. See Chapter 16 on how to unmount a file system and disable swap.

6. Execute the *vgdisplay* command and *grep* for "Cur LV" to see the number of logical volumes currently available in *vgbook*. It should show 0, as you have removed both logical volumes.

```
[user1@server2 ~]$ sudo vgdisplay vgbook | grep 'Cur LV'
  Cur LV                0
```

This concludes the exercise.

Exercise 15-8: Reduce and Remove a Volume Group

Perform this exercise on *server2* as *user1* with *sudo* where required. In this exercise, you will:

- Reduce *vgbook* by removing the *sdc2* and *sdd* physical volumes from it
- Remove the volume group
- Confirm the deletion of the volume group and the logical volumes

1. Remove *sdc2* and *sdd* physical volumes from *vgbook* by issuing the *vgreduce* command:

```
[user1@server2 ~]$ sudo vgreduce vgbook /dev/sdc2 /dev/sdd
  Removed "/dev/sdd" from volume group "vgbook"
  Removed "/dev/sdc2" from volume group "vgbook"
```

2. Remove the volume group using the *vgremove* command. This will also remove the last physical volume, *sdc1*, from it.

```
[user1@server2 ~]$ sudo vgremove vgbook
  Volume group "vgbook" successfully removed
```

You can also use the -f option with the *vgremove* command to force the volume group removal even if it contains logical and physical volumes.

Remember to proceed with caution whenever you perform reduce and erase operations.

3. Execute the *vgs* and *lvs* commands for confirmation:

```
[user1@server2 ~]$ sudo vgs
  VG   #PV #LV #SN Attr   VSize   VFree
  rhel   1   2   0 wz--n- <19.00g    0
[user1@server2 ~]$
[user1@server2 ~]$ sudo lvs
  LV   VG   Attr       LSize   Pool Origin
  root rhel -wi-ao---- <17.00g
  swap rhel -wi-ao----   2.00g
```

This concludes the exercise.

Exercise 15-9: Uninitialize Physical Volumes

Perform this exercise on *server2* as *user1* with *sudo* where required. In this exercise, you will:

- Uninitialize all three physical volumes—*sdc1*, *sdc2*, and *sdd*—by deleting the LVM structural information from them
- Confirm the above action
- Remove the partitions from the *sdc* disk
- Verify that all disks used in Exercises 15-6 to 15-10 are now in their original raw state

1. Remove the LVM structures from *sdc1*, *sdc2*, and *sdd* using the *pvremove* command:

```
[user1@server2 ~]$ sudo pvremove /dev/sdc1 /dev/sdc2 /dev/sdd
  Labels on physical volume "/dev/sdc1" successfully wiped.
  Labels on physical volume "/dev/sdc2" successfully wiped.
  Labels on physical volume "/dev/sdd" successfully wiped.
```

2. Confirm the removal using the *pvs* command:

```
[user1@server2 ~]$ sudo pvs
  PV         VG   Fmt  Attr PSize   PFree
  /dev/sda2  rhel lvm2 a--  <19.00g    0
```

The partitions and the disk are now back to their raw state and can be repurposed.

3. Remove the partitions from *sdc* using the *parted* command:

```
[user1@server2 ~]$ sudo parted /dev/sdc rm 1
[user1@server2 ~]$ sudo parted /dev/sdc rm 2
```

4. Verify that all disks used in previous exercises have returned to their original raw state using the *lsblk* command:

```
[user1@server2 ~]$ lsblk
NAME            MAJ:MIN RM  SIZE RO TYPE MOUNTPOINTS
sda               8:0    0   20G  0 disk
├─sda1            8:1    0    1M  0 part
├─sda2            8:2    0    1G  0 part /boot
└─sda3            8:3    0   19G  0 part
  ├─rhel-root   253:0    0   17G  0 lvm  /
  └─rhel-swap   253:1    0    2G  0 lvm  [SWAP]
sdb               8:16   0  400M  0 disk
sdc               8:32   0  400M  0 disk
sdd               8:48   0  400M  0 disk
sr0              11:0    1  7.9G  0 rom  /mnt
```

5. Clear partition and LVM signatures from the *sdc* and *sdd* disks using the *wipefs* command. This is to ensure that you do not see any warning messages the next time you use these disks:

```
[user1@server2 ~]$ sudo wipefs -a /dev/sdc
[user1@server2 ~]$ sudo wipefs -a /dev/sdd
```

This brings the exercise to an end.

We will recreate logical volumes and construct file system and swap structures in them in the next chapter.

Chapter Summary

This chapter delved into foundational storage management, beginning with a comparison of the MBR and GPT partitioning schemes to clarify their use cases. We then introduced two common storage management solutions in RHEL, with a focus on the Logical Volume Manager (LVM).

We explored advanced concepts like thin provisioning and its operational benefits. Hands-on exercises included partitioning disks using both MBR and GPT. The core of the chapter was dedicated to LVM, where we examined its architecture and components. A series of hands-on exercises demonstrated the end-to-end management of physical volumes, volume groups, and logical volumes—including creation, expansion, reduction, and deletion.

Review Questions

1. What is the main advantage of thin provisioning over regular LVM allocation?
2. Where is the partition table information stored on BIOS-based systems?
3. What would *sdd3* represent?
4. Provide the command to add physical volumes */dev/sdm1* and */dev/sdn* to *vg20* volume group.
5. What are the two commands that you can use to add logical extents to a logical volume?
6. Provide the command to create a volume group called *vg20* on */dev/sdd* disk with physical extent size 64 MB.
7. Thin provisioning allows us to create logical volumes of sizes larger than the actual physical storage size. True or False?
8. What is the maximum supported number of usable partitions on a GPT disk?
9. What would the command *parted /dev/sdx mkpart pri 1 200m* do?
10. What is the maximum number of usable partitions that can be created on an MBR disk?
11. What does the command *parted /dev/sdd mklabel msdos* do?
12. Which file in the */proc* file system stores the in-memory partitioning information?
13. The *parted* utility may be used to create LVM logical volumes. True or False?
14. What are the two commands that you can use to reduce the number of logical extents from a logical volume?
15. A single disk can be used by both parted and LVM solutions at the same time. True or False?
16. Provide the command to erase */dev/sdd1* physical volume from *vg20* volume group.
17. Provide the command to remove *vg20* along with logical and physical volumes it contains.
18. What is the default size of a physical extent in LVM?
19. What is the default name for the first logical volume in a volume group?
20. If a volume group has a PE size of 32 MB, what would be the minimum size of a logical volume created in it?
21. What is one difference between the *pvs* and *pvdisplay* commands?
22. When can a disk or partition be referred to as a physical volume?
23. Provide the command to remove *webvol* logical volume from *vg20* volume group.
24. It is necessary to create file system structures in a logical volume before it can be used to store files in it. True or False?
25. Physical and logical extents are typically of the same size. True or False?
26. What is the purpose of the *pvremove* command?
27. What does the command *pvcreate /dev/sdd* do?
28. A disk or partition can be added to a volume group without being initialized. True or False?
29. Provide the command to create a logical volume called *webvol* of size equal to 100 logical extents in *vg20* volume group.
30. A volume group can be created without any physical volume in it. True or False?

31. A partition can be used as an LVM object. True or False?
32. Which command would you use to view the details of a volume group and its objects?

Answers to Review Questions

1. Thin provisioning allows to create LVs whose total size exceeds the physical pool capacity.
2. The partition table information is stored in MBR on the first sector of the disk.
3. *sdd3* represents the third partition on the fourth disk.
4. *vgextend vg20 /dev/sdm1 /dev/sdn*
5. The *lvextend* and *lvresize* commands.
6. *vgcreate -s 64 vg20 /dev/sdd*
7. True.
8. 128.
9. The command provided will create a primary partition of size 200 MB on *sdx* disk starting at 1 MB.
10. 14.
11. The command provided will create an MBR partition table on *sdd*, destroying any existing partition table.
12. The *partitions* file.
13. False.
14. The *lvreduce* and *lvresize* commands.
15. True. A single disk can be shared between parted-created partitions and LVM.
16. *vgreduce vg20 /dev/sdd1*
17. *vgremove -f vg20*
18. The default PE size is 4 MB.
19. *lvol0* is the default name for the first logical volume created in a volume group.
20. 32 MB
21. The *pvs* command lists basic information about physical volumes whereas the *pvdisplay* command shows the details.
22. After the *pvcreate* command has been executed on it successfully.
23. *lvremove /dev/vg20/webvol*
24. True.
25. True.
26. The *pvremove* command is used to remove LVM information from a physical volume.
27. The command provided will prepare the */dev/sdd* disk for use in a volume group.
28. False. A disk or partition must be initialized before it can be added to a volume group. The *vgcreate* command initializes a disk or partition if it is not already initialized with *pvcreate*.
29. *lvcreate -l 100 -n webvol vg20*
30. False.
31. True.
32. The *vgdisplay* command with the -v option.

Do-It-Yourself Challenge Labs

The following labs are designed to reinforce most of the concepts and skills covered in this chapter. You are expected to complete these labs without external assistance. A step-by-step guide is not provided, as the required knowledge has already been presented in the chapter; however, each lab includes hints pointing to the relevant major topic(s).

Use the lab environment created specifically for the end-of-chapter labs. See the sub-section "Lab Environment for End-of-Chapter Labs" in Chapter 01 "Local Installation" for details.

Add more storage to *server4* if required.

Lab 15-1: Create and Remove Partitions with parted

As *user1* with *sudo* on *server4*, create a 150 MB primary partition on one of the available 400 MB disks (*lsblk*) using the *parted* utility directly at the command prompt. Create a GPT partition table if the disk is new. Create a 240 MB partition by running *parted* interactively while ensuring that the second partition does not overlap the first. Verify the label and the partitions. Remove both partitions at the command prompt. (Hint: MBR Storage Management with parted).

Lab 15-2: Create Volume Group and Logical Volumes

As *user1* with *sudo* on *server4*, initialize 1 x 400 MB disk for use in LVM (use *lsblk* to identify available disks). Create volume group *vg100* with PE size 8 MB and add the physical volume. Create two logical volumes *lvol0* and *swapvol* of sizes 160 MB and 180 MB. Use the *vgs*, *pvs*, *lvs*, and *vgdisplay* commands for verification. (Hint: Logical Volume Manager).

Lab 15-3: Expand Volume Group and Logical Volume

As *user1* with *sudo* on *server4*, create a partition on an available 400 MB disk and initialize it for use in LVM (use *lsblk* to identify available disks). Add the new physical volume to *vg100*. Expand the *lvol0* logical volume to size 300 MB. Use the *vgs*, *pvs*, *lvs*, and *vgdisplay* commands for verification. (Hint: Logical Volume Manager).

Lab 15-4: Remove Volume Group and Physical Volumes

As *user1* with *sudo* on *server4*, remove the volume group and uninitialize the physical volumes. Confirm the deletion with *vgs*, *pvs*, *lvs*, and *vgdisplay* commands. Use the *lsblk* command and verify that the disks used for the LVM labs no longer show LVM information. (Hint: Logical Volume Manager).

Chapter 16

Local File Systems and Swap Space

By the end of this chapter, you will be able to:

- Describe and Differentiate Key File System Types: Ext4, XFS, VFAT, and ISO9660
- Configure Persistent File System Mounting Using Device Names, UUIDs, and Labels
- Create, Mount, and Resize File Systems in Partitions and Logical Volumes
- Monitor Storage Utilization and Calculate Disk Usage
- Implement and Manage Swap Space in Partitions and Logical Volumes

RHCSA Objectives:

34. Configure systems to mount file systems at boot by Universally Unique ID (UUID) or label
35. Add new partitions and logical volumes, and swap to a system non-destructively (the first part is covered in detail in Chapter 15)
36. Create, mount, unmount, and use vfat, ext4, and xfs file systems
39. Extend existing logical volumes (more details in Chapter 15)

File systems are the most common structures you create in partitions and volumes regardless of the underlying storage management solution you employ. They are logical containers you use for file storage that you can optimize, resize, mount, and unmount independently. You must connect them to the directory hierarchy for users and applications to access them. You can accomplish this automatically at system boot or manually as required. File systems can be mounted or unmounted using their unique identifiers, labels, or device files. There is a whole slew of commands available for file system creation and administration; some of them are file system type specific while others are general.

The other common structure created in partitions and logical volumes is the swap space. Swapping provides a mechanism to move out and in pages of idle data between physical memory and swap. Swap areas act as extensions to the physical memory, and they may be activated or deactivated independent of swap spaces located in other partitions and volumes.

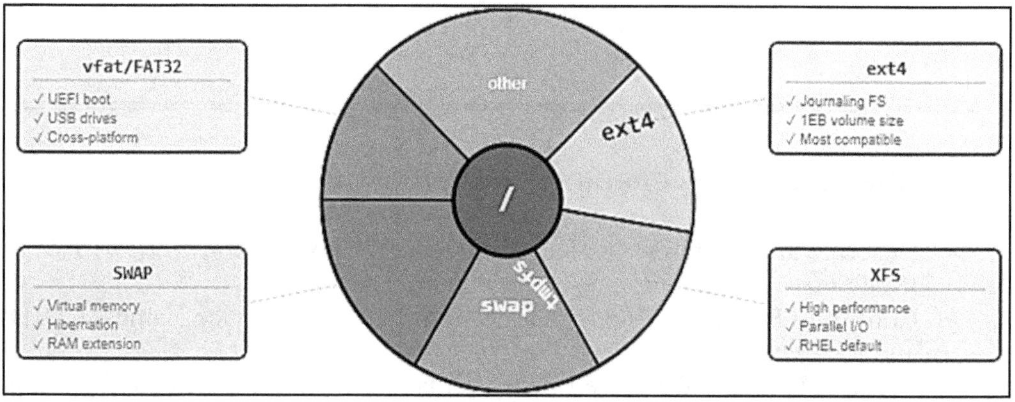

This chapter elaborates on file systems and swap, and demonstrates their creation and management in several exercises. It also highlights the tools to monitor their usage.

File Systems and File System Types

A *file system* is a logical container that stores files and directories. Each file system is created in a discrete partition or logical volume. A typical production RHEL system usually has numerous file systems. During OS installation, two file systems—*/* and */boot*—are created in the default disk layout. However, you can design a custom disk layout with separate containers for different types of data. Common additional file systems created during installation include */home*, */opt*, */tmp*, */usr*, and */var*. The */* and */boot* file systems are mandatory for installation and booting.

Storing disparate data in distinct file systems versus storing all data in a single file system offers the following advantages:

- **Independent mounting/unmounting:** Make any file system accessible (mount) or inaccessible (unmount) to users independent of other file systems. This hides or reveals information contained in that file system.
- **Targeted maintenance:** Perform file system repair activities on individual file systems
- **Data segregation:** Keep dissimilar data in separate file systems

- **Independent optimization:** Optimize or tune each file system independently for performance
- **Flexible sizing:** Grow or shrink a file system independent of other file systems

RHEL supports several file system types that may be categorized in three groups: *disk-based*, *network-based*, and *memory-based*. They are described below:

- **Disk-based:** created on physical drives using SATA, USB, Fibre Channel, and other technologies to store information persistently.
- **Network-based:** disk-based file systems or directories shared over the network for remote access.
- **Memory-based (or virtual):** created at system startup, maintained during runtime, and destroyed at system shutdown.

Table 16-1 lists and explains various common disk- and network-based supported file system types.

File System Type	Category	Description
Ext4	Disk	The fourth generation of the extended file system. It supports metadata and quota journaling, an unlimited number of subdirectories, larger file system sizes, bigger file sizes, and better handling of extended user attributes than its predecessors.
XFS	Disk	XFS is a highly scalable and high-performing 64-bit file system. It supports metadata journaling for faster crash recovery, and online defragmentation, expansion, quota journaling, and extended user attributes. XFS is the default file system type in RHEL 10.
VFAT	Disk	This file system is used for post-Windows 95 file system formats on hard disks, USB drives, and floppy disks.
ISO9660	Disk	This is used for optical file systems such as CD and DVD.
NFS	Network	Network File System. A shared directory or file system for access by remote Linux systems.
AutoFS	Network	Auto File System. An NFS file system configured to mount and unmount automatically on remote client systems.

Table 16-1 File System Types

This chapter covers Ext4, XFS, and VFAT file systems at length. It also touches upon mounting and unmounting ISO9660. For a brief discussion on memory-based file systems, see Chapter 02 "Initial System Interaction". NFS and AutoFS are discussed in Chapter 18 "Network File System".

Extended File Systems

Extended file systems have been part of RHEL for many years. The first generation is obsolete and no longer supported. The second generation is partly supported. The third and fourth generations are currently fully supported. The fourth generation is the latest in the series and is superior in features and enhancements to its predecessors.

The structure of an extended file system is built on a partition or logical volume at the time of file system creation. This structure is divided into two sets. The first set holds the file system's metadata and is very tiny. The second set stores the actual data, and it occupies almost the entire partition or the LVM logical volume space.

The metadata includes the *superblock*, which maintains vital structural information, such as the type, size, and status of the file system, and the number of data blocks it contains. Since the superblock holds such critical information, it is automatically replicated and maintained at multiple locations throughout the file system. The superblock at the beginning of the file system is referred to as the *primary superblock*, and all of its copies as *backup superblocks*. If the primary superblock becomes corrupted, it renders the file system inaccessible. One of the backup superblocks is then used to replace the corrupted primary superblock to bring the file system back to its normal state.

The metadata also contains the *inode table*, which maintains a list of *index node* (*inode*) numbers. Each file is assigned an inode number at its creation, and the inode number holds the file's attributes such as its type, permissions, ownership, size, and last access/modification time. The inode also holds and keeps track of the pointers to the actual data blocks where the file contents are located.

The Ext4 file system supports a journaling mechanism that helps it recover swiftly following a system crash. It keeps track of recent changes in its metadata in a *journal* (or log). Each metadata update is written in its entirety to the journal after completion. During reboot following a system crash, the system checks the journal of each file system to determine if there are any inconsistencies, and it recovers the file system rapidly using the latest metadata information stored in its journal.

Ext4 supports file systems up to 1EiB (ExbiByte) and files up to 16TiB (TebiByte) in size. Additionally, Ext4 uses a series of contiguous physical blocks on the hard disk called *extents*, resulting in improved read and write performance with reduced fragmentation. Ext4 supports extended user attributes, metadata and quota journaling, etc.

XFS File System

The *X File System* (XFS) is a high-performing 64-bit extent-based journaling file system type. XFS supports file systems and files up to 8EiB (ExbiByte) in size. It does not run file system checks at system boot; rather, it relies on you to use the *xfs_repair* utility to manually fix any issues. XFS sets the extended user attributes and certain mount options by default on new file systems. It enables defragmentation on mounted and active file systems to keep as much data in contiguous blocks as possible for faster access. The only major limitation with using XFS is its inability to shrink.

Like Ext4, XFS also uses journaling for metadata operations, guaranteeing the consistency of the file system against abnormal or forced unmounting. The journal information is read, and any pending metadata transactions are replayed when the XFS file system is remounted.

XFS uses sophisticated techniques in its architecture for speedy I/O performance. It can be snapshot in a mounted, active state. The snapshot can then be used for backup or other purposes.

VFAT File System

VFAT (*Virtual File Allocation Table*) is an extension of the legacy *FAT16* file system type, that was introduced in early versions of MS-DOS. The support for FAT16 was later added to Microsoft Windows, macOS, and some UNIX versions, enabling them to read and write files written in that format. FAT16 had significant limitations; it was designed to use no more than 8.3 characters in filenames, limiting filenames to a maximum of eight characters plus three characters as an extension. Moreover, it only allowed filenames to begin with a letter or number and to not contain spaces. FAT16 treated lowercase and uppercase letters alike.

VFAT was introduced with Microsoft Windows 95 and it has since been available. It supports 255 characters in filenames including spaces and periods; however, it still does not differentiate between lowercase and uppercase letters. VFAT support was added to Linux several years ago. While it can be created on hard drives, it is primarily used on removable media, such as USB flash drives, for data transfers between Linux and Windows.

ISO9660 File System

This file system type conforms to the ISO 9660 standard, hence the name. It is used for removable optical disc media such as CD/DVD drives for transporting software and patches, and operating system images in ISO format between computers. The ISO9660 format originated from the *High-Sierra File System* (HSFS) format, and it has now been enhanced to include innovative features.

File System Management

Managing file systems involves such operations as creating, mounting, labeling, viewing, resizing, unmounting, and removing them. These management tasks are common to both Extended and XFS types. Most of these functions are also applicable to VFAT and a few to optical file systems.

In Chapter 15, you created several partitions and logical volumes. However, you did not initialize them with a file system type, and therefore you could not mount or use them. Later, you destroyed all those partitions, volumes, and the LVM volume group. All the disks were returned to their unused state after the completion of the exercises.

Here is a listing of the block devices to confirm the current state of the disks:

```
[user1@server2 ~]$ lsblk
NAME              MAJ:MIN RM   SIZE RO TYPE MOUNTPOINTS
sda                 8:0    0    20G  0 disk
├─sda1              8:1    0     1M  0 part
├─sda2              8:2    0     1G  0 part /boot
└─sda3              8:3    0    19G  0 part
  ├─rhel-root     253:0    0    17G  0 lvm  /
  └─rhel-swap     253:1    0     2G  0 lvm  [SWAP]
sdb                 8:16   0   400M  0 disk
sdc                 8:32   0   400M  0 disk
sdd                 8:48   0   400M  0 disk
sde                 8:64   0   400M  0 disk
sr0                11:0    1   7.9G  0 rom  /mnt
```

The output verifies the unused state and availability status for all the disks—*sdb* through *sde*. You will be reusing them in exercises in this chapter.

File System Administration Commands

To create and manage file systems, RHEL offers commands of which some are limited to their operations on the Extended, XFS, or VFAT file system type, while others are general and applicable to all file system types. Table 16-2 describes common file system administration commands.

Command	Description
	Extended File System
e2label	Modifies the label of a file system
tune2fs	Tunes or displays file system attributes
	XFS
xfs_admin	Tunes file system attributes
xfs_growfs	Extends the size of a file system
xfs_info	Exhibits information about a file system
	VFAT
	General File System Commands
blkid	Displays block device attributes including their UUIDs and labels
df	Reports file system utilization
du	Calculates disk usage of directories and file systems
fsadm	Resizes a file system. This command is automatically invoked when the lvresize command is run with the -r switch.
lsblk	Lists block devices and file systems and their attributes including their UUIDs and labels
mkfs	Creates a file system. Use the -t option and specify ext4, vfat, or xfs file system type.
mount	Mounts a file system. Displays currently mounted file systems.
umount	Unmounts a file system

Table 16-2 File System Management Commands

Most of these commands are used in this chapter.

Mounting and Unmounting File Systems

To enable users to access files and application programs in a file system, you must connect the file system to the directory structure at a desired attachment point, which is referred to as the *mount point*. A mount point in essence is any empty directory that you create and use for this purpose.

There are many file systems already mounted on your system, such as the root file system on */* and the boot file system on */boot*. Both of them are empty directories and are reserved to connect the two file systems to the directory hierarchy. You can use the *mount* command to view information about mounted file systems. The following shows the XFS file systems only:

```
[user1@server2 ~]$ mount -t xfs
/dev/mapper/rhel-root on / type xfs (rw,relatime,seclabel,attr2,inode64,logb
ufs=8,logbsize=32k,noquota)
/dev/sda1 on /boot type xfs (rw,relatime,seclabel,attr2,inode64,logbufs=8,lo
gbsize=32k,noquota)
```

The "-t xfs" option makes the command to only show the file systems initialized with the XFS type.

The *mount* command is also used for mounting a file system on a mount point, and this action is performed with *root* privileges. The command requires the absolute pathnames of the file system block device and the mount point name. It also accepts the file system UUID or label in lieu of the block device name. Options are available with this command to mount all or a specific type of file system. The *mount* command is also used to mount other types of file systems such as those located in removable media. Upon successful mount, the kernel places an entry for the file system in the */proc/self/mounts* file.

A mount point should be empty when an attempt is made to mount a file system on it, otherwise the content of the mount point will hide. As well, the mount point must not be in use or the mount attempt will fail.

The *mount* command supports numerous options that may be used as required to override its default behavior. We can also specify multiple comma-separated options. Table 16-3 describes some common options.

Option	Description
_netdev	Used for a file system that requires network connectivity in place before it can be mounted. NFS is an example.
auto (noauto)	Mounts (or does not mount) the file system when the -a option is specified
defaults	Mounts a file system with all the default values (async, auto, rw, etc.)
remount	Remounts an already mounted file system to enable or disable an option
ro (rw)	Mounts a file system read-only (read/write)

Table 16-3 Common mount Command Options

The opposite of the *mount* command is *umount*, which is used to detach a file system from the directory hierarchy and make it inaccessible to users and applications. This command expects the absolute pathname to the block device containing the file system or its mount point name to detach it. Options are available with *umount* to unmount all or a specific type of file system. The kernel removes the corresponding file system entry from the */proc/self/mounts* file after it has been successfully disconnected.

Determining the UUID of a File System

Every Extended and XFS file system has a 128-bit (32 hexadecimal characters) UUID (*Universally Unique IDentifier*) assigned to it at creation. In contrast, a vfat file system uses a shorter 32-bit (8 hexadecimal characters) UUID. Assigning a UUID makes the file system unique among many other file systems that potentially exist on the system. The primary benefit of using a UUID is the fact that it always stays persistent across system reboots. UUIDs are used by default in RHEL 10 in the */etc/fstab* file for any file system that is created by the system in a standard partition.

RHEL attempts to mount all file systems listed in the */etc/fstab* file at reboots. Each file system has an associated device file and UUID, but may or may not have a corresponding label. The system checks for the presence of each file system's device file, UUID, or label, and then attempts to mount it.

The */boot* file system, for instance, is located in a partition and the device file associated with it on *server2* is */dev/sda2*. You can use the *xfs_admin* command, the *blkid* command, or the *lsblk* command as follows to determine its UUID:

```
[user1@server2 ~]$ sudo xfs_admin -u /dev/sda2
UUID = 95e86c71-539f-4579-b119-6da362f89974
[user1@server2 ~]$
[user1@server2 ~]$ sudo blkid /dev/sda2
/dev/sda2: UUID="95e86c71-539f-4579-b119-6da362f89974" BLOCK_SIZE="512"
 TYPE="xfs" PARTUUID="671d53eb-c479-45e8-897f-ee3fc6b2ed61"
[user1@server2 ~]$
[user1@server2 ~]$ sudo lsblk -f /dev/sda2
NAME FSTYPE FSVER LABEL UUID                                 FSAVAIL FS
USE% MOUNTPOINTS
sda2 xfs                95e86c71-539f-4579-b119-6da362f89974  625.8M
 35% /boot
```

The UUID reported by the above commands for the */boot* file system is "95e86c71-539f-4579-b119-6da362f89974". If you *grep* for the string "boot" on the */etc/fstab* file, you will see that the system uses this UUID to mount */boot*. A discussion on the */etc/fstab* file is provided later in this chapter.

For extended file systems, you can use the *tune2fs* command in addition to the *blkid* and *lsblk* commands to determine the UUID.

A UUID is also assigned to a file system that is created in an LVM logical volume; however, it need not be used in the *fstab* file, as the device files associated with the logical volumes are always unique and persistent.

Labeling a File System

A unique label may be used instead of a UUID to keep the file system association with its device file exclusive and persistent across system reboots. A label is limited to a maximum of 12 characters on the XFS file system and 16 characters on the Extended file system. By default, no labels are assigned to a file system at the time of its creation.

The */boot* file system is located in the */dev/sda2* partition and its type is XFS. You can use the *xfs_admin* or the *lsblk* command as follows to determine its label:

```
[user1@server2 ~]$ sudo xfs_admin -l /dev/sda2
label = ""
[user1@server2 ~]$ sudo lsblk -f /dev/sda2
NAME FSTYPE FSVER LABEL UUID                                 FSAVAIL FS
USE% MOUNTPOINTS
sda2 xfs                95e86c71-539f-4579-b119-6da362f89974  625.8M
 35% /boot
```

The output shows that there is currently no label assigned to the */boot* file system.

A label is not needed on a file system if you intend to use its UUID or if it is created in a logical volume; however, you can still apply one using the *xfs_admin* command with the -L option. Labeling an XFS file system requires that the target file system be unmounted.

The following example demonstrates the steps to unmount */boot*, set the label "bootfs" on its device file, and remount it:

```
[user1@server2 ~]$ sudo umount /boot
[user1@server2 ~]$ sudo xfs_admin -L bootfs /dev/sda2
writing all SBs
new label = "bootfs"
[user1@server2 ~]$ sudo mount /boot
```

You can confirm the new label by executing **sudo xfs_admin -l /dev/sda2** or **sudo lsblk -f /dev/sda2**.

For extended file systems, use the *e2label* command to apply a label and the *tune2fs*, *blkid*, or *lsblk* command to view and verify.

Now you can replace the UUID="95e86c71-539f-4579-b119-6da362f89974" for */boot* in the *fstab* file with LABEL=bootfs, and unmount and remount */boot* as demonstrated above for confirmation.

A label can also be applied to a file system created in a logical volume; however, it is not recommended for use in the *fstab* file, as the device files for logical volumes are always unique and remain persistent across system reboots.

Automatically Mounting a File System at Reboots

File systems defined in the */etc/fstab* file are mounted automatically at reboots. This file must contain proper and complete information for each listed file system. An incomplete or inaccurate entry might leave the system in an undesirable or unbootable state. Another benefit of adding entries to this file is that you only need to specify one of the four attributes—block device name, UUID, label, or mount point—of the file system that you wish to mount manually with the *mount* command. The *mount* command obtains the rest of the information from this file. Similarly, you only need to specify one of these attributes with the *umount* command to detach it from the directory hierarchy.

The default *fstab* file contains entries for file systems created at installation. On *server2*, for instance, this file currently has the following three entries:

```
UUID=e6ee0b10-d853-4ef5-898c-14480c6516ba /      xfs   defaults 0 0
LABEL=bootfs                              /boot  xfs   defaults 0 0
UUID=959fe3fa-0d2e-44e7-9ae3-ea76f936c108 none   swap  defaults 0 0
```

EXAM TIP: Any missing or invalid entry in this file may render the system unbootable. You will have to boot the system in emergency mode to fix this file. Ensure that you understand each field in the file for both file system and swap entries.

The format of this file is such that each row is broken out into six columns to identify the required attributes for each file system to be successfully mounted. Here is what the columns contain:

Column 1: Defines the physical or virtual device path where the file system is resident, or its associated UUID or label. There can be entries for network file systems here as well.
Column 2: Identifies the mount point for the file system. For swap partitions, use either "none" or "swap".

Column 3: Specifies the file system type such as Ext4, XFS, VFAT, or ISO9660. For swap, the type "swap" is used. You can use "auto" instead to leave it up to the *mount* command to determine the type.
Column 4: Identifies one or more comma-separated options to be used when mounting the file system. See Table 15-3 for a description of some of the options, consult the manual pages for the *mount* command or the *fstab* file for additional options and details.
Column 5: this field is used by the *dump* utility to ascertain the file systems that need to be dumped. A value of 0 (or the absence of this column) disables this check. This field is applicable only on Extended file systems; XFS does not use it.
Column 6: Expresses the sequence number in which to run the *e2fsck* (file system check and repair utility for Extended file system types) utility on the file system at system boot. By default, 0 is used for memory-based, remote, and removable file systems, 1 for */*, and 2 for */boot* and other physical file systems. 0 can also be used for */*, */boot*, and other physical file systems that you do not want to be checked or repaired. This field is applicable only on Extended file systems; XFS does not use it.

A 0 in columns 5 and 6 for XFS, virtual, remote, and removable file system types is meaningless. You do not need to add them for these file system types.

This file is edited manually, so care must be observed to circumvent syntax and typing errors.

Monitoring File System Usage

On a live system, you often need to check file system usage to know if a mounted file system requires an expansion for growth or a clean up to generate free space. This involves examining the used and available spaces for a file system. The *df* (*disk free*) command is used for this purpose. By default, this command reports the usage in KBs unless the -m or -h option is specified to view the numbers in MBs or human-readable format.

Run this command with the -h option on *server2*:

```
[user1@server2 ~]$ df -h
Filesystem             Size  Used Avail Use% Mounted on
/dev/mapper/rhel-root   17G  4.1G   13G  25% /
devtmpfs               4.0M     0  4.0M   0% /dev
tmpfs                  853M   84K  853M   1% /dev/shm
tmpfs                  342M  6.9M  335M   2% /run
tmpfs                  1.0M     0  1.0M   0% /run/credentials/systemd-journald.
ervice
tmpfs                  171M  144K  171M   1% /run/user/1000
/dev/sr0               7.9G  7.9G     0 100% /mnt
/dev/sda2              960M  335M  626M  35% /boot
```

The output shows the file system device file or type in column 1, followed by the total, used, and available spaces in columns 2, 3, and 4, and the usage percentages and mount points in the last two columns.

This command has a few other useful flags that can produce modified output. These flags include:

-T to add the file system type to the output (example: **df -hT**)
-x to exclude the specified file system type from the output (example: **df -hx tmpfs**)

-t to limit the output to a specific file system type (example: **df -t xfs**)
-i to show inode information (example: **df -hi**)

You can use -h with any of these examples to print information in human-readable format.

Calculating Disk Usage

In contrast to the *df* command that returns usage information for an entire file system, the *du* command reports the amount of space a file or directory occupies within the file system. By default, it shows the output in KBs; however, you can use the -m or -h option to view the numbers in MBs or human-readable format. In addition, you can view a usage summary with the -s switch and a grand total with -c.

Run this command on the */usr/bin* directory to view the usage summary:

```
[user1@server2 ~]$ du -sh /usr/bin
234M     /usr/bin
```

To add a "total" row to the output and with numbers displayed in KBs:

```
[user1@server2 ~]$ du -sc /usr/bin
238912   /usr/bin
238912   total
```

Try this command using different options on the */usr/sbin/lvm* file and observe the output.

Exercise 16-1: Create and Mount Ext4, VFAT, and XFS File Systems in Partitions

Perform this exercise on *server2* as *user1* with *sudo* where required. In this exercise, you will:

- Create 2 x 150 MB partitions on the */dev/sdb* disk
- Initialize partition 1 with the Ext4 and partition 2 with VFAT file system types
- Create an XFS file system on the entire */dev/sdc* disk
- Identify UUIDs for the three file systems
- Define file systems for persistence using UUIDs
- Create mount points called */ext4fs1*, */vfatfs1*, and */xfsfs1*
- Mount all three file systems
- Verify the mount and their current usage

1. Create a GPT partition table on *sdb* using the *parted* command:

```
[user1@server2 ~]$ sudo parted /dev/sdb mklabel gpt
Warning: The existing disk label on /dev/sdb will be destroyed and all
data on this disk will be lost. Do you want to continue?


Yes/No? Yes
```

2. Create 2 x 150 MB primary partitions on *sdb* with *parted*:

```
[user1@server2 ~]$ sudo parted /dev/sdb mkpart pri 1 151m
[user1@server2 ~]$ sudo parted /dev/sdb mkpart pri 152 302m
```

3. Initialize the first partition (*sdb1*) with Ext4 file system type using the *mkfs* command:

```
[user1@server2 ~]$ sudo mkfs -t ext4 /dev/sdb1
mke2fs 1.47.1 (20-May-2024)
Creating filesystem with 146432 1k blocks and 36576 inodes
Filesystem UUID: bb6bce01-97ec-41de-981b-84c864e643c7
Superblock backups stored on blocks:
        8193, 24577, 40961, 57345, 73729

Allocating group tables: done
Writing inode tables: done
Creating journal (4096 blocks): done
Writing superblocks and filesystem accounting information: done
```

4. Initialize the second partition (*sdb2*) with VFAT file system type using the *mkfs* command:

```
[user1@server2 ~]$ sudo mkfs -t vfat /dev/sdb2
mkfs.fat 4.2 (2021-01-31)
```

5. Initialize the whole disk (*sdc*) with the XFS file system type using the *mkfs.xfs* command. The -f option forces creation, overwriting any existing data.

```
[user1@server2 ~]$ sudo mkfs.xfs /dev/sdc -f
meta-data=/dev/sdc               isize=512    agcount=4, agsize=25600 blk
s
         =                       sectsz=512   attr=2, projid32bit=1
         =                       crc=1        finobt=1, sparse=1, rmapbt=
1
         =                       reflink=1    bigtime=1 inobtcount=1 nrex
t64=1
         =                       exchange=0
data     =                       bsize=4096   blocks=102400, imaxpct=25
         =                       sunit=0      swidth=0 blks
naming   =version 2              bsize=4096   ascii-ci=0, ftype=1, parent
=0
log      =internal log           bsize=4096   blocks=16384, version=2
         =                       sectsz=512   sunit=0 blks, lazy-count=1
realtime =none                   extsz=4096   blocks=0, rtextents=0
```

6. View UUIDs of the new file systems using the *lsblk* command:

```
[user1@server2 ~]$ sudo lsblk -f /dev/sdb /dev/sdc
NAME FSTYPE FSVER LABEL UUID
E% MOUNTPOINTS
sdb

├─sdb1
│    ext4   1.0          bb6bce01-97ec-41de-981b-84c864e643c7

└─sdb2
     vfat   FAT16        CCBA-0825

sdc  xfs                 d0eb85dc-3625-4d43-b9dd-3d5e31234486
```

7. Open the */etc/fstab* file, go to the end of the file, and add entries for the file systems using their UUIDs:

```
UUID=bb6bce01-97ec-41de-981b-84c864e643c7 /ext4fs1 ext4 defaults 0 0
UUID=CCBA-0825 /vfatfs1 vfat defaults 0 0
UUID=d0eb85dc-3625-4d43-b9dd-3d5e31234486 /xfsfs1 xfs defaults 0 0
```

8. Create mount point directories */ext4fs1*, */vfatfs1*, and */xfsfs1* for the three file systems:

```
[user1@server2 ~]$ sudo mkdir /ext4fs1 /vfatfs1 /xfsfs1
```

9. Mount the new file systems using the *mount* command. This command will fail if there are any invalid or missing information in the file.

```
[user1@server2 ~]$ sudo mount -a
```

Always validate the fstab file by running the above command after modifying the file and before rebooting the system. This command attempts to mount all entries and will report errors if it finds inconsistencies in the file, allowing you to fix them without risking an unbootable system.

10. Run the *systemctl* command to notify the *systemd* daemon to use the updated *fstab* file:

```
[user1@server2 ~]$ sudo systemctl daemon-reload
```

11. View the mount and availability status as well as the types of all three file systems using the *df* command:

```
[user1@server2 ~]$ df -hT
........
/dev/sdb2          vfat      143M     0  143M   0% /vfatfs1
/dev/sdc           xfs       336M   27M  310M   8% /xfsfs1
/dev/sdb1          ext4      129M   14K  119M   1% /ext4fs1
```

The output verifies the creation and current usage of the three file systems. They are added to the *fstab* file for persistence. A system reboot at this point will remount them automatically. These file systems can now be used to store files.

Exercise 16-2: Create and Mount Ext4 and XFS File Systems in LVM Logical Volumes

Perform this exercise on *server2* as *user1* with *sudo* where required. In this exercise, you will:

- Create a volume group called *vgfs* using *sdd* disk as a physical volume with PE size 8 MB
- Create a logical volume called *ext4vol* of size 70 MB
- Create a logical volume called *xfsvol* of size 320 MB
- Initialize the first logical volume with the Ext4 file system type
- Initialize the second logical volume with the XFS file system type

- Ensure both file systems are persistently defined using their logical volume device filenames
- Create mount points called */ext4fs2* and */xfsfs2*
- Mount the file systems
- Verify the mount and their current usage

1. Initialize the *sdd* disk for use in LVM using the *pvcreate* command. Ignore any warning message that appears.

```
[user1@server2 ~]$ sudo pvcreate /dev/sdd
  Physical volume "/dev/sdd" successfully created.
```

2. Create the volume group *vgfs* with a PE size of 8 MB using the physical volume:

```
[user1@server2 ~]$ sudo vgcreate -s 8 vgfs /dev/sdd
  Volume group "vgfs" successfully created
```

The PE size is not easy to alter after a volume group creation, so ensure it is defined as required at creation.

3. Create a logical volume *ext4vol* of size 70 MB in *vgfs* using the *lvcreate* command:

```
[user1@server2 ~]$ sudo lvcreate -n ext4vol -L 70 vgfs
  Rounding up size to full physical extent 72.00 MiB
  Logical volume "ext4vol" created.
```

4. Create a logical volume *xfsvol* of size 320 MB in *vgfs* using the *lvcreate* command:

```
[user1@server2 ~]$ sudo lvcreate -n xfsvol -L 320 vgfs
  Logical volume "xfsvol" created.
```

5. Format the *ext4vol* logical volume with the Ext4 file system type using the *mkfs.ext4* command:

```
[user1@server2 ~]$ sudo mkfs.ext4 /dev/vgfs/ext4vol
mke2fs 1.47.1 (20-May-2024)
Creating filesystem with 73728 1k blocks and 18432 inodes
Filesystem UUID: 6ea77fc0-da69-4e94-a4a0-74bbbf2768d4
Superblock backups stored on blocks:
        8193, 24577, 40961, 57345

Allocating group tables: done
Writing inode tables: done
Creating journal (4096 blocks): done
Writing superblocks and filesystem accounting information: done
```

You may alternatively use **sudo mkfs -t ext4 /dev/vgfs/ext4vol**.

6. Format the *xfsvol* logical volume with the XFS file system type using the *mkfs.xfs* command:

```
[user1@server2 ~]$ sudo mkfs.xfs /dev/vgfs/xfsvol
meta-data=/dev/vgfs/xfsvol       isize=512    agcount=4, agsize=20480 blks
         =                       sectsz=512   attr=2, projid32bit=1
         =                       crc=1        finobt=1, sparse=1, rmapbt=1
         =                       reflink=1    bigtime=1 inobtcount=1 nrext64=1
         =                       exchange=0
data     =                       bsize=4096   blocks=81920, imaxpct=25
         =                       sunit=0      swidth=0 blks
naming   =version 2              bsize=4096   ascii-ci=0, ftype=1, parent=0
log      =internal log           bsize=4096   blocks=16384, version=2
         =                       sectsz=512   sunit=0 blks, lazy-count=1
realtime =none                   extsz=4096   blocks=0, rtextents=0
```

You may use **sudo mkfs -t xfs /dev/vgfs/xfsvol** instead.

7. Open the */etc/fstab* file, go to the end of the file, and append entries for the file systems for persistence using their device files:

```
/dev/vgfs/ext4vol /ext4fs2 ext4 defaults 0 0
/dev/vgfs/xfsvol  /xfsfs2  xfs  defaults 0 0
```

8. Create mount points */ext4fs2* and */xfsfs2* using the *mkdir* command:

```
[user1@server2 ~]$ sudo mkdir /ext4fs2 /xfsfs2
```

9. Mount the new file systems using the *mount* command. This command will fail if there is any invalid or missing information in the file.

```
[user1@server2 ~]$ sudo mount -a
```

Fix any issues in the file if reported.

10. Run the *systemctl* command to notify the *systemd* daemon to use the updated *fstab* file:

```
[user1@server2 ~]$ sudo systemctl daemon-reload
```

11. View the mount and availability status as well as the types of the new LVM file systems using the *df* command:

```
[user1@server2 ~]$ lsblk /dev/sdd
NAME              MAJ:MIN RM  SIZE RO TYPE MOUNTPOINTS
sdd                 8:48   0  400M  0 disk
├─vgfs-ext4vol    253:2    0   72M  0 lvm  /ext4fs2
└─vgfs-xfsvol     253:3    0  320M  0 lvm  /xfsfs2
[user1@server2 ~]$
[user1@server2 ~]$ df -hT | grep fs2
/dev/mapper/vgfs-ext4vol ext4      63M   14K   58M   1% /ext4fs2
/dev/mapper/vgfs-xfsvol  xfs      256M   22M  235M   9% /xfsfs2
```

The *lsblk* command output illustrates the LVM logical volumes (*ext4vol* and *xfsvol*), the disk they use (*sdd*), the sizes (72 MB and 320 MB), and the mount points (*/ext4fs2* and */xfsfs2*) where the file systems are connected to the directory structure.

The *df* command shows the size and usage information. Both file systems are added to the *fstab* file for persistence, meaning future system reboots will remount them automatically. They can now be used to store files.

Exercise 16-3: Resize Ext4 and XFS File Systems in LVM Logical Volumes

Perform this exercise on *server2* as *user1* with *sudo* where required. In this exercise, you will:

- Create a 100 MB partition on *sdb* disk and add it to the *vgfs* volume group created in Exercise 16-2
- Extend the *ext4vol* logical volume along with the file system it contains by 40 MB using two separate commands
- Extend the *xfsvol* logical volume along with the file system it contains by 40 MB using a single command
- Verify the new sizes

1. Add a 100 MB partition to *sdb* disk and confirm:

```
[user1@server2 ~]$ sudo parted /dev/sdb mkpart pri 303 404
[user1@server2 ~]$ sudo parted /dev/sdb pri
Model: ATA VBOX HARDDISK (scsi)
Disk /dev/sdb: 419MB
Sector size (logical/physical): 512B/512B
Partition Table: gpt
Disk Flags:

Number  Start   End    Size   File system  Name  Flags
 1      1049kB  151MB  150MB  ext4         pri
 2      152MB   302MB  150MB  fat16        pri
 3      303MB   404MB  101MB               pri
```

The new partition is *sdb3*.

2. Initialize the new partition and add it to *vgfs*:

```
[user1@server2 ~]$ sudo pvcreate /dev/sdb3
  Physical volume "/dev/sdb3" successfully created.
[user1@server2 ~]$ sudo vgextend vgfs /dev/sdb3
  Volume group "vgfs" successfully extended
```

3. Confirm the new size of *vgfs* using the *vgs* and *vgdisplay* commands:

```
[user1@server2 ~]$ sudo vgs
  VG    #PV #LV #SN Attr   VSize   VFree
  rhel    1   2   0 wz--n- <19.00g      0
  vgfs    2   2   0 wz--n- 480.00m 88.00m
[user1@server2 ~]$
[user1@server2 ~]$ sudo vgdisplay vgfs
  --- Volume group ---
  VG Name               vgfs
  System ID
  Format                lvm2
  Metadata Areas        2
  Metadata Sequence No  4
  VG Access             read/write
  VG Status             resizable
  MAX LV                0
  Cur LV                2
  Open LV               2
  Max PV                0
  Cur PV                2
  Act PV                2
  VG Size               480.00 MiB
  PE Size               8.00 MiB
  Total PE              60
  Alloc PE / Size       49 / 392.00 MiB
  Free  PE / Size       11 / 88.00 MiB
  VG UUID               v3m7td-1a31-oiqH-gXdn-sSds-NMPC-TAqWe1
```

There are now two physical volumes in the volume group and the total size increased to 480 MB.

4. Extend *ext4vol* as well as the file system it contains by 40 MB using the *lvextend* and *fsadm* command pair. Make sure to use uppercase L to specify the size. The default unit is MB. The plus sign (+) signifies an addition to the current size.

```
[user1@server2 ~]$ sudo lvextend -L +40 /dev/vgfs/ext4vol
  Size of logical volume vgfs/ext4vol changed from 72.00 MiB (9 extents) to 112
.00 MiB (14 extents).
  Logical volume vgfs/ext4vol successfully resized.

[user1@server2 ~]$ sudo fsadm resize /dev/vgfs/ext4vol
resize2fs 1.47.1 (20-May-2024)
Filesystem at /dev/mapper/vgfs-ext4vol is mounted on /ext4fs2; on-line resizing
required
old_desc_blocks = 1, new_desc_blocks = 1
The filesystem on /dev/mapper/vgfs-ext4vol is now 114688 (1k) blocks long.
```

The *resize* subcommand instructs the *fsadm* command to grow the file system to the full length of the logical volume.

5. Extend *xfsvol* and the file system (-r) it holds by (+) 40 MB using the *lvresize* command:

```
[user1@server2 ~]$ sudo lvresize -rL +40 /dev/vgfs/xfsvol
  File system xfs found on vgfs/xfsvol mounted at /xfsfs2.
  Size of logical volume vgfs/xfsvol changed from 320.00 MiB (40 extent
s) to 360.00 MiB (45 extents).
  Extending file system xfs to 360.00 MiB (377487360 bytes) on vgfs/xfs
vol...
xfs_growfs /dev/vgfs/xfsvol
meta-data=/dev/mapper/vgfs-xfsvol isize=512    agcount=4, agsize=20480
blks
........
data blocks changed from 81920 to 92160
xfs_growfs done
  Extended file system xfs on vgfs/xfsvol.
  Logical volume vgfs/xfsvol successfully resized.
```

6. Verify the new extensions to both logical volumes using the *lvs* command. You can also use the *lvdisplay* or *vgdisplay* command instead.

```
[user1@server2 ~]$ sudo lvs | grep vol
  ext4vol vgfs -wi-ao---- 112.00m

  xfsvol  vgfs -wi-ao---- 360.00m
```

7. Check the new sizes and the current mount status for both file systems using the *df* and *lsblk* commands:

```
[user1@server2 ~]$ df -hT | grep -E 'ext4vol|xfsvol'
/dev/mapper/vgfs-ext4vol ext4      100M   14K   93M   1% /ext4fs2
/dev/mapper/vgfs-xfsvol  xfs       296M   23M  274M   8% /xfsfs2
[user1@server2 ~]$
[user1@server2 ~]$ lsblk /dev/sdd /dev/sdb
NAME                MAJ:MIN RM  SIZE RO TYPE MOUNTPOINTS
sdb                   8:16   0  400M  0 disk
├─sdb1                8:17   0  143M  0 part /ext4fs1
├─sdb2                8:18   0  143M  0 part /vfatfs1
└─sdb3                8:19   0   96M  0 part
  ├─vgfs-ext4vol 253:2   0  112M  0 lvm  /ext4fs2
  └─vgfs-xfsvol  253:3   0  360M  0 lvm  /xfsfs2
sdd                   8:48   0  400M  0 disk
├─vgfs-ext4vol     253:2   0  112M  0 lvm  /ext4fs2
└─vgfs-xfsvol      253:3   0  360M  0 lvm  /xfsfs2
```

The outputs reflect the new sizes for both file systems. The discrepancy in file system sizes reported by the two commands is normal.

This concludes the exercise.

Swap Space and its Management

Physical memory (or RAM) is a finite, volatile storage resource employed for loading the kernel and running user programs and applications. *Swap space* is a dedicated area on a storage device used for holding idle data until it is needed. The operating system splits physical memory into small, fixed-size logical blocks called *pages*. This mechanism allows the system to handle more processes than can fit in physical memory simultaneously. This physical-to-virtual mapping of pages is stored in a data structure called *page table*, and it is maintained by the kernel.

Paging Process

When a process is launched, it requires space in physical memory to run and be processed. While multiple processes can run concurrently, physical memory cannot accommodate all their pages at once. The kernel monitors the memory usage. When free memory drops below a defined threshold, the system starts moving selected idle pages of data from physical memory to the swap space to make room for additional processes. This operation is referred to as *paging out* (or *swapping out*). When a process needs data that has been paged out, a *page fault* occurs, triggering the system to page the data back into physical memory from swap. This operation is called *paging in* (or *swapping in*). The overall mechanism of moving pages between physical memory and swap is known as *demand paging*.

Thrashing

Systems with insufficient physical memory for their workload may become overly busy with paging activity. When this happens, they do not have enough cycles to carry out other useful tasks, resulting in degraded system performance. This excessive paging, which severely degrades performance, is called *thrashing*.

When thrashing occurs or free memory falls below a critical threshold, the kernel may deactivate idle processes and throttle new processes creation. Normal operation resumes only when available memory rises above the threshold and thrashing diminishes.

Determining Current Swap Usage

While traditional guidance suggested swap space equal to or double the memory size, modern systems with large physical memory (e.g., 64 GB+) may require little to no swap for typical workloads.

Use the *free* command to view memory and swap space utilization. It displays the following information:

- **Total:** total installed memory
- **Used:** memory currently in use
- **Free:** completely unused memory
- **Shared:** memory used by tmpfs and shared memory
- **Buff/cache:** sum of (1) memory holding metadata and data waiting to be written to disk (buffers) and (2) memory storing frequently accessed data from disk (cached)
- **Available:** Memory available for starting new processes without swapping

Specify the -h flag with the command to list the values in human-readable format. The -t option adds a "Total" line at the bottom of the output. Here is a sample output from *server2*:

```
[user1@server2 ~]$ free -ht
               total        used        free      shared  buff/cache   available
Mem:           1.7Gi       766Mi       596Mi        10Mi       502Mi       938Mi
Swap:          2.0Gi          0B       2.0Gi
Total:         3.7Gi       766Mi       2.6Gi
```

The output indicates that the system has 1.7 GB of total memory, of which 766 MB is in use, 596 MB is free, and 938 MB is available. It also shows 10 MB of shared memory and 502 MB used by kernel buffers and page cache.

On the subsequent row, it reports the total swap space (2.0 GB) with 0 Bytes in use. The last line prints the combined utilization of both memory and swap.

Try **free -hts 3** and **free -htc 2** to refresh the output every three seconds (-s) and to display the output twice (-c).

The *free* command reads data from the */proc/meminfo* file . Values in this file are in KBs and provide more details than *free* does. Here are the relevant fields from this file:

```
[user1@server2 ~]$ cat /proc/meminfo | grep -E 'Mem|Swap'
MemTotal:          1746496 kB
MemFree:            610828 kB
MemAvailable:       961352 kB
SwapCached:              0 kB
SwapTotal:         2097148 kB
SwapFree:          2097148 kB
```

This data depicts the usage of the system's runtime memory and swap.

Prioritizing Swap Spaces

Production systems often use multiple swap areas to meet the workload demand. By default, the kernel uses swap areas in the order they appear in the */proc/swaps* file. You can set swap priorities using the "pri" option in the *fstab* file. Priorities range from -1 to 32767. Higher numbers indicate higher priority. Without pri, the default is -1. Swap areas with equal priority are used in a round-robin fashion. The swap space created at system installation gets priority -2.

Swap Space Administration Commands

RHEL provides three primary commands for swap management: *mkswap*, *swapon*, and *swapoff*. Use *mkswap* to initialize a partition or logical volume for use as swap space. Once created, you can activate it with the *swapon* command or deactivate it with *swapoff*. For persistent activation across reboots, add an entry to the *fstab* file using the swap area's device file, UUID, or label.

Exercise 16-4: Create and Activate Swap in Partition and Logical Volume

Perform this exercise on *server2* as *user1* with *sudo* where required. In this exercise, you will:

- Create one swap area in a new 120 MB *sde1* partition using the *mkswap* command
- Create another swap area in a 250 MB logical volume called *swapvol* in *vgfs*. Create a partition called *sde2* and add it to *vgfs*.
- Add their entries to *fstab* file for persistence using the UUID and priority 1 for the partition swap and the device file and priority 2 for the logical volume swap
- Activate both swap areas and verify activation

EXAM TIP: Use the lsblk command to determine available disk space before performing any storage management tasks.

1. Use *parted* to label the *sde* disk as it has not been used so far:

```
[user1@server2 ~]$ sudo parted /dev/sde mklabel gpt
```

2. Create two partitions of sizes 120 MB and 250 MB, and confirm:

```
[user1@server2 ~]$ sudo parted /dev/sde mkpart pri 1 121

[user1@server2 ~]$ sudo parted /dev/sde mkpart pri 122 371

[user1@server2 ~]$ sudo parted /dev/sde print
Model: ATA VBOX HARDDISK (scsi)
Disk /dev/sde: 419MB
Sector size (logical/physical): 512B/512B
Partition Table: gpt
Disk Flags:

Number  Start   End    Size   File system  Name  Flags
 1      1049kB  121MB  120MB               pri
 2      122MB   371MB  250MB               pri
```

The output confirms the creation of two partitions.

3. Initialize the second partition and add it to *vgfs*:

```
[user1@server2 ~]$ sudo pvcreate /dev/sde2
  Physical volume "/dev/sde2" successfully created.
[user1@server2 ~]$
[user1@server2 ~]$ sudo vgextend vgfs /dev/sde2
  Volume group "vgfs" successfully extended
```

4. Create logical volume *swapvol* in *vgs* using the *lvcreate* command. There should be 29 x 8 MB LEs available from the *sde2* physical volume. Use **sudo vgdisplay -v vgfs** to confirm.

```
[user1@server2 ~]$ sudo lvcreate -l 29 -n swapvol vgfs
  Logical volume "swapvol" created.
```

5. Construct swap structures in *sde1* and *swapvol* using the *mkswap* command:

```
[user1@server2 ~]$ sudo mkswap /dev/sde1
Setting up swapspace version 1, size = 114 MiB (119533568 bytes)
no label, UUID=7f28d4cb-bf5e-46d9-b65b-358d4fc9617b
[user1@server2 ~]$
[user1@server2 ~]$ sudo mkswap /dev/vgfs/swapvol
Setting up swapspace version 1, size = 232 MiB (243265536 bytes)
no label, UUID=009e34ff-a1bf-4fc6-a760-10710ebffe68
```

6. Edit the *fstab* file and add entries for both swap areas for auto-activation on reboots. Obtain the UUID for partition swap with **lsblk -f /dev/sde1** and use the device file for logical volume. Specify their priorities.

```
UUID=7f28d4cb-bf5e-46d9-b65b-358d4fc9617b swap swap pri=1 0 0
/dev/vgfs/swapvol                         swap swap pri=2 0 0
```

> **EXAM TIP:** You will not be receiving any credits for this work if you forget to add correct entries to the fstab file.

7. Determine the current amount of swap space using the *swapon* command:

```
[user1@server2 ~]$ sudo swapon
NAME      TYPE      SIZE USED PRIO
/dev/dm-1 partition   2G   0B   -2
```

There is one 2 GB swap area.

8. Activate the new swap regions using the *swapon* command:

```
[user1@server2 ~]$ sudo swapon -a
```

The command will display errors if it finds any syntax or other issues with the swap entries in the *fstab* file.

9. Confirm the activation using the *swapon* command or by viewing the */proc/swaps* file:

```
[user1@server2 ~]$ sudo swapon
NAME      TYPE      SIZE USED PRIO
/dev/dm-1 partition   2G   0B   -2
/dev/sde1 partition 114M   0B    1
/dev/dm-4 partition 232M   0B    2
[user1@server2 ~]$
[user1@server2 ~]$ cat /proc/swaps
Filename     Type         Size      Used  Priority
/dev/dm-1    partition    2097148   0     -2
/dev/sde1    partition    116732    0     1
/dev/dm-4    partition    237564    0     2
```

Both swap spaces are active. Their sizes and priorities are also visible. The device mapper device files for the logical volumes and the device file for the partition swap are also exhibited.

10. Issue the *free* command to view the reflection of swap numbers on the Swap and Total lines:

```
[user1@server2 ~]$ free -ht
          total     used      free    shared  buff/cache   available
Mem:      1.7Gi    764Mi     603Mi      10Mi       497Mi       941Mi
Swap:     2.3Gi       0B     2.3Gi
Total:    4.0Gi    764Mi     2.9Gi
```

The total swap is now 2.3 GB. This concludes the exercise.

Chapter Summary

This chapter provided a comprehensive guide to managing two critical storage structures: file systems and swap space. These structures are created in partitions or LVM logical volumes irrespective of the underlying storage management solution used to build them.

We began with an in-depth exploration of file systems, covering their concepts, types, benefits, administration and monitoring commands, and the concepts of mounting them manually and persistently using their UUIDs and labels. Hands-on exercises reinforced these concepts, demonstrating file system creation, management, labeling, and usage monitoring within both partitions and LVM logical volumes.

The second half of this chapter focused on the concepts of swapping and paging. We explained the mechanisms of how they work, followed by hands-on exercises for creating, activating, and managing swap spaces. This included configuring swap in both partition and logical volume, and ensuring their persistence across system reboots.

Review Questions

1. What information does the *blkid* command display about block devices?
2. What does the command *xfs_admin -L bootfs /dev/sda1* accomplish?
3. The *lsblk* command cannot display file system UUIDs. True or False?
4. Which two file systems are created during a default RHEL 10 installation?
5. What does *lvresize -r -L +30 /dev/vg02/lvol2* do?
6. XFS is the default file system type in RHEL 10. True or False?
7. What is the process of paging out and paging in known as?
8. What does the command *mkswap /dev/sdz2* do?
9. What would happen if you tried to mount a file system on a directory that already contains files in it?
10. A UUID is always assigned to a file system at its creation time. True or False?
11. Arrange the activities to create and activate a swap space while ensuring persistence: (a) swapon, (b) update fstab, (c) mkswap, and (d) reboot?
12. The primary superblock contains pointers to file data blocks, while backup superblocks do not. True or False?
13. What does *mkfs.ext4 /dev/vgtest/lvoltest* do?
14. Arrange in logical order: umount file system, mount file system, create file system, remove file system.
15. Which of these statements is wrong with respect to file systems: (a) optimize each file system independently, (b) keep dissimilar data in separate file systems, (c) grow and shrink a file system independent of other file systems, and (d) file systems cannot be expanded independent of other file systems.
16. Which command applies a label to an XFS file system?
17. Which virtual file contains information about the current swap?
18. The */etc/fstab* file can be used to activate swap spaces automatically at system reboots. True or False?
19. What is the standard file system type for optical media?
20. The *xfs_repair* command requires the target file system to be mounted. True or False?
21. Provide two commands that can be used to activate and deactivate swap spaces manually.
22. Provide the *fstab* file entry for an Ext4 file system located in device */dev/mapper/vg20-lv1* and mounted with default options on the */ora1* directory.

23. Which virtual file contains information about currently mounted file systems?
24. What does *mount -a* do?
25. What does *df -t xfs* display?
26. Which command reports total and used physical memory and swap space?
27. Name three commands that can display the UUID of an XFS file system.

Answers to Review Questions

1. The *blkid* command displays block device attributes including file system type, UUID, and label.
2. The command provided will apply the specified label to the XFS file system in */dev/sda1*.
3. False.
4. The root (*/*) and boot (*/boot*) file systems.
5. The command provided will expand the logical volume *lvol2* in volume group *vg02* and its file system by 30 MB.
6. True.
7. The process of paging out and in is known as demand paging.
8. The command provided will create swap structures in the */dev/vdz2* partition.
9. Existing files in the directory become inaccessible (hidden) until the file system is unmounted.
10. True.
11. Correct sequence: c/a/b or c/b/a.
12. False. Both primary and backup superblocks contain identical metadata; neither contains file data pointers.
13. The command provided will format */dev/vgtest/lvoltest* logical volume with Ext4 file system type.
14. Create, mount, unmount, and remove.
15. d is incorrect.
16. The *xfs_admin* command can be used to create a label for an XFS file system.
17. The */proc/swaps* file lists active swap areas and their usage.
18. True.
19. The default file system type for optical devices is ISO9660.
20. False. The command requires the file system to be unmounted.
21. The *swapon* and *swapoff* commands.
22. /dev/mapper/vg20-lv1 /ora1 ext4 defaults 0 0
23. The */proc/self/mounts* file.
24. The command provided will mount all file systems listed in */etc/fstab* that are not already mounted.
25. The command provided will display all mounted file systems of type XFS.
26. The *free* command.
27. You can use the *xfs_admin*, *lsblk*, and *blkid* commands to view the UUID of an XFS file system.

Do-It-Yourself Challenge Labs

The following labs are designed to reinforce most of the concepts and skills covered in this chapter. You are expected to complete these labs without external assistance. A step-by-step guide is not provided, as the required knowledge has already been presented in the chapter; however, each lab includes hints pointing to the relevant major topic(s).

Use the lab environment created specifically for the end-of-chapter labs. See the sub-section "Lab Environment for End-of-Chapter Labs" in Chapter 01 "Local Installation" for details.

Lab 16-1: Create VFAT, Ext4, and XFS File Systems in Partitions and Mount Persistently

As *user1* with *sudo* on *server4*, create three 70 MB primary partitions on one of the available 400 MB disks (*lsblk*) using the *parted* utility directly at the command prompt. Create an MBR partition table if the disk is new. Initialize partition 1 with VFAT, partition 2 with Ext4, and partition 3 with XFS file system types. Create mount points */vfatfs5*, */ext4fs5*, and */xfsfs5*, and mount all three manually. Determine the UUIDs for the three file systems, and add them to the *fstab* file. Unmount all three file systems manually, and execute *mount -a* to mount them all. Run *df -h* for verification. (Hint: File System Management).

Lab 16-2: Create Ext4 and XFS File Systems in LVM Volumes and Mount Persistently

As *user1* with *sudo* on *server4*, initialize an available 400 MB disk for use in LVM (*lsblk*). Create volume group *vg200* with PE size 8 MB and add the physical volume. Create two logical volumes *lv200* and *lv300* of sizes 120 MB and 100 MB. Use the *vgs*, *pvs*, *lvs*, and *vgdisplay* commands for verification. Initialize the volumes with Ext4 and XFS file system types. Create mount points */lvmfs5* and */lvmfs6*, and mount them manually. Add the file system information to the *fstab* file using their device files. Unmount the file systems manually, and execute *mount -a* to mount them back. Run *df -h* to confirm. (Hint: File System Management).

Lab 16-3: Extend Ext4 and XFS File Systems in LVM Volumes

As *user1* with *sudo* on *server4*, initialize an available 400 MB disk for use in LVM (*lsblk*). Add the new physical volume to volume group *vg200*. Expand logical volumes *lv200* and *lv300* along with the underlying file systems to 200 MB and 250 MB. Use the *vgs*, *pvs*, *lvs*, *vgdisplay*, and *df* commands for verification. (Hint: File System Management).

Lab 16-4: Create Swap in Partition and LVM Volume and Activate Persistently

As *user1* with *sudo* on *server4*, create two 100 MB partitions on an available 400 MB disk (*lsblk*) using the *parted* utility directly at the command prompt. Create an MBR partition table if the disk is new. Initialize one of the partitions with swap structures. Apply label *swappart* to the swap partition, and add it to the *fstab* file. Execute *swapon -a* to activate it. Run *swapon -s* to confirm activation.

Initialize the other partition for use in LVM. Expand volume group *vg200* (Lab 14-3) by adding this physical volume to it. Create logical volume *swapvol* of size 180 MB. Use the *vgs*, *pvs*, *lvs*, and *vgdisplay* commands for verification. Initialize the logical volume for swap. Add an entry to the *fstab* file for the new swap area using its device file. Execute *swapon -a* to activate it. Run *swapon* to confirm activation. (Hint: Swap and its Management).

Chapter 17

Networking Essentials and Network Connections

By the end of this chapter, you will be able to:

- Define Fundamental Networking Concepts: Hostnames, Protocols, Ports, and Ethernet Addresses
- Change System Hostname Persistently Using Multiple Methods
- Compare IPv4 and IPv6 Addressing
- Explain Classful and Classless Network Addressing, and Subnetting
- Describe Consistent Device Naming
- Differentiate Between Physical Network Device and Logical Connection Profile
- Analyze the Structure of a Network Connection Profile
- Manage Network Interfaces and Connections
- Configure Static IP Addresses
- Utilize the hosts Table for Hostname-to-IP Resolution
- Verify Network Configuration and Test Connectivity

RHCSA Objectives:

47. Configure IPv4 and IPv6 addresses

At the heart of every modern IT infrastructure lies the network—a system that allows computers to communicate, share resources, and access data. A computer network is formed when you connect two or more physical or virtual computers together via wired or wireless means. To work effectively with network configuration and troubleshooting, you need a solid understanding of fundamental concepts and terms.

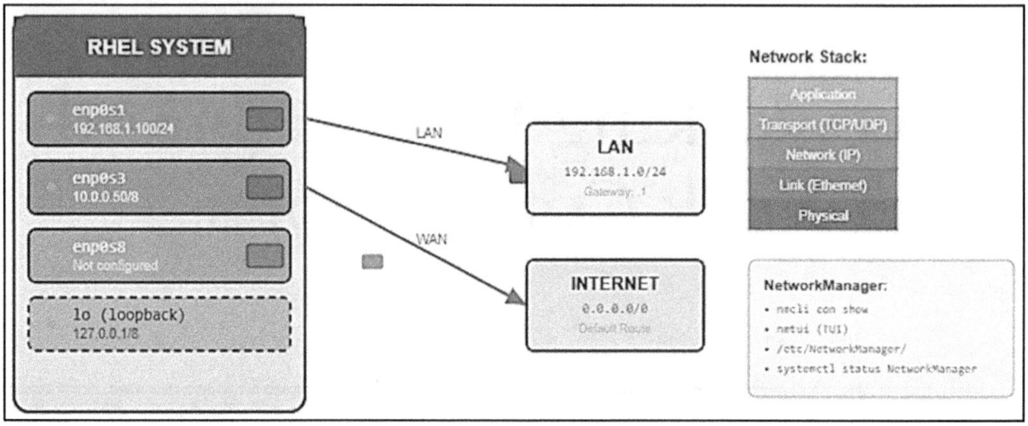

This chapter is structured to build this knowledge systematically. It begins by establishing a foundation in networking fundamentals, covering core concepts such as hostnames, key protocols, and hardware addressing. The discussion progresses to IP addressing, exploring the specifics of IPv4 and IPv6, followed by the evolution from classful to the classless (CIDR) addressing scheme. The chapter then details network devices and connections, including the NetworkManager service, the nmcli tool, and hands-on configuration of interfaces and connections.

For a system to communicate on a network, it must be configured with a unique IP and hostname. These parameters are stored within a connection profile attached to a network device. This chapter demonstrates how these assignments can be configured statically, modified using commands, and tested to confirm successful communication.

Networking Fundamentals

The primary purpose of computer networks is to allow users to share data and resources. A simple network is formed when two computers are interconnected. Using a networking device such as a *switch*, this network can be expanded to include additional computers, as well as printers, scanners, storage, and other devices (collectively referred to as *nodes*). A computer on the network can be configured to act as a file server, storage server, or a gateway to the Internet for the rest of the networked computers. Nodes may be interconnected using wired or wireless media. A corporate network may have thousands of nodes linked via a variety of data transmission media. The Internet is the largest network of networks with millions of nodes.

There are many elementary concepts and terms that you need to grasp before being able to configure network interfaces, connection profiles, and client/server setups that are covered in this and other chapters. There are also many configuration files and commands related to various network services that you need to understand thoroughly to manage a RHEL-based environment effectively. Some of these concepts, terms, configuration files, and commands are explained in this chapter.

Hostname

A *hostname* is a unique label that is assigned to a node to identify it on the network. It can consist of up to 63 alphanumeric characters including letters, digits, and hyphens. It is normally assigned based on the purpose and primary use of the system. In RHEL, the hostname is stored in the */etc/hostname* file.

The hostname can be viewed with several different commands, such as *hostname*, *hostnamectl*, *uname*, and *nmcli*, or by displaying the contents of the */etc/hostname* file. Run these commands on *server1*:

```
[user1@server1 ~]$ hostname
server1.example.com
[user1@server1 ~]$ hostnamectl --static
server1.example.com
[user1@server1 ~]$ uname -n
server1.example.com
[user1@server1 ~]$ nmcli general hostname
server1.example.com
[user1@server1 ~]$ cat /etc/hostname
server1.example.com
```

All the above commands displayed the same output.

Exercise 17-1: Change System Hostname

Perform this exercise on both *server1* and *server2* as *user1* with *sudo* where required. In this exercise, you will:

- Change the hostnames of both lab servers persistently
- Rename *server1.example.com* to *server10.example.com* by editing a file and restarting the corresponding service daemon
- Rename *server2.example.com* to *server20.example.com* using a command
- Validate the change on both systems

On *server1*:

1. Open the */etc/hostname* file in a text editor and change the current entry to the following:

```
server10.example.com
```

2. Execute the *systemctl* command to restart the *systemd-hostnamed* service and verify the new hostname with the *hostname* command:

```
[user1@server1 ~]$ sudo systemctl restart systemd-hostnamed
[user1@server1 ~]$ hostname
server10.example.com
```

3. To view the new hostname in the command prompt, log off and log back in as *user1*. The new prompt will look like:

```
[user1@server10 ~]$
```

On *server2***:**

1. Execute the *hostnamectl* command to change the hostname to *server20.example.com*:

```
[user1@server2 ~]$ sudo hostnamectl set-hostname server20.example.com
```

2. To view the new hostname in the command prompt, log off and log back in as *user1*. Use the *hostname* command to view the new name:

```
[user1@server20 ~]$
[user1@server20 ~]$ hostname
server20.example.com
```

You can also change the system hostname using the *nmcli* command. For instance, you could have used **nmcli general hostname server20.example.com** to rename *server2.example.com*. The *nmcli* command is explained in detail later in this chapter.

EXAM TIP: You need to know only one of the available methods to change the system hostname.

Going forward, you will be using the new hostnames *server10* and *server20*.

Protocol

A *protocol* is a set of rules governing the exchange of data between two network nodes. These rules include how data is formatted, coded, and controlled. The rules also provide error handling, speed matching, and data packet sequencing. In other words, a protocol is a common language that all nodes on the network speak and understand. Protocol numbers and their names are defined in the */etc/protocols* file. An excerpt from this file is provided below:

```
[user1@server10 ~]$ cat /etc/protocols
ip        0       IP          # internet protocol, pseudo protocol number
hopopt    0       HOPOPT      # hop-by-hop options for ipv6
icmp      1       ICMP        # internet control message protocol
igmp      2       IGMP        # internet group management protocol
ggp       3       GGP         # gateway-gateway protocol
ipv4      4       IPv4        # IPv4 encapsulation
........
```

Column 1 in the output lists the name of a protocol, followed by the associated protocol number, alias, and a short description in columns 2, 3, and 4.

Some common protocols include TCP, UDP, IP, and ICMP.

TCP and UDP Protocols

TCP (*Transmission Control Protocol*) and UDP (*User Datagram Protocol*) are transport-layer protocols responsible for carrying data between network nodes. TCP is reliable, connection-oriented, and point-to-point. It checks for errors and correct sequencing upon packet arrival at the destination node and returns an acknowledgement to the source, maintaining a reliable point-to-point connection between the communicating hosts. If the packet is received with an error or if it is lost in transit, the destination node requests a resend of the packet. This behavior ensures reliable data delivery. Due to its reliability and connection-oriented nature, TCP is widely implemented in network applications.

UDP, in contrast, is unreliable and connectionless. If a packet is lost or contains errors upon arrival at the destination, the source node is unaware of it. The destination node does not send an acknowledgment back to the source node. A common use of this protocol is in applications where low latency is preferred and reliability is not required.

Well-Known Ports

Both TCP and UDP use ports for data transmission between a client and its server program. Ports are categorized as well-known, registered, or dynamic (ephemeral). A well-known port is reserved for a specific service and is standardized across operating systems, while registered ports are assigned by IANA (*Internet Asigned Numbers Authority*) to vendor-specific or user applications. Well-known ports are defined in the */etc/services* file, an excerpt of which is presented below:

```
[user1@server10 ~]$ cat /etc/services
........
ftp             21/tcp
ftp             21/udp          fsp fspd
ssh             22/tcp                          # The Secure Shell (SSH) Protocol
ssh             22/udp                          # The Secure Shell (SSH) Protocol
telnet          23/tcp
telnet          23/udp
# 24 - private mail system
lmtp            24/tcp                          # LMTP Mail Delivery
lmtp            24/udp                          # LMTP Mail Delivery
smtp            25/tcp          mail
........
```

Column 1 lists the official name of a network service, followed by the port number and transport layer protocol the service uses, optional aliases, and comments in successive columns.

Some common services and the ports they listen on include FTP (*File Transfer Protocol*) 21, SSH (*Secure Shell*) 22, SMTP (*Simple Mail Transfer Protocol*) 25, DNS (*Domain Name System*) 53, HTTP (*HyperText Transfer Protocol*) 80, NTP (*Network Time Protocol*) 123, secure HTTP (*HyperText Transfer Protocol Secure*) 443, and rsyslog 514.

A dynamic (ephemeral) port is an automatically assigned port number used by a client application when initiating a communication session with a server. This port number is released after the session has ended.

ICMP Protocol

The *Internet Control Message Protocol* (ICMP) is a key protocol. It is primarily used for testing and diagnosing network connections. Commands such as *ping* use this protocol to send control messages to remote network devices to test connectivity and report statistical and diagnostic information. The report includes the number of packets transmitted, received, and lost; a round-trip time for individual packets with an overall average; a percentage of packets lost during the communication; and so on. See a sample below that shows two packets (-c2) sent from *server10* to the IP address of *server20*:

```
[user1@server10 ~]$ ping -c2 192.168.0.120
PING 192.168.0.120 (192.168.0.120) 56(84) bytes of data.
64 bytes from 192.168.0.120: icmp_seq=1 ttl=64 time=0.325 ms
64 bytes from 192.168.0.120: icmp_seq=2 ttl=64 time=0.402 ms

--- 192.168.0.120 ping statistics ---
2 packets transmitted, 2 received, 0% packet loss, time 45ms
rtt min/avg/max/mdev = 0.325/0.363/0.402/0.042 ms
```

Other commands, such as *traceroute*, also employ ICMP for route discovery and debugging.

Ethernet Address

An *Ethernet* address is a unique 48-bit address that is used to identify the correct destination node for data packets transmitted from the source node. The data packets include hardware addresses for the source and the destination node. The Ethernet address is also known as the *hardware* address, *physical* address, *link layer* address, or *MAC* address.

You can use the *ip* command to list all network interfaces available on the system along with their Ethernet addresses:

```
[user1@server10 ~]$ ip addr | grep ether
    link/ether 08:00:27:5f:fd:43 brd ff:ff:ff:ff:ff:ff
```

IP and hardware addresses work together, and a combination of both is critical to identifying the correct destination node on the network. A network protocol called *Address Resolution Protocol* (ARP) is used to enable IP and hardware addresses to work in tandem. ARP determines the hardware address of the destination node when its IP address is known.

IP Addressing: IPv4 and IPv6

Every device on a network requires a unique identifier to communicate, which is provided by an *Internet Protocol* (IP) address. Two versions of this protocol are in use today: the widely deployed IPv4 and its successor, IPv6. This section covers the structure, characteristics, and key differences between the two protocols.

IPv4 Address

IPv4 stands for *Internet Protocol version 4* and represents a unique 32-bit logical address that a node uses to communicate with other network nodes. It was the first version of IP that was released for public use. IPv4 addresses are commonly referred to as *dotted-decimal* (or *dotted-quad*) addresses, and they can be assigned on a temporary or permanent basis. Temporary addresses are referred to as *dynamic* addresses and are typically leased from a DHCP server for a defined period of time. Permanent addresses, on the other hand, are called *static* addresses and they are manually set.

You can use the *ip* command with the addr argument to view the current IP assignments on the system. Run this command on *server10* and see what it returns:

```
[user1@server10 ~]$ ip addr
1: lo: <LOOPBACK,UP,LOWER_UP> mtu 65536 qdisc noqueue state UNKNOWN
 group default qlen 1000
    link/loopback 00:00:00:00:00:00 brd 00:00:00:00:00:00
    inet 127.0.0.1/8 scope host lo
       valid_lft forever preferred_lft forever
    inet6 ::1/128 scope host noprefixroute
       valid_lft forever preferred_lft forever
2: enp0s3: <BROADCAST,MULTICAST,UP,LOWER_UP> mtu 1500 qdisc fq_code
l state UP group default qlen 1000
    link/ether 08:00:27:71:ef:78 brd ff:ff:ff:ff:ff:ff
    altname enx08002771ef78
    inet 192.168.0.110/24 brd 192.168.0.255 scope global noprefixro
ute enp0s3
       valid_lft forever preferred_lft forever
    inet6 2001:1970:5383:4b00:354c:1c7a:2c63:bf21/128 scope global
dynamic noprefixroute
       valid_lft 2228sec preferred_lft 2228sec
    inet6 2001:1970:5383:4b00:a00:27ff:fe71:ef78/64 scope global dy
namic noprefixroute
       valid_lft 604766sec preferred_lft 86366sec
    inet6 fe80::a00:27ff:fe71:ef78/64 scope link noprefixroute
       valid_lft forever preferred_lft forever
```

The output indicates one configured network connection (number 2 above) called *enp0s3* with IPv4 address 192.168.0.110 assigned to it. The other connection (number 1 above), represented as *lo*, is a special-purpose software device present on every Linux system. Its IPv4 address is typically 127.0.0.1, and it is known as the system's *loopback* (or *localhost*) address. Network programs and applications that communicate with the local system employ this interface.

IPv6 Address

With the explosive growth of the Internet, the presence of an extremely large number of network nodes requiring an IP, and an ever-increasing demand for additional addresses—the conventional IPv4 public address space, which provides approximately 4.3 billion addresses—has largely been exhausted. To meet the future demand, a new version of IP is now available and its use is expanding. This new version is referred to as IPv6 (*Internet Protocol version 6*), originally referred to as IPng (*Internet Protocol next generation*). By default, IPv6 is enabled in RHEL 10 on all configured network connections.

IPv6 is a 128-bit software address, providing access to approximately 340 undecillion (340 followed by 36 zeros) addresses. This is an extremely large space, and it is expected to fulfill the IP requirements for several decades to come.

IPv6 uses the *Neighbor Discovery Protocol* (NDP) to probe the network to discover neighboring IPv6 devices, determine their reachability, and map their associations. This protocol also includes enhanced functionalities (provided by ICMP and ARP in IPv4 networks) for troubleshooting issues pertaining to connectivity, address duplication, and routing.

Unlike IPv4 addresses, which are represented as four dot-separated octets, IPv6 addresses contain eight colon-separated 16-bit hexadecimal fields (hextets). A sample IPv6 address is 2001:1970:5383:4b00:a00:27ff:fe5f:fd43/64. To simplify representation, leading zeros in a hextet can be omitted, and a single contiguous sequence of hextets containing only zeros can be replaced with a double colon (::).

The *ip addr* command also shows IPv6 addresses for the interfaces:

```
[user1@server10 ~]$ ip addr | grep inet6
    inet6 ::1/128 scope host
    inet6 2001:1970:5383:4b00:a00:27ff:fe5f:fd43/64
```

It returns two IPv6 addresses. The first one belongs to the loopback interface (::1/128), and the second one is assigned to the *enp0s3* connection.

Major Differences between IPv4 and IPv6

There are several differences between IPv4 and IPv6 protocols. Some of the major ones are highlighted in Table 17-1.

IPv4	IPv6
Uses 4x8-bit, period-separated decimal number format. Example: 192.168.0.100	Uses 8x16-bit, colon-separated hexadecimal number format. Example: fe80::a00:27ff:feae:f35b
Number of address bits: 32	Number of address bits: 128
Maximum number of addresses: ~4.3 billion.	Maximum number of addresses: virtually unlimited
Common testing tools: ping, traceroute, tracepath, and others	Common testing tools are the same as for IPv4 (they auto-detect the IP version)
Support for IP autoconfiguration: limited (manual or DHCP)	Support for IP autoconfiguration: yes (via SLAAC)
Minimum packet size: 576 bytes	Minimum packet size: 1280 bytes
Built-in IPSec support: optional	Built-in IPsec support: optional and standardized

Table 17-1 IPv4 vs IPv6

The 127.0.0.0/8 range is reserved for loopback testing and cannot be assigned to nodes.

These and other differences not listed here are due to enhancements and new features added to IPv6.

IP Addressing: From Classful to Classless

The evolution of IP addressing has been driven by the need for greater efficiency and flexibility in a rapidly expanding internet. This section traces that journey, beginning with the original classful system, moving through the intermediary step of subnetting, and concluding with the modern Classless Inter-Domain Routing (CIDR) standard that is foundational to networking today.

Classful Addressing – The Historical Foundation

The original IPv4 address space was divided into five classes (A, B, C, D, and E) to accommodate networks of varying sizes and purposes. Classes A, B, and C were used for general network assignments, while class D was reserved for multicasting, and class E was set aside for experimental use.

Each address consisted of two parts: the *network* portion, which identified the destination network, and the *node* (or *host*) portion, which identified a specific device on that network.

The key characteristic of classful addressing was the fixed boundary between the network and node portions.

Table 17-2 summarizes the primary classes:

Class	Address Range	Default Mask	Max Networks	Max Hosts per Network	Typical Network Size
A	1.0.0.0 - 126.255.255.255	255.0.0.0	126	~16 million	Large
B	128.0.0.0 - 191.255.255.255	255.255.0.0	16,384	65,534	Medium
C	192.0.0.0 - 223.255.255.255	255.255.255.0	~2 million	254	Small

Table 17-2 Classful Network Addressing

The 127.0.0.0/8 range is reserved for loopback testing and cannot be assigned to nodes.

The rigid boundaries of classful addressing led to significant inefficiency and rapid IPv4 address exhaustion. A single large organization might get a full class A block but only use a fraction of it, while another organization might outgrow a class C block that only supported 254 nodes. These limitations created the need for a more flexible addressing solution.

Subnetting and the Subnet Mask

Subnetting is the process of dividing a large network address space into multiple smaller, logical subnetworks known as *subnets*. It helps reduce network congestion, improve performance, and simplify administration.

Technically, subnetting borrows bits from the node portion of the address to create additional network identifiers. The original network bits remain unchanged.

The following are key points to remember when dealing with subnetting:

- ✓ Subnetting reduces the number of usable node addresses.
- ✓ All devices within a subnet share the same subnet mask.
- ✓ Each subnet functions as an independent network and requires a router to communicate with other subnets.
- ✓ The first and last addresses in a subnet are reserved. The first identifies the subnet itself, and the last is the broadcast address.

A *subnet mask* (or *netmask*) defines which bits of an IP address represent the network and which represent the node. Routers use the mask to distinguish the boundary between network and node portions.

Like IP addresses, subnet masks can be written in binary or dotted-decimal notation. The 1s in the mask represent network or network bits, while the 0s represent node bits.

The default masks for the classful networks are provided in Table 17-2 (above).

Classless Addressing – The Modern Standard

Classless Inter-Domain Routing (CIDR) was designed to replace classful addressing to prevent the quick depletion of IPv4 addresses and reduce the size of global routing tables. CIDR eliminates the fixed class boundaries (8, 16, or 24 bits) and allows the network/node division to occur at any bit in the 32-bit address. This enables address allocation in variable-size blocks, improving efficiency and scalability.

CIDR notation expresses an IP address and its subnet mask compactly using a trailing slash (/) followed by the number of bits in the network portion (called the *prefix length*). For example, 192.168.1.10/24 is equivalent to the IP 192.168.1.10 with a subnet mask of 255.255.255.0. A /27 mask (255.255.255.224) creates smaller subnets of 32 addresses each, allowing for much more efficient use of address space than was possible with classful addressing.

While CIDR was introduced for IPv4, its prefix notation and hierarchical routing concepts are also used by IPv6.

Network Devices and Connections

Network Interface Cards (NICs) are hardware adapters that provide one or more Ethernet ports for network connectivity. NICs may also be referred to as *network adapters* and individual ports as *network interfaces* or *network devices*. NICs may be built-in to the system board or may be add-on adapters. They are available in one-, two-, and four port designs on a single adapter.

Individual interfaces (devices) can have one or more connection profiles associated with them, each containing different configuration settings. Each connection profile has a unique name and includes settings such as the device name, UUID, hardware address, IP address, and so on. A connection profile can be configured by editing configuration files or by using command-line tools. A device can have multiple connection profiles attached, but only one of them can be active at a time.

Consistent Network Device Naming

In RHEL versions 6 and earlier, network interfaces used *eth* (Ethernet), *em* (embedded), and *wlan* (wireless LAN) naming and were numbered starting at 0 as the interfaces were discovered during system boot. This was the default scheme that had been in place for network device naming for years. Given multiple interfaces located onboard and on add-on NICs, the number assignments could change on the next boot due to detection failures or errors, potentially resulting in connectivity and operational issues.

As of RHEL 7, the default naming scheme is based on a set of rules implemented by *systemd-udevd*. The default ruleset assigns names based on the device's physical location, topology, and firmware settings. The underlying virtualization platform—VMware, VirtualBox, KVM, Hyper-V—can also influence interface naming. Sample device names include *enp0s3* and *ens160*.

This advanced ruleset has resulted in consistent and predictable naming, eliminating the risk of interface re-enumeration during hardware rescans. Moreover, the designated names are not affected by the addition or removal of interface cards. This naming scheme helps in identifying, configuring, troubleshooting, and replacing the correct adapter without disruption.

Exercise 17-2: Add Network Devices to server10 and server20

This exercise adds one network interface to *server10* and one to *server20* using VirtualBox. In this exercise, you will:

- Shut down *server10* and *server20*
- Launch VirtualBox and add one network interface to each server
- Power on both servers and confirm the new interfaces

1. Execute **sudo shutdown now** on *server10*.
2. Start VirtualBox on your Windows/macOS computer and select *RHEL10-VM1*.
3. Click Settings at the top, and then select Network in the window that opens. Click on "Adapter 2" and check the "Enable Network Adapter" box. Select "Internal Network" from the drop-down list next to "Attached to". See Figure 17-1.

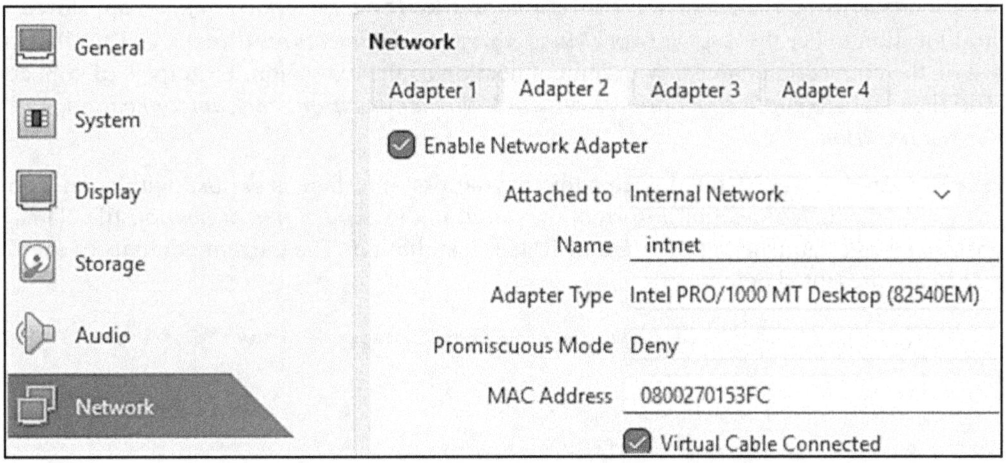

Figure 17-1 VirtualBox | Add Network Interface

4. Click OK to return to the main VirtualBox interface.
5. Power on *RHEL10-VM1*.
6. When the server is up, log on as *user1* and run the *ip a* command to verify the new interface:

```
[user1@server10 ~]$ ip a
........
 3: enp0s8: <BROADCAST,MULTICAST,UP,LOWER_UP> mtu 1500 qdisc fq_codel state UP gr
 oup default qlen 1000
     link/ether 08:00:27:01:53:fc brd ff:ff:ff:ff:ff:ff
     altname enx0800270153fc
```

The output reveals a new network device named *enp0s8*. This is the interface that you just added to the VM.

7. Repeat steps 1 through 6 to add a network interface to *server20* and verify the addition.

This completes the addition of new network interfaces to *server10* and *server20*. You are now ready to use them in the upcoming exercises.

The NetworkManager Service

NetworkManager is the default service used in RHEL 10 for configuring, administering, and monitoring network interfaces and connections. This service includes a daemon called *NetworkManager*, which is responsible for keeping available interfaces and connections active. It offers a powerful command-line tool called *nmcli* to manage interfaces and connections, and to control the service. This utility offers many options for effective management. The *NetworkManager* service also furnishes a text-based interface called *nmtui* and a graphical connection editor called *nm-connection-editor* that you may use in lieu of *nmcli*.

Understanding Interface Connection Profiles

Each network connection is defined by a configuration file that specifies IP assignments and other relevant parameters. The networking subsystem reads this file and applies the settings when the connection is activated. Connection configuration files (or *connection profiles*) are stored in a central location under the */etc/NetworkManager/system-connections* directory. The filenames are based on the connection names, with .nmconnection as the extension. Examples of connection profile files include *enp0s3.nmconnection*, *ens160.nmconnection*, *em1.nmconnection*, and *eth0.nmconnection*.

On *server10* and *server20*, the device name for the first interface is *enp0s3* with connection name *enp0s3* and relevant connection information stored in the *enp0s3.nmconnection* file. This connection was established at the time of RHEL installation. The current contents of the file from *server10* are presented below:

```
[user1@server10 ~]$ sudo cat /etc/NetworkManager/system-connections/enp0s3.nmcon
nection
[connection]
id=enp0s3
uuid=a3ca28ab-2cf0-3a27-84cf-8ccb0b693ec9
type=ethernet
autoconnect-priority=-999
interface-name=enp0s3
timestamp=1761572561

[ethernet]

[ipv4]
address1=192.168.0.110/24
gateway=192.168.0.1
method=manual

[ipv6]
addr-gen-mode=eui64
method=auto

[proxy]
```

The file has multiple sections. Each section defines a set of networking properties for the connection. The output above shows five sections—connection, ethernet, ipv4, ipv6, and proxy.

There are no settings defined under the ethernet and proxy sections. The other three have a few properties defined and they are outlined in Table 17-3 in the order in which they are listed.

Property	Description
id	Any description given to this connection. The default matches the interface name.
uuid	The UUID associated with this connection
type	Specifies the type of this connection
autoconnect-priority	If the connection is set to autoconnect, connections with higher priority will be preferred. A higher number means higher priority. The range is between -999 and 999 with 0 being the default.
interface_name	Specifies the device name for the network interface
timestamp	The time, in seconds since the Unix Epoch that the connection was last activated successfully. This field is automatically populated each time the connection is activated.
address1/method	Specifies the static IP for the connection if the method property is set to manual. /24 represents the subnet mask.
addr-gen-mode	Generates an IPv6 address based on the hardware address of the interface.

Table 17-3 Network Connection Configuration Directives

There are hundreds of other properties that may be defined in connection profiles depending on the type of interface and requirements. Run **man nm-settings** for a description of additional properties.

Network Device and Connection Administration Tools

There are a few tools and methods available for configuring and administering network interfaces, connections, and connection profiles. The *NetworkManager* service includes a toolset for this purpose as well. Table 17-4 lists the basic tools for network interface and connection management.

Command	Description
ip	A powerful and versatile tool for displaying, monitoring, and managing interfaces, connections, routing, traffic, etc.
nmcli	Creates, updates, deletes, activates, and deactivates connection profiles and manages devices.
nmtui	Text-equivalent for the nmcli command.
nm-connection-editor	Graphical tool for the management of network devices and connections.

Table 17-4 Network Interface and Connection Management Tools

You can manually create a connection profile and attach it to a network device; however, a discussion on that is beyond the scope of this book.

The ifup, ifdown, and ifconfig commands, and storing interface profiles in the /etc/sysconfig/network-scripts directory are deprecated and should no longer be used. The NetworkManager service and associated tools are the replacements.

The nmcli Command

nmcli is a NetworkManager command-line tool used to create, view, modify, remove, activate, and deactivate network connections, and to control and report network device status. It operates on seven different object categories, with each category supporting several options to form a complete command. The seven categories are general, networking, connection, device, radio, monitor, and agent. This discussion focuses only on the connection and device object categories. They are described in Table 17-5 along with management operations that they can perform.

Object	Description
Connection: activates, deactivates, and administers network connections	
show	Lists connections
up / down	Activates/deactivates a connection
add	Adds a connection
edit	Edits an existing connection or adds a new one
modify	Modifies one or more properties of a connection
delete	Deletes a connection
reload	Instructs NetworkManager to re-read all connection profiles
load	Instructs NetworkManager to re-read a connection profile
Device: displays and administers network interfaces	
status	Exhibits device status
show	Displays detailed information about all or the specified interface

Table 17-5 nmcli Subcommands

Object categories and their subcommands may be written in abbreviated form. For instance, the connection category may be abbreviated as a "c" or "con" and the device category as a "d" or "dev". The same rule applies to object names as well. For instance, add may be specified as an "a", delete as a "d", and so on. Refer to the *nmcli-examples* manual page for additional examples.

The *nmcli* command supports tab completion to make its use easier. Run a few examples on *server10* to understand the command's usage.

To show (s) all available connections (c):

```
[user1@server10 ~]$ nmcli c s
NAME    UUID                                  TYPE      DEVICE
enp0s3  a3ca28ab-2cf0-3a27-84cf-8ccb0b693ec9  ethernet  enp0s3
lo      9bc6b340-bd13-47ac-b056-12d92663ea04  loopback  lo
```

The output lists two connection profiles (NAME) and the devices (DEVICE) they are attached to. It also shows their UUID and type.

To display the status (s) of all available network devices (d):

```
[user1@server10 ~]$ nmcli d s
DEVICE  TYPE      STATE                   CONNECTION
enp0s3  ethernet  connected               enp0s3
lo      loopback  connected (externally)  lo
enp0s8  ethernet  disconnected            --
```

The output shows three devices and their types, states, and the connection profiles attached to them. The loopback interface is not managed by *NetworkManager*.

Exercise 17-3: Configure New Network Connections

Perform this exercise on *server10* and *server20* as *user1* with *sudo* where required. In this exercise, you will:

- Create a connection profile using the *nmcli* command for the new network interface *enp0s8* that was added to *server10* and *server20* in Exercise 17-2
- Assign IP 172.10.10.110/24 to *server10* and 172.10.10.120/24 to *server20*, and assign gateway 172.10.10.1 and DNS 172.10.10.1 to both
- Confirm new assignments

1. Check the presence of the new interface:

```
[user1@server10 ~]$ sudo nmcli d status | grep enp
enp0s3   ethernet   connected                     enp0s3
enp0s8   ethernet   disconnected                  --
```

The output signifies the existence of a new network device named *enp0s8*. It does not have a connection profile attached at the moment.

2. Add (a) a connection profile (c) and attach it to the new interface. Use the type Ethernet, device name (ifname) *enp0s8* with a matching connection name (con-name), CIDR (ip4) 172.10.10.110/24, gateway (gw4) 172.10.10.1, and DNS (ipv4.dns) 172.10.10.1:

```
[user1@server10 ~]$ sudo nmcli c a type ethernet ifname enp0s8 con-nam
e enp0s8 ip4 172.10.10.110/24 gw4 172.10.10.1 ipv4.dns 172.10.10.1
Connection 'enp0s8' (882e08b0-cf23-4822-ab5d-c58562954949) successfull
y added.
```

A new connection has been added, attached to the new interface, and activated. In addition, the command has saved the connection information in a new file called *enp0s8.nmconnection* and stored it in the */etc/NetworkManager/system-connections* directory.

3. Confirm the new connection status:

```
[user1@server10 ~]$ sudo nmcli d status | grep enp
enp0s3   ethernet   connected                     enp0s3
enp0s8   ethernet   connected                     enp0s8
```

The output indicates the association of the new connection with the network device.

4. Check the content of the *enp0s8.nmconnection* file:

```
[user1@server10 ~]$ sudo cat /etc/NetworkManager/system-connections/en
p0s8.nmconnection
[connection]
id=enp0s8
uuid=882e08b0-cf23-4822-ab5d-c58562954949
type=ethernet
interface-name=enp0s8

[ethernet]

[ipv4]
address1=172.10.10.110/24
dns=172.10.10.1;
gateway=172.10.10.1
method=manual

[ipv6]
addr-gen-mode=default
method=auto

[proxy]
```

There are many default directives added to the connection profile in addition to the configuration items you entered with the *nmcli* command above.

5. Check IP assignments for the new connection:

```
[user1@server10 ~]$ ip a show enp0s8
3: enp0s8: <BROADCAST,MULTICAST,UP,LOWER_UP> mtu 1500 qdisc fq_codel s
tate UP group default qlen 1000
    link/ether 08:00:27:01:53:fc brd ff:ff:ff:ff:ff:ff
    altname enx0800270153fc
    inet 172.10.10.110/24 brd 172.10.10.255 scope global noprefixroute
 enp0s8
       valid_lft forever preferred_lft forever
    inet6 fe80::6b18:cbd9:ac39:3841/64 scope link noprefixroute
       valid_lft forever preferred_lft forever
```

The IP is assigned to the interface. The connection will be tested later in this chapter.

Repeat steps 1 through 5 to configure a connection for *enp0s8* on *server20.*

This brings the exercise to a conclusion.

> **EXAM TIP:** You need to know only one of the available methods to configure IP assignments.

Understanding Hosts Table

Each IP address used on the system should have a hostname assigned to it. In an environment with multiple systems on the network, it is prudent to have some sort of a hostname to IP address resolution method in place to avoid repeatedly typing destination IP addresses when accessing systems. DNS is one such method. It is designed for scalable networks such as enterprise networks and the Internet. For small, internal networks, the use of a local hosts table (the */etc/hosts* file) is also common. This file is used to maintain static hostname-to-IP mappings for systems on a local network, allowing us to access a system by simply employing its hostname. In this book, there are two systems in place: *server10.example.com* with IP 192.168.0.110 and alias *server10*, and *server20.example.com* with IP 192.168.0.120 and alias *server20*. You can append this information to the */etc/hosts* file on both *server10* and *server20* as shown below:

```
192.168.0.110     server10.example.com     server10
192.168.0.120     server20.example.com     server20
```

Each row in the file contains an IP address in column 1 followed by the *official* (*canonical*) hostname in column 2, and one or more optional aliases thereafter. The official hostname and one or more aliases give users the flexibility of accessing the system using any of these names.

> **EXAM TIP:** In the presence of an active DNS where all hostnames are resolvable, updating the /etc/hosts file is usually unnecessary.

As expressed above, the use of the *hosts* file is common on small networks, and it should be updated on each individual system to reflect any changes for best inter-system connectivity experience.

Testing Network Connectivity

RHEL includes the *ping* command to examine network connectivity between two systems. It uses the IP address of the destination system to send a series of ICMP Echo Request packets to it. A response from the remote system validates connectivity and health. With the -c option, you can specify the number of packets to transmit.

The following sends two packets from *server10* to 192.168.0.120 (*server20*):

```
[user1@server10 ~]$ ping 192.168.0.120 -c 2
PING 192.168.0.120 (192.168.0.120) 56(84) bytes of data.
64 bytes from 192.168.0.120: icmp_seq=1 ttl=64 time=0.406 ms
64 bytes from 192.168.0.120: icmp_seq=2 ttl=64 time=0.418 ms

--- 192.168.0.120 ping statistics ---
2 packets transmitted, 2 received, 0% packet loss, time 38ms
rtt min/avg/max/mdev = 0.406/0.412/0.418/0.006 ms
```

Under "192.168.0.120 ping statistics," the output shows the number of packets transmitted, received, and lost. The packet loss should be 0%, and the round-trip time should not be too high for a healthy connection. In general, you can use this command to test connectivity with the system's own IP, the loopback IP (127.0.0.1), a static route, the default gateway, and any other address on the local or remote network.

If a *ping* response fails, you need to check that the NIC is present and recognized by the system, its driver is installed, network cable is secured appropriately, IP and netmask values are set correctly, and the default or static route is accurate.

Exercise 17-4: Update Hosts Table and Test Connectivity

Perform this exercise on *server10* and *server20* as *user1* with *sudo* where required. In this exercise, you will:

- Update the */etc/hosts* file on *server10* and *server20*
- Add the IP addresses assigned to both network connections and map them to the hostnames *server10*, *server10s8*, *server20*, and *server20s8* appropriately
- Test connectivity from *server10* to *server20* and from *server10s8* to *server20s8* using their IP addresses and then their hostnames

On *server10*:

1. Open the */etc/hosts* file and add the following entries:

```
192.168.0.110 server10.example.com server10
192.168.0.120 server20.example.com server20
172.10.10.110 server10s8.example.com server10s8
172.10.10.120 server20s8.example.com server20s8
```

On *server20*:

2. Open the */etc/hosts* file and add the following entries:

```
192.168.0.110 server10.example.com server10
192.168.0.120 server20.example.com server20
172.10.10.110 server10s8.example.com server10s8
172.10.10.120 server20s8.example.com server20s8
```

3. Send two ICMP packets from *server10* to the IP address of *server20*:

```
[user1@server10 ~]$ ping -c2 192.168.0.120
PING 192.168.0.120 (192.168.0.120) 56(84) bytes of data.
64 bytes from 192.168.0.120: icmp_seq=1 ttl=64 time=0.369 ms
64 bytes from 192.168.0.120: icmp_seq=2 ttl=64 time=0.446 ms

--- 192.168.0.120 ping statistics ---
2 packets transmitted, 2 received, 0% packet loss, time 45ms
rtt min/avg/max/mdev = 0.369/0.407/0.446/0.043 ms
```

4. Issue two ICMP packets on *server10* to the hostname of *server20*:

```
[user1@server10 ~]$ ping -c2 server20
PING server20.example.com (192.168.0.120) 56(84) bytes of data.
64 bytes from server20.example.com (192.168.0.120): icmp_seq=1 ttl=64 time=0.351 ms
64 bytes from server20.example.com (192.168.0.120): icmp_seq=2 ttl=64 time=0.422 ms

--- server20.example.com ping statistics ---
2 packets transmitted, 2 received, 0% packet loss, time 26ms
rtt min/avg/max/mdev = 0.351/0.386/0.422/0.040 ms
```

5. Send one ICMP packet from *server10* to the IP address associated with *server20s8*:

```
[user1@server10 ~]$ ping -c1 172.10.10.120
PING 172.10.10.120 (172.10.10.120) 56(84) bytes of data.
64 bytes from 172.10.10.120: icmp_seq=1 ttl=64 time=4.56 ms

--- 172.10.10.120 ping statistics ---
1 packets transmitted, 1 received, 0% packet loss, time 0ms
rtt min/avg/max/mdev = 4.558/4.558/4.558/0.000 ms
```

6. Issue one ICMP packet on *server10* to the hostname of *server20s8*:

```
[user1@server10 ~]$ ping -c1 server20s8
PING server20s8.example.com (172.10.10.120) 56(84) bytes of
64 bytes from server20s8.example.com (172.10.10.120): icmp_s
31 ms

--- server20s8.example.com ping statistics ---
1 packets transmitted, 1 received, 0% packet loss, time 0ms
rtt min/avg/max/mdev = 2.313/2.313/2.313/0.000 ms
```

Steps 3 through 6 verified the connectivity to the remote server over both connections. Each server has two IP addresses, and each IP address is mapped to a unique hostname.

This concludes the exercise.

Chapter Summary

This chapter discussed the rudiments of networking. It began by providing an understanding of various essential networking terms and concepts to build the foundation for networking topics going forward. Topics such as hostname, protocols, network ports, Ethernet addresses, IPv4, IPv6, classful and classless network addressing, subnetting, and consistent device naming were covered in sufficient detail.

We modified hostnames on both lab servers by modifying a configuration file and restarting the hostname service on one server and using a single command on the other. We employed two methods to demonstrate multiple ways of doing the same thing. A third method was also mentioned to rename a hostname.

Next, we described the terms network devices and network connections, and realized the difference between the two. We examined a connection profile and looked at directives that can be defined for a network connection. We added a new network device to each lab server and configured them. We activated the new connections and performed a ping test for functional validation. Lastly, we populated the hosts tables with the IP and hostname mapping on both lab servers.

Review Questions

1. Name four commands that can be used to display the hostname.
2. Which service is responsible for maintaining consistent device naming?
3. Define protocol.
4. What is the functional difference between a network device and a network connection in RHEL?

5. List two key differences between TCP and UDP protocols.
6. What would the *ip addr* command produce?
7. What is the significance of the NAME and DEVICE directives in a connection profile?
8. Which command can you use to display the hardware address of a network device?
9. Which directory stores the network connection profiles?
10. What would the command *nmcli c s* do?
11. True or False. A network device is a network port and a network connection is a configuration file attached to it.
12. IPv4 is a 32-bit logical address. How many bits does an IPv6 address have?
13. What would the command *hostnamectl set-hostname host20* do?
14. Name the file that stores the hostname of the system.
15. The */etc/hosts* file maintains hostname-to-hardware address mappings. True or False?
16. Which file would you consult to identify the port number and protocol associated with a network service?

Answers to Review Questions

1. The *hostname*, *uname*, *hostnamectl*, and *nmcli* commands can be used to view the system hostname.
2. The *systemd-udevd* service handles consistent naming of network devices.
3. A set of rules that govern the exchange of information between two network nodes.
4. A network device is the physical or virtual network interface (for example, enp0s3), while a network connection is a configuration profile that defines how the device is configured and used.
5. TCP is connection-oriented and reliable; UDP is connectionless and unreliable.
6. This command provided will display detailed information about network interfaces, including IP assignments, interface state, and hardware (MAC) address.
7. The NAME directive sets the name for the network connection, and the DEVICE directive defines the network device the connection is associated with.
8. The *ip* command.
9. The */etc/NetworkManager/system-connections* directory.
10. The command provided will display the status information for all network connections.
11. True.
12. 128.
13. The command provided will set the system hostname to host20 by updating the */etc/hostname* file and immediately applies the change via the *systemd-hostnamed* service.
14. The */etc/hostname* file.
15. False. This file maintains the hostname-to-IP address mappings.
16. The */etc/services* file.

Do-It-Yourself Challenge Labs

The following labs are designed to reinforce most of the concepts and skills covered in this chapter. You are expected to complete these labs without external assistance. A step-by-step guide is not provided, as the required knowledge has already been presented in the chapter; however, each lab includes hints pointing to the relevant major topic(s).

Use the lab environment created specifically for the end-of-chapter labs. See the sub-section "Lab Environment for End-of-Chapter Labs" in Chapter 01 "Local Installation" for details.

Lab 17-1: Add a New Interface and Configure Connection Profile

Add a third network interface to *RHEL10-VM3* in VirtualBox.

As *user1* with *sudo* on *server30*, run *ip a* and verify the addition of the new interface. Use the *nmcli* command and assign IP 192.168.0.230/24, gateway 192.168.0.1, and DNS 192.168.0.1. Deactivate and reactivate this connection manually. (Hint: Exercise 17-2 and Exercise 17-3).

Lab 17-2: Add a New Interface, Configure Connection Profile, and Test Connectivity

Add a third network interface to *RHEL10-VM4* in VirtualBox.

As *user1* with *sudo* on *server40*, run *ip a* and verify the addition of the new interface. Use the *nmcli* command and assign IP 192.168.0.240/24, gateway 192.168.0.1, and DNS 192.168.0.1. Deactivate and reactivate this connection manually. Add entries for both *server30-3* and *server40-3* to the *hosts* table of both systems. Run ping tests between the two systems using hostnames and then IP addresses. (Hint: Exercise 17-2, Exercise 17-3, and Exercise 17-4).

Chapter 18

Network File System and AutoFS

By the end of this chapter, you will be able to:

- Describe the Core Concepts and Architecture of the Network File System (NFS) Service
- Explain the Advantages of NFS and the Difference Between its Versions
- Configure an NFS Server to Share a Directory with Specific Clients
- Mount an NFS Share on a Client Manually and Persistently
- Discover the AutoFS Service: Learn How it Works, its Benefits over Static Mounts, and Key Components
- Analyze AutoFS Maps to Control Automount Behavior
- Mount NFS Shares On-Demand Using Direct and Indirect Mapping Techniques
- Configure NFS and AutoFS to Centrally Store and Automatically Mount User Home Directories

RHCSA Objectives:

37. Mount and unmount network file systems using NFS
38. Configure autofs

Sharing files seamlessly between servers is a common requirement in any environment. You can mount shares on RHEL and accessed them the same way as local file systems. You can do this manually using the same tools that you employ for mounting and unmounting local file systems. An alternative solution is to implement the AutoFS service to automatically mount and unmount them without the need to execute any commands explicitly. AutoFS monitors activities in mount points based on which it triggers a mount or unmount action.

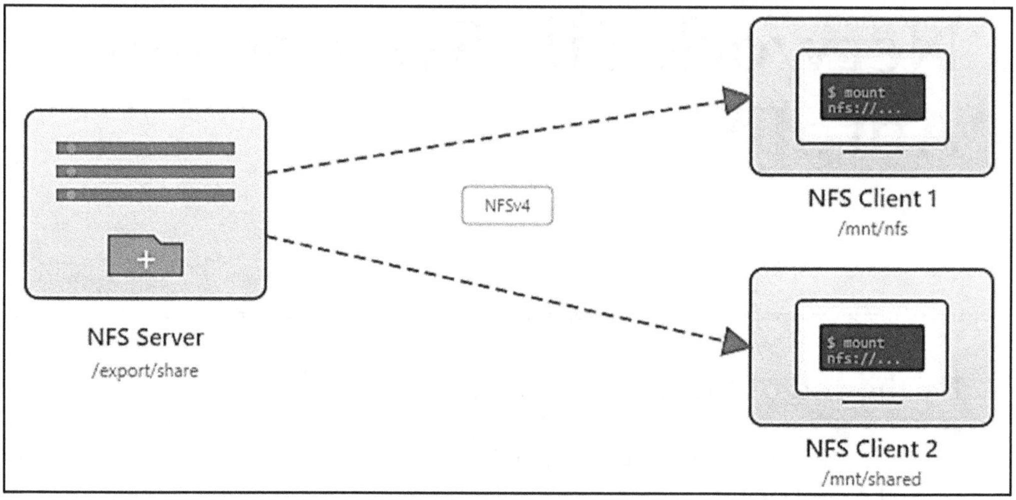

RHEL exports shares using the Network File System service for remote mounting on clients. A combination of this service and AutoFS/standard mount is prevalent in real world scenarios. This chapter elaborates on the benefits of the file sharing solution and expounds upon AutoFS. It demonstrates a series of exercises to detail the server-side and client-side configurations. It also explores the automatic mounting of user home directories on clients.

Network File System

Network File System (NFS) is a distributed file system protocol that allows file sharing over a network. The Network File System service is based upon the client/server architecture whereby users on one system access files, directories, and file systems (collectively called *shares*) that reside on a remote system as if they are mounted locally on their system. The remote system that makes its shares available for network access is referred to as an NFS server, and the process of making the shares accessible is referred to as *exporting*. The shares the NFS server exports may be accessed by one or more systems. These systems are called NFS clients, and the process of making the shares accessible on clients is referred to as *mounting*. See Figure 18-1 for a simple NFS client/server arrangement that shows two shares—*/export1* and */export2*—exported on the network to a remote system, which has them mounted there.

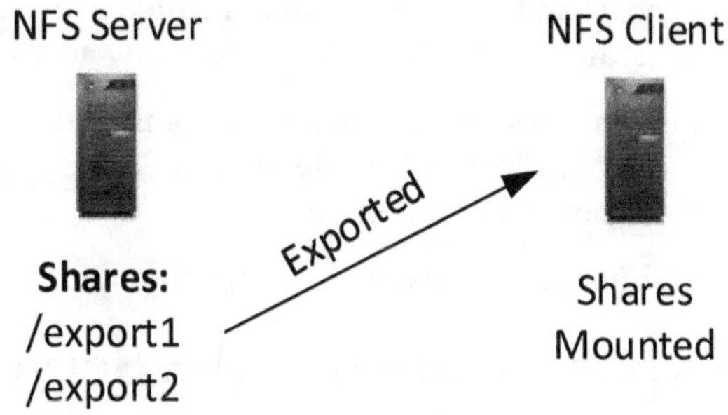

Figure 18-1 NFS Server/Client

A system can provide both server and client functionality concurrently. When a directory or file system share is exported, the entire directory structure beneath it becomes available for mounting on the client. A subdirectory or the parent directory of a share cannot be re-exported if they exist in the same file system. Similarly, a mounted share should not be re-exported, as this configuration is unsupported and can lead to unpredictable behavior. A single exported file share is mounted on a directory mount point.

Benefits of Using NFS

The use of NFS provides several benefits, some of which are highlighted below:

- ✓ Supports a variety of operating system platforms including Linux and UNIX, and can interoperate with Microsoft Windows through additional services.
- ✓ Multiple NFS clients can access a single share simultaneously.
- ✓ Enables the sharing of common application binaries and other read-only information, resulting in reduced administration overhead and storage cost.
- ✓ Gives users access to uniform data.
- ✓ Allows the consolidation of scattered user home directories on the NFS server and then exporting them to the clients. This way users will have only one home directory to maintain.

NFS Versions

RHEL 10 provides support for NFS versions 3, 4.0, 4.1, and 4.2, with version 4.2 being the default. NFSv3 supports both TCP and UDP transport protocols, asynchronous writes, and 64-bit file sizes, which give clients the ability to access files larger than 2 GB.

NFSv4.x are *Internet Engineering Task Force* (IETF) series of protocols that provide all the features of NFSv3, plus the ability to transit firewalls and work on the Internet. They provide enhanced security and support for encrypted transfers, as well as greater scalability, better cross-platform interoperability, and better system crash handling. They use usernames and group names mapped to UIDs and GIDs for files located on network shares. NFSv4.0 and NFSv4.1 use TCP by default. UDP support exists only for limited backward compatibility and is rarely used. In contrast, NFSv4.2 only supports TCP.

NFS Server and Client Configuration

This section presents two exercises, one demonstrating how to export a share on a server (NFS server) and the other outlines the steps on mounting and accessing a share on a remote system (NFS client). The basic setup of the NFS service is straightforward. It requires adding an entry of the share to a file named */etc/exports* and using a command called *exportfs* to make it available on the network. It also requires the addition of a firewall rule to allow access to the share by NFS clients.

The *mount* command used on an NFS client is the same command used in Chapter 16 "Local File Systems and Swap Space" to mount local file systems. Moreover, the *fstab* file requires an entry for the NFS share on the client for persistent mounting.

The exercises in this section illustrate the usage of both commands and the syntax of both files.

Exercise 18-1: Export Share on NFS Server

Perform this exercise on *server20* as *user1* with *sudo* where required. In this exercise, you will:

- Create a directory called */common*
- Export */common* to *server10* in read/write mode
- Ensure that NFS traffic is allowed through the Linux firewall
- Confirm the export

1. Install the NFS software called *nfs-utils*:

```
[user1@server20 ~]$ sudo dnf -y install nfs-utils
Last metadata expiration check: 0:00:09 ago on Wed 17 Dec 2025 10:38:
58 AM.
Dependencies resolved.
======================================================================
 Package              Arch        Version             Repository  Size
======================================================================
Installing:
 nfs-utils            x86_64      1:2.8.2-3.el10      BaseOS     487 k
Installing dependencies:
 gssproxy             x86_64      0.9.2-10.el10       BaseOS     118 k
 libev                x86_64      4.33-14.el10        BaseOS      56 k
 libnfsidmap          x86_64      1:2.8.2-3.el10      BaseOS      67 k
 libverto-libev       x86_64      0.3.2-10.el10       BaseOS      15 k
 rpcbind              x86_64      1.2.7-3.el10        BaseOS      63 k
 sssd-nfs-idmap       x86_64      2.10.2-3.el10       BaseOS      39 k

Transaction Summary
======================================================================
Install  7 Packages

Total size: 845 k
Installed size: 2.0 M

........
Installed:
  gssproxy-0.9.2-10.el10.x86_64
  libev-4.33-14.el10.x86_64
  libnfsidmap-1:2.8.2-3.el10.x86_64
  libverto-libev-0.3.2-10.el10.x86_64
  nfs-utils-1:2.8.2-3.el10.x86_64
  rpcbind-1.2.7-3.el10.x86_64
  sssd-nfs-idmap-2.10.2-3.el10.x86_64

Complete!
```

Follow the instructions outlined in "Exercise 10-1: Mount RHEL 10 ISO Persistently" and "Exercise 11-1: Configure Access to dnf Repositories" to ensure the above software installation works.

2. Create */common* directory to be exported as a share:

```
[user1@server20 ~]$ sudo mkdir /common
```

3. Add full permissions to */common*:

```
[user1@server20 ~]$ sudo chmod 777 /common
```

4. Add the NFS service persistently to the Linux firewall to allow the NFS traffic to pass through it, and load the new rule:

```
[user1@server20 ~]$ sudo firewall-cmd --permanent --add-service nfs
success
[user1@server20 ~]$ sudo firewall-cmd --reload
success
```

Refer to Chapter 21 "The Linux Firewall" for details around the Linux firewall service.

5. Start the NFS service and enable it to autostart at system reboots:

```
[user1@server20 ~]$ sudo systemctl --now enable nfs-server
Created symlink /etc/systemd/system/multi-user.target.wants/nfs-server.service
→ /usr/lib/systemd/system/nfs-server.service.
```

6. Verify the operational status of the NFS service:

```
[user1@server20 ~]$ sudo systemctl status nfs-server
● nfs-server.service - NFS server and services
     Loaded: loaded (/usr/lib/systemd/system/nfs-server.service; ena>
     Active: active (exited) since Wed 2025-12-17 10:44:50 EST; 21s >
 Invocation: e01528eb3f4b4507a8fcc661028ec7c2
       Docs: man:rpc.nfsd(8)
             man:exportfs(8)
    Process: 3292 ExecStartPre=/usr/sbin/exportfs -r (code=exited, s>
    Process: 3294 ExecStart=/bin/sh -c /usr/sbin/nfsdctl autostart |>
    Process: 3322 ExecStart=/bin/sh -c if systemctl -q is-active gss>
   Main PID: 3322 (code=exited, status=0/SUCCESS)
   Mem peak: 1.6M
        CPU: 101ms

Dec 17 10:44:49 server20.example.com systemd[1]: Starting nfs-server>
Dec 17 10:44:50 server20.example.com systemd[1]: Finished nfs-server>
```

7. Open the */etc/exports* file in a text editor and add an entry for */common* to export it to *server10* with read/write option:

```
/common server10(rw)
```

8. Export the entry defined in the */etc/exports* file. The -a option exports all the entries listed in the file and -v displays verbose output.

```
[user1@server20 ~]$ sudo exportfs -av
exporting server10.example.com:/common
```

The NFS service is now set up on *server20* with the */common* share available for mounting on *server10* (NFS client in this case).

For practice, you can unexport the share by issuing the *exportfs* command with the -u flag as follows:

```
[user1@server20 ~]$ sudo exportfs -u server10:/common
```

Before proceeding, re-export the share using **sudo exportfs -av**.

Exercise 18-2: Mount Share on NFS Client

Perform this exercise on *server10* as *user1* with *sudo* where required. In this exercise, you will:

- Mount the */common* share exported in Exercise 18-1
- Create a mount point called */local*
- Mount the remote share manually
- Confirm the mount
- Add the remote share to the file system table for persistence
- Remount the share and confirm
- Create a test file in the mount point
- Confirm the file creation on the NFS server

1. Install the NFS software called *nfs-utils*:

```
[user1@server10 ~]$ sudo dnf -y install nfs-utils
```

2. Create */local* mount point:

```
[user1@server10 ~]$ sudo mkdir /local
```

3. Mount the share manually using the *mount* command:

```
[user1@server10 ~]$ sudo mount server20:/common /local
```

The remote share is successfully mounted on *server10*, and it can be accessed as any other local file system.

4. Confirm the mount using either the *mount* or the *df* command:

```
[user1@server10 ~]$ mount | grep local
server20:/common on /local type nfs4 (rw,relatime,vers=4.2,rsize=26214
4,wsize=262144,namlen=255,hard,fatal_neterrors=none,proto=tcp,timeo=60
0,retrans=2,sec=sys,clientaddr=192.168.0.110,local_lock=none,addr=192.
168.0.120)
[user1@server10 ~]$
[user1@server10 ~]$ df -h | grep local
server20:/common          17G  4.1G   13G  25% /local
```

The *mount* command output displays the NFS protocol version (NFS4.2) and the default mount options used for the share.

5. Open the */etc/fstab* file and append the following entry for persistence:

```
server20:/common   /local   nfs   _netdev   0  0
```

The _netdev option instructs the system to wait for networking to be available before attempting to mount the share.

A mount point should be empty and must not be in use when an attempt is made to mount a share to it.

6. Unmount the share manually using the *umount* command and remount it via the *fstab* file to validate the accuracy of the entry placed in the file:

```
[user1@server10 ~]$ sudo umount /local
[user1@server10 ~]$ sudo mount -a
```

7. Run **mount** and **df -h** again to verify the remounting.
8. Create a file called *nfsfile* under */local* and verify:

```
[user1@server10 ~]$ touch /local/nfsfile
[user1@server10 ~]$ ls -l /local/
total 0
-rw-r--r--. 1 user1 user1 0 Dec 17  2025 nfsfile
```

9. Confirm the file creation on the NFS server (*server20*):

```
[user1@server20 ~]$ ls -l /common/
total 0
-rw-r--r--. 1 user1 user1 0 Dec 17 10:54 nfsfile
```

EXAM TIP: Do not forget to update the /etc/fstab file on the client.

This completes the setup and testing of mounting, unmounting, and remounting of an NFS share on the client.

Auto File System (AutoFS)

In the previous section, you learned how to attach (mount) an NFS share to the Linux directory tree manually for access by users and applications on an NFS client. Once attached, the share was treated just like any other local file system. You also learned how to manually detach (unmount) an NFS share from the directory tree to make it inaccessible to users and applications. To ensure that the share is remounted after a system reboot, you added it to the *fstab* file.

RHEL provides an alternative method for mounting and unmounting shares dynamically at runtime and automatically across system reboots. This feature is delivered by a service called the *Auto File System* (AutoFS). AutoFS is a client-side service that automatically mounts a network file system, such as an NFS share, on-demand. With a proper entry placed in AutoFS configuration files, the AutoFS service automatically mounts a share upon detecting activity in its mount point with a command such as *ls* or *cd*. Similarly, AutoFS unmounts the share automatically if it has not been accessed for a predefined period of time.

To prevent inconsistencies, mounts managed by AutoFS must not be mounted or unmounted manually or defined in the /etc/fstab file.

The use of AutoFS prevents the kernel from maintaining unused mounts, resulting in reduced resource usage and improved reliability.

Benefits of Using AutoFS

There are several benefits associated with using the AutoFS service over placing entries in the */etc/fstab* file. Some of the key benefits are described below:

- ✓ AutoFS requires NFS shares to be defined in text configuration files called *maps*, located in the */etc* or */etc/auto.master.d* directory. AutoFS does not make use of the */etc/fstab* file.
- ✓ AutoFS does not require users to have *root* privileges to access a mounted NFS share; manual mounting and mounting via *fstab* do require that privilege.
- ✓ AutoFS prevents an NFS client from hanging if an NFS server is down or inaccessible. With the other method, the unavailability of the NFS server may cause the NFS client to hang.
- ✓ With AutoFS, a share is unmounted automatically if it is not accessed for a configurable timeout period (300 seconds by default). With the *fstab* method, the share stays mounted until it is either manually unmounted or the client shuts down.
- ✓ AutoFS supports wildcard characters and environment variables, features that the other method does not support.

How AutoFS Works

The AutoFS service runs a user-space daemon called *automount*, which is responsible for automatically mounting and unmounting NFS file systems. The daemon starts at system boot and reads the master map but does not mount any shares immediately.

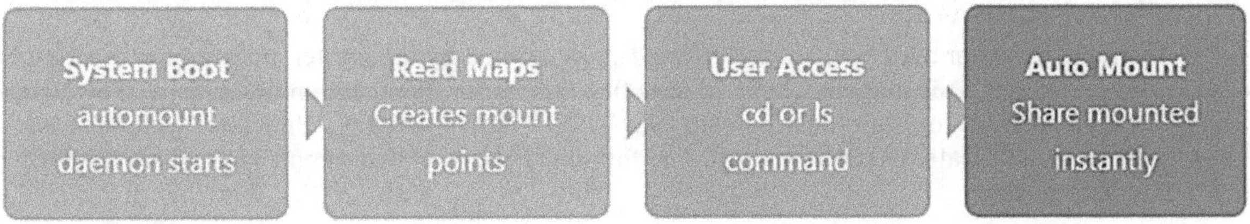

When the service detects user activity under a mount point during runtime, it mounts the requested file system at that time. If a share remains idle for a certain time period, *automount* unmounts it by itself.

AutoFS Configuration File

The primary configuration file for the AutoFS service is */etc/autofs.conf*, which AutoFS reads at service startup. Some key directives from this file are shown below along with their preset values:

```
master_map_name = auto.master
timeout = 300
negative_timeout = 60
mount_nfs_default_protocol = 4
logging = none
```

There are additional directives available in this file and more can be added to modify the default behavior of the AutoFS service. Table 18-1 describes the above directives.

Directive	Description
master_map_name	Defines the name of the master map. The default is auto.master located in the /etc directory.
timeout	Specifies, in seconds, the maximum idle time after which a share is automatically unmounted. The default is five minutes.
negative_timeout	Expresses, in seconds, a timeout value for failed mount attempts. The default is one minute.
mount_nfs_default_protocol	Sets the default NFS protocol version used when mounting shares.
logging	Configures a logging level. Options are none, verbose, and debug. The default is none (disabled).

Table 18-1 AutoFS Directives

The directives in the *autofs.conf* file are normally left at their default values, but you can alter them if required.

AutoFS Maps

AutoFS needs to know which NFS shares to mount, where to mount them, and which mount options to apply. This information is stored in configuration files called *maps*. There are three common map types: *master*, *direct*, and *indirect*.

The Master Map

The default master map file is */etc/auto.master*, as defined by the master_map_name directive in */etc/autofs.conf*. This map may be used to define entries for direct and indirect maps. However, it is recommended to store user-defined map files in the */etc/auto.master.d* directory, which the AutoFS service automatically parses at startup. The following presents two samples to explain the format of the map entries:

```
/-        /etc/auto.master.d/auto.direct        # Line 1
/misc     /etc/auto.misc                        # Line 2
```

The two entries are explained below.

The Direct Map

The direct map is used to mount shares automatically on any number of unrelated mount points. Some key points to note when working with direct maps are:

- ✓ Direct mounted shares are always visible to users.
- ✓ Local and direct mounted shares can coexist under one parent directory.
- ✓ Accessing a directory containing multiple direct mount points may trigger mounting of all shares.

Each direct map entry places a separate share entry in the mount table */proc/self/mounts*, historically */etc/mtab*. This file is updated whenever a local file system, removable file system, or network share is mounted or unmounted.

Line 1 from above defines a direct map and points to the */etc/auto.master.d/auto.direct* file for mount details.

You may append options to the line entry in *auto.master*; however, any options specified there applies to all subentries in the referenced map file.

The Indirect Map

The indirect map is preferred when you want to mount all shares under a common parent directory. Some key points to note when working with indirect maps are:

- ✓ Indirect mounted shares become visible only after the corresponding subdirectory is accessed.
- ✓ Local and indirect mounted shares cannot coexist under the same parent directory.
- ✓ Each indirect map puts only one entry in the */etc/mtab* mount table.
- ✓ Accessing a directory containing many indirect mount points shows only the shares that are already mounted.

Line 2 from above represents an indirect map, notifying AutoFS to refer to the */etc/auto.misc* file for mount details. The umbrella mount point */misc* will precede all mount point entries listed in the */etc/auto.misc* file. This indirect map entry is normally used to automount removable file systems, such as CDs, DVDs, external USB disks, and so on. Any custom indirect map file should be located in the */etc/auto.master.d* directory.

You may append an option to the corresponding line entry in the *auto.master* file above; however, that option will apply to all subentries in the specified map file.

Direct Map vs. Indirect Map

Both direct and indirect maps have their own advantages and limitations.

Direct Map	Indirect Map
✓ Mounts on unrelated mount points	✓ Mounts under common parent directory
✓ Always visible to users	✓ Visible only after access
✓ Can coexist with local shares	✓ Cannot coexist with local shares
✓ Each mount = separate /etc/mtab entry	✓ Single entry in /etc/mtab
✓ Example: /- /etc/auto.direct	✓ Example: /misc /etc/auto.misc

In general, indirect maps are preferred for automounting NFS shares because they provide cleaner organization and simpler management.

Exercise 18-3: Access NFS Share Using Direct Map

Perform this exercise on *server10* as *user1* with *sudo* where required. In this exercise, you will:

- Configure a direct map to automount the NFS share */common* from *server20*
- Install the relevant software
- Create a local mount point */autodir*
- Set up AutoFS maps to support the automatic mounting
- Test access to the mount

Note that */common* is already mounted on the */local* mount point via the *fstab* file. This setup should remain intact.

1. Install the AutoFS software package called *autofs*:

```
[user1@server10 ~]$ sudo dnf install -y autofs
........
Running transaction
  Preparing        :                                          1/1
  Installing       : libsss_autofs-2.10.2-3.el10.x86_64       1/2
  Installing       : autofs-1:5.1.9-11.el10.x86_64            2/2
  Running scriptlet: autofs-1:5.1.9-11.el10.x86_64            2/2
Installed products updated.

Installed:
  autofs-1:5.1.9-11.el10.x86_64   libsss_autofs-2.10.2-3.el10.x86_64

Complete!
```

2. Create a mount point */autodir* using the *mkdir* command:

```
[user1@server10 ~]$ sudo mkdir /autodir
```

3. Edit the */etc/auto.master* file and add the following entry at the beginning of the file. This entry will point the AutoFS service to the *auto.dir* file for additional information.

```
/-   /etc/auto.master.d/auto.dir
```

4. Create */etc/auto.master.d/auto.dir* file and add the mount point, NFS server, and share information to it:

```
/autodir   server20:/common
```

5. Start the AutoFS service now and set it to autostart at system reboots:

```
[user1@server10 ~]$ sudo systemctl enable --now autofs
Created symlink /etc/systemd/system/multi-user.target.wants/autofs.service → /u
sr/lib/systemd/system/autofs.service.
```

6. Verify the operational status of the AutoFS service. Use the -l and --no-pager options to show full details without piping the output to a pager program (the *pg* command in this case).

```
[user1@server10 ~]$ sudo systemctl status autofs -l --no-pager
● autofs.service - Automounts filesystems on demand
     Loaded: loaded (/usr/lib/systemd/system/autofs.service; enabled;
preset: disabled)
     Active: active (running) since Wed 2025-12-17 08:03:33 EST; 16s a
go
 Invocation: fa3eb559bbc24212b4d2ba615f5e3129
   Main PID: 3873 (automount)
      Tasks: 6 (limit: 10665)
     Memory: 1.7M (peak: 2.4M)
        CPU: 101ms
     CGroup: /system.slice/autofs.service
             └─3873 /usr/sbin/automount --systemd-service --dont-check
-daemon

Dec 17 08:03:33 server10.example.com systemd[1]: Starting autofs.servi
ce - Automounts filesystems on demand...
Dec 17 08:03:33 server10.example.com (utomount)[3873]: autofs.service:
 Referenced but unset environment variable evaluates to an empty strin
g: OPTIONS
Dec 17 08:03:33 server10.example.com systemd[1]: Started autofs.servic
e - Automounts filesystems on demand.
```

7. Run the *ls* command on the mount point */autodir* and then issue the *mount* command to verify that the share is automounted and accessible:

```
[user1@server10 ~]$ ls /autodir/
nfsfile
[user1@server10 ~]$ mount | grep autodir
/etc/auto.master.d/auto.dir on /autodir type autofs (rw,relatime,fd=6,
pgrp=4111,timeout=300,minproto=5,maxproto=5,direct,pipe_ino=28873)
server20:/common on /autodir type nfs4 (rw,relatime,vers=4.2,rsize=262
144,wsize=262144,namlen=255,hard,fatal_neterrors=none,proto=tcp,timeo=
600,retrans=2,sec=sys,clientaddr=192.168.0.110,local_lock=none,addr=19
2.168.0.120)
```

Observe the above outcomes. An activity in the mount point (the *ls* command) caused AutoFS to mount the share */common* on */autodir*. The *mount* command output depicts the path of the AutoFS map (*/etc/auto.master.d/auto.dir*), the file system type (autofs), and the options used during the mount process. Wait for five minutes and run the *mount* command again. You will see that the AutoFS-managed mount has been automatically unmounted. A *cd*, *ls*, or another activity in the mount point will bring it back.

This completes the AutoFS setup for an NFS share using a direct map.

Exercise 18-4: Access NFS Share Using Indirect Map

Perform this exercise on *server10* as *user1* with *sudo* where required. In this exercise, you will:

- Configure an indirect map to automount the NFS share */common* from *server20*
- Install the relevant software
- Set up AutoFS maps to support automatic mounting
- Observe that the specified mount point "autoindir" is created automatically under */misc*.

Note that */common* is already mounted on the */local* mount point via the *fstab* file and it is also configured via a direct map for automounting on */autodir*. This setup should remain intact.

1. Install the *autofs* software package if it is not already there:

```
[user1@server10 ~]$ sudo dnf -y install autofs
Last metadata expiration check: 2:27:30 ago on Wed 17 Dec 2025 05:52:3
3 AM.
Package autofs-1:5.1.9-11.el10.x86_64 is already installed.
Dependencies resolved.
Nothing to do.
Complete!
```

2. Confirm that the entry for the indirect map */misc* in the */etc/auto.master* file exists:

```
[user1@server10 ~]$ grep ^/misc /etc/auto.master
/misc   /etc/auto.misc
```

3. Edit the */etc/auto.misc* file and add the mount point, NFS server, and share information to it:

```
autoindir   server20:/common
```

4. Start the AutoFS service now and set it to autostart at system reboots:

```
[user1@server10 ~]$ sudo systemctl enable --now autofs
Created symlink /etc/systemd/system/multi-user.target.wants/autofs.service → /u
sr/lib/systemd/system/autofs.service.
```

5. Verify the operational status of the AutoFS service. Use the -l and --no-pager options to show full details without piping the output to a pager program (the *pg* command in this case):

```
[user1@server10 ~]$ sudo systemctl status autofs -l --no-pager
● autofs.service - Automounts filesystems on demand
     Loaded: loaded (/usr/lib/systemd/system/autofs.service; enabled; vendor pr
eset: disabled)
     Active: active (running) since Sun 2023-02-05 18:35:13 EST; 10s ago
   Main PID: 3872 (automount)
      Tasks: 6 (limit: 10944)
     Memory: 1.8M
        CPU: 76ms
     CGroup: /system.slice/autofs.service
             └─3872 /usr/sbin/automount --systemd-service --dont-check-daemon

Feb 05 18:35:13 server10.example.com systemd[1]: Starting Automounts filesystem
s on demand...
Feb 05 18:35:13 server10.example.com systemd[1]: Started Automounts filesystems
 on demand.
```

6. Run the *ls* command on the mount point */misc/autoindir* and then *grep* for both *auto.misc* and *autoindir* on the *mount* command output to verify that the share is automounted and accessible:

```
[user1@server10 ~]$ ls /misc/autoindir
nfsfile
[user1@server10 ~]$
[user1@server10 ~]$ mount | grep -E 'auto.misc|autoindir'
/etc/auto.misc on /misc type autofs (rw,relatime,fd=8,pgrp=4306,timeou
t=300,minproto=5,maxproto=5,indirect,pipe_ino=29964)
server20:/common on /misc/autoindir type nfs4 (rw,relatime,vers=4.2,rs
ize=262144,wsize=262144,namlen=255,hard,fatal_neterrors=none,proto=tcp
,timeo=600,retrans=2,sec=sys,clientaddr=192.168.0.110,local_lock=none,
addr=192.168.0.120)
```

Observe the above outcomes. An activity in the mount point (*ls* command in this case) caused AutoFS to mount the share */common* on */misc/autoindir*. The *mount* command output illustrates the path of the AutoFS map (*/etc/auto.misc*), the auto-generated mount point (*/misc/autoindir*), file system type (autofs), and the options used during the mount process. You can use the same umbrella mount point */misc* to mount additional auto-generated mount points.

This mount point will automatically disappear after five minutes of idling. You can verify that by issuing the *mount* command again. A *cd, ls,* or another activity in the mount point will bring it back.

This completes the AutoFS setup for an NFS share on the client using an indirect map.

Automounting User Home Directories

AutoFS allows us to automount user home directories by exploiting two special characters in indirect maps. The asterisk (*) replaces the references to specific mount points and the ampersand (&) substitutes the references to NFS servers and shared subdirectories. With user home directories located under */home* on one or more NFS servers, the AutoFS service dynamically mounts the required home directory when a user attempts to access it. The service will mount only that specific user's home directory rather than the entire */home*. The indirect map entry for this type of substitution is defined in an indirect map, such as */etc/auto.master.d/auto.home*, and will look like:

```
*    -rw    &:/home/&
```

With this entry in place, there is no need to update any AutoFS configuration files if additional NFS servers with */home* shared are added or removed. Similarly, if user home directories are added or deleted, there will be no impact on the functionality of AutoFS. If there is only one NFS server sharing the home directories, you can simply specify its name in lieu of the first & symbol in the above entry.

Exercise 18-5: Automount User Home Directories Using Indirect Map

There are two portions for this exercise. Perform the first portion on *server20* (NFS server) and the second portion on *server10* (NFS client) as *user1* with *sudo* where required.

In the first portion, you will:

- Create a user account named *user30* with UID 3000
- Add the */home* directory to the list of NFS shares so that it becomes available for remote mount

In the second portion, you will:

- Create a user account named *user30* with UID 3000, base directory */nfshome*, and no home directory
- Create an umbrella mount point called */nfshome* for mounting the user home directory from the NFS server
- Install the relevant software
- Establish an indirect map to automount the remote home directory of *user30* under */nfshome*
- Observe that the home directory is automounted under */nfshome* when you sign in as *user30*

On NFS server *server20*:

1. Create a user account called *user30* with UID 3000 (-u) and assign password "password1":

```
[user1@server20 ~]$ sudo useradd -u 3000 user30
[user1@server20 ~]$ echo password1 | sudo passwd --stdin user30
Changing password for user user30.
passwd: all authentication tokens updated successfully.
```

2. Edit the */etc/exports* file and add an entry for */home* (do not modify or remove the previous entry):

```
/home server10(rw)
```

3. Export all the shares listed in the */etc/exports* file:

```
[user1@server20 ~]$ sudo exportfs -avr
exporting server10.example.com:/home
exporting server10.example.com:/common
```

On NFS client *server10*:

1. Install the *autofs* software package if it is not already there:

```
[user1@server10 ~]$ sudo dnf install -y autofs
```

2. Create a user account called *user30* with UID 3000 (-u), base home directory location */nfshome* (-b), no home directory (-M), and password "password1":

```
[user1@server10 ~]$ sudo useradd -u 3000 -b /nfshome -M user30
[user1@server10 ~]$ echo password1 | sudo passwd --stdin user30
Changing password for user user30.
passwd: all authentication tokens updated successfully.
```

This is to ensure that the user's UID is consistent across both the server and the client, thereby avoiding access issues.

3. Create the umbrella mount point */nfshome* to automount the user's home directory:

```
[user1@server10 ~]$ sudo mkdir /nfshome
```

4. Edit the */etc/auto.master* file and add the mount point and indirect map location to it:

```
/nfshome   /etc/auto.master.d/auto.home
```

5. Create the */etc/auto.master.d/auto.home* file and add the following information to it:

```
*   -rw   server20:/home/user30
```

For multiple user setup, you can replace "user30" with the & character, but ensure that those users exist on both the server and the client with consistent UIDs.

6. Start the AutoFS service now and set it to autostart at system reboots. This step is not required if AutoFS is already running and enabled.

```
[user1@server10 ~]$ sudo systemctl enable --now autofs
Created symlink /etc/systemd/system/multi-user.target.wants/autofs.service → /u
sr/lib/systemd/system/autofs.service.
```

7. Verify the operational status of the AutoFS service. Use the -l and --no-pager options to show full details without piping the output to a pager program (the *pg* command):

```
[user1@server10 ~]$ sudo systemctl status autofs -l --no-pager
● autofs.service - Automounts filesystems on demand
     Loaded: loaded (/usr/lib/systemd/system/autofs.service; enabled;
preset: disabled)
     Active: active (running) since Wed 2025-12-17 09:11:05 EST; 14s a
go
 Invocation: 69981b14fe39408a96fd7cf0f240747b
   Main PID: 4632 (automount)
      Tasks: 8 (limit: 10665)
     Memory: 1.9M (peak: 2.3M)
        CPU: 53ms
     CGroup: /system.slice/autofs.service
             └─4632 /usr/sbin/automount --systemd-service --dont-check
-daemon

Dec 17 09:11:05 server10.example.com systemd[1]: Starting autofs.servi
ce - Automounts filesystems on demand...
Dec 17 09:11:05 server10.example.com (utomount)[4632]: autofs.service:
 Referenced but unset environment variable evaluates to an empty strin
g: OPTIONS
Dec 17 09:11:05 server10.example.com systemd[1]: Started autofs.servic
e - Automounts filesystems on demand.
```

8. Log in as *user30* and run the *pwd*, *ls*, and *df* commands for verification:

```
[user1@server10 ~]$ su - user30
Password:
[user30@server10 ~]$ pwd
/nfshome/user30
[user30@server10 ~]$ ls -l
total 0
[user30@server10 ~]$ df -h .
Filesystem              Size  Used Avail Use% Mounted on
server20:/home/user30    17G  4.1G   13G  25% /nfshome/user30
```

The user is successfully logged in with their home directory automounted from the NFS server. The *pwd* command confirms the path. The *df* command verifies the NFS server name and the source home directory path for *user30*, as well as the mount location. You can also use the *mount* command and pipe the output to *grep* for *user30* to view mount details (**mount | grep user30**).

> **EXAM TIP:** You must understand how to configure AutoFS for automounting remote user home directories.

This completes the setup for an automounted home directory share for a user.

Chapter Summary

This chapter covered the sharing and mounting of remote file systems using the Network File System (NFS) protocol. We explored the core concepts, benefits, and versions of NFS, along with the essential commands and configuration files for both servers and clients.

The practical portion began with configuring an NFS server to export a directory, followed by exercises on an NFS client to mount the share both manually and persistently. We then introduced the AutoFS service for on-demand mounting, detailing its components and map types. Exercises demonstrated how to automount shares using both direct and indirect maps. The chapter concluded with a specific configuration for automounting user home directories from a central NFS server.

Review Questions

1. What command can be used to reload AutoFS maps without rebooting the system?
2. The name of the AutoFS service daemon is *autofs*. True or False?
3. What would the line entry */dir1 *(rw)* in the */etc/exports* file mean?
4. In AutoFS, what happens if a mounted share remains idle beyond the configured timeout?
5. Which directory is recommended for storing custom AutoFS master map files?
6. What file lists all currently mounted file systems, including AutoFS mounts?
7. Which NFS protocol version is used by default by AutoFS unless otherwise specified?
8. What type of AutoFS map would have the */- /etc/auto.media* entry in the *auto.master* file?
9. AutoFS requires *root* privileges to automatically mount a network file system. True or False?
10. What is the default timeout value for a file system before AutoFS unmounts it automatically?
11. Name the three common types of maps that AutoFS supports.
12. Arrange the tasks in three different correct sequences to export a share using NFS: (a) update */etc/exports*, (b) add service to firewall, (c) run *exportfs*, (d) install *nfs-utils*, and (e) start nfs service.
13. What would the entry * *server10:/home/&* in an AutoFS indirect map imply?
14. Which command is used to export a share?
15. An NFS server exports a share and an NFS client mounts it. True or False?
16. Which command would you use to unexport a share?
17. What is the name of the NFS service configuration file?
18. What is the name of the AutoFS configuration file and where is it located?
19. Which AutoFS map file is read first when the AutoFS service starts?
20. True or False. AutoFS mounts defined in indirect maps are visible immediately after the AutoFS service starts.

Answers to Review Questions

1. The *systemctl reload autofs* or *systemctl restart autofs* command.
2. False. The name of the AutoFS service daemon is *automount*.
3. The line entry would export */dir1* in read/write mode to all client systems.
4. The share is automatically unmounted by AutoFS.
5. The */etc/auto.master.d* directory.
6. The */proc/self/mounts* file (*/etc/mtab* points to it).
7. NFS version 4.
8. A direct map.
9. False.
10. Five minutes.
11. The three common AutoFS maps are master, direct, and indirect.
12. d/e/b/a/c, d/e/a/c/b, or d/e/a/b/c.
13. This indirect map entry would dynamically mount individual user home directories from *server10* under the parent mount point.
14. The *exportfs* command.

15. True.
16. The *exportfs* command with the -u switch.
17. The */etc/nfs.conf* file.
18. The AutoFS configuration file is *autofs.conf*, and it is located in the */etc* directory.
19. The master map file (by default */etc/auto.master*) is read first.
20. False. Indirect map mounts become visible only after they are accessed.

Do-It-Yourself Challenge Labs

The following labs are designed to reinforce most of the concepts and skills covered in this chapter. You are expected to complete these labs without external assistance. A step-by-step guide is not provided, as the required knowledge has already been presented in the chapter; however, each lab includes hints pointing to the relevant major topic(s).

Use the lab environment created specifically for the end-of-chapter labs. See the sub-section "Lab Environment for End-of-Chapter Labs" in Chapter 01 "Local Installation" for details.

Lab 18-1: Automount NFS Share using Direct Map

As *user1* with *sudo* on *server30*, share directory */sharenfs* (create it) in read/write mode using NFS. On *server40* as *user1* with *sudo*, install the AutoFS software and start the service. Configure the master and a direct map to automount the share on */mntauto* (create it). Run *ls* on */mntauto* to trigger the mount. Use *df -h* to confirm. (Hint: NFS Server and Client Configuration, and Auto File System).

Lab 18-2: Automount NFS Share using Indirect Map

As *user1* with *sudo* on *server40*, configure the master and an indirect map to automount the share under */autoindir* (create it). Run *ls* on */autoindir/sharenfs* to trigger the mount. Use *df -h* to confirm. (Hint: Auto File System).

Lab 18-3: Automount Multiple NFS Shares using Indirect Map

As *user1* with *sudo* on *server30*, create and export two directories named */sharenfs1* and */sharenfs2* in read/write mode using NFS. As *user1* with *sudo* on *server40*, configure the AutoFS master and an indirect map to automount both shares under a common parent directory */multishare* (create it). Trigger the mounts using *ls* on each directory and confirm the mounts using *df -h*. (Hint: AutoFS maps: The Indirect Map).

Lab 18-4: Verify AutoFS Timeout Behavior

As *user1* with *sudo* on *server40*, ensure an NFS share is automounted using AutoFS. Trigger the mount by running *ls* on the AutoFS mount point and confirm the mount using the *mount* or *df -h* command. Wait at least five minutes without accessing the mount point and verify that the share is automatically unmounted. Trigger the mount again using *ls* and confirm that it is remounted successfully. (Hint: AutoFS Configuration File).

Chapter 19

Hostname Resolution and Time Synchronization

By the end of this chapter, you will be able to:

- Explain the Domain Name System (DNS) and its Role in Hostname Resolution
- Identify the Different Roles a System can Play in a DNS Architecture
- Analyze Entries in Resolver Configuration Files
- Employ a Suite of Lookup Tools to Test and Troubleshoot Name Resolution
- Describe the Importance of Time Synchronization and the Network Time Protocol (NTP)
- Characterize Key NTP Concepts: Time Sources, NTP Roles, and Stratum Levels
- Examine the Structure of the Chrony Configuration File and its Key Directives
- Configure NTP/Chrony Client and Verify its Synchronization Status
- View, Set, and Adjust the Date and Time

RHCSA Objectives:

48. Configure hostname resolution
44. Configure time service clients

Two services are fundamental to the stability and usability of any networked system: hostname resolution and time synchronization. Domain Name System is an OS- and hardware-independent network service you employ for determining the IP address of a system when its hostname is known, and vice versa. You implement this mechanism to map human-friendly hostnames to their assigned numeric IP addresses by consulting one or more servers offering the hostname resolution service. This service has been used on the Internet and corporate networks as the de facto standard for this purpose. DNS clients use this service to communicate with remote systems. There are several lookup programs that use DNS to obtain information.

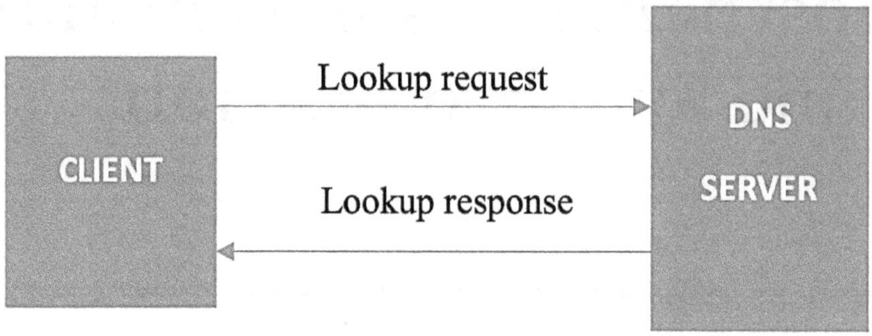

The Chrony service, an implementation of the Network Time Protocol, maintains the clock on the system and keeps it synchronized with a more accurate and reliable source of time. Providing accurate and uniform time for systems on the network allows time-sensitive applications such as monitoring software, backup tools, scheduling utilities, billing systems, file sharing protocols, and authentication programs to perform correctly and precisely. It also aids logging and auditing services to capture and record messages and alerts in log files with accurate timestamps.

DNS and Name Resolution

Domain Name System (DNS) is an inverted tree-like structure employed on the Internet and private networks (including home and corporate networks) as the de facto standard for resolving hostnames to their numeric IP addresses. DNS is platform-independent with support integrated in every operating system. DNS is commonly implemented using BIND (*Berkeley Internet Name Domain*), which has historically been the most widely used DNS server software. *Name resolution* is the technique that uses DNS/BIND for hostname lookups.

To understand DNS, a brief discussion of its components and roles is imperative. The following subsections provide a look at the client-side configuration files and commands, along with examples on how to use the tools for resolving hostnames.

DNS Name Space and Domains

The DNS *name space* is a hierarchical organization of all the domains on the Internet. The root of the name space is represented by a period (.). The hierarchy directly below the root (.) consists of *top-level domains* (TLDs) such as .com, .net, .edu, .org, .gov, .ca, and .de. A DNS *domain* is a collection of one or more systems. Subdomains fall under their parent domains and are separated by a period (.). For example, *redhat.com* is a second-level domain that falls under the *.com* top-level domain, and *bugzilla.redhat.com* is a third-level domain that falls under *redhat.com.*

Figure 19-1 exhibits a sample hierarchy of the name space, showing the top three domain levels.

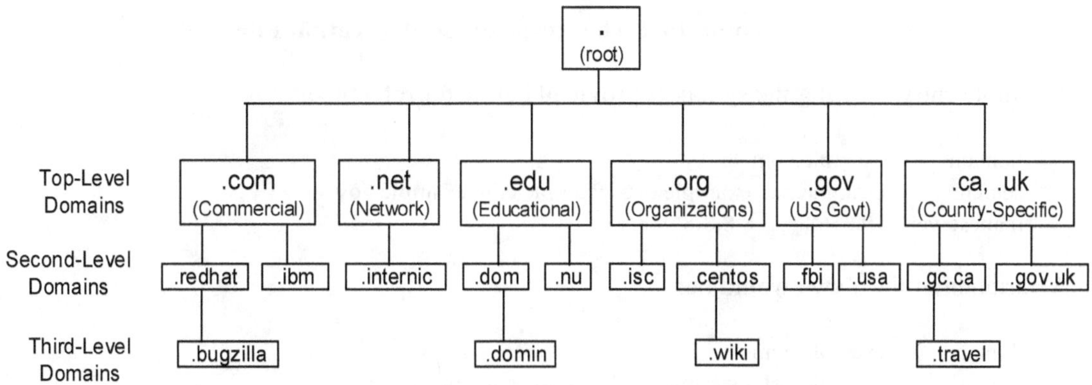

Figure 19-1 Sample DNS Hierarchy

At the deepest level of the hierarchy are the *leaves* (systems, nodes, or any device with an IP address) of the name space. For example, a network switch *net01* in *.travel.gc.ca* subdomain will be known as *net01.travel.gc.ca.* When a period (.) is appended to the end of this name (*net01.travel.gc.ca.*), it represents the *Fully Qualified Domain Name* (FQDN).

DNS Roles

From a DNS perspective, a system can be configured to operate as a primary server, secondary server, or client. A DNS server is commonly referred to as a *nameserver*.

A *primary server* is responsible for its domain (or subdomain). It maintains a master database of all the hostnames and their associated IP addresses that are included in that domain. All changes in the database are done on this server. Each domain must have one primary server, with one or more optional *secondary* servers for redundancy and load distribution. A secondary server also stores an updated copy of the master database, and it continues to provide name resolution service in the event the primary server becomes unavailable or inaccessible.

A *DNS client* queries nameservers for name lookups. Every system with access to the Internet or other external networks will have the DNS client functionality configured and operational. Setting up a DNS client on Linux primarily involves two text files that are discussed in the next two subsections.

Understanding Resolver Configuration File

The *resolv.conf* file under */etc* is the DNS resolver configuration file where you define information to support hostname lookups. You may edit this file manually with a text editor. Resolver utilities reference it to construct and transmit queries. Three key directives may be defined in this file: domain, nameserver, and search; they are described in Table 19-1.

Directive	Description
domain	Identifies the default domain name to be searched for queries
nameserver	Declares one or more DNS server IP addresses to be queried one at a time in the order in which they are listed. Nameserver entries may be defined as separate line items with this directive or on a single line.
search	Specifies up to six domain names, of which the first must be the local domain. No need to define the domain directive if the search directive is used.

Table 19-1 The Resolver Configuration File

A sample entry showing the syntax is provided below for reference:

```
domain      example.com
search      example.net  example.org  example.edu  example.gov
nameserver  192.168.0.1  8.8.8.8  8.8.4.4
```

A variation of the above would be:

```
domain      example.com
search      example.net  example.org  example.edu  example.gov
nameserver  192.168.0.1
nameserver  8.8.8.8
nameserver  8.8.4.4
```

On *server10* and *server20*, the *resolv.conf* file currently contains two search entries and three nameserver entries. These entries are automatically placed by the NetworkManager service.

```
[user30@server10 ~]$ cat /etc/resolv.conf
# Generated by NetworkManager
search cgocable.net example.com
nameserver 2001:18c0:ffe0:28::1
nameserver 2001:18c0:ffe0:28::2
nameserver 172.10.10.1
```

If this file is absent, resolver utilities may default to querying a local caching resolver, such as 127.0.0.53, or rely on system-managed DNS configuration.

Viewing and Adjusting Name Resolution Sources and Order

The *nsswitch.conf* file under */etc* directs the lookup utilities to the correct source to get hostname information. In the presence of multiple sources, this file also identifies the order in which to consult them and an action to be taken next. Four status keywords—success, notfound, unavail, and tryagain—control this behavior, and they are described along with default actions in Table 19-2.

Keyword	Meaning	Default Action
success	Information found in source and provided to the requester	return (do not try the next source)
notfound	Information not found in source	continue (try the next source)
unavail	Source down or not responding; service disabled or not configured	continue (try the next source)
tryagain	Source busy, retry later	continue (try the next source)

Table 19-2 Name Service Source and Order Determination

The following example entry shows the syntax of a relevant entry from the *nsswitch.conf* file. It shows two sources for name resolution: files (*/etc/hosts*) and DNS (*/etc/resolv.conf*).

```
hosts:   files   dns
```

Based on the default behavior, the search will terminate if the requested information is found in the *hosts* table. However, you can alter this behavior and instruct the lookup programs to return if the requested information is not found there. The modified entry will look like:

```
hosts:   files [notfound=return]   dns
```

This modified entry prevents DNS from being consulted if the hostname is not found in the local hosts file.

See Chapter 17 "Networking Essentials and Network Connections" for details on the /etc/hosts file.

Once the *resolv.conf* and *nsswitch.conf* files are configured appropriately, you can use any of the native client resolver tools for lookups. Common query tools available in RHEL 10 include *dig*, *host*, *nslookup*, and *getent*.

Performing Name Resolution with dig

dig (*domain information groper*) is a DNS lookup utility. It queries the nameserver specified at the command line or consults the *resolv.conf* file to determine the nameservers to be queried. This tool may be used to troubleshoot DNS issues due to its flexibility and verbosity. The following shows a few usage examples.

To get the IP for *redhat.com* using the nameserver listed in the *resolv.conf* file:

```
[user1@server10 ~]$ dig redhat.com
........
;; ANSWER SECTION:
redhat.com.                3600    IN      A       52.200.142.250
redhat.com.                3600    IN      A       34.235.198.240

;; Query time: 470 msec
;; SERVER: 2001:18c0:ffe0:28::1#53(2001:18c0:ffe0:28::1) (UDP)
;; WHEN: Wed Dec 17 12:35:30 EST 2025
;; MSG SIZE  rcvd: 71
```

The output shows the total time (470 milliseconds) it took to get the result, the IP addresses (52.200.142.250 and 34.235.198.240) of redhat.com, the IPv6 address of the nameserver used for the query (2001:1970:xxxxxx), query timestamp, the size of the received message (71 bytes), and other information.

To perform a reverse lookup on the redhat.com IP (52.200.142.250), use the -x option with the command:

```
[user30@server10 ~]$ dig -x 52.200.142.250
........
;; ANSWER SECTION:
250.142.200.52.in-addr.arpa. 300 IN     PTR     ec2-52-200-142-250.com
pute-1.amazonaws.com.

;; AUTHORITY SECTION:
142.200.52.in-addr.arpa. 256    IN      NS      ns1-24-us-east-1.ec2-r
dns.amazonaws.com.
142.200.52.in-addr.arpa. 256    IN      NS      ns2-24-us-east-1.ec2-r
dns.amazonaws.com.
142.200.52.in-addr.arpa. 256    IN      NS      ns3-24-us-east-1.ec2-r
dns.amazonaws.com.
142.200.52.in-addr.arpa. 256    IN      NS      ns4-24-us-east-1.ec2-r
dns.amazonaws.com.

;; Query time: 22 msec
;; SERVER: 2001:18c0:ffe0:28::1#53(2001:18c0:ffe0:28::1) (UDP)
;; WHEN: Wed Dec 17 12:37:41 EST 2025
;; MSG SIZE  rcvd: 245
```

Reference the command's manual pages for details and options.

Performing Name Resolution with host

host is a basic DNS lookup utility that works on the same principles as the *dig* command in terms of nameserver determination. This tool produces lesser data in the output by default; however, you can add the -v option for verbosity.

To perform a lookup on *redhat.com*:

```
[user1@server10 ~]$ host redhat.com
redhat.com has address 52.200.142.250
redhat.com has address 34.235.198.240
redhat.com mail is handled by 10 us-smtp-inbound-2.mimecast.com.
redhat.com mail is handled by 10 us-smtp-inbound-1.mimecast.com.
```

Rerun the above with -v added. The output will be similar to that of the *dig* command.

To perform a reverse lookup on the IP of *redhat.com* using the -v flag to add details:

```
[user30@server10 ~]$ host -v 52.200.142.250
........
;; ANSWER SECTION:
250.142.200.52.in-addr.arpa. 300 IN     PTR     ec2-52-200-142-250.com
pute-1.amazonaws.com.

;; AUTHORITY SECTION:
142.200.52.in-addr.arpa. 300    IN      NS      ns1-24-us-east-1.ec2-r
dns.amazonaws.com.
142.200.52.in-addr.arpa. 300    IN      NS      ns2-24-us-east-1.ec2-r
dns.amazonaws.com.
142.200.52.in-addr.arpa. 300    IN      NS      ns3-24-us-east-1.ec2-r
dns.amazonaws.com.
142.200.52.in-addr.arpa. 300    IN      NS      ns4-24-us-east-1.ec2-r
dns.amazonaws.com.

Received 234 bytes from 2001:18c0:ffe0:28::1#53 in 46 ms
```

Refer to the command's manual pages for options and more information.

Performing Name Resolution with nslookup

nslookup queries the nameservers listed in the *resolv.conf* file or those specified explicitly on the command line. The following shows a few usage examples.

To get the IP for *redhat.com* using nameserver 8.8.8.8 instead of the nameserver defined in *resolv.conf*:

```
[user1@server10 ~]$ nslookup redhat.com 8.8.8.8
Server:         8.8.8.8
Address:        8.8.8.8#53

Non-authoritative answer:
Name:   redhat.com
Address: 52.200.142.250
Name:   redhat.com
Address: 34.235.198.240
```

To perform a reverse lookup on the IP of *redhat.com* using the nameserver from the resolver configuration file:

```
[user30@server10 ~]$ nslookup 52.200.142.250
250.142.200.52.in-addr.arpa     name = ec2-52-200-142-250.compute-1.am
azonaws.com.

Authoritative answers can be found from:
142.200.52.in-addr.arpa nameserver = ns1-24-us-east-1.ec2-rdns.amazona
ws.com.
142.200.52.in-addr.arpa nameserver = ns2-24-us-east-1.ec2-rdns.amazona
ws.com.
142.200.52.in-addr.arpa nameserver = ns3-24-us-east-1.ec2-rdns.amazona
ws.com.
142.200.52.in-addr.arpa nameserver = ns4-24-us-east-1.ec2-rdns.amazona
ws.com.
```

Consult the command's manual pages on how to use it in interactive mode.

Performing Name Resolution with getent

The *getent* (*get entries*) command is a rudimentary tool that can fetch matching entries from the databases defined in the *nsswitch.conf* file. This command reads the corresponding database and displays the information if found. For name resolution, it uses the *hosts* database to resolve the specified hostname or IP address. For instance, run the following for forward and reverse lookups:

```
[user1@server10 ~]$ getent hosts redhat.com
34.235.198.240  redhat.com
52.200.142.250  redhat.com
[user1@server10 ~]$
[user1@server10 ~]$ getent hosts 34.235.198.240
34.235.198.240  ec2-34-235-198-240.compute-1.amazonaws.com
```

Check the command's manual pages for available flags and additional information.

Time Synchronization

Network Time Protocol (NTP) is a networking protocol for synchronizing the system clock with remote time servers for accuracy and reliability. This protocol has been in use with tens of millions of computing devices employing it to synchronize their clocks with tens of thousands of time servers deployed across the globe. Having steady and exact time on networked systems allows time-sensitive applications, such as authentication and email applications, backup and scheduling tools, financial and billing systems, logging and monitoring software, and file and storage sharing protocols, to function with precision.

NTP exchanges timestamped packets with configured time servers and selects sources based on delay, jitter, and clock stability rather than physical distance. The client system records the clock drift rate in a drift file, which Chrony uses to compensate for systematic clock inaccuracies over time.

RHEL 10 has an implementation of NTP called *Chrony*. Chrony uses the UDP protocol over the well-known NTP port 123. If enabled, it starts at system boot and continuously operates to keep the system clock in sync with a more accurate source of time.

Chrony performs well on computers that are intermittently connected to the network, operate on busy networks, do not run continuously, or experience temperature-related clock drift.

Time Sources

A *time source* is any reference device that acts as a provider of time to other devices. The most precise sources of time are the atomic clocks. They provide highly precise time signals that are used to generate *Coordinated Universal Time* (UTC). They produce radio signals that radio clocks use for time propagation to computer servers and other devices that require correctness in time. When choosing a time source for a network, preference should be given to the one that takes the least amount of time to respond. This server may or may not be closest physically.

The common sources of time employed on computer networks are the local system clock, an Internet-based public time server, and a radio clock.

The local system clock can be used as a provider of time. This requires manual administrative correction or precise synchronization using an external reference. Keep in mind that this server has no way of synchronizing itself with a more reliable and precise external time source. Therefore, using the local system clock as a time server is the least recommended option.

Several public time servers are available over the Internet for general use (visit *www.ntp.org* for a list). These servers are typically operated by government agencies, research and scientific organizations, large software vendors, and universities around the world. One of the systems on the local network is identified and configured to receive time from one or more public time servers. This option is preferred over the use of the local system clock.

The official *ntp.org* site also provides a common pool called *pool.ntp.org* for vendors and organizations to register their own NTP servers voluntarily for public use. Examples include *rhel.pool.ntp.org* and *ubuntu.pool.ntp.org* for distribution-specific pools, and *ca.pool.ntp.org* and *oceania.pool.ntp.org* for country and continent/region-specific pools. Each pool consists of multiple time servers maintained by volunteers, identified using enumerated hostnames such as *0.rhel.pool.ntp.org*, *1.rhel.pool.ntp.org*, *2.rhel.pool.ntp.org*, and so on.

A radio clock is regarded as a highly accurate provider of time, as it receives time updates straight from an atomic clock. *Global Positioning System* (GPS), WWVB, and DCF77 are some popular radio clock methods. A direct use of signals from these sources requires connectivity of some hardware to the computer identified to act as an organizational or site-wide time server.

NTP Roles

From an NTP standpoint, a system can be configured to operate as a primary server, secondary server, peer, or client.

A *primary* server gets time from a time source and provides time to secondary servers or directly to clients.

A *secondary* server receives time from a primary server and can be configured to furnish time to a set of clients to offload the primary or for redundancy. The presence of a secondary server on the network is optional but highly recommended.

A *peer* reciprocates time with an NTP server. Peers typically operate at the same stratum level and exchange time information to improve accuracy and reliability.

A *client* receives time from a primary or a secondary server and adjusts its clock accordingly.

Stratum Levels

As mentioned, there are different types of time sources available so you can synchronize the system clock. These time sources are categorized hierarchically into several levels that are referred to as *stratum levels* based on their distance from the reference clocks (atomic, radio, and GPS). The reference clocks operate at stratum level 0 and are the most accurate provider of time with little to no delay. Besides stratum 0, there are fifteen additional levels that range from 1 to 15. Of these, servers operating at stratum 1 are highly accurate, as they receive time directly from stratum 0 reference clocks. See Figure 18-2 for a sample hierarchy.

A stratum 0 device cannot be used on the network directly. It is attached to a computer, which is then configured to operate at stratum 1. Servers functioning at stratum 1 are called *time servers* and they can be set up to deliver time to stratum 2 servers. Similarly, a stratum 3 server can be configured to synchronize its time with a stratum 2 server and deliver time to the next lower-level servers, and so on. Servers sharing the same stratum can be configured as peers to exchange time updates with one another.

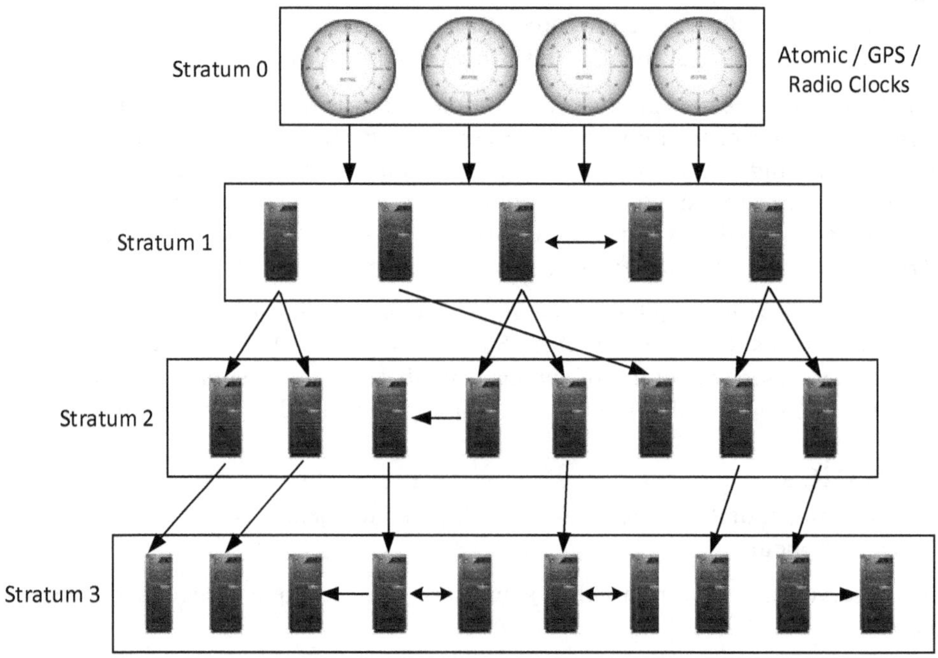

Figure 19-2 NTP Stratum Levels

There are numerous public NTP servers available for free that synchronize time. They normally operate at higher stratum levels such as 2 and 3.

Chrony Configuration File

The key configuration file for the Chrony service is *chrony.conf* located in the */etc* directory. This file is referenced by the Chrony daemon at startup to determine the sources to synchronize the clock, the log file location, and other details. This file can be modified by hand to set or alter directives as required. Some common directives used in this file along with real or mock values are presented below:

```
driftfile    /var/lib/chrony/drift
logdir       /var/log/chrony
pool         0.rhel.pool.ntp.org  iburst
server       server20s8.example.com  iburst
server       127.127.1.0
peer         prodntp1.abc.net
```

Table 19-3 describes these directives.

Directive	Description
driftfile	Indicates the location and name of the drift file to be used to record the rate at which the system clock gains or losses time. This data is used by Chrony to maintain local system clock accuracy.
logdir	Sets the directory location to store the log files in
pool	Defines the hostname that represents a pool of time servers. Chrony binds itself with one of the servers to get updates. In case of a failure of that server, it automatically switches the binding to another server within the pool. The iburst option dictates the Chrony service to send the first four update requests to the time server every 2 seconds. This allows the daemon to quickly bring the local clock closer to the time server at startup.
server	Defines the hostname or IP address of a single time server. The IP 127.127.1.0 represents the local system clock and should be used only in isolated or fallback scenarios.
peer	Identifies the hostname or IP address of a time server running at the same stratum level. A peer provides time to a server as well as receives time from the same server.

Table 19-3 Chrony Directives

There are plenty of other directives and options available with Chrony that may be defined in this file. Use **man chrony.conf** for details.

Chrony Daemon and Command

The Chrony service runs as a daemon program called *chronyd* that handles time synchronization in the background. It uses the configuration defined in the */etc/chrony.conf* file at startup and sets its behavior accordingly. If the local clock requires a time adjustment, Chrony normally slews the clock gradually to minimize time offsets instead of stepping the clock abruptly. There are additional options available that may be passed to the service daemon if required.

The Chrony service has a command-line program called *chronyc* available that can be employed to monitor the performance of the service and control its runtime behavior. There are a few subcommands available with *chronyc*; the *sources* subcommand displays current time sources, and the *tracking* subcommand reports synchronization and performance statistics.

Exercise 19-1: Configure NTP Client

Perform this exercise on *server10* as *user1* with *sudo* where required. In this exercise, you will:

- Install the Chrony software package if it is not already installed
- Activate the Chrony service using the default configuration file
- Validate the binding and operation

1. Install the Chrony package using the *dnf* command:

```
[user1@server10 ~]$ sudo dnf install -y chrony
Last metadata expiration check: 1:41:09 ago on Wed 17 Dec 2025 1:
:01:46 PM.
Package chrony-4.6.1-1.el10.x86_64 is already installed.
Dependencies resolved.
Nothing to do.
Complete!
```

The software is already installed on the system.

2. Ensure that preconfigured public time server entries are present in the */etc/chrony.conf* file:

```
[user1@server10 ~]$ grep -E 'pool|server' /etc/chrony.conf | grep -v ^#
pool 2.rhel.pool.ntp.org iburst
```

There is a single pool entry set in the file by default. This pool name is backed by multiple NTP servers behind the scenes.

3. Start the Chrony service and set it to autostart at reboots:

```
[user1@server10 ~]$ sudo systemctl --now enable chronyd
Created symlink /etc/systemd/system/multi-user.target.wants/chronyd.service → /usr/li
b/systemd/system/chronyd.service.
```

4. Examine the operational status of the Chrony service:

```
[user1@server10 ~]$ sudo systemctl status chronyd --no-pager -l
● chronyd.service - NTP client/server
     Loaded: loaded (/usr/lib/systemd/system/chronyd.service; enabled; pre
set: enabled)
     Active: active (running) since Wed 2025-12-17 13:45:37 EST; 4h 57min
ago
 Invocation: af38e29164f947cf94eac1b1100bcd22
       Docs: man:chronyd(8)
             man:chrony.conf(5)
    Process: 5615 ExecStart=/usr/sbin/chronyd $OPTIONS (code=exited, statu
s=0/SUCCESS)
   Main PID: 5621 (chronyd)
      Tasks: 1 (limit: 10665)
     Memory: 1.3M (peak: 3M)
        CPU: 187ms
     CGroup: /system.slice/chronyd.service
             └─5621 /usr/sbin/chronyd -F 2
........
```

The service has started successfully, and it is set for autostart.

5. Inspect the binding status using the *sources* subcommand with *chronyc*:

```
[user1@server10 ~]$ chronyc sources
MS Name/IP address         Stratum Poll Reach LastRx Last sample
===============================================================================
^+ time2.mbix.ca                 1   6   377    16  +2807us[+2807us] +/-  27ms
^- 2a02:c6c1:1:201:0:2:0:3       2   6   377    16  +1141us[+1141us] +/-  49ms
^- zero.gotroot.ca               3   6   377    18   -822us[ -822us] +/-  54ms
^* vps-yul1.orleans.ddnss.de     2   6   377    84  -2708us[-1767us] +/-  14ms
```

The output typically displays information across eight columns. Columns 1 to 4—M, S, Name/IP address, and Stratum—illustrate the mode, state, hostname/IP, and stratum level of the source. The ^ means the source is a server and the * implies current association with the source.

Columns 5 to 8—Poll, Reach, LastRx, and Last sample—display the polling rate (6 means 64 seconds), reachability register (377 indicates a valid response was received), how long ago the last sample was received, and the offset between the local clock and the source at the last measurement. Check out the manual pages for the *chronyc* command and search for the section 'sources' for additional details.

The time source, *vps-yul1.orleans.ddnss.de*, at the bottom in the output indicates that *server10* is currently synchronized with that server. This association is identified with an asterisk character (*) beside the time server name.

6. Display the clock performance using the *tracking* subcommand:

```
[user1@server10 ~]$ chronyc tracking
Reference ID    : 48496BED (vps-yul1.orleans.ddnss.de)
Stratum         : 3
Ref time (UTC)  : Wed Dec 17 23:54:27 2025
System time     : 0.001122145 seconds fast of NTP time
Last offset     : +0.000789378 seconds
RMS offset      : 0.019141512 seconds
Frequency       : 5.022 ppm slow
Residual freq   : +0.245 ppm
Skew            : 8.688 ppm
Root delay      : 0.024125827 seconds
Root dispersion : 0.003914248 seconds
Update interval : 129.4 seconds
Leap status     : Normal
```

Rows 1 and 2 in the above output identify the current source of time (Reference ID) and the stratum level it is configured at (Stratum). Row 3 shows the reference time at which the last measurement from the time source was processed (Ref time). Row 4 displays the local time offset from the NTP time (System time). Row 5 depicts the last reported offset from the NTP server (Last offset). Row 6 shows the clock frequency adjustments (in parts per million) used to compensate for drift (Frequency). The rest of the rows show additional information. Check out the manual pages for the *chronyc* command and search for the section "tracking" for additional details.

EXAM TIP: You will not have access to the outside network during the exam. You must point your system to an NTP server available on the exam network. Comment out the default server and pool directives and add a single directive "server <hostname>" to the file. Replace <hostname> with the NTP server name or its IP address as provided.

This concludes the exercise.

Displaying and Setting System Date and Time

System date and time can be viewed and manually adjusted with native Linux tools such as the *timedatectl* command. This command can modify the date, time, and time zone. When executed without any option, as shown below, it outputs the local time, Universal time, RTC time (*real-time clock*, a battery-backed hardware clock located on the system board), time zone, and the status of the NTP service:

```
[user1@server10 ~]$ timedatectl
               Local time: Wed 2025-12-17 19:01:11 EST
           Universal time: Thu 2025-12-18 00:01:11 UTC
                 RTC time: Thu 2025-12-18 00:01:11
                Time zone: America/Toronto (EST, -0500)
System clock synchronized: yes
              NTP service: active
          RTC in local TZ: no
```

Manual date and time adjustments require the NTP/Chrony service to be disabled. Run the *timedatectl* command as follows to turn off NTP and verify:

```
[user1@server10 ~]$ sudo timedatectl set-ntp false
[user1@server10 ~]$ timedatectl | grep NTP
              NTP service: inactive
```

To modify the current date to March 28, 2026, and confirm:

```
[user1@server10 ~]$ sudo timedatectl set-time 2026-03-28
[user1@server10 ~]$ timedatectl
               Local time: Sat 2026-03-28 00:00:06 EDT
           Universal time: Sat 2026-03-28 04:00:06 UTC
                 RTC time: Sat 2026-03-28 04:00:05
                Time zone: America/Toronto (EDT, -0400)
System clock synchronized: no
              NTP service: inactive
          RTC in local TZ: no
```

To change both date and time in one command (March 31, 2026 at 11:20 p.m.):

```
[user1@server10 ~]$ sudo timedatectl set-time "2026-03-31 23:20"
[user1@server10 ~]$ timedatectl
               Local time: Tue 2026-03-31 23:20:02 EDT
           Universal time: Wed 2026-04-01 03:20:02 UTC
                 RTC time: Wed 2026-04-01 03:20:01
                Time zone: America/Toronto (EDT, -0400)
System clock synchronized: no
              NTP service: inactive
          RTC in local TZ: no
```

To reactivate NTP:

```
[user1@server10 ~]$ sudo timedatectl set-ntp true
[user1@server10 ~]$ timedatectl | grep NTP
              NTP service: active
```

Check out the manual pages for the *timedatectl* command for more subcommands and usage examples.

Chapter Summary

This chapter focused on two critical network services: hostname resolution and time synchronization. We began by exploring the Domain Name System (DNS), analyzing the resolver configuration file, and the source determination file. We added DNS entries for hostname lookup and validated the configuration using client tools.

The second half of the chapter covered the Network Time Protocol (NTP) and its implementation via the Chrony service. We examined the roles of time sources and clients, the hierarchy of strata, and the key directives in Chrony's configuration file. Through a hands-on exercise, we configured an NTP client, monitored its time synchronization status, and used RHEL tools to query and manage the system clock.

Review Questions

1. Provide the maximum number of nameservers that can be defined in the resolver configuration file.
2. What is the purpose of a drift file in Chrony/NTP?
3. The Chrony client is preconfigured when the *chrony* software package is installed. You just need to start the service to synchronize the clock. True or False?
4. List any three DNS lookup tools.
5. List the utility that you can use to change system time.
6. What does the asterisk (*) symbol indicate in the output of chronyc sources?
7. What would you add to the Chrony configuration file if you want to use the local system clock as the provider of time?
8. BIND is an implementation of Domain Name System. True or False?
9. Define time source.
10. Name the three DNS roles that a RHEL system can play.
11. Chrony is an implementation of the Network Time Protocol. True or False?
12. What is the name and location of the DNS resolver file?
13. What stratum level do two peer time sources operate on a network?
14. What would you run to check the NTP synchronization status with time servers?

15. Define DNS name space.
16. Name the four Chrony/NTP roles that a RHEL system can play.
17. Which file defines the name resolution sources and controls the order in which they are consulted?
18. What is the filename and directory location for the Chrony configuration file?

Answers to Review Questions

1. Three.
2. The purpose of a drift file is to keep track of the rate at which the system clock gains or loses time.
3. True.
4. Name resolution tools include *dig*, *host*, *getent*, and *nslookup*.
5. The *timedatectl* command can be used to modify the system time.
6. The asterisk (*) indicates the currently selected time source that Chrony is synchronized with.
7. Add "server 127.127.1.0" to the Chrony configuration file and restart the service.
8. True.
9. A time source is a reference device that provides time to other devices.
10. From a DNS perspective, a RHEL system can be a primary server, a secondary server, or a client.
11. True.
12. The DNS resolver file is called *resolv.conf* and it is located in the */etc* directory.
13. Peers operate at the same stratum level.
14. Run *chronyc sources* to check the synchronization status.
15. The DNS name space is a hierarchical organization of all domains on the Internet.
16. From a Chrony/NTP standpoint, a RHEL machine can be a primary server, a secondary server, a peer, or a client.
17. The */etc/nsswitch.conf* file.
18. The name of the Chrony configuration file is *chrony.conf* and it is located in the */etc* directory.

Do-It-Yourself Challenge Labs

The following labs are designed to reinforce most of the concepts and skills covered in this chapter. You are expected to complete these labs without external assistance. A step-by-step guide is not provided, as the required knowledge has already been presented in the chapter; however, each lab includes hints pointing to the relevant major topic(s).

Use the lab environment created specifically for the end-of-chapter labs. See the sub-section "Lab Environment for End-of-Chapter Labs" in Chapter 01 "Local Installation" for details.

Lab 19-1: Configure Chrony

As *user1* with *sudo* on *server40*, install Chrony and configure the service to start automatically at system boot. Edit the Chrony configuration file and comment out all lines that begin with "pool" or "server". Go to the end of the file, and add a new line "server 127.127.1.0". Start the Chrony service and run *chronyc sources* to verify the time source binding. (Hint: Time Synchronization).

Lab 19-2: Modify System Date and Time

As *user1* with *sudo* on *server40*, execute the *date* and *timedatectl* commands to check the current system date and time. Identify the distinctions between the two outputs. Use *timedatectl* and change the system date to a future date. Observe the new date and time. Re-enable NTP using the *timedatectl* command to reset the date and time to the current system time. (Hint: Time Synchronization).

Chapter 20

The Secure Shell Service

By the end of this chapter, you will be able to:

- Describe the OpenSSH Service, its Versions, and Supported Algorithms
- Examine Core Encryption Techniques and Authentication Methods
- Explain OpenSSH Configuration Files
- Use OpenSSH Administration Commands
- Implement Public/Private Key-Based Authentication for Enhanced Security
- Run Commands on Remote Linux Systems
- Transfer Files Security between Linux Systems

RHCSA Objectives:

04. Access remote systems using ssh
29. Securely transfer files between systems
54. Configure key-based authentication for SSH

Secure Shell is a network service that delivers a secure mechanism for data transmission between source and destination systems over insecure network paths. It provides a set of utilities that allows you to generate key pairs and use them to set up trusted logins between systems for themselves. Additional utilities in the set gives remote users the ability to log in, execute commands, and transfer files securely over encrypted network channels. These tools have predominantly supplanted their insecure counterparts in the corporate world.

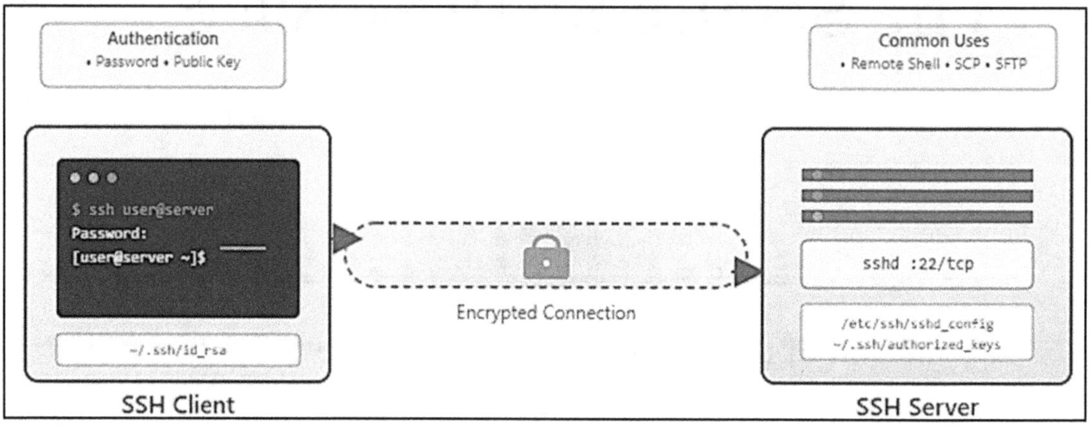

The OpenSSH Service

Secure Shell (SSH) delivers a secure mechanism for data transmission between source and destination systems over IP networks. It was designed to replace legacy remote login and file transfer programs—*telnet*, *rsh*, and *ftp*—which transmitted user credentials in clear text and did not encrypt data in transit.

SSH uses strong encryption to secure the communication channel and supports multiple authentication mechanisms, including passwords and cryptographic keys. It also employs *message authentication codes* (MACs) to ensure data integrity throughout a session. These protections make it extremely difficult for unauthorized users to intercept passwords or tamper with transmitted data.

The OpenSSH suite includes utilities such as *ssh* and *sftp*, which allow users to securely log in to remote systems, execute commands, and transfer files.

Common Encryption Techniques

Encryption is the process of transforming information into an unreadable format to prevent unauthorized access. OpenSSH uses a combination of *symmetric* and *asymmetric* encryption techniques during a client and server session. These techniques are also referred to as *secret key encryption* and *public key encryption*, respectively.

Symmetric Technique

Symmetric encryption uses a single shared secret, known as the *session key*, to encrypt and decrypt data. This key is generated dynamically during the initial key exchange when the SSH client and server establish a connection.

Because symmetric encryption is computationally efficient, it is used to encrypt the bulk of data transferred during an SSH session.

Asymmetric Technique

Asymmetric encryption uses a *public key* and a *private key* that are mathematically related. The public key is shared freely, while the private key must remain confidential.

In SSH, asymmetric encryption is primarily used during key exchange and user authentication. Data encrypted with a public key can only be decrypted using the corresponding private key. This mechanism allows secure identity verification without transmitting sensitive information such as passwords.

Authentication Methods

After an encrypted channel is established, the client and server negotiate an authentication method. OpenSSH supports multiple authentication mechanisms, which are typically attempted in the following order (depending on server configuration):

- GSSAPI-based authentication
- Host-based authentication
- Public key-based authentication
- Challenge-response authentication
- Password-based authentication

Let's review each one briefly.

GSSAPI-Based Authentication

GSSAPI (*Generic Security Service Application Program Interface*) provides a framework for integrating security mechanisms such as *Kerberos*. When enabled, OpenSSH uses Kerberos tokens to authenticate users without requiring passwords to be transmitted.

Host-Based Authentication

Host-based authentication allows users to authenticate based on the trust relationship between client and server systems. For each user that requires an automatic login to the server, a *~/.shosts* file is set up containing the client name or IP address.

The same rule applies to a group of users or all users on the client that require access to the server. In that case, the setup is done in the */etc/ssh/shosts.equiv* file on the server.

This method is rarely used today due to security concerns and is disabled by default in RHEL.

Private/Public Key-Based Authentication

This method uses a private/public key combination for user authentication. The user on the client has a private key and the server stores the corresponding public key. During login, the server challenges the client to prove possession of the private key. If the key is protected by a passphrase, the user must supply it locally. No passwords are transmitted to the server.

Challenge-Response Authentication

This method requires users to answer one or more authentication challenges correctly. It is often used with one-time passwords (OTP) or multi-factor authentication systems.

Password-Based Authentication

This is the last fall back option. The server prompts the user to enter their password. It checks the password against the stored entry in the *shadow* file and allows the user in if the password is confirmed. This method is typically enabled by default but is considered less secure than key-based authentication.

Of the five authentication methods, the password-based method is common and requires no further explanation. The GSSAPI-based, host-based, and challenge-response methods are beyond the scope of this book. The public/private key method, being the preferred and recommended method, will be the focus in the remainder of this chapter.

OpenSSH Protocol Version and Algorithms

OpenSSH currently supports SSH protocol version 2, which is the default and only supported version in RHEL 10. OpenSSH supports various cryptographic algorithms for data encryption and user authentication, including RSA, DSA, and ECDSA. RSA is the most commonly used algorithm, partly because it supports both encryption and digital signatures. In contrast, DSA and ECDSA are typically used only for authentication (key-based login) in SSH implementations. These algorithms generate public and private key pairs for asymmetric cryptography.

ECDSA is a modern alternative of DSA.

RSA stands for *Rivest-Shamir-Adleman*, who first published this algorithm, DSA for *Digital Signature Algorithm*, and ECDSA is an acronym for *Elliptic Curve Digital Signature Algorithm*.

OpenSSH Packages

OpenSSH provides three primary software packages:

- **openssh:** includes the *ssh-keygen* command and core library routines
- **openssh-clients:** includes commands, such as *sftp*, *ssh*, and *ssh-copy-id*, and a client configuration file */etc/ssh/ssh_config*
- **openssh-server:** contains the *sshd* service daemon, server configuration file */etc/ssh/sshd_config*, and additional library routines.

All three packages are installed by default during RHEL installation.

OpenSSH Server Daemon and Client Commands

The OpenSSH server program, *sshd*, is enabled and operational by default on RHEL systems, allowing remote users to log in to the system using an SSH client program such as PuTTY or the *ssh* command. This daemon listens on TCP port 22, as documented by the Port directive in the */etc/ssh/sshd_config* file.

The client software includes plenty of utilities such as those listed and described in Table 20-1.

Command	Description
sftp	A secure remote file transfer program
ssh	A secure remote login command
ssh-copy-id	Installs public key on remote systems
ssh-keygen	Generates and manages SSH key pairs

Table 20-1 OpenSSH Client Tools

The use of these commands is demonstrated in the following subsections.

Server Configuration File

The OpenSSH server configuration file is */etc/ssh/sshd_config*. This file defines global settings that control how the *sshd* daemon behaves. The authentication events are logged to the */var/log/secure* file.

A few directives with their default values from the *sshd_config* file are displayed below:

```
[user1@server10 ~]$ sudo cat /etc/ssh/sshd_config
#Port                        22
ListenAddress                0.0.0.0
SyslogFacility               AUTH
#LogLevel                    INFO
PermitRootLogin              prohibit-password
#PubkeyAuthentication        yes
AuthorizedKeysFile           .ssh/authorized_keys
PasswordAuthentication       yes
#PermitEmptyPasswords        no
UsePAM                       no
X11Forwarding                no
```

The above directives are elaborated in Table 20-2.

Directive	Description
Port	Specifies the port number to listen on. Default is 22.
ListenAddress	Sets the local addresses the sshd service should listen on. Default is to listen on all local addresses.
SyslogFacility	Defines the facility code to be used when logging messages to the /var/log/secure file. This is based on the configuration in the /etc/rsyslog.conf file. Default is AUTH.
LogLevel	Identifies the level of criticality for the messages to be logged. Default is INFO.
PermitRootLogin	Allows or disallows the root user to log in directly to the system with a password. Default is prohibit-password.
PubKeyAuthentication	Enables or disables public key-based authentication. Default is yes.
AuthorizedKeysFile	Sets the name and location of the file containing a user's authorized keys. Default is ~/.ssh/authorized_keys.
PasswordAuthentication	Enables or disables local password authentication. Default is yes.

Directive	Description
PermitEmptyPasswords	Allows or disallows the use of null passwords. Default is no.
UsePAM	Enables or disables user authentication via PAM. If enabled, only root will be able to run the sshd daemon. Default is no.
X11Forwarding	Allows or disallows remote access to graphical applications. Default is no.

Table 20-2 OpenSSH Server Configuration File

Any updates to this file must be followed by running **sudo systemctl restart sshd** for the changes to take effect.

There are many more settings available that may be added to the file for additional control. Check out the manual pages for the *sshd_config* file (**man 5 sshd_config**) for details.

Client Configuration File

The OpenSSH client configuration file is */etc/ssh/ssh_config*. This file controls how outbound SSH connections behave. Users can define custom settings for themselves and store them in the *~/.ssh/config/ssh_config* file.

A few directives with their default values from the *ssh_config* file are displayed below:

```
[user1@server10 ~]$ sudo more /etc/ssh/ssh_config
# Host  *
# ForwardX11                no
# PasswordAuthentication    yes
# StrictHostKeyChecking     ask
# IdentityFile              ~/.ssh/id_rsa
# IdentityFile              ~/.ssh/id_dsa
# IdentityFile              ~/.ssh/id_ecdsa
# IdentityFile              ~/.ssh/id_ed25519
# Port                      22
```

The above directives are described in Table 20-3.

Directive	Description
Host	Container that declares directives applicable to one host, a group of hosts, or all hosts. It ends when another occurrence of Host or Match is encountered. Default is *, which sets global defaults for all hosts.
ForwardX11	Enables or disables automatic redirection of X11 traffic over SSH connections. Default is no.
PasswordAuthentication	Allows or disallows password authentication. Default is yes.
StrictHostKeyChecking	Controls (1) whether to add host keys (host fingerprints) to $HOME/.ssh/known_hosts when accessing a host for the first time, and (2) what to do when the keys of a previously accessed host mismatch with what is stored in ~/.ssh/known_hosts. Options are:

Directive	Description
	no: adds new host keys and ignores changes to existing keys. **yes:** adds new host keys and disallows connections to hosts with non-matching keys. **accept-new:** adds new host keys and disallows connections to hosts with non-matching keys. **ask (default):** prompts whether to add new host keys and disallows connections to hosts with non-matching keys.
IdentityFile	Defines the name and location of a file that stores a user's private key for their identity validation. Supported values are id_rsa, id_dsa, id_ecdsa, and id_ed25519 based on the type of algorithm used. Their corresponding public key files with .pub extension are also stored at the same directory location. Default is id_ed25519.
Port	Sets the port number to listen on. Default is 22.

Table 20-3 OpenSSH Client Configuration File

The *~/.ssh* directory does not exist by default; it is created when a user executes the *ssh-keygen* command for the first time to generate a key pair or connects to a remote OpenSSH server and accepts its host key for the first time. In the latter case, the client stores the server's host key locally in a file called *known_hosts* along with its hostname or IP address. On subsequent access attempts, the client will use this information to verify the server's authenticity.

There are many more settings available that may be added to the file for additional control. Check out the manual pages for the *ssh_config* file (**man 5 ssh_config**) for details.

System Access and File Transfer

A user must log in to a Linux system to use it or transfer files. The login process identifies the user to the system. For accessing a RHEL system remotely, use the *ssh* command, and for copying files, use the *sftp* command. These tools require either a resolvable hostname of the target system or its IP address. Both commands are secure and can operate over secure and unsecured network channels for data exchange.

The following subsections and exercises demonstrate multiple access scenarios, including:

- Accessing a RHEL system from another RHEL system
- Accessing a RHEL system from a Windows computer (already covered in Chapter 01)
- Accessing a RHEL system using SSH keys
- Transferring files using *sftp*

Exercise 20-1: Access RHEL System from Another RHEL System

Perform this exercise on *server10* and *server20* as *user1*.

This exercise works under two assumptions: *user1* exists on both *server10* and *server20* (Chapter 01) and correct hostname-to-IP mappings are placed in the */etc/hosts* file (Chapter 17).

In this exercise, you will:

- Issue the *ssh* command as *user1* on *server10* to access *server20*
- Run basic commands on *server20* for validation
- Log off and return to the originating system

1. Issue the *ssh* command as *user1* on *server10*:

```
[user1@server10 ~]$ ssh server20
The authenticity of host 'server20 (192.168.0.120)' can't be established.
ED25519 key fingerprint is SHA256:WNhc1xN4MEcjIIlwE/BHxeSUv37uu0lqseBhYHpH2V8
.
This key is not known by any other names.
Are you sure you want to continue connecting (yes/no/[fingerprint])? yes
Warning: Permanently added 'server20' (ED25519) to the list of known hosts.
user1@server20's password:
Activate the web console with: systemctl enable --now cockpit.socket

Register this system with Red Hat Insights: rhc connect

Example:
# rhc connect --activation-key <key> --organization <org>

The rhc client and Red Hat Insights will enable analytics and additional
management capabilities on your system.
View your connected systems at https://console.redhat.com/insights

You can learn more about how to register your system
using rhc at https://red.ht/registration
Last login: Wed Dec 17 07:46:03 2025 from 192.168.0.91
[user1@server20 ~]$
```

Answer 'yes' to the question presented and press `Enter` to continue. This step adds the hostname of *server20* to the */home/user1/.ssh/ known_hosts* file on the originating computer (*server10*). This message will not reappear on subsequent login attempts to *server20* for this user. Enter the correct password for *user1* to be allowed in. You will be placed in the home directory of *user1* on *server20*. The command prompt reflects that information.

2. Issue basic Linux commands *whoami*, *hostname*, and *pwd* to confirm that you are logged in as *user1* on *server20* and placed in the correct home directory:

```
[user1@server20 ~]$ whoami
user1
[user1@server20 ~]$ hostname
server20.example.com
[user1@server20 ~]$ pwd
/home/user1
[user1@server20 ~]$
```

3. Run the *logout* or *exit* command or simply press the key combination `Ctrl+d` to log off *server20* and return to *server10*:

```
[user1@server20 ~]$ exit
logout
Connection to server20 closed.
[user1@server10 ~]$
```

This concludes the exercise.

If you want to log in as a different user such as *user2* (assuming *user2* exists on the target server *server20*), you may run the *ssh* command in either of the following ways:

```
[user1@server10 ~]$ ssh -l user2 server20
[user1@server10 ~]$ ssh user2@server20
```

The above will allow you to log in if the password entered for *user2* is valid.

Exercise 20-2: Generate, Distribute, and Use SSH Keys

Perform this exercise on *server10* and *server20* as *user1* and *sudo* where required. In this exercise, you will:

- Generate a passwordless SSH key pair using RSA algorithm for *user1* on *server10*
- Display private and public file contents
- Distribute the public key to *server20*
- Attempt to log in to *server20* from *server10*
- Show the log file message for the login attempt

1. Log in to *server10* as *user1*.
2. Generate RSA keys without a password (-N) and without detailed output (-q). Press `Enter` when prompted to provide the filename to store the private key.

    ```
    [user1@server10 ~]$ ssh-keygen -N "" -q
    Enter file in which to save the key (/home/user1/.ssh/id_ed25519):
    ```

The contents of the *id_ed25519* (private key) file are shown below:

```
[user1@server10 ~]$ cat .ssh/id_ed25519
-----BEGIN OPENSSH PRIVATE KEY-----
b3BlbnNzaC1rZXktdjEAAAAABG5vbmUAAAAEbm9uZQAAAAAAAAABAAAAMwAAAAtzc2gtZW
QyNTUxOQAAACDfr6LCEXaTAZNqqKz7XxUU7NUo8Ut3mQOTCsG155gouAAAAKAwKGvdMChr
3QAAAAtzc2gtZWQyNTUxOQAAACDfr6LCEXaTAZNqqKz7XxUU7NUo8Ut3mQOTCsG155gouA
AAAEAUCsgrOxuMNJEigyCaiZyKoKffjUi4GAmDiWayrR/B0N+vosIRdpMBk2qorPtfFRTs
1SjxS3eZA5MKwbXnmCi4AAAAGnVzZXIxQHNlcnZlcjEwLmV4YW1wbGUuY29tAQID
-----END OPENSSH PRIVATE KEY-----
```

The contents of the *id_ed25519.pub* (public key) file are displayed below:

```
[user1@server10 ~]$ cat .ssh/id_ed25519.pub
ssh-ed25519 AAAAC3NzaC1lZDI1NTE5AAAAIN+vosIRdpMBk2qorPtfFRTs1SjxS3eZA5MKwbXnm
Ci4 user1@server10.example.com
```

3. Install the public key to *server20* under */home/user1/.ssh* directory. Accept the fingerprint for *server20* when prompted (only presented on the first login attempt). Enter the password for *user1* set on *server20* to continue. The public key will be installed in a file called *authorized_keys*.

```
[user1@server10 ~]$ ssh-copy-id server20
/usr/bin/ssh-copy-id: INFO: Source of key(s) to be installed: "/home/user1/.s
sh/id_ed25519.pub"
/usr/bin/ssh-copy-id: INFO: attempting to log in with the new key(s), to filt
er out any that are already installed
/usr/bin/ssh-copy-id: INFO: 1 key(s) remain to be installed -- if you are pro
mpted now it is to install the new keys
user1@server20's password:

Number of key(s) added: 1

Now try logging into the machine, with: "ssh 'server20'"
and check to make sure that only the key(s) you wanted were added.
```

At the same time, this command also creates or updates the *known_hosts* file on *server10* and stores the fingerprint for *server20* in it. Here is what the previous step stored in it:

```
[user1@server10 ~]$ cat .ssh/known_hosts
server20 ssh-ed25519 AAAAC3NzaC1lZDI1NTE5AAAAIOCPUFdQ9faLdeUK6PJS6v/0j3hdo5dk
9h57koEPKopi
```

4. On *server10*, run the *ssh* command as *user1* to connect to *server20*. You will not be prompted for a password because there was none assigned to the SSH keys.

```
[user1@server10 ~]$ ssh server20
. . . . . . . . .
Last login: Thu Dec 18 16:37:24 2025 from 192.168.0.110
[user1@server20 ~]$
```

5. On *server20*, view this login attempt in the */var/log/secure* file:

```
[user1@server20 ~]$ sudo tail /var/log/secure

........
Dec 18 17:31:00 server20 sshd-session[6774]: Accepted publickey for user1 fro
m 192.168.0.110 port 60700 ssh2: ED25519 SHA256:mfmM987ndA8IHqRmWrJRPQHMIrOjq
5WciPDT2/7KQtU
Dec 18 17:31:00 server20 sshd-session[6774]: pam_unix(sshd:session): session
opened for user user1(uid=1000) by user1(uid=0)
```

The log entries show the timestamp, hostname, process name and PID, username and source IP, and other relevant information. This file will log all future login attempts for this user.

Executing Commands Remotely Using ssh

The *ssh* command allows you to securely log in to a remote system or execute commands without an interactive session. Exercise 20-2 demonstrated how a user can log in using this command. The following shows a few basic examples on how to use *ssh* to execute a command on a remote system.

Invoke the *ssh* command on *server10* to execute the *hostname* command on *server20*:

```
[user1@server10 ~]$ ssh server20 hostname
server20.example.com
```

Run the *nmcli* command on *server20* to show (s) active network connections (c):

```
[user1@server20 ~]$ ssh server20 nmcli c s
NAME     UUID                                  TYPE      DEVICE
enp0s3   c8b405de-1e1f-3c5a-a650-e02456537fff  ethernet  enp0s3
enp0s8   c9f3059a-03a3-4d3a-9d68-b4a42dbe92c6  ethernet  enp0s8
lo       853d1894-4a4b-4c68-9449-87f18bb47b3f  loopback  lo
```

You can run any command on *server20* this way without a full login session.

Transferring Files Remotely Using sftp

The *sftp* command is an interactive file transfer tool. This tool can be launched as follows on *server10* to connect to *server20*:

```
[user1@server10 ~]$ sftp server20
Connected to server20.
sftp> ?
```

Type ? at the sftp> prompt to list available commands along with a short description:

```
sftp> ?
Available commands:
bye                                Quit sftp
cd path                            Change remote directory to 'path'
chgrp [-h] grp path                Change group of file 'path' to 'grp'
chmod [-h] mode path               Change permissions of file 'path' to 'mode'
chown [-h] own path                Change owner of file 'path' to 'own'
copy oldpath newpath               Copy remote file
cp oldpath newpath                 Copy remote file
df [-hi] [path]                    Display statistics for current directory or
                                   filesystem containing 'path'
exit                               Quit sftp
get [-afpR] remote [local]         Download file
help                               Display this help text
lcd path                           Change local directory to 'path'
lls [ls-options [path]]            Display local directory listing
lmkdir path                        Create local directory
ln [-s] oldpath newpath            Link remote file (-s for symlink)
lpwd                               Print local working directory
ls [-1afhlnrSt] [path]             Display remote directory listing
lumask umask                       Set local umask to 'umask'
mkdir path                         Create remote directory
progress                           Toggle display of progress meter
put [-afpR] local [remote]         Upload file
pwd                                Display remote working directory
quit                               Quit sftp
........
```

As shown in the above output, there are many common commands available at the sftp> prompt. These include *cd* to change directory, *get/put* to download/upload a file, *ls* to list files, *pwd* to print working directory, *mkdir* to create a directory, *rename* to rename a file, *rm* to remove a file, and *bye/quit/exit* to exit the program and return to the command prompt. These commands will run on the remote server (*server20*). The following demonstrates some of these commands:

```
sftp> mkdir /tmp/dir10-20
sftp> cd /tmp/dir10-20/
sftp> pwd
Remote working directory: /tmp/dir10-20
sftp> put /etc/group
Uploading /etc/group to /tmp/dir10-20/group
group                                             100%  908      2.6MB/s   00:00
sftp> ls -l
-rw-r--r--    ? user1    user1          908 Dec 18 17:45 group
sftp> cd ..
sftp> pwd
Remote working directory: /tmp
sftp> cd /home/user1
sftp> get /usr/bin/gzip
Fetching /usr/bin/gzip to gzip
gzip                                              100%  102KB   8.7MB/s   00:00
sftp>
sftp> quit
[user1@server20 ~]$
```

Furthermore, there are four commands beginning with an 'l'—*lcd*, *lls*, *lpwd*, and *lmkdir*—available at the sftp> prompt. They are intended to be run on the source server (*server10*). Other Linux commands are also available at the sftp> prompt that you can use for basic file management operations on the remote server.

Type *quit* at the sftp> prompt to exit the program when you are done.

Consult the manual pages for the *sftp* command for options and additional details.

Chapter Summary

This chapter provided a comprehensive overview of the OpenSSH service. We explored its core components, including the underlying symmetric and asymmetric encryption techniques that protect data in transit.

The chapter detailed the various authentication methods available, with a strong emphasis on configuring key-based authentication as a more secure alternative to passwords. We examined the client and server configuration files, and learned how to control aspects of the OpenSSH daemon's behavior.

Through hands-on exercises, we demonstrated how to access a remote system using SSH, generate and distribute key pairs for passwordless login, execute commands remotely, and use sftp for secure file transfers. The knowledge gained here is fundamental for performing daily administrative tasks securely across a network.

Review Questions

1. What does the StrictHostKeyChecking directive control in the OpenSSH client configuration?
2. Name the OpenSSH client-side configuration file.
3. What would the command *ssh server10 ls* do?

4. What is the difference between symmetric and asymmetric encryption?
5. What does the command *ssh-keygen -N ""* do?
6. What is the default location for storing user SSH keys?
7. What does the command *ssh-copy-id* do?
8. Which two of the five authentication methods discussed in this chapter are most commonly used?
9. Where are failed SSH login attempts recorded on a RHEL system?
10. What is the purpose of the *ssh-keygen* command?
11. Name the default algorithm used with SSH.
12. The primary OpenSSH server configuration file is *ssh_config*. True or False?
13. What kind of information does the *$HOME/.ssh/known_hosts* file store?
14. List the two encryption techniques described in this chapter.
15. What is the default port used by the secure shell service?
16. Which log file stores authentication messages?
17. The *ssh* tool provides a non-secure tunnel over a network for accessing a RHEL system. True or False?

Answers to Review Questions

1. It controls whether new host keys are automatically added to the known_hosts file and how mismatched host keys are handled.
2. The client-side OpenSSH configuration file is */etc/ssh/ssh_config*.
3. The command provided will run the *ls* command on the specified server without requiring a full interactive login session.
4. Symmetric encryption uses a single shared key to encrypt and decrypt data, while asymmetric encryption uses a public/private key pair where the public key encrypts data and the private key decrypts it.
5. The command provided will generate a passwordless SSH key pair using the default ED25519 algorithm.
6. SSH keys are stored under the *$HOME/.ssh* directory.
7. The *ssh-copy-id* command distributes the public key to remote systems.
8. Public key-based and password-based authentication methods are most commonly used.
9. Failed SSH login attempts are logged in /var/log/secure.
10. The *ssh-keygen* command generates a public/private key combination for use with SSH.
11. The default algorithm used with OpenSSH is ED25519.
12. False. The primary OpenSSH server configuration file is *sshd_config*.
13. The *$HOME/.ssh/known_hosts* file stores fingerprints of remote servers that the client has previously accessed.
14. The two encryption techniques are symmetric (secret key) and asymmetric (public/private keys).
15. The default port used by the secure shell service is 22.
16. Authentication messages are logged to the */var/log/secure* file.
17. False. The *ssh* command provides a secure tunnel over the network.

Do-It-Yourself Challenge Labs

The following labs are designed to reinforce most of the concepts and skills covered in this chapter. You are expected to complete these labs without external assistance. A step-by-step guide is not provided, as the required knowledge has already been presented in the chapter; however, each lab includes hints pointing to the relevant major topic(s).

Use the lab environment created specifically for the end-of-chapter labs. See the sub-section "Lab Environment for End-of-Chapter Labs" in Chapter 01 "Local Installation" for details.

Lab 20-1: Establish Key-Based Authentication

As *user1* with *sudo* on *server30* and *server40*, create a user account *user20* and assign a password. As *user20* on *server40*, generate a private/public key pair without a passphrase using the *ssh-keygen* command. Distribute the public key to *server30* with the *ssh-copy-id* command. Log in to *server30* as *user20* and accept the server fingerprint. On subsequent login attempts from *server40* to *server30*, *user20* should not be prompted for their password. (Hint: System Access and File Transfer).

Lab 20-2: Test the Effect of PermitRootLogin Directive

As *user1* with *sudo* on *server40*, edit the */etc/ssh/sshd_config* file and change the value of the directive PermitRootLogin to "no". Use the *systemctl* command to activate the change. As *root* on *server30*, run *ssh server40* (or use its IP). You should see a "Permission denied" message. Reverse the change on *server40*, restart the service, and try *ssh server40* again. You should be able to log in. (Hint: The OpenSSH Service).

Lab 20-3: Remote File Transfer with SFTP

As *user1* on *server40*, use *sftp* to connect to *server30*. Enter the password for *user1* if prompted. At the sftp> prompt, upload a test file from *server40* using the *put* command, and verify that the verify the upload with *ls*. Download a file from *server30* to *server40* using the *get* command and verify it on *server40*. Exit the sftp session using *quit*. (Hint: System Access and File Transfer).

Lab 20-4: Local File Transfer with SFTP

As *user1* on *server30*, use *sftp* to connect to *server40*. Enter the password for *user1* if prompted. At the sftp> prompt, use the *lcd* command to change the local directory on *server30*, *lput* to upload a file from *server30* to *server40*, and *lget* to download a file from *server40* to *server30*. Exit the sftp session using the *bye* command. (Hint: System Access and File Transfer).

Chapter 21

The Linux Firewall

By the end of this chapter, you will be able to:

- Implement Host-Based Security Control with the Linux Firewall
- Describe the firewalld Service and its Purpose
- Explain the Concepts of firewalld Zones and Services
- Analyze the Structure of Zone and Service Configuration Files
- Control Access to Network Services and Ports Using firewalld
- Manage Firewall Rules with the firewall-cmd Command

RHCSA Objectives:

50. Restrict network access using firewall-cmd/firewall
55. Configure firewall settings using firewall-cmd/firewalld

Running a system in a networked or an Internet-facing environment requires that you take security measures to tighten access to the system in general and individual services in particular. You can accomplish this by implementing a firewall and restricting inbound traffic to allowed ports from valid source IP addresses only. We discuss a host-based firewall solution in this chapter.

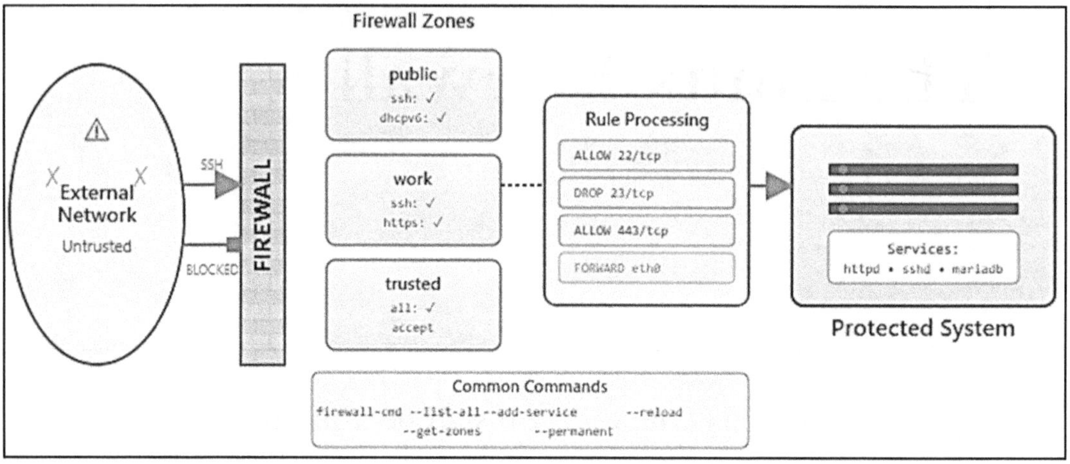

Firewall Overview

A *firewall* is a security system, implemented in hardware, software, or both, that monitors and controls network traffic based on predefined rules. There are two categories of firewall systems—network firewalls and host-based firewalls. *Network* firewalls protect entire networks and are typically deployed at network perimeters, while *host-based* firewalls run on individual servers to protect local traffic.

RHEL is shipped with a host-based firewall solution that works by filtering data packets. A data packet is formed as a result of a process called *encapsulation* whereby the header information is attached to a message (called *payload*) during packet formation. The header includes information such as source and destination IP addresses, port, and type of data. Based on predefined *rules*, a firewall intercepts each inbound and outbound data packet, inspects its header, and decides whether to allow the packet to pass through.

Port numbers are standardized identifiers used by network services to communicate. In RHEL, common port assignments are listed in the */etc/services* file. Some common services and their assigned port numbers are: FTP (*File Transfer Protocol*) uses port 21, SSH (*Secure Shell*) 22, Postfix (an email service) 25, HTTP (*HyperText Transfer Protocol*) 80, and NTP (*Network Time Protocol*) uses port 123.

RHEL's host-based firewall is built on the *netfilter* framework in the Linux kernel, which provides packet filtering, *Network Address Translation* (NAT), and packet classification. It uses *nftables* as the modern user-space interface for defining and managing filtering rules, replacing the older *iptables* system.

Together, Netfilter and nftables inspect, modify, drop, forward, and enforce packets according to defined rule sets. RHEL uses the *firewalld* service to dynamically manage nftables rules via the *firewall-cmd* command, without requiring a service restart.

Overview of the firewalld Service

firewalld is the default host-based firewall management service in RHEL 10. One of the major advantages is its ability to add, modify, or delete firewall rules immediately without disrupting current network connections or restarting the service process. This is especially useful in testing and troubleshooting scenarios. *firewalld* also allows rules to be saved persistently so they are automatically applied at system reboots.

The *firewalld* service lets you perform management operations at the command line using the *firewall-cmd* command, graphically using the web console, or manually by editing rules files. *firewalld* stores the default rules in files located in the */usr/lib/firewalld* directory, and those that contain custom rules in the */etc/firewalld* directory. The default rules files may be copied to the custom rules directory and modified.

firewalld Zones

firewalld uses the concept of *zones* for easier and transparent traffic management. Zones define policies based on the trust level of network connections and source IP addresses. A network connection can be part of only one zone at a time; however, a zone can have multiple network connections assigned to it. Zone configuration may include services, ports, and protocols that may be open or closed. It may also include rules for advanced configuration items such as masquerading, port forwarding, NAT'ing, ICMP filters, and rich language. Rules for each zone are defined and manipulated independent of other zones.

firewalld inspects each incoming packet to determine the source IP address and applies the rules of the zone that has a match for the address. In the event that no zone configuration matches the address, it associates the packet with the zone that has the network connection defined, and applies the rules of that zone. If neither works, *firewalld* associates the packet with the default zone, and enforces the rules of the default zone on the packet.

The *firewalld* software installs several predefined zone files that may be selected or customized. These files include templates for traffic that must be blocked or dropped, and for traffic that is public-facing, internal, external, home, public, trusted, and work-related. Of these, the *public* zone is the default zone, and it is activated by default when the *firewalld* service is started. Table 21-1 lists and describes the predefined zones sorted based on the trust level from trusted to untrusted.

Zone	Description
trusted	Allow all incoming traffic
internal	Reject all incoming traffic except for what is allowed. Intended for use on internal networks.
home	Reject all incoming traffic except for what is allowed. Intended for use in homes.
work	Reject all incoming traffic except for what is allowed. Intended for use at workplaces.
dmz	Reject all incoming traffic except for what is allowed. Intended for use in publicly accessible demilitarized zones.

Zone	Description
external	Reject all incoming traffic except for what is allowed. Outgoing IPv4 traffic forwarded through this zone is masqueraded to look like it originated from the IPv4 address of an outgoing network interface. Intended for use on external networks with masquerading enabled.
public	Reject all incoming traffic except for what is allowed. It is the default zone for any newly added network interfaces. Intended for use in public places.
block	Reject all incoming traffic with icmp-host-prohibited message returned. Intended for use in secure places.
drop	Drop all incoming traffic without responding with ICMP errors. Intended for use in highly secure places.

Table 21-1 firewalld Default Zones

By default, outgoing traffic is allowed for all predefined zones, unless restricted by specific rules.

Zone Configuration Files

firewalld stores zone rules in XML format at two locations: the system-defined rules in the */usr/lib/firewalld/zones* directory, and the user-defined rules in the */etc/firewalld/zones* directory. System-defined XML files serve as templates that can be copied, modified, or applied immediately to network connections. They are automatically copied to the */etc/firewalld/zones* directory if modified with a management tool. Alternatively, you can copy the required zone file to the */etc/firewalld/zones* directory manually, and make the necessary changes. The *firewalld* service reads the files saved in this location, and applies the rules defined in them. A listing of the system zone files is presented below:

```
[user1@server10 ~]$ ls -l /usr/lib/firewalld/zones/
total 40
-rw-r--r--. 1 root root 312 Jan 14  2025 block.xml
-rw-r--r--. 1 root root 306 Jan 14  2025 dmz.xml
-rw-r--r--. 1 root root 304 Jan 14  2025 drop.xml
-rw-r--r--. 1 root root 317 Jan 14  2025 external.xml
-rw-r--r--. 1 root root 410 Jan 14  2025 home.xml
-rw-r--r--. 1 root root 425 Jan 14  2025 internal.xml
-rw-r--r--. 1 root root 729 Feb 28  2025 nm-shared.xml
-rw-r--r--. 1 root root 356 Jan 14  2025 public.xml
-rw-r--r--. 1 root root 175 Jan 14  2025 trusted.xml
-rw-r--r--. 1 root root 352 Jan 14  2025 work.xml
```

The default *public* zone file is displayed below:

```
[user1@server10 ~]$ cat /usr/lib/firewalld/zones/public.xml
<?xml version="1.0" encoding="utf-8"?>
<zone>
  <short>Public</short>
  <description>For use in public areas. You do not trust the other computers
on networks to not harm your computer. Only selected incoming connections ar
 accepted.</description>
  <service name="ssh"/>
  <service name="dhcpv6-client"/>
  <service name="cockpit"/>
  <forward/>
</zone>
```

As depicted in the above output, the zone has a name and description, and it contains a list of all the allowed services—*ssh*, *dhcpv6-client*, and *cockpit*. See the manual pages for *firewalld.zone* for details on zone configuration files.

firewalld Services

In addition to the concept of zones, *firewalld* also uses the idea of *services* for easier activation and deactivation of specific rules. *firewalld* services are preconfigured firewall rules delineated for various services and stored in different files. The rules consist of necessary settings, such as the port number, protocol, and possibly helper modules, to support the loading of the service. *firewalld* services can be added to a zone. By default, *firewalld* blocks all traffic unless a service or port is explicitly opened.

Service Configuration Files

firewalld stores service rules in XML format at two locations: the system-defined rules in the */usr/lib/firewalld/services* directory, and the user-defined rules in the */etc/firewalld/services* directory. System-defined XML files serve as templates that can be copied, modified, or applied immediately. They are automatically copied to the */etc/firewalld/services* directory if modified with a management tool. Alternatively, you can copy the required service file to the */etc/firewalld/services* directory manually, and make the necessary changes. The *firewalld* service reads the files saved in this location, and applies the rules defined in them. A listing of the system service files is presented below:

```
[user1@server10 ~]$ ls -l /usr/lib/firewalld/services/
total 1044
-rw-r--r--. 1 root root 433 Jan 14  2025 0-AD.xml
-rw-r--r--. 1 root root 352 Jan 14  2025 afp.xml
-rw-r--r--. 1 root root 381 Jan 14  2025 alvr.xml
-rw-r--r--. 1 root root 399 Jan 14  2025 amanda-client.xml
-rw-r--r--. 1 root root 427 Jan 14  2025 amanda-k5-client.xml
-rw-r--r--. 1 root root 283 Jan 14  2025 amqps.xml
-rw-r--r--. 1 root root 273 Jan 14  2025 amqp.xml
-rw-r--r--. 1 root root 465 Jan 14  2025 anno-1602.xml
-rw-r--r--. 1 root root 431 Jan 14  2025 anno-1800.xml
........
```

The following shows the content of the *ssh* service file:

```
[user1@server10 ~]$ cat /usr/lib/firewalld/services/ssh.xml
<?xml version="1.0" encoding="utf-8"?>
<service>
  <short>SSH</short>
  <description>Secure Shell (SSH) is a protocol for logging into and executing c
ommands on remote machines. It provides secure encrypted communications. If you
plan on accessing your machine remotely via SSH over a firewalled interface, ena
ble this option. You need the openssh-server package installed for this option t
o be useful.</description>
  <port protocol="tcp" port="22"/>
</service>
```

As depicted in the above output, the service has a name and description, and it defines the port and protocol for the service. See the manual pages for *firewalld.service* for details on service configuration files.

Firewalld Management

Managing the *firewalld* service involves operations such as listing, querying, adding, changing, and removing zones, services, ports, IP sources, and network connections. There are three methods available in RHEL to perform these management tasks: the *firewall-cmd* utility for command line administration, a web interface for graphical administration, and manual editing of zone and service templates. We use the command-line method in this book.

The firewall-cmd Command

The *firewall-cmd* command is a powerful tool to manage the *firewalld* service at the command prompt. This tool can be used to add or remove rules from the runtime configuration or save modifications persistently for use across system reboots. It supports numerous options for managing zones, services, ports, network connections, and other firewall settings; Table 21-2 lists and describes only the most common options.

Option	Description
General	
--state	Displays the running status of firewalld
--reload	Reloads firewall rules from zone files. All runtime-only changes are lost, while permanent rules remain intact.
--permanent	Stores a change persistently. The change becomes active only after the firewall service is reloaded or restarted.
Zones	
--get-default-zone	Shows the name of the default/active zone
--set-default-zone	Changes the default zone for both runtime and permanent configuration
--get-zones	Prints a list of available zones
--get-active-zones	Displays the active zone and the assigned interfaces
--list-all	Lists all settings for a zone
--list-all-zones	Lists the settings for all available zones
--zone	Specifies the name of the zone to work on. Without this option, the default zone is used.
Services	
--get-services	Prints predefined services
--list-services	Lists services for a zone
--add-service	Adds a service to a zone
--remove-service	Removes a service from a zone
--query-service	Queries for the presence of a service
Ports	
--list-ports	Lists network ports
--add-port	Adds a port or a range of ports to a zone
--remove-port	Removes a port from a zone
--query-port	Queries for the presence of a port

Option	Description
Network Interfaces	
--list-interfaces	Lists network interfaces assigned to a zone
--add-interface	Binds a network interface to a zone
--change-interface	Changes the binding of a network interface to a different zone
--remove-interface	Unbinds a network interface from a zone
IP Sources	
--list-sources	Lists IP sources assigned to a zone
--add-source	Adds an IP source to a zone
--change-source	Changes an IP source
--remove-source	Removes an IP source from a zone

Table 21-2 Common firewall-cmd Options

With most --add and --remove options, the --permanent switch may be specified to store the rule persistently in the zone configuration files under the */etc/firewalld/zones* directory. Some of the options from Table 21-2 are used in the upcoming exercises; the rest are beyond the scope of this book. Consult the manual pages for the command for details on the usage of these and other options.

Querying the Operational Status of firewalld

You can check the running status of the *firewalld* service using either the *systemctl* or the *firewall-cmd* command. Both commands produce different outputs, but the objective is to verify that the service is running.

```
[user1@server10 ~]$ sudo firewall-cmd --state
running
[user1@server10 ~]$ sudo systemctl status firewalld -l --no-pager
● firewalld.service - firewalld - dynamic firewall daemon
     Loaded: loaded (/usr/lib/systemd/system/firewalld.service; enabled; pres
et: enabled)
     Active: active (running) since Wed 2025-12-17 03:04:22 EST; 1 day 17h ag
o
 Invocation: 568fd689d6e8427f945c0293642afa8e
       Docs: man:firewalld(1)
   Main PID: 891 (firewalld)
      Tasks: 2 (limit: 10665)
     Memory: 50.2M (peak: 51.8M)
        CPU: 2.994s
     CGroup: /system.slice/firewalld.service
             └─891 /usr/bin/python3 -sP /usr/sbin/firewalld --nofork --nopid

Dec 17 03:04:16 server10.example.com systemd[1]: Starting firewalld.service -
 firewalld - dynamic firewall daemon...
Dec 17 03:04:22 server10.example.com systemd[1]: Started firewalld.service -
firewalld - dynamic firewall daemon.
```

The output indicates that the *firewalld* service is running on *server10*. The other command outcome also reports that the service is marked for autostart at system reboots. If *firewalld* is not enabled or is inactive, issue **sudo systemctl --now enable firewalld** to start it immediately and enable it for autostart at system reboots.

You are now ready to perform the exercises presented next.

Exercise 21-1: Add Services and Ports, and Manage Zones

Perform this exercise on *server10* as *user1* with *sudo* where required. In this exercise, you will:

- Determine the current default zone
- Add and activate a permanent rule to allow HTTP traffic on port 80
- Add a runtime rule for traffic intended for TCP port 443 (the HTTPS service)
- Add a permanent rule to the *internal* zone for TCP port range 5901 to 5910
- Confirm the changes
- Display the contents of the affected zone files
- Switch the default zone to *internal* and activate it.

1. Determine the current default zone:

```
[user1@server10 ~]$ sudo firewall-cmd --get-default-zone
public
```

2. Add a permanent rule to allow HTTP traffic on its default port:

```
[user1@server10 ~]$ sudo firewall-cmd --permanent --add-service http
success
```

The command copied the *public.xml* file from the */usr/lib/firewalld/zones* directory to the */etc/firewalld/zones* directory, and added the rule for the HTTP service.

3. Activate the new rule:

```
[user1@server10 ~]$ sudo firewall-cmd --reload
success
```

4. Confirm the activation of the new rule:

```
[user1@server10 ~]$ sudo firewall-cmd --list-services
cockpit dhcpv6-client http ssh
```

5. Display the content of the default zone file to confirm the addition of the permanent rule:

```
[user1@server10 ~]$ sudo cat /etc/firewalld/zones/public.xml
<?xml version="1.0" encoding="utf-8"?>
<zone>
  <short>Public</short>
  <description>For use in public areas. You do not trust the
 networks to not harm your computer. Only selected incoming
epted.</description>
  <service name="ssh"/>
  <service name="dhcpv6-client"/>
  <service name="cockpit"/>
  <service name="http"/>
  <forward/>
</zone>
```

6. Add a runtime rule to allow traffic on TCP port 443 and verify:

```
[user1@server10 ~]$ sudo firewall-cmd --add-port 443/tcp
success
[user1@server10 ~]$ sudo firewall-cmd --list-ports
443/tcp
```

7. Add a permanent rule to the *internal* zone for TCP port range 5901 to 5910:

```
[user1@server10 ~]$ sudo firewall-cmd --add-port 5901-5910/tcp --permanent --zone internal
success
```

8. Display the content of the *internal* zone file to confirm the addition of the permanent rule:

```
[user1@server10 ~]$ sudo cat /etc/firewalld/zones/internal.xml
<?xml version="1.0" encoding="utf-8"?>
<zone>
  <short>Internal</short>
  <description>For use on internal networks. You mostly trust
rs on the networks to not harm your computer. Only selected in
s are accepted.</description>
  <service name="ssh"/>
  <service name="mdns"/>
  <service name="samba-client"/>
  <service name="dhcpv6-client"/>
  <service name="cockpit"/>
  <port port="5901-5910" protocol="tcp"/>
  <forward/>
</zone>
```

The *firewall-cmd* command makes a backup of the affected zone file with a *.old* extension whenever an update is made to a zone.

9. Switch the default zone to internal and confirm:

```
[user1@server10 ~]$ sudo firewall-cmd --set-default-zone internal
success
[user1@server10 ~]$ sudo firewall-cmd --get-default-zone
internal
```

10. Activate the rules defined in the *internal* zone and list the port range added earlier:

```
[user1@server10 ~]$ sudo firewall-cmd --reload
success
[user1@server10 ~]$ sudo firewall-cmd --list-ports
5901-5910/tcp
```

This completes the exercise.

Exercise 21-2: Remove Services and Ports, and Manage Zones

Perform this exercise on *server10* as *user1* with *sudo* where required. In this exercise, you will:

- Remove the two permanent rules that were added in Exercise 21-1
- Switch the *public* zone back as the default zone
- Confirm the changes

1. Remove the permanent rule for HTTP from the *public* zone:

```
[user1@server10 ~]$ sudo firewall-cmd --remove-service=http --zone public --permanent
success
```

Notice the optional equal sign (=) used with the --remove-service option. The *firewall-cmd* command supports the specification of add, remove, change, and zone options with and without an equal sign (=). The --zone option is used to specify the *public* zone, as it is currently not the default.

2. Remove the permanent rule for ports 5901 to 5910 from the *internal* zone:

```
[user1@server10 ~]$ sudo firewall-cmd --remove-port 5901-5910/tcp --permanent
success
```

The --zone option is not used, as 'internal' is currently the default zone.

3. Switch the default zone to *public* and validate:

```
[user1@server10 ~]$ sudo firewall-cmd --set-default-zone=public
success
[user1@server10 ~]$ sudo firewall-cmd --get-default-zone
public
```

4. Activate the *public* zone rules, and list the current services:

```
[user1@server10 ~]$ sudo firewall-cmd --reload
success
[user1@server10 ~]$
[user1@server10 ~]$ sudo firewall-cmd --list-services
cockpit dhcpv6-client ssh
```

The *public* zone reflects the removal of the HTTP service. This concludes the exercise.

Exercise 21-3: Test the Effect of Firewall Rule

Perform this exercise on *server10* and *server20* as *user1* with *sudo* where required. In this exercise, you will:

- Remove the *sshd* service rule from the runtime configuration on *server10*
- Access *server10* from *server20* using the *ssh* command

1. Remove the rule for the *sshd* service on *server10*:

```
[user1@server10 ~]$ sudo firewall-cmd --remove-service ssh
success
```

2. Issue the *ssh* command on *server20* to access *server10*:

```
[user1@server20 ~]$ ssh server10
ssh: connect to host server10 port 22: No route to host
```

The error is displayed because the firewall on *server10* blocked the SSH connection. Put the rule back on *server10* and try accessing it from *server20* again:

3. Add the rule back for *sshd* on *server10*:

```
[user1@server10 ~]$ sudo firewall-cmd --add-service=ssh
success
```

4. Issue the *ssh* command on *server20* to access *server10*. Enter "yes" if prompted to accept the host key, and then enter the password for *user1*.

```
[user1@server10 ~]$ ssh server20
Activate the web console with: systemctl enable --now cockpit.socket
Register this system with Red Hat Insights: rhc connect
Last login: Thu Dec 18 21:25:51 2025 from 192.168.0.110
[user1@server20 ~]$
[user1@server20 ~]$ ssh server10
Activate the web console with: systemctl enable --now cockpit.socket
Register this system with Red Hat Insights: rhc connect
Last login: Thu Dec 18 21:24:42 2025 from 192.168.0.120
```

This brings the exercise to an end.

Chapter Summary

This chapter equipped you with the skills to manage the host-based firewall using firewalld. We began by understanding the foundation: the kernel's netfilter framework and the nftables subsystem that firewalld controls.

We demystified the key concepts of zones, which define trust levels for network connections, and services, which are pre-defined rules for common daemons. You learned how to use the powerful firewall-cmd command-line tool to query the firewall state, manage runtime and permanent rules, and assign interfaces and sources to zones.

The exercises provided hands-on experience in adding and removing services and ports, switching the default zone, and witnessing the immediate effect of firewall rules on network accessibility. Configuring firewalld is a fundamental administrative task for securing any RHEL system exposed to a network.

Review Questions

1. What is the purpose of the *drop* zone?
2. What is the process of data packet formation called?
3. What type of traffic is allowed by default for all zones?
4. What would the command *firewall-cmd --remove-port=5000/tcp* do?
5. What is the effect of using the --permanent option with *firewall-cmd*?
6. What is the primary command-line tool for managing firewalld called?
7. What would the command *firewall-cmd --permanent --add-service=nfs --zone=external* do?
8. If you have a set of firewall rules defined for a service stored under both */etc/firewalld* and */usr/lib/firewalld* directories, which of the two sets will take precedence?
9. What is the kernel module in RHEL 10 that implements the host-level protection called?
10. *firewalld* is the firewall management solution in RHEL 10. True or False?
11. Which directory stores the configuration file for modified zones?
12. Name the default firewalld zone.
13. What is the purpose of service configuration files?
14. What command would you use to list all services allowed in the active zone?
15. Which command reloads configuration files without restarting the service?
16. What happens to runtime firewall rules after a system reboot?
17. A firewall can be configured between two networks but not between two hosts. True or False?
18. After changing the default firewalld zone to internal, what would you run to verify?
19. What command would you use to list all active zones and their assigned interfaces?
20. What is the difference between adding a service and adding a port?

Answers to Review Questions

1. The *drop* zone drops all incoming traffic without sending any response, providing a high level of security.
2. The process of data packet formation is called encapsulation.
3. Outgoing traffic is allowed by default in all zones.
4. The command provided will remove the runtime firewall rule for TCP port 5000 from the default zone.
5. The --permanent option stores the rule in the zone configuration file so that it persists across reboots. The change becomes active only after a reload or restart.
6. The primary command-line tool for managing *firewalld* is called *firewall-cmd.*
7. The command provided will add the *nfs* service to the *external* firewalld zone persistently.
8. The ruleset located in the */etc/firewalld* directory will have precedence.
9. The host-level packet filtering framework implemented in the Linux kernel is called netfilter.
10. True.
11. The modified zone files are stored under the */etc/firewalld/zones* directory.
12. The default *firewalld* zone is the *public* zone.
13. Service configuration files store service-specific port numbers, protocols, and related settings, making it easy to activate and deactivate services.
14. You would run *firewall-cmd --list-services* to list all services allowed in the active zone.
15. The *firewall-cmd --reload* command reloads configuration files without restarting the service.
16. Runtime firewall rules are lost after a system reboot unless they are saved as permanent rules.
17. False. A firewall can also be configured between two host computers.
18. You run *firewall-cmd --get-default-zone* for validation.

19. You would run *firewall-cmd --get-active-zones* to list all active zones and their assigned interfaces.
20. Adding a service opens a predefined set of ports and protocols associated with that service, while adding a port opens a specific port or range of ports.

Do-It-Yourself Challenge Labs

The following labs are designed to reinforce most of the concepts and skills covered in this chapter. You are expected to complete these labs without external assistance. A step-by-step guide is not provided, as the required knowledge has already been presented in the chapter; however, each lab includes hints pointing to the relevant major topic(s).

Use the lab environment created specifically for the end-of-chapter labs. See the sub-section "Lab Environment for End-of-Chapter Labs" in Chapter 01 "Local Installation" for details.

Lab 21-1: Add Service to Firewall

As *user1* with *sudo* on *server30*, add and activate a permanent rule to allow HTTPS traffic in the default zone. Confirm the change by viewing the zone's XML file and by running the appropriate *firewall-cmd* command. (Hint: Firewall Management).

Lab 21-2: Add Port Range to Firewall

As *user1* with *sudo* on *server30*, add and activate a permanent rule to allow the UDP port range 8000 to 8005 in the *trusted* zone. Confirm the change by viewing the zone's XML file and by running the appropriate *firewall-cmd* command. (Hint: Firewall Management).

Lab 21-3: Remove a Firewall Service

As *user1* with *sudo* on *server30*, remove the runtime rule that allows the SSH service from the default zone. Verify that SSH access is blocked from *server40*. Restore the rule and confirm that SSH access works again. (Hint: Firewall Management).

Lab 21-4: Test Firewall Rule Persistence

As *user1* with *sudo* on *server30*, add a runtime-only rule to allow TCP port 9000. Reboot the system and verify that the rule is no longer present. Then add the same rule permanently and confirm that it persists after another reboot. (Hint: The firewall-cmd command).

Chapter 22

Security Enhanced Linux

By the end of this chapter, you will be able to:

- Describe Security Enhanced Linux (SELinux) and its Key Terminology
- Explain SELinux Contexts for Users, Processes, Files, and Network Ports
- Copy, Move, and Archive Files with and without SELinux Context
- Describe How Domain Transitioning Works
- Define SELinux Booleans
- Query and Manage SELinux Using Command-Line Tools
- Modify SELinux Contexts for Files and Network Ports
- Add New SELinux Rules to the Policy Database
- View and Analyze SELinux Alert Messages

RHCSA Objectives:

58. Set enforcing and permissive modes for SELinux
59. List and identify SELinux file and process context
60. Restore default file contexts
61. Manage SELinux port labels
62. Use Boolean settings to modify system SELinux settings

Security Enhanced Linux is a mechanism that controls who can access and do what on the system. It is part and parcel of the Linux kernel. It handles access beyond what the traditional access control system delivers including file and directory permissions, user and group-level permissions, and shadow password and password aging mechanisms.

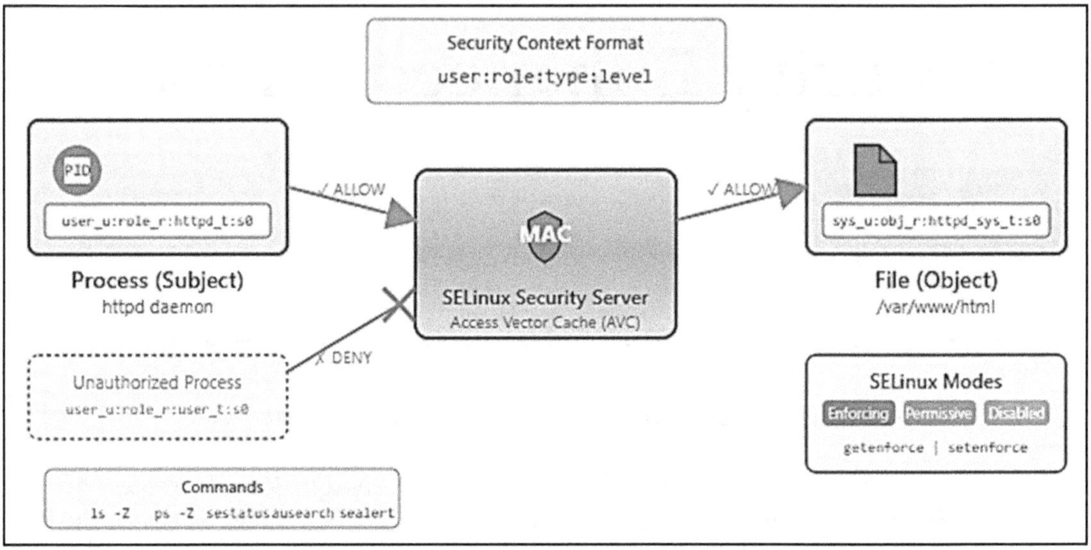

The goal of SELinux is to limit the possible damage that could occur to the system due to unauthorized user or program access. This chapter covers SELinux in reasonable detail.

Security Enhanced Linux

Security Enhanced Linux (SELinux) is an implementation of the *Mandatory Access Control* (MAC) security architecture that provides flexible, granular, and policy-driven access controls for Linux systems. MAC is integrated directly into the Linux kernel, enabling the kernel to enforce additional security mechanisms beyond the traditional permission model.

SELinux complements the standard Linux *Discretionary Access Control* (DAC) security architecture. DAC includes traditional file and directory permissions, ownership, *Access Control Lists* (ACLs), extended attributes, and privilege escalation mechanisms such as *su* and *sudo*.

MAC introduces an additional layer of protection by restricting how *subjects* interact with *objects*, even when DAC permissions would otherwise allow access.

A subject is a Linux user or process, and an object is any resource the subject attempts to access. Objects include files, directories, file systems, hardware devices, network interfaces or connections, ports, pipes, and sockets.

MAC limits the actions a subject can perform on an object according to system-wide security policy. This significantly reduces the potential damage that can occur if a service, application, or user account is compromised through the exploitation of vulnerabilities.

Access Control List (ACL) provides fine-grained permissions beyond the traditional owner/group/other (rwx) model. A discussion is beyond the scope of this book and the RHCSA exam.

The key difference between DAC and MAC lies in who controls access:

- **DAC (Discretionary Access Control):** The owner of a resource (e.g., a user who creates a file) determines who can access it by setting permissions such as read, write, and execute. For example, a user who owns a file can grant write access to everyone, even if doing so introduces a security risk.
- **MAC (Mandatory Access Control – SELinux):** A system-wide security policy governs access decisions. Ownership and DAC permissions alone are insufficient. Even if a user owns a file, SELinux will deny access unless the policy explicitly permits the requesting process to access that object.

This model prevents compromised services or users from accessing resources beyond their defined purpose.

Policy Enforcement and Protection Model

MAC controls are fine-grained and designed to protect the system as a whole. If one service is compromised, SELinux confines the damage to only those resources explicitly allowed to that service.

For example, if the HTTP service (*httpd*) is compromised, the attacker can only access files and resources permitted to the *httpd* process by SELinux policy—not arbitrary system files or other services' data.

SELinux enforces this behavior using a set of authorization rules collectively known as a *policy*. When a subject attempts to access an object, SELinux examines the security *contexts* (also called *labels*) assigned to both the subject and the object and determines whether the action is allowed.

Access Vector Cache (AVC)

SELinux access decisions are cached in a special area called the *Access Vector Cache* (AVC). Each time a process attempts an action, SELinux first checks the AVC to see whether the request has already been evaluated. If a cached decision exists, SELinux uses it immediately instead of re-evaluating the policy rules. This mechanism improves performance while maintaining strong security enforcement.

Default SELinux State

By default, SELinux is enabled and enforcing at the time of RHEL installation. The default configuration confines system services and daemons to the minimum privileges for correct operation, while allowing administrators to customize enforcement as needed.

Terminology

Understanding SELinux requires familiarity with key terms. These terms explain the concepts and functionality covered throughout this chapter.

Subject

A *subject* is a user or process that attempts to access an object. Examples include system_u for SELinux system user, and unconfined_u for SELinux user not restricted by policy. The subject component is stored in field 1 of the SELinux context.

Object

An *object* is a resource—file, directory, file system, hardware device, network interface, network connection, network port, pipe, or socket—that a subject attempts to access. Examples include object_r for general objects, system_r for system-owned objects, and unconfined_r for objects not restricted by the policy.

Access

An *access* is an action performed by a subject on an object. Access examples include reading a file, writing to a directory, executing a program, and listening on a network port.

Policy

A *policy* is a comprehensive set of rules that SELinux enforces system-wide. SELinux does not rely on user discretion; it consults the policy to determine whether an access attempt is permitted. Any action not explicitly allowed by the policy is denied. RHEL provides three predefined SELinux policies: *targeted*, *mls (Multi-Level Security)*, and *minimum*, with targeted being the default.

- **targeted:** This policy confines selected system services while allowing other processes to run unconfined. For instance, system services like *httpd* run in confined domains, while logged-in users typically run in unconfined domains.
- **mls:** This policy enforces strict, hierarchical security controls and is used primarily in highly regulated environments.
- **minimum:** This policy is a lightweight version of the targeted policy and protects only a limited set of services.

Context (Label)

A *context* (or *label*) is a tag that stores security attributes for subjects and objects. Every SELinux context consists of four components: SELinux user, role, type (or domain), and sensitivity level. SELinux uses this information to make access control decisions.

Labeling

Labeling refers to assigning contexts to files, directories, processes, and other objects.

SELinux User

SELinux defines several SELinux user identities, each authorized for specific roles and security levels. Linux users are mapped to SELinux users through policy rules, which determine the roles and security levels that processes launch by those users may enter.

For instance, a Linux user mapped to the SELinux user user_u runs in confined domains and is typically restricted from performing administrative actions such as using the *su* and *sudo* commands or executing programs located in their home directories. These restrictions are enforced by the SELinux policy and help limit the impact of a compromised user account.

Role

A *role* is an attribute of SELinux's *Role-Based Access Control* (RBAC) model. It classifies who (subject) is allowed to access what (domains or types). SELinux users are authorized for roles, and roles are authorized for domains and types. Each subject has an associated role to ensure that the system and user processes are separated. A subject can transition into a new role to gain access to other domains and types. Example roles include user_r for ordinary users, sysadm_r for administrators, and system_r for processes that initiate under the system_r role. The role is stored in field 2 of the context.

Type Enforcement

Type enforcement (TE) is the primary access control mechanism in SELinux. It defines rules that control how processes running in specific domains (subjects) are allowed to access objects labeled with particular types, such as files, directories, devices, and network resources. These access decisions are made by evaluating the SELinux contexts assigned to both the subject and the object.

Type and Domain

A *type* is an attribute used by type enforcement to classify objects based on their security requirements. Objects such as files, directories, devices, and other system resources that share common security characteristics are grouped under the same type. Examples include user_home_dir_t for objects located in user home directories and usr_t for most objects stored under the */usr* directory. The type is stored in field 3 of a file context.

A *domain* defines the access permissions of a process. Processes with common security requirements are grouped within the same domain type and run confined within that domain according to SELinux policy rules. Examples include init_t for the *systemd* process, firewalld_t for the *firewalld* process, and unconfined_t for processes that are not bound by SELinux policy. The domain is stored in field 3 of a process context.

SELinux policy rules specify how domains may interact with object types, which domain transitions are permitted, and how domains may interact with one another. Access is allowed only if explicitly permitted by the policy; all other access attempts are denied by default.

Level

A *level* is an attribute used by *Multi-Level Security* (MLS) and *Multi-Category Security* (MCS). It consists of a sensitivity:category pair that defines the security level within an SELinux context. A category may be specified as a single value or as a range, such as c0.c4, which represents categories c0 through c4. In RHEL, the targeted policy is used by default, which enforces MCS, not full MLS. Under MCS, all processes operate at a single sensitivity level (s0), but may be assigned 0 to 1023 categories to provide additional isolation.

SELinux Contexts for Users

SELinux contexts define security attributes applied to both subjects and objects. Each context consists of four components: user, role, type (or domain), and security level. The following example shows the context for *user1* using the *id* command with -Z option:

```
[user1@server10 ~]$ id -Z
unconfined_u:unconfined_r:unconfined_t:s0-s0:c0.c1023
```

The output indicates that *user1* is mapped to the SELinux user unconfined_u, which means that there are no SELinux policy restrictions placed on processes launched by this user. In a default RHEL configuration, this is the case for all Linux users, including *root*. This entails that user-initiated processes run in the unconfined domain, and access to system resources is governed primarily by DAC. Under this default configuration, SELinux enforcement mainly targets system services and daemons, rather than interactive user sessions.

In addition to the unconfined user with unlimited privileges, SELinux includes seven confined user identities that enforce restricted access to system objects. These users are mapped to Linux users via SELinux policy and are designed to limit what roles, domains, and security levels a user's processes may enter. This confinement helps protect the system from accidental or malicious damage caused by user actions.

To list the SELinux users defined in the policy, you can use the *seinfo* command. Note that the *setools-console* package must be installed before this command can be used.

```
[user1@server10 ~]$ sudo seinfo -u

Users: 8
   guest_u
   root
   staff_u
   sysadm_u
   system_u
   unconfined_u
   user_u
   xguest_u
```

The output shows the eight predefined SELinux users available in the policy. You can view the mapping between Linux users and SELinux users using the *semanage* command:

```
[user1@server10 ~]$ sudo semanage login -l

Login Name           SELinux User         MLS/MCS Range        Service

__default__          unconfined_u         s0-s0:c0.c1023       *
root                 unconfined_u         s0-s0:c0.c1023       *
```

The output displays Linux users in column 1 (Login Name) and SELinux users they are mapped to in column 2 (SELinux User). Columns 3 and 4 show the associated security level (MLS/MCS Range), and the context for the Linux user (the * represents all services). By default, all non-*root* Linux users are represented as __default__, which is mapped to the unconfined_u user in the policy.

SELinux Contexts for Processes

You can determine the context assigned to processes using the *ps* command with the -Z flag. The following example shows only the first two lines of the command output:

```
[user1@server10 ~]$ ps -eZ
LABEL                               PID TTY          TIME CMD
system_u:system_r:init_t:s0           1 ?        00:00:04 systemd
```

In the output, the SELinux user (system_u) identifies the SELinux identity under which the process is running and is typically mapped to the Linux *root* user for system services. The role (system_r) indicates the role associated with the process. The domain (init_t) represents the SELinux type applied to the process and defines the permissions and restrictions enforced by SELinux. The security level (s0) reflects the MLS/MCS level.

Processes that are not confined by SELinux policy run in the unconfined_t domain and are not subject to domain-based SELinux restrictions.

SELinux Contexts for Files

You can view the context assigned to files and directories using the *ls* command with the -Z switch. The following example shows the four context attributes applied to the */etc/passwd* file:

```
[user1@server10 ~]$ ls -lZ /etc/passwd
-rw-r--r--. 1 root root system_u:object_r:passwd_file_t:s0 2889 Dec 17 09:09
/etc/passwd
```

The output indicates the SELinux user (system_u), role (object_r), type (passwd_file_t), and security level (s0) associated with the *passwd* file. The type is the most significant component for access control decisions involving files, as it is used by type enforcement rules to determine which domains may access the file.

Contexts for system-installed and user-created files are stored in the *file_contexts* and *file_contexts.local* policy files located in the */etc/selinux/targeted/contexts/files* directory. These context definitions can be viewed and managed using the *semanage* command.

Copying, Moving, and Archiving Files with SELinux Contexts

As mentioned earlier, all files in RHEL are labeled with an SELINUX security context by default. New files inherit the context of their parent directory at the time of creation. However, three common file management operations—copying, moving, and archiving—require special attention. Special rules must be observed to ensure that files retain or receive correct contexts. These rules are as follows:

1. **Copying to a different directory:** If a file is copied to a different directory, the destination file receives the destination directory's context, unless the --preserve=context switch is specified with the *cp* command to retain the source file's original context.
2. **Overwriting an existing file during a copy:** If a copy operation overwrites an existing destination file in the same or a different directory, the copied file inherits the context of the overwritten file, unless the --preserve=context switch is specified with the *cp* command to preserve the source file's original context.
3. **Moving a file:** If a file is moved to the same or a different directory, the SELinux context remains unchanged, even if it differs from the destination directory's context.
4. **Archiving a file:** If a file is archived with the *tar* command, use the --selinux option to preserve the context within the archive.

Later in the chapter, you will perform an exercise to confirm the behavior of these operations.

SELinux Contexts for Ports

SELinux contexts also define security attributes for network ports, which can be viewed with the *semanage* command. The following example illustrates a subset of the output:

```
[user1@server10 ~]$ sudo semanage port -l
SELinux Port Type              Proto    Port Number
chronyd_port_t                 udp      323
dns_port_t                     tcp      53, 853
ftp_port_t                     tcp      21, 989, 990
http_port_t                    tcp      80, 81, 443, 488, 8008, 8009, 8443, 9000
ntp_port_t                     udp      123
syslogd_port_t                 udp      514, 601, 20514
```

The output is displayed in three columns. Column 1 shows the SELinux type, column 2 indicates the protocol, and column 3 lists the port number(s). By default, SELinux allows services to listen only on a restricted, predefined set of network ports. Any attempt by a service to bind to a port that is not explicitly permitted by SELinux policy will be denied, even if traditional firewall rules allow the traffic.

Domain Transitioning

SELinux allows a process running in one domain to transition into another domain to execute an application that is restricted to run within that domain, provided that an explicit rule exists in the policy to permit the transition. Domain transitions are a fundamental mechanism that enables privileged system utilities to function securely without granting excessive access to user processes.

SELinux defines a permission setting called *entrypoint* in its policy to control which executable files may be used to transition a process into another domain. In simple terms, entrypoint determines which executable files are allowed to trigger a domain change.

To understand how domain transition works, consider the following example, which illustrates what happens when a Linux user changes their password using the */usr/bin/passwd* command.

The *passwd* command is labeled with the passwd_exec_t type, which can be confirmed as follows:

```
[user1@server10 ~]$ ls -lZ /usr/bin/passwd
-rwsr-xr-x. 1 root root system_u:object_r:passwd_exec_t:s0 91584 Nov  3  2024
 /usr/bin/passwd
```

The *passwd* command requires access to the */etc/shadow* file in order to modify a user's password. The *shadow* file is protected by SELinux and has a different type assigned to it, known as shadow_t:

```
[user1@server10 ~]$ ls -lZ /etc/shadow
----------. 1 root root system_u:object_r:shadow_t:s0 1971 Dec 17 09:09
/etc/shadow
```

The SELinux policy contains rules that specifically allow processes running in the passwd_t domain to read from and write to files labeled with the shadow_t type, and permit the executable file labeled with the passwd_exec_t type to serve as an entrypoint into the passwd_t domain.

When a user executes the *passwd* command, the user's shell process (typically running in an unconfined or user domain) executes the *passwd* binary. Because the policy explicitly allows this executable to act as an entrypoint, the process transitions into the passwd_t domain. Once in this domain, the process is permitted to modify the */etc/shadow* file.

To observe this behavior, open two terminal windows.

In window 1, issue the *passwd* command as *user1* and wait at the password prompt:

```
[user1@server10 ~]$ passwd
Changing password for user user1.
Current password: _
```

In window 2, run the *ps* command to inspect the process context:

```
[user1@server10 ~]$ ps -eZ | grep passwd
unconfined_u:unconfined_r:passwd_t:s0-s0:c0.c1023 3836 pts/1 00:00:00
 passwd
```

As shown in the output, the *passwd* command (process) has transitioned into the passwd_t domain. Processing running in this domain are explicitly authorized by policy to modify the contents of the */etc/shadow* file, while remaining restricted from accessing unrelated system resources.

SELinux Booleans

Booleans are on/off switches that are used to enable or disable specific conditional rules within the SELinux policy. Booleans allow you to modify SELinux behavior dynamically and immediately, without recompiling or reloading the policy. For instance, the ftpd_anon_write Boolean can be turned on to enable anonymous users to upload files. This privilege can be revoked by turning this Boolean off. Boolean values are stored in virtual files located in the */sys/fs/selinux/booleans* directory. Each file corresponds directly to a Boolean name. A listing of this directory typically reveals hundreds of Boolean entries on a standard RHEL system:

```
[user1@server10 ~]$ ls -l /sys/fs/selinux/booleans/
total 0
-rw-r--r--. 1 root root 0 Feb  5 22:02 abrt_anon_write
-rw-r--r--. 1 root root 0 Feb  5 22:02 abrt_handle_event
-rw-r--r--. 1 root root 0 Feb  5 22:02 abrt_upload_watch_anon_write
-rw-r--r--. 1 root root 0 Feb  5 22:02 antivirus_can_scan_system
-rw-r--r--. 1 root root 0 Feb  5 22:02 antivirus_use_jit
-rw-r--r--. 1 root root 0 Feb  5 22:02 auditadm_exec_content
........
```

The manual pages for Booleans are provided by the *selinux-policy-doc* package. Once installed, use the -K option with the *man* command to bring the pages up for a specific Boolean. For instance, issue **man -K abrt_anon_write** to view the manual pages for the abrt_anon_write Boolean.

Boolean values can be viewed, and flipped temporarily or permanently. Temporary changes are stored as a "1" or "0" in the corresponding Boolean file under the */sys/fs/selinux/booleans* directory and permanent changes are saved in the policy database. The new value takes effect right away in both cases.

One of the exercises in the next section demonstrates how to list, modify, and persist Boolean values.

SELinux Administration

Managing SELinux involves plentiful administrative tasks, including controlling the activation mode, checking operational status, managing security contexts for subjects and objects, and switching Boolean values. RHEL provides a set of commands to perform these operations. These commands are available through multiple packages, such as:

- **libselinux-utils:** provides *getenforce*, *setenforce*, and *getsebool* commands
- **policycoreutils:** contains *sestatus*, *setsebool*, and *restorecon* commands
- **policycoreutils-python-utils:** provides the *semanage* command
- **setools-console:** includes the *seinfo* and *sesearch* commands

For viewing alerts and debugging SELinux-related issues, RHEL also provides a graphical tool called *SELinux Alert Browser*, which is part of the *setroubleshoot-server* package.

To fully manage SELinux, ensure that these packages are installed on the system. Additional utilities exist for specialized tasks, but they are used less frequently and are beyond the scope of this book.

Management Commands

SELinux provides a variety of commands for effective administration. Table 22-1 lists and describes the primary management commands mentioned above plus a few more under various management categories.

Command	Description
	Mode Management
getenforce	Displays the current mode of operation
grubby	Updates and displays GRUB2 boot loader configuration
sestatus	Shows SELinux runtime status and Boolean values
setenforce	Switches the operating mode between enforcing and permissive temporarily
	Context Management
chcon	Changes file contexts (changes do not survive file system relabeling)
restorecon	Restores default contexts on files using policy definitions
semanage	Changes file contexts (changes survive file system relabeling)
	Policy Management
seinfo	Provides information on policy components
semanage	Manages the policy database
sesearch	Searches rules within the policy database
	Boolean Management
getsebool	Displays Booleans and their current settings
setsebool	Modifies Boolean values temporarily or permanently
semanage	Modifies Boolean values persistently
	Troubleshooting
sealert	The graphical troubleshooter program

Table 22-1 SELinux Management Commands

Most of these commands are used throughout this chapter.

Viewing and Controlling SELinux Operational State

One of the key configuration files that controls the SELinux operational state and default policy type is the */etc/selinux/config* file. The default contents of this file are displayed below:

```
[user1@server10 ~]$ cat /etc/selinux/config

# This file controls the state of SELinux on the system.
# SELINUX= can take one of these three values:
#     enforcing - SELinux security policy is enforced.
#     permissive - SELinux prints warnings instead of enforcing.
#     disabled - No SELinux policy is loaded.
........
SELINUX=enforcing
# SELINUXTYPE= can take one of these three values:
#     targeted - Targeted processes are protected,
#     minimum - Modification of targeted policy. Only
 are protected.
#     mls - Multi Level Security protection.
SELINUXTYPE=targeted
```

The SELINUX directive sets its activation mode:

- *Enforcing* activates it and allows or denies actions based on policy rules
- *Permissive* activates SELinux, but permits all actions. This mode is useful for troubleshooting and testing.
- *Disabled* completely turns SELinux off

When running in enforcing mode, the SELINUXTYPE directive dictates the type of policy to be enforced. The default is targeted.

To determine the current operating mode, issue the *getenforce* command:

```
[user1@server10 ~]$ getenforce
Enforcing
```

The output displays enforcing as the current active mode. You may flip the state to permissive using the *setenforce* command, and verify the change with *getenforce*:

```
[user1@server10 ~]$ sudo setenforce permissive
[user1@server10 ~]$ getenforce
Permissive
```

You may alternatively use "1" for enforcing and "0" for permissive.

The change takes effect at once; however, it will be lost at the next system reboot. To make it persistent, edit the */etc/selinux/config* file and set the SELINUX directive to a desired mode.

EXAM TIP: You can switch SELinux to permissive for troubleshooting a non-functioning service. Don't forget to change it back to enforcing when the issue is resolved.

To disable SELinux persistently, use the *grubby* command as follows:

```
[user1@server10 ~]$ sudo grubby --update-kernel ALL --args selinux=0
```

The above command appends the selinux=0 setting to the end of the "options" line in the bootloader configuration file located in the */boot/loader/entries* directory:

```
[user1@server10 ~]$ sudo cat /boot/loader/entries/cde21919216441f8ab5a8
c30cdc4e38-6.12.0-124.16.1.el10_1.x86_64.conf
title Red Hat Enterprise Linux (6.12.0-124.16.1.el10_1.x86_64) 10.0 (Co
ghlan)
version 6.12.0-124.16.1.el10_1.x86_64
linux /vmlinuz-6.12.0-124.16.1.el10_1.x86_64
initrd /initramfs-6.12.0-124.16.1.el10_1.x86_64.img $tuned_initrd
options root=/dev/mapper/rhel-root ro crashkernel=2G-64G:256M,64G-:512M
resume=UUID=b1103e6a-18ac-407b-815f-cf03d3096091 rd.lvm.lv=rhel/root rd
lvm.lv=rhel/swap rhgb quiet $tuned_params selinux=0
grub_users $grub_users
grub_arg --unrestricted
grub_class rhel
```

To revert the above, simply re-run the *grubby* command with the --remove-args option as shown below:

```
[user1@server10 ~]$ sudo grubby --update-kernel ALL --remove-args selinux=0
```

A system reboot is required for either change to take effect.

Querying Status

The current SELinux runtime status can be viewed with the *sestatus* command. This command also displays the location of principal directories, the policy in effect, and the activation mode.

```
[user1@server10 ~]$ sestatus
SELinux status:                 enabled
SELinuxfs mount:                /sys/fs/selinux
SELinux root directory:         /etc/selinux
Loaded policy name:             targeted
Current mode:                   enforcing
Mode from config file:          enforcing
Policy MLS status:              enabled
Policy deny_unknown status:     allowed
Memory protection checking:     actual (secure)
Max kernel policy version:      33
```

The output reveals that SELinux is enabled (SELinux status), and it is running in enforcing mode (Current mode) with the targeted policy in effect (Loaded policy name). It also indicates the current mode setting in the *config* file (Mode from config file) along with other information.

The *sestatus* command can be invoked with the -v switch to report on security contexts assigned for files and processes, as listed in the */etc/sestatus.conf* file. The default contents of this file are shown below:

```
[user1@server10 ~]$ cat /etc/sestatus.conf
[files]
/etc/passwd
/etc/shadow
/bin/bash
/bin/login
/bin/sh
/sbin/agetty
/sbin/init
/sbin/mingetty
/usr/sbin/sshd
/lib/libc.so.6
/lib/ld-linux.so.2
/lib/ld.so.1

[process]
/sbin/mingetty
/sbin/agetty
/usr/sbin/sshd
```

Run the *sestatus* command with -v:

```
[user1@server1 ~]$ sestatus -v
SELinux status:                 enabled
SELinuxfs mount:                /sys/fs/selinux
SELinux root directory:         /etc/selinux
Loaded policy name:             targeted
Current mode:                   enforcing
Mode from config file:          enforcing
Policy MLS status:              enabled
Policy deny_unknown status:     allowed
Memory protection checking:     actual (secure)
Max kernel policy version:      33

Process contexts:
Current context:                unconfined_u:unconfined_r:unconfined_t:s0-s0:c0
c1023
Init context:                   system_u:system_r:init_t:s0

File contexts:
Controlling terminal:           unconfined_u:object_r:user_devpts_t:s0
/etc/passwd                     system_u:object_r:passwd_file_t:s0
/etc/shadow                     system_u:object_r:shadow_t:s0
/bin/bash                       system_u:object_r:shell_exec_t:s0
/bin/login                      system_u:object_r:login_exec_t:s0
/bin/sh                         system_u:object_r:bin_t:s0 -> system_u:object_r
shell exec t:s0
........
```

With -v included, the command reports the contexts for the current process (Current context) and the *init* (*systemd*) process (Init context) under Process Contexts. It also reveals the file contexts for the controlling terminal and associated files under File Contexts.

Exercise 22-1: Modify SELinux File Context

Perform this exercise on *server10* as *user1* with *sudo* where required. In this exercise, you will:

- Create a directory *sedir1* under */tmp* and a file *sefile1* under *sedir1*
- Check the context on the directory and file
- Change the SELinux user and type to user_u and public_content_t on both using a single command
- Verify the changes

1. Create the hierarchy *sedir1/sefile1* under */tmp*:

```
[user1@server10 ~]$ cd /tmp
[user1@server10 tmp]$ mkdir sedir1
[user1@server10 tmp]$ touch sedir1/sefile1
```

2. Determine the contexts on the new directory and file:

```
[user1@server10 tmp]$ ls -ldZ sedir1
drwxr-xr-x. 2 user1 user1 unconfined_u:object_r:user_tmp_t:s0 21 Feb  6
11:30 sedir1
[user1@server10 tmp]$ ls -ldZ sedir1/sefile1
-rw-r--r--. 1 user1 user1 unconfined_u:object_r:user_tmp_t:s0 0 Feb  6
1:30 sedir1/sefile1
```

The directory and the file get unconfined_u and user_tmp_t as the SELinux user and type.

3. Modify the SELinux user (-u) on the directory to user_u and type (-t) to public_content_t recursively (-R) with the *chcon* command:

```
[user1@server10 tmp]$ sudo chcon -vu user_u -t public_content_t sedir1 -R
changing security context of 'sedir1/sefile1'
changing security context of 'sedir1'
```

4. Validate the new context:

```
[user1@server10 tmp]$ ls -ldZ sedir1
drwxr-xr-x. 2 user1 user1 user_u:object_r:public_content_t:s0 21 Feb  6
 11:30 sedir1
[user1@server10 tmp]$ ls -ldZ sedir1/sefile1
-rw-r--r--. 1 user1 user1 user_u:object_r:public_content_t:s0 0 Feb  6
11:30 sedir1/sefile1
```

Changing the SELinux user on files is rarely required in real-world administration; type enforcement is what primarily controls access.

This concludes the exercise.

Exercise 22-2: Add and Apply File Context

Perform this exercise on *server10* as *user1* with *sudo* where required. In this exercise, you will:

- Add a custom file context mapping for *sedir1* to the SELinux policy database persistently to ensure a relabeling will not reset it to its previous value (see Exercise 22-1)
- Change the context on the directory to some random values
- Restore the default context from the policy database back to the directory recursively

1. Determine the current context on the directory and file:

```
[user1@server10 tmp]$ ls -ldZ sedir1
drwxr-xr-x. 2 user1 user1 user_u:object_r:public_content_t:s0 21 Feb  6
 11:30 sedir1
[user1@server10 tmp]$ ls -ldZ sedir1/sefile1
-rw-r--r--. 1 user1 user1 user_u:object_r:public_content_t:s0 0 Feb  6
11:30 sedir1/sefile1
```

The output indicates that SELinux user (user_u) and type (public_content_t) are currently applied to the directory and the file.

2. Add (-a) the directory recursively to the policy database using the *semanage fcontext* command:

```
[user1@server10 tmp]$ sudo semanage fcontext -a -s user_u -t public_con
tent_t '/tmp/sedir1(/.*)?'
```

The regular expression (/.*)? instructs the command to include all files and subdirectories under */tmp/sedir1*. This expression is needed only if recursion is required.

The above command added the context to the */etc/selinux/targeted/contexts/files/file_contexts.local* file. You can use the *cat* command to view the content.

3. Validate the addition by listing (-l) the recent changes (-C) in the policy database:

```
[user1@server10 tmp]$ sudo semanage fcontext -Cl | grep sedir
/tmp/sedir1(/.*)?  all files    user_u:object_r:public_content_t:s0
```

4. Change the current context on *sedir1* to something random (staff_u/etc_t) with the *chcon* command:

```
[user1@server10 tmp]$ sudo chcon -vu staff_u -t etc_t sedir1 -R
changing security context of 'sedir1/sefile1'
changing security context of 'sedir1'
```

5. The security context is changed successfully. Confirm with the *ls* command:

```
[user1@server10 tmp]$ ls -ldZ sedir1 ; ls -lZ sedir1/sefile1
drwxr-xr-x. 2 user1 user1 staff_u:object_r:etc_t:s0 21 Feb  6 11:30
 sedir1
-rw-r--r--. 1 user1 user1 staff_u:object_r:etc_t:s0 0 Feb  6 11:30
sedir1/sefile1
```

6. Reinstate the context on the *sedir1* directory recursively (-R) as stored in the policy database using the *restorecon* command:

```
[user1@server10 tmp]$ sudo restorecon -Rv sedir1
Relabeled /tmp/sedir1 from staff_u:object_r:etc_t:s0 to staff_u:obj
ect_r:public_content_t:s0
Relabeled /tmp/sedir1/sefile1 from staff_u:object_r:etc_t:s0 to sta
ff_u:object_r:public_content_t:s0
```

The output confirms the restoration of the default context on the directory and the file.

> **EXAM TIP:** Use the combination of semanage and restorecon commands to add a custom file context to the SELinux policy and then apply it. This will prevent the file context from resetting to its original value in the event of SELinux relabeling (disabled to enforcing/permissive).

Exercise 22-3: Add and Delete Network Ports

Perform this exercise on *server10* as *user1* with *sudo* where required. In this exercise, you will:

- Add a non-standard network port (8010) to the SELinux policy database for use by the *httpd* service
- Confirm the addition
- Remove the port from the policy
- Verify the deletion

1. List (-l) ports for the *httpd* service as defined in the SELinux policy database:

```
[user1@server10 ~]$ sudo semanage port -l | grep ^http_port
http_port_t    tcp    80, 81, 443, 488, 8008, 8009, 8443, 9000
```

The output reveals eight network ports the *httpd* process is currently allowed to listen on.

2. Add (-a) port 8010 with type (-t) http_port_t and protocol (-p) tcp to the policy:

```
[user1@server10 ~]$ sudo semanage port -at http_port_t -p tcp 8010
```

3. Confirm the addition:

```
[user1@server10 ~]$ sudo semanage port -l | grep ^http_port
http_port_t  tcp  8010, 80, 81, 443, 488, 8008, 8009, 8443, 9000
```

The new network port is visible in the outcome.

4. Delete (-d) port 8010 from the policy and confirm:

```
[user1@server10 ~]$ sudo semanage port -dp tcp 8010
[user1@server10 ~]$ sudo semanage port -l | grep ^http_port
http_port_t  tcp  80, 81, 443, 488, 8008, 8009, 8443, 9000
```

The port is removed from the policy database.

EXAM TIP: Any non-standard port you want to use for any service, make certain to add it to the SELinux policy database with the correct type.

Exercise 22-4: Copy Files with and without Context

Perform this exercise on *server10* as *user1* with *sudo* where required. In this exercise, you will:

- Create a file called *sefile2* under */tmp* and display its context
- Copy this file to the */etc/default* directory
- Observe the change in the context
- Remove *sefile2* from */etc/default*, and copy it again to the same destination, ensuring that the target file receives the source file's context

1. Create file *sefile2* under */tmp* and show context:

```
[user1@server10 ~]$ touch /tmp/sefile2
[user1@server10 ~]$ ls -lZ /tmp/sefile2
-rw-r--r--. 1 user1 user1 unconfined_u:object_r:user_tmp_t:s0 0 Feb
  6 11:48 /tmp/sefile2
```

The context on the file includes unconfined_u (user), object_r (role), user_tmp_t (type), and s0 (level).

2. Copy this file to the */etc/default* directory, and check the context again:

```
[user1@server10 ~]$ sudo cp /tmp/sefile2 /etc/default/
[user1@server10 ~]$ ls -lZ /etc/default/sefile2
-rw-r--r--. 1 root root unconfined_u:object_r:etc_t:s0 0 Feb  6 11:
49 /etc/default/sefile2
```

The target file (*/etc/default/sefile2*) received the default context of the destination directory (*/etc/default*).

3. Erase the */etc/default/sefile2* file, and copy it again with the --preserve=context option:

```
[user1@server10 ~]$ sudo rm /etc/default/sefile2
[user1@server10 ~]$ sudo cp --preserve=context /tmp/sefile2 /etc/de
fault
```

4. List the file to view the context:

```
[user1@server10 ~]$ ls -lZ /etc/default/sefile2
-rw-r--r--. 1 root root unconfined_u:object_r:user_tmp_t:s0 0 Feb
6 11:50 /etc/default/sefile2
```

The original context (user_tmp_t) is preserved on the target file after the copy operation has finished.

Exercise 22-5: View and Toggle SELinux Boolean Values

Perform this exercise on *server10* as *user1* with *sudo* where required. In this exercise, you will:

- Display the current state of the Boolean nfs_export_all_rw
- Toggle its value temporarily
- Reboot the system
- Flip its value persistently after the system has rebooted

1. Display the current setting of the Boolean nfs_export_all_rw using three different commands—*getsebool*, *sestatus*, and *semanage*:

```
[user1@server10 ~]$ sudo getsebool -a | grep nfs_export_all_rw
nfs_export_all_rw --> on
[user1@server10 ~]$ sudo sestatus -b | grep nfs_export_all_rw
nfs_export_all_rw                 on
[user1@server10 ~]$ sudo semanage boolean -l | grep nfs_export_
all_rw
nfs_export_all_rw   (on , on)  Allow nfs to export all rw
```

2. Turn off the value of nfs_export_all_rw using the *setsebool* command by simply furnishing "off" or "0" with it and confirm:

```
[user1@server10 ~]$ sudo setsebool nfs_export_all_rw 0
[user1@server10 ~]$ sudo getsebool -a | grep nfs_export_all_rw
nfs_export_all_rw --> off
```

3. Reboot the system and rerun the *getsebool* command to check the Boolean state:

```
[user1@server10 ~]$ sudo getsebool -a | grep nfs_export_all_rw
nfs_export_all_rw --> on
```

The value reverted to its previous state.

4. Set the value of the Boolean persistently (-P or -m as needed) using either of the following:

```
[user1@server10 ~]$ sudo setsebool -P nfs_export_all_rw off
[user1@server10 ~]$ sudo semanage boolean -m -0 nfs_export_all_rw
```

5. Validate the new value using the *getsebool*, *sestatus*, or *semanage* command:

```
[user1@server10 ~]$ sudo getsebool nfs_export_all_rw
nfs_export_all_rw --> off
[user1@server10 ~]$ sudo sestatus -b | grep nfs_export_all_rw
nfs_export_all_rw             off
[user1@server10 ~]$ sudo semanage boolean -l | grep nfs_export_
all_rw
nfs_export_all_rw    (off , off)  Allow nfs to export all rw
```

The command outputs confirm the permanent change.

Chapter Summary

This chapter provided a deep dive into SELinux, demystifying its core concepts and practical administration. We started by establishing the fundamental terminology—subjects, objects, policies, and contexts—and contrasting Mandatory Access Control with Discretionary Access Control.

We learned that contexts are the heart of SELinux, and we practiced viewing them for users, processes, files, and ports. The chapter covered critical administrative tasks: controlling the operational state (enforcing vs. permissive), modifying file contexts persistently, and managing network port labels.

We explored advanced concepts like domain transitioning and the use of Booleans as dynamic policy switches. Finally, we highlighted the essential management commands that form the toolkit for any administrator needing to diagnose and configure SELinux on a system. Understanding SELinux is key to implementing and maintaining robust security.

Review Questions

1. What two tasks must be done to completely disable SELinux?
2. What is the purpose of the command *sestatus*?
3. What would the command *semanage login -a -s user_u user10* do?
4. Name the two commands that can be used to modify a Boolean value.
5. Which option is used with the *ps* command to view the security contexts for processes?
6. Which option with the *cp* command must be specified to preserve SELinux contexts?
7. What would the command *restorecon -F /etc/sysconfig* do?
8. What is the name of the default SELinux policy used in RHEL 10?
9. Name the four parts of a process context.
10. Name the directory that stores SELinux Boolean files.
11. What are the two commands to display and modify the SELinux mode?
12. Name the two SELinux subjects.
13. What is the name and location of the SELinux configuration file?
14. What would the command *semanage fcontext -Cl* do?
15. Which command can be used to ensure modified contexts will survive file system relabeling?
16. SELinux is an implementation of discretionary access control. True or False?
17. Where are SELinux denial messages logged in the absence of the *auditd* daemon?
18. With SELinux running in enforcing mode and one of the services on the system is compromised, all other services will be affected. True or False?
19. What would the command *sestatus -b | grep nfs_export_all_rw* do?
20. Name the command that starts the SELinux Troubleshooter program.

Answers to Review Questions

1. SELinux must be disabled in the configuration file, and the system must be rebooted.
2. The *sestatus* command displays SELinux status information.
3. This command provided will map Linux user *user10* with SELinux user user_u.
4. The *semanage* and *setsebool* commands.
5. The -Z option.
6. The --preserve=context option.
7. The command provided will force restoration of the default SELinux contexts on the specified directory, even if the current contexts appear correct.

8. The default SELinux policy used in RHEL 10 is targeted.
9. The four parts of a process context are user, role, type/domain, and sensitivity level.
10. The */sys/fs/selinux/booleans* directory.
11. The *getenforce* command displays the mode and the *setenforce* command modifies it temporarily.
12. User and process are the two SELinux subjects (processes act on behalf of users).
13. The SELinux configuration file is */etc/selinux/config*.
14. The command provided will list all locally defined custom file context rules from the SELinux policy database.
15. The *semanage* command with *fcontext*.
16. False. SELinux is an implementation of mandatory access control.
17. The SELinux denial messages are logged to the */var/log/messages* file.
18. False.
19. The command provided will display the current value of the specified Boolean.
20. The command name is *sealert*.

Do-It-Yourself Challenge Labs

The following labs are designed to reinforce most of the concepts and skills covered in this chapter. You are expected to complete these labs without external assistance. A step-by-step guide is not provided, as the required knowledge has already been presented in the chapter; however, each lab includes hints pointing to the relevant major topic(s).

Use the lab environment created specifically for the end-of-chapter labs. See the sub-section "Lab Environment for End-of-Chapter Labs" in Chapter 01 "Local Installation" for details.

Lab 22-1: Disable and Enable the SELinux Operating Mode

As *user1* with *sudo* on *server30*, check and make a note of the current SELinux operating mode. Modify the configuration file and set the mode to disabled. Reboot the system to apply the change. Run *sudo getenforce* to confirm the change when the system is up. Restore the directive's value to enforcing in the configuration file, and reboot to apply the new mode. Run *sudo getenforce* to confirm the mode when the system is up. (Hint: SELinux Administration).

Lab 22-2: Modify Context on Files

As *user1* with *sudo* on *server30*, create directory hierarchy */tmp/d1/d2*. Check the contexts on */tmp/d1* and */tmp/d1/d2*. Change the SELinux type on */tmp/d1* to etc_t recursively with the *chcon* command and confirm. Add */tmp/d1* to the policy database with the *semanage* command to ensure the new context is persistent for the directory hierarchy. Run the *restorecon* command recursively on */tmp/d1* to confirm the context is preserved. (Hint: SELinux Administration).

Lab 22-3: Add Network Port to Policy Database

As *user1* with *sudo* on *server30*, add network port 9005 to the SELinux policy database for the secure HTTP service using the *semanage* command. Verify the addition. (Hint: SELinux Administration).

Lab 22-4: Copy Files with and without Context

As *user1* with *sudo* on *server30*, create file *sef1* under */tmp*. Copy the file to the */usr/local* directory. Check and compare the contexts on both the source and destination files. Create another file *sef2* under */tmp* and copy it to the */var/local* directory using the --preserve=context option with the *cp* command. Check and compare the contexts on both source and destination files. (Hint: SELinux Administration).

Lab 22-5: Flip SELinux Booleans

As *user1* with *sudo* on *server30*, check the current value of Boolean *ssh_use_tcpd* using the *getsebool* and *sestatus* commands. Use the *setsebool* command and toggle the value of the Boolean. Confirm the new value with the *getsebool*, *semanage*, or *sestatus* command. (Hint: SELinux Administration).

Appendix A: RHCSA Practice Exam 1

Time Duration: 3 hours
Passing Score: 70% (210 out of 300)
Instructions: The RHCSA exam, EX200, is offered electronically on a physical computer running RHEL 10 as the base operating system. The computer has two virtual machines with RHEL 10 running in each one of them. The exam presents two sets of tasks that are to be completed within the stipulated time in the identified virtual machine. Firewall and SELinux must be taken into consideration for all network services. All settings performed in the virtual machines must survive system reboots, or you will lose marks. Access to the Internet, printed and electronic material, and electronic devices is prohibited during the exam.

Setup for Practice Exam 1:

Build a virtual machine with RHEL 10 Server with GUI (Exercises 1-1 and 1-2). Use a 20 GB disk for the OS with default partitioning. Add 1 x 500 MB disks and a network interface. Do not configure the network interface or create a normal user account during installation.

Instructions:

01: The following tasks are in addition to the exercises and labs presented in the book. No solutions are furnished, but hints to applicable exercises, chapters, or topics are provided in parentheses for reference.

02: Do not browse the Internet or seek help from other sources. However, you can refer to the manual pages, and the documentation under the /usr/share/doc directory. This rule does not apply to the kernel download task if included.

03: All exam tasks must be executed in a terminal window using only the command-line interface (no GUI).

04: You can reboot the VM whenever you want during this exam but retest the configuration after each reboot for verification.

05: Use your knowledge and judgement for any missing configuration in task description.

Tasks:

Task 01: Assuming the root user password is lost, and your system is running in multi-user target with no current root session open. Reboot the system into an appropriate systemd target and reset the root user password to root1234. (Exercise 13-2). After completing this task, log in as the root user and perform the remaining tasks presented below.

Task 02: Configure a network connection on the primary network device with IP address 192.168.0.241/24, gateway 192.168.0.1, and nameserver 192.168.0.1. Use different IP assignments based on your lab setup. (Exercise 17-3).

Task 03: Using a manual method (modify file by hand), set the system hostname to rhcsa1.example.com and alias rhcsa1. Update the hosts table. Make sure that the new hostname is reflected in the command prompt. (Exercises 17-1 and 17-4).

Task 04: Set the default boot target to multi-user. (Chapter 14, topic: Managing Target Units).

Task 05: Set the SELinux operating mode to permissive persistently. (Chapter 22, topic: Viewing and Controlling SELinux Operational State).

Task 06: Perform a case-insensitive search for all lines in the /usr/share/dict/linux.words file that begin with the pattern "essential". Redirect the output to /var/tmp/pattern.txt file. Make sure that empty lines are omitted. (Chapter 07, topic: Pattern Matching using Regular Expressions).

Task 07: Change the primary command prompt for the root user to display the hostname, username, and current working directory information in that order. Update the per-user initialization file for permanence. (Exercise 7-1).

Task 08: Create user accounts called user10, user20, and user30. Set their passwords to Temp1234. Make user10 and user30 accounts to expire on December 31, 2027. (Exercise 5-1; Exercise 6-1 or 6-2). Create a group called group10 and add user20 and user30 as secondary members. (Exercise 6-4). Create a user account called user40 with UID 2929. Set the password to user1234. (Exercise 5-2).

Task 09: Install Flatpak software packages. Add the Flathub repository to the system. Verify that the repository is available by listing applications and runtimes available from it. Search and install the Calculator application for all users. Verify that the application is installed by launching it on the desktop. (Exercises 12-1 and 12-2).

Task 10: Remove the Flatpak Calculator application and reinstall it for group10. Configure the system so that only the members of group10 can run the Calculator application. (Exercise 12-1, 12-2, 12-3, topic: The flatpak Command).

Task 11: Attach the RHEL 10 ISO image to the VM and mount it persistently to /mnt/cdrom. Define access to both repositories and confirm. (Exercise 10-1).

Task 12: Create a logical volume called lvol1 of size 220 MB in vgtest volume group. Mount the ext4 file system persistently to /mnt/mnt1. (Exercises 15-6, 15-7, and 16-2).

Task 13: Create a logical volume called lvswap of size 220 MB in vgtest volume group. Initialize the logical volume for swap use. Use the UUID and place an entry for persistence. (Exercises 15-6, 15-7, and 16-4; Chapter 16, topic: Automatically Mounting a File System at Reboots).

Task 14: Use the combination of tar and bzip2 commands to create a compressed archive of the /usr/lib directory. Store the archive under /var/tmp as usr.tar.bz2. (Exercise 3-1).

Task 15: Create a directory hierarchy /dir1/dir2/dir3/dir4 and apply the same SELinux file contexts used by /etc recursively. (Chapter 03, topic: Creating Files and Directories; and Exercise 22-2).

Task 16: Enable access to the atd service for user20 and deny for user30. (Chapter 09, topic: Controlling User Access).

Task 17: Add a custom message "This is RHCSA practice exam on $(date) by $LOGNAME" to the /var/log/messages file as the root user. Use a regular expression to confirm the message entry to the log file. (Chapter 14, topic: Logging Custom Messages; Chapter 07, topic: Pattern Matching using Regular Expressions).

Task 18: Allow user20 to use sudo without being prompted for their password. (Chapter 06, topic: Substituting Users and Doing as Substitute User).

Task 19: Write a bash shell script to create three user accounts—user555, user666, and user777—with no login shell and passwords matching their usernames. The script should also extract the three usernames from the /etc/passwd file and redirect them into /var/tmp/newusers. (Chapter 08, Script12; Chapter 07, topic: Pattern Matching using Regular Expressions, and Redirection).

Task 20: Configure the firewall to allow permanent access via port range 7590 to 7599. Verify that the rule is active. Reboot the system and confirm that access via the ports is still in effect. Remove the port range permanently and confirm. (Exercise 21-1 and 21-2).

Reboot the system and validate the configuration.

Appendix B: RHCSA Practice Exam 2

Time Duration: 3 hours
Passing Score: 70% (210 out of 300)
Instructions: The RHCSA exam, EX200, is offered electronically on a physical computer running RHEL 10 as the base operating system. The computer has two virtual machines with RHEL 10 running in each one of them. The exam presents two sets of tasks that are to be completed within the stipulated time in the identified virtual machine. Firewall and SELinux must be taken into consideration for all network services. All settings performed in the virtual machines must survive system reboots, or you will lose marks. Access to the Internet, printed and electronic material, and electronic devices is prohibited during the exam.

Setup for Practice Exam 2:

Build a virtual machine with RHEL 10 Server with GUI (Exercises 1-1 and 1-2). Use a 20 GB disk for the OS with default partitioning. Add 2 x 500 MB disk and a network interface. Do not configure the network interface or create a normal user account during installation.

Instructions:

01: The following tasks are in addition to the exercises and labs presented in the book. No solutions are furnished, but hints to applicable exercises, chapters, or topics are provided in parentheses for reference.

02: Do not browse the Internet or seek help from other sources. However, you can refer to the manual pages, and the documentation under the /usr/share/doc directory. This rule does not apply to the kernel download task if included.

03: All exam tasks must be executed in a terminal window using only the command-line interface (no GUI).

04: You can reboot the VM whenever you want during this exam but retest the configuration after each reboot for verification.

05: Use your knowledge and judgement for any missing configuration in task description.

06: Read all the storage tasks and set your strategy for disk partitioning prior to attempting them.

Tasks:

Task 01: Configure a network connection on the primary network device with IP address 192.168.0.242/24, gateway 192.168.0.1, and nameserver 8.8.8.8. Use different IP assignments based on your lab environment. (Exercise 17-3).

Task 02: Set the system hostname to rhcsa2.example.com and alias rhcsa2. Update the hosts table. Make sure that the new hostname is reflected in the command prompt. (Exercises 17-1 and 17-4).

Task 03: Create a user account called user70 with UID 7000 and comments “I am user70”. Set the maximum allowable inactivity for this user to 30 days. (Exercises 5-2; Exercise 6-1 or 6-2).

Task 04: Create a user account called user50 with a non-interactive shell. (Exercise 5-4).

Task 05: Attach the RHEL 10 ISO image to the VM and mount it persistently to /mnt/dvdrom. Define access to both repositories and confirm. (Exercise 10-1).

Task 06: Create a logical volume called lv1 of size equal to 35 LEs in vg1 volume group (create vg1 with PE size 8 MB in a partition on a disk). Initialize the logical volume with XFS type and mount it on /mnt/lvfs1. Create a file called lv1file1 in the mount point. Set the file system to automatically mount at each system reboot. (Exercises 15-6, 15-7, and 16-2; Chapter 16, topic: Automatically Mounting a File System at Reboots).

Task 07: Extend the file system in the logical volume lv1 by 60 MB without unmounting it and without losing any data. Confirm the new size for the logical volume and the file system. (Exercise 16-3).

Task 08: Create a swap partition of size 85 MB. Use its UUID and ensure it is activated after every system reboot. (Exercise 16-5; Chapter 16, topic: Automatically Mounting a File System at Reboots).

Task 09: Create a partition of size 200 MB and format it with Ext4 file system structures. Assign label stdlabel to the file system. Mount the file system on /mnt/stdfs1 persistently using the label. Create file stdfile1 in the mount point. (Exercise 15-2 or 15-4; Chapter 16, topic: Labeling a File System; and Exercise 16-1).

Task 10: Create a Bash shell script named /usr/local/bin/search.sh that executes the command "find / -perm /4000 -type f -exec cp {} /root/search/ \;". Ensure the script copies all files with setuid permission bit set on them into a directory /root/search/ (create this directory before running the script). Create a systemd service unit that runs this script. Create a systemd timer unit that executes this service every 5 minute. Enable and start the timer. Verify that the timer is active and that the script executes successfully. Reboot the system and confirm that the timer remains enabled and continues to execute as scheduled. (Exercise 4-5, Chapter 08; Chapter 14, topic: Rotating log files, plus do your own research).

Task 11: Create a directory /direct01 and apply SELinux contexts for /root to it. (Exercise 22-2).

Task 12: Set up a cron job for user70 to search for files owned by user70 in the entire directory structure and copy them to the directory /var/tmp/coredir1. This job should run every Monday at 1:20 a.m. (Chapter 04, topics: Using the find Command and Using find with -exec and -ok Flags; and Exercise 9-3).

Task 13: Search for all files in the entire directory structure that have been modified in the past 30 days and save the file listing in the /root/modfiles.txt file. (Chapter 04, topics: Using the find Command and Using find with -exec and -ok Flags).

Task 14: Modify the bootloader program and set the default autoboot timer value to 2 seconds. (Exercise 13-1).

Task 15: Determine the recommended tuning profile for the system and apply it. (Exercise 14-2).

Task 16: Configure Chrony to synchronize system time using the local hardware clock (127.127.1.0) as the reference source. Remove all other NTP sources. (Exercise 19-1).

Task 17: Install the "Development Tools" package group and capture its information in /var/tmp/systemtools.out file. (Chapter 03, topic: Pattern Matching using Regular Expressions; and Exercise 11-3).

Task 18: Lock user account user70. Use regular expressions to capture the line that shows the lock and store the output in file /var/tmp/user70.lock. (Chapter 03, topic: Pattern Matching using Regular Expressions; and Exercise 6-3).

Task 19: Configure the firewall and add a runtime rule to allow access to the HTTP service. Verify the rule, and reboot the system. After the restart, check whether the rule still exists. Re-add the rule permanently and reboot the system. Confirm the rule is still active following the restart. Now remove the rule and confirm the removal after a reboot. (Exercises 21-1 and 21-2).

Task 20: Write a bash shell script so that it prints RHCSA when RHCE is passed as an argument, and vice versa. If no argument is provided, the script should print a usage message and quit with exit value 5. (Chapter 08: Script10).

Reboot the system and validate the configuration.

Appendix C: RHCSA Practice Exam 3

Time Duration: 3 hours
Passing Score: 70% (210 out of 300)
Instructions: The RHCSA exam, EX200, is offered electronically on a physical computer running RHEL 10 as the base operating system. The computer has two virtual machines with RHEL 10 running in each one of them. The exam presents two sets of tasks that are to be completed within the stipulated time in the identified virtual machine. Firewall and SELinux must be taken into consideration for all network services. All settings performed in the virtual machines must survive system reboots, or you will lose marks. Access to the Internet, printed and electronic material, and electronic devices is prohibited during the exam.

Setup for Practice Exam 3:

Build two virtual machines with RHEL 10 Server with GUI (Exercises 1-1 and 1-2). Use a 20 GB disk for the OS with default partitioning. Add 1 x 400 MB disk and a network interface to both virtual machines. Do not configure the network interfaces or create a normal user account during installation.

Instructions:

01: The following tasks are in addition to the exercises and labs presented in the book. No solutions are furnished, but hints to applicable exercises, chapters, or topics are provided in parentheses for reference.

02: Do not browse the Internet or seek help from other sources. However, you can refer to the manual pages, and the documentation under the /usr/share/doc directory. This rule does not apply to the kernel download task if included.

03: All exam tasks must be executed in a terminal window using only the command-line interface (no GUI).

04: You can reboot the VM whenever you want during this exam but retest the configuration after each reboot for verification.

05: Use your knowledge and judgement for any missing configuration in task description.

Tasks:

Task 01: On VM1, set the system hostname to rhcsa3.example.com and alias rhcsa3 using a command. Update the hosts table. Make sure that the new hostname is reflected in the command prompt. (Exercises 17-1 and 17-4).

Task 02: On rhcsa3, configure a network connection on the primary network device with IP address 192.168.0.243/24, gateway 192.168.0.1, and nameserver 192.168.0.1 (use different IP assignments based on your lab environment). (Exercise 17-3).

Task 03: On VM2, set the system hostname to rhcsa4.example.com and alias rhcsa4 using a manual method (modify file by hand). Make sure that the new hostname is reflected in the command prompt. (Exercises 17-1 and 17-4).

Task 04: Run "ping -c2 rhcsa4" on rhcsa3. Run "ping -c2 rhcsa3" on rhcsa4. You should see 0% loss in both outputs. (Exercise 17-4).

Task 05: On rhcsa3 and rhcsa4, attach the RHEL 10 ISO image to the VM and mount it persistently to /mnt/sr0. Define access to both repositories and confirm. (Exercise 10-1).

Task 06: On rhcsa3, install httpd software, update SELinux policy database to allow traffic on port 80, create file /var/www/html/file1 and add the system hostname to it, set proper SELinux context on /var/www/html recursively, enable and start the HTTP service, run curl http://rhcsa3/file1 at the command prompt to access the page. (Exercises 22-1, 22-2, and 22-3).

Task 07: Configure NFS service on rhcsa3 and share /rh_share3 with rhcsa4. Configure AutoFS direct map on rhcsa4 to mount /rh_share3 on /mnt/rh_share4. User user80 (create on both systems) should be able to create files under the share on the NFS server as well as under the mount point on the NFS client. (Exercises 5-1, 18-1, and 18-3).

Task 08: Configure NFS service on rhcsa4 and share the home directory for user60 (create user60 on both systems) with rhcsa3. Configure AutoFS indirect map on rhcsa3 to automatically mount the home directory under /nfsdir when user60 logs on to rhcsa3. (Exercises 5-1, 18-1, 18-4, and 18-5).

Task 09: On rhcsa3, search for all manual pages for the description containing the keyword "password" and redirect the output to file /root/search.out. (Chapter 02, topic: Searching by Keyword; Chapter 07, topic: Redirections).

Task 10: On rhcsa3, create file lnfile1 under /var/tmp and create one hard link /var/tmp/lnfile2 and one soft link /boot/file1. Edit lnfile1 using one link at a time and confirm. (Exercises 3-2 and 3-3).

Task 11: On rhcsa3, install software group called "Legacy UNIX Compatibility". (Exercise 11-3).

Task 12: On rhcsa3, add the http service to "external" firewalld zone persistently. (Exercise 21-1).

Task 13: On rhcsa3, set SELinux type shadow_t on a new file testfile1 in /usr and ensure that the context is not affected by a SELinux relabeling. Add HTTP port 8400/UDP to the public firewall zone persistently. (Chapter 03, topic: File and Directory Operations; Exercises 22-1 and 22-2).

Task 14: Configure passwordless ssh access for user60 from rhcsa3 to rhcsa4. (Exercise 20-2).

Task 15: Write a bash shell script that checks for the existence of files (not directories) under the /usr/bin directory that begin with the letters "ac" and display their statistics (the stat command). (Chapter 08: Table 8-1 and Script07).

Task 16: On rhcsa3, configure a cron job to log the current date and time to /var/log/cron.log every day at 12:05 a.m. Ensure the job persists across reboots. (Exercise 9-3).

Task 17: On rhcsa3, create a directory /data3, set ownership to user80, and configure permissions so only the owner can access it. (Exercise 4-1 and 4-2).

Task 18: On rhcsa3, create a single partition on the entire disk, format it with XFS, mount it persistently at /mnt/xfs, set up read and write permissions for the owner, owning group, and everyone else, and mount the file system. Confirm the file system creation using the disk free command. (Exercise 16-1).

Task 19: On rhcsa4, set SELinux to permissive mode temporarily. Verify the change, then restore enforcing mode. (Chapter 22: topic: viewing and controlling SELinux operating state).

Task 20: On rhcsa3, create a compressed archive of /etc using tar and gzip, and store it under /var/tmp/etcbackup.tar.gz. (Exercise 3-1).

Reboot the system and validate the configuration.

Appendix D: RHCSA Practice Exam 4

Time Duration: 3 hours
Passing Score: 70% (210 out of 300)
Instructions: The RHCSA exam, EX200, is offered electronically on a physical computer running RHEL 10 as the base operating system. The computer has two virtual machines with RHEL 10 running in each one of them. The exam presents two sets of tasks that are to be completed within the stipulated time in the identified virtual machine. Firewall and SELinux must be taken into consideration for all network services. All settings performed in the virtual machines must survive system reboots, or you will lose marks. Access to the Internet, printed and electronic material, and electronic devices is prohibited during the exam.

Setup for Practice Exam 4:

Build two virtual machines with RHEL 10 Server with GUI (Exercises 1-1 and 1-2). Use a 20 GB disk for the OS with default partitioning. Add a network interface to both virtual machines. Do not configure the network interfaces or create a normal user account during installation.

Instructions:

01: The following tasks are in addition to the exercises and labs presented in the book. No solutions are furnished, but hints to applicable exercises, chapters, or topics are provided in parentheses for reference.

02: Do not browse the Internet or seek help from other sources. However, you can refer to the manual pages, and the documentation under the /usr/share/doc directory. This rule does not apply to the kernel download task if included.

03: All exam tasks must be executed in a terminal window using only the command-line interface (no GUI).

04: You can reboot the VM whenever you want during this exam but retest the configuration after each reboot for verification.

05: Use your knowledge and judgement for any missing configuration in task description.

Tasks:

Task 01: On VM1, assuming the root user password is lost, and your system is running in multi-user target with no current root session open. Reboot the system into an appropriate systemd target and reset the root user password to root1234. (Exercise 13-2). After completing this task, log in as the root user to verify.

Task 02: On VM1, set the system hostname to rhcsa5.example.com and alias rhcsa5. Update the hosts table. Make sure that the new hostname is reflected in the command prompt. (Exercises 17-1 and 17-4).

Task 03: On rhcsa5, configure a network connection on the primary network device with IP address 192.168.0.245/24, gateway 192.168.0.1, and nameserver 192.168.0.1. Use different IP assignments based on your lab environment. (Exercise 17-3).

Task 04: On VM2, set the system hostname to rhcsa6.example.com and alias rhcsa6 manually (modify file by hand). Make sure that the new hostname is reflected in the command prompt. (Exercises 17-1 and 17-4).

Task 05: On rhcsa6, configure a network connection on the primary network device with IP address 192.168.0.246/24, gateway 192.168.0.1, and nameserver 192.168.0.1. Use different IP assignments based on your lab environment. (Exercise 17-3).

Task 06: Run "ping -c2 rhcsa6" on rhcsa5. Run "ping -c2 rhcsa5" on rhcsa6. You should see 0% loss in both outputs. (Exercise 17-4).

Task 07: On rhcsa5 and rhcsa6, attach the RHEL 10 ISO image to the VM and mount it persistently to /mnt/sr0. Define access to both repositories and confirm. (Exercise 10-1).

Task 08: Export /share5 on rhcsa5 and mount it to /share6 persistently on rhcsa6. (Exercises 18-1 and 18-2).

Task 09: Use NFS to export home directories for all users (u1, u2, and u3) on rhcsa6 so that their home directories become available under /home1 when they log on to rhcsa5. Create u1, u2, and u3. (Exercises 5-1, 18-1 and 18-5).

Task 10: Configure passwordless ssh access for u1 from rhcsa5 to rhcsa6. Copy the directory /etc/sysconfig from rhcsa5 to rhcsa6 under /var/tmp/remote securely. (Exercise 20-2; Chapter 20, topic: Transferring Files Remotely Using sftp).

Task 11: On rhcsa6, flip the value of the Boolean nfs_export_all_rw persistently. (Exercise 22-5).

Task 12: On rhcsa5 and rhcsa6, set the tuning profile to powersave. (Exercise 14-2).

Task 13: On rhcsa5, create file lnfile1 under /var/tmp and create three hard links called hard1, hard2, and hard3 for it. Identify the inode number associated with all four files. Edit any of the files and observe the metadata for all the files for confirmation. (Exercise 3-2).

Task 14: On rhcsa6, list all files that are part of the "setup" package, and use regular expressions and I/O redirection to send the output lines containing "hosts" to /root/setup.pkg. (Exercise 10-2; Chapter 07, topics: Pattern Matching using Regular Expressions, and Redirections).

Task 15: On rhcsa5, check the current version of the Linux kernel. Download and install the latest version of the kernel from Red Hat website. Ensure that the existing kernel and its configuration remain intact. Reboot the system and confirm the new version is loaded. (Exercise 13-3; Chapter 02, topic: Viewing System Information).

Task 16: On rhcsa5, configure journald to store messages permanently under /var/log/journal and fall back to memory-only option if /var/log/journal directory does not exist or has permission/access issues. (Exercise 14-1).

Task 17: Write a bash script that defines an environment variable called ENV1=book1 and creates a user account that matches the value of the variable. (Chapter 07, topic: Setting and Unsetting Variables; Exercise 5-1; Chapter 08: Script02).

Task 18: On rhcsa6, write a message "RHCSA Practice Exam" to /var/log/messages file. (Chapter 14: Managing Services).

Task 19: On rhcsa5, install Flatpak support. Add the Flathub repository to the system. Verify that the repository is available by listing applications and runtimes available from it. Search and display all text editing Flatpak applications in the flathub repository, show metadata of any one of them and install it for system-wide use. Verify that the application is installed by launching it on the desktop. (Exercises 12-1 and 12-2).

Task 20: On rhcsa6, install Flatpak support. Add the Flathub repository to the system. Search and display all Flatpak applications in the flathub repository. Create a user account called flatuser and install any application just for this user. Verify that the application is installed by launching it on the desktop. (Exercises 12-1 and 12-2).

Reboot the system and validate the configuration.

Bibliography

The following websites, forums, and guides were referenced in writing this book:

1. www.virtualbox.org
2. docs.redhat.com/docs/en-US
3. developers.redhat.com
4. www.redhat.com
5. www.opensource.org
6. www.systemd.io
7. www.tldp.org
8. wiki.archlinux.org
9. www.ibm.com
10. www.wikipedia.org
11. www.linux.org
12. www.firewalld.org
13. www.gnome.org
14. www.isc.org
15. www.netfilter.org
16. www.nftables.org
17. www.nsa.gov/research/selinux
18. www.ntp.org
19. www.chrony.tuxfamily.org
20. www.openssh.org
21. www.pathname.com/fhs
22. RHCSA Red Hat Enterprise Linux 9 by Asghar Ghori
23. RHCSA Red Hat Enterprise Linux 8 (UPDATED) by Asghar Ghori
24. RHCSA Red Hat Enterprise Linux 8 by Asghar Ghori
25. Red Hat Certified System Administrator & Engineer for RHEL 7 by Asghar Ghori
26. Red Hat Certified System Administrator & Engineer for RHEL 6 by Asghar Ghori

Glossary

. (single dot)	Represents current directory.
.. (double dots)	Represents parent directory of the current directory.
Absolute mode	A method of permission allocation to a file or directory.
Absolute path	A pathname that begins with a /.
Access mode	See Permission mode.
Access permission	See File permission.
Access right	See File permission.
Access Vector Cache	A special cache area that SELinux uses to store its decisions.
Address Resolution Protocol	A protocol used to determine a system's Ethernet address when its IP address is known.
Address space	Memory location that a process can refer.
Administrator	See Superuser.
Algorithm	A set of well-defined but complex mathematical instructions used for data encryption and decryption.
Alias	A short name to refer to a lengthy command.
Alias substitution	See Alias.
Anaconda	RHEL's installation program.
Apache	A popular HTTP web server software.
Application stream	A method of making multiple versions of a software application available for installation from the same repository.
AppStream	One of the dnf repositories in RHEL 10 that provides add-on software applications along with some core operating system components.
Archive	A file that contains one or more files.
Argument	A value passed to a command or program.
ARP	See Address Resolution Protocol.
ASCII	An acronym for American Standard Code for Information Interchange.
Asymmetric encryption technique	A technique that uses a combination of public/private keys to allow two network nodes to communicate privately.
Auditing	System and user activity record and analysis.
Authentication	The process of identifying a user to a system.

AutoFS	The NFS client-side service that automatically mounts and unmounts an NFS share on an as-needed basis.
AutoFS maps	Configuration files to define the directory location to automount a remote share.
Automounter	See AutoFS.
AVC	See Access Vector Cache.
Background process	A process that runs in the background.
Backup	Process of saving data on an alternative media such as a tape or another disk.
BaseOS	One of the dnf repositories in RHEL 10 that includes the foundational RHEL components.
Bash shell	A feature-rich default shell available in Red Hat Enterprise Linux.
Berkeley Internet Name Domain	A University of California at Berkeley implementation of DNS for Linux and UNIX platforms. See also Domain Name System.
Binary package	A software package available in a format that dnf/rpm can recognize and install.
BIND	See Berkeley Internet Name Domain.
BIOS	Basic I/O System. Software code that sits in the computer's non-volatile memory and is executed when the system is booted. Also see Firmware.
Block	A collection of bytes of data transmitted as a single unit.
Block device file	A file associated with devices that transfer data randomly in blocks. Common examples are disk, CD, and DVD.
Bluetooth	A wireless technology for communication.
Boolean	The on/off switch to permit or deny an SELinux rule for a service.
Boot	See Boot process.
Bootloader	A small program that loads the operating system in memory.
Boot order	The sequence in which to try devices to boot the system.
Boot process	The process of starting up a system to a usable state.
Bourne Again Shell	See Bash shell.
Bus	Data communication path among devices in a computer system.
Cache	A temporary storage area on the system where frequently accessed information is duplicated for quick future access.
Calling process	See Parent process.
CentOS	Community Enterprise Operating System. A 100% unsponsored rebuild of Red Hat Enterprise Linux OS available for free.
Cgroup	See Control group.
Challenge-response authentication	An authentication method that presents one or more arbitrary challenge questions to the user.
Character special file	A file associated with devices that transfer data serially, one character at a time. Common examples are disk, tape, and mouse.
Child directory	A directory one level below the current directory.

Child process	A sub-process started by a process.
Child shell	A child shell is spawned by the current shell as needed.
Chrony	An implementation of Network Time Protocol for time synchronization on network devices.
CIDR	See Classless Inter-Domain Routing.
Classless Inter-Domain Routing	A technique for better use of IP addresses. It also results in smaller and less cluttered routing tables.
Command	An instruction given to the system to perform a task.
Command aliasing	See Alias.
Command history	See History substitution.
Command interpreter	See Shell.
Command-line argument	See Positional parameter.
Command-line completion	See Tab completion.
Command-line editing	A shell feature that allows editing at the command line.
Command-line mode	See Last-line mode.
Command mode	A vim mode that allows navigational and text operations.
Command prompt	The OS prompt where you type commands.
Command substitution	A shell feature that allows the assignment of the output of an executed command to a variable.
Compression	The process of compressing data.
Context (SELinux)	A set of SELinux attributes applied to SELinux subjects and objects.
Contiguous data blocks	A series of data blocks.
Control group	A process management technique.
Core	A core is a processor that shares the chip with other cores. Multi-core processor chips are common.
CPU-intensive	A program or application that heavily uses system processors.
Crash	An abnormal system shutdown caused by electrical outage or kernel malfunction, etc.
Crontable	A table of cron jobs scheduled for a user. Commonly abbreviated as crontab.
Current directory	The present working directory.
Current shell	The shell where a program is launched. Compare with Child shell.
DAC (SELinux)	See Discretionary Access Control.
Daemon	A server process that runs in the background and responds to client requests.
Database	A collection of data.

D-bus	Desktop Bus. Another communication method that allows multiple services running in parallel on a system to talk to one another on the same or remote system. Compare with Socket.
De-encapsulation	The reverse of encapsulation. See Encapsulation.
Default	Predefined values or settings that are automatically accepted by commands or programs.
Default permissions	Permissions assigned to a file and directory at creation.
Defunct process	See Zombie process.
Desktop bus	See D-bus.
Desktop environment	Software such as GNOME that provides graphical environment for users to interact with the system.
Device	A peripheral such as a printer, disk drive, or a CD/DVD device.
Device driver	The software that controls a device.
Device file	See Special file.
DHCP	See Dynamic Host Configuration Protocol.
Directory structure	Inverted tree-like Linux/UNIX directory structure.
Discretionary Access Control	A rich set of traditional access controls in Linux.
Disk-based file system	A file system created on a non-volatile storage device.
Disk partitioning	Creation of partitions on a given storage device so as to access them as distinct, independent logical containers for data storage.
Display manager	Application that is responsible for the presentation of graphical login screen.
Dnf	A major enhancement to yum.
Dnf repository	See Repository.
DNS	See Domain Name System.
DNS name space	See Name space.
Domain	A group of computers configured to use a service such as DNS or NIS.
Domain Name System	The de facto hostname resolution service used on the Internet and corporate networks.
Domain (SELinux)	It ascertains the type of access that a process has.
Domain transitioning	The ability of a process running in one SELinux domain to enter another domain to execute a task in that domain.
Driver	See Device driver.
Dynamic Host Configuration Protocol	A networking service that provides IP assignments to devices.
Edit mode	See Insert mode.
Encapsulation	The process of forming a packet through the seven OSI layers.

Encryption	A method of scrambling information for privacy. See asymmetric encryption technique and symmetric encryption technique.
Encryption keys	A single secret key or a pair of private/public keys that is used to encrypt and decrypt data for private communication between two network nodes.
Environment variable	A variable whose value is inherited by programs in sub-shells.
EOF	Marks the End OF File.
Error redirection	A shell feature that allows forwarding error messages generated during a command execution to an alternative destination (file, printer, etc.).
Escape mode	See Command mode.
Ethernet	A family of networking technologies designed for LANs.
Ethernet address	See MAC address.
Exit code	A value returned by a command when it finishes execution.
Exit value	See Exit code.
Export	See Share.
Exporting	The process of making a directory or file system available over the network for sharing.
Extended file system	A type of file system that has been around in Linux for decades and currently has the fourth generation included and widely used in recent Linux distributions.
Extended mode	See Last-line mode.
Extension	Additional functionality provided to desktop applications and runtimes in Flatpak.
Extent	The smallest unit of space allocation in LVM. It is always contiguous. See Logical extent and Physical extent.
External command	A command external to the shell.
Fedora	Red Hat sponsored community project for collaborative enhancement of Red Hat Enterprise Linux OS.
Fibre channel	A family of networking technologies designed for storage networking.
File descriptor	A unique, per-process integer value used to refer to an open file.
Filename expansion	A series of characters used in matching filenames. Also see Metacharacters and Wildcard characters.
Filename globbing	See Filename expansion.
File permission	Read, write, execute or no permission assigned to a file or directory at the user, group, or public level.
File system	A grouping of files stored in special data structures.
File Transfer Protocol	A widely used protocol for file exchange.
Filter	A command that performs data transformation on the given input.
Firewall	A software or hardware appliance used for blocking inbound unauthorized access.

Firewalld	A dynamic firewall manager.
Firewalld zone	A method of segregating incoming network traffic.
Firmware	The BIOS or the UEFI code in x86-based systems.
Flathub	A popular public remote (repository) that hosts thousands of Flatpak applications, runtimes, and extensions.
Flatpak	An application packaging and distribution framework for desktop application deployments across Linux distributions.
FTP	See File Transfer Protocol.
Full path	See Absolute path.
Gateway	A device that connects two networks.
Gateway address	An IP address that allows a system to communicate with computers on a different network.
GECOS	General Electric Comprehensive Operating System. The comments field in the /etc/passwd file.
GID	See Group ID.
Globally Unique Identifier	See Universally Unique Identifier.
Globbing	See Regular expression.
GNOME	GNU Object Model Environment. An intuitive graphical user environment.
GNU	GNU Not Unix. A project initiated to develop a free Unix-like operating system.
GPG	Gnu Privacy Guard. An open-source implementation of PGP. See PGP.
GPL	General Public License that allows the use of software developed under GNU project to be available for free to the general public.
GPT	See GUID Partition Table.
Graphical User Interface	An interface that allows users to interact with the operating system or application graphically.
Group	A collection of users that requires same permissions on files and directories.
Group ID	A numeric identifier assigned to a group.
GRUB2	Grand Unified Bootloader version 2. The second generation of the GRUB bootloader program that loads the operating system in memory.
GSSAPI-based authentication	An authentication method that provides a standard interface for security mechanisms to be plugged in.
Guest	An operating system instance that runs in a virtual machine.
GUI	See Graphical User Interface.
GUID	See Universally Unique Identifier.
GUID Partition Table	A small disk partition on a UEFI system that stores disk partition information.
Hard link	A mapping between a filename and its inode number.
Hardware address	See MAC address.

Hardware clock	See Real-Time Clock.
Hashing	See Password hashing.
History expansion	See History substitution.
History substitution	A shell feature that enables the storage of previously executed commands.
Home directory	A directory where a user lands when he logs into the system.
Host-based firewall	A firewall service that runs on the Linux system.
Host-based authentication	An authentication method that allows a single user, a group of users, or all users on the client to be authenticated on the server.
Hostname	A unique name assigned to a network node.
Hostname resolution	See Name resolution.
Host table	A file that maintains IP and hostname mappings.
HTTP	See HyperText Transfer Protocol.
HTTPS	See HyperText Transfer Protocol Secure.
HyperText Transfer Protocol	HyperText Transfer Protocol. Allows access to web pages.
HyperText Transfer Protocol Secure	Secure cousin of HTTP. Allows access to secure web pages.
Hypervisor	Software loaded on a computer to virtualize its hardware.
ICMP	See Internet Control Message Protocol.
Index node	An index node number holds a file's properties including permissions, size and creation/modification time as well as contains a pointer to the data blocks that actually store the file data.
Init	An older method of system initialization. It has been replaced by systemd in RHEL versions 7 and up.
Initialization files	See Shell startup files.
Initial permissions	Predefined permission settings that are used to calculate default permissions for new files and directories.
Initial Setup	Program that starts at first system reboot after a system has been installed to customize authentication, firewall, network, time zone and other services.
Inode	See Index node.
Inode table	A table in a file system that keeps a record of inode numbers.
Input mode	See Insert mode.
Input redirection	A shell feature that allows supplying input to a command from an alternative source (file, etc.).
Insert mode	A vim mode that allows entering text.
Installable package	See Binary package.
Installer program	A program that is launched to install an operating system or application.
Interface card	See Network device.
Internet	A complex network of computers and routers.

Internet Control Message Protocol	A well-known networking protocol that is primarily used for testing and debugging.
Internet Protocol	A protocol that is responsible for relaying traffic between network nodes.
Inter-Process Communication	Allows processes to communicate directly with each other by sharing parts of their virtual memory address space, and then reading and writing data stored in that shared virtual memory.
I/O redirection	A shell feature that allows getting input from a non-default location and sending output and error messages to non-default locations.
IP	See Internet Protocol.
IP address	A unique 32- or 128-bit software address assigned to a network node.
IPC	See Inter-Process Communication.
ISO9660	A file system type used to mount optical devices.
Job	A process started in the background.
Job scheduling	Execution of commands, programs, or scripts in future.
Journald	A systemd-based logging service for collecting and storing logging data.
Journaled file system	A file system that uses the journaling mechanism for swift recovery after a system crash.
Journaling	A file system feature that allows it to maintain a journal (log) of its metadata changes to be used to fix any potential anomalies that may arise due to an abnormal system shutdown.
Kerberos	A networking protocol used for user authentication over unsecure networks.
Kernel	Software that controls the entire system including all hardware and software.
Kernel-based Virtual Machine	An open-source hypervisor software used for host virtualization.
KVM	See Kernel-based Virtual Machine.
Label (storage)	A unique partition identifier that may be used instead of a UUID or device file.
Label (SELinux)	See Context.
Labeling	The process of mapping files with their stored SELinux contexts.
Last-line mode	A vim mode to perform advanced search and editing operations.
Latency	The time it takes for a data packet to travel between two network nodes.
Link	An object that associates a filename to any type of file.
Link count	Number of links that refers to a file.
Link layer address	See MAC address.
Linux	A UNIX-like, open-source operating system.
Load balancing	A technique whereby more than one server serve client requests to share the load.
Localhost	A reserved, non-networked hostname assigned to every device. It represents the device itself.
Local variable	A variable whose value is private to the shell (current shell) it is defined in.

Logical extent	A unit of space allocation for logical volumes in LVM.
Logical volume	A logical container in LVM that holds a file system or swap.
Login Manager	See Display manager.
Logging	A process of capturing desired alerts and forwarding them to preconfigured locations.
Logical construct	Controls the flow of a script via test conditions.
Logical Volume Manager	A widely used disk partitioning solution.
Login	A process that begins when a user enters a username and password at the login prompt.
Login directory	See Home directory.
Loopback	A reserved IP address assigned to a device for testing and troubleshooting local issues.
Looping construct	Performs an action on a list of elements or repeatedly until a condition becomes true or false.
LVM	See Logical Volume Manager.
MAC address	A unique 48-bit hardware address of a network interface. Also called physical address, Ethernet address, and hardware address.
MAC (SELinux)	See Mandatory Access Control.
Machine	A computer, system, workstation, desktop, or server.
Major number	A number that points to a device driver.
Mandatory Access Control	A rich set of policies for granular access controls.
Map	See AutoFS map.
Masquerading	A variant of NAT.
Master Boot Record	A small region on the disk that stores disk partition information.
MBR	See Master Boot Record.
Memory-based file system	A kernel-managed virtual file system created in memory at system boot and destroyed at system shutdown.
Memory-intensive	A program or application that heavily uses memory.
Metacharacters	A series of characters that have special meaning to the shell and are used in pattern matching and filename globbing. Also see Wildcard characters.
Minor number	A unique number that points to an individual device controlled by a specific device driver.
MLS	See Multi-Level Security.
Module (kernel)	Device drivers used to control hardware devices and software components.
Mounting	Attaching a device (a file system, a CD/DVD) to the directory structure.
Multi-Level Security	One of the two standard SELinux policies that controls access at deeper levels.

Named pipe	Allows two unrelated processes running on the same system or on two different systems to communicate with each other and exchange data.
Name resolution	A technique to determine IP address by providing hostname.
Namespace	A layer of isolation between process groups and the rest of the system.
Name space	A hierarchical organization of DNS domains on the Internet.
NAT	See Network Address Translation.
NDP	See Neighbor Discovery Protocol.
Neighbor Discovery Protocol	A networking protocol that is used to discover Ipv6 devices and troubleshoot networking issues.
Netfilter	A framework that provides a set of hooks within the kernel to enable it to intercept and manipulate data packets.
Netmask	See Subnet mask.
Network	Two or more computers joined together to share resources.
Network Address Translation	Allows systems on an internal network to access external networks using a single IP address.
Network classes	Ranges of IP addresses classified into five distinct categories.
Network connection	A connection profile attached to a network device (interface).
Network device	A physical or virtual network interface assigned to a system for network connectivity.
Network File System	A networking protocol that allows Linux systems to share resources (files, directories, and file systems) on the network.
Network interface	See Network device.
Network interface card	See Network device.
NetworkManager	A Linux service that is used to configure, administer, and monitor network devices and connections.
Network mask	See Subnet mask.
Network Time Protocol	A networking protocol that is used to synchronize the system clock with a reliable time source.
NIC	See Network device.
NFS	See Network File System.
NFS client	A system that mounts an exported Linux resource.
NFS server	A system that exports (shares) a resource for mounting by an NFS client.
Nftables	A packet classification framework to monitor network traffic.
Niceness	It determines the priority of a process.
Nice value	See Niceness.
Node	A network device with a hostname and IP address.
Node name	A unique name assigned to a node.

Nologin (user) account	A user without the ability to log in to the system.
Normal (user) account	A user account with limited privileges on the system.
NTP	See Network Time Protocol.
NTP client	A system that receives time from a primary or secondary NTP server for its clock adjustments.
NTP peer	Two or more time servers that operate at the same stratum level.
NTP pool	A pool of time servers.
NTP server	See Primary NTP server and Secondary NTP server.
Object (SELinux)	A file, directory, file system, device, network connection, network interface, network socket, network port, etc.
Octal mode	A method for setting permissions on a file or directory using octal numbering system.
Octal numbering system	A 3-digit numbering system that represents values from 0 to 7.
On-demand activation	A systemd way of activating a service when needed.
Open source	Any software whose source code is published and is accessible at no cost to the public under GNU GPL for copy, modification and redistribution.
OpenSSH	A free implementation of secure shell services and utilities.
Orphan process	An alive child process of a terminated parent process.
OSTree	In Flatpak, OSTree is the underlying technology used to store and deliver application files efficiently.
Output redirection	A shell feature that allows forwarding a command output to an alternative destination (file, printer, etc.).
Owner	A user who has ownership rights on a file, directory, or process.
Owning user	The owner of a file or directory.
Owning group	The group of a file or directory.
Package	A set of necessary files and metadata that makes up a software application.
Package credibility	The authenticity or originality of a package.
Package database	A directory location that stores metadata for installed packages.
Package dependency	Additional required packages for a successful installation or functioning of another package.
Package group	A group of similar applications that can be managed as a single entity.
Package integrity	A state of being complete and error-free.
Paging	The process of transferring data between memory and swap space.
PAM	See Pluggable Authentication Module.
Parent directory	A directory one level above the current directory.
Parent process	A process with one or more child processes spawned.

Parent process ID	The ID of a process that starts a child process.
Parallelism	A systemd way of starting multiple services concurrently at system boot.
Partition	A partition created on a storage device.
Password aging	A mechanism that provides enhanced control on user passwords.
Password-based authentication	An authentication method that prompts users to enter their passwords to be signed in.
Password hashing	A one-way process of converting a legible text string into a random but unique string of characters using one of the several available password hashing algorithms.
Pattern matching	See Regular expression.
Peer	See NTP peer.
Per-user startup files	A set of initialization files that defines custom settings for an individual user upon logging in.
Performance-based	Hands-on implementation.
Performance monitoring	The process of acquiring data from system components for analysis and decision-making purposes.
Permission	Right to read, write, or execute.
Permission class	Access rights on files and directories based on an individual user, a group of users, or everyone else on the system.
Permission type	Read, write, or execute permission bits set on files or directories.
Permission mode	Add, revoke, or assign a permission type to a permission class.
PGP	Pretty Good Privacy. An encryption program to ensure data privacy and secrecy.
Physical address	See MAC address.
Physical extent	A unit of space allocation on physical volumes in LVM.
Physical volume	A disk or a partition logically brought under LVM control.
PID	See Process ID.
Pipe	Sends output of one command as input to the second command.
Pipeline	A command construction with the pipe character used multiple times.
Pluggable Authentication Module	A set of library routines that allows using any authentication service available on a system for user authentication, password modification and user account validation purposes.
Policy (SELinux)	A set of rules enforced system-wide for analysis of security attributes on subjects and objects.
Pool	See Thin pool.
Pool (NTP)	See NTP pool.
Port	A number appended to an IP address. This number could be associated with a well-known service or is randomly generated.
Portal	A secure intermediary layer in Flatpak that allows a sandboxed application to interact with the host system in a controlled, permission-based way.

Port forwarding	A method of directing incoming network traffic to an alternative network port.
Positional parameter	An argument supplied to a script at the time of its invocation, and its position is determined by the shell based on location with reference to the calling script.
POST	Power-On-Self-Test that runs at system boot to test hardware. See BIOS, Firmware, and UEFI.
Postfix	A mail transfer application used for sending and receiving mail.
PPID	See Parent process ID.
Primary DNS	A system that acts as the primary provider of DNS zones.
Primary NTP server	A system that gets time from a more reliable source and provides time to secondary servers or clients.
Primary prompt	The symbol where commands and programs are typed for execution.
Priority	See Process priority.
Private key	A randomly generated portion of the private/public key combination that is used to decode the messages encrypted with the paired public key.
Privilege	An extra right to accomplish something.
Process	Any command, program, or daemon that runs on a system.
Process ID	A numeric identifier assigned by kernel to each process spawned.
Process niceness	See Niceness.
Process priority	The value at which a process is running. This value is determined based on the current niceness setting.
Process state	One of multiple states in which a process is held during its lifecycle.
Processor	A CPU. It may contain more than one cores.
Profile (module)	A list of recommended packages that are organized for purpose-built convenient installations.
Prompt	See Primary prompt and Secondary prompt.
Protocol	A common language that communicating nodes understand.
Proxy	A system that acts on behalf of other systems to access network services.
Public key	A randomly generated portion of the private/public key combination that is used to encode messages destined for a specific user.
Public key-based authentication	An authentication method that uses a public/private key pair for user authentication.
Public key encryption	See Asymmetric encryption technique.
Quoting	Treats the specified special character as a regular character by disabling their special meaning.
Real-Time Clock	A battery-backed hardware clock on the system.
Recovery	A function that recovers a crashed system to its previous normal state. It may require restoring lost data files.
Redhat Package Manager	A file format used for packaging software for RHEL and its clones.

Red Hat Subscription Management	A comprehensive management service provided by Red Hat to its clients.
Redirection	Getting input from and sending output to non-default destinations.
Regex	See Regular expression.
Regular expression	A string of characters commonly used for pattern matching and filename globbing.
Relative path	A path to a file relative to the current user location in the file system hierarchy.
Remote	A flatpak repository that contains desktop applications, runtimes, and extensions.
Repository	A URL location that provides access to software packages for installation.
Rescue mode	A special boot mode for fixing and recovering an unbootable system.
Resolver	The client-side of DNS.
Return code	See Exit code.
RHCE	Red Hat Certified Engineer. A designation that may be earned by passing a performance based RHCE exam.
RHCSA	Red Hat Certified System Administrator. A designation that may be earned by passing a performance based RHCSA exam.
RHEL	Red Hat Enterprise Linux.
RHSM	See Red Hat Subscription Management.
Role (SELinux)	It controls who (SELinux subject) is allowed to access what (SELinux domains or types).
Root (user) account	See Superuser.
Router	A device that routes data packets from one network to another.
Routing	The process of choosing a path over which to send a data packet.
Root servers	The thirteen most accurate root DNS servers.
RPM	See RedHat Package Manager.
Rsyslog	Essential Linux service for capturing system messages and forwarded them to various destinations for storage.
RTC	See Real-Time Clock.
Runtime	The operational state of an operating system.
Runtime	In Flatpak, base libraries and dependencies that desktop applications require to run successfully.
Sandbox	An isolated environment where flatpak applications run.
SAS	Serial Attached SCSI. See Small Computer System Interface.
SATA	Serial Advanced Technology Attachment. This disk technology is a successor to the PATA drives.
Script	A text program written to perform a series of tasks.
SCSI	See Small Computer System Interface.

Search path	A list of directories where the system looks for the specified command.
Seccomp	See Secure Computing Mode.
Secondary DNS	A system that acts as an alternate provider of DNS zones.
Secondary NTP server	A system that gets time from a primary NTP server and provides time to NTP clients.
Secondary prompt	A prompt indicating that the entered command needs more input.
Secret key encryption	See Symmetric encryption technique.
Secure Computing Mode	A Linux feature that impose security constraints to protect processes.
Secure shell	A set of tools that gives secure access to a system.
Security context	SELinux security attributes set on files, processes, users, ports, etc.
Security Enhanced Linux	An implementation of Mandatory Access Control architecture for enhanced and granular control on files, processes, users, ports, etc.
SELinux	See Security Enhanced Linux.
Server (hardware)	Typically, a larger and more powerful system that offers services to network users.
Server (software)	A process or daemon that runs on the system to serve client requests.
Service (user) account	A user account that is used to control an installed application or service.
Shadow password	A mechanism to store passwords and password aging data in a secure file.
Share	A directory or file system shared over the network.
Shared memory	A portion in physical memory created by a process to share it with other processes that communicate with that process.
Sharing	See Exporting.
Shell	The Linux command interpreter that sits between a user and kernel.
Shell parameter	An entity that holds a value such as a name, special character, or number.
Shell program	See Script.
Shell script	See Script.
Shell scripting	Programming in a Linux shell to automate one or a series of tasks.
Shell startup files	A set of files that are used to define the environment for a user upon logging in.
Shell variable	See Local variable.
Signal	A software interrupt sent to a process.
Simple Mail Transfer Protocol	A networking protocol used for email transfer over the Internet.
Single user mode	An operating system state in which the system cannot be accessed over the network.
Skeleton directory	A directory location where user default configuration templates are stored.

Small Computer System Interface	A parallel interface used to connect peripheral devices to the system.
SMTP	See Simple Mail Transfer Protocol.
Snapshot	The state of a system at a certain point in time.
Socket	A communication method that allows a process to talk to another process on the same or remote system.
Soft link	See Symbolic link.
Source package	A software package that can be modified and repackaged for a specific purpose.
Special characters	See Metacharacters.
Special file	A file that points to a specific device.
SSH	See Secure Shell.
Standard error	A standard location to forward error messages to. Also see Error redirection.
Standard input	A standard location to receive input from. Also see Input redirection.
Standard output	A standard location to forward output to. Also see Output redirection.
Startup files	See Shell startup files.
Stderr	See Standard error.
Stdin	See Standard input.
Stdout	See Standard output.
Stratum level	The categorization of NTP time sources based on reliability and accuracy.
String	A series of characters.
Subject (SELinux)	A process or user.
Subnet	One of the smaller networks formed using the process of subnetting. See Subnetting.
Subnet mask	Segregates the network bits from the node bits in an IP address.
Subnetting	The process of dividing an IP address into several smaller subnetworks.
Sub-shell	See Child shell. Compare with Current shell.
Substituting users	See Switching users.
Sudo	A method of delegating a portion of superuser privileges to normal users.
Superblock	A small portion in a file system that holds the file system's critical information.
Superuser	A user with full powers on the system.
Swap	Alternative disk or file system location for paging.
Switch	A network device that looks at the MAC address and switches the packet to the correct destination port based on the MAC address.
Switching users	The ability to switch to a different user account provided the target user's password is known.
Symbolic link	A shortcut that points to a file or directory located somewhere in the directory hierarchy. Compare with hard link.

Symbolic mode	A method of setting permissions on a file using non-decimal values.
Symlink	See Symbolic link.
Symmetric encryption technique	A technique that employs a secret key for private communication between two network nodes.
Syslog	See rsyslog.
System	A computer or a logical partition in a computer that runs an operating system.
System Administrator	Person responsible for installing, configuring and managing a RHEL system.
System call	A mechanism that applications use to request service from the kernel.
System console	A display terminal that acts as the system console.
Systemd	System daemon. The default method of system initialization and service management starting at RHEL 7.
System recovery	The process of recovering an unbootable system.
System tuning	A service in RHEL 10 to monitor connected devices and dynamically adjust their parameters for performance improvement.
System-wide startup files	A set of initialization files that defines common settings for all users upon logging in.
Tab completion	A shell feature that allows completing a file or command name by typing a partial name at the command line and then hitting the Tab key twice for additional matching possibilities.
Target	A logical collection of systemd units. All units within a target are treated as a single entity.
Targeted policy	An SELinux policy.
TCP	See Transmission Control Protocol.
TCP/IP	Transmission Control Protocol / Internet Protocol. A stacked, standard suite of protocols for computer communication.
Terminal	A window where commands are executed.
Test condition	Used in logical constructs to decide what to do next.
Thin pool	A pool of storage that uses the thin provisioning technology to allow the creation of volumes much larger than their actual physical size.
Thin provisioning	An economical technique of storage allocation and utilization.
Thrashing	Excessive amount of paging.
Throughput	The amount of data transferred between two network nodes within a specified period of time.
Tilde expansion	See Tilde substitution.
Tilde substitution	A shell feature that uses the tilde character as a shortcut to navigate within the directory tree.
Time source	A reference device that provides time to other devices.
Transmission Control Protocol	A stateful and reliable transport protocol. Compare with UDP.

Tty	Refers to a terminal.
Tuning profile	A set of attributes that can be applied to a system for improving performance of certain components.
Type enforcement	It controls the ability of an SELinux subject to access domains and types.
Udevd	Dynamic device management service.
UDP	See User Datagram Protocol.
UEFI	See Unified Extensible Firmware Interface.
UID	See User ID.
Umask	See User mask.
Unified Extensible Firmware Interface	Software code used in computers for pre-boot system management. Also see Firmware.
Universally Unique IDentifier	A unique alphanumeric software identifier used to identify an object, such as a disk or disk partition.
Unmounting	Detaching a mounted file system or a CD/DVD from the directory structure.
Unit	A systemd object used to organize service startups, socket creation, etc.
Universal Time Coordinated	The reference time used around the world to determine the local time and time zone.
USB	Universal Serial Bus. A bus standard to connect peripheral devices.
User Datagram Protocol	A stateless and unreliable transport protocol. Compare with TCP.
User ID	A numeric identifier assigned to a user.
User mask	A value used in calculating default access rights on new files and directories.
User Private Group	Referred to the GID that matches with the user's UID for safeguarding the user's private data from other users.
UTC	See Universal Time Coordinated.
UUID	See Universally Unique IDentifier.
Variable	A temporary storage of data in memory.
Variable substitution	A shell feature that allows the value of a variable to be used in a command.
VFAT	See Virtual File Allocation Table.
VirtualBox	A type II hypervisor to virtualize an operating system.
VirtualBox Manager	The management interface for VirtualBox.
Virtual console	One of several consoles available for system access.
Virtual File Allocation Table	An MSDOS-compatible file system type.
Virtual file system	See memory-based file system.
Virtual host	An approach to host more than one website on a single system using unique or shared IP addresses.

Virtualization	A technology that allows a single physical computer to run several independent logical computers (called virtual machines) with complete isolation from one another.
Virtual machine	A logical computer running within a virtualized environment.
Volume group	A logical container in LVM that holds physical volumes, logical volumes, file systems, and swap.
Wayland	A graphical display protocol that provides a point-and-click interface to launch applications.
Web	A system of interlinked hypertext documents accessed over a network or the Internet via a web browser.
Web server	A system or service that provides web clients access to website pages.
Wildcard characters	A subset of metacharacters used for character matching in strings. See also Metacharacters.
Workload	Any application, database, program, or a combination that runs on the system.
XFS	eXtended File System. A high-performance journaling file system type.
Yum repository	See Repository.
Zero-block elimination	A technique to remove empty (zero-byte) data blocks from storage.
Zombie process	A child process that terminated abnormally and whose parent process still waits for it.
Zone (DNS)	A delegated portion of a DNS name space.
Zone (Firewalld)	A firewalld zone for traffic management.

Index

D

E

F

G

O

P

Q

R

S

T

U

V

W

X

www.ingramcontent.com/pod-product-compliance
Lightning Source LLC
LaVergne TN
LVHW082018200926
848481LV00010B/2883
9781775062189